Dictionary of
BANKING
and
FINANCE

Dictionary of
BANKING
and
FINANCE

by

LEWIS E. DAVIDS

*Illinois Bankers Professor of Bank Management
at the College of Business and Administration,
Southern Illinois University at Carbondale;
Editor of The Bank Board Letter*

1980

LITTLEFIELD, ADAMS & CO.

Copyright © 1978
LITTLEFIELD, ADAMS & CO.
81 Adams Drive, Totowa, N.J. 07512

Reprinted 1980

Library of Congress Cataloging in Publication Data

Davids, Lewis E
    Dictionary of banking and finance

    (A Littlefield, Adams quality paperback ; 336)
    1. Banks and banking--Dictionaries
2. Finance--Dictionaries. I. Title.

HG151.D365   332'.03   78-13985
ISBN 0-8226-0336-5

PRINTED IN THE UNITED STATES OF AMERICA

CONTENTS

PREFACE

There are a number of contemporary developments that make a work of this type essential. Since the mid-nineteen sixties there has been a banking revolution due to the increased freedom and options that have been permitted banks. For example, banks have been allowed to lease goods, to establish foreign operations, and bank holding companies have been permitted a broadening of their services. Furthermore, the Eurodollar market has recently attracted financial institutions to it, in addition to which multinational corporations, predominately from the United States, have called upon banks to provide them with a broad spectrum of financial services.

Other developments also have emphasized the need for this dictionary: in schools of higher learning there has been a distinct shifting in emphasis from what may be called empirical learning to that which is more quantitatively oriented, along with the adoption of the case method of learning. For these reasons many of the textbooks and case books in banking and finance simply do not provide the type of information that is found in this work.

Banking and finance may be viewed from different directions. One is the actual operations of banks per se and their related financial institutions such as stock markets, commodity markets, investment companies, and the like. Conversely, banking and finance may be viewed from the businessman's need for financial accomodation and his use of their services.

Needless to say there is a good deal of judgmental decision making as to what terms should be included in a dictionary of this type. Words like bank, member bank, check, money, stock, and bond obviously are very closely related to banking and finance. However, there are other terms that are very important for analysis of the literature and cases involving financial institutions. For example, a good deal of banking today involves statement analysis and ratio analysis of financial statements. Thus, there is the need to know the type of accounting terminology that bankers would be concerned about in analyzing financial statements. Furthermore, banking increasingly is involved with trusts and many of the terms and phrases used in trust administration are of a legal nature. Those terms that are specifically related to trust administration are included here. To a much lesser extent certain terms that are associated with other fields such as taxation and government are covered as they are considered essential for the understanding of banking and finance.

Some dictionaries in their search for accuracy have devoted literally pages of explanation to the definition of a single word or phrase. Such dictionaries may properly be called encyclopedic. This dictionary has not adopted such a technique but has tried to define terms briefly and succinctly so that students and people in the financial field may be able to comprehend the meaning of the words and phrases used in texts, publications, and conversations concerning the field of banking and finance.

Lewis E. Davids, Ph.D.

NOTES ON ARRANGEMENT

This dictionary has been compiled to serve as a reference for those concerned with banking and finance terminology. A significant proportion of terms defined have been obtained from authoritative agencies in the financial field.

Entries in bold face type are interfiled in strict alphabetical order—letter by letter (i.e. **Auditor** preceding **Audit program** followed by **Audit report.**)

Abbreviations of terms and organizations are listed alphabetically at the beginning of each letter.

Cross references to related or comparative definitions are supplied for many of the entries and are introduced by the word "See" following the entries.

Sources from which entries have been obtained are identified by key numbers in parenthesis after definitions for entries. A list of the sources arranged numerically by key numbers appears in the section ACKNOWLEDGEMENTS on page 227

A

A Class "A" or Series "A" when accompanied by other letters and printed on the top line of the ticker tape.

A.B.A. American Bankers Association. The national organization of banking. A voluntary association of banks and other bank organizations. "To promote the general welfare and usefulness of banks and financial institutions."

A.B.A. Numerical system. The system of bank numbers whereby each bank in the United States and its territories is provided with a definite number of its own which constitutes a numerical name used only by that bank.

ABW Advise by wire.

A/C Account.

A.C. Assistant Cashier.

ACC. Accept, accepted.

Accrd. Int. Accrued Interest.

Ack. Acknowledge, acknowledgment.

Acpt. Acceptance.

A/CS PAY. Accounts Payable.

A/CS REC. Accounts Receivable.

A.C.V. Actual cash value.

A/D After Date.

Adj. Adjustment.

ADR's American Depository Receipts. See that term.

A.D.S. Autographed Document Signed. Document completely handwritten by the signer.

Adv. Advise, advice.

Ad Val. Ad Valorem.

A & F Semi-annual interest payments in August and February.

Agt. Agent.

Agy. Agency.

A.I.M.A. As interest may appear.

A.J.O.J. Quarterly interest payments or dividends in April, July, October and January.

A1 Highest class.

AMW Average Monthly Wage.

A/N Account number.

A.N.F.M. Quarterly interest payments or dividends in August, November, February and May.

Ann. Annual, annuity.

A & O Semi-annual interest payments in April and October.

AO Area Office.

A.O. Account of.

A/O Account of.

A.O.G. Arrival of goods. Trade discounts may be stated "A.O.G." which means that the discount period is determined from the time the goods arrive or are received.

A/P Authority to purchase or authority to pay.

ASAP As soon as possible.

ASE American Stock Exchange.

Assn. Association.

Asst. Cash. Assistant Cashier.

Astd. Assented.

Atty. Attorney.

Aud. Auditor, Audit.

Auth. Authority.

accommodation bill of lading A bill of lading issued by a common carrier prior to receipt of the goods for shipment.

accommodation charge Usually a single purchase for which credit is arranged on a temporary basis without the routine of opening a regular credit account. Also described as "This Transaction Only" and other designations.

accommodation endorsement When a person signs or endorses a note or draft solely for the purpose of inducing a bank to lend money to a borrower whose credit is not substantial enough to warrant a loan, such an endorsement is called an accommodation endorsement. The endorser, while being liable to repay the amount in full, ordinarily does not expect to do so. He derives no benefit from the transaction, but acts as a guarantor or surety for the borrower. Another form of accommodation endorsement is the practice among banks of endorsing the acceptances of other banks for a fee, in order to make them acceptable for purchase in the acceptance market.

accommodation endorser One who endorses a negotiable instrument for the accommodation of another party, having no right of ownership but simply guaranteeing fulfillment of the contract to subsequent holders of the instrument. See Endorsement; Endorser.

accommodation note A note which has received an Accommodation Endorsement. See Note; Accommodation Endorsement.

accommodation paper A note or similar obligation, the payment of which is guaranteed by some party other than the one who receives the benefit. Thus, before advancing funds, a bank may require the endorsement of a director of known means upon the note of a corporation of doubtful strength.

accord and satisfaction The settlement of a dispute by an executed agreement between the parties whereby the aggrieved party takes something different from his claim.

account A contractual agreement between a bank and its customer, allowing the customer to use bank services for a fee. A record of all the financial transactions and the date of each, expressed in debits and credits, evaluated in money, and showing the current balance. See also Bank Account.

accountabilities Assets, liabilities, items held in trust, and other items for which an individual, firm, corporation, or other legal entity must render an accounting. For example, certain officials and/or other employees of a bank are frequently entrusted with funds and legal documents for which a final accounting must be made. Even though a trust officer has disbursed all funds entrusted to his care, and has fulfilled all financial obligations pertaining thereto, he is still obligated to give an accounting of the items affecting the trust. Therefore, these items are known as accountabilities.

account activity Transactions on an account or group of accounts, i.e., media, such as debits or credits, or change in status, such as alerts, holds, etc.

account analysis The process of analyzing a checking account to determine the profit or loss incurred by the bank for servicing the account over a given period, usually one month. If the analysis shows that the customer is not maintaining a sufficient balance to pay for the services rendered, a service charge is usually applied to offset the difference. The objective of an account analysis and service charge is to obtain fair and reasonable compensation for services rendered to a customer. See Service Charge.

account and risk The limitation found on broker's statements of confirmation which calls attention to the condition that the broker is not assuming any risk and is acting for the "Account and Risk" of his customer.

accountant An individual who is competent in accounting, systems, audits, balance sheets, profit and loss statements and bookkeeping. Some accountants are Certified or Registered Public Accountants.

account balance The amount of money payable to a bank (loans) or by a bank (Time or Demand Deposits) on a customer's account. See Balance.

account day That day designated by such organizations as stock and commodity exchanges for settlement of the accounts between members. Also called Settlement Day.

account in balance An account in which the debit and credit footings are equal.

accounting The art of recording, classifying, and summarizing in a significant manner and in terms of money, transactions and events which are, in part, of a financial character, and interpreting the results thereof.

accounting method A taxpayer's accounting method is usually the "cash" or the "accrual" basis of accounting by which his records are kept. Special methods of reporting income such as the installment basis are variations of these two methods.

accounting period An accounting period is the 12 month period on the basis of which the taxpayer's records are kept. If his books are kept on the basis of a 12 month period ending with a month other than December, his accounting period is a "fiscal" year. A special 52-53 week accounting period is also recognized for income tax purposes.

account in trust An account opened by an individual to be held in trust and maintained for the benefit of another. In the absence of a legally constituted trust fund, withdrawals from the account are subject to the approval of the party establishing the account. An example is an educational fund established by an individual for the benefit of a minor.

account number The numerical identification given to an account within a given institution or business, such numerical identification being a part of and in direct harmony with the whole system of numerical description given to the accounts as a whole which are found within that institution or business. Such a system of numeri-

cal description is termed the "Code" or "Code of Accounts."

To facilitate proof, bookkeeping, and sorting procedure within the separate departments (particularly the Commercial Bookkeeping Department) of a bank, many banks have adopted a system for numerically describing all individual accounts on deposit. Account numbers may describe type of account, branch designation, amount of activity, location of the account in the file, etc., or it may have no special significance at all.

To insure that the individual depositor's number appears on all checks written, many institutions are furnishing the depositor with books and blank checks bearing the individual depositor's account number. See Terminal Digit Control; Code of Accounts.

account reconciliation plan (A.R.P.) A program using the Auxiliary On-Us field on MICR checks to furnish high volume accounts with a list and total of checks in numerical serial sequence and to aid in balancing the bank's statement to the customer's check register.

accounts current A statement of account in which are posted the debits and credits of a customer and the balance at the end of the accounting period or time of cyclical billing.

accounts payable A current liability representing the amount owed by an individual or a business to a creditor for merchandise or services purchased on open account or short term credit.

accounts payable account An account in the general ledger that shows the total amount owed to creditors for merchandise purchased on account; the title of the general ledger controlling account that controls the accounts payable ledger and that shows the total amount owed to creditors on account.

accounts receivable Money owed a business enterprise for merchandise bought on open account (i.e., without the giving of a note or other evidence of debt).

accounts receivable account The title of the general ledger controlling account that controls the accounts receivable ledger and that shows the total amount to be collected on account from all the customers of the business.

account stated The understanding and liability of a debtor that a bill or account rendered is accurate if it has not been questioned by the debtor within a reasonable time.

accrual The accumulation of income earned or expense incurred over a period, regardless of its actual receipt of payment. For example, interest on a loan accrues from the date of the note until the interest is paid.

accrual of discount Annual addition to book value of bonds purchased below par. See Amortization.

accrued dividends The customary, regular dividend considered to be earned but not declared or payable on legally issued stock or other instruments of part ownership of a legally organized business or financial institution.

accrued interest Interest accumulated on a bond since the last interest payment was made. The buyer of the bond pays the market price plus accrued interest. Exceptions include bonds which are in default and income bonds. See Flat; Bond, Income.

accrued liability The present monetary value, actuarially determined, of the estimated cost of pensions and benefits, payable to active and retired members. It covers service rendered prior to the date of an actuarial valuation and constitutes the difference between the values of future benefits and the value of prospective employee and employer contributions related to future service.

accumulate Buying by traders who expect to hold the contracts for a more or less extended period.

accumulate at interest To increase the principal by the amount of interest due thereby forming a new basis for the calculation of interest.

accumulated surplus The excess of profits accumulated by a corporation.

accumulation The purchase of a security or securities in such a way that securities are obtained without causing the price to materially increase. The purchase orders are frequently executed when the market is soft and on the down side. If the orders to purchase are expertly executed the price is not "run up" and additional accumulation may be made at relatively favorable prices. The term also refers to the spread between the face amount of a bond and the discount price.

accumulation plan An arrangement which enables an investor to purchase mutual fund shares regularly in large or small amounts, usually with provisions for the investment of income dividends and the acceptance of capital gains distributions in additional shares. Plans are of two types, voluntary and contractual.

"acid test" ratio One of the most important credit barometers used by lending institutions as it indicates the ability of a business enterprise to meet its current obligations. The formula used to determine the ratio is as follows:

$$\frac{\text{Cash plus Receivables plus Marketable Securities}}{\text{Current Liabilities}}$$
$$\frac{C + R + M.S.}{C.L.}$$

Frequently, a 1 to 1 ratio is deemed necessary.

acknowledgment A wired or written notification that an item has been received and that funds are, or are not, available for its immediate payment. See also Wire Fate Items.

acquisition cost The cost to the company of securing business, including commissions to agents and brokers, and in some companies field supervision costs.

acquittance A document giving written evidence of the discharge of, or freedom from, a debt or financial obligation.

action 1 The term used in France for a share of stock. 2. Pertains to the volume and price movements in securities.

active account In the parlance of a bank bookkeeping department, an active account is one on which there is currently activity (i.e., one which has a posting of checks or deposits on the day upon which it is referred to as an active account). An active account may also denote an account which has unusual or excessive activity over a given period.

active assets That portion of total assets which are in continuous productive use in a business.

active capital Working capital.

active corporation One which maintains an organization for operating property or administering its financial affairs.

active market A situation in which the market for securities, futures or other commodities has experienced a large volume of orders.

active partner An officer or partner of a firm who actively engages in the operation of the firm for the benefit of all associates.

active securities Those securities which may be readily purchased and sold and for which daily quotations are available.

active stock A security which enjoys a broad and continuous market and thus may be bought or sold with ease.

active trust A trust regarding which the trustee has some active duty to perform; opposed to bare, dry, naked, or passive trust.

activity charge A service charge imposed on checking account depositors by banks for check or deposit activity, where the average balances maintained are not enough to compensate for the cost of handling the items.

acts of bankruptcy Any act enumerated under Section 3 of the National Bankruptcy Act, the most common being the inability to pay debts of not less than one thousand dollars as they mature and voluntarily appearing in a bankruptcy court or involuntary bankruptcy in which creditors who are unpaid petition the bankruptcy court.

actual A physical commodity.

actually outstanding Applied to securities actually issued and not reacquired by or for the issuing corporation.

actuals The actual physical commodity as distinguished from the futures.

addition An addition to a fixed asset already recorded in the property ledger (as distinguished from a newly acquired asset). Examples are additional floor space added to an existing building, and new attachments to a piece of equipment.

add-on purchase Combining a new purchase with an older one, adding it to an existing installment contract. (59)

add-on rate An installment finance method by which the Rate is computed on the advance. The factor for each maturity is pro rata per annum of the Rate. 6% Add-On means $6 per $100 for one year, $9 per $100 for 18 months, $12 per $100 for 24 months, etc., on monthly and seasonal contracts.

addresser A device used in connection with a charge-plate to imprint the customer's name, address, and other data, on the salescheck. (26)

adjudication The decision of a competent court with regard to matters in dispute; to be distinguished from arbitration. (74)

adjustable currency See Elastic Money.

adjusted gross estate The value of an estate after all allowable deductions have reduced the gross estate, but before federal estate taxes. (95)

adjusted trial balance A merger of the trial balance columns of the work sheet with the adjustment columns. The adjusted trial balance represents the trial balance that would be obtained if it were prepared immediately after the adjusting entries are posted. (73)

adjusting entries General journal entries that are made at the end of the fiscal period to bring the asset, liability, income, and expense accounts up to date. (73)

adjustment bond A debt security issued in the recapitalization of a distressed corporation. Since they are income bonds they are sold on a flat basis. See Flat.

adjustment mortgage A mortgage that has been issued out of a reorganization.

adjustments Those deductions made to charge off losses such as from sales of securities or bad debts.

ad litem For the purpose of the suit. (74)

administration The care and management of an estate by a trustee or a guardian; to be distinguished from the settlement of an estate by an executor or an administrator. (74)

administrative board A retirement board or a retirement committee charged with the policy direction of a retirement system. The board may consist of representatives of the employer and employees, and sometimes pensioners. An administrative board is also frequently referred to as the "Pension Board" or "Retirement Board" (32)

administrative employees Management workers exempt from the wage-hour law if administrative regulations are met. (12)

administrative expense budget An estimate of the cash expenditures that will be required for the expenses of the administrative division of the business during the budget year. (73)

administrative law As distinguished from common law or statute law, administrative law results from the regulations of a governmental body, either state or federal, which is responsible for carrying out statute law.

administrative provisions Provisions in a will or trust agreement setting forth the duties and powers of the executor or the trustee regarding the care and management of the property; to be distinguished from dispositive provisions. (74)

administrator A qualified individual or trust company who is appointed by a court of law to manage and distribute the estate of a deceased person where such deceased person died intestate (without leaving a will), or where a will fails to name an Executor. The administrator must carry out the decisions of the court of law having jurisdiction over the estate of the deceased until relieved of the administrative duties upon final distribution of the estate to all claimants approved and recognized by the court. (1)

administrator ad colligendum An administrator appointed to collect foreign assets. (74)

administrator ad litem An administrator appointed by the court to supply a party to an action at law or in equity in which the decedent or his representative was, or is, a necessary party. (74)

administrator cum testamento annexo (Administrator with the will annexed) An individual or a

trust institution appointed by a court to settle the estate of a deceased person in accordance with the terms of his will when no executor has been named in the will or when the one named has failed to qualify. (74)

administrator cum testamento annexo de bonis non (Administrator with the will annexed as to property not yet distributed) An individual or a trust institution appointed by a court to complete the settlement of the estate of a deceased person in accordance with the terms of his will when the executor or the administrator with the will annexed has failed to continue in office. (74)

administrator de bonis non (Administrator as to property not yet distributed) An individual or a trust institution appointed by a court to complete the settlement of the estate of a person who has died without leaving a valid will when the administrator originally appointed has failed to continue in office. (74)

administrator de son tort An individual or corporation charged with the duties and liabilities of an administrator, although not appointed one, because of his or its own wrongdoing with respect to assets in his or its possession. (74)

administrator durante absentia An administrator appointed by the court to serve during the absence of the executor or administrator. (74)

administrator pendente lite An individual or a trust institution appointed by a court to take over and safeguard an estate during a suit over an alleged will, or over the right of appointment of an executor or administrator. (74)

administrator's deed The legal instrument given by a person who is legally vested with the right of administration of an estate, especially of an estate such as that of a minor, or incompetent such as a lunatic, or of a testator having no competent executor. (54 t)

administrator with the will annexed An individual or a trust institution appointed by a court to settle the estate of a deceased person in accordance with the terms of his will when no executor has been named in the will or when the one named has failed to qualify. (74)

administratrix Feminine derivation of the male Administrator.

admission by investment Term meaning that a new partner is admitted into a partnership by contributing additional cash to the business, thereby increasing the assets and the proprietorship of the business. (73)

admitted to dealings Means that official approval by an exchange and the SEC has been granted a security, and it is "admitted to the list", i.e., has the privilege of being traded on that particular exchange. (105)

ad valorem Designates an assessment of taxes against property. Literally, according to the value. (54)

advance 1. A loan, either secured or unsecured. 2. See Overdraft. (31, 74, 92)

advance bill A bill of exchange drawn in advance of the shipment of goods.

advance-decline line An index of comparison between the general market and the Dow-Jones Industrial Average. It is computed by taking an arbitrary number as a base; from this is subtracted the net difference in advances and declines on New York Stock Exchange each day, if declines are predominate, or adding the net difference if advances are predominant. For example, if the base selected is 1000, and there are 600 declines and 400 advances that day, the index would be 800. This index is then plotted on a chart with the D-J averages. If it coincides, it is said to be conforming; if it moves downward while the industrials are advancing, it indicates a deteriorating market; or vice versa, strength is indicated when the Line moves upward and the industrials are declining. (105)

advance funding A method for making contributions to a pension plan in advance of the date when the funds are actually required to meet payments for benefits. Actuarial reserve financed pension plans imply advance funding. (32)

adverse claim As applied to a bank account, a claim to ownership by a person other than the one in whose name the account stands. (90)

adverse possession A possession inconsistent with the right of the true owner. (5)

advice book That record of incoming and outgoing advices.

advice department The department of a bank which processes advices. See also Advices.

advices The term "advices" connotes several types of forms used in the banking field. Generally speaking, an advice is a form of letter that relates or acknowledges a certain activity or result with regard to a depositor's relations with a bank. Examples are: credit advice, debit advice, advice of payment, advice of execution, etc. In commercial transactions, information on a business transaction such as a shipment of goods. (1)

affiant A person who makes an affidavit or statement under oath or affirmation. (74)

affidavit A written, notarized, dated, sworn statement of the facts pertaining to a financial transaction or happening. Such statements must show the name and address, and be signed by the party making the statement, and bear the signature of the attesting official. (1)

affidavit of claim A form required when a claim is filed. In general, it contains the facts on which the claim is based.

affiliate A legal term fully defined in the Banking Act of 1933. Generally, the term pertains to any organization which a bank owns or controls through stock holdings, or which the bank's shareholders own, or whose executive officers are also directors of the bank.

affiliated company Under the Investment Company Act, a company in which there is any direct or indirect ownership of 5 per cent or more of the outstanding voting securities. (3)

As defined under I.C.C., Account 706, the term included companies:
  (a) solely controlled by the accounting company or jointly controlled by the accounting company and others under a joint agreement,
  (b) solely controlling the accounting company or jointly controlling the accounting company under a joint agreement.

  (c) controlled by controlled companies,
  (d) controlled by controlling companies.
By "control" is meant the ability to determine the action of a corporation. (19)

affinity Relationship by marriage; to be distinguished from consanguinity which is relationship by blood. (74)

affreightment A bill of lading. A contract to transport goods by sea; either a charter party or a bill of lading. (51)

afghani Monetary unit of Afghanistan.

after acquired clause That portion of a mortgage which states that any additional property which the mortgagor acquires after the mortgage is drawn will also be security for the loan.

after-acquired property Property acquired by a corporation subsequent to the execution of a mortgage or by a testator subsequent to the making of his will. (74)

after-born child A child born after the execution of the parent's will; to be distinguished from posthumous child. (74)

after date When used in notes or bills the term "after date" refers to the date the document is drawn. Thus, a note dated July 10 bearing the words or figures of "fifteen days after date" would refer to July 25, and the time would be the normal business hours of the community.

against actuals See Exchange of Spot or Cash Commodity for Futures.

against the box A short sale by a holder of a long position in the same security. Several reasons for selling "Against the Box" include: 1. Attempt to not reveal his true position (he can't be caught short). 2. Tax considerations. 3. Inaccessibility of the long shares to make delivery within the required time.

agency A term used to describe certain types of accounts in trust institutions. The main distinguishing characteristic of an agency is that the title to the property does not pass to the trust institution but remains in the name of the owner of the property, who is known as the principal. (88)

agency coupled with an interest An agency in which the agent has a legal interest in the subject matter. Such an agency is not terminated, as are other agencies, by the death of the principal but continues in effect until the agent can realize upon his legal interest. (74)

agenda The order or schedule of doing business at a meeting of an organization.

agent A person who acts for another person by the latter's authority. The distinguishing characteristics of an agent are: (1) that he acts on behalf, and subject to, the control of his principal. (2) that he does not have title to the property of his principal, and (3) that he owes the duty of obedience to his principal's orders. (88)

Called a broker in the securities market. One who is an intermediary between buyers and sellers and charges a commission for his services. (105)

agent de change The French term for stockbroker. (105)

aggregate The total of several values, possessions, obligations. (59)

aggregate balance The calculated accumulation of account balances during the statement period. Used to determine the Average Daily Balance. (83)

aggregate corporation An incorporated venture having more than one stockholder.

aggressive portfolio A securities portfolio held primarily for appreciation rather than defensive quality or yield possibility. (105)

aging accounts receivable A technique for making an analysis of the accounts of a business by segregating them into classes such as those accounts which are current, those which are 30, 60, 90, or over 90 days past due. By comparing the percentages of accounts which are in each classification with those which were in the same classification last month and one year ago a business administrator is able to judge the relative performance of his credit department and the state of his accounts receivable.

agio A premium in the form of interest or some other valued differential. Full bodied gold coins of two different nations might be identical in weight and fineness yet not be traded at identical prices in the foreign exchange markets due to the market preference for one compared to the other. The differential is the agio.

agricultural loans Loans to farmers except those secured by real estate. (4)

agricultural paper Those acceptances, notes and similar documents which have arisen out of agricultural, farming or ranching transactions rather than trade, commerce or industry.

air pocket A sharp, sudden weakness in a particular issue in which the selling is not orderly and the normal range of fluctuation for that security is exceeded.

alienate Transfer title to property. (66)

alimony An allowance made to a woman for her support out of the estate or income of her husband upon her legal separation or divorce from him or during a suit for the same. (35)

allied members The partners or voting stockholders in an exchange member organization who are subject to all of the regulations of the exchange, but do not have the privilege to transact business on the exchange floor other than through their associate who is the exchange member. (105)

allocated expense Proportioned expense, usually by company or function. (42)

allocation The crediting of a receipt in its entirety or the charging of a disbursement in its entirety to one account, as to the principal account or to the income account; to be distinguished from apportionment. (88)

allonge A piece of paper attached to a negotiable instrument so that additional endorsements may be added.

all, or any part A discretionary privilege given to a broker by his client to transact his original buy or sell order in any amount the broker deems proper, limited only by the client's specified price. (105)

all, or none In connection with buy and sell orders, it is understood that the transaction must be executed only for the number of shares stipulated, and no less. In the underwriting business it means that sales of a new issue will become final, only if the entire issue is sold within a specified time. (105)

allot To divide an appropriation (q.v.) into amounts for certain periods or for specific purposes. (29)

allotment The amount of a new issue that is assigned or alloted to a subscriber by a member of the sales organization or syndicate. (105)

allotment ledger A subsidiary ledger which contains an account for each allotment showing the amount allotted, expenditures, encumbrances, the net balance and other related information. See Appropriation Ledger. (29)

allotment notice The document prepared by an investment banker or syndicate manager which states the amount and related details of price and time of payment for securities and is transmitted to the subscriber. It may be for the full amount of securities requested by the subscriber or less.

allottee That individual or firm which has subscribed to purchase securities and has been assigned a share or allotment.

allowance The sum or sums awarded a fiduciary by a court as compensation for its services; to be distinguished from charge, commission, and fee. See Widow's Allowance. (88)

allowance for bad debts Same as "Reserve for Bad Debt"; an account for showing the estimated loss on uncollectable debts as an offset against the value shown for accounting receivable. (73)

allowance for depreciation See Reserve for Depreciation. (73)

alteration Any change involving an erasure or rewriting in the date, amount, or payee of a check or other negotiable instrument. In accounting records, necessary alterations are best made by crossing out the "old" figure, leaving it legible, and writing the correct one above or below the original. (83)

altered check One on which the date, payee, or amount has been changed or erased. A bank is responsible for paying a check as it is originally drawn; consequently, it may refuse to pay a check which has been altered. (1)

alternate account An account in the name of two or more persons, any of whom may draw against the account without further authority from the others. See Joint Account and Survivorship Account. (85)

alternate depositors Holders of a joint account. (A deposit account made out in the names of husband and wife or of two partners which is payable to either or to the survivor is a joint account.)

alternative payee One of two parties to whom an account or negotiable instrument or other bill or draft is payable. Payment to either removes the payor of that extent of his obligation to both or either. In a joint account in the name of a husband or wife the financial institution may pay either as holder of the draft, passbook or other financial instrument.

amalgamation The uniting or combining of two or more businesses. (105)

amendment An addition, deletion, or change in a legal document. (74)

American Bankers Association (A.B.A.). The national organization of banking organized in 1875 to "promote the general welfare and usefulness of banks and financial institutions." The Association consists of about eighty working groups, including four divisions, seven commissions, and a number of councils and committees. The A.B.A. (as it is generally known) has over 16,000 members, representing over 98% of all the banks in the United States and over 99% of the banking resources. (85)

American depository receipts A. document similar to a stock certificate which is registered in the holder's name. The certificate represents a certain number of shares in an alien corporation. Such shares are held by an alien bank that acts as the agent for a domestic commercial bank which has issued the depository receipt.

American Institute of Banking. The educational section of the American Bankers Association, organized in 1900 to provide educational opportunity in banking for bank people. The Institute's activities are carried on through numerous chapters and study groups in many cities and towns. In addition to its regular classes, the Institute conducts correspondence courses. Membership is open only to employees and officers of A.B.A. member institutions. (1)

Americans Term for American securities on the London Stock Exchange. Also called "Yankees." (105)

American Stock Exchange A leading securities exchange located in New York City. Formerly known as the Outdoor Market or New York Curb Exchange because it initially conducted operations outdoors at Wall and Hanover Streets. Moved indoors at 86 Trinity Place in 1921. Present name was adopted in 1953. It is the largest market for foreign securities in the United States. (105)

amortization The gradual reduction of debt by equal periodic payments sufficient to pay current interest plus a portion of the principal which will liquidate the debt at maturity. Also used to indicate the periodic "writing-off" of premiums on investment. (83)

amortization of discount on funded debt A charge to income each fiscal period for a proportion of the discount and expense on funded debt obligations applicable to that period. This proportion is determined according to a rule, the uniform application of which through the interval between the date of sale and date of maturity will extinguish the discount and expense on funded debt. However, the accounting company may, at its option, charge to profit and loss all or any portion of discount and expense remaining unextinguished at any time. (19)

amortization reserve A balance sheet account in which are recorded the net accumulated provisions for the extinguishment of an asset at the end of a predetermined period. (21)

amortized mortgage loan A mortgage loan that provides for repayment within a specified time by means of regular payments at stated intervals (usually monthly, quarterly, or semiannually) to reduce the principal amount of the loan and to cover interest as it is due. (89)

amortized value The investment value of a security determined by the process of Amortization. This value is appropriate for use in connection with bonds which are fully secured, and are not in default as to either principal or interest. (42)

amount at interest Principal sum deposited for the purpose of earning interest. (42)

analysis department The statistical part of an institution concerned with interpretation and preparation of operating data and cost accounting.

analysis history record A statement which contains the profits or losses and other historical conditions concerning the account over a period of time, usually month by month. (83)

analysis paper Paper that is used to analyze the trial balance and to assemble information for the profit and loss statement and the balance sheet. It is ruled with six or more money columns. (73)

analysis, systems The examination of an activity, procedure, method, technique, or a business to determine what must be accomplished and how the necessary operations may best be accomplished. (104)

analyst In the securities business, a trained person who investigates all of the facts concerning a security, company, or industry under study and advises his firm and/or its clients with regard to his conclusions about the merits and/or defects, and the action which should be taken. Analysts may specialize in certain industries as part of an investment research department within their firm. (105)

ancestor One who precedes another in the line of descent. At common law the term ancestor is applied only to a person in direct line of ascent (father, grandfather, or other forebear), but by statute it has been broadened to apply also to a person of collateral relationship (uncle or aunt, for example) from whom property has been acquired. (88)

ancillary Designating or pertaining to a document, proceeding, officer, or office; etc., that is subordinate to, or in aid of, another primary or principal one; as, an ancillary attachment, bill or suit presupposes the existence of another principal proceeding. (54)

Subordinate or auxiliary to something or someone else; used in such terms as ancillary administration, ancillary administrator, and ancillary guardian. (74)

ancillary letters testamentary Letters subordinate or auxiliary to letters testamentary, as, for example, those issued in one jurisdiction for probate of property owned by a nonresident decedent. (74)

ancillary receiver That individual appointed to assist a receiver. Generally, the receiver is handling a foreign corporation (one domiciled outside the state) and the ancillary receiver helps liquidate and handle the claims within his own domestic state reporting to and taking direction from the receiver who is in the foreign state.

and interest (also) and accrued interest A reference to a bond quotation which means that to the quoted price which is given must be added interest at the rate given on the bond to the delivery date.

annual basis The statistical manipulation of data which is for a period of less than a year, to estimate the total results for an entire year. To be accurate, the processing should take into consideration the impact of the seasonal variation.

annual report The formal financial statement issued yearly by a corporation to its share owners. The annual report shows assets, liabilities, earnings — how the company stood at the close of the business year and how it fared profit-wise during the year. (2)

annual return See Yield.

annual statement The annual report made by a company at the close of the fiscal year, stating the company's receipts and disbursements, assets and liabilities. Such a statement usually includes an account of the progress made by the company during the year. (51, 50)

annuity A series of periodic payments for a fixed future period or for life, payable monthly, semiannually, annually or at other specified intervals. It is frequently used to describe a part of the retirement allowance derived from the accumulated contributions made by the member, as distinguished from that part of the retirement allowance financed by employer's contributions which is called a "pension." (32)

annuity, apportionable An annuity that provides for a pro rata fractional payment covering the period from the date of the last regular premium payment to the date of death. (5)

annuity bond An investment, usually one not providing a maturity date. (42)
See Serial Annuity Bonds. (29)

annuity certain An annuity payable for a specified period of time, regardless of the time of death of the annuitant. (32)

annuity certain and life An annuity payable for a specified period of time and for as long thereafter as the annuitant may live. (32)

annuity, consolidated An investment, specifically British Government Bonds or "Consols". (42)

annuity deferred An annuity, commencing more than one year from the payment of a lump sum, or from the commencement of periodic payments, to the insurer. (51)

annuity due An annuity whose first payment is made at the beginning of each period (i.e., month, quarter, year et al.) rather than at the end. (58)

annuity, equity Term formerly used for variable annuities. The annuity is based on investments, mostly in common stocks, which are not guaranteed as to income or liquidation value but are expected or intended to provide a hedge against the impact of inflation on the purchasing power of the fixed annuities. (5)

annuity, group A pension plan providing annuities at retirement to a group of persons under a master contract. It is usually issued to an employer for the benefit of employees. The individual members of the group hold certificates as evidence of their coverage. The most common

type of group annuity provides for the purchase each year of a paid-up deferred annuity for each member, the total amount received by the member at retirement being the sum of these deferred annuities. Another type is the deposit administration plan. (53)

annuity, immediate life A life annuity commencing one month, three months, six months, or one year after purchase, depending on the frequency of the periodic payments. (51)

annuity, installment refund A life annuity with an agreement that the insurer will, on the death of the annuitant, continue payments to a beneficiary until the total of the payments to annuitant and beneficiary equals the consideration paid to the insurer. (51)

annuity, joint and survivor An annuity payable as long as any one of two or more persons survives. (51)

annuity, life An annuity payable as long as the annuitant or annuitants live. (51)

annuity method of depreciation See Depreciation Methods; Annuity. (28)

annuity reserve A monetary sum equal to the actuarial value of future payments to be made on account of an annuity. (32)

annuity reserve fund An amount of sum set aside in a reserve to provide for the payment of annuities. Usually derived from the members' accumulated contributions, or contributions by the members and the employer. (32)

annuity, retirement A deferred annuity for which the premiums, less loading, are accumulated at interest and are used to purchase an annuity at a specified age. Prior to that age the annuitant is entitled to a cash surrender value. In case of death the surrender value is paid to his beneficiary. (51)

annuity, survivorship An annuity payable to the annuitant for the period during which he survives the insured. (51)

annuity table A listing of the present values of $1.00 per year or month payable for life, or for a term of years at specified ages for each sex, computed on the basis of assumed rates of mortality and interest. (32)

annulment A judicial decree that a marriage was void from the beginning. (35)

annunciator boards The large boards on the wall of a stock exchange by which the telephone clerk can get the attention of the firm's Floor Broker. Each broker has a number which is flashed on the board to call the broker, or his messenger, to the firm's booth on the rim of the trading floor. (105)

antecedents In credit analysis this term refers to the business history of the company or individual under investigation. Some credit files have a section labeled "Antecedents Report," which contains the above mentioned history.

antedated check A check which is dated prior to the date on which it is issued — that is, delivered or mailed to the payee. If a check dated July 15, for example, is not issued until July 20, it is an antedated check. (85)

anticipated acceptance An acceptance which is paid prior to the stated terms of payment.

anticipation and intentions data Provide information on the plans of businessmen and consumers regarding their economic activities in the near future. These plans are considered valuable aids to economic forecasting, either directly or as an indication of the state of confidence concerning the economic outlook. In recent years, much progress has been made in compiling such information, and a number of surveys by various private organizations and government agencies now ascertain anticipations and intentions of businessmen and consumers. (124)

anticipation rate A discount or rebate for payment prior to the stated terms of payment.

anticipation, right of The privilege given the mortgagor, by a provision in the mortgage instruments to pay all or any portion of the outstanding balance of the obligation prior to its due date without penalty. (89)

antitrust An action against monopolistic conditions. Opposed to trusts or large combinations of capital. (93)

application-for-loan form A printed form used by most financial institutions which contains a prospective borrower's request for a loan. (31, 92)

application of funds statement Also called Statement of Source and Use of Funds or Where Got-Where Gone Statement. Made from balance sheets to two periods, the statement permits an analysis of the changes which have developed during the period chosen.

appointment Act of authorizing an agent to act for his company. (5)

apportionment The division or distribution of a receipt of a disbursement of property between or among two or more accounts, as between principal and income; to be distinguished from allocation. (74)

appraisal Evaluation of a specific piece of personal or real property, or the property of another as a whole. The value placed on the property evaluated. (1)

appraisal of business An examination to decide how much a business is worth. (93)

appraisal report A written report of the factors considered in arriving at a valuation of a particular piece of property. (31, 93)

appraisal surplus The excess of appraised values over book values. (54)

appraise To make an estimate of value, particularly of the value of the property.
NOTE: If the property is valued for purposes of taxation the inclusive term "assess" is substituted for the above term. (29)

appraiser An individual who makes appraisals.

appreciation The increase in the value of an asset in excess of its depreciable cost which is due to economic and other conditions, as distinguished from increases in value due to improvements or additions made to it. (1)
Term generally used when changes occur in an exchange rate that is not a par value. It makes the currency concerned more expensive in terms of other currencies. Appreciation may involve either discrete or gradual changes in value. See Depreciation. (130)

appreciation rate The index figure used against the actual or estimated cost of a property in computing its cost of reproduction, new as of a different date or under different conditions of a higher price level. (54)

appropriation An authorized sum of money set aside, frequently in a separate fund, to pay certain known or anticipated costs of a given item or service. (1)

appropriation ledger A subsidiary ledger containing an account with each appropriation. Each account usually shows the amount originally appropriated, transfers to or from the appropriation charged against the appropriation, the net balance, and other related information. If allotments are made and a separate ledger is maintained for them, each account in the appropriation ledger usually shows the amount appropriated, transfers to or from the appropriation, the amount allotted, and the unallotted balance. See also Allotment Ledger. (29)

appropriation of income or surplus An action by the board of directors setting aside amounts for specific purposes, such as payment of dividends, allotments to sinking funds, and additional investment. (19)

approved list A list, statutory or otherwise, which contains the authorized investments that a fiduciary may acquire. (74)

approved plan The term used to denote a plan which has been accepted by the U.S. Internal Revenue Service, for tax deduction of contributions thereunder. (32)

arbitrage A technique employed to take advantage of differences in price. If, for example, XYZ stock can be bought in New York for $10 a share and sold in London at $10.50, an arbitrageur may simultaneously purchase XYZ stock here and sell the same amount in London, making a profit of 50 cents a share, less expenses. Arbitrage may also involve the purchase of rights to subscribe to a security, or the purchase of a convertible security—and the sale at or about the same time of the security obtainable through exercise of the rights or of the security obtainable through conversion. See Convertible; Rights. (2)

arbitrage house A financial organization such as private banker, foreign exchange dealer or broker which does business in arbitrage.

arbitrager also **arbitrageur** One who engages in the activity of arbitrage. See Arbitrage.

arbitragist Also called an Arbitrager, or one who conducts an Arbitrage business, i.e., a business for profit in securities whereby a purchase is made in one market and a simultaneous sale in another market at a different (higher) price. (105)

arbitration of exchange The prices of bills of exchange payable in foreign currency varies in different financial centers in the world. Therefore a person in country A may find it profitable to purchase a bill of exchange in country B for payment in country C. This is arbitration of exchange.

array A series of items arranged in a meaningful pattern. (104)

arrears Amount due and unpaid. A bond or preferred stock is "in arrears" when interest or dividends have fallen due but have not been paid. Money due but unpaid. Includes dividends or cumulative preferred stock that have been passed. (3, 116)

arrival draft A draft with shipping documents that is payable upon the arrival of the goods described in the documents. The arrival draft is presented upon receipt to the drawee as a means of preparing him to pay when the goods arrive.

articles of association A certificate similar to one of incorporation which is used by non-stock companies such as charitable, eleemosynary and mutual corporations. It sets forth the pertinent data on the organization and is filed with the appropriate governmental agencies upon approval and becomes part of the public record.

articles of copartnership The written agreement by which a partnership is formed. (73)

articles of incorporation A certificate of incorporation which sets forth the pertinent data on a corporation. The certificate is filed with the appropriate governmental agencies upon approval and becomes part of the public record.

asked price 1. In the case of open-end shares, the price (including the selling charge or load) at which the buyer may purchase stock from the investment company. In the case of closed-end shares, the lowest price at which the stock is then offered for sale in the public market. 2. That price at which a commodity or security is offered for sale either over the counter or on an exchange. 3. The price an owner asks for his stock when he offers it for sale. 4. The lowest offer or quoted round-lot price which any potential seller will accept for a security at any given time. 5. A term used by many newspapers to describe the price per share at which mutual fund shares are being offered to the public. It is synonymous with "offering price." The "offering price" is usually the net asset value per share plus a sales charge. (3, 116, 105, 65)

as per advice Words found on some bills of exchange and drafts that show that the drawee has or is to be informed that the draft has been drawn.

assay The chemical testing or analysis of ores or metals to learn the contents and purity of them.

assay office A place designated for the testing of ore, commodities and bullion as well as foreign coin.

assemblage The act of bringing two or more individuals or things to form an aggregate whole; specifically, the cost or estimated cost of assembling two or more parcels of land under a single ownership and unit of utility over the normal cost or current market prices of the parcels held individually. (54)

assented securities Securities whose holders have agreed to some change in the terms or status of the securities. (Such changes may involve a lower interest rate, a postponement of payment of principal, a reduction in the security or collateral used to back the bond.)

assented stocks or bonds See Assented Securities. (105)

assess To value property officially for the purpose of taxation.
NOTE: The term is sometimes used to denote the levy of taxes, but such usage is not recommended since it fails to distinguish between

the valuing process and the tax levying process. The term is also used erroneously as a synonym for "special assessment". (29)

assessable securities Securities such as common stock or classified A or B stock which stockholders may be forced to pay an amount over the par value. Few securities since the banking acts of the 1930's have this liability. Prior to that time it was found in securities issued by national banks.

assessable stock See Assessable Securities. (105)

assessed value The valuation placed on property by public authority for purposes of taxation. (89)

assessment The attempt to raise additional capital by making a levy on a security. The assumption being that without such assessment for additional capital the corporation will experience difficulties but with additional capital the projected success of the corporation will more than compensate for the levy. A tax assessment consists of placing a value on real or personal property for tax purposes.

assessment (overcall) Additional amounts of capital which an investor may be called upon to furnish beyond the original subscription amount. Overcalls may be mandatory or optional. (125)

assessor The designated public official who makes the official estimate of value. (5)

asset Something represented by a debit balance that is or would be properly carried forward upon a closing of books of account according to the rules or principles of accounting (provided such debit balance is not in effect a negative balance applicable to a liability), on the basis that it represents either a property right or value acquired, or an expenditure made which has created a property right or is properly applicable to the future. Thus, plant, accounts receivable, inventory, and a deferred charge are all assets in balance-sheet classification. (17)

asset, capital Those which are not readily convertible into cash and in the ordinary course of business are not so converted, more often termed "fixed assets." Included in this category are real estate, leaseholds, natural resource lands, machinery and equipment, furniture and fixtures, patterns, drawings, etc. (66)

asset, contingent Those whose realization depends upon future events which may or may not occur. (66)

asset coverage *Direct*-The extent to which net assets (after all prior claims) cover a specific senior obligation, whether bank loans, debentures or preferred stock. It may be expressed in either dollar, percentage or ratio terms.
Overall-The ratio of total assets to the sum of all prior obligations including that of the specific issue under consideration taken at liquidating value. (3)

asset currency Bank notes which are not secured by any specific assets but rather by the general assets of the issuing bank. Several nations have such characteristics. More correctly termed General Asset Currency.

asset, current Those which are readily convertible into cash without substantial loss; also termed quick assets. Included are cash, investments, notes and accounts receivable, and inventories. (66)

asset, dead Those assets which are not productive of income under normal operations. A stand-by machine tool or a high cost facility that is not used except in emergencies is a dead asset during those periods it is not in use.

asset, deferred Assets which are not readily convertible into cash, or subject to current settlement. (19)

asset, fixed Any physical unit necessary for the conduct of a business. It is distinguished from a Current Asset in that it is of a permanent nature and is not consumed in Production. The acquisition of a Fixed Asset, whether purchased or constructed, represents a "Capital Expenditure." (For example, buildings, machinery, furniture and fixtures, trucks and autos, etc.) The gradual decrease in value of fixed assets is recognized as "Depreciation." (28)

asset, fixed register A record (book, card, or sheet) that contains the details of the cost price and the depreciation of the fixed assets. (73)

asset, fixed test Ratio of Fixed Assets to Fixed Liabilities. (1)

asset, fixed to tangible net worth Fixed Assets represent depreciated book values of buildings, leasehold improvements, machinery, furniture, fixtures, tools, and other physical equipment, plus land, if any, and valued at cost or appraised market value. The ratio is obtained by dividing Fixed Assets by Tangible Net Worth. Ordinarily, the relationship between Fixed Assets and Tangible Net Worth should not exceed 100 percent for a manufacturer, and 75 percent for a wholesaler or retailer. Beyond these limits, so disproportionate an amount of capital is frozen into machinery or "bricks and mortar" that the necessary margin of operating funds for carrying receivables, inventories and day-to-day cash outlays, as well as maturing obligations becomes too narrow. This not only exposes the business to the hazards of unexpected developments, such as a sudden change in the business climate, but creates possible drains on income in the form of heavy carrying and maintenance charges should a serious portion of Fixed Assets lie idle for any length of time. (61)

asset, floating A quick asset such as cash, government bonds or prime listed securities.

asset, fluid See Current Assets.

asset, frozen Any asset, which cannot be used by its owner because of legal action. The owner cannot use it, nor can he dispose of the asset until the process of the law has been completed and a decision passed down from the courts.

A motor car which has been impounded by law because of a driving violation is a frozen asset. A building which has been condemned as a public detriment or hazard cannot be occupied nor can it be sold until the restriction of its use has been lifted by process of law. This is also a frozen asset. (1)

asset, gross All property in possession of a company. Gross Assets are the total of the Ledger and Non-Ledger Assets. (42)

asset, hypothecated Things pledged without transferring possession or title. (93)

asset, inactive That portion of total assets which are not in continuous productive use in a business. An emergency pump or storage facility which is not used for an extended period could be an inactive asset.

asset, intangible An asset which has no substance or physical body; it is incorporeal. The most widely known types of intangible assets are known as "Goodwill" and "Patent Rights." These assets are purchased, sometimes for very substantial outlays of capital. Their value to the purchaser lies in the use he can make of them although they cannot be seen. A purchaser buys "Goodwill" in order to take over a business which has enjoyed a fine business reputation for several years. The purchase price of "Goodwill" is determined by the profits a business has enjoyed due to business ethics, quality of the product handled, or desirable location. "Patent Rights" permit a manufacturer to use a patent to his advantage, the patent right being transferred for a consideration by the inventor or holder of the patent right. (1)

asset, ledger Those assets for which accounts are maintained in the General Ledger. (42)

asset, liquid Those assets, generally current assets, which may be quickly turned into cash.

asset, minus A term applied to the amount that must be subtracted from the original value of an asset in order that the present value of the asset may be known. (73)

asset, net Generally used to describe total assets at market value less current liabilities. (3)

asset, net value A term usually used in connection with investment trusts, meaning net asset value per share. It is common practice for an investment trust to compute its assets daily, or even twice daily, by totaling the market value of all securities owned. All liabilities are deducted, and the balance divided by the number of shares outstanding. The resulting figure is the net asset value per share. See Assets; Investment Trust. (2)

asset, nominal An asset whose value is inconsiderable, doubtful or difficult to evaluate such as judgments or claims in reorganization. Accounting conventions generally recommend that nominal assets be written down and carried at some token value. The customary amount is one dollar. This calls attention to the asset but also conservatively values it. Goodwill, copyrights and such assets may be considered at times to be nominal assets.

asset, non-accrual An asset, such as a loan, which has been questioned upon bank examination, or which is known to be a "slow" or "doubtful" loan. A reserve is set up or applied on this type of loan, and it is excluded from the earning or accrual assets. As funds are collected on these loans, they are applied to the principal until the principal is fully collected. The remaining payments are applied to interest.

asset, non-ledger Assets not carried in the General Ledger, such as accrued dividends, uncollected and deferred premiums, and excess of Market Value of securities over Book Value. (42)

asset, ordinary Any asset that is purchased and sold as a regular part of a continuing business activity. What may be an ordinary asset to one business may be a capital asset to another. A real estate broker-developer who sells land would be selling an ordinary asset but a retail merchant would be selling a capital asset if he sold land. The term has significance for tax purposes in regard to capital gains as compared to income.

asset, original Stocks, bonds, or other property received in a trust at the time of its creation, or an estate at the time of appointment of the executor or administrator. (74)

asset, permanent A capital or fixed asset. See both terms.

asset, personal An asset that is owned for personal use. (73)

asset, physical See Assets, Tangible. (66)

asset, pledged Securities owned by a bank, generally United States government bonds and obligations, specified by law, which must be pledged as collateral security for funds deposited by the United States government, or state or municipal governments. (1)

asset, quick Those current assets which can be immediately converted to cash; does not include inventories or other current assets that might take some time to convert to cash.

asset, risk (National Bank Examiners' terminology). In its most restricted sense, all bank assets except cash and U.S. government obligations; under a somewhat broader definition (also used by the examiners), all bank assets except cash, direct U.S. government obligations, obligations of federal agencies, loans secured by an equal par value of direct U.S. obligations, and government guaranteed loans (including FHA Title II loans, but not FHA Title I loans). (33, 103)

asset, tangible Those assets which are of a physical and material nature (perceptible to touch) as distinguished from intangible assets which are imperceptible to touch. Examples of tangible assets are: cash, land, buildings, etc. (1)

assets, total All money, equipment, real estate, and credits owned by a business.

asset, value *Per Common Share*-company's net resources (after deduction of all liabilities, preferred stocks' liquidating value and accrued dividends, if any), divided by the number of common shares outstanding.

Per Preferred Share-another way of showing asset coverage, company's net resources (after deduction of all liabilities, any prior preferred stocks' liquidating value and accrued dividends, if any), divided by the number of preferred shares outstanding. (3)

asset, wasting Mines, timber lands, quarries, and other like assets which diminish in value by the removal of their product. (29)

asset, working Those assets invested in securities that can be expected to fluctuate more or less with common stock prices generally. Corrections may be made to eliminate an investment company's holdings of cash and high-grade senior securities and to give weight to holdings of junior issues. (3)

assign To transfer to another. A person to whom property is assigned. (35)

assignat Paper money issued during the French Revolution which was backed by land that was taken from the church and aristocracy. The money was later repudiated.

assigned account An account, usually receivable, which has been assigned to a bank as security for a loan by a borrower. In theory, the bank takes possession of the account pledged. In actual practice, however, in order not to jeopardize the relationship between the borrower and his customer (whose account has been pledged), the bank will allow the account to be paid by the customer in the normal manner, and will rely upon the integrity of the borrower to apply this payment against the loan balance. (83)

assigned book account See Assigned Account.

assigned expense Expense incurred by a particular function. (42)

assigned in blank Space for name of new owner is left blank upon formal transfer, or assignment, of title to a security or other property. (105)

assignee One to whom property, or a limited interest, is transferred. (42)

assignment The transfer of the legal right or interest in a policy to another party, generally in connection with the sale of property. In many kinds of insurance it is valid only with the consent of the insurer. In life insurance, usually binding on the insurer only if filed with the insurer. The transfer, after an event insured against, of one's right to collect an amount payable under an insurance contract. (52, 51, 50)

assignment in blank The transfer of title signed by the previous owner in which the name of the new owner is not filled in but rather left blank. A Street Certificate is an example of a security in which the assignment is in blank. See Street Certificate.

assignment of leases Additional security often taken in connection with mortgages of commercial properties. (121)

assignment of rents A written document which transfers to a mortgagee on default, the owner's right to collect rents. (31, 92)

assignment separate from certificate Refers to a detached assignment or stock (bond) power. This document is identical to the back part of the security, and includes a description of the security. This enables the holder to transfer the certificate safely by sending the unsigned certificate and properly filled out stock power under separate cover. One without the other has no value, so little harm would result if one happened to be lost or stolen. (105)

assignment to creditors The transfer of property in trust or for the benefit of creditors. (35)

assignor The person who assigns a mortgage or insurance agreement. (5)

assimilation The successful distribution of new securities to the public by the underwriters of the issue and the members of their syndicate.

associated banks Banks which are associated through membership in a clearing house association.

Associated Credit Bureaus of America, Inc. Membership organization of credit bureaus and collection service departments throughout the nation. Facilities inter-bureau credit reporting by means of a "coupon" system. (26)

association A savings association, savings and loan association, building and loan association, co-operative bank or homestead association. (31, 92)

assumpsit An action to recover damages for a breach or non-performance of a contract or promise, oral or in writing. (35)

assumption of debt Taking on another's debt. (93)

at a discount A security selling in the market place below par value. (105)

at a premium A security selling in the market place above par value. May also refer to an extra amount charged for borrowing a stock for delivery on a short sale due to scarcity of particular security. If the redemption price of a security is higher than market price or face value, it is said to be redeemed at a premium. (105)

at call A transaction in the call money market.

at or better Instructions to a broker to purchase a stated number of shares at the price instructed or if the market conditions permit at a better, more favorable (lower) price for the purchaser.

at par A security price which equals par or face value. (105)

at seller's option See Seller's Option.

at sight A term used in drafts, and bills of exchange, indicating that payment is due on demand or presentation. (83)

attached account An account against which a court order has been issued, permitting disbursement of the attached balance ONLY with the consent of the court. (83)

attachment A transfer of the right to receive payments or other benefits under a contract. The one who transfers the right is the "Assignor"; the one to whom the right is transferred is the "Assignee". (89)

attachment ledger Attached accounts are usually separated from free accounts, since they require court orders to pay out funds. The book or ledger in which these accounts are kept is called the "attachment ledger." (1)

attest To bear witness to; as, to attest a will or other document. (88)

attestation clause The clause of a document containing the formal declaration of the act of witnessing; in the case of a will, the clause immediately following the signature of the testator and usually beginning, "Signed, sealed, published, and declared by the said ⁚ . ." (74)

attested wills The most common form of will. It is in writing, handwritten or typewritten, signed by the testator or by someone for him and acknowledged by him. His signature must be witnessed by two or more adults at the time of execution.

attesting witness One who testifies to the authenticity of a document, as the attesting witness to a will; to be distinguished from subscribing witness. (74)

at the close An order to be executed at the best price attainable at the close of the market on the day it is entered, except on the American Stock Exchange where Rule 130 would be violated. (105)

at the market An order to buy or sell a security or commodity "at the market" calls for its execu-

tion at the best possible price when the order reaches the trading floor. See Floor; GTC; Limited Order; Stop Limit Order. (2)

at the opening An order that is to be executed at the best price attainable at the opening of the market, without a set price limit. Odd-lot orders at the opening are dependent upon the opening price for the round-lot. (105)

In the case of round-lots, an order to purchase or sell must be executed at the opening of the trading session. In the case of an odd-lot, an order to purchase or sell must be executed at the regular odd-lot differential from the round-lot. A purchase of an odd-lot would be at ⅛ of a point or 12 & ½ cents per share higher than the round-lot opening price in most cases while a sale would be at ⅛ of a point or 12½ cents per share lower than the opening price.

at thirty days sight Term meaning that the drawee is allowed thirty days' time on a time draft from the date of his acceptance in which to pay the paper. (73)

attorney at law A person who is legally qualified and authorized to represent and act for clients in legal proceedings; to be distinguished from attorney in fact. (74)

attorney in fact A person who, acting as agent, is given written authorization by another person to transact business for him out of court; to be distinguished from attorney at law. See also Power of Attorney. (74)

auction A sale by verbal bids to the individual making the highest bid.

auction market A market where goods are freely sold to the highest bidder. The New York Stock Exchange is the largest securities auction. Brokers on the floor exchange bids and offers until an agreement is reached as to price and the transaction is effected. (105)

audit In general, an examination of accounting documents and of supporting evidence for the purpose of reaching an informed opinion concerning its propriety. An examination intended to serve as a basis for an expression of opinion regarding the fairness, consistency, and conformity with accepted principles, of statements prepared by a corporation or other entity for submission to the public or to other interested parties. (17)

audit committee A committee that the president or board of directors of an organization appoints to check and report upon the accuracy of the treasurer's records. (73)

audited voucher A voucher which has been examined and approved for payment. See Accounts Payable. (29)

auditor An officer of a bank who is in charge of the regular examination and checking of accounts or financial records. In some banks he is directly responsible to the Board of Directors. (83)

auditor's certificate A statement signed by an auditor in which he states that he has examined the financial statements, the system of internal control, the accounting records, and supporting evidence in accordance with generally accepted auditing standards and in which he expresses his opinion, based on such examination, regarding the financial condition of the governmental unit or any of its enterprises, the results from operations, and any facts which he has investigated in his professional capacity. (29)

audit program A detailed outline of work to be done and the procedure to be followed in any given audit. (29)

audit report The report prepared by an auditor covering the audit or investigation made by him. As a rule, the report should include: (a) a statement of the scope of the audit; (b) summary of findings; (c) recommendations; (d) certificate; (e) financial statements; and (f) sometimes statistical tables. (29)

audit trail An auditing concept that provides, in a step-by-step fashion, the history of an account by carrying in the account master file, the date and serial number of the last previous transaction. This allows the auditor to trace back all transactions affecting the account. (83)

authenticated copy A copy of an instrument on which is an attestation in the manner required by law by an official authorized to make such certification, as by the certification and seal of a specified public official. (74)

authentication Applied to bonds, the signing, by the trustee, of a certificate on a bond for the purpose of identifying it as being issued under a certain indenture, thus validating the bond. (74)

authority to purchase (letter of credit). This term is generally used in connection with Far Eastern Trade. It is a substitute for a "Commercial Letter of Credit" and permits the bank to which it is directed to purchase drafts drawn on an importer rather than on a bank. Drafts drawn under authority to purchase have to be marked with the "A/P" number and must conform to the conditions of the letter of authority to purchase. Drafts drawn under "A/Ps" are usually confined to United States dollar transaction and branch or correspondent banks in the cities where such drafts originate. (1)

authorization index Listing of credit customers by name and address, credit limits, and other instructions or restrictions. Can be arranged alphabetically or geographically. In the latter case the street number is the primary key to the index. (26)

authorized capital stock The total amount of stock that a corporation is permitted by its charter to issue. (73)

authorized investment An investment that is authorized by the trust instrument; to be distinguished from legal investment. (74)

authorized issue The amount of a security issue stipulated in the corporation charter which can be changed only by amendment. (105)

authorizer Person in credit office designated to approve or disapprove requests for purchases to be charged to credit accounts. (26)

automatic currency See Elastic Money.

autonomous investment The formation of new capital without regard for the cost of the investment in terms of interest rate or of national income. Most investments by public agencies are autonomous while most investments by private profit seeking individuals or agencies would be induced.

auxiliary account A contra, offset or adjunct account which is associated with a principal account.

availability date The date on which checks payable at out-of-town banks are considered collected and converted into cash. It is determined by the geographical location of the drawee bank, in relation to time and distance from the sending bank. Many banks have charts specifying the date on which a depositor may draw against checks deposited and payable at out-of-town points. (1)

available assets Those assets of an individual or firm which may be easily sold to meet a need. Such assets normally would not be mortgaged or pledged.

available balance The book balance less any hold, uncollected funds, and restrictions against an account. (83)

available fund The amount of cash or damand deposits which an individual or firm may obtain to meet a need. Such assets normally would not be pledged.

avails The proceeds of a discounted note. The amount which a borrower receives on a note which is discounted.

average annual bill per customer Annual revenue (exclusive of discounts and penalties) from a class of service divided by the average annual number of customers for that class of service. (21)

average balance The total of the daily balances in an account during a month divided by the number of days in the month (or period). In banking, a high average balance for an account (all things being equal—such as number of checks drawn) generally indicates a more profitable account than one with a low balance.

average book The record kept by a lender such as a bank in which various averages such as the average balance, average loan, by customer are posted as a means of statistical analysis and to provide management with essential data for decision making.

average collected balance The average collected balance of a depositor's account is usually determined on a monthly basis. It is arrived at by adding the daily balances of the account, and deducting the sum of the float, or uncollected items, from the formal total, and dividing the remainder by the number of days in the month. (1)

average daily balance The average amount of money that a customer keeps on deposit, determined by adding the daily balances of his account for a given length of time and dividing the total by the number of days covered, (the mean average). (83)

average hourly earnings As distinguished from hourly wage rate, the average hourly earnings takes total monetary compensation and divides it by the number of hours worked. Whereas average hourly wage rate is based upon regular hours of employment and does not include premium for overtime or bonuses. The average hourly earnings does include all such premiums including the shift differential.

average loan file See Average Book.

average number of customers The average of the number of customers counted regularly once in each of twelve consecutive months. (21)

average out To conclude a trade or commitment in the market without loss, or at a profit, by the process of averaging; i.e., buying securities at different prices, but selling at a time when price is equal to, or better than, the average price of purchases. (105)

average price The mean, or average, price of a security obtained in the purchase or sale of a security by the process of averaging; i.e., buying or selling securities at various prices to establish an average price on the total transaction. (105)

average revenue The total amount received from sales divided by the number of items sold.

averages Various ways of measuring the trend of securities prices on a stock exchange, the most popular of which is the Dow-Jones average of 30 industrial stocks. The term average has led to considerable confusion. A simple average for, say, 50 leading stocks would be obtained by totaling the prices of all and dividing by 50. But suppose one of the stocks in the average is split. The price of each share of that stock is then automatically reduced because more shares are outstanding. Thus, the average would decline even if all other issues in the average were unchanged. That average thus becomes useless as an indicator of the market's trend.

Various formulas—some very elaborate—have been devised to compensate for stock splits and stock dividends and thus give continuity to the average. Averages and individual stock prices belong in separate compartments.

In the case of the Dow-Jones industrial average, the prices of the 30 stocks are totaled and then divided by a divisor which is intended to compensate for past stock splits and dividends and which is changed from time to time. As a result, point changes in the average have only the vaguest relationship to dollar price changes in stocks included in the average. See Point; Split. (2)

averaging up or down The practice of making purchases of the same security at different price levels, thereby arriving at a higher or a lower average cost than the first commitment. (103)

award 1. The acceptance by a borrower of a competitive bid for a security issue in the form of notification to the high bidder investment banker or syndicate. 2. The findings of a competent court or board on a matter to be settled by such a body in favor of one of the parties to the case.

B

B Class B bonds or stocks.

B. Means Class "B" or Series "B" when accompanied by other letters and printed on the top line of the ticker tape. Means "bid" or "buyer" when printed on the bottom line of the tape, preceding prices. (105)

Bal. Balance.

B.B.B. Banker's blanket bond. (5)

Bd. Bond; Board.

B/D Bills discounted.

B/E. Bill of exchange.

Bel. Fcs. Belgian Francs.

BFCU Bureau of Federal Credit Unions. (67)

B.F.P. Bona fide purchaser.

B.I.S. Bank for International Settlements.

Bk. Bank.

Bkg Banking.

Bkr Broker.

Bks Books.

Bk Town Banking Town.

B/L Bill of Lading.

B. & L. Assn. Building and Loan Association.

B/L Atchd. Bill of Lading attached.

Bo. Bonding. (5)

B. of L. or B/L Bill of Lading.

B/P Bills Payable.

B/P Burden of proof.

B/R Bills Receivable.

Br. Branch.

B. S. Bill of sale; balance sheet.

B/S Bill of sale.

Bt. Bought.

B/V Book value.

backdoor listing The practice of a company making itself eligible for listing on an exchange by acquiring a listed company and merging itself into acquisition, after failing to meet the listing requirements of an exchange by itself. (105)

backlog The existence and accumulation of unfilled orders on a company's books. (105)

backspread That less than normal price difference in an arbitrage transaction. If a spread of 5% between a currency, commodity or security is the general and long standing difference in one market compared with another for such reasons as costs of insurance, telegrams, interest, etc., and the spread drops below 5% it is termed "backspread".

bad debts Commercially speaking, bad debts are the amounts due on open account that have been proved to be uncollectable. Financial institutions, as well as commercial enterprises, charge current operations with an amount (usually a given per cent of the total outstanding) which past experience indicates to be the amount (or percentage) of the accounts or loans outstanding that will be uncollectable. The amount charged to current operations is credited to an account termed "Reserve for Bad Debts." See Reserve. (1)

bad debts collected Amounts previously written off as uncollectable that are subsequently collected; a financial income account that shows by its credit entries the collections of accounts that had been previously written off as uncollectable. (73)

bad debts expense The expense account in which the amount of loss on uncollectable debts is debited. (73)

bad delivery Security and commodity exchanges have specific regulations on delivery of certificates, titles, payment, etc. When delivery does not comply with these regulations it constitutes Bad Delivery.

bad loans See Bad Debts.

baht Monetary unit of Thailand.

bailee A "legal entity" (see definition) which is entrusted with an article for safekeeping. Under the terms of the agreement, the bailee receives the article, shows due care and caution in its protection, and returns the article to the lawful owner in exactly the same state and condition in which it was received for safekeeping. The owner pays a fee to the bailee for this protective service. (1)

bailee's receipt That document used instead of a Trust Receipt by a bailee which is given to the holder of title. Used generally by banks in those cases where the credit standing of the bailee is poor, instead of the less effective Trust Receipt.

bailment Delivery of personal property for a particular purpose with the intent that the property will be returned to the person who originally delivered it. Storage of goods, the pledge of securities as collateral are examples of bailments. (5)

bailor The individual who delivers personal property to another in trust. Title to the property is retained by the bailor subject to the claim for services of the bailee.

balance The amount standing to the credit of a customer's account, representing the amount he is entitled to withdraw. The difference between total debits and credits, whether against or in favor of a bank at the clearinghouse. (83)

balance as a whole A form of proof method employed in banks, usually in the bookkeeping department. A control total is established for several books or ledgers. Each bookkeeper processes her work by posting to her accounts. At the end of the posting run, several bookkeepers will add their combined totals, and will "balance as a whole" to the control total for their group of ledgers. (1)

balance changes See Account Activity. (83)

balance-column ledger ruling Three column ledger ruling that provides a debit column, a credit column, and a balance column. The balance column is used for showing the balance of the account after each entry has been posted. (73)

balanced funds Refers to Investments Companies that diversify their holdings among a wide list of bonds, preferred stocks and common stock. For example, during generally high market periods they would increase their holdings in defensive issues, or bonds and preferreds; and in low market periods, more aggressive issues, such as common stocks, would be sought. (105)

balance due Amount still owing. (93)

balance of account The amount required to equalize the total debits and total credits posted to a given account. Balances are of three types: *Zero*—indicating that total debits and total credits are equal; *Debit Balance*—indicating the excess of total debits; and *Credit Balance*—indicating the excess of total credits over total debits, at a given moment of time. (1)

balance of payments In international finance, the difference between all visible and invisible trade payments made by a nation to foreign creditors and the visible and invisible items paid by foreign debtors during a stated period of time. Invisible items would include such payments of foreign exchange for insurance, shipping and immigrant remittances.

balance of trade In international finance, the relationship, expressed in monetary units between the nations exports and imports. If the exports exceed the imports the term favorable balance of trade is used. If imports exceed the exports it is termed unfavorable balance of trade. Annual figures are generally used.

balance on goods and services The algebraic sum of exports and imports of goods and services. It includes merchandise trade (exports and imports of goods) and the so-called "invisible" items—shipping charges, income on investments, rents, royalties, payments for insurance, donations, and travel.

A surplus balance on goods and services is compatible with an export of capital or an accumulation of foreign exchange reserves. On the other hand, a deficit balance on goods and services must be financed by an import of capital or a drawing down of foreign exchange reserves. (124)

balance on goods and services excluding transfers under military grants Is given in order to show the relationship between flows of goods and services and capital plus reserve movements. Transfers made under military grants are accounted for in two, exactly offsetting entries and, therefore, have no net effect on the other flows in the balance of payments.

The balance on goods and services, excluding transfers under military grants, corresponds to the net exports of goods and services in the National Income and product accounts. (124)

balance on goods, services, and unilateral transfer The balance on goods, services, and unilateral transfers represents the balance on current account which—except for errors and omissions—must be counterbalanced by capital movements, a change in official reserves, or both.

All transactions involving transfers of goods and services are included in the current account, with the exception of monetary gold transactions, which are recorded as a component part of U.S. official reserve assets.

The balance on goods, services, and unilateral transfers is net foreign investment by the United States. (124)

balance sheet A condensed statement showing the nature and amount of a company's assets, liabilities and capital on a given date. In dollar amounts the balance sheet shows what the company owned, what it owed, and the ownership interest in the company of its stockholders. See Assets; Earnings Report. (2)

balance sheet tests The application of ratio and statement analysis to a firm's balance sheet. Generally, comparison is made with model statements such as are available from Dun & Bradstreet, Robert Morris Associates and trade associations, as well as other ratios as the quick ratio, the iron ratio, the current ratio.

balance slip An itemized list prepared daily of coin and paper money to verify the correctness of the cash register audit tape strip. (73)

balances with domestic banks The total amounts that reporting member banks have on deposit in other commercial banks. (4)

balance transfer The process of forwarding the balance from an old to a new ledger sheet. All or part of the old ledger becomes a statement of account which will be sent to a customer. (83)

balancing The ultimate act of bringing two sets of related figures into agreement. As in proof work—the total of deposits being in agreement with the totals of all items making up the deposits—this is "balance" in banking parlance. All work in banks must be in balance, all debits equalling all credits, etc. Minor errors that develop from large volumes are carried into "difference" or "suspense" accounts (see definitions) until uncovered by audits, or customers' discrepancies reported and located. Adjustments are then made, and the difference account properly adjusted. (1)

balancing an account The process of determining the balance of an account, writing it on the smaller side, totaling and ruling the account, and bringing the balance into the new section of the account below the double lines. (73)

balboa Monetary unit of Panama.

ballooning A stock market level or quotation which is considered to be too high to be maintained.

An outlawed practice of manipulation by which prices of stocks, groups of stocks or the market would be forced to over-inflated levels far beyond their intrinsic value. (105)

balloon loan A loan in which small periodic payments are made during the term of the loan. These sums are not sufficient to pay the full loan so that at the end of the period there is a need to refinance the loan since the last payment is a balloon or large amount that was not expected to be paid in full. Credit insurance of level term or decreasing term life may be written. The latter is more appropriate for a balloon loan. (5)

bank An organization, normally a corporation, chartered by the state or federal government, the principal functions of which are:
1. To receive demand deposits and pay customers' checks drawn against them.
2. To receive time deposits and pay interest thereon.
3. To discount notes, make loans, and invest in government or other securities.
4. To collect checks, drafts, notes, etc.
5. To issue drafts and cashier's checks.
6. To certify depositor's checks.
7. When authorized by a chartering government, it may act in a fiduciary capacity. (83)

bankable bill A document that may easily be discounted at a bank.

bankable paper Sometimes called "bank paper" Any paper which meets the credit standards for acceptance or endorsement by a bank. See Bankable Bill.

bank acceptance A draft drawn on a bank and accepted by the bank. (85)

bank account Accounts may be established in the name of individuals or firms. They may be time or demand. They may be single name, multiname, joint, or trustee. They may be general or for some specific purpose such as Travel or a Christmas account. They may require a minimum balance or they may be drawn upon by check or may require a pass book. They may, if time accounts, be paid interest, but if demand, are not usually paid interest.

bank balance The amount in a depositor's account after adding all deposits to the previous balance and subtracting the depositor's checks and service charges. (73)

bank book A passbook used by banks to post entries such as deposits, withdrawals, and interest for a customer. The customer retains possession of the book with the bank teller making the entries upon its presentation.

bank books A bank's records of the status of other banks' deposits with them and vice versa. (Sometimes called "Banks and Bankers" or "B and B.") Term "Bank Book" sometimes used in lieu of "Passbook." (83)

bank call The demand made upon a bank by a supervisory authority for a sworn statement of the bank's condition as of a certain date. Synonym: Call Report. (83)

bank charge plans A relatively new and important development in the general field of consumer credit. Usually a copyrighted plan brought to a community by a bank or private organization under charter or franchise for providing a complete credit service including credit authorization, billing, and collection of 30-day accounts for representative stores. Most banks charge 5% or less of total credit sales for their service. (26)

bank check (Also called treasurer's check, officer's check, or cashier's check.) A check drawn by a bank on itself and signed by an authorized officer. Savings banks do not usually draw such checks. (90)

bank clearing See Clearings. (1)

bank credit The credit created by commercial banks through the media of loans and discounts—granted with or without collateral. The amount of credit so extended is controlled in part by the rediscount rates established by the Federal Reserve Board. A specified sum up to which one will be allowed to draw money from a bank upon the deposit of security. (1, 93)

bank credit proxy The average deposit liability (including demand and time deposits and individuals, businesses and governments) of member banks. This data is available daily to the Federal Reserve Banks and is used as a relative correlation of the loans and investments of member banks. The latter figure is not available daily.

bank debits The sum total of all debits (made up of sight drafts honored and checks and other instruments) drawn against deposited funds of individuals, partnerships, corporations and other legal entities during a given period of time—usually reported by banks daily. The total volume of bank debits for a given subdivision of the nation, and the nation as a whole, is used by statisticians and economists to forecast economic trends. (1)

bank deposit The placing of money or other valuables in a bank for safekeeping.

bank directors Persons selected by the stockholders of a bank from among their own number. The directors are responsible to the stockholders for profitable management and to government supervisory authority for operation of the bank according to law and sound banking principles. (85)

bank discount The charge, generally expressed as a percent of the face amount of the commercial paper or personal note which is made by a bank for payment before maturity of a note. (i.e. A note for $1,000 dollars due in one month might be "discounted" by the bank and the holder paid $980. This would be a 6% discount or ½% per month. (½% x 12 months equals 6%.)

bank draft A check drawn by one bank on its funds on deposit in another bank. The usual purpose is to aid collection of the check by draft on a bank in the area in which it will be negotiated. (83)

bank-eligible issues (Government bond terminology.) Issues of U.S. Treasury obligations eligible for immediate purchase by commercial banks—mainly those due or callable within ten years. (103)

bank endorsement An endorsement stamped on the back of items passing through the bank. This endorsement is stamped on the items either by a hand stamp or by endorsing machines. Banks either endorse or identify all items taken in through the teller's window or deposited through the mail except, "On Us" checks cashed, or coming into the bank from clearing house exchanges or in cash letters. The banks in the larger cities may use endorsing equipment whereby they can delete a portion of the bank endorsement, and show only the date and A.B.A. transit number of the bank sending in the items. In this way, these banks can identify any item as to the bank which sent it to them. Bank endorsements contain the following legend: "Pay to the order of any bank, banker, or trust company. All prior endorsements guaranteed." The endorsement will show the date, the bank's name in full, and the bank's transit number, usually in two places. Bank endorsements are very important to all bankers, in that they provide a means of tracing items through the collection channels of the banking system. In this connection, see also definitions of Examine for Bank Endorsement and Return Item. (1)

bankers acceptance An acceptance, the payment of which has been guaranteed by a bank. (83)

banker's pool The combination of prominent financial and banking interests during the 1929 market break to support key issues, but which ended in a futile effort to stabilize the market. (105)

banker's shares Management Shares. Shares issued to the investment bankers which frequently in the past were able to control or manage the company because of voting features which the banker's shares had as compared to the lack of vote or fractional vote of other shares such as Class A stock.

bank examination An examination made by representatives of a federal or state bank supervisory authority, to make certain that a bank is solvent and is operating in conformity with banking laws and sound banking principles. (85)

bank examiner A person who, as the representative of a federal or state bank supervisory authority, examines the banks under its jurisdiction with respect to their financial condition, management, and policies. (83)

bank exchanges Those items such as checks, notes, drafts, etc., which are collected through a clearing house system.

bank for cooperatives A financial institution created as part of the Farm Credit Administration to provide credit to farm cooperatives.

bank for international settlements Financial institution in Basel, Switzerland formed to help settle the financial claims resulting from World War I.

bank holding company In general usage, any company which owns or controls one or more banks. However, a bank holding company as defined in the Bank Holding Company Act of 1956 is one which controls *two* or more banks. Such companies must register with the Board of Governors of the Federal Reserve System and are commonly referred to as "registered bank holding companies." (128)

bank holiday Any day so designated by competent state authority or national authority. Most bank holidays are determined by state custom and may not be celebrated outside a state or region. (For example Gen. Lee's and Jefferson Davis' birthdays are observed in some southern states as bank holidays but not in the rest of the country.) About five holidays are observed in all states, New Year's, Washington's Birthday, 4th of July, Labor Day, and Christmas. During emergencies some states and the national government have declared bank holidays for the purpose of preventing runs.

bank indorsement See Bank Endorsement.

banking business Primarily the business of receiving funds on deposit and making loans. (1)

banking department That part of a state or federal agency which is concerned with the enforcement of the respective banking code.

banking house The physical building that is used by a bank in its regular function of banking.

banking legislation Those state and federal statutes which regulate banking. Of major importance are the National Banking Act, The Federal Reserve Banking Act with amendments, The Bank Deposit Insurance Act, the Banking Act of 1933, of 1934 and 1935.

banking power The ability of a bank or a system of banks to expand the supply money by the making of loans up to the maximum permitted by a fractional reserve system.

banking syndicate The association of a group of banks for the purpose of underwriting and selling of an issue of securities.

banking system The type, structure, and method of operation of a nation's or state's banks.

bank insolvency That situation in which the capital of a bank is impaired and the proper authorities (in national banks, the Comptroller of the Currency; in state banks, the State Banking Commissioner or the Superintendent of Banking) decide to close and liquidate a bank. If insured by the Federal Deposit Insurance Corporation, they take steps to reduce losses by such devices as loans, encouraging merger or sale of the insured banks assets.

bank ledger See Due to Banks. (1)

bank note A noninterest-bearing promissory note of a bank issued for general circulation as money and payable to the bearer on demand. In the United States only the Federal Reserve Banks now issue bank notes. (85)

bank number See A.B.A. Number. (83)

bank of circulation See Bank of Issue.

bank of deposit In one sense, any bank which accepts any type of deposit (time, demand, escrow, etc.) is a bank of deposit. However, it is generally used to refer to commercial banks which accept deposits subject to demand check withdrawal.

bank of discount Those banks, generally commercial banks, which will extend credit on acceptances, bills of exchange and notes. Such financial institutions as Mortgage Banks, Investment Banks, and Savings Banks are not generally considered to be banks of discount though they may extend credit on notes which often are secured. While Federal Reserve Banks engage in discounting it is properly known as rediscounting since the notes already have been discounted by the borrowing commercial bank.

bank of issue A bank that is legally permitted to issue money such as bank notes.

bank paper 1. Any paper which bears acceptance or endorsement by a bank. 2. Any paper which meets the credit standards for acceptance or endorsement by a bank.

bank passbook Small book issued by the bank to a depositor to record his deposits. (73)

bank post remittance Any bill of exchange of foreign origin which a bank has honored and pays through the use of the mail either by money order or by cash.

bank premises Book value of building and equipment. (4)

bank rate The interest rate charged by the bank on typical loans. Also the discount rate established by a central bank. This is the rate that the commercial bank must pay to discount or borrow from the central bank.

bank reconciliation A technique for comparing the balance shown in a checking account with the monthly statement received from the bank. If there are not bookkeeping errors the balance shown in the check book will exceed the bank statement by the amount of the checks which have been drawn but not presented to the bank for payment.

bank reference Many creditors require a new account or debtor to provide them with the name and permission to inquire of their bank. The "bank reference" given by the new account is contacted and requested to furnish broad credit information about the subject of the inquiry.

bank reserves Commercial banks that are mem-

bers of the Federal Reserve System are required to keep a proportion of their deposit liabilities in the form of reserves with the Federal Reserve District Bank or till cash. Non-member state banks must comply with their individual state banking law requirements.

bank return A statement of a check clearinghouse.

bank run A situation in which abnormally large withdrawals are made on a bank out of fear that the bank may close.

bankrupt Insolvent, unable to pay debts. The Bankruptcy Act is a federal statute, providing for distribution of assets of a bankrupt to specified creditors. A voluntary petition in bankruptcy is one filed by a person, persons, firm or corporation, seeking relief from debts. An involuntary petition in bankruptcy is one filed by a group of creditors against a person, firm or corporation believed involved to the extent of being bankrupt. (35)

bankruptcy A state of conditions in which the financial position of an individual, corporation or other legal entity is such as to cause them to be actually or legally bankrupt. Such condition is commonly referred to as a condition of insolvency. (1)

Bankruptcy Act The National Bankruptcy Act governing Bankruptcy. (1)

bank service charge A monthly charge made by a bank when a depositor's balance is less than a fixed sum in order to compensate the bank for the expense of handling a small account. (73)

bank stamp See Bank Endorsement.

bank statement A monthly statement of account which a bank renders to each of its depositors. It shows in detail the amounts deposited, the checks paid by the bank, and the balance on hand at the end of the month. (73)

bank statement of condition See Statement of Condition. (90)

bank wire A private wire service offered financial institutions which speeds and facilitates the transfer of funds and the reporting of security transactions, quotations, the payment or nonpayment of items, and credit information on individuals and organizations. (1)

bar chart A chart of the price action of a security, the patterns of which are used by analysts to help in formulating their opinion about future movements. Either daily, weekly or monthly charts of the price ranges and associated volume are studied. (105)

bar graph A graph with solid bars that shows clearly the comparisons of two or more amounts. (73)

barometers Those business indices which are used to evaluate the condition of a market or economy. Industrial production, total employment, freight car loadings, etc., are among some of the statistical series which are considered to be barometers.

barometer stock A security which moves in the same direction as the market and for this reason is considered to be representative of the market. U.S. Steel is an example of a barometer stock.

barren money Money which is not being put to

productive use such as in the case of hoarding in a safe deposit box as compared with money which may be productively used in a banking system.

Barron's Confidence Index The ratio of *Barron's Magazine's* highest-grade corporate bond yield average to the Dow-Jones composite bond yield average (which includes lower-grade bonds). The Index changes with corresponding changes in these yields. The Index can be related to prices since they move in the opposite direction of yields. Thus, users of the Index can watch the action of bond prices. If high-grade bond prices rise, their yield falls and the C.I. falls, which indicates that professional investors are placing their money in relatively safe investments because financial prospects are dim. If low-grade bond prices out perform the higher-grade bond prices, the yield on them falls and the C.I. rises, which indicates a more optimistic outlook for the future. (105)

barter The exchange, without the use of money, of one item or service for another.

base coins Minor coins made of copper, nickel, zinc, or aluminum as distinguished from gold and silver.

base period Many statistical series choose a "base period" or normal period which is given the weight or value of 100. As the time series are computed, the current data is related to the base. If the measurement in the base period, for example, was 200 units and current measurement is 300 units, one could express the base as 100 and current as 150. By reducing the data to a percentage of the base period, complex data may be more easily evaluated.

base stock inventory plan See Inventory Plans. (28)

basic rating Standard classification under the Numerical System for selection of risks. (42)

basic stock The minimum amount in inventory required at the lowest level of sales for a business during a given period of time.

basic trend Main direction. (93)

basic yield A concept similar to pure interest, that is, the annual rate of return in percent on a risk-free investment such as a long term U.S. government bond. Even in this illustration there is some risk including the effect of inflation on purchasing power of the future income from the bond.

basing point A technique for quoting prices of products. The buyer figures his delivered cost from the geographic point used as the base even though the product is not necessarily shipped from there.

basis The yield to maturity of a bond. The annual yield or percentage return on an equity.

The spread between the price for a product sold by a futures contract and the price for the spot commodity. Also, the actual standard grade for a futures contract.

The difference between futures, quotations, and actuals prices. (123)

basis, adjusted Cost including allowable capital improvements minus depreciation previously allowed or allowable. (120)

basis, allocation of Proportionment of the origi-

nal cost or basis of a property to land, improvements (building) and personal property. (120)

basis, new Basis to new owner after purchase or exchange. In exchange, composed of old basis plus loan assumed and/or boot and/or cash paid plus recognized gain minus loan relief, cash or boot received. (120)

basis point (Municipal bond terminology.) A measure for small differences in yields; 100 basis points cqualing 1%. For example, there is a 20 basis point spread (difference) between bonds quoted at yields of 1.30% and 1.10%. (103)

batch A group of deposits, incoming clearings, or other items assembled for proving purposes and for facilitating balancing. Normally, a batch contains about 150 items, which is approximately the pocket capacity of a proof machine. However, there is no minimum or maximum limitation to a batch size. (83)

A group of deposits, or a group of other items, which are proved in one operation. Also termed "block". (90)

batch number The number assigned to a batch of items being processed through the proof department. It is placed in the account number field of the Batch Ticket and on the back of the remainder of the items in the batch. (83)

batch processing Collection of data over a period of time to be sorted and processed as a group during a particular machine run. (83)

batch proof A system for proving deposits, usually performed in the following sequence: (a) deposits are assembled in groups of various sizes, (b) deposit tickets are sorted into one group, (c) checks are sorted into several classifications, such as clearings, transit, bookkeeping, etc., (d) cash release tickets are sorted according to tellers, (e) deposit tickets, checks, and cash release tickets are listed on a "batch" or "block" sheet in their respective columns, (f) the total of the deposits and other credits should equal the recapitulation of the checks and other debits. (1)

batch sheet A "proof sheet" used in the Batch Proof system (see definition). The batch sheet is arranged in columns for deposits, various classifications of checks and other debits, and cash release tickets. After sorting, all items in the batch are listed in their respective columns, the totals recapped and proved. The batch sheet then becomes a permanent record of the bank, and is used by bank auditors to check back any errors arising from transactions. (1)

batch system See Batch Proof.

batch ticket When used in an MICR system the batch ticket is a control document which is encoded with the total amount of a batch and is identified by a special transaction code. The batch ticket can also contain such encoded information as batch number, source number, and/or proof machine number. This ticket accompanies the items from the Proof Department to the Document Processing Center. (83)

bay Space on a selling floor between four columns—a recess or opening in walls. (33)

bear A person who thinks security prices will fall. A bear market is one that goes down over a period of time. (116)

bear account A short account.

bear campaign Also Bear Raiding, which refers to the practice of selling securities short to depress prices, and then attempting to close out the short sales at a profit. (105)

bear clique An informal group of people who combine their attempts to depress security or commodity prices by the practice of short selling. (105)

bearer Holder or person in possession of money, or of a check, bill, note, or other instrument. "The person in possession of a bill or note which is payable to bearer" (Negotiable Instruments Law). (85)

bearer bond A bond which is presumed to be owned by the person who holds it; the owner's name is not on record with the issuer.

bearer form In a form payable to bearer, the security having no registered owner. (103)

bearer instrument Any negotiable instrument which is payable to the individual who has physical possession of it.

bearing the market A form of manipulation, also known as "bear raiding", which artificially depresses prices by short selling. The one-eighth rule makes continuous short sales impossible. (106)

bearish and bullish When conditions suggest lower prices, a bearish situation is said to exist. If higher prices appear warranted, the situation is said to be bullish. (9)

bear market (Stock market terminology.) A period of generally declining market prices. (103)

bear pool A form of manipulation now prohibited which consisted of a formally organized fund contributed by operators who desired prices to be forced downward. The fund was usually entrusted to a manager. The agreement usually stipulated the amount of profits and losses to be shared, and that none of the members should make individual transactions in the particular security being manipulated. (105)

bear position Means a "short position" or the prevailing market position of a pessimist; i.e., one who has sold securities short in hopes that the market will turn downward, at which point securities will be bought at a lower price to give a net profit. (105)

bear raid The attempt to depress the price of a security or good by heavy selling. Prior to 1933 this was accomplished by short sales. Today it is much more difficult to do because of changes in the rules for short sales.

bear raiding A prohibited, as well as impossible, form of manipulation in which a group of bear operators conduct an intense short selling campaign to depress the price of a security or group of securities; thereby frightening other security holders into selling or forcing liquidation of inadequate margin accounts. Once the prices have been driven down, the Bear Raiders can close out their short contracts (buy the security at a lower price than they received in the sale of it) at a profit. (105)

bear squeeze, or panic The condition brought about when securities advance in price, rather than decline, to the dismay of the Bears (short interest holders). This may force the bears to close out their positions at a loss. (105)

beating the gun Any attempt to sell or do a thing prior to the approved or agreed upon time.

below par A quotation or transaction at a price less than the amount on the face of the instrument. A $1,000 face amount bond which is quoted at $950 is being offered at $50 below par.

benchmark statistics Comprehensive data (compiled at infrequent intervals) which are used as a basis for developing and adjusting interim estimates made from sample information. Many of the monthly and quarterly estimates of economic data published by the Bureau of the Census and the Office of Business Economics make use of the various decennial, quinquennial, and annual censuses and surveys for benchmark purposes.

Census or other benchmark data are used both in the design and interpretation of subsequent samples and in the revision of interim estimates that may have developed systematic errors between census or survey periods. An example of this process may be seen in the Census Bureau's series on manufacturer's shipments, inventories, and new orders. These series are collected and estimated from monthly sample reports for approximately 55 detailed industry categories. The monthly estimates are periodically adjusted— usually in July or August of each year—to reflect developments in the *Annual Survey of Manufacturers*, a more comprehensive survey —the benchmark statistics—of all manufacturing activity in the economy. (124)

beneficiary 1. The person who, unless the trustee has later indicated a change in his intentions, will receive the balance of a trust account upon the death of the trustee. 2. The person in whose favor a letter of credit is issued. 3. The person designated to receive the income or principal of a trust estate. 4. The person who is to receive the proceeds of or benefits accruing under an insurance policy or annuity. (90, 93)

beneficiary, change of Process of altering the beneficiary endorsement to provide for payment to one other than originally named, or to provide for payment in a different manner. (42)

beneficiary, contingent A beneficiary who is entitled to benefits only after the death of a primary beneficiary. (51)

beneficiary endorsement An endorsement placed on (or attached to in rider form) the policy setting forth the names of the beneficiaries, relationship to the insured, manner in which policy proceeds are to be paid each, and conditions upon which each beneficiary's right to receive such payment is based. (42)

beneficiary, irrevocable A beneficiary for whom another may not be substituted by the insured. (51)

beneficiary, primary A beneficiary who is first entitled to benefits on death of an insured. (51)

benefit formula A formula for computing the amount of annuity, pension or other benefit payable under a retirement plan, usually based upon salary, or wages, length of service, and age. (32)

bequeath To give personal property by will; to be distinguished from devise. (74)

bequest A gift of personal property made by a decedent in his or her will. The party receiving the gift is called a legatee. See also Legacy. (1)

best bid The highest price anyone is willing to pay for something offered for sale. This bid is the relevant one in establishing the market for a stock. (105)

betterment 1. A physical improvement in or to an existing property which changes its original attributes and character, and which increases its reproduction cost, desirability, utility and value, without enlargement or expansion of the property; not to be confused with maintenance, repairs, or replacements. 2. Improvements in the nature of installations which are wholly new to the property, such as: air conditioning, a dishwasher, oil burner, indirect lighting, heavy duty wiring, restaurant booths (if affixed so as to become an integral part of the real estate), street curbs, public sewage disposal system, where none existed before. 3. Improvements in existing facilities or equipment, such as: substitution of a circulating hot water heating system for a one pipe, warm air furnace, installation of additional kitchen cabinets, enlargement or increase in the number of catch basins in a public (or private, storm drainage system to increase the efficiency of the system. (66)

Biannual Occurring twice a year. (93)

bid A price offered, subject unless otherwise stated, to immediate acceptance for a specific amount of commodity. (9)

bid ahead The term used in explaining to a prospective security buyer that bids at the same price or at a higher price arrived on the trading floor before his, and that they have precedence over his bid for the same stock. (105)

bid and asked price The price at which an owner offers to sell (asked) and the price at which someone has agreed to buy (bid). Said of unlisted stocks and bonds buy may apply to any property in which there is an active trade. See Quotation. (85)

bidding up The act of sucessively raising the price bid for a security or commodity to higher levels for fear of failing to have an order executed before an advance is under way. (105)

bid price In the case of open-end shares, the price at which the holder may redeem his shares; in most cases it is the current net asset value per share. In the case of closed-end shares, the highest price then offered for stock in the public market. (3)

bids and offers A "bid" is the quotation of a prospective buyer for the purchase; and an "offer" is the quotation of a seller for the sale of a trading unit or other specified amount of a security. Some of the established methods of trading in securities are:
For Cash—delivery and payment must be made on the same day.
Regular Way—securities must be delivered and paid for on the third full business day after sale.
Seller's Option—trading of securities in this way gives the seller the right to deliver the securities within a period of not less than 4 nor more than 60 days. (1)

bid wanted A request by a security holder who would like to sell and wants to find a buyer. (105)

big board The New York Stock Exchange.

big steel Nickname for United States Steel Corporation or its common stock; formerly applied to the company's preferred stock. (105)

big three The three largest firms in any industry. (105)

bilateral Between two parties, individuals, companies or nations.

bilateral payments agreement Is an agreement between two countries or their central banks to channel all or specified settlements between themselves through special accounts, normally subject to a reciprocal credit margin (swing). Arrangements of this nature usually imply that the use of convertible foreign currencies or gold between the partner countries is avoided except when the credit margin is exceeded or net balances are settled. (130)

bill A note or bill of exchange. A document showing the amount that is due a creditor which is given or sent to a debtor. A bill of sale, a way bill, a due bill, or paper money such as a ten dollar bill.

bill adjuster Person employed in credit office. Receives and investigates complaints made by customers of errors on bills. (26)

bill book A Liability Ledger.

bill broker An individual or firm which acts as a middle man and sells commercial paper to financial institutions. The bill broker was much more active and important during the 19th century than he is today.

bill discounted A promissory note or bill of exchange from which the bank deducts, in advance, its fee or interest for lending the money (usually to the holder or endorser). (1)

biller Person trained in operation of bookkeeping or billing machines and responsible for posting all debit and credit transactions to a group of individual customer's accounts. (26)

bill for payment That instrument which is presented to a debtor or his agent for the purpose of being paid as differentiated from one which was presented for acceptance.

billing The act of sending out bills or statements to customers. (59)

bill of credit A written instrument in which the drawer requests the firm or individual addressed to advance credit to the bearer or named firm or individual at the risk of the drawer.

bill-of-exchange An order drawn by one person on another, directing him to pay money to some third person. (93)

bill of lading Order Bill of Lading. A negotiable document by which a transportation line acknowledges receipt of freight and contracts for its movement. Surrender of the original Order Bill of Lading, properly endorsed, is required by transportation lines upon delivery of the freight, in accordance with the terms of the Bill of Lading. (19)

bill of materials Form which lists descriptive information such as name of parts, numbers of parts, quantity and related data. This form is typically used in assembly, planning, scheduling, cost and production activities.

bill of sale A written document whereby a seller transfers to a buyer the title to certain goods; resembles a deed to real property. (31, 92)

bills discounted The notes, bills of exchange and acceptances which a bank has discounted for its customers.

bills discounted ledger A Liability Ledger.

bills discounted overdue Those bills, notes acceptances and similar obligations which have passed their due date or matured and are still not paid. Representing past due accounts of doubtful value they are segregated from other assets.

bills of credit Archaic term found in U.S. Constitution for paper money issued by the government.

bills payable A comprehensive term that includes the sum total of notes and trade acceptances which a business owes to trade creditors and which the business must pay at their maturity. The term also refers to the sum of money which a member bank has borrowed, on its own collateral note, from the Federal Reserve Bank. (1)

bills receivable A comprehensive term that includes the total of all notes and trade acceptances given by customers, usually in payment of merchandise, which the debtors must pay at maturity. (1)

bimetallism The "free" or unlimited coinage of two metals, generally of gold and silver. The coins have full legal tender value and an established relationship or ratio of value such as sixteen ounces of silver of a standard fineness or purity to one ounce of gold of a standard fineness or purity.

Black Friday September 24, 1869 when the attempt to corner the gold market was broken. The excesses resulted in a business panic and depression. Since then a number of sharp drops in the securities markets have occurred on Friday and the term has been carried forward to indicate a sharp drop approaching panic proportions.

black market A place where illegal transactions take place. Generally these violations involve rationing, price or exchange controls.

blank bill A bill of exchange with no payee designated.

blank endorsement The endorsement or signature of an individual or company on an instrument such as a check or note making it payable to the bearer and thus negotiable without restrictions.

blanket mortgage A mortgage that takes in or "covers" all the assets or property of the debtor.

blanket position bond Protects the employer from loss caused by dishonesty on the part of his employees. The most that is payable for a single embezzlement is the face amount of the bond times the number of dishonest employees involved in the embezzlement. (5)

blank transfer See Assignment in Blank.

blind pool A speculative device at times used in the securities markets in which a group of speculators let one of their members handle the operation or management of their obligated funds. The pool's membership, other than the one selected member, is generally not revealed to the public. The pool operates for a stated period of time or until a specific goal has been reached. See Bob Tail Pool.

block A large number of shares of stocks or large number of bonds. See Batch. (1)

blockage Designating the administration of an account as subject to United States Treasury control because of enemy or suspected enemy interest. A discount from the established market for which a large block of stock of a single corporation would have to be sold if the entire holding were placed on the market at a given date (a term used in connection with federal estate tax). (74)

blocked account Any account in a bank the handling of which is closely circumscribed by government regulations. The term in this country is used to designate any account whose administration is subject to United States Treasury license because of enemy or suspected enemy interest. (74)

blocked currency A device used by some nations to discriminate against certain types of holders of the claims against a nation. It is generally used to try to control foreign exchange rates and the balance of payments as well as trade movement. Blocked currencies are quoted at discounts from the unblocked or regular currency of a nation. At times the blocked currency may be used only in certain regulated ways and may involve the need for special permits from the monetary authorities.

block system See Batch Proof.

blotter A term used in many banks to describe a form of journal. The blotter is usually arranged in columns so that like entries can be listed in a chronological order in the correct column, and then add-listed for settlement at the end of the business day. Many banks use a "blotter" of this type for the original pen-and-ink entry of all loans made. Many banks not mechanized at the teller's window have the tellers use a sheet of this type to record all cash-in and cash-paid-out transactions to obtain individual teller's settlement. (1)

blow off A heavy volume selling or buying climax after an extended movement up or down. (105)

blue chip Common stock in a company known nationally for the quality and wide acceptance of its products or services and for its ability to make money and pay dividends in good times and bad. Usually such stocks are relatively high priced and offer relatively low yields. (2)

blue list The trade offering sheets of bond dealers, listing dealers' offerings of municipal bonds for sale all over the country.

A composite list published five days a week by The Blue List Publishing Company, New York City, showing current municipal bond offerings by banks and municipal bond houses all over the country. (103)

blue sky laws A popular name for laws various states have enacted to protect the public against securities frauds. The term is believed to have originated when a judge ruled that a particular stock had about the same value as a patch of blue sky. (2)

State statutes regulating the issuance and sale of securities. S.E.C. regulations and the Federal Securities Act of 1933 are the Federal counterpart. (125)

board The directors of an association. (31, 92)

board lot A round lot. The regular unit of trade for the designated exchange. The board or round lot on the New York Stock Exchange is generally 100 shares of stock or $1,000 par value for a bond unless an exception is made.

board of directors Those individuals elected by the stockholders of a corporation to manage the business. An "inside" board has the directors who are also active in the day-to-day operation of the firm while an "outside" board is made up of individuals who do not make active day-to-day decisions in the business but are rather concerned with policy and broad general direction.

Board of Governors of the Federal Reserve System This is a government agency located in Washington, D.C., which supervises, coordinates, and controls the operations of the twelve Federal Reserve banks, and has regulatory power with respect to member banks. The Board of Governors consists of seven members appointed by the President of the United States and affirmed by the Senate. The term of office is fourteen years, and no two members may be appointed from the same Federal Reserve District. The terms are staggered, so the Board changes one member every two years. (1)

board of managers A term given in some states to the board of trustees of a mutual savings bank. (90)

board of trade A chamber of commerce or a produce exchange.

board of trustees The body in a mutual savings bank which manages the institution, establishes the policies under which it is to be operated, appoints the officers, etc. (90)

board room A room for customers in a broker's office where opening, high, low and last prices of leading stocks are posted on a board throughout the day. (2)

bob tail pool A group of speculators who act independently of each other but with a common goal and agreement in mind. The commitments made by each member are his own responsibility. See Blind Pool.

boerse Dutch and German word for Stock Exchange.

boiler room High pressure peddling over the telephone of stocks of dubious value. A typical boiler room is simply a room lined with desks or cubicles, each with a salesman and telephone. The salesmen telephone what are known in the trade as "sucker lists". (2)

boiler room operation A dubious operation involving the sale of very speculative and frequently valueless securities through the use of high pressure phone techniques and misleading literature. The appeal of quick profit and rapid price change is used to stimulate the unsophisticated to purchase the security without making a proper investigation as to the merits of the security.

bolivar Monetary unit of Venezuela.

boliviano Monetary unit of Bolivia.

bolsa A stock exchange in Latin America and Spain.

bona fide purchaser One who purchases property in good faith, without notice of any defect in the title, and for a valuable consideration. (74)

bonanza Any unusually profitable investment.

bond An interest-bearing certificate of debt, usually issued in series by which the issuer (a government or corporation) obligates itself to pay the principal amount and interest at a specified time, usually five years or more after date of issue. Bonds may be distinguished from promissory notes or other evidences of debt because of their formal execution under seal and certification by a bank or trust company that they are authorized by the board of directors of a corporation, or other governing body. Corporate bonds are usually secured by a lien against certain specified property. Bonds may be issued in "bearer" form or "registered". (1)

bond, adjustment The term used for income bonds that have been issued out of a reorganization. See Bond, Income.

bond amortization Any of several systems of providing a rational way of writing down the premium over par which has been paid for a bond. A bond bought at 105 (which is $1050) and maturing in five years would have to be amortized for $50 since at maturity the holder will only receive $1000. One way would be to write off $10 each year so that this would not all fall due at one period.

bond anticipation notes Short-term notes of a municipality sold in anticipation of bond issuance which are full faith and credit obligations of the governmental unit and are to be retired from the proceeds of the bonds to be issued. See Interim Borrowing. (29)

bond, approved In some states "legal lists" are prepared for fiduciaries. Such bonds named in the "legal list" are approved bonds. See Legal List.

bond, assumed Bonds which originally were the obligation of one corporation but which for some reason such as a subsidiary relationship have been assumed as obligations as well by another corporation. Most assumed bonds are found in the area of railway divisional bonds in which the parent company has assumed the interests and principal obligation of the original debtor, which is a division of a system.

bond, authority Bonds payable from the revenues of a specific authority. Since such authorities usually have no revenue other than charges for services, their bonds are ordinarily revenue bonds.

NOTE: Such bonds differ from other revenue bonds (q.v.) in that the protections offered the bondholder, in addition to the pledges written into the bond contract, are often partially embodied in the statute which creates the authority. (29)

bonds authorized and unissued Bonds which have been legally authorized but have not been issued and which can be issued and sold without further authorization.

NOTE: This term must not be confused with the terms "margin or borrowing power" or "legal debt margin" either one of which represents the difference between the legal debt limit of a governmental unit and the debt outstanding against it. (29)

bond, baby A bond of less than $1,000 which is the regular unit for most non-governmental bonds.

bond, bail A bond guaranteeing appearance in court of the principal named in the bond. (51)

bond, banker's blanket Type of business insurance coverage. A broad form of bond guaranteeing banks against loss due to dishonest, fraudulent, or criminal acts of their employees, and insuring against loss due to robbery, larceny, burglary, theft, hold-up, forgery, misplacement, and mysterious unexplained disappearances. (5)

bond, bearer Bonds whose proceeds (principal and interest) are payable to the bearer, that is, to whoever has physical possession. Since there is no identification, such bonds always have attached coupons, which are cut and presented to collect the interest. (103)

bond, bid A guarantee that the contractor will enter into a contract, if it is awarded to him, and furnish such contract bond (sometimes called performance bond) as is required by the terms of the bond. (50)

bond, blanket Used in banks and related institutions to cover losses caused by robbery, burglary, or the dishonesty of employees and officers of the financial institution. (5)

bond, blanket fidelity Covers losses to an employer by dishonest acts of his employee or employees. (5)

bond, bonus 1. A security which was issued to veteran soldiers for service to their country and was in addition to their rated pay.

2. A rather rare device in bond form given for the same reasons as are stated in Bonus Stock.

bond, borrowed Brokers and banks at times borrow bonds so that they may meet certain requirements. Brokers borrow to make delivery on short sales while banks borrow bonds to comply with collateral requirements of government agencies.

bond, bridge Securities which have been issued for the construction of a bridge.

bond, callable Bonds which the issuing corporation or body may redeem before their maturity. Generally some premium is paid by the issuing corporation to the holder of the bond should it be called. Interest stops when a bond is called.

bond, called A bond which the debtor has declared to be due and payable on a certain date, prior to maturity, in accordance with the provisions of an issue to be redeemed, the bonds to be retired are usually drawn by loss. (74)

bond, circular A detailed description of a bond offering which is used as a means of publicizing the pertinent facts about the issue. The circular is brought out by the underwriters and sent to interested individuals and firms.

bond, city Those municipal bonds which are issued by cities. The income of such securities is exempt from present federal income tax.

bond, civil Bonds of any governmental agency.

bond, classified A debt security which is given a designation such as Series A or B or to differentiate it from some other bond of the same debtor.

bond, clean A bond of the coupon type which has

not been altered by any endorsement or modification of the original contract such as the words "assented" or "extended."

bond, collateral Additional security for a loan. (5)

bond, collateral trust An issue of bonds for which collateral has been pledged to guarantee repayment of the principal. This type of bond usually arises out of intercompany transactions where the parent company will issue bonds with securities of a subsidiary as the underlying collateral. Railroads often do this type of financing. (84)

bond, commercial blanket Bond issued for stated amount on all regular employees of the covered company insuring against loss from employee's dishonest acts. (5)

bond, completion A bond guaranteeing the construction of an improvement in connection with which and prior to the completion of which, a mortgagee or other lender advances money to the owner. (5)

bond, consolidated A debt instrument issued to take the place of two or more previously issued bonds. This may be done to simplify a debt structure or to take advantage of a lower prevailing interest rate.

bond, construction Type of business insurance coverage that protects the insured from those particular risks associated with construction. (5)

bond, continued A debt instrument that does not have to be redeemed at maturity but can continue to earn interest. The Series E bonds have been "Continued". Extended Bonds.

bond, contract A guarantee of the faithful performance of a construction contract and the payment of all labor and materials bills incident thereto. In those situations where two bonds are required, one to cover performance and the other to cover payment of labor and material, the former is known as a performance bond and the latter as a payment. (50)

bond, convertible Bonds having the special provision for being converted into stock at a certain time and at a specified price. (74)

bond, corporate Those obligations of corporations as distinguished from civil bonds which are obligations of a national, state, or local government or agency.

bond, coupon Bonds with interest coupons attached. The coupons are clipped as they come due and are presented by the holder for payment of interest. See Bearer Bond; Bond, Registered. (2)

bond, court All bonds and undertakings required of litigants to enable them to pursue certain remedies of the courts. (50)

bond crowd Those members of a securities exchange who specialize in dealing and trading in bonds. Since bonds are traded in a special area of the exchanges it refers to those who concentrate and deal in that area.

bond, currency Prior to the "Gold Clause" decision of the U.S. Supreme Court in 1934, some bonds were payable in gold and others in any lawful money. The latter are designated as Currency Bonds. Since 1934 all bonds, even those with gold clauses are payable in lawful currency.

bond, customhouse Bonds required by the United States Government in connection with payment of duties or to produce bills of lading.

bond, debenture Any unsecured promissory note or obligation issued under the terms of a formal indenture or agreement between the debtor corporation and the bondholder creditor. (19)

bond, deferred Also called an extended bond, or one which has had its maturity date extended by mutual consent of issuer and holder. (105)

bond, definitive A permanent bond issued by a corporation; to be distinguished from a temporary bond issued pending the preparation of the definitive bond. (74)

bond, depository A bond guaranteeing payment of funds to depositors in accordance with the terms of a deposit in a bank. Not the same as federal deposit insurance. (51+)

bond discount That amount below the par or face amount of a bond at which a bond is sold. A bond with a face amount of $1,000 which is sold for $950 has a $50 discount. If it matures in five years it will or should pay $1,000. Thus the holder will receive in addition to his investment and the rate of return on it (which will be higher than the face interest rate), the discount.

bond, escrow Those bonds held in escrow. See Escrow.

bond, extended Continued bonds; bonds which have matured without the debtor paying the principal but which the debtor agrees to extend or continue to pay at some future date. If the creditor accepts such an extension of maturity, the bonds may be stamped to indicate such agreement.

bond, external Bonds issued by a country or business for purchase outside that country. These bonds are frequently denominated in the currency of the purchaser. At times the option is given the purchaser to elect in which currency he wishes to receive payment of interest and principal. See Bond, Internal.

bond, fidelity A promise to make good, financial loss due to the dishonesty of employees; a financial guarantee of the performance of an implied obligation. (51)

bond, fiduciary A bond, in behalf of a person appointed by a court to a position of trust, as executor of an estate. (42)

bond, foreign Foreign bonds may take even more forms than domestic bonds by being moved from their country of origin. Foreign bonds which are deliberately sold abroad are external bonds; those that are payable in dollars are called foreign dollar bonds. Some foreign bonds are payable in more than one currency at the option of the holder and some are tied to price indexes as to value of principal. Foreign bonds that have defaulted may be assented or stamped. Those still in default are sold flat. They may be obligations of nations, states, municipalities or of foreign corporations.

bond, forgery Insurance against loss due to forgery or alteration of, on, or in checks or other instruments. (51)

bond, fraud Type of business insurance protection against loss caused by fraud. (5)

bond fund A fund established to receive and disburse the proceeds of a governmental bond issue. (29)

An investment company, the portfolio of which consists primarily of bonds. (65)

bond, funding Bonds issued to retire outstanding floating debt and to eliminate deficits. (29)

bond, gold A debt instrument which gives the legal holder the option of being paid principal and/or interest in gold. This type of bond is still found in the United States in issues originally distributed prior to the Supreme Court decision in 1935 which invalidated the gold clause option. However, such bonds are not paid in gold but with legal currency.

bond, government Obligations of the U.S. Government regarded as the highest grade issues in existence. Obligations of governments other than the United States are generally designated as foreign government bonds. (2)

bond, guaranteed A bond which has interest or principal, or both, guaranteed by a company other than the issuer. Usually found in the railroad industry when large roads, leasing sections of trackage owned by small railroads, may guarantee the bonds of the smaller road. (2)

bond, improvement A bond issued by a municipality for the purpose of financing a public improvement.

bond, improvement mortgage A bond issued for the purpose of financing improvements of the debtor firm and which are secured by a general mortgage.

bond, income An obligation upon which interest is payable to the extent earned in each year except that interest not earned and unpaid may be either fully or partially cumulative according to the terms of the contract. The income bond may or may not be secured by the pledge of either real or personal property. (19)

An obligation in which the promise to pay interest is conditional upon the earnings of the obligor. Usually interest is to be paid in any year only if it is earned. (74)

bond, indemnity A written instrument under seal by which the signer, usually together with his surety or bondsman, guarantees to protect another against loss. An indemnity bond in which the obligation assumed by the surety is not a fixed amount is known as an open penalty form of indemnity bond. (88)

bond indenture The contract describing the interest and maturity date and other important terms under which bonds are issued. (105)

bond, indeterminate A callable bond which has no established maturity date. The call feature generally is not effective until some stated period has elapsed.

bond, indorsed Endorsed Bond. 1. A bond which has been extraneously endorsed or signed so that it may not be considered for normal or proper delivery according to the rules of the exchange and for this reason must be sold and described as an "Endorsed Bond". 2. A bond which has been endorsed by some other firm or individual besides the maker generally for such purposes as to improve the stature of the bond or as one phase of a movement of consolidation.

bond, installment More commonly called "Serial Bonds". See Bonds, Serial.

bond, insular Any bond issued by an insular part of the United States such as Hawaii.

bond, interchangeable A bond in either coupon or registered form which may be converted to the other form or its original form at the option of the holder. There may be some service charge for such conversion.

bond interest The interest on bonds is paid according to the terms of the bond, generally twice a year. It may be by the use of a coupon if the security is a bearer bond, or it may be by check if the bond is registered. The interest is computed as a percentage of the face amount which is generally $1,000 thus a 6% bond interest would result in the payment of $60 per year. The $60 is divided into the payment periods. If payment is semi-annual, $30 is paid each period, if payment is quarterly $15 is paid each quarter.

bond, interim The temporary paper certificate, generally printed and not engraved, to be exchanged for the definitive and engraved certificate. The engraving is for purposes of preventing forgery and alteration.

bond, internal A bond issued by a country payable in its own currency; to be distinguished from an external bond, which is a bond issued by one country and sold in another country and payable in the currency of that other country. (74)

bond, internal revenue Bonds required by the United States Government, which guarantee payment of federal taxes and compliance with government regulations. (50)

bonds issued Bonds sold. (29)

bond, jeopardy assessment Bond to stay in jeopardy assessment pending appeal; Form 1129. A bond required to guarantee payment of federal income taxes which are due or are claimed to be due. Form 1129 is the Treasury Department form. (5)

bond, joint and several A debt instrument in which the holder may look to payment from more than one company up to the full face amount of the security. These securities are mostly associated with railroad financing for such facilities as terminals used by more than one railroad. The users of the terminal agree to be responsible for the payment in the event the others default. The holder may only collect the face amount once, but he may collect from all or only one of the obligors.

bond, joint control A bond required before the assets of an estate are transferred to the custody of the principal. (5)

bond, junior Bonds which are not senior; that is, are secondary or subordinate to another issue which in the event of liquidation would have a prior claim to the junior bonds. See Bond, Senior; Senior Interest; Senior Securities.

bond, legal Bonds that state or federal law prescribe as suitable and legal investments for fiduciary institutions. In an number of states a "legal list" states by name and issue those investments that a fiduciary or trustee may purchase and hold for beneficiary.

Bond, Liberty Those issues, since matured, which were issued by the United States government during World War I were denominated in amounts that were attractive to many citizens. The sales of these bonds were attended with rallies, theatrical appeals and had not only the purpose of raising funds but also of reducing purchasing power and thus inflation.

bond, maintenance A bond guaranteeing against defects in workmanship or materials for a stated time after acceptance of work. (51)

bond market 1. The place where bonds are bought and sold. Most bonds are sold over the counter though substantial amounts are sold on the various exchanges.

2. Those financial institutions which purchase bonds such as insurance companies, trust funds, banks.

bond, mortgage A bond secured by a mortgage on a property. The value of the property may or may not equal the value of the so-called mortgage bonds issued against it. See Bond, Debenture. (2)

bond, municipal A bond issued by a state or a political subdivision, such as county, city, town, or village. The term also designates bonds issued by state agencies and authorities. In general, interest paid on municipal bonds is exempt from federal income taxes. (2)

bond of indemnity A written instrument under seal by which the signer, usually together with his surety or bondsman, guarantees to protect another against loss. It is generally required to protect the drawee bank when the drawer issues a stop-payment order against a certified check. Such an agreement without sureties and not under seal is called an indemnity agreement. (85)

bond, open-end A mortgage bond of an issue which does not have a limitation on the number or amounts of bonds which may be issued under the mortgage though some relationship may be required of the number and amount of bonds to the value of the property mortgaged.

bond, optional See Callable Bond. (29)

bond, optional payment A bond which gives the holder the choice to receive payment of interest or principal or both in the currency of one or more foreign countries, as well as in domestic funds. (74)

bond ordinance or resolution An ordinance or resolution authorizing a bond issue. (29)

bond, participating A relatively rare bond which after receiving a stated rate of periodic interest also shares in a profit known by the issuing firm. The profit sharing is determined by a formula.

bond, passive A bond which does not bear any interest; such bonds may be issued as a result of reorganization or where normal economic forces are subordinated to some charitable or eleemosynary purpose.

bond, performance A bond supplied by one party to another protecting that party against loss in the event of improper performance or completion of the terms of an existing contract. (1)

bond, permit A bond guaranteeing that the person to whom a permit is, or is to be issued will comply with the law or ordinance regulating the privilege for which the permit is issued. (51)

bond, perpetual A bond which has no maturity. The French Rentes and some British Consols are perpetual bonds. Few such bonds have been issued in the United States.

bond power A form of assignment executed by the owner of registered bonds which contains an irrevocable appointment of an attorney-in-fact to make the actual transfer on the books of the corporation. See Power of Attorney; Stock Power. (74)

bond, preference An adjustment or income bond. See those terms.

bond, premium In the United States, a bond which is selling above its face value. In Europe, a bond having a lottery feature. When called, as distinguished from regular maturity, a premium bond generally pays substantially more than face amount.

The excess of the price at which a bond is acquired or sold, over its face value. NOTE: The price does not include accrued interest at the date of acquisition or sale. (29)

bond, prior lien A bond which takes precedence over other bonds issued by the same company.

bonds, privileged Convertible bonds or bonds which have attached warrants are known at times as privileged bonds.

bond, public Any bond which is issued by a government or governmental agency be it federal, state, municipal, domestic or foreign. In contrast, non-governmental organizations such as commercial corporations issue private bonds.

bond, purchase money A bond which has as security a Purchase Money Mortgage. See that term.

bond quality ratings The system of assigning symbolic ratings to the various levels of investment qualities of bonds. The bonds are measured according to their investment risk. Standard & Poor's Corporation use the symbols A1+ for the highest quality bond down thru D for bonds with little recoverable value. Moody's Investor Service uses the symbols Aaa down thru C. (105)

bond, quasi-municipal Also called Semi-municipal bond. A bond of a type such as irrigation, reclamation, levee, sewerage, drainage, paving bonds which are limited in their source of receipts to a restricted number of tax payers in the municipality, generally those receiving the benefits as distinguished from the entire body of tax payers in the municipality.

bond ratings A number of agencies and organizations evaluate securities. The three best known are Standard and Poor's, Moody's, and Fitch's. State banking departments also rate bonds. While the technique and basis of judgment for each rating service varies somewhat from other services, the main effort is to break down into similar risk classes the various securities. In this way the relative investment stature of each issue may be measured. Figures such as A & 1 indicate higher evaluation than B & 2, etc.

bond, redeemable A callable bond. See Callable; Bond, Called.

bond, redemption A refunding bond.

bond, redemption value Guaranteed face amount of a bond payable at maturity. (42)

bonds, refunding Bonds issued to retire bonds already outstanding. The refunding bonds may be sold for cash and outstanding bonds redeemed in cash, or the refunding bonds may be exchanged with holders of outstanding bonds. (29)

bond register A book of original entry, in bound or loose-leaf form, in which is recorded the details relative to the purchase and sale of bonds for the firm's own investment account. (1)

bond (registered) A registered bond is one in which the name of the owner is designated, and the proceeds are payable only to him. Bonds may be registered as to principal and interest, or to principal only. Interest on a bond registered as to both principal and interest, is paid to the owner by check as it becomes due. Bonds registered as to principal only, have coupons attached which are detached and collected as the interest becomes due. (1)

bond, reorganization An adjustment bond. A debt security issued in the recapitalization of a distressed corporation.

bond, revenue Bonds the principal of and interest on which are to be paid solely from earnings; usually those of a municipally owned utility or other public service enterprise the revenues and possibly the properties of which are pledged for this purpose. (29)

Bond, Savings A bond issued by the Treasury Department of the United States government for the encouragement of thrift. This bond may be purchased by the public in post offices, banks, and in the personnel offices of most large businesses. The government has encouraged "Payroll Deduction" plans, whereby employees can authorize a deduction from their pay each pay period. When the bond has been paid for, it is issued to the employee. Banks also encourage this type of investment by establishing a plan whereby a depositor may authorize the bank to deduct from his checking account each month the price of a Savings Bond, and mail it to him. Savings Bonds come in several series. (1)

bond, schedule A bond listing the names and positions of employees included as principals. See Bond, Fidelity. (42)

bond, school A type of municipal bond used to finance construction and purchase equipment of a school.

bond, second mortgage A bond which is issued on property which already has a first mortgage outstanding on it.

bond, secured A bond secured by a pledge of assets (plant or equipment), the title to which should be transferred to bondholders in the event of foreclosure. (105)

bond, senior Bonds which have first or prior claim to the assets of the debtor in the event of liquidation.

bond, serial Issues redeemable by installments, each of which is to be paid in full ordinarily out of revenues of the year in which it matures, or revenues of the preceeding year.

NOTE: Some state laws or regulations have further defined serial bonds to include some or all of the following features:

1. The payments must be in installments.

2. The installments must be consecutive.
3. Payments must be made during at least two-thirds of the life of the whole issue.
4. No one year's installment may be more than three times the amount of the smallest yearly installment unless the bonds are serial annuity bonds. (29)

bond, serial annuity Serial bonds in which the annual installments of the bond principal are so arranged that the payments for principal and interest combined are approximately the same each year. (29)

bond, sewer A type of municipal bond issued for the purpose of financing the construction of sewers.

bond, sinking fund Bonds issued under an agreement which requires the governmental unit to set aside periodically, ordinarily out of its revenues, a sum which, with earnings thereon, will be sufficient to redeem the bonds at their stated date of maturity.
NOTE: Sinking Fund bonds are usually also term bonds. (29)

bond, special district Bonds of a local taxing district which have been organized for a special purpose, such as road, sewer, fire, drainage, irrigation, and levee districts. (29)

bond, special lien Special assessment bonds which are liens against particular pieces of property. (29)

bond, stamped When the debtor on a bond issue becomes distressed he may default and then offer to resume payment at a much lower rate of interest or a delayed maturity. If the holder of the bond accepts this offer his bonds are stamped to signify his assenting to the terms. Thus two types of bonds are outstanding, those stamped and assented bonds and the original unassented and unstamped bond. When a purchaser buys the bonds in such a situation, he must instruct his broker which of the two types to buy.

bond, sterling A bond denominated in British pounds sterling as distinguished from a bond denominated in other currency units such as United States dollars.

bonds, straight serial Serial bonds in which the annual installments of bond principal are approximately equal. (29)

bond, surety A written promise to pay damages or to indemnify against losses caused by the party or parties named in the document, through non-performance or through defalcation; for example, a surety bond given by a contractor or by an official handling cash or securities. (29)

bond, tax anticipation Longer term debt instruments than Tax Anticipation Notes, but possessing the same general features. See Tax Anticipation Notes.

bond, tax exempt The securities of states, cities, and other public authorities specified under federal law, the interest on which is either wholly or partly exempt from federal income taxes. (2)

bond, temporary A bond which is the same as the definitive bond except that it is printed rather than engraved. Since some exchanges require engraving to prevent counterfeiting on listed securities, the temporary bond may be issued until the engraved definitive bond is ready. At that time they will be exchanged.

bonds, term Bonds of the same issue usually maturing all at one time and ordinarily to be retired from Sinking Funds. NOTE: Sometimes a term bond has more than one maturity date; for example, a serial issue having postponed maturities in only a few late years of its term. (29)

bond, terminable A bond which has a stated maturity. Most bonds in the United States have stated maturity however in France the Rentes and in Britain the Consols are perpetual, that is have no maturity.

bond, terminal Bonds secured by property in the form of railroad terminals or grain terminals.

bond, territorial A bond of a United States dependency or insular possession.

bond, treasury Coupon issues having original maturities of more than five years. (115)

bond, underlying Bonds that have a senior lien where subsequent claims also exist.

bond, unified A Consolidated Bond. See Bond, Consolidated.

Bond, United States Savings A non-negotiable bond issued in different series such as E, F, & G. The most commonly issued being the series E. Such bonds are issued in small, odd units such as $18.75 with a maturity value of $25 or $37.50 with a maturity value of $50. The typical period such bonds were originally issued for was 10 years, but because of changed interest rates, the maturity has been altered rather than the redemption amount.

bond, unsecured A bond which is backed up by the faith and credit of the issuer rather than the pledging of assets. (105)

bond value tables Since most securities are not sold exactly at par, but the interest is computed on the par or face value when one purchases such securities it is important to know what the price paid for the security will yield if held to maturity (or sometimes the call date). Various companies have prepared printed tables of such values so that one may simply look up such yields without going through the labor of computing the yields. Most banks and financial institutions use such tables as labor saving devices.

bond, warehouse customs Bonds furnished only on forms prescribed by the United States Treasury Department that are required by federal laws and regulations in connection with the importation of dutiable merchandise. (5)

bond yield The rate of return on bonds. (74)

bonded debt That portion of indebtedness represented by outstanding bonds. That amount of the debt of a company or government which is represented by bonds. NOTE: If there are Sinking Fund bonds, this term should be replaced by "gross bonded debt" and "net bonded debt" (29)

bonded goods Any goods stored in a bonded warehouse. The owner of the goods has deposited a bond with the government which guarantees that the tax or duty on the goods will be paid upon withdrawal of the goods.

bonded indebtedness See Bonded Debt. (29)

bonded warehouse A warehouse owned by persons approved by the U.S. Treasury Department and under bond or guarantee for the strict observance of the revenue laws; utilized for storing goods until duties are paid or goods are otherwise properly released. (19)

bondholder One who owns bonds and therefore is a creditor of the issuer. (85)

bond house An institution doing business primarily in bond sales. (105)

bonus An additional dividend paid to savers who have met all the conditions of a special savings account contract. (31, 92)

bonus stock A sweetening device used to encourage the sale of another class of securities. For example, the issuing of a share or shares of common stock for each unit of purchase of preferred stock. The bonus stock may be given to the ultimate purchaser, the salesman or the underwriter of the issue.

book A notebook the specialist in a stock exchange uses to keep a record of the buy and sell orders at specified prices, in strict sequence of receipt, which are left with him by other brokers. See Specialist. (2)

book account Same as Open Account. See that term.

book cost The amount at which property is recorded in plant accounts without deduction of related reserves or other accounts. (21)

book credit Those items shown on the ledger accounts which represent obligations of firms and individuals which are not secured by notes or other security. Also described as book accounts or open book accounts.

book crowd Those traders in inactive bonds on the New York Stock Exchange. Sometimes the term "Cabinet Crowd" is used in the same sense since the information on the inactive bonds is kept in cabinets.

book depreciation The amount reserved upon books of record to provide for the retirement or replacement of an asset. (54)

bookkeeper Person who posts debits and credits on a bank's record of a depositor's account, whether by hand or by machine. (83)

bookkeeping cycle The entire bookkeeping process applicable to a fiscal period (journalizing, posting, preparing a trial balance, preparing financial statements, etc.). (73)

bookkeeping department A department of a bank where the records of all depositors' checking accounts are posted and kept. In the larger banks there may be found several bookkeeping departments, such as: commercial, corporation accounts, special checking, general ledger, bank ledger, foreign accounts, stock transfer, and trust bookkeeping. (1)

bookkeeping equation A one-line summary of the balance sheet in mathematical form. The fundamental bookkeeping equation is:

Assets = Liabilities + Proprietorship   (73)

book liability The amount at which securities issued or assumed by the carrier and other liability items are recorded in the accounts of the carrier. (19)

book of final entry A book to which information is transferred from a book of original entry. (73)

book of original entry The record in which the various transactions are formally recorded for the first time, such as the cash journal, check register, or general journal. Where machine bookkeeping is used, it may happen that one transaction is recorded simultaneously in several records, one of which may be regarded as the book of original entry.

NOTE: Memorandum books, check stubs, files of duplicate sales invoices, etc., whereon first or prior business notations may have been made, are not books of first (original) entry in the accepted meaning of the term, unless they are also used as the media for direct posting to the ledgers. (29)

book of secondary entry Ledgers as distinguished from books of original entry such as Journals.

books 1. The journals, ledgers or records containing the accounts of a business. 2. A record kept by the specialist in a particular stock of all the orders which can not be executed because they are limited to a price other than the one prevailing in the market. (105)

books (close) The date the Transfer Agent closes the transfer books of a corporation and checks the stockholder list to determine those eligible to vote or receive dividends. See Transfer Books. (105)

books (open) The date the Transfer Agent opens a corporation's transfer books to resume the normal business of transferring stocks after they had been closed to check the stockholder list. See Transfer Books. (105)

book-sort The method of sorting all checks and deposits into the books or ledgers within the bookkeeping department's alphabetical breakdown by a "rough sort." Example: all items going to the A-B-C-D book or ledger are rough-sorted into this four letter breakdown. This is to be distinguished from "fine-sort," wherein each bookkeeper sorts the items according to the alphabetical arrangement within each book or ledger. (1)

book value An accounting term. Book value of a stock is determined from a company's records, by adding all assets (generally excluding such intangibles as good will), then deducting all debts and other liabilities, plus the liquidation price of any preferred issues. The sum arrived at is divided by the number of common shares outstanding and the result is book value per common share. Book value of the assets of a company or a security may have little or no significant relationship to market value. (1)

boom A period of rapidly rising prices, characterized by substantial excess of demand for goods and services, full employment, sharply increasing demand for and supply of luxury items, inflation, rising interest rates, abnormal commercial and industrial plant expansion, and profitable use of marginal (and even submarginal) agents of production, and a care-free attitude by a substantial part of the public. (66)

boot Payments by or to the Treasury that may be necessary in an advance refunding in order to align more closely the respective values of the eligible issues and the issues offered. (115)

Fair market value (FMV) of assets other than "like" real property, used to equate the equities in an exchange. (IRS also considers cash as boot.) (120)

booth An area on the outside rim of an exchange trading floor occupied by a member firm and used to transmit orders from the firm's offices to the trading floor. (105)

borrowed reserves Discounts and advances from Federal Reserve Banks; mainly advances secured by U.S. government securities or eligible paper. (117)

borrowed stocks Brokers at times borrow stock for the purpose of providing delivery on short sales made for their clients.

borrower Any legal entity (see definition)—an individual, proprietorship, partnership, corporation, or organization—who obtains funds from the lender by the extension of credit for a period of time for a consideration. The borrower signs a note as evidence of the indebtedness. See Negotiable Instrument; Maker. (1)

borrowing power The ability of a firm or individual to obtain a loan from an individual or firm such as a bank.

borrowings The amount borrowed by reporting member banks; the breakdown shows the amounts borrowed from the Federal Reserve Banks, and from others—mostly other commercial banks. (4)

boston bookkeeping or ledger A single entry system. A progressive ledger.

bottom That phase of a projection of a time series on a chart which is the lowest point of the series. The term is generally associated with the depression phase of a cycle.

bottom dropped out of Refers to the market condition of a security when it declines so abruptly and suddenly that it appears the price may drop to zero. (105)

bottom out A condition in which a time series which has been graphically plotted after reaching a low point or phase has started to rise or improve.

bottom price That lowest price for a security or commodity for a period of time such as a day, week, season, year or cyclical phase.

bottomry A combination of money lending and insurance on hulls associated with early marine insurance. (5)

bourse A stock exchange in Europe.

box Term for a safe deposit box, or metal container in which valuables, such as securities, may be safely kept. (105)

branch bank See Branch Banking. (85)

branch banking Any bank which maintains complete banking facilities in offices away from its main office, or head office, may be considered as carrying on branch banking business. The separated units are called branches or offices and are permitted among the various classes of banks in the several states under certain conditions. Generally speaking, national banks are allowed to have branches in a state under the same conditions granted to a state-chartered bank. That is, if a state is permitted to have state-wide branches, then the same privilege is afforded national banks. At present, a few states permit

state-wide banking. The majority do, however, permit branches within city limits. (1)

brassage The charge made by the government mint for coining bullion which is the cost to the government for that service. If a charge is greater than the cost, it is known as seigniorage.

breach The art of breaking, used in such phrases as "breach of peace," "breach of promise," "breach of trust." (5)

breach of trust Violation of a duty of a trustee to a beneficiary. (74)

break A more or less sharp price decline. (9)

break even point Where the income from the business just equals the cost of doing business leaving neither a profit or a loss. (93)

break in the market An unusually sharp drop in the price for a product.

breakout The market action of a security or a market average in penetrating either above an apparent resistance level (supply) or below an apparent support level (accumulation). (105)

break up price or value The liquidating price or value of the firm.

break-up value The amount, or value, of the available assets, including the value of the marketable securities of a holding company or investment trust. (105)

brick A term used in banks to describe a package of new currency which is banded with steel straps, the straps being sealed at the joining points. New currency is shipped from the Federal Reserve Bank by this method of packaging. (1)

bring out The public offering of a new security issue by an underwriter.

broad market A situation permitting the sale and purchase of a large number and types of securities or commodities.

broad tape An enlarged form of the ticker tape machine operated by Dow Jones & Co. which prints all the important news, especially financial. Many financial businesses have a broad tape, but they are not allowed on the floors of stock exchanges because floor traders would be given too much of an advantage. (105)

broke 1. Refers to the price action of a declining security. 2. Means to lack funds. (105)

broken lot An odd lot. Generally, less than one hundred shares of stock or the usual unit of measurement and unit of sale.

broker An agent, often a member of a Stock Exchange firm or an Exchange member himself, who handles the public's orders to buy and sell securities or commodities. For this service a commission is charged. (2)

A middleman who brings together buyers and sellers of the same security or commodity and executes their orders, charging a commission for the service. See Commission; Dealer. (85)

brokerage The business of a broker. (54)

The fee or commission paid by a client to a broker for the execution of his order. (105)

brokerage account A client's account which is managed by the broker on behalf of and subject to the client's order. The broker buys and sells securities or commodities either for cash or on margin. (105)

broker-agent While generally one is either a broker or an agent, some individuals maintain two offices, one as a broker the other as an agent. One who is licensed to act both as broker and as agent. (51+)

broker's free credit balance The idle amount of money in brokerage accounts which is reported monthly by the New York Stock Exchange. (105)

broker's loan Loans made to stock brokers and secured by stock exchange collateral. Statistics on this type of loan are tabulated by the Federal Reserve Banks and others as a guide to the investing public. (1)

bubble A speculative situation in which the capitalization of the future value of the activity is so high that there is little probability of the venture making a reasonable profit on such high valuations. When this is recognized the bubble bursts and prices fall. The most famous bubbles include the Mississippi Bubble, the East India Bubble, and the Tulip Bubble.

bucketeer One who is associated with a Bucket Shop.

bucketing Operation of a Bucket Shop.

bucket shop An illegal operation now almost extinct. The bucket shop operator accepted a client's money without actually ever buying or selling securities as the client ordered. Instead he held the money and gambled that the customer was wrong. When too many customers were right, the bucket shop closed its doors and opened a new office. (2)

buck the trend To go contrary to "the crowd", for example, selling short in an advancing market, or buying long in a declining market. (105)

budget A plan of financial operation embodying an estimate of proposed expenditures for a given period or purpose and the proposed means of financing them.

NOTE: The term "budget" is used in two senses in practice. Sometimes it designates the financial plan presented to the appropriating body for adoption and sometimes the plan finally approved by that body. It is usually necessary to specify whether the budget under consideration is preliminary and tentative or whether it has been approved by the appropriating body. The term is also sometimes confused with the budget document. (29)

budgetary accounts Those accounts necessary to reflect budget operations and conditions, such as estimated revenues, appropriations, and encumbrances, as distinguished from proprietary accounts. See Proprietary Accounts. (29)

budgetary control A plan to control all operations in order to secure maximum profit from a minimum capital investment. This is accomplished by setting standards against which actual performance can be measured. An efficient Budgetary Control program not only detects inefficiencies but also definitely fixes responsibility upon the proper person or persons. (28)

budget calendar A step-by-step listing of the component requirements of a complete budget together with the specified date on which each of the component parts should be completed. The calendar is used to assure that the total budget requirements are accurately known and will be completed by a given date. (1)

budget, cash A summary of anticipated receipts and disbursements for a forthcoming period. It is generally used in forecasting cash requirements to meet future bond redemptions, dividends, plant expansion, etc. (28)

budget document The instrument used by the budget making authority to present a comprehensive financial program to the appropriating body. The budget document usually consists of three parts. The first part contains a message from the budget-making authority together with a summary of the proposed expenditures and the means of financing them. The second consists of schedules supporting the summary. These schedules show in detail the proposed expenditures and means of financing them together with information as to past years' actual revenues and expenditures and other data used in making the estimates. The third part is composed of drafts of the appropriation, revenue, and borrowing measures necessary to put the budget into effect. (29)

budget, fixed An estimate of receipts and expenditures, unalterable once established. Effects of changes in sales or production volume or in product mix are not recognized.

budget, flexible A scientific measure of actual results which provides for varying levels of activity. For example, a Flexible Expense Budget would allow various amounts for supervision depending upon the level of normal plant capacity (see Plant Capacity, Normal). In the case of material moving, the allowance might be based on tons or pieces actually moved, etc. (28)

budget, forecast A scientific estimate of anticipated results. It is usually established from previous experience, weighted to reflect expected future trends. It generally does not provide for varying levels of activity. This type of budget is used to forecast future sales, expenses, production, etc. (28)

budget plan (Installment plan) A system of buying or making expenditures in divided equal payments over a period of time. (59)

budget, production A scientific estimate of the required normal plant capacity (see Plant Capacity, Normal) necessary to meet the anticipated sales volume. (28)

budget, purchase A scientific estimate prepared by the purchasing department for the purpose of forecasting purchases required in line with company policy. (28)

budget, static See Budget, Forecast. (28)

budget, summary A recap of the functional or departmental budgets into an all-plant master budget. (28)

budget surplus or deficit The difference between net budget receipts and net budget expenditures in a given year. (Cash balances, appropriation balances, and surpluses and deficits of previous years are not a part of the calculation.) (7)

budget, variable See Budgets, Flexible. (28)

building and loan association A co-operative or stock society for the saving, accumulation, and lending of money. Deposits is an institution of this kind may be represented by shares issued in the name of the depositor. (83)

building loan A mortgage loan which is made to finance the construction of a building. It is advanced in stages as the construction work progresses. See Construction Loan. (90)

bulge A more or less sharp price advance. (9)

bulk line costs Those costs in any industry at which over 80% of the goods are produced. On the basis of such bulk line costs, price fixing or stabilization programs can be established.

bull A person who believes security prices will rise. (116)

bull account 1. That part of the market which believes prices will advance. 2. The total amount of securities held for anticipated appreciation. (105)

bull campaign An informal concentrated effort by a group of market operators or financial interest to push security prices upward. (105)

bull clique An informal group of people or interests that conduct a "bull campaign", i.e., attempt to push prices upward. (105)

bullion Precious metals such as platinum, gold, or silver which are cast in ingots or bars and considered merely as metal. (5)

bullion broker An individual or firm which deals in precious metals.

bull market (Stock market terminology) A period of generally increasing market prices. (103)

bull pool A form of manipulation now prohibited which consisted of a formally organized fund contributed by financial interests who desired prices to advance. A pool manager was selected and an agreement entered upon which stipulated the division of profits or losses and that none of the members should make individual transactions in the particular security being manipulated. (105)

bull position Refers to the prevailing status of market optimists, or bulls. If most of the market is on the buying side, i.e., leading securities are being acquired by institutions and individual investors, this is said to be a strong bull position. (105)

bunched 1. Refers to the appearance on the ticker tape of consecutive sales of the same security at identical or different prices. 2. Also may refer to one order sent to an exchange floor by a broker who has combined two or more orders from different customers. This eliminates the odd-lot orders, but round-lot was made of two odd-lot orders, and Stock Exchange rules specify that the regular commission must be paid on each odd-lot contributing to the round-lot order. (105)

bunco A swindle.

bunco game Any of a number of methods of swindling.

buoyant A condition in which prices or business conditions are advancing.

burden of proof The duty of proving a position taken in a court of law. Failure in the performance of that duty calls for judgment against the person on whom the duty rests. Thus, the burden of proof that the paper writing is not the valid will of the testator is upon the person who contests the will. (74)

burglar alarm A warning device to signal if entry is made by unlawful person or persons. The use of such alarms will permit certain reductions on premiums. (5)

business barometer A composite of weighted index numbers used to estimate the level of business. It may also be a single index of a business activity which is considered to be reflective of business activity such as total employment.

business cycle The fluctuation of business activity during which the stages of recovery, prosperity, recession, and depression are observed. Some cycles may have a period of panic between prosperity and recession.

business failures The number of business firms which cease doing business for such reasons as assignment for creditors, bankruptcy, attachment, court action and compromise settlements. Dun & Bradstreet regularly publish figures on Business Failures which some economists consider as significant economic indicators of the direction of business.

business forecasting All business executives must engage in some form of business forecasting which is an attempt to anticipate economic conditions at some future time. Many economists attempt to use scientific methods in their forecasting. The National Bureau of Economic Research has done more in this field than any other agency and, among other contributions, has developed a number of time series which lead or anticipate a business fluctuation. A number of companies and consultants sell their services as forecasters of business. While some of these are helpful, no infallible method has been perfected to forecast business.

business index (indices) A business index is a time series which presents economic data. Among the more important indices are: The Federal Reserve Board's, Index of Industrial Production; The Bureau of Labor's, Index of Employment; The Department of Commerce's time series found in the Survey of Current Business. In addition, a number of private agencies such as financial periodicals, regularly publish business indices.

business insurance trust A trust of life insurance policy contracts created in connection with a business enterprise. The term is applied both to a trust created for the liquidation of business interests and to a trust created for credit purposes or otherwise for the benefit of a business enterprise. (88)

businessman's risk A designation for a class of securities in which the investor is supposed to be able to assume risks similar to a businessman and to follow the developments with the economic background of a businessman. A securities salesman would not be criticised for recommending certain investment situations to a businessman but would be if he recommended the same securities to a widow or orphan.

business paper See Commercial Paper.

business risk There are a number of different risks which are involved in granting credit. These include insurable risks, moral risks, and the risk from acts of God such as floods, and earthquakes. One major risk, the business risk, involves the ability of a businessman to operate his business in an efficient and profitable manner.

business solvency That situation in which a firm has more assets than liabilities. Since some of the assets may not be available for paying maturing debts a firm or individual which possesses business solvency may none the less be financially insolvent.

business transaction An act of business involving buying or selling or other exchanges in value. (73)

business transfer payments Represent money paid by the business sector to persons for which no goods or services are received in return. Thus, there is no offsetting contribution to the economy's productive process. Major items included in this line are corporate gifts to nonprofit institutions, consumer bad debts, and personal injury payments by business to persons other than employees. Estimates of unrecovered thefts of cash and capital assets and cash prizes are also included. (124)

business trust 1. Massachusetts trust or common law trust. A form of business organization wherein the assets are conveyed or transferred to a board of trustees for management and operation for the benefit of the holders of transferable trust certificates representing shares which resemble closely the shares of stock in a corporation. 2. Voting trust. A form of business organization wherein the owners of a part or all of the stock of a company transfer their shares to trustees for the purpose of voting them. They receive in return transferable voting trust certificates which entitle them to any dividends on the stock. (74)

buttonwood tree The tree associated with the founding of the New York Stock Exchange. Twenty-four men gathered under such a tree on May 17, 1792, at 68 Wall Street and established themselves as brokers for the purchase and sale of public stocks. (105)

buy and put away An old Wall Street maxim that claims a successful stock market practice is to buy stocks then put them away and forget about them. This, of course, is not always true because all securities will not advance in price as hoped. However, in an inflationary period this might be a successful practice for most stocks. (105)

buy back The purchase of a long contract to cover a short position. Generally associated with covering a security or commodity which was sold short.

buyers' market The period of a contracting demand; prices are on a downward trend. (5)

buyer's monopoly A market situation characterized by many sellers and one buyer.

buyers option The legal right the buyer has to acquire a security, commodity, or other thing within the terms of the option contract.

buyers' strike A situation in which the buyers of a product stop their purchases. This may be because the price is simply too high, or it may be caused by a concerted attempt by organisers to exert pressure on the sellers to force price reductions.

buyer's surplus An economic concept to recognize that many buyers would pay more for a product than the seller has asked. The difference between what the buyer pays and what he would pay if he had to is known as the buyer's surplus.

buy in To cover or liquidate a sale. Shorts are

said to "cover" when they repurchase the contracts they sold originally. (9)

buying motives Real reasons why people purchase goods and services. The motives may be logical or emotional.

buying on a shoestring The practice of buying securities on very thin margin (the value of a shoestring). (105)

buying on balance That situation in which a broker's orders to buy exceed the orders he has to sell. In a market the sales equal the purchases, but for a brokerage firm they need not equal each other.

buying on margin Many items are bought without the purchaser immediately paying the whole price. Examples of buying on margin include purchase of a home with a mortgage or of a security with a partial payment and borrowing the difference from a broker or bank. Margin refers to the proportion of down payment that is made by the purchaser. The Board of Governors of the Federal Reserve Board has the right to establish margin requirements for the purchase of listed securities. This is a selective credit control.

buying on scale A method used in purchasing securities in which the broker is instructed to buy a given number of shares at given intervals of a price decline. Since the buyer does not know how low the price will drop, by buying on scale as the price drops his average cost per share also drops.

buying order The instructions to buy such things as securities and commodities which are given to a broker. There are many restrictions that may be made part of an order such as time of execution, place of execution, limit on authority, market orders, day orders, good till cancelled, etc.

buying outright The purchase of a thing without mortgage or use of margin. Buying long.

buying power The capacity to purchase possessed by an individual buyer, a group of buyers, or the aggregate of the buyers in an area or a market. "Purchasing power" is preferred. (13)

buying rate That publicized quotation for purchasing such things as foreign exchange, commodities, and bills of exchange which a bank, manufacturer or other purchaser uses to let the trader know of his willingness to buy.

buying under the rule See Under the Rule.

buy on bid A method by which someone can buy a listed stock from an odd-lot trader who is selling at the bid price rather than waiting to execute an odd-lot sale after the next round-lot sale, which may be an indefinite time. (105)

buy on close or opening To buy at the end or beginning of the session at a price within the closing or opening range. (9)

buy on the offer A method of buying an odd-lot which avoids the delay which might be involved with a market order. Rather than waiting for the next round-lot sale to establish the price of the odd-lot transaction, a "buy on the offer" order will be executed at the lowest quoted asking price plus the odd-lot differential. (105)

buy-sell agreement An agreement wherein owners of a business arrange to transfer their respective ownership interests upon the death of one, or upon some other event, so as to provide continued control of the business or some other desired end. (74)

buy ticket A form prepared in multiple copies, used by the investment department to instruct the order department to purchase a security. (74)

by-laws Generally, specific provisions supplementing and implementing the charters or constitutions of private organizations such as corporations and labor unions. (12)

Rules adopted by a bank for the conduct of its affairs, pursuant to the powers and authority given in its charter. (90)

Those rules adopted by the board of directors of a corporation which are subordinate to a constitution or charter which give the general duties of the officers and their powers, as well as a general statement of operation policy.

C

C Carat. (37)

C. Means "cash" when printed on the lower line of the ticker tape preceding prices. (105)

C/A Cause of action.

C. A. D. Cash against documents.

¢ Cent in U.S. and Canada.

c% Cents per cent. (5)

C Centigrade.

C Class C bonds and stocks.

C. A. Current assets; Chartered Accountant.

C. A. F. Cost, assurance, freight.

Can. Cancel.

Cap. Capital; Capitalization.

Cash. Cashier.

C/B Cash book.

C. B. D. Cash before delivery.

C. C. Cashier's check; contra credit.

C.C.I.A. Consumer Credit Insurance Association. (5)

C. D. Cash Discount.

C.D. See Certificate of Deposit. (1)

CEA Commodity Exchange Authority; Council of Economic Advisers.

CED Committee for Economic Development.

Cert. Certification.

C and F Cost and freight are included in the price quoted. It does not include the cost of insurance. If insurance cost is included then the abbreviation C.I.F. is quoted.

C. H. Clearing House.

Chgs. Charges.

Chq. Cheque.

C. & I. Cost and insurance.

C.I.D. Compound Interest Deposit. A type of savings account. See Special Interest Account. (1)

C.I.F. Cost, insurance, and freight. (5)

C. I. F. & C. Cost, insurance, freight and commissions (or charges).

Ck. Check.

C/L Cash letter.

Cl Clause.

C. L. Current liabilities; Car load lots.

C.L. Common law.

Cmn. Commission.

Co. Coinsurance. (5)

Co. Company.

COB Close of Business. (67)

C.O.D. Cash on Delivery. The seller requires full payment at time of delivery to point specified by purchaser. (24)

C.O.D. Account A general ledger account that is maintained to show the amount to be collected on C.O.D. sales. It is debited for all C.O.D. sales. It is credited for all C.O.D. collections and for all returned C.O.D. shipments. (73)

C.O.D. Delivery Sheet A form that is filled out daily to show the details and the totals of the C.O.D. sales, collections, and returns for the day. (73)

Coll. Collateral; collection.

Coll/L Collection Letter.

Coll. Tr. Collateral Trust.

Com. Common; Commerce.

Com'l. Ppr. Commercial paper.

Comm. Commission.

Comp. Compound; composite.

Comp't. Comptroller.

Con. Cr. Contra credit.

Cond. Condition.

Cons. Consolidated.

Consid. Consideration.

Cont. Contract.

Conv. Convertible.

Cor. Corpus; correspondent.

Corp. Corporation; corporate.

C/P Condition precedent.

C/P Contract price. (5)

C. P. A. Certified Public Accountant.

Cps. Coupons.

Cr. Credit, Creditor.

C. S. Capital Stock.

C/S Condition subsequent.

C/T Cable Transfer.

Ctfs. Certificates.

Cts. Cents; Centimes.

Cum. Cumulative.

C.U.N.A. Credit Union National Association. (5)

Curr. Current; currency.

Cvt. Convertible; convert.

Cy. Currency.

cabinet crowd Also called the Inactive or Book Crowd. Those individuals who trade in inactive bonds on the floor of the New York Stock Exchange.

cable rate A term used in foreign exchange to refer to the rates quoted for a cable transfer of foreign exchange. The Cable Rate is higher than the check, demand, 30; 60; or 90-day bill of exchange rate.

cable transfer The transfer of funds in a foreign country through instructions sent by cable. (85)

calculator A device that performs primarily arithmetic operations based upon data and instructions inserted manually or contained on punch cards. It is sometimes used interchangeably with computer. (104)

call This word has five different connotations:

1. To demand payment of an installment of the price of bonds or stocks which have been subscribed for. The date of call is discretionary with the issuing corporation, or may have been prearranged. The subscribed capital of a corporation which is uncalled, may, according to arrangements made with subscribers, be called at any time in conformity with the agreement made when the stock was allotted.

2. To demand payment of a loan secured by collateral (a demand loan, see definition) because of failure on the part of the borrower to comply with the terms of the loan. This may be caused by failure to provide additional margin due to falling value of the collateral, or to liquidate the loan in accordance with a prearranged schedule.

3. Comptroller's Call (See definition).

4. Margin Call (See definition).

5. Call Options (See Puts and Calls).

callable A bond issue, all or part of which may be redeemed by the issuing corporation under definite conditions before maturity. The term also applies to preferred shares which may be retired by the issuing corporation. (2)

call back The act of reading back posting media to the postings, or checks making up a list, to the listing of the items. One person reads the amounts to another person who is checking the "run" for accuracy. Call backs are often made when a balance or settlement is not accomplished, the call back being one form of proving the accuracy of a run of items. Call backs are frequently used in connection with the "Dual Plan" of posting, wherein statement balances are called back to ledger balances.

call loan A loan made on a day-to-day basis, callable on twenty-four hours' notice. Typically, loans made to members of the New York Stock Exchange to facilitate the exchange of securities. (85)

call money Money loaned by banks to brokers which is subject to call (demanded payment) at the discretion of the lender. See Call Loan. (1)

call money market Those financial institutions which are active in providing call money. Today brokers individually arrange with the big banks for their day-to-day money needs to finance margin purchases.

called preferred stock Preferred stock, containing call provisions, which is redeemed by a corporation. (74)

call price A term generally used in connection with preferred stocks and debt securities having a fixed claim. It is the price which an issuer must pay in order to voluntarily retire such securities. Often call price exceeds par or liquidating price in order to compensate the holder of the called security for his loss of income and investment position resulting from the call. (3)

call provision A bond with a call provision may be redeemed at the option of the issuer before maturity, usually at a premium.

call purchase A technique for purchasing commodities in which the seller has some option of pricing in the future within a stated range of the present price.

call report Banking authorities such as the Comptroller of the Currency, Federal Reserve Banks, Federal Deposit Insurance Corporation and State Superintendent of Banking call a minimum of three times and sometimes four times a year for the banks under their supervision to provide statements of condition as of the call date. The actual date is not released prior to the "call" so that banks may not engage in "window dressing" activities.

call sale A technique for selling commodities in which the buyer has some option of pricing in the future within a stated range of the present price.

cambism or cambistry The technique of engaging in foreign exchange.

cambist A specialist in foreign exchange or a publication tabulating rates of foreign exchange and associated regulations.

cancel To mark or perforate; make void. (93)

cancellation, flat Cancellation as of the date of inception, and without charge. (42)

cancellation, pro rata Cancellation with a return of premium proportionate to the unexpired period for which premiums were paid. (42)

cancellation, short-rate Cancellation upon request of an insured, with a return of less than the proportionate amount. (42)

cancelled checks Checks which have been paid and charged to the depositor's account, then stamped or perforated with the date of the payment and the drawee bank's name or clearinghouse number. These checks are retained in the files of the bank until a statement of the depositor's account is sent to him. (83)

cancelling machine 1. (Sometimes called a "perforator.") A machine used for cancelling checks, pass books, and other records in a bank. It is accomplished by a series of dies which perforate either the word "cancelled" or the word "paid" through the inserted record. The date of cancellation and the bank's transit number may also be perforated in the record. 2. Machine through which mail is run for the purpose of effacing stamps and placing postmarks on letters. (1, 39)

canon of ethics Written and unwritten standards of conduct expected by certain groups, especially professional groups, in the pursuit of their specialized activities. (74)

capital The amount subscribed and paid by stockholders to permit a bank to function as such. Capital requirements of banks, both national and state, are governed by the size of the community in which they are chartered to operate. Supervisory authorities determine the amount of capital necessary for a bank to start operations in a given locality. In all cases, capital must be fully paid in cash before a bank is allowed to open for business. Shareholders of national banks and some state banks must pay a premium for the capital stock purchased, this premium being applied to the establishment of a paid-in surplus. (1)

In an a counting sense, the excess of assets over liabilities. In a corporation, it is the sum of the various capital stock accounts, surplus, and undivided profits; hence capital is synonymous with net worth. See Surplus. (85)

capital account An account maintained in the name of the owner, or owners, of a business which indicates his or their equity in that business—usually at the close of the last accounting period. (1)

capital assets A collective term which includes all fixed assets, consisting of furniture and fixtures, land, buildings, machinery, etc. (1)

capital budget An improvement program and the methods of its financing.

NOTE: This term is frequently limited to a longterm budget for improvements but is sometimes also used to designate that part of the current budget which deals with improvements. See also Long-Term; Budget. (29)

capital charges Sums required to satisfy interest upon, and amortization of, monies invested in an enterprise. (54)

capital costs Cost of improvements which extend the useful life of property and/or add to value. Not deductible for tax purposes in the year incurred but depreciable over their useful lives. (120)

capital distribution See Liquidating Dividend. (74)

capital expenditure Investments of cash or other property or the creation of liability in exchange for property to remain permanently in the business; usually land, buildings, machinery, and equipment. (54)

capital expenditures budget An estimate of cash expenditures for purchases of new equipment or other fixed assets during a future fiscal period of a business. (73)

capital, fixed The amount of money expended on permanent investment in fixed assets. (66)

capital formation The creation of capital through savings. In this sense capital is not money or securities or land but a productive good such as machinery which may be purchased with the money savings.

capital gain (or loss) Profit or loss resulting from the sale or exchange of a capital asset; for F.I.T. purposes, it is the difference between sales price and the cost basis remaining at the time of sale after deducting normal depreciation, cost depletion, abandonments and other write-offs. The recapture as ordinary income may be required of the excess of "fast depreciation" over normal depreciation, statutory depletion over cost depletion, and other preferential tax items. (125)

capital gains distribution A distribution to investment company shareholders from net long-term capital gains realized by a "regulated investment company" on the sale of portfolio securities. (3)

capital growth An increase in market value of securities; a long-term objective many investment companies pursue. (65)

capital investments A collective term representing the amounts invested in capital, fixed assets, or in long-term securities as contrasted with those funds invested in current assets or short-term securities. Generally speaking, capital investments include all funds invested in assets which, during the normal course of business, are not expected to be realized upon during the ensuing fiscal period. (1)

capital issues Those issues of bonds and stocks which are more or less permanent and fixed as compared with short-term notes and accounts payable.

capitalization Total amount of the various securities issued by a corporation. Capitalization may include bonds, debentures, preferred and common stock. Bonds and debentures are usually carried on the books of the issuing company in terms of their par or face value. Preferred and common shares may be carried in terms of par or stated value. Stated value may be an arbitrary figure decided upon by the directors or may represent the amount received by the company from the sale of the securities at the time of issuance. See Par. (2)

capitalization rate 1. The relationship of income to capital investment or value, expressed as a percentage. 2. The (percentage) rate at which an anticipated future income stream is discounted to present worth, i.e., market value. (66)

capitalization rate (S), basis for split Justification of the use of split rates is confined to two basic assumptions, as follows:

1. Investment in land and investment in building represent different degrees of risk and, therefore, require the application of different rate in the capitalization of the income attributed to each: (a) Land value is presumed to be stable and to earn a constant return to perpetuity. (b) Terminable lives of buildings require a higher rate to insure return of capital investment within their estimated economic life, in addition to a return on the investment or capital value. 2. Income attributable to land and return to building are predictable, separable and identifiable. (66)

capitalization rate (S), methods of selection of 1. Band of Investment, sometimes designated Synthetic—in which the current mortgage rate and rate for equity capital are combined in the same proportion as each (mortgage and equity) bears to the total value estimate. For example:

662/3% mortgage loan X 6.0% rate = 0.40 or 4.00%

331/3% equity capital X 12.0% rate = 0.40 or 4.00%

Synthetic (net) rate developed = 0.80 or 8.00%

The accuracy of this method depends upon the correctness of the appraiser's estimate of the availability of mortgage money at the rate and loan-value ratio set forth, and the degree to which the rate of return on equity capital has been verified by reference to comparable sales. (66)

2. Comparative—under which an over-all rate is developed through the process of dividing the sales prices of comparable properties into the net income (s), before depreciation, being produced (or capable of being produced under competent management) at time of sale of these properties. The over-all, or composite, rate so produced includes provision for return on and of capital investment in both land and improvements, and is applied to net income before depreciation. This is the best known, and most

commonly used and accepted method of selection of a capitalization rate because it is a reflection of the doings of buyers and sellers in the market place.

3. Summation or Component Rate—in which the net rate is fabricated or built up adding together the subrates applicable to the various factors which influence the size of the whole. Under this technique, a specific rate is assigned to each factor presumed to influence investors in their determination of the final rate. The most commonly accepted influencing factors are the (a) safe rate, (b) rate for risk, (c) rate for non-liquidity, (d) rate for management, to which is sometimes added (e) rate for regularity of payment. Such a fabricated rate might be illustrated as follows:

Safe rate	3.5%
Rate for risk	2.0%
Rate for non-liquidity	2.0%
Rate for management	0.5%
Total rate	8.0%

This is the least desirable method for the selection of capitalization rates, as it depends upon proper evaluation of each of several components, at least two of which cannot be said to have market support. (66)

capitalization rate (S), net 1. The rate of interest expected to be earned on an investment. 2. The rate of interest at which anticipated future net income is discounted, exclusive of provision for recapture of capital investment. (66)

capitalization rate (S), over-all Net (capitalization) rate plus provision for recapture of total investment, i.e., land and improvements. This is the rate used in the Property Residual Technique and is applied to net income before depreciation. (66)

capitalization rate (S), safe The net rate of return on a virtually riskless and completely liquid investment, generally accepted as the savings bank interest rate or interest being paid on long-term government bonds in a stable market; usually known as the "Safe Rate." (66)

capitalization rate (S), source of The market is the only source of capitalization rates which provides provable support for those rates. (66)

capitalization rate (S), split A term used in the capitalization process denoting the application of different rates to portions of total net income presumed to be earned by fractional parts of an improved property, e.g., one rate applied to claimed earnings of land and another applied to net income said to be earned by the building; commonly known as "Split Rates." (66)

capitalization ratios The percent that each of the following or its components is of total capitalization: Bonds, Other Long-Term Debt, Preferred Stock, Common Stock and Retained Income, Capital Surplus, and Premium on Capital Stock. (21)

capitalize 1. To include in the investment account expenditures for purchase or construction of property, or for organization. 2. To issue securities to represent such investment. 3. To divide income by a rate of interest to obtain principal. (19)

capitalized cost The original cost of an asset plus

all the net charges incurred to ready or complete it for its intended use. (29)

capitalized value The asset value (principal) of a given number of income dollars determined on the basis of an assumed rate of return. For example, the capitalized value of a $500 perpetual income at a rate of 5% is $10,000 (Obtained by dividing $500 by .05). (103)

capital loan A loan which cannot be repaid without disposing of capital assets, in contrast to a loan, for example, to purchase merchandise, the sale of which will provide funds to repay the loan. (85)

capital movement The liquidation of capital investment in one area and its reinvestment in another area.

capital outlay Expenditures for the acquisition of or addition to fixed assets. Included are amounts for replacements and major alterations, but not for repair. (7)

capital paid in The amount paid in for Federal Reserve Bank stock owned by member banks. (4)

capital rating Many mercantile agencies divide their evaluation of a credit risk into two phases; one being an estimation of the net worth of a business which is called the Capital Rating and the second phase which refers to the payment record of the subject as to his practice of discounting, paying on time or of being slow.

capital requirements The total monetary investment essential to the establishment and operation of an enterprise. The appraised investment in plant facilities and normal working capital. It may or may not include appraised cost of business rights such as patents, contracts, and charter. (54)

capital resources Resources of a fixed or permanent character, such as land and buildings, which cannot ordinarily be used to meet expenditures. (29)

capital stock (Commercial Business) The specified amount of stock which a corporation may sell as authorized by the state granting the corporation charter. If the stock has a stated value per share, such value is known as "par value." Stock without a designated value is referred to as "no par value" stock. Such authorized stock is commonly recorded on the books of account in the following manner:

Unissued Stock (Debit) $500,000.00
Authorized Capital Stock (Credit) . . . $500,000.00

As the stock is sold, such sales are commonly recorded in the following manner:

Cash, or other Assets (Debit) $100,000.00
Unissued Stock (Credit) $100,000.00

Each stockholder, upon purchasing the stock, is issued a certificate showing the stockholder's name and number of shares purchased, and the value (par value, if any) assigned to each share. This certificate of stock is a contract between the stockholder and the corporation issuing the stock, granting the stockholder his proportionate share (or equity) in the capital and in the future earnings of the corporation. See Stock; Stock Certificate. (1)

capital stock discount and expense A balance

sheet account. The excess of par value over the price paid in by the shareholder is capital stock discount. Expenses incurred in connection with the issuance and sale of capital stock which are not properly chargeable to Organization, and which have not been charged to Surplus are included in Capital Stock Discount and Expense. (21)

capital stock subscribed A temporary capital account that contains a record of capital stock subscribed for but not issued because the subscriptions have not been fully paid. (73)

capital structure The distribution of a corporation's capital among its several component parts, such as stock, bonds, and surplus. (90)

capital surplus All surplus not properly classifiable as retained income. It may include credit from sales by the utility of reacquired capital stock, surplus arising from the retirement and cancellation of the company's capital stock, from donations by stockholders of the company's capital stock, from a reduction of the par or stated value of the company's capital stock, and from forgiveness of debt of the company; also, surplus recorded at a reorganization or in connection with a recapitalization. (21)

capital turnover A term commonly used by the Credit Department of a lending institution which represents the number of times the outstanding capital has "turned over" in relation to the net sales for a given period of time, frequently a year.

carat A unit of weight for gems equal to about 3.2 grains. A twenty-fourth part of pure gold. Pure gold with no alloy is 24 carat gold but would be too soft for practical handling and thus generally some alloy is added.

care of securities The action of an investor after buying and paying for a security. Safekeeping practices include registering the security in his own name, using only registered mail when transferring the certificate, endorsing the back of the certificate only when necessary, keeping a separate and identical record such as the transfer agent keeps, and either leaving the certificate with a bank or securities firm. (105)

carrier's lien Right of carrier to retain property which it has transported as security for the collection of charges. (19)

carry 1. To renew a matured note. 2. To purchase securities on a long rather than short basis. 3. To provide the difference between a partial down payment and the total price of a product or service.

carryback A corporate income tax term which refers to the right of a corporation to apply a deficit in one year's earnings against profits in a previous year or years. In this manner the corporation may then obtain a rebate on the taxes paid in the profitable period.

carrying broker A broker which is supplying funds for a customer who is trading on margin.

carrying charge The fee charged by a broker for carrying a customer's securities on margin. See Margin. (2)

Those charges incurred in carrying the actual commodity for one or more days, weeks or months, generally including interest, insurance and storage but sometimes including other pertinent items. (9)

carrying market A market in which more distant positions are quoted at a premium over the nearby positions, and where this premium is high enough to compensate for the carrying charges. (123)

carrying value The value of a fixed asset remaining after its accumulated depreciation reserve has been deducted from its original depreciable cost. (29)

carry-over That portion of the production of a good that has not been consumed during the period and thus is available for later consumption.

carry-overs and carry-backs There are two kinds of carry-overs and carry-backs available to corporations for federal income tax purposes: (1) Net Operating Loss; (2) Unused Excess Profits Credit. The net operating loss carry-over or carry-back is the excess of the deductions allowed under the income tax law over the statutory gross income, with certain exceptions, additions and limitations. The excess profits credit carry-over or carry-back is the excess of the excess profits credit over the excess profits net income. It is to be understood that an operating deficit will not necessarily produce a carry-over or a carry-back for income tax purposes. (19)

cartel An attempt to stabilize prices or a commodity or industry by the allocation of territory or quotas to the members of the cartel. These members agree to not compete with each other under the terms of the cartel understanding. A combination in restraint of trade similar to the "trusts" of the 1890s.

cash Currency, checks, postal and express money orders, and bankers' drafts on hand or on deposit with an official or agent designated as custodian of cash; and bank deposits.

NOTE: All cash must be accounted for as a part of the fund to which it belongs. Any restrictions or limitations as to its availability must be indicated in the records and statements. It is not necessary, however, to segregate the cash itself; for example, it is not necessary to have a separate bank account for each fund. (29)

cash account A ledger account which has debits which show receipts and credits which show payments and the debit difference is the amount of cash on hand.

cash assets The amount of bank deposits and cash on hand as shown by a financial statement.

cash audit An audit of the cash transactions for a stated period, for the purpose of determining that all cash received has been recorded, that all disbursements have been properly authorized and vouched, and that the balance of cash is either on hand or on deposit. A cash audit can be limited from a complete inquiry into all cash transactions (a complete cash audit) to one involving only some of them (a limited cash audit). Such an audit establishes the accountability of the persons responsible for cash. (29)

cash balance The amount of cash on hand. (73)

cash basis The system of accounting under which revenues are accounted for only when received in cash, and expenditures are accounted for only when paid. (29)

cashbook A book of original entry in which the cash receipts journal and the cash payments journal are brought together to form one book. (73)

cash budget An estimate of cash receipts and disbursements for a future fiscal period of a business; a budget in which the estimated expenditures for the coming year are allocated to the months in such a manner that the expenditures planned for any given month do not exceed the cash that will be available (from collections or borrowing) for that month. (73)

cash bus A cabinet on wheels where tellers store cash in the teller's cage or wicket during the day. This cabinet has sufficient room for the "cash till" and also storage under lock and key for packaged specie money that may be required for making change in large orders. The teller wheels the cash bus into the vault after balancing the cash at the end of the day. (1)

cash buying The purchase of a thing such as a commodity or security by payment in full as contrasted with a margin purchase.

cash commodity Same as "Spot Commodity"; originally referred to a commodity on the spot, which may be put in a position for delivery, now used to also include a commodity bought or sold "to arrive" or to be delivered at a later date. A spot commodity as distinguished from a futures contract. (9)

cash credit The British custom of permitting check overdrafts to an amount which is called the cash credit.

cash credit discount In installment cash credit, the discount is the charge for the credit service which is deducted from the total amount of the loan before the borrower received the balance in cash. (131)

cash discount An allowance received or given if payment is completed within a stated period.
  NOTE: The term is not to be confused with "trade discount". (29)

cash dividend Declared dividends that are payable in cash. In this case cash would include checks as distinguished from a stock or commodity dividend. (1)

cash earnings The net income or profits of a corporation including accrued depreciation and amortization. (105)

cashed check Check accepted by a bank in exchange for cash. Usually such an item can be identified by a teller's stamp or cash out symbol. (83)

cash flow The way a business receives funds. The money that is made available by the operation of the firm. For example, the payment of a large debt by a past due debtor will increase the cash flow of the creditor. The taking of depreciation while a business has earnings will also provide a cash flow if the depreciation is not funded.

cashier An officer of a bank who is charged with the custody of the bank's assets, and whose signature is necessary on official documents. He may not delegate this authority, so that in large banks where his duties are too numerous, assistant cashiers are appointed by the board of directors to perform specific duties.

cashier's account That ledger account of a bank which is mostly used to record cashier's checks.

cashier's check A bank's own check drawn upon itself, and signed by the cashier, or other authorized official. It is a direct obligation of the bank. It is used to pay obligations of the bank; to disburse the proceeds of a loan to the borrower in lieu of credit to his deposit account; and is sold to customers for domestic remittance purposes where a personal check is not acceptable. (1)

cash-ins Redemptions of investment company shares. (105)

cash in vault Coin and currency actually held by the banks on their own premises. (4)

cash items 1) Any items for which a depositor may be given immediate ledger credit. To be distinguished from "Collection Items." 2) Any unpaid item being held prior to disposition or conversion into cash. (83)

cash letter Transit check with listing tapes, transmitting items from one bank to another for collection. Frequently, the items contained in the cash letter are grouped into several batches with a listing tape attached to each batch. The totals are recapped on the transmittal form letter. Generally, these are associated with mail deposits received from other banks. Cash letters are sometimes referred to as "transit letters" or "transmittal letters." (83)

cash letter of credit A letter addressed by a bank to its correspondent bank to make available to the party named in the letter, funds up to a specified amount within certain time limitations. The sum named in the letter is deposited with the bank before the letter is issued, hence the designation "cash letter of credit." (1)

cash loan See Policy Loan. (42)

cash market The spot market as contrasted with the futures market.

cash method of handling purchases The method of recording purchases only when they are paid by recording the invoice in the cash payments journal. (73)

cash on delivery Purchases must be paid for on delivery to customer. (26)

cash over A general ledger account to which tellers' cash overages are credited. See Cash Over and Short. (1, 73)

cash over and short The variation of the cash on hand from the balance of the cash account or cashbook. If the cash on hand is more than the balance of the cash account or cashbook, the cash is over. If the cash on hand is less than that of the balance, the cash is short; the title of the account in which a record is kept of the variations of the cash on hand from the balance of the cash account or cashbook as revealed by the daily cash proof. The account is debited for all shortages in the cash and is credited for all overages. (73)

cash payments journal A special journal in which all cash payments, and only cash payments, are recorded. (73)

cash receipts journal A special journal in which all cash receipts, and only cash receipts, are recorded. (73)

cash register A business machine that is used to provide an immediate record of each cash transaction; a business machine that provides quickly an immediate record of transactions. It also provides a convenient place for sorting and keeping the money used in daily transactions. (73)

cash register totals The daily totals for each type of transaction, such as cash sales, charge sales, receipts on account, and paid outs. (73)

cash release ticket A slip either hand-written or machine printed by which a teller charges himself for the amount of cash on a deposit. When these slips are hand-written, a duplicate is made so that the teller will have a copy available to arrive at a cash balance. Machine printed tickets are in original only, because the amount of cash is added to a "cash in" total in the machine, which provides the teller with a balancing figure. The original tickets accompany the deposits to the proof department, and are used to prove the total of the deposit along with checks of other items deposited. (1)

cash reserve An amount of cash, or very liquid securities quickly convertible to cash, kept in reserve for special purposes or to protect against sudden emergency need. (59)

Those legal requirements for banks to maintain legal reserves. Banks that are members of the Federal Reserve System keep their cash reserves on deposit with their district Federal Reserve Bank and are permitted to count some of their till cash also as part of their legal reserves. The cash reserves of state nonmember banks is determined by the individual state law.

cash sale 1. One in which cash is received for the full amount at the time of the sale. 2. A transaction on the floor of the Stock Exchange which calls for delivery of the securities the same day. In "regular way" trades, the seller is allowed four business days for delivery. See Regular Way Delivered. (73, 2)

cash short A general ledger account to which tellers' cash shortages are charged. (1)

cash substitution ticket See Cash Release Ticket. (1)

cash ticket A slip or ticket used as a substitute for cash included in a deposit. The teller verifies and retains the cash, recording the amount on the cash ticket. (83)

cash till A tray built with compartment bins to help tellers sort and have ready for easy access the various denominations of currency. The till usually contains bins for each of the denominations, such as $1.00, $5.00, $10.00, $20.00, and $50.00 and $100.00. The $2.00 bills are generally segregated and carried in the back portion of the cash till. If the teller is authorized to carry larger denominations these will also be carried in the rear portion of the till. (1)

cash trade An exchange of a good or thing for payment in full in the form of money.

cash transactions As used in the cash accounts:

Cash Deposits: cash receipts from all sources by the Treasury, the public, and from seigniorage.

Cash Withdrawals: budget expenditures, trust and deposit fund expenditures, and government-sponsored enterprise expenditures (net) less intragovernmental and other expenditures.

Net Cash Borrowing: when the sale of securities to the public exceeds the redemption of securities by the public. It excludes sale of securities to trust account, and government enterprises.

Net Cash Repayment of Borrowing: when the redemption of securities by the public exceeds the sale of securities to the public. (7)

cats and dogs (securities) Stocks and bonds of dubious value. Lenders such as banks will not accept such securities as collateral for loans.

causa mortis See Gift Cause Mortis. (74)

caveat A notice not to do an act, given to a person by a party having an interest in the matter, until that party is heard in the matter. (66)

caveat emptor A Latin phrase for, "Let the buyer beware".

caveator An interested party who gives notice to some officer not to do a certain act until the party is heard in opposition, as the caveator of a will offered for probate. (74)

caveat venditor A Latin phrase for, "Let the seller beware".

cease-and-desist order Order issued by a court or government agency directing an employer or a union to end an unfair practice.

cedule The European designation for the duplicate copy of a warehouse receipt.

cemetery trust A trust which has as its purpose, the upkeep of a grave, burial plot, or cemetery. (74)

cent One hundredth part of a dollar.

central bank A bank which deals chiefly with other banks in holding the banking reserves of its country or district and normally government agencies or government related agencies and operates in the broad public interest. In the United States, central banking functions are carried on by the twelve regional Federal Reserve Banks under the supervision of the Board of Governors of the Federal Reserve System. In many other countries there is but a single institution that functions as a central bank, e.g., Bank of England. (8)

central charge plan See Bank Charge Plans. (26)

central file Those records of a firm in which information on the customers of the firm is maintained in a form to permit an evaluation of the profitability and services provided the customer.

central proof A system for effecting economy of operation by centralizing all proof and distributing functions in a single department of a bank. See Proof Department. (1, 83)

central rate A rate established under a temporary regime (based on an Executive Board decision of December 18, 1974) by a country which temporarily does not maintain rates based on a par value in accordance with the relevant Fund rules but does maintain transactions in its territories. Central rates are in certain respects treated as par values, and the concept was introduced primarily to allow Fund members who, prior to August 15, 1971, had an effective par value to base their exchange rates on a stable rate subject to specified margin requirements during the period when the par value of the U.S. dollar was not effective. The temporary regime provides for the possibility of margins of 2-¼ per cent either side of the central rate. After the change in the par value of the U.S. dollar on May 8, 1974, a number of countries have replaced their central rates with new par values. (130)

central reserve city bank A member bank in New York City or Chicago. At one time St. Louis also was a Central Reserve City. Banks in these money centers frequently held the legal reserves of state banks and for this reason were considered unique. In recent years this special treatment, especially in the form of reserve requirements, has declined.

central wholesale market The collecting points for agricultural products in which large scale storage, processing, credit and similar facilities are available.

certificate The actual piece of paper which is evidence of ownership of stock in a corporation. Watermarked paper is finely engraved with delicate etchings to discourage forgery. Loss of a certificate may at the least cause a great deal of inconvenience—at the worst, financial loss. (2)

certificate of accounts That document and statement which is issued by a certified public accountant which states the accountant's evaluation of the books of accounts of a firm which he has audited or from which he has audited or from which he has prepared statements.

certificate of analysis That document which a seller may be obliged to tender to an importer with a bill of exchange which is used to establish the quality, fineness and other characteristics of a shipment.

certificate of beneficial interest A legal instrument which is issued to owners of a business. The document describes the owner's equity and is commonly used in voting trusts.

certificate of claim A contingent promise of the Federal Housing Administration to reimburse an insured mortgagee for certain costs incurred during foreclosure of an insured mortgage provided the proceeds from the sale of the property acquired are sufficient to cover those costs. (89)

certificate of deposit A formal receipt for funds left with a bank as a special deposit, generally interest-bearing. Such deposits may bear interest and be payable at a definite date in the future, or they may be non-interest bearing demand deposits. These deposits are payable only upon surrender of the formal receipt properly indorsed, and they are carried on the general ledger of the bank under heading "Certificate of Deposit" rather than on the individual ledgers under the name of the person to whom the certificate was originally issued. (85)

certificate of incorporation The franchise or charter issued by the state to the original petitioners of an approved corporation. Such franchise or charter constitutes the authority granted by the state for the organization to transact business as a corporation. (1)

certificate of indebtedness 1. Government issues of short-term, unsecured notes used to raise funds for current expenses. 2. United States Treasury Certificate. A short-term obligation of

less maturity length than a bond but more than Treasury Bills or Notes. (105)

certificate of protest That document which a notary public prepares when a dishonored negotiable instrument is again presented but not paid. The certificate is legal evidence that presentation has been made and refused.

certificate of stock A Stock Certificate. See that term.

certificated stock A commodity that has been examined, classified, and found to be tenderable and thus has had a certificate issued. The commodity may thus be traded as being of a specified class or quality.

certification The acceptance of a check or draft by the drawee bank, evidenced by a stamp placed on the face of the instrument and signed by an officer or some other authorized employee of the drawee bank. On certification, the instrument ceases to be a liability of the maker and becomes a liability of the acceptor. Thus, the drawee bank's credit is substituted for the credit of the maker. By its certifications the bank guarantees that sufficient funds have been set aside from the depositor's account to pay the check when payment is demanded. (90)

certification department That part of a bank in which the certification tellers process checks and record regarding checks which are certified.

certification teller A teller whose duty is to certify or accept checks of depositors. In large banks this may be his only duty, but in smaller banks it is usually combined with other duties. (1)

certified check A depositor's check across the face of which an officer of the bank or some other authorized person has stamped the word "certified" and the bank's name and then signed his own name. By its certification the bank guarantees that sufficient funds have been set aside from the depositor's account to pay the check when payment is demanded. (85)

certiorari A proceeding to review in a competent court the action of an inferior tribunal, board, or officer exercising judicial functions, when such action is alleged to be without jurisdiction or otherwise illegal. (5)

certiorari, writ of The method used to direct inferior courts, officers, boards or tribunals to certify to the superior court the record of their proceedings for inspection and review. (66)

cestui The beneficiary of a trust.

cestui que trust (pl., cestuis que trust) A person for whose benefit a trust is created; the same as a beneficiary. A person having a beneficial interest in property held in trust. (88, 5)

cestui que vie The person on whose life, insurance is written. The applicant for the insurance is properly called the insured whether the applicant be the person whose life is insured or not. Where the beneficiary applies for a policy and retains all the incidences of ownership, the person (other than the beneficiary) on whose life the policy is issued is not a party to the contract and has no rights in it. (58)

ceteris paribus All other things being equal. (Latin)

chain banking In the states that prohibit branch

banking the same goal can be achieved by controlling a number of banks through stock ownership of the individual banks and then dictating a common policy. This is also known as Group Banking as well as Chain Banking. Technically at least three banks are needed to be considered a chain. Some authorities distinguish between Group Banking and Chain Banking by restricting the term "Group" to three or more banks controlled by means of a holding company as compared with the "Chain" banks which are controlled by common stock ownership by an individual or group of individuals.

chain of title The succession of conveyances from some accepted starting point whereby the present holder of real property derives his title. (54)

chancellor of the exchequer That individual in Great Britain whose function is similar to the United States Secretary of the Treasury, and who is in charge of the receipts and payments of the government of the United Kingdom.

change in business inventories Often referred to as inventory investment. It represents the value of the increase or decrease in the physical stock of goods held by the business sector valued in current period prices. These inventories are in three stages of production: raw materials, semifinished goods, and finished goods ready for sale or shipment.

An inventory increase is regarded as investment because it represents production not matched by current consumption; an inventory decrease is regarded as "negative investment" because it reflects consumption in excess of current production. (124)

change of beneficiary See Beneficiary, Change of. (42)

character 1. As applied to an expenditure classification, this term refers to certain important groups of expenditures which are distinguished on the basis of the periods they are presumed to benefit. The three chief classes are expenses, provisions for the retirement of debt, and capital outlays. Expenses are presumed to benefit primarily the current fiscal period. Provisions for the retirement of debt involve expenditures on account of benefits received at least in part in prior fiscal periods although their benefits may extend to the present period and future periods. Capital outlays represent expenditures for durable assets the benefit of which applies both to this fiscal period and to some subsequent period or periods. (29)

2. The ways in which any person feels, thinks, and acts, considered as good or bad. Moral nature, moral strength or weakness. (93)

charge As applied to trust business, the price fixed or demanded by a trust institution for a trust department service. It is compensation which a trust institution has a legal right to fix (in the form of either a commission or a fee), in contrast to an allowance which is granted by a court. See also Allowance; Commission; Fee. (88)

charge account Credit arrangement whereby customer is permitted to charge purchases according to previous arrangements. The customer is expected to pay in full during the month following purchase or on cycle billing due date. Has no

service or carrying charge. Occasionally such accounts arranged on 30, 60, 90 day basis for larger purchases. One-third or more of the total amount being payable each month. (26)

charge authorization phone system Equipment permitting direct contact from sales department to credit office for the purpose of authorizing charges. Equipment is often selective so that calls may be directed to the individual in charge of a particular alphabetical group. (26)

charge customer A customer to whom merchandise is sold on account. (73)

charged-off paper See Write-Offs. (1)

charge notice See Debit Memo. (1)

charge-off The action of transferring an account from accounts receivable to "Suspense" or "Profit and Loss" accounts. The act of writing off an account to its present value. This may be to zero or some amount lower than the amount the account is being carried at prior to the writing down or off. It is the result of the recognition of the change in value of an asset. Thus, an account receivable which has proven not to be collectable may be charged off. (26)

charge-out A term used to designate the release of debits or credits to other departments for further handling. Before releasing such items their package totals are recorded on a charge-out sheet. Later, the totals are included in the final proof. It is sometimes necessary to remove large checks or deposits for further processing before certain groups of items are proved or balanced. A memorandum record of each item removed is substituted in its place in order to complete the proving. This memorandum record is called a "charge-out" or "substitution ticket." (83, 1)

charge-plate Trade name describing device bearing the name of credit customer together with other descriptive data. (26)

charges, carrying Those fixed expenses which must be paid to support an idle property such as taxes, insurance premiums, standby water and sewer rents, and, on occasion, watchmen's or other protective service. (66)

charge-send Authorized credit purchase of merchandise taken by the customer. (26)

charge-ticket That written memorandum which a bookkeeper uses as a guide in posting a debit item to an account. Same as debit ticket. (83)

charitable bequest A gift of personal property to a legal charity by will. See Charity. (74)

charitable devise A gift of real property to a legal charity by will. See Charity. (74)

charitable remainder An arrangement wherein the remainder interest goes to a legal charity upon the termination or failure of a prior interest. (74)

charitable trust A trust created for the benefit of a community, ordinarily without a definite beneficiary; as, a trust for educational purposes. The same as a public trust; opposed to a private trust. (88)

charity An agency, institution, or organization in existence and operation for the benefit of an indefinite number of persons and conducted for educational, religious, scientific, medical, or other beneficent purposes. (74)

A gift of real or personal property (or both) to

be applied, consistently with existing laws, "for the benefit of an indefinite number of persons, either by bringing their hearts under the influence of education or religion, by relieving their bodies from disease, suffering or constraint, by assisting them to establish themselves in life, or by creating or maintaining public buildings or works, or otherwise lessening the burden of government." (88)

charter A document issued by a national or state supervisory agency granting a bank the right to do business. The terms and conditions under which the bank may operate are enumerated in the charter. As a general rule, state charters permit more latitude in the banking field than do national charters. (1)

chartered accountant A member of an Institute of Chartered Accountants in the British Empire. Admission to such institutes is dependent upon serving a period of apprenticeship and passing an entrance examination. (29)

chartist An individual, interested in economic data such as price movements, supply and demand, and volume of trading, who plots and interprets charts constructed from such data. The term is mostly associated with security and commodity trading.

chartist's liability The estimated risk involved in buying a stock or selling it short as derived from analyzing the chart patterns. (105)

chart of accounts A list of account titles showing the order of arrangement and the classification of accounts in the general ledger; a classified list of accounts used by a business as a guide in recording transactions. (73)

charts Records of price changes in a stock or market average kept on graph paper with the associated volume of transactions. Analysts utilize these in trying to determine future market action and the resulting actions they should take. (105)

chattel Every species of property, movable or immovable, which is less than a life estate in land. (5)

chattel mortgage A legal document in which personal property (chattels) is made security for payment of a debt but is left in the hands of the debtor so long as payments are kept up as contracted. (59)

chattel mortgage agreement A legal agreement with a purchaser of merchandise on an installment basis. Provides that buyer accepts title to goods on delivery but gives seller a mortgage on such merchandise that may be foreclosed under certain conditions and by prescribed legal procedure. (26)

chattel, personal Any item of movable property besides real estate. (54)

chattel, real An interest in land, such as a leasehold, which is less than a freehold estate. See Tenancy at Sufferance; Tenancy at Will; Tenancy for Years. (88)

cheap money The economic condition characterized by low interest rates and high price level. Inflationary.

check A bill of exchange drawn on a bank payable on demand; a written order on a bank to pay on demand a specified sum of money to a named

person, to his order, or to bearer out of money on deposit to the credit of the maker.
NOTE: A check differs from a warrant in that the latter is not necessarily payable on demand and may not be negotiable; and it differs from a voucher in that the latter is not an order to pay. A vouchercheck combines the distinguishing marks of a voucher and a check; it shows the propriety of a payment and is an order to pay. (29)

check book A book containing blank checks furnished by banks to depositors to permit them to withdraw funds from their checking accounts. A customer may keep a complete record of his deposits, his withdrawals, and his balance, by means of stubs or a register book. (83)

check collection department See Proof Department. (1)

check currency Demand deposits created by a bank loan and subject to withdrawal by check as contrasted with paper money or coin.

check desk That section of a bookkeeping department through which all incoming and outgoing debit and credit items pass. It assembles and controls all final proof figures for the bookkeeping department. The term is also applied to a proof department for incoming and outgoing items. (1)

check files The files in which all paid and cancelled checks are stored until they are ready to be returned to the depositors with their statements. Check files may simply be drawers in a bookkeeper's desk, or in large banks a section of the bookkeeping department charged with the responsibility of filing checks and proving them with the statements before mailing. (1)

check filing The process of placing cancelled checks in storage to facilitate the periodic mailing of customer's statements. (83)

checking account Amounts of money kept with a financial institution subject to immediate withdrawal on personal demand or by use of checks or "orders to pay". (59)

check list An adding machine list of depositor's checks which are to be charged to his checking account. The number of checks used to make a list varies with the individual bank. The number of checks attached to a list is usually indicated on the list to be used for account analysis. The object of a list is to cut down on the number of items posted to a depositor's account, since only the total of the list appears on the depositor's statement. This saves the bookkeeper's time, since the making of lists may be assigned to a new or less experienced clerk. (1)

check on us Checks drawn on a bank and presented to it for deposit or payment. (85)

check out When a block does not prove and the difference is not located by verifying the addition of the deposit tickets and comparing the check amounts with the listings, it is necessary to re-sort to what is termed as "check out." This consists of matching each item shown on the deposit tickets with a similar amount appearing on the block listing tapes. This will establish that the depositor has done one of the following: included a check without listing it, listed a check but failed to include it, or listed a check incorrectly. (83)

check protection Any of a number of devices to prevent alteration or forgery of checks. Many checks are printed on paper which reacts to erasures or chemical bleach. Other safety devices include printing devices which actually emboss figures on the paper as well as print the figures.

check rate The Demand Rate or most common rate used in foreign exchange quotation which generally is lower than a cable rate but higher than the time bill rate.

check register The name frequently used to describe the form of the cash payments journal that is used with the voucher system. (73)

check routing system A device to facilitate the handling and routing of transit items through banks that remit at par all over the United States. The check routing symbol is the denominator of a fraction, the numerator being the A.B.A. transit number. The entire fraction is located in the upper right-hand corner of a check. The check routing symbol is composed of three or four digits. The first digit in a denominator of three figures or the first two digits in a denominator of four figures identify the Federal Reserve District (1-12) in which the drawee bank is located. The next to the last digit designates the Federal Reserve Bank head office or branch through which the item should be cleared and also any special clearing arrangement. (The head office is indicated by the figure 1. Branches, if any, arranged alphabetically are indicated by figures 2 to 5. Figures 6 to 9 are used to designate special collection arrangements.) The last digit shows whether the item is acceptable for immediate or deferred credit. (Figure 0 designates items which are receivable for immediate credit. All other numbers, 1 to 9 inclusive, in the last position do not indicate the number of days of deferred availability but designate the state in alphabetical progression in which the drawee bank is located.) An example of a check routing symbols followings:

83-1016
1011

83 is the prefix number for the State of Kansas; 1016 is the A.B.A. suffix number for the Richland State Bank; in the denominator, the 10 shows that this bank is in the 10th Federal Reserve District; the next number (1) means that the item is cleared through the head office of the Federal Reserve Bank of Kansas City, Missouri; the last number (1) indicates that items drawn on the Richland State Bank are received by the Head Office of Federal Reserve Bank of Kansas City for deferred rather than immediate (0) Credit. It also indicates that Kansas is the first State in alphabetical progression in the territory served by the Head Office of the Federal Reserve Bank of Kansas City. (1)

check, selection A check, usually automatic, to verify that the correct register or other device has been selected in the performance of an instruction. (104)

check serial number The magnetic characters imprinted in the auxiliary On-Us field. These figures correspond to the number on each check used by the maker as identification. See Account Reconciliation Plan (A.R.P.). (83)

check stub That part of the check form that is bound permanently in the checkbook. It is used for retaining a record of the check that is attached to it. (73)

check the market 1). In the over-the-counter market, this refers to asking for price quotations from several firms to determine the best quotes and the depth of the market. 2). When used to refer to any stock, it is for the purpose of finding out if the market for the stock has changed since the last time it was sold or quoted. (105)

cheque The designation of a check in Canada and other foreign countries. See Check. (1)

chermatistic The pursuit of wealth or profit.

Chicago Board of Trade The largest grain exchange in the world where spot or futures contracts are made in a large range of agricultural products.

chief clerk Usually a junior officer or a senior clerk whose duties consist of handling various transactions of an important nature, such as notary work, protests, wire transfers, and technical negotiable instruments. In branch banking, the chief clerk is a junior officer who is charged with the supervision of personnel and the general operations of the branch. He is the administrative assistant to the Branch Manager. (1)

chose Anything that is personal property. (74)

chose action A right to personal property which has not been reduced to possession or enjoyment but which is recoverable in an action at law—for example, a patent right, a copyright, a royalty right, a right growing out of a contract or out of damage to person or to property, or a right under a life insurance policy. While the right itself is the chose in action, the evidence of the right, such as the life insurance policy, sometimes is referred to as if it were the chose in action. To be distinguished from a chose in possession. (88)

chose in action That claim for personal property not in one's possession such as a suit to collect on an account receivable which is past due.

chose in possession Any article of tangible personal property in actual, rightful possession, such as a watch, an automobile, or a piece of furniture; to be distinguished from a chose in action. (88)

Christmas club account A savings account whereby a customer deposits a specified sum each week in order to accumulate a lump sum for Christmas expenditures. Usually does not bear interest. (83)

churning 1. Continuous buying and selling of securities which does not move the market very much in either direction. 2. An illegal practice referring to a broker's frequent attempts to buy and sell securities for his clients in order to generate commissions. (105)

cipher code Those messages sent by business firms which utilize a system of signals or words which convey a meaning to the receiver other than the apparent literal translation. Such codes accomplish several valuable goals such as saving some of the cost of transmission of telegraph or other commercial communication since one arbitrary word or phrase can be given a much more lengthy meaning. It provides some assurance of authenticity since a code word may be used to identify the sender.

cipher-proof A method of balancing whereby

certain figures are automatically subtracted from a control total. If the balance results in zero, it is proved that all figures were added and listed correctly. Sometimes referred to as "Zero Balance." (83)

circle graph (or pie graph) A graph in the form of a circle that is divided into pieces or sections that indicate proportions. (73)

circular A prospectus. A publication for general circulation such as information on a security. (73)

circular letter of credit A document, usually issued by a bank, that is not addressed to any specific bank or agency. The bank agrees to accept drafts upon it if they are within the terms of the letter.

circulating assets Current assets. See that term.

circulating capital As contrasted with Fixed Capital which is relatively permanent, circulating capital is used synonymously with working capital.

circulating medium Money; an item of exchange which is generally accepted without endorsement.

circulation statement The monthly report of the Treasury of the United States which gives the amount of money outstanding, and the amount of currency which is held by the Federal Reserve Banks and the U.S. Treasury.

city collection department A department in a bank which handles the collection of items payable within a city, and receives and collects these items by messenger. As a general rule, those items which cannot be collected through the local clearing house due to their being drawn on non-members, or drafts with documents attached which require special handling, pass through this department. (1)

city items Those checks, notes and other negotiable items which are drawn upon individuals or institutions located in the same city in which they were deposited.

civil corporation An artificial being, created by law for the purpose of engaging in the business purposes stated in its charter which is granted by the state.

civil law The legal system prevailing in the European, Asiatic, Central American, and South American countries which inherited their legal systems from Rome—in other words, in practically all except the English-speaking countries of the United States of America and the British Commonwealth. See Common Law. (74)

civil loans Those loans made by any governmental agency.

claim The right to any debts, privileges, or other things in possession of another; also, the titles to anything which another should concede to, or confer on, the claimant. (74)

claim against estate A demand made upon the estate to do or to forebear some act as a matter of duty. A common example would be the claim submitted by a creditor for a debt owed him by the decedent at the time of his death. (74)

claim agent Individual authorized by an insuring underwriter to pay a loss or losses. (5)

claimant Individual asserting a right or presenting a claim for a suffered loss. One who makes or presents a claim. (5)

claim audit A survey of a policy record to determine the payment due an insured under a claim. (42)

claim, contested or resisted Validity of a claim disputed. (42)

claim ratio See Loss Ratio. (42)

claims reported by U.S. banks: long-term Long-term claims reported by U.S. banks represent commercial bank loans to foreigners. These loans may go to private business, individuals, or foreign governments. A large part of these comprise loans for foreign corporations, including loans to finance ship mortgages, U.S. exports, plant expansion, and to refinance debts outstanding. A loan is considered long-term if its repayment schedule is for more than one year.

The flow in the opposite direction appears in Long-term liabilities reported by U.S. banks. (124)

claims reported by U.S. banks: short-term Short-term claims include loans extended to foreigners with a maturity of less than one year. Loans to foreign banks for the purpose of financing general trade transactions on foreign accounts and short-term bank claims in foreign currencies that represent correspondent balances held in the bank's own account abroad are included.

Nonbank claims such as outstanding collections held in the bank's custody or short-term investments in foreign money market assets are also included. (124)

claims reported by U.S. residents other than banks: long-term Those claims reported by private business firms resulting from their export transactions. These claims assume various forms. A common example is "supplier's credit." This is the long-term financing extended to a foreigner by a U.S. corporation in order that it may sell its product abroad. Long-term loans made to foreigners by insurance companies are also included. (124)

claims reported by U.S. residents other than banks: short-term Includes those claims reported by U.S. brokerage houses. These claims may be in the form of a cash account held by the broker. Also included are other short-term financial assets held abroad such as the unused proceeds of loan flotations by U.S. corporations in foreign capital markets. (124)

classified Term referring to any security which has been divided into two or more classifications. (105)

classified stock Equity security divided into groups such as Class A and Class B. The difference between the two classes will be determined by the provisions of the charter and by-laws. Typically the difference between A & B class of stock is in the right of voting.

class system A stagger system for the election of members of a board of directors. Each group or "class" has a term of more than one year. Only one class would be voted upon for election in any one year. This permits a perpetuation of control and makes it difficult to unseat the existing management or administration of a corporation.

clean bill of exchange A Bill of Exchange which has no other documents attached to it such as a bill of lading.

clean bill of lading A Bill of Lading which has not been changed or modified by such limitation clauses as may be added by a carrier such as "shipper's load and count".

clean draft A sight or time draft which has no other documents attached to it. This is to be distinguished from "Documentary Draft". (1)

clean letter of credit A letter of credit which does not require such documents as bills of lading as a condition of acceptance by a bank. Such letters are issued only to prime risks.

clean up To make a large profit. (105)

clean-up fund Amount payable to an estate or a principal beneficiary for the purpose of cleaning up debts that may occur or remain as of the date of death. (42)

clear This term has three meanings in banking circles:
1. The clearing of a check is the collection and final payment of it through a clearing house; 2. The clearing of active securities through a stock exchange clearing house; 3. A legal term meaning "free from encumbrances," such as "clear title" referring to title of property or goods.

In transportation, the term refers to the certification given by Customs that a vessel may depart since it has complied with the customs requirements. (1)

clearance papers The certificate issued to a vessel's captain which shows that custom requirements have been met.

cleared Refers to the time when a person who has contracted for a security, actually pays for it and receives delivery. Some brokerage firms make a specialty of clearing transactions, charging other firms for this service, the fee dependent upon whether the other firm is a member of the same exchange (lower fee) or a non-member (higher fee). (105)

clearing Domestic clearing (clearing within a country) is the offsetting of bank counterclaims and the settlement of balances; it may be either local or nationwide. International clearing is the settlement of balances between countries through the medium of foreign exchange. (85)

clearing account An account designed to facilitate the distribution of certain items which usually affect more than one class of accounts, such as those for the production and distribution of power, the production and handling of materials and supplies, and for shop operations. (19)

clearing agreement Accord between participating nations whereby buyers of foreign goods or services pay for them with their own domestic currency. Periodically the central banks of the agreeing nations will balance at the previously agreed upon rates of exchange.

clearing house A place where representatives of the banks in the same locality meet each day at an agreed time to exchange checks, drafts, and similar items drawn on each other and to settle the resulting balances. (85)

clearing house agent Redemption Agent. A member of a clearing house that will clear items for a non-member of the clearing house.

clearing house association A voluntary association of banks, located in the same city, that is formed to facilitate the daily exchange of checks, drafts, and notes among its members and to set-

tle balances caused by these exchanges. Its members agree upon policies and rules for their mutual benefit. (83)

clearing house balance The sum of the credit and debit totals or balances as of the close of the banking day.

clearing house certificate Prior to the formation of the Federal Reserve System, debit balances resulting from clearing house exchanges were settled in gold. In times of financial stress member banks pooled their securities with the clearing house, to be used for the settlement of balances in lieu of gold. Clearing house certificates were issued against this pool of securities by the manager of the clearing house association to settle the exchange balances of debtor banks whose own resources were inadequate. The New York Clearing House Association resorted to the use of clearing house certificates ten times in its history, the first being at the outbreak of the Civil War in 1860. (1)

clearing house statement A weekly statement published by large clearing house associations, showing the capital, surplus, undivided profits, average net demand deposits, and average time deposits of its member banks. (1)

clearing member A member of a clearing house who is also a member of an exchange. Some exchange members are not members of a clearing house and thus clear their trades through a clearing member.

clearing price Also known as Settlement Price. A price, usually the closing price which is established daily by the clearing house administration to adjust the margin payments for transactions between the members and the clearing house.

clearings The incoming cash letters of items which must be proved, sorted, returned if necessary, and for which settlement must be made. (83)

climax Also called a blow-off, which means a large volume of trading accompanying the culmination of an extended upward or downward movement in the price of a security or market average. (105)

clique A gentlemen's agreement by a number of individuals to manipulate stock by such techniques as matched orders and short or wash sales. There is no formal organization but rather reliance on concerted action. The action of a clique is today illegal.

clock stamp A mechanical or electric time-recording device for imprinting upon an inserted document the time of arrival, and frequently the date upon which the item was received or transmitted. Such devices are frequently used in Safe Deposit and Security Deposit vaults. (1)

close The last price recorded of a sale of a security during a trading day. In the case of commodities "close" refers to the period just before the end of a trading day at which all trades which are designated for execution "at the close" are transacted.

close corporation A corporation whose shares of stock are held by a few persons, usually officers, employees, or others close to the management. These shares are rarely offered to the public. (74)

closed account An account with equal debits and credits; that is, with no balance. To indicate that an account is closed, it should be totaled and ruled. (73)

closed corporation A corporation whose shares are not held by the general public but rather by a small group such as members of a family or the management of a company. The term "Close Corporation" means the same but is used less frequently.

closed-end company An investment company with a relatively fixed amount of capital whose securities are traded on a securities exchange of in the over-the-counter market, in the same way as ordinary corporate securities. (3)

closed-end investment company A management investment company which has raised its capital by means of a public offering, over a limited period of time, of a fixed amount of common stock (and which may also have raised capital by the issuance of senior securities). The stock of a closed-end investment company is bought and sold on securities exchanges or over-the-counter markets, as are the securities of business corporations. (65)

closed-end investment trust An investment fund which allows only the original prescribed number of shares to be distributed. (74)

closed mortgage A corporate trust indenture under which bonds have been authenticated and delivered (as an original issue) to the extent authorized under the indenture. Compare Open-End Mortgage. (74)

closed out That condition in which a margin purchaser or short seller has not been able to "cover" or make up the new amount of margin which has resulted from the price fluctuation of his securities. Under such circumstances he is "Closed Out" or sold out by his broker.

closed trade The consummation of a transaction by selling a security which had been purchased long previously, or covering a short sale, i.e., buying a security previously sold short. (105)

closely held Stock which is not likely to come onto the market in the immediate future, especially that stock held by a family or another company for long-term investment purposes. (105)

close market Refers to bid and asked quotations that are relatively near together. (105)

close money A condition in the economy where interest rates are higher than normal and loans are difficult to obtain but the interest rates are not as high or loans as difficult to make as under a "Tight Money" condition.

close prices That condition in the securities or commodity markets in which prices fluctuate only minor amounts and the "Spread" between bid and asked prices is narrow.

closing a mortgage loan The consummation of a loan transaction in which all appropriate papers are signed and delivered to the lender, the making of the mortgage becomes a completed transaction, and the proceeds of the mortgage loan are disbursed by the lender to the borrower or upon the borrower's order. (89)

closing charges The expenses or costs incurred in the sale, transfer, or pledging of property, such as recording fees and title examination fees, which must be provided for and distributed between the parties upon the consummation of the transaction. (89)

closing entries General journal entries that are made at the end of the fiscal period to transfer the income, cost, and expense accounts to the profit and loss summary account and to transfer the net profit or the net loss to the proprietor's drawing account; an entry or entries made in the general journal at the end of the fiscal period to transfer the balance of one or more accounts into another account. (73)

closing of the exchange Refers to the hours of an exchange, particularly the closing hour. (105)

closing price Securities and commodity exchanges release daily the "closing price" of the items traded. This price is the last quotation for a completed transaction during the trading day. If an inactive security has only one transaction the closing and opening price are the same. See Closing Range.

closing range Commodities, unlike securities, are often traded at several prices at the opening or close of the market. Buying or selling orders at the opening might be filled at any point in such a price range for the commodity.

closing the books 1. Those entries made by a bookkeeper at the end of a period which permits balancing and preparation of financial statements. See Closing Entries. 2. When dividends are declared to stockholders of record of a particular date the Transfer Agent closes the books which record the stock transfer so he may compile the list of stockholders who are to receive the dividend. Stocks sell "ex-dividend" the day after the closing of the books.

closing the ledger The process of recording the closing entries in the general journal, posting them to the ledger, and ruling and balancing the ledger accounts; the entire process of summarizing the income and the expense accounts and transferring the net profit or the net loss to the capital account. (73)

cloud on title A defect in the owner's title to property arising from a written instrument or judgment or from an order of court purporting to create in someone else an interest in or lien upon the property and therefore impairing the marketability of the owner's title. (74)

club account The popularity of the Christmas Club account has led banks to open other types of club accounts on the same basis. It is a convenient method of saving small amounts regularly for a definite purpose. Popular names for the newer club accounts are "Budget Savings", "Vacation Club," "Travel Club," and "All Purpose Club." Many depositors are using these club accounts to accumulate savings for annual premiums on life insurance, taxes, and vacations. (1)

co-assignee An individual or firm to whom some property right has been assigned jointly with some other firm or individual.

code ("Telegraphic," "Cipher," "Secret") The sending of telegraphic or wireless messages in a numerical, alphabetical, or numerical and alphabetical arrangement in order to reduce the cost of sending the message and/or for secrecy. See Cipher Code. (1)

code, dictionary An alphabetical arrangement of English words and terms, associated with their code representations. (104)

codicil An amendment or a supplement to a will, executed with the same formalities as the will itself. A codicil is a definite part of the will and is probated with it. (74)

co-executor An individual or trustee who acts jointly with another executor. See Executor.

cognovit note A form of note (legal evidence of indebtedness) which is both a promissory note and chattel mortgage. The borrower, within the wording of the instrument, waives his right of action to the chattel property in case of his default in any payments agreed to in the transaction. (1)

coin The term used in banks applicable to all metallic money to distinguish it from paper money and bullion. (1)

A piece of metal stamped and issued by the authority of the government for use as money. (93)

coinage The minting of coins from strips of metal. The coins are used as money.

coin counting machine A machine used in banks to count accurately and swiftly large volumes of specie, or coins. The machine has a hopper into which are fed all denominations of coins. The machine is regulated to sort out coins from the smallest size (dime) to the largest (half dollar). The coins are automatically counted as they are sorted, one denomination at a time, and are then packaged in coin wrappers. (1)

coining rate The Mint Ratio.

collate To merge two or more ordered sets of data, or cards in order to produce one or more ordered sets which still reflect the original ordering relations. The collation process is the merging of two sequences of cards, each ordered on some mutual key; into a single sequence ordered on the mutual key. (104)

collateral Specific property which a borrower pledges as security for the repayment of a loan, agreeing that the lender shall have the right to sell the collateral for the purpose of liquidating the debt if the borrower fails to repay the loan at maturity. In the case of a loan against real property, the lender usually must go through what is often a lengthy and legally involved procedure in order to acquire title to the real estate which is collateral for the loan. (89)

collateral heir A person not in the direct line of the decedent from whom he inherits real property, as, for example, a nephew of the decedent who receives a share of his uncle's estate. See Direct Heir; Heir. (74)

collateral loan A loan for which the borrower has deposited with the lender certain property as a pledge of payment. The lender usually has the right to sell the property to pay off the debt if it is not paid according to its terms. (31, 92)

collateral note A promissory note which is secured by the pledge of specific property. (85)

collateral security Real or personal property which is put up or pledged for a loan as to be distinguished from a co-endorsement.

collateral surety Commercial paper, such as stocks or bonds, which is placed with the lender as security for the payment of a loan. (73)

collateral trust notes Bonds secured by the deposit of other bonds or stocks, usually issued by holding companies, investment trusts, and railroads. (74)

collateral value That estimate of value of the thing put up as security for a loan which is made by the lender. In the case of securities and traded commodities, the lender may be further restricted in his valuation by regulations of an appropriate body such as the exchange or Federal Reserve Board.

collection agent That individual, firm, or bank which handles checks, drafts, coupons and similar items for another individual, bank or firm and attempts to collect such instruments.

collection analyst Person in the collection division of the credit office, responsible for determining status and subsequent collection procedure of customers' past-due accounts. (26)

collection basis of reporting A method of reporting the receipts of takes by the Internal Revenue Service at the time of receipt of returns by collecting officers in the field (as compared with Treasury statements of receipts on the basis of reports of deposits made in Treasury accounts). The collections basis provides detail of collections by type of tax. (7)

collection charges Those fees charged for collecting drafts, notes, coupons and accounts receivable. Since most banks are on a "par" collection system for checks there is no direct charge from such banks. However, in some rural areas there still are "non-par banks"; these banks do charge a fee for paying checks that are not directly presented to them.

collection clerk A clerk that works in the Collection Department. See that term.

collection correspondent Person in the collection division of a credit office, responsible for handling collection matters by mail. (26)

collection department The department which handles checks, drafts, coupons, and other items received from a customer for collection. Depositor's account is credited only after final payment has been received; payment is remitted to a non-depositor. (83)

collection expense The expense incurred in the collection of notes, drafts, or accounts. (73)

collection fee The percentage paid an agent for his services in collecting premiums. (42)

collection item (As distinguished from a cash item) Items (drafts, notes, acceptances, etc.) received for collection and credited to a depositor's account after final payment. Collection items are usually subject to special instructions regarding delivery of documents when attached, protest, etc., and in most banks are subject to a special fee for handling which is called a collection charge. Also termed collections. (83, 85)

collection ledger That record or book in which are recorded items that have been placed for collection.

collection letter A letter of transmittal containing special handling instructions which accompanies items to be handled for collection and credit after payment. (83)

collection manager Supervisor of the collection division of the credit office. Usually (although not always) responsible to the credit manager. Handles all collection matters. (26)

collection percentage The amount collected during a given period, usually one month, expressed percentage-wise against the total amount owing by all customers at the beginning of a period. (26)

collection period 1. The period of time that it takes such items as checks and notes to clear. Most banks use a "deferred availability schedule" which is provided through their Federal Reserve Bank and gives the typical time needed to collect transit checks. The difference between the actual time and the time estimated by the deferred availability schedule gives rise to "float".
2. Credit men use the "collection period" of their accounts receivable as one measurement of their efficiency.

Obtained by dividing annual net sales made on credit terms by 365 days to obtain average daily credit sales, then dividing the average daily credit sales into notes and accounts receivable, including any discounted. (Example: A concern makes annual sales of $365,000 on open account terms. Average daily credit sales are therefore $1,000. If the total notes and accounts receivable of this concern are $32,000, the collection period is 32 days.) (61)

collection ratio The ratio of receivables (accounts, notes, and interest) to net sales which indicates the efficiency of a business in collecting its accounts with customers. (73)

collection reminder Reminder to customer that payment or payments are past due. Can be printed, typed, or in the form of a statement or sticker insert. (26)

collection teller A teller whose regular duty is the handling of collections. See Collection Department. (1)

collective investment fund A pooled investment trust under which the funds of pension and profit sharing plans that are approved by the Internal Revenue Service are commingled for investment. (74)

collective ownership Possession of a good in common with no particular part or proportion assigned to anyone. A public building or road is owned by the taxpayers of the district or subdivision; however, no one taxpayer can identify or claim any particular part.

collusion A secret agreement between two or more persons to defraud another person of his rights or to obtain an unlawful object. (88)

colon Monetary unit of Costa Rica and El Salvador.

color of title An appearance of title founded upon a written instrument which, if valid, would convey title. (5)

columnar cash payments journal A cash payments journal in which special columns are provided. (73)

columnar cash receipts journal A cash receipts journal in which special columns are provided. (73)

columnar general journal A general journal in which special columns are provided. (73)

columnar journal A journal with special columns for the classification of transactions. (73)

columnar purchases journal A purchases journal in which special columns are provided. (73)

columnar returned purchases and allowances journal A returned purchases and allowances journal in which special columns are provided. (73)

columnar returned sales and allowances journal A returned sales and allowances journal in which special columns are provided. (73)

columnar sales journal A sales journal in which special columns are provided. (73)

co-maker A person who signs the note of another as an additional maker for the purpose of strengthening the credit of the principal maker. (85)

combination The merger of two or more companies for the purpose of controlling and lessening competition or to achieve economies.

combination in restraint of trade Any agreement or understanding between individuals or companies with the objective of restricting competition in the sale, production or the distribution of a good or service.

combination journal See Combined Cash Journal. (73)

combined cash journal A combination of the cash receipts journal and the cash payments journal with one or more of the other journals. (73)

combined cash journal and daily financial statement The standard bookkeeping forms that have been devised by manufacturers for use in accounting systems which omit the use of a ledger. (73)

combined entry One that contains more than two bookkeeping elements. Such an entry may consist of two or more debits and one credit, or one debit and two or more credits. It may also consist of several debits and several credits. (73)

commercial account In general, this term is associated with a checking account. However, in many banks the bookkeeping department is divided into two sections to afford greater control in handling different types of activity. One section handles the regular checking accounts of individuals, while the other section handles the checking accounts for all types of businesses. (1)

commercial agency A firm which provides facilities in the area of credit and collections. Also known as Mercantile Agency. The agency may be general, that is, not limited as to geographic area or line of trade, or a special agency which is limited to a particular trade or area. Dun and Bradstreet Inc. is the largest general commercial agency.

commercial and industrial loans Loans for business purposes except those secured by real estate. (4)

commercial bank A banking corporation which accepts demand deposits subject to check and makes short term loans to business enterprises, regardless of the scope of its other services. (85)

commercial bar That bar, or brick of precious metal such as gold or silver, which is designed for use in the arts and industry area as distinguished from one designed for monetary use. A jeweler's bar, generally smaller than the bar used for monetary purposes is an example of a commercial bar.

commercial bill Those bills of exchange which have resulted from a commercial business transaction as compared to the non-commercial bills such as a banker's bill. In theory, a commercial bill, if discounted, will provide a desirable expansion of the money supply while a bill arising out of, say, a financial speculation, would generally be undesirable and inflationary, if rediscounted.

commercial borrower One who borrows for some purpose having to do with business or commerce. (59)

commercial borrowing Those loans which are made to retailers and wholesalers as distinguished from industrial or manufacturing loans. However the term is loosely used and frequently takes in the latter type of borrower. It is also used to differentiate between loans made to private individuals such as personal loans and auto loans as compared to loans made to business firms.

commercial credit That credit used by manufacturers, retailers, wholesalers, jobbers and commission agents for the production and distribution of goods. It is distinguished from investment, agricultural, bank, and personal credit.

commercial credit company A finance or credit company. One which buys and sells installment contracts and open book accounts which are obtained from retailers and wholesalers. At times they also engage in factoring.

commercial credit documents A general expression for those papers and documents such as bills of lading and warehouse receipts which accompany an extention of commercial credit.

commercial discounts That discount which is given to encourage prompt payment of a commercial account. Probably the most common commercial discount is expressed 2/10 net 30 which means that a discount of 2% may be taken from the face of the bill if paid within ten days but if paid after the tenth through the thirtieth day the bill is paid in full or net. After the thirtieth day the bill is considered past due.

commercial draft A written order signed by one person or firm requesting another person or firm to pay a stated sum of money to a third party. (73)

commercial failures Those business firms which have terminated for adverse economic reasons. Dun & Bradstreet releases weekly figures on the number of firms that have failed in the United States. This time series is considered a valuable business barometer. D & B uses companies that have made assignments, or filed petitions of bankruptcy. In a strict sense some business firms may "fail" and sell out without court action.

commercial forgery policy Contract of insurance to protect one who accepts checks in payment for services or goods. (5)

commercial letter of credit An instrument by which a bank lends its credit to a customer to enable him to finance the purchase of goods. Addressed to the seller, it authorizes him to draw drafts on the bank under the terms stated in the letter. (85)

commercial loan See "Loan" for general definition. Commercial loans are principally loans made to businesses for the financing of inventory purchases and the movement of goods, as distinguished from personal loans or consumer credit loans. Commercial loans are short-term loans or acceptances (time drafts accepted). (1)

commercial paper Notes and acceptances arising out of commercial transactions, usually received by business enterprises in payment for goods or services. Also, a concern with prime credit rating desiring to obtain funds through the open market may make arrangements with a commercial paper (promissory notes) wherever buyers can be found. The dealer sells these notes to banks and other investors at a rate of discount slightly lower than that which he charged the borrower. (83)

commercial paper house Those principals and dealers who buy commercial paper at one rate and attempt to sell it at another. See Broker.

commercial paper names Those well-known borrowers who are frequently in the commercial paper market.

commercial report See Credit Report. (50)

commercial stocks Those figures periodically released by the United States Department of Agriculture on the volume of grain at the major grain centers.

commercial teller An employee whose prime function is paying and receiving funds for bank customers. (83)

commingled fund A common fund in which the funds of several accounts are mixed. (74)

commingled investment fund A bank-operated trust fund in which accounts of individual customers are commingled and lose their identity. Each customer, in effect, owns a share of the entire fund. Such a fund differs only in detail from a mutual fund. (128)

commission 1. Fee charges by a broker for performance of a specific operation such as the buying or selling of commodities. 2. A percentage of the principal of a trust account or of the income (or of both) which a trust institution acting in a fiduciary capacity receives as compensation for its services; to be distinguished from allowance and fee. Thus, income commission is a percentage of the total amount of income collected. (9, 74)

commission broker An agent who executes the public's orders for the purchase or sale of securities or commodities. See Dealer. (2)

commission, contingent A commission, the amount of which is dependent on the profitableness (or some other characteristic) of the business written by an agent or reinsurer. (51)

commission house The investing public's main contact with the securities business, otherwise known as a brokerage firm which furnishes investment information, accepts and executes orders, and receives and delivers securities. (105)

commission merchant An agent, transacting business in his own name, who usually exercises physical control over the goods consigned to him and negotiates their sale. The commission merchant usually enjoys broader powers as to prices, methods, and terms of sale than does the broker although he must obey instructions issued by his principal. He generally arranges delivery, extends necessary credit, collects, deducts his fees, and remits the balance to his principal. Comment: Most of those who have defined the commission merchant state that he has possession of the goods he handles. In its strict meaning the word "possession" connotes to some extent the idea of ownership; in its legal meaning it involves a degree of control, somewhat of a misnomer when applied to an agent; that fact is disregarded in this definition since this usage is commonly accepted in the trade. (13)

commission trade Those transactions in securities or commodities in which the brokerage firm receives a commission as distinguished from those transactions, generally over the counter, in which it acts as a principal and buys and sells for its own account and does not charge a commission.

Commissioner of Banking That state executive heading the Banking Department who enforces and regulates the state chartered banks in his state. The term Superintendent of Banking is used in some states for the same function.

commissioners' values The values of securities as determined by the National Association of Insurance Commissioners to be used by insurers for valuation purposes when preparing financial statements. (42)

commitment An agreement or a promise to do something (such as making a loan or insuring a mortgage) in the future upon the fulfillment of specified conditions. (89)

committee for incompetent An individual or a trust institution appointed by a court to care for the property or the person (or both) of an incompetent; similar to a guardian, conservator, or curator. (88)

committee in lunacy See Committee for Incompetent.

committees In reference to stock exchange, those bodies which function to aid in the operation of the exchange, such as the Admissions, Business Conduct, and Stock List Committees of the New York Stock Exchange. (105)

commodity dollar A non-realized economic concept which would stabilize the value of money by removing the metallic base and freeze the value of the dollar to an index of commodity prices.

commodity exchange An association of member traders in agricultural products which have standards of quality. The typical exchange deals primarily in futures which provide the opportunity of hedging. Spot or actual commodity transactions may also take place on some exchanges but the proportionate volume is much smaller than the futures contracts. The Chicago Board of Trade is the largest commodity exchange in the world.

Commodity Exchange Act The 1936 act creating the Commodity Exchange Commission which regulates trading in the contract markets and other broad powers to prevent fraud and manipulation in covered commodities and establish limits in trading for the purpose of preventing excessive speculation.

Commodity Exchange Authority The unit within the U.S. Department of Agriculture which enforces the Commodity Exchange Act of 1936.

Commodity Exchange Commission The Secretary of Agriculture, the Secretary of Commerce, and the Attorney General are designated by the Commodity Exchange Act of 1936 as the Commodity Exchange Commission.

commodity paper Any note, draft, or other document with warehouse receipts or bills of lading for commodities. In the event of default, the lender may sell the commodities up to the value of the loan and the expense of collection.

commodity prices Prices may be on actual, spot, cash commodities or on a futures contract. In addition, the U.S. Department of Agriculture computes commodity prices in the various markets and publishes them in a monthly study "Agricultural Prices". These prices are averages of the various grades as of the middle of the month.

commodity rate That interest rate charged by banks on notes, bills of exchange, drafts and similar documents issued on stable commodities.

commodity standard An occasionally proposed monetary system which would substitute a commodity or commodities for the precious metal or other base of a currency.

commodity theory of money A proposed explanation of the value of money which holds that money is valued by the value of its base such as gold or silver. While it is recognized that there is a relationship between the base and the value of money, it is further recognized that other factors also have a deep influence on the value of money.

common capital stock (Common Stock) Represents the funds invested by the residual owners whose claims to income and assets are subordinated to all other claims. (21)

common expense An expense arising from two or more forms of operation, the portion resulting from each form of operation not being distinguishable. For expenses common to freight and passenger service prescribed rules are in effect with regard to their apportionment. (19)

common law The legal system prevailing in the English-speaking countries—that is, the United States of America and the British Commonwealth of Nations. It originated in England and its form of development was different from that of Roman (civil) law. See Civil Law. (74)

common law defenses Pleas which would defeat an injured workman's suit against his employer (and which are still effective in the absence of Workmen's Compensation or Employers' Liability legislation). They are: 1. Contributory negligence on employee's part; 2. Injury caused by fellow servant; 3. Assumption of risk by the employee in the course of his work. (50)

common law trust See Massachusetts Trust.

common machine language (MICR) The common machine language for mechanized check handling is a specially designed group of ten Arabic numbers and four special symbols printed in magnetic ink in designated field locations along the bottom edge of a check. The Bank Management Commission of the American Bankers Association, in their 1959 publication number 147, stated the original intention of the MICR program as follows: "The concept of the Common Machine Language, of course, is for the amount to be encoded by the first bank receiving the item for collection. This would permit all further handling in intermediate and paying banks to be primarily mechanical, resulting in tremendous economies in the banking system." The above quotation assumes that eventually all banks will at least have their transit number routing symbol encoded on their own checks, regardless of whether they intend to use equipment which will read the magnetic ink characters or not. The following as an explanation of the established fields:

1. Transit Number Field is used to encode the abbreviated routing symbol (1234) and the transit number (7890) of the drawee bank. The prefix number (56) is not used. The printing of this field does not discontinue the use of the familiar routing symbol transit number which will continue to appear in the upper right corner on checks. For non-par banks, the number 9 is encoded in the high-order digit position of the routing symbol. Field length: 11 characters.

2. On-Us Field is reserved for encoded information which is of use only to the drawee bank. Such information as account number and transaction code would appear in this area. Field length: 18 to 19 characters.

3. Amount Field is a universal field to be used for encoding the amount of the check as a by-product of the proof function. The first bank receiving the check in a deposit or for collection may encode this field. Field length: 10 characters. (83)

common property Land generally, or a tract of land, considered as the property of the public in which all persons enjoy equal rights; a legal term signifying an incorporeal hereditament consisting of a right of one person in the land of another, as common of estovers, of pasture, of piscary, property not owned by individuals or government, but by groups, tribes, or in formal villages. (54)

common size statement This refers to the device used in comparing statements, especially a statement from a small-sized concern with a statement of a concern many times larger in a similar line of business. To avoid misinterpretation and confusion frequently encountered while dealing with large amounts, the device operates as follows:

The total value of each individual item (asset) is divided by the total of all like items (total assets), thus reducing each figure to a percentage of the whole.

These computations are made for all items appearing on all statements (or reports) being compared, and then the resulting percentages are used for comparison rather than their dollars and cents values.

Frequently, there is a need for analyzing a statement for which there are no figures from like concerns available. Various market research organizations furnish percentages considered to be the "normal" or "average" for a large number of similar businesses which they have analyzed to obtain the normal or average of a given industry and territory as a whole. (1)

common stock Securities which represent an ownership interest in a corporation. If the company has also issued preferred stock, both common and preferred have ownership rights, but the preferred normally has prior claim on dividends and, in the event of liquidation, assets. Claims of both common and preferred stockholders are junior to claims of bondholders or other creditors of the company. Common stockholders assume the greater risk, but generally exercise the greater control and may gain the greater reward in the form of dividends and capital appreciation. The terms common stock and capital stock are often used interchangeably when the company has no preferred stock. See Capital Stock; Preferred Stock. (2)

common stock dividends Dividends declared on common stock during the year whether or not they were paid during the year. Unless otherwise qualified, it is the amount of such dividends charged to Retained Income (Earned Surplus) and includes those payable in cash or stock. (21)

common stock fund An investment company, the portfolio of which consists primarily of common stocks. Such a company may reserve the right to take defensive positions in cash, and in bonds, and other senior securities, whenever existing conditions appear to warrant such action. (65)

common trust fund A fund maintained by a bank or a trust company exclusively for the collective investment and reinvestment of money contributed to the fund by the bank or trust company in its capacity as trustee, executor, administrator, or guardian and in conformity with the rules and regulations of the Board of Governors of the Federal Reserve System pertaining to the collective investment of trust funds by national banks, as well as with the statutes and regulations (if any) of the several states. (74)

community property Under Spanish law as it developed in eight states, spouses have equal interest in assets and income obtained by either during the period of the marriage. Thus, in the event of death or divorce only half of the assets of the married couple are subject to such factors as taxation, or separation from the estate. The other system found in the majority, about 42 states, is known as "Separate Property."

community property law Law regarding property owned jointly by a man and wife. Insurance policies are often considered community property. (42)

community trust A trust ordinarily composed of gifts made by many people to a trustee for educational, charitable, or other benevolent purposes in a community. The property of the trust is trusteed, and distribution of the funds is under the control of a selected group of citizens who act as a distribution committee. There may be one trustee or, as is more often the case, several trustees (usually trust institutions of the community), each serving under identical declarations of trust in the administration of the property committed to its care and management. Some community trusts are known as foundations. See Foundation. (74)

comparative balance sheet A balance sheet that shows information for more than one fiscal period. (73)

comparative profit and loss statement A profit and loss statement that shows information for more than one fiscal period. (73)

comparative reports Financial reports that show the figures for more than one fiscal period. (73)

comparative statement The income, expense, profit and loss, balance sheet or other financial statement of the same concern for two or more consecutive years that are analyzed to determine the increase or decrease in their component items, frequently for credit purposes. (1)

comparisons That mutual exchange of data between two brokers or one broker and his bank which helps verify that each party's records of collateral held against loan are accurate and in agreement. If the comparisons do not agree the two parties can quickly trace down any difference.

compensated dollar A monetary unit in which the gold content would be changed from time to time to keep the purchasing power level with some commodity index.

compensating balance The amount of a commercial loan which the banker requires his borrower to keep with the bank. The range varies but frequently is between 10 and 20%. The purpose of the balance is two-fold: 1. To serve as a nest egg for emergencies the borrower may have. 2. To increase the earnings of the bank. Small banks generally do not require such balances, large city banks do.

compensation As applied to trust business, this general term covers four specific terms — allowance, charge, commission, and fee — which should be differentiated. See each of these terms for definitions. (88)

competition The market situation where no one trader can materially affect the market price of a product.

complete audit An audit in which an examination is made of the system of internal control and of the details of all of the books of account, including subsidiary records and supporting documents, as to legality, mathematical accuracy, complete accountability, and application of accepted accounting principles. One of the main features of a complete audit is that the auditor is not expected to make any qualifications in his report except such as are imposed by lack of information, that is, physical inability to get the facts. See Limited Audit. (29)

completes A term in a floor report which indicates that an order to buy, or sell, a block of securities has been accomplished or completed. (105)

complete special audit A complete audit of some particular phase of a governmental unit's activities, such as Sinking Fund transactions or a complete audit of all of a governmental unit's transactions for a shorter or longer period of time than the usual audit period. (29)

complex trust A trust in which the trustee is not required to distribute income currently, or distribute amounts other than income, or make a charitable contribution. (74)

composite demand The complete schedule of demand for a good or service. The composite demand for sugar would include not only confec-

tioners, bakers, and housewives, but all who might use it.

composite supply The complete supply schedule for a good or service, or function. The composite supply of heat would include not only all the coal, oil, and electricity but would include atomic energy, solar energy, etc.

composition An agreement among creditors and with their debtor whereby each creditor is to be paid less than the amount of his claim. (35)

composition settlement The acceptance by a creditor of an amount smaller than that which he is legally entitled to from a debtor. In doing this he waives his right to the full amount.

compound See Tables, Discount; Tables, Interest. (42)

compound entry See Combined entry.

compound interest Interest payable on the interest of a debt and on accrued interest from the time such interest fell due. The interest paid on the principal sum plus the interest on the interest, as it falls due and, remaining unpaid, is added to the principal. (54)

comptroller 1. The official of the business whose approval of the payment of a voucher must be obtained before the check may be issued. 2. In large firms this office is often held by a vice president with the title "Vice President and Comptroller". The duties of a comptroller generally embrace the audit functions of the firm, and the establishment and control over all systems in use in operations. The comptroller also is one of the key officers in the future planning of the firm's operations. (73, 1)

Comptroller of the Currency An appointed official who is responsible for the chartering, supervision, and liquidation of national banks. His office is located in the Treasury Department. (85)

comptroller's call The Comptroller of the Currency may "call" upon all national banks to submit a complete financial report of their activities at any given date. Reports must, according to law, be submitted at his call at least three times a year. These "called reports" must also be published in all local newspapers in the town nearest to the bank.

Quoting in part from Section 5211, the Federal Reserve Act: "The Comptroller shall also have the power to call for special reports from any particular association when ever, in his judgment, the same are necessary in order to obtain a full and complete knowledge of its condition. (1)

concern 1. A business establishment, company or firm. 2. To be interested or anxious. (93)

concession A deviation from higher regular terms or conditions. The right to use property for a stated purpose or purposes.

condensed statement A financial statement in which many of the minor details are grouped together so that it may be more easily read by the general public.

conditional endorsement An endorsement which states and imposes conditions upon the transferee. The instrument may still be negotiated within the terms of the condition but the individual who has made the conditional endorsement has the right to the proceeds of the instrument should the conditions not be fulfilled.

conditional gift A gift of property by will which is subject to some condition specified in the will or in the trust instrument; opposed to an absolute gift. (88)

conditional indorsement See Conditional Endorsement.

conditional sale contract Legal agreement with purchaser of goods on an installment basis. To be legally effective it must be filed in most states at the county court house or other designated place. Provides that the seller retains title to goods until payment is made in full. Repossession of goods is made by proper legal procedure, which differs in various states. (26)

conditional sales Sales under a payment contract where title remains with the seller until final payment is made, but the property is transferred to the buyer at once. (59)

conditional will This form of will meets all the requirements of a valid will, but the validity does not become effective until the occurrence of some condition. The condition, such as the birth of a child, must be perfectly clear in the wording of the instrument. The condition must be fulfilled before the will becomes operative.

condition of weekly reporting member banks That release by the Federal Reserve System which shows the changes in the reporting banks from one week to the next. This financial information is of interest not only to bankers but to economists since it shows the changes in banks which represent over half the banking resources of the country.

condition subsequent A condition, by the failure or non-performance of which an estate already vested is defeated. (74)

condominium The common ownership of a piece of property by one or more individuals, each of whom owns an absolute undivided interest in the property. It is an interest which has all of the characteristics associated with free ownership, such as alienability, mortgageability, divisability and inheritability. (84)

confession of judgment An admission by a party to whom an act or liability is imputed. (35)

confidence man An individual who cheats and defrauds. A swindler.

confirmation The report of all relevant data sent by a broker to a client as a formal memorandum of any securities contract assumed by the client. (105)

confirmed letter of credit A foreign bank wishing to issue a letter of credit to a local concern may request a local bank in the city in which the beneficiary is located to confirm this credit to the beneficiary. The purpose of this confirmation is to lend the prestige and responsibility of the local bank to the transaction because the status of the foreign bank may be unknown to the beneficiary. The confirming bank assumes responsibility for the payment of all drafts drawn under the credit and usually charges a fee for doing so. (1)

conflict of laws That branch of the law which is concerned with the legal principles applicable in a situation wherein the law of two or more jurisdictions is claimed to be applicable by the parties

to the controversy and the laws of the two or more jurisdictions are in conflict with one another.

conformed copy A copy of an original document with the signature, seal, and other such features being typed or otherwise noted. (74)

congeneric Meaning "of the same kind," this term has been used to designate one-bank holding companies that have diversified into areas beyond the traditional bounds of banking, but within the financial field. This term distinguishes them from the conglomerates, which are corporations which include business enterprises of all descriptions. (128)

conglomerate In the field of banking, the term is used to designate one-bank holding companies whose subsidiaries engage in activities totally unrelated to banking or financial areas. (128)

consanguinity Blood relationship; to be distinguished from affinity. (74)

consent decree The settlement of equity cases whereby the defendent agrees to stop certain actions that caused the case to be brought. This agreement is expressed as a judicial decree and the legal suit is dropped.

consent trust A trust in which the consent of the settlor or some designated person is required before specified action by the trustee. (74)

consequential damage The impairment of value which does not arise as an immediate result of an act, but as an incidental result of it. The impairment of value to private property caused by the acts of public bodies or caused by the acts of neighboring property owners. The term "consequential damage" applied only in the event no part of land is actually taken. The damage resulting from the taking of a fraction of the whole, that is, over and above the loss reflected in the value of the land actually taken is commonly known as severance damage. (54)

conservator Generally, an individual or trust institution appointed by a court to care for property; specifically, an individual or a trust institution appointed by a court to care for and manage the property of an incompetent, in much the same way that a guardian cares for and manages the property of a ward. (88)

consideration The price or subject matter which induces a contract. It may be money, commodity exchange, or a transfer of personal effort. In appraising, usually the actual price at which the property is transferred. In insurance, the consideration may be the statements made on the application and payment of premium. (54)

consignee One with whom a shipment of goods is placed to be sold for the owner (consignor). (73)

consignment The act of an individual or company of delivery or transfer of goods to an agent to be cared for or sold. (5)

consignment ledger A subsidiary ledger containing the individual accounts with consignors. (73)

consignment sale A sales transaction completed by a consignee whereby goods are sold for a consignor. (73)

consignor The owner of goods sent to a consignee. (73)

consolidate To bring together several obligations under one agreement, contract or note. (59)

consolidated The results obtained when the accounts of a parent company and its subsidiary companies are combined to reflect the financial position and results of operations of the group as if operated as a single entity. Such a consolidation involves proper intercompany eliminations and minority interest adjustments. (21)

consolidated balance sheet A balance sheet showing the financial condition of a corporation and its subsidiaries. See Balance Sheet. (2)

consolidated mortgage A mortgage on several separate units of property which are covered by the consolidated mortgage. Railroads for example, find that it is more economical to take many small pieces of property and finance them with one consolidated mortgage than issuing a separate mortgage for each property.

consolidated sinking fund One sinking fund that is established to serve two or more bond issues. (29)

consolidated statement of financial position Summarizes the company's financial position at a particular moment in time.

consolidated statement of income A financial summary of the operations of the company for a specified period of time. "Consolidated" means that the statement includes the operations of all subsidiary companies in which a company has a controlling interest.

consolidation The surrender of two or more small denominations of a security for a larger denomination: This type of transaction frequently follows the receipt of small lots of securities resulting from stock dividends or the exercise of rights. (74)

consols Originally referred to a three per cent bond issue of Great Britain which had no stated maturity. Since the consols have no maturity and bear a fixed rate of interest the price they sell at may be converted into a yield rate which in turn approaches what economists refer to as "pure" interest. See Pure Interest.

constant, annual The percentage which, when applied directly to the face value of a debt or capital value of an asset, develops the annual amount of money necessary to pay a specified net interest rate on the reducing balance and to liquidate the debt or value of the asset in a certain period of time. This is the percentage equivalent of the level payment mortgage plan or the annuity factors developed in the Inwood Tables, whereby the annual payment (or return) is applied first to interest on the reducing balance of the debt, or value of the asset, with the remainder applied to principal reduction. (66)

constant dollar estimates Represent an effort to remove the effects of price changes from statistical series reported in dollar terms. In general, constant dollar series are derived by dividing current dollar estimates by appropriate price indexes. The result is a series as it would presumably exist if prices were the same throughout as in the base year—in other words, as if the dollar had constant purchasing power. Any changes in such a series would reflect only changes in the real (physical) volume of output. (124)

constant factor That periodic amount of principal and interest needed to retire a loan.

constant payment A fixed or invariable payment, a continually recurring payment. (54)

constant yield rate An installment finance method by which the Rate is computed on the total note as in the True Discount Rate, but for a contract of 12 monthly payments only. The Factor for each maturity is not pro rata per annum of the Rate, but all other monthly maturities and all seasonal maturities are computed to produce the same Simple Interest Yield as a contract for 12 monthly payments. 6% Constant Yield means $6 per $94 for 1 yr, only when repaid monthly, which converts to 11.78% Simple Interest. The 6% Factor for each other monthly maturity, or any seasonal maturity produces 11.78% Simple Interest. This method (sometimes called Gross Charge) was developed by FHA for Title I Loans. Note that it is the same as True Discount for a contract of 12 monthly payments only. (70)

construction loan Funds extended on the security of real property for the purpose of constructing or improving a building. See Building Loan. (90)

constructive side of the market A long purchase of a security with the expectation that the market price will advance. A "bullish" position.

constructive trust A trust imposed by a court of equity as a means of doing justice, without regard to the intention of the parties, in a situation in which a person who holds title to property is under a duty to convey it to another person; to be distinguished from an express trust and a resulting trust. (74)

consul The United States Foreign Service officer located in a foreign nation who represents the American tourists, businessmen and other traveling nationals of the U.S.

consular invoice An invoice covering a shipment of goods certified (usually in triplicate) by the Consul of the country for which the merchandise is destined. This invoice is used by customs officials of the country of entry to verify the value, quantity, and nature of the merchandise imported. (1)

consult account A trust in which the trustee is required by the instrument to consult a designated party before taking action; to be distinguished from consent trust. (74)

consultant One with whom the fiduciary must confer in the administration of a fiduciary account. (74)

consumer credit Credit extended by a financial institution to a borrower for the specific purpose of financing the purchase of a household appliance, alteration or improvement, or piece of equipment (which may include an automobile or small aircraft). This credit is generally extended to individuals rather than to businesses. The largest field for this type of financing is in household appliances and home improvements, such as insulation work, furnaces, storm windows, and doors, etc. The loan is made for twelve, eighteen, twenty-four months, or longer, and a liquidation agreement is based upon a definite repayment in equal monthly installments. The financial institution has a chattel mortgage, a lien, or a lease agreement as collateral on the commodity purchased, and may take possession of the property at any time that the liquidation agreement is not carried out by the borrower. (1)

consumer finance companies Companies licensed by state for the special purpose of providing consumers with a reliable service for installment cash loans. (131)

consumer goods Commodities whose ultimate use is to contribute directly to the satisfaction of human wants or desires—such as shoes and food—as distinguished from producers' or capital goods. (89)

consumer loan Loans to individuals or families, the proceeds to be used for consumer, as contrasted to business or investment purposes. (59)

consumer plant and equipment The still unused service and uses that are built into the possession of a people as individuals and families, a form of personal and family wealth. (59)

consumers' cooperative An association of ultimate consumers organized to purchase goods and services primarily for use by or resale to the membership.

Comment: According to this definition the term applies only to the cooperative purchasing activities of ultimate consumers and does not embrace collective buying by business establishments, industrial concerns, and institutions. (13)

contest of a will An attempt by legal process to prevent the probate of a will or the distribution of property according to the will. (74)

continental rate The rate charged on bills of exchange and on foreign exchange for those nations on the continent of Europe.

contingency reserve An excess of the monetary value of assets over actuarial reserve requirements which is available to provide for possible future deficits arising from an adverse experience. It is frequently used to denote an excess of assets over current liabilities without regard to accrued actuarial liabilities. (32)

contingency surplus See Contingency Reserve. (51)

contingent assets Items without value to the accounting company until the fulfillment of conditions regarded as uncertain. (19)

contingent beneficiary The beneficiary whose interest is conditioned upon a future occurrence which may or may not take place. Unless or until the condition takes place, the interest is only contingent. (74)

contingent executor An executor named in a will whose capacity as executor is dependent upon the action or nonaction of the principal executor. (74)

contingent fees Remuneration based or conditioned upon future occurrences or conclusions, or results of services to be performed. (54)

contingent fund Assets or other resources set aside to provide for unforeseen expenditures, or for anticipated expenditures of uncertain amount.

NOTE: The term should not be used to describe a reserve for contingencies. The latter is set aside out of the appropriated surplus of a fund but does not constitute a separate fund. Similarly, an appropriation for contingencies is not a contingent fund since an appropriation is not a fund. (29)

contingent interest A future interest in real or personal property that is dependent upon the fulfillment of a stated condition. Thus the interest may never come into existence. To be distinguished from vested interest. (74)

contingent liabilities Items which may become liabilities as a result of conditions undetermined at a given date, such as guarantees, pending law suits, judgments under appeal, unsettled disputed claims, unfilled purchase orders, and incompleted contracts.

NOTE: All contingent liabilities should be shown on the face of the balance sheet or in a footnote thereto. (29)

contingent order An order to buy or sell a security at a certain price dependent upon the execution of a prior order. (105)

contingent remainder A future interest in property that is dependent upon the fulfillment of a stated condition before the termination of a prior estate; to be distinguished from vested remainder. See Remainder. (74)

contingent reserve See Contingency Reserve.

contingent trustee A trustee whose appointment is dependent upon the failure to act of the original or a successor trustee. (74)

continuing account An open book account which is periodically settled by the debtor but, since purchases are continually being made, is not closed out.

continuing agreement That phase of a broker's loan agreement with his bank which simplifies his borrowing since the broker does not have to make a loan application and sign a note every time he borrows. Once the continuing agreement is signed the broker may borrow within the terms of the contract on a continuing basis.

continuing guaranty A form given to a bank by a person to guarantee repayment of a loan to another party. This guaranty promises payment by the guarantor in the event of default by the borrower, and is so worded that it may apply to a current loan, or to one made at a later date. The guaranty may or may not pledge collateral as security for the loan. (1)

continuity of coverage A clause attached or contained in a fidelity bond which takes the place of another bond and agrees to pay the losses that would be recoverable under the first bond except that the discovery period has expired. This would be in a case where losses have been caused by a dishonest employee and have not been discovered, though they had occurred at various times stretching over a period of time, that time being a period under which several bonds had been insured. This may involve a chain of several bonds, each one superseding a prior obligation. Those losses will be covered if the chain of bonds is unbroken and each has included continuity of coverage clause. (52)

continuous audit An audit in which the detailed work is performed either continuously or at short, regular intervals throughout the fiscal period, usually at the shortest intervals (for example, weekly or monthly) at which subsidiary records are closed and made available for audit in controllable form. Such "continuous" work leads up to the completion of the audit upon the closing of the accounting records at the end of the fiscal year.

A continuous audit differs from a periodic audit, even though the detailed work may be performed, for example, monthly, in that no report is made in the case of the former, except of irregularities detected and adjustments found to be necessary, until the end of a complete fiscal period, and, further, in that the certification of balance-sheet and operating-statement figures, as such, may be deferred until the end of the fiscal period. A continuous audit is not necessarily a complete audit, but may be limited in scope according to understanding and to meet the requirements of the case.

continuous market The market for a security or commodity which is so broad that normal amounts may be sold with little difficulty and small price variation.

contra This simply means that the account has an offsetting credit or debit entry. (31, 92)

contra balances Balances in accounts that are the opposite of the normal balances of such accounts (as an account payable with a debit balance). (73)

contract An agreement entered into by two or more parties by the terms of which one or more of the parties, for a consideration, undertakes to do or to refrain from doing some act or acts in accordance with the wishes of the other party or parties. A contract to be valid and binding must be entered into by competent parties, be bound by a consideration, possess mutuality, represent an actual meeting of minds, and cover a legal and moral act. (54)

contract account General term describing a long-term credit arrangement for purchase of specific items described in the contract. Usually includes a service or carrying charge. See Chattel Mortgage Agreement; Conditional Sales Contract. (26)

contract for deed An agreement by the seller to deliver the deed to the property when certain conditions have been fulfilled, such as the completion of certain payments and provision of insurance. It has similar features to a mortgage. (5)

contract grades Those grades or types of the commodity which may be delivered on the futures contract. Differentials based on federal standards have been established by the various commodity exchanges which provide premiums for superior grades or discounts for lower grades. (9)

contract market Any commodity exchange which may engage in the business of futures contracts and is approved by the Secretary of Agriculture subject to the Commodity Exchange Administration supervision.

contract of sale A written document whereby an owner agrees to convey title to a property when the purchaser has completed paying for the property under the terms of the contract. (31, 92)

contractor A person who contracts to perform work or to supply materials under specified conditions. (89)

contract payable Sums due on contracts.
    NOTE: Amounts withheld as guarantees on contracts should be shown separately; for example, "Contracts Payable—Retained Percentage." See Accounts Payable. (29)

contractual plan By common usage, an accumulation plan with a stated paying-in period and provision for regular investments at monthly or quarterly dates. Substantially synonymous with prepaid charge plan. (3)

contrary market Market movement in a generally unexpected direction. (105)

contributory pension A retirement system in which the employer and the employee both make payments for the benefit of the employee. The system may in addition be vested, that is, subject to tenure; the employee, upon termination of employment, may take his and his employers contribution with him. A non-vested pension would not have the employer's contribution go with the employee until actual retirement.

control A system under which all transactions or balances of a given type are included in a single total, so that the accuracy of their recording may be proved. (85)

control account An account in the general ledger used to carry the total of several subsidiary accounts. Whenever any subsidiary account is affected, the same will be reflected in the control account total. Control accounts are also used as "total" accounts, controlling the accounts within a "book" or "ledger" in the bookkeeping department and the savings department. (1)

control, budget See Budget, Flexible. (28)

control card A card which indicates the total dollar amount on deposit and the total number of accounts in a single ledger. Control cards are debited and credited according to each day's transactions and are used as a basis of proof when trial balances are taken. In addition to the control card for each ledger or section, there is a master control card for each unit, or for the bank as a whole. (90)

controlled account 1.) A discretionary account. A trading account in securities or commodities in which the principal does not necessarily instruct his broker to buy or sell but rather gives a power of attorney for his broker to exercise his own discretion. 2.) An account which the salesman is able to take with him in the event he changes firms.

controlled commodities Those commodities which are agricultural products domestically produced and are subject to the Commodity Exchange Authority under the Commodity Exchange Act.

controlled company Any firm that is under the control of another company such as a holding company or a parent company.

controlled economy The administration of the means of production and consumption by a large amount of government planning and controls with only nominal use of the price system.

control, ledger A major ledger which contains the sum of the balances of more than one account in a subsidiary ledger. For example, the All-Plant Expense Account for Supervision in the Control Ledger controls the individual Departmental Supervision accounts in the Factory Ledger. (28)

controlled inflation That economic situation in which the monetary and fiscal authorities of a nation deliberately create inflationary conditions, generally through increasing the supply of money. The objective is to pull the economy out of a recession or period of deflation into prosperity. By such controls as the authorities have over the money supply they are able to reduce the increase in inflation as they approach their goal.

History shows that some nations that thought they could control inflation have been unsuccessful.

controlling account An account, usually kept in the general ledger, which receives the aggregate of the debit and of the credit postings to a number of identical, similar, or related accounts called subsidiary accounts so that its balance equals the aggregate of the balance in these accounts.

NOTE: It serves as a check upon the mathematical accuracy of the detail ledger account postings and frees the control ledger of a mass of detail. (29)

controlling company A company may be controlled by another company through many devices. Several of them are: Through stock ownership, through interlocking boards of directors, by use of a holding company, through leases, patents, copyrights and common management.

controlling interest In a legal sense slightly over fifty per cent of the voting stock will control any corporation. However, in a de facto sense, many corporations may be controlled by a much smaller percentage of voting stock if the rest of the stock is widely dispersed and not active in voting.

controlling records Those types of records which are used to control subsidiary ledgers.

convenience goods Those consumers' goods which the customer usually purchases frequently, immediately, and with the minimum of effort. Examples of merchandise customarily bought as convenience goods are: tobacco products, soap, most drug products, newspapers, magazines, chewing gum, small packaged confections, and many grocery products.

Comment: These articles are usually of small unit value and not bulky. The definition, however, is based on the method of purchase employed by the typical consumer. Its essence lies in consumer attitude and habit. The convenience involved may be in terms of nearness to the buyer's home, easy accessibility to some means of transport, or close proximity to places where people go during the day or evening, for example, downtown to work. (13)

convenient payment account Installment payment arrangement for purchase of either soft or hard goods. Usually carries a service or carrying charge. Specific payments required on specified dates. Also known as "Deferred Payment Account" and a variety of other terms. (26)

conventional billing System of rendering to customer itemized, descriptive statement of all purchases, cash payments, merchandise returned and allowances, made during a specific period, usually one calendar month. Original sales-checks, and other billing media, retained by store. (26)

conventional mortgage loan A mortgage loan made directly to the borrower without government insurance of guaranty. (89)

conversion 1. The appropriation of, dealing with, or using the property of another without right or consent as though it were ones own. 2. The exchange of personal or real property of one nature for that of another nature. 3. The exchange of one type of security for another, as example— the exchange of bonds for stock. 4. The exchanging of a charter granted by the State for a Federal Charter, etc. (1)

conversion charge The specified cost of converting from one class or series of an open-end fund to another issued by the same company or group of companies having the same sponsor. It is usually lower than the regular sales charge. (3)

conversion price That amount or rate at which a holder of a convertible bond may exchange it for the stock of the same corporation. This price may be fixed or determinable.

conversion ratio The number of shares of common stock which may be received in exchange for a convertible bond or convertible preferred stock of the same corporation. The conversion price is usually stated at the issue date of the bond or preferred stock, and will not necessarily be the same as the market price when the conversion privilege is exercised. (105)

conversion value Value created by changing from one state, character, form, or use to another. (54)

convertible A bond, debenture or preferred share which may be exchanged by the owner for common stock or another security, usually of the same company, on accordance with the terms of the issue. (2)

convertible currencies Include the U.S. Treasury and Federal Reserve holdings of foreign currencies that are counted as part of official U.S. reserve assets.

Changes in U.S. holdings of foreign currencies result primarily from reciprocal currency arrangements. The U.S. has reciprocal currency arrangements under which the U.S. may exchange dollars for other currencies under certain conditions and up to agreed upon limits with a number of countries and the Bank for International Settlements. After a stated period of time, the transaction may be reversed. These arrangements are commonly referred to as "swap arrangements." Their purpose is to provide a mechanism to absorb the initial shock of unusually heavy movements of funds in international exchanges, thereby permitting gold or SDR's (special drawing rights) to play a much less active role in the settlement of temporary imbalances. While a swap agreement does not affect the surplus or deficit in the balance of payments, it allows the U.S. (or other participating country) to finance a deficit for a short period without reducing its gold and foreign exchange assets. (124)

convertible money Any money which may be exchanged at par for the standard or legal money.

convertible preferred stock See Convertible Securities.

convertible securities Securities carrying the right (either unqualified or under stated conditions) to exchange the security for other securities of the issuer. Most frequently applies to preferred stocks carrying the right to exchange for given amounts of common stock. (3)

conveyance Broadly speaking, this term is used to describe the transfer by mortgage, deeds, bill of sale, etc., of title of property from one party (the seller) to another (the buyer). (1)

conveyancing The technique and steps taken in transferring title to real property.

cooperative A type of business enterprise that is owned by its customers. (73)

cooperative bank A term given in some states to an institution that operates as a savings and loan association. See Savings and Loan Association. (90)

cooriginator In bonding, where the clients of more than one surety company join for a specific contract. Such surety is known as cooriginator for its client's share. (50)

co-partnership (or partnership) A company of partners, as distinguished from a proprietorship or a corporation. (35)

copper a tip To take a position opposite to the recommendation. Since some tips are circulated for the purpose of stimulating the hearers to do something, if the hearer suspects that the tip is designed for that purpose, he may personally gain by doing the opposite.

(A tip to buy a stock may be made because of the desire on the part of the tipster to unload it on the public without loss. A short sale under such circumstances would be profitable and the seller has coppered a tip.)

cordoba Monetary unit of Nicaragua.

corner Buying of a stock or commodity on a scale large enough to give the buyer, or buying group, control over the price. A person who must buy that stock or commodity, for example, one who is short, is forced to do business at an arbitrarily high price with those who engineered the corner. See Short. (2)

corporate agent Trust companies act as agents for corporations, governments, and municipalities for various transactions. In each case, a fee is charged for the particular service rendered. These services are listed below:

Coupon and Bond Paying Agent—The Trust Company pays all maturing coupons or bonds of its principal. Funds are provided by the principal (bond issuing legal entity) and a statement is rendered to the principal periodically showing all receipts and disbursements. When the indenture requires it, paid coupons and bonds are cremated and a cremation certificate is returned to the principal along with the statement. Otherwise the paid coupons and bonds are returned with statement to the principal.

Dividend Disbursing Agent The Trust Company pays all dividends to stockholders of record and renders a report to the corporation of such disbursement.

Fiscal Agent-Tax Withholdings As fiscal agent for a government, a Trust Company is required to report to the government for whom it acts as fiscal agent, all taxes withheld that may be deposited with it for the account of the government.

Stock Redemption Agent—Handles the redemption of stock under a reorganization, or retirement of preferred stock by a corporation. (1)

corporate chain That form of business organiza-

tion in which a central office exercises a great deal of control over branch operations.

corporate depositary A trust institution serving as the depositary of funds or other property. See also Depositary; Depository. (74)

corporate fiduciary A trust institution serving in a fiduciary capacity, such as executor, administrator, trustee, or guardian. (74)

corporate profits after taxes The earnings of U.S. corporations organized for profit after liability for federal and state taxes has been deducted. (124)

corporate profits before taxes The net earnings of corporations organized for profit measured before payment of federal and state profit taxes. They are, however, net of indirect business taxes. They are reported without deduction for depletion charges and exclusive of capital gains and losses and intercorporate dividends. (124)

corporate profits tax liability Reflects federal and state taxes levied on corporate earnings. In the national accounts, taxes on corporate profits are recorded on an accrual basis. In other words, they are assigned to the period when the taxes are actually paid to the Internal Revenue Service or state governments. These two periods may or may not be the same. (124)

corporate records The documents such as the certificate of incorporation, the by-laws, the secretary's minutes of the meetings of the board of directors, the list of shareholders, and such other records required by the state in which the corporation is incorporated and such other appropriate bodies such as the Securities Exchange Commission, and listing exchange may require.

corporate resolution A document given to a bank by a corporation defining the authority vested in each of its officers who may sign and otherwise conduct the business of the corporation with the bank. Corporate resolutions usually are given with or without borrowing powers. These powers are granted by the board of directors of the firm. (1)

corporate shell A company that exists without fixed assets aside from cash but may have an exchange listing. (105)

corporate stock The equity shares of a corporation. These shares may be common, preferred, or classified. The term corporate stock is also used to occasionally refer to bonds of some municipalities.

corporate surety Insurance provided by a surety company as compared to surety provided by an individual. The writing of bonds by a corporation as obligor. (5)

corporate surplus As of the date of the balance sheet, the equity in the assets not offset by the capitalization, current or deferred liabilities, or unadjusted credits. It includes appropriations for additions to property, for retirement of funded debt, reserves for sinking and other funds, and other appropriations not specifically invested. (19)

corporate trust A trust created by a corporation, typical of which is a trust to secure a bond issue. (74)

That part of a trust company's operations which is devoted to acting as trustee for corporations, and their security issues. Among the more important corporate trust functions are acting as transfer agent and as a registrar, paying interest on bonds and processing coupons, handling a corporation's sinking fund, receiving subscriptions to various issues and handling escrow funds.

corporate trustee A trust institution serving as a trustee. (74)

corporation A corporation has been defined as "an invisible, intangible, artificial entity, existing only in contemplation of the law." (Chief Justice John Marshall in "Trustees of Dartmouth College vs. Woodward.") (1)

corporation finance That area of business which is concerned with providing the funds needed by a business. This would include the technique of organizing and raising the initial capital of the corporation, the provision of working capital through proper cash flow practices, the emergency steps needed in the event of insolvency or bankruptcy as well as those techniques such as dividend policies which will permit a corporation to obtain needed capital for expansion.

corporation income tax A progressive tax levied on earnings of corporations and Massachusetts trusts by either the federal or state government.

corporation securities Business corporation securities as distinguished from Government or Municipal Securities. (105)

corporation sole A one-man corporation, the authority, duties, and powers of which are attached to and go with the office and not the natural person who for the time being holds the office. (74)

corporators The group which in certain states elects the trustees of a mutual savings bank. The number of corporators is not limited, and the group is self-perpetuating. (90)

corporeal Pertaining to a right or group of rights of a visible and tangible nature. (54)

corporeal hereditament See Hereditament. (74)

corpus A term used in trust companies and trust accounting to describe all the property in a trust, also referred to as the "body" of the trust. A corpus may consist of real estate, stocks, bonds, and other personal property, cash in the form of bank accounts, and any items that the donor may wish to have included. (1)

correcting entries Entries made in the general journal to correct errors in the bookkeeping records that have been discovered after the trial balance has been prepared. (73)

correction Refers to a price reaction in the general market or a specific security which may retrace as much as one-third to two-thirds of the previous gain. (105)

correspondency system Origination and administration of mortgage loans for investors by independent loan correspondents. (121)

correspondent bank A depository bank, generally located in a large business center, that has direct connection or friendly service relations with other banks for the purposes of issuing drafts payable in that center and routing transit items for collection in that area. (83)

correspondent firm A brokerage firm that maintains a mutually advantageous business and firm. This quite often occurs between one firm located in a city where there is an exchange and another out-of-town firm which has business executed and cleared by the member firm. (105).

cost The amount, measured in money, of cash expended or other property transferred, capital stock issued, services performed, or a liability incurred, in consideration of goods or services received or to be received. (17)

The amount of money or money's worth given for property or services.

NOTE: Cost may be incurred even before money is paid, that is, as soon as liability is incurred. Ultimately, however, money or money's worth must be given in exchange. Again, the cost of some property or service may in turn become a part of the cost of another property or service. For example, the cost of part or all of the materials purchased at a certain time will be reflected in the cost of articles made from such materials or in the cost of those services in the rendering of which the materials were used. (29)

cost, accounting plan A plan wherein the detailed Cost Accounts are prepared in such a manner that all costing and pricing information is readily available as an automatic by-product of producing the formal accounting entries. This is frequently referred to as an Interlocking Cost Plan. See Cost, Finding Plan. (28)

cost, allocation The proportionate distribution of costs and expenses to the benefiting Orders or Departments. For example, certain direct costs, such as heat treating, are often too small to be applied directly to the Order. They are then allocated on some equitable basis, such as number of units on the Order to the total number of units heat treated, etc. A large percentage of all expenses are allocated—sweeping on floor area, insurance on appraised value of fixed assets, power on horsepower of motors, etc. (28)

cost, analysis The comparison of actual with anticipated costs of production to discover what variations have occurred and what remedies may be applied. (28)

cost and freight A selling term reflecting that the price includes charges for handling costs and freight to delivery to a destination, such as a foreign port. The buyer must pay any additional charges from that point including insurance.

cost basis The original price or cost of an asset usually based on the purchase price or, in the case of assets received from an estate, on the appraised value of the assets at the death of the donor or some anniversary or other fixed date. (74)

cost, book The cost of acquisition shown in the general ledger of an individual partnership or corporation which generally includes direct and indirect costs, financing costs, and all development costs, except preliminary operating losses. (66)

cost, center A purely arbitrary division or unit of a plant set up for costing purposes only. It may be a man at a bench, a machine or group of machines, a department, a floor, or entire building. (28)

cost, conversion The value of Direct Labor and Burden Applied entering into the cost of a manufactured product. This represents the cost of converting the material from its original to its final manufactured state. See Inventory, Raw Material; Inventory, Finished Goods. (28)

cost, depreciated Cost new less accrued depreciation, as of date of appraisal. Erroneously used on occasion to reflect cost new less deterioration or physical wear-out only. (66)

cost, development The sum total of all costs, other than for actual construction, necessary to bring a property to the point of full operation including, but not necessarily limited to, financing costs, incorporation and other organizational expense, leasing commissions paid, promotional fees and advertising, loss of reasonable return on investment until anticipated occupancy is developed. Technically, all leasing commissions may be considered as part of the cost of development, but if they are paid over a period of years as rents are collected, they are usually treated as an operating expense item. (66)

cost, direct All costs directly related to site acquisition and construction of improvements generally considered to include the following: 1. Land Cost a) Purchase price, including broker's commission if paid by the buyer. b) All legal and recording charges connected with the purchase of the site. 2. Cost of Building (s) and Land Improvements a) All architects', engineers', consultants', and supervisory fees. b) Construction cost of building, equipment and fixtures, and including builder's profit, overhead, cost of performance bond, and "general conditions" items such as survey and permit fees, fencing, shoring for lateral support of adjacent land or streets, watchment, contractor's "shack" and/or temporary building for on-the-job fabrication of units and material storage, power line installation, and cost of electric power used in construction. (66)

cost, expired Costs which are not applicable to the production of future revenues and, for that reason, are treated as deductions from current revenues or are charged against retained earnings. Examples are costs of products or other assets sold or disposed of, and current expenses. (17)

cost factors The various expenses which must be met by a supplier of consumer credit, and which therefore influence the charges he will make for credit services. (131)

cost, financing Fees paid for arranging necessary financing. (66)

cost, finding plan A plan wherein separate and distinct records of costs are maintained for costing and pricing purposes only. No attempt is made to "tie-in" this information with the formal accounting entries. All purely Cost Finding Plans entail a considerable duplication of clerical effort and generally fail to provide as accurate information as that obtainable from cost accounting plans. (28)

cost, historical Past expenditures for the acquisition of a property (or construction and land costs) plus cost of betterments and permanent improvements. (66)

cost, indirect All costs necessary to the development of a property which are not construction and land acquisition items including: 1. Counsel fees and legal expenses in connection with construction problems and contracts. 2. Financing cost. 3. Insurance and taxes during construction. 4. Interest on land cost during construction and on construction loans. 5. Loss of reasonable return on investment until anticipated occupancy is developed. 6. Owner's overhead during construction. (66)

costing point See Cost Center. (28)

cost, insurance, and freight A selling term reflecting that the price includes charges for handling costs, insurance, and freight to delivery to a foreign port. The buyer must pay any additional charges from that point. (5)

cost ledger A subsidiary record wherein each project, job, production center, process, operation, product, or service is given a separate account where all items entering into its cost are posted in the required detail. Such accounts should be so arranged and kept that the results shown in them may be reconciled with and verified by a control account or in the general books. (29)

cost less depreciation, replacement Replacement cost new as of date of appraisal, minus loss from all causes, i.e., accrued depreciation. (66)

cost less depreciation, reproduction Reproduction cost new as of date of appraisal, minus loss from all causes, i.e., accrued depreciation. (66)

cost, manufacturing The value of all Direct Labor, Direct Material and Burden Applied entering into the cost of producing a finished product. It does not include administrative and selling expenses or profit; all of which are subsequently added to the manufacturing cost to obtain the total cost or wholesale price of the product. (28)

cost of goods sold A corporation's manufacturing expenses connected with the products the company sells and appearing in the profit and loss statement. (105)

cost of insurance The cost or value of net insurance protection in a given year. (42)

cost of merchandise sold The result obtained by subtracting the ending merchandise inventory from the sum of the beginning merchandise inventory and the net purchases for the month. (73)

cost of repairs 1. The estimated amount necessary to be spent to restore to a new condition those items of construction which require correction in the immediate future because of deterioration. 2. The amount actually spent to restore to a new condition those construction items which were worn-out because of deterioration. 3. Sometimes used to designate the amount to be or actually spent to restore worn-out parts to a usable condition, e.g., hot water tank with a secondhand, though serviceable, substitute unit. (66)

cost of reproduction The cost of replacing a building as of any given date (usually current). (31, 92)

cost of reproduction new As applied to Interstate Commerce Commission valuation, the estimated cost of reproducing the existing property of a carrier under price levels of a specified period. (19)

cost of sales The composite value of the product at the time it is offered for sale. This is composed of the manufacturing cost plus a proportionate percentage of selling and administrative expenses and profit. (28)

cost of occupancy The periodic expenditure of money necessary to occupy a property, exclusive of the expenses directly attributable to the conduct of a business.

1. Owner-occupant: fair rental value, including charge for betterments and/or alterations, plus utilities, heat, etc.

2. Tenant: rent, amortization of improvements' cost, heat, utilities, plus all real estate items chargeable to tenant such as portion or all non-business or non-inventory taxes, and fire and liability insurance premiums. (66)

cost plus contracts An agreement by which the buyer pays the seller or producer his costs of the product and also a percentage of the costs in addition for his profits. Contracts for production of devices of unknown costs such as a space vehicle may take this form. Where costs are better known, it is probable that a fixed price contract will be used.

cost, prime The value of Direct Material and Direct Labor only entering into the cost of a manufactured product. This represents the direct charges only and does not include any Burden Charges. (28)

cost records All ledgers, supporting records, schedules, reports, invoices, vouchers, and other records and documents reflecting the cost of projects, jobs, production centers, processes, operations, products, or services, or the cost of any of the component parts thereof. (29)

cost, re-operation The cost of repairing work which was previously rejected by an inspection department as spoilage so that it can again meet inspection requirements. The cost of performing this work is generally charged to an expense account even though it is performed by Direct Labor in a Direct Department. Examples of Re-operation are: reducing the diameter of an oversize part so that it will conform to the rest of the order, in Work in Process Inventory: Performing machining operations on much needed purchased material which would normally be rejected by the Receiving Inspection Department because it failed to meet the specifications called for on the Purchase Order. (28)

cost, replacement 1. The cost of construction new of a building (or an improvement to land) having utility equivalent to the unit under appraisal, but built with modern materials and according to current standards, design and layout. See Reproduction Cost. 2. The cost of acquisition of an equally desirable substitute property. (66)

costs and expenses The costs of doing business which must be paid from the revenues received by the company.

cost sheet A special sheet containing space for recording the detailed costs of each production order. (73)

cost, square foot 1. The result obtained by the division of the actual or estimated cost of a building by its gross floor area, or by the division of the actual or estimated cost of a land improvement by its square foot area. 2. The unit (in terms of money) which, multiplied by the number of square feet in a building or land improvement, results in the actual or estimated cost. (66)

cost systems, actual Any cost system that reveals the true cost of manufacturing, in contrast with Standard Cost Systems (see Cost System, Standard Plan). When the actual cost figures are not available until after the completion of the entire manufacturing cycle, this type of Cost System is frequently referred to as an Historical Cost System. Examples of Actual Cost Systems are: Job Order, Operation, and Process Cost Systems. See Cost Systems, Job Order, Operation and Process. (28)

cost systems, dual standard plan Both Actual and scientifically pre-determined standard amounts of Direct Labor, Direct Material and Burden Applied are debited and credited to Work in Process Inventory. However, only actual costs are entered in Finished Goods Inventory and Cost of Sales. In this case, the standards are used solely for manufacturing control purposes. It is frequently a first step towards the installation of a single or partial Standard Cost System. See Cost Systems, Partial Standard Plan and Single Standard Plan. (28)

cost systems, historical See Cost Systems, Actual. (28)

cost systems, job order All actual Direct Labor and Direct Material, plus Burden Applied are debited to Work in Process Inventory for each specific unit of production. This system is commonly in use where no standards have been established, or where large numbers of non-repetitive manufacturing processes are involved. For example, printing plants, the manufacture of heavy machinery, specialty products, etc. (28)

cost systems, normal Long term average amounts of Direct Labor, Direct Material and Burden Applied are computed for each product class. These averages are debited to the Work in Process Inventory Accounts for the current number of units of production. Frequently this is the first stage in the development of a Standard Cost System. See Cost Systems, Standard Plan. (28)

cost systems, operation The totals of actual Direct Labor, Direct Material plus Burden Applied are charged to Work in Process Inventory by operations rather than by departments as in a Process Cost System (see Cost System, Process). This type of Cost System is generally in use where the manufacturing cycle entails a considerable number of operations, and various lots of production that are not readily distinguishable, one from the other. For example, cement mills, artificial gas, rubber manufacture, etc. (28)

cost systems, partial standard plan Actual amounts of Direct Labor and Direct Material and Standard amounts of Burden Applied Inventory and charged to Finished Goods Inventory at scientifically pre-determined standard amounts for all like units of production. (28)

cost systems, process The totals of Direct Labor, Direct Material and Burden Applied are charged to Work in Process Inventory by department only. This type of Cost System is generally in use where the manufacturing cycle is of a continuous nature, and various lots of production are not readily distinguishable, one from the other. For example, flour mills, oil refineries, etc. (28)

cost systems, single standard plan Scientifically predetermined standard amounts of Direct Labor, Direct Material and Burden Applied are charged and ultimately credited to Work in Process Inventory for all like units of production. Any differences between standard and actual amounts are closed out to variance accounts. (28)

cost systems, standard plan Scientifically predetermined costs are used instead of Actual Costs (see Cost System, Actual) for valuing Work in Process Inventory and frequently for determining cost of sales. The three major types of Standard Cost Plans are: (see Cost Systems, Single, Partial, and Dual Standard). These plans are primarily used where highly repetitive manufacturing processes are involved. For example, the manufacture of pencils, electric motors, gadgets, typewriters, etc. (28)

cost, unexpired (Assets) Those costs which are applicable to the production of future revenues. Examples are inventories, prepaid expenses, plan, investments, and deferred charges. (17)

cost unit A term used in cost accounting to designate the unit of product or service whose cost is computed. These units are selected for the purpose of comparing the actual cost with a standard cost or with actual costs of units produced under different circumstances or at different places and times. (29)

co-trustee That individual or trust company or bank permitted to provide trust functions, that act with another as a trustee.

counter cash That part of the actual cash of a bank kept by the tellers in their cages. (83)

counter check A form of check provided by a bank for the convenience of the depositor. A counter check can be cashed only by the drawer personally. (85)

counter deposits A deposit presented at the teller's window by a customer. Other forms include deposits by mail, clearings, collections, or internal sources. (83)

counter-error In accounting, an error (over or short) which is offset by an error of equal amount, thus creating a balance which is correct without disclosing that two or more of the transactions apparently proved are actually in error. (83)

counterfeit currency coverage A bond that protects the insured against loss through the receipt in good faith of counterfeited or altered United States currency or coin. (5)

counterfeit money Spurious currency and specie coins which have been made to appear genuine. The act of creating counterfeit money is a felony under law, and the conspirators of making and distributing counterfeit money are subject to long prison terms and heavy fines. The United States Secret Service, a bureau of the Treasury

Department, is constantly on the alert tracking down the criminals who traffic counterfeit money. (1)

countermand The act of cancelling an order which has been given but not as yet carried out.

counterpart fund The amount of domestic currency a nation sets aside as an offset adjustment for loans or gifts from abroad. The domestic currency provision reduces the foreign exchange problem and local currency may then be expended at an appropriate time in a relatively non-inflationary way for public works, building of embassies and such. The Economic Cooperation Administration of the U.S.A. has been one of the most important users of this type of fund.

countersign The act of signing a document which requires two or more signatures, one of which already is affixed.

country bank The American Bankers' Association, for the purpose of making studies of bank operations, considers banks whose total assets are $7,500,000 or less as being, generally speaking, "Country Banks." In a geographic sense, a country bank is any bank not classified as being a Reserve City Bank. (1)

country check A transit check. An item drawn on an out of town bank. A check drawn upon a bank not located in a Central Reserve or Reserve City.

country collections A term describing all items which are being sent outside the city in which the sending bank is located. A banker will speak of "city collections," which are items drawn on banks and business houses upon whom drafts are to be collected within the city of the bank's location; and "country collections," which are sent out of the city to the bank's correspondents for collection and payment. (1)

country elevator In contrast to a terminal elevator which is situated in a major market a country elevator is situated close to the actual point of production. The farmer generally brings his grain to the country elevator, from there the grain is retransported to the terminal elevator.

coupon One of a series of promissory notes of consecutive maturities attached to a bond or other debt certificate and intended to be detached and presented on their respective due dates for payment of interest. (85)

coupon account Type of credit extension whereby books of coupons having a stated value are sold on installment payment basis. Coupons used in issuing stores as cash. Payment for coupon book is stretched over period of time. Coupon Accounts generally used for credit customer of limited responsibility, and whose buying must be closely controlled. (26)

coupon book The ledger used by a coupon paying trustee in which is recorded the receipts and disbursements and related data concerning the coupons it has processed.

coupon collection Being negotiable, coupons are collectable the same as any other negotiable instrument. The owner of the bond, from which the coupon was clipped, signs a "Certificate of Ownership" and attaches the coupon to this certificate. It is then either cashed by the bank, or deposited by the depositor as a credit to his account. Coupons are collected by banks under special transit letters which require considerably more description than is required for check collections. (1)

coupon collection department That department of a bank or trust company devoted to Coupon Collection. See that term.

coupon collection teller That individual member of a Coupon Collection Department whose function is processing the coupons presented for payment.

coupon ledger See Coupon Book.

coupon rate The interest rate specified on interest coupons attached to a bond. The term is synonymous with nominal interest rate (q.v.) (29)

coupon shell A term used in certain localities describing the envelope in which maturing coupons are enclosed for collection. (1)

court account Accounts which require court accountings and approval in their normal conduct. Probate, guardianship, conservatorship, and testamentary trust accounts are the most common. (74)

courtesy box Collection box equipped with mail chute for motorists. (39)

court of claims That federal court which handles all claims against the United States which arise out of any contract with the Government, or regulation of the President or act of Congress as well as claims directed to it by the Senate or House of Representatives.

court of equity Courts applying a system of jurisprudence more flexible than that of the common law in order to work justice where the common law, by reason of its rigidity, fails to recognize a right or is unable to enforce it. (74)

court trust A trust coming under the immediate supervision of the court such as a trust by order of court or, in some states, a trust under will. (74)

court trusts Trusts may be classified as Court Trusts or Private Trusts. The former generally is a Trust Company or a bank authorized to perform the trust function, and is designated or appointed by order of a court having such jurisdiction.

covenant A promise, incorporated in a trust indenture or other formal instrument, to perform certain acts or to refrain from the performance of certain acts. (74)

cover Shorts are said to cover when they buy back the contracts they had previously sold, thereby liquidating their position. (9)

The cancellation of a short position in any futures by the purchase of an equal quantity of the same futures. (123)

coverage As used in credit analysis, coverage is the amount of one item in a financial statement in relationship to another item. Thus, if accounts payable is shown as $1,000 and cash as $2,000, the coverage is two times. That is, there are two dollars to pay each dollar of accounts payable and thus the probability is that no difficulty would be experienced in being able to pay those accounts.

creator The trustor. One who created or established a trust.

credit 1. Used in general sense means act of allowing person or persons immediate use of goods or services with payment deferred until an agreed future date. 2. Used in bookkeeping sense means an entry on ledger signifying cash payment, merchandise returned, or an allowance. Opposite of "debit". (26)

credit acceptance Notification to customer that credit application has been accepted and account available for use. (26)

credit agency Those companies which make a business of providing credit and collection information. See Mercantile Agency.

credit application A form which the consumer must fill out when he wants to use consumer credit; it usually contains questions concerning present and previous places of residence, work history, present earnings, and other credit transactions. (131)

credit association Usually known as the Retail Credit Association. A group of local retail credit granters forming a dues-paying association. In most cases the local association with ten or more members is a unit of the National Retail Credit Association. (26)

credit authorizer See Authorizer. (26)

credit balance 1. Any account which has a larger amount of credits than debits. 2. An account with a broker which shows that the broker is indebted to the customer. Typically this results from trading in a street name and permitting the dividends to be paid to the broker which in turn are held for the customer as a credit balance.

credit barometrics Those financial ratios applied to balance sheets and profit and loss statements which permit adequate credit analysis. Among the more important are: The current ratio and the merchandise turnover ratio.

credit bureau Place where information about payment records of individuals and firms and all other relevant data are assembled. Information released to members and non-members on request. Credit Bureaus can be Merchant-owned, that is, ownership held by local merchants and others, or can be privately owned. (26)

credit card Used by oil companies, hotels, banks, and other firms as a means of identification and credit authorization. Bears the name, address, and signature of holder. Can be good for an unlimited time or with definite expiration date. (26)

credit, charge account (or credit, open account) Generally refers to credit of 30 days' duration extended by department stores and other retail outlets as a matter of convenience to customers. Typically no carrying charges. (24)

credit clearing See Credit Interchange.

credit company 1. A commercial credit company. 2. A company which operates similar to a factor but which takes paper subject to "recourse" rather than "without recourse."

credit, consumer (Short and Intermediate Term) All forms of short-term credit extended to consumers for the purchase of goods and services, or to pay debts.

credit controls Those restraints which are imposed by authoritative bodies. The Federal Reserve Board controls credit in several ways: 1.

Reserve requirements for member banks; 2. open market operations; 3. rediscount rates; 4. margin requirements. In addition, in periods of national emergency, other regulating devices were used to regulate credit such as the fiscal operation of the U.S. Treasury, gold sterilization and action by the American Bankers Association.

credit currency Any currency which does not have full convertibility into standard money. Fiduciary money.

credit declined Notification to customer that credit application has not been accepted. (26)

credit department (1) In a non-bank the department of a company which establishes lines of credit for various customers and authorizes the extension of credit. In addition most mercantile credit departments also have responsibility for the collection of the accounts. (2) A department in a bank where credit information is obtained, assembled, and retained for reference purposes. Credit applications for loans are presented to this department by a loan officer. The credit department gathers all available information on the customer, and prepares it for the confidential use of the loan officer. Based upon the findings of the credit departments, which will make an analysis of the credit information, the loan officer is in a position to make a decision as to whether the loan application should be rejected. The credit department also obtains information and answers credit inquiries for its bank correspondents, who may have a business transaction pending that will involve credit knowledge on a local business. (1)

credit entry An entry that is placed on the right-hand side of an account. (73)

credit facilities A business system set up to offer credit services to those who possess personal or business credit. (59)

credit file An assembly of facts and opinions which indicates the financial resources of an individual (or an enterprise), his character, and his record of performance, especially toward financial obligations. (89)

credit folder Same as Credit File.

credit footing of an account The columnar total that is written at the foot of the credit money column in the account. (73)

credit grantor A misused term indicating that credit is supplied to consumers by business. The true concept is that business supplies only the facilities through which those who possess credit can use it. (59)

credit information Almost any information on a subject, individual or company can be of help to a credit analyst. The information may be obtained direct, by personal interview, by telephone, or letter. It may be obtained from a credit bureau or mercantile agency. Financial institutions and businesses in the same trade also are valuable sources of information. The principal type of information may be classified a. Antecedent information b. Financial statements information c. Payment experience information including such factors as highest credit and record of discounting.

credit, installment A form of credit in which the customer purchases goods under an agreement to pay the balance due in installments. A stipulated carrying charge is made. (24)

credit instruments Any document, contract or paper which may be used to obtain credit. This would include paper money not redeemable in standard money, checks, notes, drafts, bills of exchange, travelers checks, letters of credit, coupons, money orders, and cashiers checks. The above are debt credit instruments. In addition, such things as preferred and common stock certificates may be classified as equity credit instruments.

credit interchange Information on credit may be interchanged in two ways: (1) Direct in which two creditors exchange their credit experience for mutual benefit; (2) by use of a central clearing bureau in which accounts of certain categories, such as 30-day past due accounts are listed and sent to the bureau which in turn collates the data for its members.

credit interchange bureau An organization which serves as a clearinghouse for its members credit inquiries and experience. See Credit Interchange.

credit interviewer Person who secures from credit applicant the necessary information required for establishing credit. (26)

credit investigation An inquiry which is undertaken by a financial institution to verify all the information given in a credit application. (131)

credit investigator An individual who is employed by or is an agent of a mercantile agency, a bank or a credit department and has as his function the obtaining of credit information on assigned subject, individuals or firms.

credit letter Another title for a cash letter; see definition. (1)

credit life insurance Life insurance issued by a life insurance company on the lives of borrowers to cover payment of loans (usually small loans repayable in installments) in case of death. It is usually handled through a lending office and is written on either a group or an individual basis.

credit limit Amount, established with or without agreement of customer, to which credit purchases may be authorized. (26)

credit line The maximum amount of credit a financial institution or trade firm will extend to a customer. The customer may in many cases be unaware of the trade credit line.

credit losses The money lost by a finance company or other credit-granting institution when a debt is not paid. This loss may be increased by the cost of collection activities before the debt is finally written off as uncollectable. (131)

credit mechanism See Credit Facilities. (59)

credit memo 1. A posting medium authorizing the credit to a specified account of a certain named amount which bears the complete description of the transaction, the date, and the signature of the party responsible for the authorization of the credit. 2. A detailed memorandum forwarded from one party or firm to another, granting credit for returned merchandise, some omission, overpayment, or other cause. (1)

credit memorandum A special business form that

is issued by the seller to the buyer and that contains a record of the credit which the seller has granted for returns, allowances, overcharges, and similar items. (73)

credit money Fiduciary money which is not fully backed by precious metals.

creditor One who is due money from another. (1)

creditor country See Creditor Nation.

creditor nation A country which on a net basis is owed more by foreigners than it owes to them. Such a nation would tend to have a "favorable" balance of trade.

creditors Those to whom one owes an obligation (usually financial). (59)

creditors' committee A group of persons who seek to arrange some settlement on behalf of each person or firm having claims on a business in financial difficulty; common procedure is for all claims to be assigned to this body for settlement. (35)

creditor's notice In probate the notice published stating the decedent's death and the name of the executor or administrator to whom claims should be presented for payment. (74)

creditor's position That portion of the market price of a property which is represented by or can be obtained through a first mortgage. (54)

credit proxy Total member bank deposits plus non-deposit items is sometimes referred to as the "adjusted credit proxy." Member bank deposit figures are seasonally adjusted, but non-deposit items are included in the series on a seasonally unadjusted basis due to the short period for which most items are available. Non-deposit items included in the series are as follows: gross liabilities of banks to own foreign branches and to branches in U.S. territories and possessions; Eurodollars borrowed directly from foreign banks or through brokers and dealers; commercial paper issued by bank holding companies or other bank affiliates; and loans or participations in pools of loans sold under repurchase agreement to other than banks and other than banks' own affiliates or subsidiaries.

credit rating 1. The amount, type, and terms of credit, if any, which the credit department estimates can be extended to an applicant for credit. 2. An estimate as to the credit and responsibility assigned to mercantile and other establishments by credit investigating and credit servicing organizations. (1)

credit rating book A listing of established credit users in an area together with a code letter indicating general credit rating. Distribution of Credit Rating Books is usually limited to members of issuing Credit Bureaus, revised periodically. Current legislation may make some Credit Rating Books illegal.

credit report Report secured from credit bureau, or other credit-information service, reporting on the applicant's financial and credit history. (26)

credit, revolving (or credit, continuous budget account) A consumer credit plan whereby a limit is placed on a customer's account, and charges up to the limit may be made without other special authorization. The amount payable each month is a specified fraction (often 1/10) of the credit limit. (Under a flexible chart plan, the size of the payment is related to the amount owed, instead of to the approved limit.) (24)

credit risk The chance of loss through nonperformance of a contract, nonpayment of debt. (59)

credit sales department Term recommended by the National Retail Credit Association to designate the place where credit and collection functions are carried on. (26)

credit sales manager or "Manager of Credit Sales". Title recommended by the National Retail Credit Association for the person in charge of credit and collection matters. (26)

credit sales promotion Term covering all activities and programs developed for the purpose of increasing credit sales to customers. (26)

credit service charge The charge made for the use of credit facilities. (59)

credit side The right-hand side of an account. (73)

credit standing One's present credit worthiness as determined by his past credit performance. (59)

credit tests Those relatively objective standards which may be applied to a credit risk. These include certain balance sheet and income statement relationships as well as the ratio analysis of the above. In addition, the size of credit extension may be limited to proportions of net worth.

credit ticket A bank bookkeeping memorandum or posting medium on which the transaction leading to a credit entry in a ledger account is described in detail. (83)

credit trade reference Name of business firm with which customer has had credit dealings. (26)

credit transfer Voucher giving bookkeeper authority to credit an account according to instructions on voucher. Opposite of "Debit" transfer. (26)

credit union A cooperative financial society organized within and limited to a specific group of people. Any group of people with common interests are eligible to form a credit union. Each union is self-managed and is intended to provide a convenient system of saving money and of lending funds to members in need at lawful rates of interest. It functions under either state or federal law and supervision. See Federal Credit Union. (90)

creditworthy Entitled to the use of credit facilities, possessed of good credit. (59)

cremation The act of destroying by fire certain records of the bank. The legal counsel of the bank advises the bank which records and documents may be destroyed, as a result of having outrun the Statute of Limitations according to the laws of the state in which the bank is operating. The term also applies to the destruction by fire of certain bonds and coupons which have been redeemed by a bank acting as fiscal agent for the issuing corporation or governmental agency. The cremation of paid securities is by agreement between the bank and the issuing agency. (1)

cremation certificate A trustee's sworn statement that a stated security or securities or documents were destroyed. (5)

crop year The commodity term referring to the

period from the harvest of a crop to the next year. Harvest dates vary for different crops. (105)

crossed check A drawing of two diagonal lines across the face of a check and the addition of a term or series of words which will determine the negotiability of the check such as to one's banker if his name is inserted between the lines. Crossed checks are used in some of the Latin American countries and in parts of Europe.

crossed sales Same as Crossed Trades. See that term.

crossed trades A manipulative device prohibited on both the securities exchanges and the commodity exchanges in which a broker or two brokers offset an order to buy with an offer to sell and do not execute the orders on the exchange. This prevents the trade from being recorded and may mean that one of the parties to the cross did not obtain the price which would have been obtained on the exchange.

cross of gold Statement made by William Jennings Bryan in 1896 in favor of free silver and against the gold standard—"You shall not press down upon the brow of labor this crown of thorns. You shall not crucify mankind upon a cross of gold."

cross-rate The calculation of the rate of exchange of two foreign currencies by using the rate of exchange of each currency in a third nation's currency. If A currency is quoted at ten peso to a U.S. dollar, and B currency is quoted at five rupees to a dollar, we can derive a cross rate of two peso to a rupee.

cross remainders Dispositive provisions of a will or trust agreement wherein there is provision that surviving life beneficiaries shall be entitled to receive or share in the income of the deceased beneficiary. (74)

crowd A group of securities people who deal primarily with one certain function. Specialists, Floor Traders, Odd-lot Dealers and other brokers make up the crowd on an exchange floor. A bond crowd is composed of those brokers dealing exclusively in bonds. (105)

cruzeiro Monetary unit of Brazil.

cum dividends With dividends, corporate stock may be termed ex-dividend which means that the buyer is not entitled to a declared dividend or cum-dividend which means that the buyer is entitled to the declared dividend.

cum rights With rights; corporate stock which still has the privilege of buying a stated amount of stock to be newly issued. Generally, the new stock is of a different class.

cumulative An arrangement whereby a dividend or interest which, if not paid when due or received when due, is added to that which is to be paid in the future. (74)

cumulative preferred stock A type of preferred stock on which dividends continue to accrue even though at the time no funds are available for payment. As conditions improve, the arrears must be paid before dividends on other issues may be resumed. (74)

cumulative voting A method of voting for corporate directors which enables the shareholder to multiply the number of his shares by the number of directorships being voted on and cast the total for one director or a selected group of directors.

A 10-share holder normally casts 10 votes for each of, say, 12 nominees to the board of directors. He thus has 120 votes. Under the cumulative voting principle he may do that or he may cast 120 (10 X 12) votes for only one nominee, 60 for two, 40 for three, or any other distribution he chooses. Cumulative voting is required under the corporate laws of some states and is permissive in most others. (2)

curator An individual or a trust institution appointed by a court to care for the property of a minor or an incompetent person. In some states a curator is essentially the same as a temporary administrator or a temporary guardian. (74)

curb broker The old designation for a member of the American Stock Exchange which formerly was called the Curb Exchange or New York Curb Exchange.

curb exchange Former name of the American Stock Exchange, second largest exchange in the country. The term comes from the market's origin on the streets of downtown New York. (2)

currency The term given to paper money issued by a government through an act of law. This paper money circulates freely at par in all channels of trade, and is backed by law with either precious metal owned and controlled by the government which issues the currency, or by the promise of the government to redeem the paper money with legal precious metals of the government. See Legal Tender; National Bank Note. (1)

currency shipments Currency may be shipped by armored car, registered mail or by express. Since the money paid out by a bank does not always return to it, some banks gain and some banks lose currency. Needed currency may thus be shipped from those banks with excessive amounts to those banks whose supplies are diminished. In many cases this is done indirectly by the use of the facilities of the district Federal Reserve Bank.

current account The term used for checking accounts in Canada and foreign countries. See Checking Account. (1)

current and accrued assets Generally consists of items realizable or to be consumed within one year from the date of the balance sheet. Includes cash, working funds, and certain deposits, temporary cash investments, receivables, materials and supplies including fuel, and prepayments. (21)

current and accrued liabilities Generally consists of obligations incurred, accrued or declared, including short-term borrowing, all of which are either due and payable, payable on demand or, in any event, contemplated to be paid within one year. (21)

current and collectable Money which flows or passes from hand to hand as a medium of exchange. (93)

current assets Those assets of a company which are reasonably expected to be realized in cash, or sold, or consumed during the normal operating cycle of the business. These include cash,

U.S. Government bonds, receivables and money due usually within one year, and inventories. (2)

current assets to current debt Obtained by dividing the total of Current Assets by total Current Debt. Current Assets are the sum of cash, notes and accounts receivable (less reserves for bad debts), advances on merchandise, merchandise inventories, and listed federal, state, and municipal securities not in excess of market value. Current Debt is the total of all liabilities falling due within one year. (61)

current budget (1) The budget prepared for the succeeding fiscal year, or in the case of some state governments, the budget prepared for the succeeding biennium. (2) The budget in force during the current fiscal year or biennium.

NOTE: It is assumed that the budget is prepared and adopted before the beginning of the fiscal year or biennium to which it relates. (29)

current debt to inventory Dividing the Current Debt by Inventory, yields yet another indication of the extent to which the business relies on funds from disposal of unsold inventories to meet its debts. (61)

current debt to tangible net worth Obtained by dividing Current Debt by Tangible Net Worth. Ordinarily, a business begins to pile up trouble when the relationship between Current Debt and Tangible Net Worth exceeds 80 per cent. (61)

current delivery Delivery during the present period such as this month for commodities. (9)

current income Wages, salary, profit or other income of the immediate period of time, this month, this year. (59)

current liabilities Liabilities which are payable within a relatively short period of time, usually no longer than a year. See Floating Debt. (29)

current prices Security prices prevailing in the market at a specified time. (105)

current ratio Ratio of current assets to current liabilities. The analysis of the relationship will give a good indication of the ability of the company to pay its current debts as they mature. From industry to industry and from a phase of the business cycle to another phase the current ratio will vary. There is no one proportion which is absolutely desirable such as $ 2 of current assets to $ 1 of current liabilities though the above is frequently cited as desirable.

current resources Resources to which recourse can be had to meet current obligations and expenditures. Examples are current assets, estimated revenues of a particular period not yet realized, transfers from other funds authorized but not received, and, in case of certain funds, bonds authorized and unissued. (29)

current yield The expression as a percentage of the annual income to the investment, e.g., annual income is five dollars and investment is one hundred dollars then current yield is five per cent. See Return.

curtail schedule A list of the amounts by which the principal of an obligation is to be reduced by partial payments and of the dates when these payments are to become due. (89)

custodian A banking institution that holds in cus-

tody and safekeeping the securities and other assets of an investment company. (65)

custodianship That agency relationship between a bank or trust company in which the bank controls the customer's property subject to instructions from its owner. It is differentiated from the safe depository function in which the bank does not control the customers property but simply provides a place for safe keeping.

custody account A concerning agency account where the main duties of the custodian (agent) are to safekeep and preserve the property and perform ministerial acts with respect to the property as directed by the principal. The agent has no investment or management responsibilities. To be distinguished from a managing agency account and a safekeeping account. (88)

customer's agreement and consent A form required by a member firm of the New York Stock Exchange of any client maintaining a margin account. The client's signature indicates agreement to abide by rules of the exchange, the SEC, and the Federal Reserve Board. (105)

customer's free credit balance The amount of money in a client's brokerage account, other than from a short sale, which is at the dispersal of the client. (105)

customer's man See Registered Representative.

customers' net debit balances Credit of N. Y. Stock member firms made available to help finance customers' purchases of stocks, bonds, and commodities. (2)

customer's room That part of a broker's office which is open for the use of his customers and which generally contains such things as a ticker tape, a quotation board and economic reports from reference investment services.

customhouse That place designated for the payment of import duties in the United States and for the payment of import and export duties in many other nations.

customs broker The licensed individual who for a fee handles the necessary papers and steps in obtaining clearance of goods through customs.

cut An expression used in banks to denote the taking of a total of a pack of checks sorted and going to one destination. The term is most frequently used in banks equipped with proof machines. Since these machines can list a large number of checks on a tape, it has been found more convenient to "cut a tape" by taking totals at intervals of between 100 and 200 items per total. The term also is applied to cancelling checks. (1)

cut-off In order to effect better control over huge volumes of checks passing through the proof department in large banks, these banks have periodic "settlements" or "cut-offs" of work. Each "cut-off" is balanced and items are immediately released from the proof department after each "settlement." This not only affords better control, but permits transit items to be mailed in several deliveries each business day. (1)

cut slip A slip of paper upon which is imprinted or written the total of a particular "cut". The cut slips are retained and used to "settle" a proof machine when the settlement is made. (1)

cutthroat competition Severe but independent endeavoring by two or more firms for the business patronage by the offer of very advantageous terms to the buyer. These terms may actually cause the failure of one or more of the competitors because of low profit margin.

cutting a loss Terminating a security transaction at a loss, before it becomes an even larger disaster. (105)

cutting a melon The declaration of an extra dividend or an increase in a regular rate of dividend by a board of directors.

cycle billing System of billing customer's purchases and other transactions. Statements are mailed to customers by alphabetical groups. (For example, all accounts with names starting with A might be mailed out the first of the month upon proof and posting. Accounts with names starting with B, mailed and proved on the 2nd, C on the 3rd, D on the 4th day, etc.) Each group being assigned a specific mailing date. Usually 16 cycles each month. Saleschecks and other billing media are accumulated during cycle periods in specially designed equipment. When cycle is to be billed all posting media is assembled and listed on customer's statement by amount only. Original saleschecks and other posting media are sent with statement to customer for proof and verification. (26)

cycle mailing The practice adopted by a number of banks of dividing the depositors' accounts into groups termed "Mailing Cycles", and the mailing of the statements at stipulated intervals during the month. Proponents of this practice claim that it decreases the cost and confusion experienced when all statements for all depositors are mailed at the same time (usually at the end of the month). (1)

cycle posting The practice of dividing accounts to be posted into groups termed "cycles" and posting these accounts at stipulated intervals during the month. (1)

cyclical billing See Cycle Billing.

cyclical stocks Stocks which move directly with the general business cycle, i.e., advancing when business improves and declining when business slackens. (Some stocks lead, while others lag behind the business cycle.) (105)

cyclical theory A theory reflected in the stock market which claims that there are identifiable, regular cycles in which the volume of trade rises or falls. The Major Cycle in which business and commodity prices move up or down, alternatingly, spans about 30 years. The Minor Cycle, and best known one, spans about 8-11 years within the trend of the Major Cycle. The Short-Term Cycle of approximately 2 years is a sharper fluctuation within the Minor Cycle. (105)

cy-pres doctrine Cy-pres means "as nearly as may be". The doctrine, applied in English and Scotch law and in some of the states of the United States, that where a testator or settler makes a gift to or for a charitable object that cannot be carried out to the letter, the court will direct that the gift will be made as nearly as possible, in its judgment, in conformity with the intention of the donor. (74)

cy-pres trust A trust, which the trustee cannot exactly execute but may carry out the general intent of the trustor. Thus if a charitable trust was established to provide a certain action at a specific time and place but due to no fault of the trustee this cannot be done because of changed circumstances the trustee under the cy-pres (near to it) doctrine may, with the consent of the appropriate court of jurisdiction, act to accomplish the general intent of the donor if not the exact intent.

D

d. Pence.

D. Days; delivery; or discount.

D/A Documents against acceptance.

D.A. Plan Deposit Administration Plan. (5)

D. & B. Dun and Bradstreet, Inc. (5)

D/Atchd. Draft attached.

D.B.A. Doing business as: (5)

D. D. Deferred Delivery.

D/D Days after date; Demand draft.

D.D.D. Comprehensive dishonesty, disappearance, and destruction policy. (5)

Deb. Debenture.

Def. Deficit; deferred.

Dem. Demand; demurrage.

Denom. Denomination.

Dep. Deposit; depositary.

Dir. Director.

Disc. Discount.

Div. Dividend or divisional.

D. & J. Semi-annual interest payments or dividends in December and June.

D/L Demand Loan.

Dlr. Dealer.

Dls. Dollars.

D. M. J. S. Quarterly interest payments or dividends in December, March, June, and September.

D.N.R. Do not renew (a policy). (5)

D/O Disbursing Office or Officer.

DO District Office. (67)

DOB Date of birth. (67)

Dom. Ex. Domestic Exchange.

DOS Date of shipment. (67)

D/P Documents against payment.

D.P. Due process.

D.R. Daily report. (5)

Dr. Debit; debtor.

D/S Days after sight.

daily reserve calculation A daily calculation to determine the "reserves" necessary to meet the "lawful reserve" requirements. See Lawful Reserve. (1)

daily statement A daily transcript of the balances shown on the accounts in the bank's general ledger. (83)

daily statement of condition See Statement of Condition. (1)

data A general term used to denote any or all facts, numbers, letters, and symbols, or facts that refer to or describe an object, idea, condition, situation, or other factors. It connotes basic elements of information which can be processed or produced by a computer. Sometimes data is considered to be expressible only in numerical form, but information is not so limited. Related to "information". (104)

data, master A set of data which is altered infrequently, and supplies basic data for processing operations. The data content of a Master File. Examples include: names, badge numbers, or pay rates in personnel data; or stock numbers, stock descriptions, or units of measure in stock control data. (104)

date The month, day and year in which the drawer prepared a contract or instrument. The date is important in terms of statutes of limitation, post-dated checks, presentment when due and also in terms of legality of enforcing payment in the event the due date is a holiday or Sunday. Some banks and clearing houses return checks as being "stale dated" if the date on the check's face is over six months old.

date of acceptance The date on which a time draft is honored, or accepted. (73)

date of draft The date on which a draft is drawn. (73)

date of payment of dividends The date on which declared dividends are payable. (73)

date of the note The date of issue. (73)

date of trade The execution date for an order to buy or sell a security. (105)

daybook A journal of accounts. (93)

daylight trading Effecting a purchase and sale of a commodity or a security during the same day so that one does not hold a "position" in the item traded overnight or longer. Scalpers generally engage in "daylight trading" and probably more is done in commodities than in securities.

day loan A clearance loan made to brokers by banks pending the delivery of collateral which would result as the day progressed from the clearings of the Stock Clearing Corporation. When the security clearings are delivered to the broker he in turn pledges them to the bank as collateral for a call loan. Day Loans are also called Morning Credits since they are cleared by the afternoon's stock clearings.

day order An order to buy or sell stock at a specified price which expires on the day the order is given unless executed. An investor may also specify a longer time or good until cancelled. See Limit Order; GTC (Good Until Cancelled). (2)

day points A term used in connection with transit work and the general ledger in a bank. The term is applied to the number of days required to send transit letters to distant points geographically by the best means of transportation. Due to the adequacy of transportation today, banks average their availability for collection of transit items into 1 day, 2 days, and 3 days. When transit letters are sent out, the bank knows the number of days it will take to collect the items. On the day that collection should be accomplished, the totals of all transit letters scheduled for credit

that day are transferred from a deferred account to the available asset account, "Due from Banks" (see definition). (1)

days of grace The reasonable length of time allowed, without suffering a loss or penalty, for postponed payment or for the presentment for payment of certain financial documents. (1)

day to day loans Call loans.

day to day money Call money.

ddd policy A package policy providing blanket fidelity, forgery, and broad form burglary coverage by specific insuring agreements. (50)

dead beat Refers to one who is notorious for non-payment of debts. (105)

dead hand A term used to indicate the continuing hold of a settlor or a testator, who has been dead for many years, upon living individuals or organizations that are confronted with conditions which the settler or the testator could not have forseen. See Statutes of Mortmain. (74)

dead market Description of a market undergoing few significant price changes with little attendent volume. (105)

deal To buy and sell, as to do business. (93)

dealer An individual or firm in the securities business acting as a principal rather than as an agent. Typically, a dealer buys for his own account and sells to a customer from his own inventory. The dealer's profit or loss is the difference between the price he pays and the price he receives for the same security. The dealer's confirmation must disclose to his customer that he has acted as principal. The same individual or firm may function, at different times, either as broker or dealer. For example, the specialist on the floor of the N. Y. Stock Exchange acts as a dealer when he buys or sells stock for his own account to maintain a market. He acts as a broker when he executes the orders commission brokers have left with him. See NASD; Specialist. (2)

dealer financing A dealer of commodities, such as household appliances, may make arrangements with a bank for the bank to finance the purchase of these appliances upon their sale by the dealer. The customers who purchase these items then become borrowers of the bank under "consumer credit" or "time sales" loans. The bank usually has the dealer endorse the notes of his customers as additional security for the loans, and has the dealer maintain reserves on each note with the bank as other security. These reserves are termed "Dealer Hold-Backs" or "Dealer Reserves." (1)

dear money Condition during which high interest rates prevail. Also a period when goods and services are readily available at lower prices.

debasement To reduce the quality, purity, content, or otherwise altering the accepted intrinsic value of the coinage of a realm.

The milling (serrated edges) found in coins is for the purpose of discouraging and detecting the removal of some of their metal content. (1)

debenture Certificates of indebtedness representing long-term borrowings of capital funds, secured only by the general credit of the issuing corporation. (21)

debenture stock Stock issued under a contract to pay a specified return at specified intervals. In this sense, it may be considered a special type of preferred stock. It is to be distinguished from debentures which represent a bond in form as compared with a share of stock. (19)

debit Used in a variety of senses. In the commercial bookkeeping department of the bank, as a verb, "debit" means to lower the balance in a checking account; as a noun, any check or ticket which is so posted. In the technical accounting sense, a debit is any amount in dollars and cents that, when posted, will increase the balance of an asset or expense account, and will decrease the balance of a liability or an income account. (83)

debit balance The amount by which the debit amounts exceed the credit amounts in a ledger account. That amount which is owed a broker and upon which interest is charged.

debit column The left-hand side of an account or journal column. (73)

debit entry An entry that is placed on the left-hand side of an account. (73)

debit footing of an account The columnar total that is written at the foot of the debit money column in the account. (73)

debit memo 1. A posting medium authorizing the debit to a specified account for a certain named amount which bears the complete description of the transaction, the date, and the signature of the party responsible for the authorization of the charge. 2. A detailed memorandum forwarded from one party or firm to another charging for some omitted charge, disallowed or improper payment, or other causes. (1)

debit ticket A bank bookkeeping memorandum or posting medium on which the transaction leading to a debit entry in a ledger account is described in detail. (85)

debit transfer Voucher giving bookkeeper authority to charge on account according to instructions on voucher. Opposite of "Credit Transfer". (26)

debt A contract evidencing an amount owed by one party to another for money, goods, or services. (105)

debtee A creditor.

debt financing The long-term borrowing of money by a business, usually in exchange for debt securities or a note, for the purpose of obtaining working capital or other funds necessary to operational needs or for the purpose of retiring current or other indebtedness. (118)

debt limit The legislative limitation on a city, state or other government to borrow beyond a fixed or determinable amount. This limitation is stated as a fixed dollar amount for the federal government. Many municipalities have their debt limitation set as a percentage of the assessed valuation of taxable property within their borders.

debt monetization The situation whereby the debt of a nation becomes the base for an increase in the money in circulation.

debtor One who owes money to another. (1)

debtor bank A bank which after the round of check distribution in a clearing house has less claims against other banks than the other banks have against it.

debtor nation A country which on a net basis owes more to foreigners than it is owed by them. Such a nation would tend to have an "unfavorable" balance of trade.

debtor's position That portion of the market price of property which is in excess of a prime first mortgage, or mortgagable interest; the equity holder's position. (54)

debt securities Are fixed obligations which evidence a debt, usually repayable on a specified future date or dates and which carry a specific rate or rates of interest payable periodically. They may be non-interest bearing also. (118)

debt service Interest requirements plus stipulated payments of principal on outstanding debt, usually stated as the combined amount due in a one-year period. (103)

debt service requirement The amount of money necessary periodically to pay the interest on the outstanding debt and the principal of maturing bonded debt not payable from a Sinking Fund (q.v.) and to provide a fund for the redemption of bonds payable from a Sinking Fund. (29)

deceased account An account carried on deposit in a bank in the name and title of a deceased person. As soon as the death of a depositor is ascertained, the bank segregates the account, and withholds payment until authorized by a court of law to make such payment to the legal heirs. Tax waivers and authorized claims to the deposited account are known to the bank before payment may be made. (1)

decedent A person who has died. A term used in connection with inheritance, estates, wills, etc. A decedent who had made no will is called an intestate decedent; one who had made a will is called a testator. (85)

declaration date The date on which the directors of a corporation authorize the payment of a dividend; to be distinguished from the date of payment of the dividend. (74)

declaration of dividend That action on the part of the board of directors of a corporation in which the decision is reached to pay the stockholders of the corporation a portion of the earnings or surplus of the firm.

declaration of trust An acknowledgment, usually but not necessarily in writing, by one holding or taking title to property that he holds in trust for the benefit of someone else. (88)

declaratory judgment The judgment or decision of a court interpreting an instrument or declaring what the law on the given matter is under a statutory proceeding that authorizes the court to enter such a judgment in a case that is not being litigated. (74)

declare a dividend The vote or declaration by a corporate board of directors to pay shareholders a dividend out of earned surplus. (105)

decline 1. Downward slump, trend. A lowering of the price for a commodity or a security. 2. To refuse. (93)

declining balance The decreasing amount which is owed on a debt as monthly payments are made. (131)

decreases Subtractions from an amount. Decreases are credits to asset accounts and debits to liability accounts or the proprietorship account. (73)

decreasing costs The situation in which the per unit cost of production declines. This is generally associated with increased production when a business is operating below normal capacity.

decree The decision of a court of equity, admiralty, probate, or divorce; to be distinguished from judgment of a court of law. (74)

deduction Taking away, as from a sum or amount. Discount, rebate, method of reasoning. (93)

deductions, fixed Payroll deductions which are constant in amount though not necessarily deductible every pay period. For example, insurance, union dues, hospitalization, etc. (28)

deductions, variable Payroll deductions computed as a percentage of gross earnings, hence may vary in amount from pay period to pay period. For example, F.I.C., withholding tax, annuities, etc. (28)

deed An instrument in writing under seal, duly executed and delivered, containing a transfer, a bargain, or contract, usually in conveying the title to a real property from one party to another. There are two general types of deeds—the quit-claim and the warranty. Under a quit-claim deed, the seller conveys property to the purchaser, the title being only as good as the title held by the seller, who releases all claim, interest, or right to the property as far as his own title is concerned. Under a warranty deed, the seller also releases all claim, right, and title to the property, but also warrants the title to be perfect, and guarantees the purchaser of these facts. The warranty is recognized by law as the subject for future restitution of loss to the purchaser if any defects in the title are conveyed by the seller. (1)

deed, administrator's A deed by a person lawfully appointed to manage and settle the estate of a deceased person who has left no executor. (66)

deed, bond for An executory contract for the sale of land, with title remaining with the grantor until the purchase price is paid; ordinarily binding on both parties. (66)

deed, committee A deed by a committee or commission appointed by a court of competent jurisdiction to sell a property. (66)

deed, executor's A deed by a person named by the decedent in his will to manage and settle his estate. (66)

deed in lieu (of foreclosure) The instrument conveying real estate to the mortgagee after a default by the mortgagor without going through the process of foreclosure. (5)

deed, mortgaged A deed by way of mortgage which has the effect of a mortgage on the property conveyed and imposes a lien on the granted estate. (66)

deed of assignment The document which is used to appoint an assignee such as an individual or a fiduciary institution to take over an insolvent firm. The assignment states the powers and functions of the appointed firm or individual.

deed, quit-claim A conveyance to the grantee of only the interest held by the grantor at the time of the conveyance, with no warranty as to encumbrances or condition of title. (66)

deed restrictions Provisions inserted in a deed limiting the use of the property conveyed by the deed. (89)

deed, trustee A deed by a party who holds property in trust. (66)

deed, warranty A deed conveying to the grantee title to the property free and clear of all encumbrances, except those specifically set forth in the document. (66)

defaced coins Coins that have been mutilated in some manner. See also Debasement. (1)

defalcation The misappropriation of money or property by one to whom it has been entrusted, usually, by reason of his employment. (29)

default The failure to do that which is required by law, or to perform on an obligation previously committed. The term is commonly used when some legally constituted governing body fails to pay the principal or interest on its bonds, or to meet other financial obligations on maturity. (29)

defaulted paper Any obligation whose principal or interest is in default. Such obligation, security, or investment, should be distinguished on all financial statements where they normally appear by showing those in default separately from those not in default. (29)

defeasance A clause that provides that performance of certain specified acts will render an instrument of contract void. (54 +)

defeasible Capable of being annulled or rendered void; as a defeasible title to property. (74)

defensive issue A security which will not decline in price as much as the averages during a recession.

defensive portfolio An aggregate of investments which are unlikely to fluctuate much in value either up or down; for example, high-grade bonds and preferred stocks. (105)

defensive stocks Also called Protective Stocks because they are usually slow moving in price movements, and thus not very attractive to speculators; but held by long-term investors who stress stability over growth, and usually withstand selling pressure in a declining market. (105)

deferred availability cash items Checks received for collection for which credit has not yet been given. The Reserve Banks credit the banks sending in the checks according to a time schedule based on the normal time required to collect payment on the checks. (4)

deferred charges Expenditures which are not chargeable to the fiscal period in which made but are carried on the asset side of the balance sheet pending amortization or other disposition; for example, discount on bonds issued.
NOTE: Deferred charges differ from prepaid expenses in that they usually extend over a long period of time (more than five years) and are not regularly recurring costs of operation. See also Prepaid Expenses. (29)

deferred consignment expenses Expenses recorded by a consignor that apply to consigned goods that will be sold in a future fiscal period. (73)

deferred credit A credit that has been "delayed" in posting for a reason. A deferred credit may be a depost which came into the bank after business hours, and is therefore entered on the books in the following day's business. Large banks with scattered branch operations may defer the posting of deposits until the following day because of delivery to the bookkeeping department. Deferred credits may also refer to income which has been received but not earned (from an accrual system standpoint). Examples: Funds left with a bank, the account to be credited on a specified future date. Unearned discount, where the discount is taken when the loan is made, and the earnings fully accrued when the loan is due and payable. (1)

deferred debits Accounts carried on the asset side of the balance sheet in which are recorded items being amortized as charges against income over a period of years (such as debt discount and expense) and items held in suspense pending final transfer or disposition (such as extraordinary property losses, clearing accounts (net), retirement or other work in progress, etc.). (21)

deferred dividend A dividend on preferred or common stock which is not to be paid until some action has taken place.

deferred gross profit on installment sales The gross profit on installment sales that will not be realized until a future fiscal period. (73)

deferred income The income account which is used to record income which has been paid in advance but not as yet earned. The pre-payment of rent or insurance are illustrations of items that become deferred income for the recipient.

deferred liabilities Liabilities, the settlement of which is deferred. (19)

deferred maintenance The expenditure necessary to restore a Fixed Asset to "like new" condition. This differs from ordinary maintenance or repairs which, in most cases, merely restore the asset to working order. For example, completely rebuilding a lathe by replacing all bearings (whether worn or not), regrinding the lead screw threads, repainting the castings, replating the fittings, etc. (28)

deferred payment Payment in a series of divided payments in the future, on a contract entered into in the present. (59)

deferred posting A term used to describe the posting of items in the bookkeeping department on a delayed basis. All items received during one day's business are intersorted and posted on the next business day, as of the date received. (83)

deferred serial bonds Serial bonds in which the first installment does not fall due for two or more years from the date of issue. (29)

deferred special assessments Special assessments which have been levied but not yet due. (29)

deferred stock Rare in the United States. Found in England. A security below regular common stock in priority of dividend. The dividend is not payable until a period of time or some event, such as earnings of a certain size, has come about.

deficiency judgment A court order authorizing collection from a debtor of any part of a debt that remains unsatisfied after foreclosure and sale of collateral. (89)

deficit 1. The excess of liabilities over assets (negative net worth); 2. a term used indicating obligations or expenditures for items which are in excess of the amount alloted for those items in a financial budget; 3. the excess of obligations and expenditures as a whole affecting a given budget period which is in excess of the budget established for the period. (1)

deficit financing The process or methods used to meet a deficit. The term has most frequently been used during recent years in connection with the government's procedure in meeting its operating deficits through the sale of large quantities of bonds. (90)

definitive A permanent certificate, generally engraved, which replaces a temporary stock or bond certificate which is generally printed in a way that will not meet the standards of the security exchange upon which the security may be traded.

definitive certificate See Definitive.

deflation An economic condition generally characterized by declining prices and depressed business. See Inflation.

deflationary gap The difference between the government and private spending at a given time and the amount of government and private spending needed to produce full employment. Under Keynesian economists' proposals, the government spending would be increased sufficiently to stimulate the private sector so that the two combined would eliminate the deflationary gap.

deflator A divisor or statistical device which attempts to remove the influence of some increase such as the changing value of money. To get "real" or "constant" values, changing prices must be tied to a base period and that part of change in price which is caused by inflation or similar distortion, should be removed by the use of a deflator.

defunct A business which has terminated for adverse reasons.

delayed items Items representing transactions which occurred before the current accounting year. (19)

delayed opening A situation caused by an accumulation of buy or sell orders before the opening of a stock exchange. Efforts are made to find counter-balancing offers, usually with institutions, firms, or individuals who have a large interest in the security, to prevent the opening price from varying sharply from the previous day's close. The specialist in the stock will often sell some of his inventory in the security, or "short" it, to help arrange a reasonable opening price. (105)

delcredere agent Agent who indemnifies his principal in the event of loss to the principal because of the extention of credit to a third party by the agent. (5)

delinquency Failure to pay an obligation when due; sometimes this term is extended to cover the amount of the delinquency. (31, 92)

delinquent Term commonly used in the trade, (but not recommended). "Past Due Credit Customer" or "Debtor" preferred. Designates credit customer in arrears on payments. (26)

delinquent special assessments Special assessments remaining unpaid on and after the date on which a penalty for non-payment is attached. (29)

delist The infrequent suspension or cancellation of privileges accorded a listed security. This may occur if an issue fails to maintain its listing requirements, such as the appropriate number of stockholders or number of shares outstanding. (105)

delivery The certificate representing shares bought "regular way" on the New York Stock Exchange normally is delivered to the purchaser's broker on the fourth business day after the transaction. If a seller wants to delay delivery of the certificates, he may have his broker offer the stock "seller's option", instead of "regular way", and he may specify the number of days, from 5 up to 60, for delivery. A stock offered "seller's option" may command a lesser price than if offered "regular way". See Bid; Cash Sale; Offer; Transfer. (2)

delivery month A futures contract must stipulate one of the calendar months as the month of delivery. (9)

delivery notice The notification of delivery of the actual commodity on the contract, issued by the seller of the futures to the buyer. The rules of the various exchanges require that tender notices be issued on certain days, and in some cases, at certain hours. In the vast majority of contract markets, tender notices are transferable. This means that the "long" receiving the notice may, without additional expense (if notice received during market session), sell his contract and pass such delivery notice on to the new buyer. In some markets, however, the long receiving a delivery notice must pay the storage charges on the actual commodity for one or more days, and an additional commission even if the contract is sold immediately after receipt of the delivery notice. (9)

delivery points Those locations designated by futures exchanges at which the commodity covered by a futures contract may be delivered in fulfillment of the contract. (9)

delivery price The price fixed by the Clearing House at which deliveries on futures are invoiced and also the price at which the futures contract is settled when deliveries are made. (9)

demand The amount of a good or service that will be purchased at various prices at a given time in a market. In another sense, it may be the amount of a good or services that will be purchased at the current price in a market. The first concept is one of a schedule of demand while the latter is one of a point of demand.

demand bill A sight bill of exchange.

demand, billing Billing demand is the demand upon which billing to a customer is based, as specified in a rate schedule or contract. The billing demand need not coincide with the actual measured demand of the billing period. (21)

demand, charge Demand charge is the specified charge to be billed on the basis of the billing demand, under an applicable rate schedule or contract. (21)

demand deposit These deposits are payable on demand at any time the depositor elects. The Federal Reserve Board and the various state laws define these deposits as being payable within 30 days after deposit. They are drawn against by check, and no notice of withdrawal is necessary. The great portion of demand deposits are known as commercial deposits, and are deposited in commercial banks (see definition). Because these deposits are payable on demand, member banks of the Federal Reserve system are required to maintain much higher reserve balances on them than on other types of deposits. (1)

demand deposit (adjusted) The total of customers' deposits in reporting member banks subject to immediate withdrawal (checking accounts), excluding interbank deposits and deposits of U.S. Government, less checks in the process of collection. (4)

demand draft A draft which is payable immediately upon sight or presentation to the drawee. Also termed Sight Draft or Presentation Draft. See Draft. (83)

demand loan A loan with no fixed maturity date, payable upon demand of the bank. Borrower is billed at specified intervals for the interest due the bank. (83)

demand mortgage A mortgage that may be called for payment on demand. (89)

demand note A promissory note payable on demand of the holder of the note as payee or transferee. (74)

de minimis doctrine The doctrine that "the law cares nothing for trifling matters". It has been involved in suits contesting "portal pay" under the Wage-Hour Law and the application of a federal statute to predominantly local activities. (12)

demise To convey an estate to another for life, for years or at will; surrendering the right of occupancy to a tenant; the quitting of the premium. (5)

demonetization To divert from the character of standard money.

demonstrative gift A gift, by will, or a specified sum of money to be paid from a designated fund or asset; as a gift of $1,000 from a specified bank account. (74)

demonstrative legacy A gift of a specific amount or thing which is payable out of a designated asset which, in the event that the asset is inadequate, the general assets of the estate may be used to pay the legacy.

demurrage A charge made on cars or other equipment held by or for consignor or consignee for loading or unloading, for forwarding directions or for any other purpose. (19)

demurrer A pleading which admits the facts but denies that they have legal effect. (35)

denomination 1. Securities, money, stamps, etc. are issued with different face values. The face value is expressed in a denomination. 2. The face amount of a bond in units of the currency in which it is issued, as a $1,000 bond. (74)

depreciation charge An estimate of the reduction in the value of fixed assets brought about through use, gradual obsolescence, or the effects of the elements (decay or corrosion).

To reflect national output more accurately, estimates for depreciation of fixed assets owned by corporate, non-corporate, nonprofit institutions, and homeowners are made. These charges are then subtracted from GNP as capital consumption allowances to yield Net National Product. The valuation of these depreciation charges reflects the type of accounting practices pursued under Internal Revenue Service regulations. (124)

deposit 1. Money placed with a banking or other institution or with a person either as a general deposit subject to check or as a special deposit made for some specified purpose; 2. securities lodged with a bank or other institution or with a person for some particular purpose; 3. sums deposited by customers for electric meters, water meters, etc., and by contractors and others to accompany and guarantee their bids. (29)

depositary One who receives a deposit of money, securities, instruments, or other property; to be distinguished from depository, which is the place of deposit. (74)

deposit book A passbook in which a client of a bank has entered the amounts of deposits made.

deposit correction slip A form used to notify a depositor of an error made by the depositor. When the error is located, the bank makes out a deposit correction slip showing what the error was, and the corrected new balance of the deposit. The depositor can then correct his records accordingly. (1)

deposit currency The effect of a typical loan from a bank. The bank credits the borrower's account with the amount of the loan. This, in turn, may be withdrawn by check or cash.

deposit function The business of receiving money on deposit for safekeeping and convenience. This function includes the receiving of demand deposits subject to check and the receiving of savings (time) deposits at interest. (83)

deposit funds Those funds which are established to account for collections that are either (a) held in suspense temporarily and later refunded or paid into some other fund of the government, or (b) held by the government as banker or agent for others. Such funds are not available for paying salaries, expenses, grants, or other expenditures of the government and, therefore, are excluded from total budget receipts or expenditures. (7)

deposit insurance See Federal Deposit Insurance Corporation. (1)

deposit interest rate Commercial banks are limited under Regulation Q if they are member banks of the Federal Reserve System and by Federal Deposit Insurance Corporation rulings if under FDIC insurance coverage, in the amount of interest rate they may declare on time deposits and are prohibited from paying any interest rates on demand deposits.

deposition The written testimony of a witness, under oath, before a qualified officer, to be used in place of the oral testimony of the witness at a trial or other hearing, such as the deposition of a non-resident subscribing witness to a will. (74)

deposit line That approximate average amount which a depositor tends to keep in his bank account. With a knowledge of the deposit line, a lending officer can judge not only the probable profitability of an account but also can be related to a loan application.

deposit loan Most loans are made by the banker crediting the borrower's account with a "loan deposit" in the amount of the loan as distinguished from presenting the borrower with currency when granting a loan.

depositor An individual person, a partnership, a business proprietorship, corporation, organization, or association is termed as a depositor when funds have been placed in a bank in the name of that legal entity. (1)

depositor's forgery bond Type of business insurance protection against loss due to forgery. (5)

depositor's life insurance A form of life insurance granted a depositor, without cost, by certain financial institutions, which pays the depositor's beneficiary or estate the amount on deposit — but not in excess of a certain stipulated sum — at the time of death of the depositor. Such benefits are often limited to those depositors whose accounts were opened prior to their attaining a stipulated age. (1)

depository A bank in which funds or securities are deposited by others, usually under the terms of a specific depository agreement. Also, a bank in which government funds are deposited or in which other banks are permitted by law to maintain required reserves. (85)

depository receipt 1. An abbreviation for American Depository Receipt. See that term. 2. At times also applied to Certificates of Deposit. See that term.

deposit receipt In banks where tellers' machines are now used, the machine issues a printed receipt for the deposit made. This receipt does away with the pen-and-ink entry made in the pass book used by checking account depositors. The bank furnishes a folder in which the depositor keeps his deposit receipts until he has received his bank statement. After verifying his statement for accuracy of entry of all deposits, he can destroy the receipts, since he has been properly credited by the bank as evidenced on his statement. (1)

deposits in federal reserve banks Deposit accounts held as follows: a) Member banks-deposits of member banks which are largely legal required reserves. b) U.S. Treasurer-general or checking accounts of the Treasury. c) Foreign-balances of foreign governments and central banks. d) Other-other deposits, includes those of non-member banks maintained for check-clearing purposes. (4)

deposit slip An itemized memorandum of the cash and other funds which a customer (depositor) presents to the receiving teller for credit to his account. (83)

deposit ticket A business form on which the depositor lists all the items that he wishes to deposit in the bank. (73)

depreciable cost The value of a fixed asset that is subject to depreciation. Sometimes this is, the original cost, and sometimes it is the original cost less an estimated salvage value. (Refer to Depreciation for an example.) (28)

depreciable plant Utility Plant. Usually tangible plant in service which is subject to depreciation (wearing out, inadequacy, obsolescence, and other causes). (21)

depreciated currency See Depreciated Money.

depreciated money 1. Money or currency which will not buy the same amount of goods and services that it did at some past period of time. 2. Money or currency which is at a discount from the standard money.

depreciation The gradual conversion of the depreciable cost of a fixed asset into expense spread over its remaining life. There are numerous depreciation methods in use for accomplishing this purpose. All are based on a periodical charge to an expense account and a corresponding credit to a depreciation reserve account for the amount of the current depreciation. For example, a certain machine tool has an original cost of $1,500. The estimated salvage value is $300 at the end of its estimated remaining life of 8 years. Its depreciable cost as recorded in the plant property ledger would be $1,200 ($1500–$300). If a linear rate depreciation method (see Depreciation Methods, Linear Rate) is in use, the annual depreciation would be $150 ($1200 ÷ 8) and the monthly depreciation would be $12.50 (one-twelfth of the annual depreciation). The unrecovered cost at any particular time is the difference between the depreciable cost and the depreciation reserve. In this case, after the machine tool had been in use for 3 years there would have been accumulated a depreciation reserve of $450 ($150 × 3) and its unrecovered cost would be $750 ($1200 – $450). At the same time its remaining life would be 5 years (8–3). (28)

depreciation, accelerated An approved method of computing accelerated depreciation deductions, for federal income tax purposes, as allowed under the 1954 Revenue Code. These methods permit relatively larger depreciation accruals during the earlier years of the life of the property and relatively smaller accruals during the later years, in contrast with the straight line method under which the annual accruals are the same for each year. (21)

depreciation, accrued 1. Loss from reproduction cost new as of date of appraisal. 2. The difference between cost new and market value as of date of appraisal. (66)

depreciation, allowable Amount permitted to be deducted annually as an expense resulting in a decrease in adjusted basis. (120)

depreciation book Accrued depreciation shown on books of account. (66)

depreciation charges Charges made by private business and non-profit institutions against receipts to account for the decrease in value of capital assets as a result of wear, accidental damage, and obsolescence, plus an estimate of corresponding depreciation in owner-occupied dwellings. Accepted accounting and tax practice permits certain methods of deducing estimated depreciation to account for the gradual exhaustion of durable capital assets. (7)

depreciation, cost depletion and retirements Encompass a variety of cost items which have in common the fact that they represent charges against current income for money spent in the past for capital or property items.

depreciation, curable That loss from cost new which can be recovered or offset through correction, repair, or replacement of the defective item causing the loss, providing the resultant value increase approximates the cost of the work; e.g., painting, redecoration, replacement of ceilings, oil burners, gutters and leaders, or modernization. (66)

depreciation, declining balance method One of the accelerative methods of computing depreciation deductions, usually for federal income tax purposes, applicable to plant additions with a useful life of three years or more, constructed after December 31, 1953; also applicable to property acquired after December 31, 1953 if original use began after that same date. Under this method, the depreciation rate is stated as a fixed percentage per year and the annual charge is derived by applying the rate to the net plant balance which is determined by subtracting accumulated depreciation on deductions of previous periods from the cost of the property. Since the annual depreciation deduction becomes smaller as the accumulated depreciation deductions increase, it is permissible to shift to the straight line method at any time in order to make full provision for the estimated depreciation. (21)

depreciation, future 1. That loss from present value which will occur in the future. 2. Sometimes used to indicate the future annual charge necessary to recapture the present building value over its economic life or the annual amount necessary to amortize total investment. (66)

depreciation, incurable That loss from cost new which is impossible to offset or which would involve an expenditure substantially in excess of the value increment resulting therefrom; e.g., loss due to detrimental neighborhood influences, loss due to over- and under-sized rooms, excessive ceiling heights, poor design and/or layout, and loss caused by gradual deterioration of the "bone structure", i.e. skeleton or structural members of a building which are rarely replaced unless they happen to be exposed such as uncovered floor joists. (66)

depreciation methods, annuity A plan for depreciating fixed assets based on the theory that an investment of capital in a current asset of like value, would earn interest. This estimated interest amount is added to the depreciable cost of the fixed asset and the whole depreciated in equal amounts. This plan is seldom encountered because it overstates both the fixed asset and burden charges accounts. (28)

depreciation methods, composite rate A plan for depreciating fixed assets, in total only. Its aim is to secure a single rate for several groups of assets having varying remaining life expectancies. One method is to add the depreciable cost of all assets and divide this figure by the sum of the annual depreciation charges for each life expectancy group. While simple in operation, this plan is inadequate in that no detailed information is available. (28)

depreciation methods, compound interest A plan for depreciating fixed assets based on the theory of adding compound interest amounts to each year's annual depreciation charge. This results in an increasing charge each year until the asset is fully depreciated. This plan is seldom encountered because of the vast amount of clerical effort involved. (28)

depreciation methods, linear rate A plan for depreciating fixed assets based on equal depreciation charges for each year of the expected life of the asset. The annual charge is arrived at by dividing the depreciable cost by the remaining life. (Occasionally an estimated salvage value is deducted from the depreciable cost before making this division.) This is by far the most common and practical method encountered. (28)

depreciation methods, machine hour rate A plan for depreciating fixed assets based on the estimated number of useful hours of production available from the machine. The hourly rate is determined by dividing the depreciable cost by the estimated number of life hours. This plan is useful where the high depreciation on valuable equipment represents one of the major elements of burden applied.

depreciation methods, service output A plan for depreciating fixed assets based on the estimated number of units of production expected from the machine during its remaining life. The charge is arrived at by dividing the depreciable cost of the fixed asset by the total expected number of units of production. The depreciation in any period is the number of units produced, times this unit rate. This plan is more widely used in the case of natural resources than in industry because of the difficulty of estimating the total number of units of production. (28)

depreciation methods, straight line See Depreciation Methods, Linear. (28)

depreciation methods, unit rate A plan for depreciating fixed assets based on the individual depreciable cost and remaining life of each unit as reflected in the plant property ledger. This is one of the most practical methods of accounting for depreciation as it permits greater freedom in the determination of rates and insures against over-depreciating a fixed asset. In addition, it provides complete information at all times on each unit. (28)

depreciation reserve An account which is credited with the periodic depreciation amounts at the time they are charged to expense. For balance sheet purposes this depreciation reserve is deducted from the depreciable cost of the associated group of fixed assets in order to determine their unrecovered cost. (Refer to Depreciation for an example.)

depreciation, sum of the year's digits (syd) method One of the accelerated methods of computing depreciation deductions, usually for federal income tax purposes, applicable to plant additions, with a useful life of three years or more, constructed after December 31, 1953. Also applicable to property acquired after December 31, 1953 if original use began after that same date. Under this method the annual deduction is derived by multiplying the cost of the property less estimated net salvage, by the estimated number of years of service life. For a property with an assumed twenty-five year life the sum of the digits would be $25 + 24 + 23 + 22 + \ldots + 3 + 2$

$+ 1$ or 325. The first year's full depreciation deduction would be 25/325ths; the second year's would be 24/325ths, etc., of the cost of the property. (21)

depression A sustained period of falling prices, characterized by excess of supply over demand, accumulating inventories, falling employment and rising welfare costs, deflation, abnormal commercial and industrial plant contraction, uneven drop in personal incomes, and fear and caution on the part of the public. (65)

derelict Personal property which has been abandoned by the owner. (35)

derivation deposit The typical result of a commercial loan is the action of the bank in crediting the account of the borrower with the amount of the loan. This deposit is derived from the loan.

derived demand That need for a good or service which has come about as a result of the demand for another good or service. Because of the demand for automobiles, there is derived demand for such things as gasoline and automobile insurance.

descendant One who is descended in a direct line from another, however remotely (child, grandchild, great-grandchild). (74)

descent The passing of real property by inheritance. See also Devolution. (74)

description Items are sometimes described on the deposit ticket, by the teller or another clerk, as to the city or bank of payment. This provides a source reference record and assists in the calculation of uncollected funds. (83)

description, deed A recitation of the legal boundaries of a parcel of land as contained in a deed of conveyance. (66)

description, metes and bounds A representation of the boundaries of a parcel of land by reference to courses and distances expressed in engineering terms, such as; "Beginning at a point in the easterly line of Stag Rock Road 67.24 ft. southeasterly of a Connecticut Highway Department merestone, thence north 58°18'10" east a distance of 200.0 feet to a point; thence in a straight line north 37°53'10" west 67.24 feet to a point; thence north 29°24'0" west 196.39' thence south 59°15'50" west 199.90 ft. to a point in the easterly line of Stag Rock Road 74.0 feet southerly from an iron pin marking the southwest corner of land now or formerly of Wilbur C. Jones and Robert W. Jones; thence south 60°36'00" east 199.75 ft. along the easterly line of Stag Rock Road to a Connecticut Highway Department merestone; thence south 51°6'50" east 67.24 ft. to a point or place of beginning." (66)

description, recorded map A description of the location and boundaries of a parcel of land by reference to a map filed in the office of the official recorder of such documents. While the technical reporting will vary according to jurisdictional requirements, one method might be illustrated as follows: ". . . a piece or parcel of land, with the buildings thereon, being known as lot 10, block 5A, section 3, map of 'Bluefields, Property of the Smith Brothers, John Doe, C. E., June 1917, Scale 1 inch=50 feet' filed in Map Book 7, Page 64, in the Town Clerk's Office, Town of Southfield, County of Duchess, State of Vermont." (66)

description, U.S. public land A description of a tract of land by reference to its position in the Public Land Survey of the General Land Office. (66)

de son tort "Of his own wrongdoing." An expression found in such phrases as executor de son tort and guardian de son tort. (88)

deutshe mark Monetary unit of Germany.

devaluation The reduction in the value of the precious or semiprecious metal content of a monetary unit or the reduction in the exchange value of a nation's currency as a result of action by some agency such as a central bank, an exchange stabilization fund or the International Monetary Fund. See also Revaluation. (130)

devise A gift of real property by will; to be distinguished from bequest. (74)

devisee A person to whom a devise is given. (74)

devisor One who bequeaths real estate in his or her will.

devolution The passing of property by inheritance; a general term that includes both descent of real property and distribution of personal property. (74)

diary A record device either in ledger or book form in which information is entered regarding the time items or instruments are received or mature or should be processed in some way.

difference account An account carried in the general ledger where all differences from the true balances, such as averages and shortages, of the firm are recorded.

differential Refers to the odd-lot differential, or compensation, received by an odd-lot broker for his services. A differential is added to the price of buy orders and subtracted from the price of sell orders. Such as the differential amounts to one-eighth point per share for stocks selling below 55, and one-quarter point per share for stocks selling at 55 and above. (105)

differentials The premiums paid for the grades higher than the Standard Growths (basic grades) and the discounts allowed for the grades lower than the basic grades. These differentials are fixed by the contract terms. (123)

digested securities Stocks and bonds that have been sold to investors who are not expected to sell the securities in the near future.

dilution The reduction in the value of an asset such as a stock. See Watered Stock.

dinar Monetary unit of Iraq and Yugoslavia.

direct cost An expense that is free from any intervening conditions. An immediate cost as compared with an indirect cost.

direct debt The debt which a governmental unit has incurred in its own name or assumed through the annexation of territory. (29)

direct, department Those departments or Cost Centers which normally perform work specifically identified with orders or processes resulting in the finished product. For example, the foundry, screw machine and assembly departments, etc. (28)

direct earnings In cases where a firm has subsidiary companies, the direct earnings of the parent company are the amounts earned by it

without the upstream dividends of the subsidiaries.

direct financing The obtaining of equity or debt capital without the use of a middleman or underwriter.

direct heir A person in the direct line of ascent or descent of the decedent; as, father, mother, son, daughter. See also Collateral Heir; Heir. (74)

direct inquiry Generally speaking, an inquiry about a person's credit standing made by one firm to another. As distinct from an inquiry to a credit bureau. (26)

direct investments The flow of U.S. capital into foreign business enterprise in which U.S. residents have significant control. Hence the capital movements are deemed to be foreign extensions of the management interests of the parent corporation. The distinction between long-term investments in equity securities and direct investment is made on the basis of ownership. Investment is considered direct when the U.S. individual or company owns more than ten percent of the foreign concern.

The flows included in the balance-of-payments report are: a) Short-and-long-term funds invested by the U.S. parent corporation. b) Transfers by the U.S. parent corporation to the foreign affiliate (or to foreign residents as compensation for the acquisition of equity interests) of funds that had been borrowed abroad by the U.S. parent or its U.S. affiliates.

The flows not included in the balance-of-payments report (although they may affect the net worth of the investments) are: a) Depreciation allowances and reinvested earnings of foreign subsidiaries. b) Changes in foreign assets that result from political actions or natural causes abroad.

These latter transactions involve no transfer of funds between the U.S. parent and its foreign affiliate.

Portfolio capital flows are recorded in the balance of payments. The flow in the opposite direction appears in Direct investments. (124)

direct leasing A lease transaction in which the funds required to purchase the equipment are provided by the lessor.

direct obligation An obligation of the drawer or maker of the instrument as distinguished from the indirect obligation of an endorser of the instrument.

directorate Refers to a corporation's Board of Directors. (105)

directors Persons elected by shareholders at the annual meeting to direct company policies. The directors appoint the president, vice presidents and all other operating officers. Directors decide, among other matters, if and when dividends shall be paid. (2)

direct reduction loan A loan repayable in consecutive equal monthly payments of interest and principal sufficient to retire the debt within a definite period. "Direct" actually means that after the monthly interest payment has been taken out of the payment, the balance of the loan payment is applied directly to the reduction of the principal of the loan. (31, 192)

direct reduction mortgage (d.r.m.) A direct reduction mortgage is liquidated over the life of the mortgage in equal monthly payments. Each monthly payment consists of an amount to cover interest, reduction in principal, taxes and insurance. The interest is computed on an outstanding principal balance monthly. As the principal balance is reduced the amount of interest becomes less thereby providing a larger portion of the monthly payment to be applied to the reduction of principal. As taxes and insurance are paid by the mortgagee (lending association), these disbursements are added to the principal balance. This procedure follows throughout the life of the mortgage. (1)

direct sendings Items that are drawn on a particular bank, and sent directly to that drawee bank by another bank, are known as direct sendings. This is to be distinguished from a transit letter which may be sent to a "correspondent bank" and containing items on many drawee banks within a certain area. (1)

direct verification A method of bank audit whereby the auditor of a bank sends a request for the verification of the balances of deposits or loans as of a stated date to the depositors or borrowers. Verifications are returned directly to the auditor confirming the correctness of balances or listing discrepancies. (1)

dirham Monetary unit of Morocco.

disagio European term for a discount such as results from the reluctance of nationals of a nation in accepting paper money when the standard money is desired. It may be related to Gresham's Law in that preference is given to full bodied coins as compared to ones which are worn or abrased.

disburse To pay out money; to expend. (93)

disbursement Money paid out in discharge of a debt or an expense; to be distinguished from distribution. (88)

disbursement schedule A list or tabular statement of the amounts to be disbursed on specific dates in accordance with agreements entered into in a mortgage loan transaction. (89)

disbursement voucher A standard order for making payments. (73)

discharge of bankruptcy An order which terminates bankruptcy proceedings, usually relieving the debtor of all legal responsibility for certain specified obligations. (35)

disclaimer A document, or a clause within a document, which renounces or repudiates the liability of an otherwise responsible party, in the event of a noncompliance on the part of another party to other certain conditions within the instrument, or in the event of named external conditions, or losses incurred due to the delivery of goods being in disagreement with the weight or count made by the shipper. (1)

discontinuous market A market which exists for unlisted securities as distinguished from the supposedly continuous market for listed securities, such as those on the New York Stock Exchange. (105)

discount 1. The amount of money deducted from the face value of a note. The borrower receives the net amount after the discount has been deducted. The discount is computed at the rate of interest agreed upon. Technically this is called "banker's discount" for it includes "interest on interest." True discount offers the borrower a very small advantage over "banker's discount." The term may also be used as a noun, the banker referring to his portfolio of "discounts", meaning his discounted notes. The term discount also refers to discounts on securities. Securities are bought and sold either at a discount (at less than par value); they are purchased at par (at face value); or they are purchased at a premium (the buyer pays a price higher than the face or par value in order to acquire them). In foreign exchange, the term "discount" is used to describe the relationship of one currency to another. As an example: Canadian currency may be at a discount to United States currency. 2. Common Stock—The percentage below asset value at which the stock sells. 3. Preferred Stock—The percentage below asset coverage or the amount to which stock is entitled in liquidation (whichever is less), at which the stock sells. (1, 3)

discount, cash A deduction from the total of an account due, allowed in return for payment within a specified period. One typical cash discount is expressed as 2/10 net 30, meaning that a 2 percent reduction from the total amount due in 30 days is permitted if payment is made within 10 days. Another is expressed as 2/10 E.O.M. (End of Month), which allows a 2-percent reduction in the total amount due if payment is made within 10 days, but provides for the credit period to begin at the end of the month in which the goods are purchased, thus permitting buyers who make many purchases during the month to pay their bills once a month and still take advantage of the regular cash discount. (24)

discounted value Present value of future payments due or receivable, computed on the basis of a given rate of interest. (42)

discount from asset value The percentage expression of the price of a stock divided by its asset value. (105)

discount, functional (or discount, trade) A deduction from the list or suggested retail price of a product provided to a certain class of customers—retail, wholesale, etc.—to cover the cost of performing certain marketing functions. (24)

discount house A retail establishment whose key policy is to sell nationally advertised consumer goods consistently at substantial discounts from customary or list prices; also handles private and other brands. Generally gives limited service and enjoys a high turnover at a low dollar markup per unit of sale. (24)

discounting a note receivable Selling a note receivable to a bank or to someone else. (73)

discounting the news The adjustment in stock prices which takes place in anticipation of prospects and developments. Thus when the development occurs as expected, the prices are not affected as they might have been. (105)

discount on purchases A cash discount taken by the buyer. (73)

discount on sales A cash discount granted by the seller. (73)

discount on securities The amount or percentage by which a security (a bond or a share of stock) is bought or sold for less than its face or par value; opposed to premium on securities. (74)

discount rate 1. The interest rate paid by member banks for loans from Federal Reserve Banks. This is often used as a signal for tighter or easier money. 2. That interest rate which a lender charges when it discounts an obligation such as a note or bill of exchange. The Discount Rate will vary by type of borrower, security, maturity, the supply and demand for funds in the market and the policy of the lender. (105)

discounts and advances Outstanding loans of the Reserve Banks, primarily to member banks. (4)

discovery proceedings Legal proceedings by which an executor or administrator procures possession or control of estate assets wrongfully concealed or withheld from him. (74)

discretionary account An account in which the customer gives the broker or someone else discretion, which may be complete or within specific limits, as to the purchase and sale of securities or commodities including selection, timing and price to be paid or received. (2)

discretionary order The customer specifies the stock or the commodity to be bought or sold, and the amount. His agent is free to act as to time and price. (2)

discretionary pool A combination of individuals given authority by others to act on their behalf in the buying or selling of securities or commodities. (105)

discretionary trust 1. A trust which entitles the beneficiary to only so much of the income or principal as the trustee in its uncontrolled discretion shall see fit to give him or to apply for his use. 2. An investment company which is not limited in its policy to any one class, or type, of stock or security but may invest in any or all of a broad range of securities. (74)

dishoarding The consumption from a stockpile which had been increased previously above its normal level.

dishonor If the maker of a note refuses to pay the note upon its legal presentation to him, he is said to have "dishonored" the note to the holder. If a drawee refuses to accept or to pay for a check, draft, or bill of exchange, the drawee is also said to "dishonor the instrument." The holder must then notify the guarantors of such instruments, if any, to be reimbursed. Proof of presentation is obtained through "Protest". (1)

disinflation The attempt to reduce the price level to a normal and not deflated level.

disintermediation The loss of deposits by commercial and mutual savings banks and of share accounts by savings and loan associations and credit unions to higher or safer yielding market instruments.

disinvestment Negative Investment. The disposal of a piece of capital or the failure to maintain a capital good that is being worn out or used up.

dispositive provisions The provisions of a will or trust agreement relating to the disposition and distribution of the property in the estate or trust; to be distinguished from administrative provisions which relate to the handling of the property while it is in the hands of the executor or trustee. (74)

dispossess To deprive one of the use of real estate. (5)

dissaving The reduction in net worth by spending more than current income.

dissent The act of disagreeing. Thus, a widow's refusal to take the share provided for her in her husband's will and assertion of her rights under the law is known as her dissent from the will. See Dower. (88)

dissolution The liquidation of a business which in theory should follow the concept of "absolute priority." See that term.

distant delivery Delivery during one of the more distant months and at least two months away. (9)

distressed sale A forced liquidation of a thing. The assumption is that the seller does not receive as high a price for his goods as he would under normal selling conditions.

distributee A person to whom something is distributed; frequently applied to the recipient of personal property under intestacy; to be distinguished from heir—a person who inherits real property. (88)

distributing syndicate Those brokerage firms, investment bankers who have formed a joint venture for the purpose of selling an issue of securities. See Distribution.

distribution Selling, over a period of time, of a large block of stock without unduly depressing the market price. See also Exchange Distribution; Liquidation; Secondary Distribution; Special Offering. (2)

distribution cost analysis The study and evaluation of the relative profitability or costs of different marketing operations in terms of customers, marketing units, commodities, territories, or services. (13)

distribution in kind Distribution of the assets of an estate in their original form and not the cash value of the property. Stocks and bonds are generally distributed among those entitled to receive them instead of being converted into cash for the purpose of effecting distribution. (74)

distributive share The share of a person in the distribution of an estate. (74)

distributor A person or company that purchases open-end investment company shares directly from the issuer for re-sale to others. Same as Principal Underwriter. (3)

diversification Spreading investments among different companies in different fields. Diversification is also offered by the securities of many individual companies because of the wide range of their activities. See Investment Trust. (2)

diversified investment company An investment company which practices diversification. The Investment Company Act of 1940 requires such a company to have at least 75% of its assets represented by cash, government securities, securities of other investment companies and other securities limited in respect of any one issuer to an amount not greater than 5% of the value of the total assets of such investment company and not more than 10% of the outstanding voting securities of such issuer. (65)

divided-column journal A journal in which the debit amount columns are at the left of the account titles and explanation column and the credit amount columns are at the right of the account titles and explanation column. (73)

dividend A portion of the net profits which has been officially declared by the Board of Directors. A dividend is paid upon a per cent of the par value of the stock, or if the stock does not have a par value, then upon a certain amount for each share of stock held by each stockholder. Dividends come under the following classifications: a) Regular dividends—described above. b) Extra dividends—distribution of excess profits over and above the regular dividend. c)Scrip dividend—a promissory dividend payable in the future—(the directors vote to withold actual cash dividend until a certain future event has taken place). d) Stock dividend—a payment of a portion of stock in lieu of the cash dividend on the same pro rata basis as the stock held by each stockholder. The National Bank Act requires a national bank to carry at least ten per cent of the net earnings for each previous six months to its surplus account before it may pay dividends. State laws in many instances have followed this same general pattern in their control over state chartered banks. (1)

dividend appropriations Amounts declared payable out of Retained Income (Earned Surplus) as dividends on actually outstanding preferred or common stock, or the amount credited to a reserve for such dividends. (21)

dividend check A negotiable instrument in the form of a check drawn on a depository bank of the corporation issuing the dividend. It is signed by the secretary of the corporation. It is dated for the day set for payment of dividends as passed by the Board of Directors. The payee is the stockholder of record in the registrar agent's office at the time of the dividend. The amount is the declaration as passed by the Board of Directors on a per-share basis. (1)

dividend claim A request made by the purchaser of stock upon the registered holder for the amount of a dividend where the transaction took place prior to the ex-dividend date, but the transfer could not be effected prior to the record date. (74)

dividend on The sale of a stock with the understanding that the buyer will receive the next dividend. (105)

dividend order A form which, when properly filled out, instructs a corporation to forward dividend checks to a specified address. (74)

dividend payer A company or security which pays dividends as contrasted with those companies and their securities which, because of poor earnings or the process of plowing back their earnings do not pay dividends.

dividend-paying agent The agent of a corporation charged with the duty of paying dividends on the stock of the corporation out of funds supplied by the corporation. (74)

dividend, pegging of Normal yearly dividend increase eliminated. (42)

dividend requirements The amount of annual earnings required to pay preferred dividends in full. (3)

dividends paid Shows the amount of cash dividends paid and the dollar value of stock dividends distributed to shareholders during the period.

divisional bond A debt instrument secured by the assets or credit of a division of a company or system. Most such bonds are of railroad divisions.

document 1. A form, voucher, or written evidence of a transaction. 2. To instruct, as by citation of reference. 3. To substantiate, as by listing of authorities. (104)

documentary bill See Documentary Draft.

documentary draft A draft accompanied by a shipping document, bill of lading, insurance certificate, etc., these documents having intrinsic value. Instructions for disposition of the document usually accompany the draft. (83)

documentary evidence Evidence in the form of written or printed papers. (5)

documentary stamp A revenue stamp issued for the payment of a tax on documents, as deeds, checks, or wills. (54)

documentation The group of techniques necessary for the orderly presentation, organization and communication of recorded specialized knowledge, in order to maintain a complete record of reasons for changes in variables. Documentation is necessary not so much to give maximum utility as to give an unquestionable historical reference record. (104)

dollar Monetary unit of Canada, Ethiopia, Liberia and the United States.

dollar acceptance A bill of exchange or acceptance which may be drawn in a foreign or domestic country but is payable in dollars. While Canada, Ethiopia, Liberia and the United States all have the dollar as their monetary unit, it is generally assumed that the dollar is a United States dollar.

dollar averaging See Dollar Cost Averaging.

dollar bill of exchange See Dollar Acceptance.

dollar control A technique for guiding inventory by means of amount of money rather than by the number of physical items.

dollar cost averaging A system of buying securities at regular intervals with a fixed amount of dollars invested over a considerable period of time, regardless of the prevailing prices of the securities. It is frequently used by institutional investors. Under this system the investor acquired not 10 shares of ABC every month or every six months but $50 worth of ABC. When ABC is selling at a low price he gets more shares than when it is selling at a high price. Over the long-term, if the price trend of a stock is upward, and periodic investments are maintained in good times and bad, dollar cost averaging may be a rewarding investment technique. See Scale Buying; Formula Investing. (2)

dollar credit A letter of credit or a credit balance which is payable in dollars.

dollar deficit See Dollar Gap.

dollar exchange See Dollar Acceptance.

dollar gap Dollar Deficit. The difference in dollars for a nation which has not earned as many dollars as it has spent in a given period of time.

dollar stabilization 1. Those acts by monetary authorities such as the International Monetary Fund, the Exchange Stabilization Fund, The Federal Reserve Board, and The United States Treasury which have as their purpose the reduction in the fluctuation of the international exchange value of the dollar. 2. It also has been used to designate an idea of Economist Irving Fisher which would result in a compensated dollar which would be tied to commodities rather than gold.

domestic acceptance In a strict sense, any acceptance which has the drawer, the drawee and the place of payment within the same state. However, the term is generally loosely used to refer to any acceptance which has the drawer, drawee and the place of payment in the United States.

domestic bill Any of numerous documents such as sight or time drafts which are drawn and payable within the same state. In a looser sense, any of numerous documents which are drawn and payable in the United States.

domestic bill of exchange Same as inland bill of exchange. (85)

domestic exchange As distinguished from Foreign Exchange, any acceptance, check, draft or similar document which is drawn and payable in the United States. In a foreign nation, any acceptance, check, draft or similar document which is drawn and payable in that nation would be considered as domestic exchange.

domicile The place where one has his true, fixed and permanent home, and to which, whenever he is absent, he has the intention of returning. (5)

domiciled company A company whose head office is in the same state as the person referring to it. (5)

domiciliary administration The settlement of that portion of a decedent's estate which is located in the state of his domicile; to be distinguished from ancillary administration which relates to property elsewhere than in the state of the decedent's domicile. (74)

domiciliary trustee The trustee of that portion of a decedent's or settlor's property which is located in the state of his domicile; to be distinguished from ancillary trustee that administers property elsewhere than in the state of the decedent's or settlor's domicile. (74)

donated stock Capital stock which is fully paid and has been returned as a gift to the issuing corporation.

donated surplus A capital surplus account that contains a record of the par value of donated stock that is in the treasury of the corporation and of the proceeds from donated stock that have been sold. (73)

donative interest An interest in property that is subject to gift. (74)

donee One who receives a gift. (74)

donor One who makes a gift. See Settlor. (74)

donor (trust) A living person who creates a "voluntary trust" (see definition). (1)

don't know (d.k.) Refers to an attempted confirmation or comparison of a securities transaction by one firm, with another firm denying knowledge of its existence. The comparison is marked "D.K." and returned. A member firm must in-

form the executing broker of this fact, and then the floor broker concerned must investigate the situation immediately. (105)

dormant account An account which has little or no activity for a period of time. Many states have set up escheat law placing the statute of limitations on dormant accounts. The bank is required to publish the names of all dormant account depositors for a specified period of time, after which the funds are transferred to the state for disposition. (83)

dormant partner One who is not known to the public as a member of the firm and who does not take an active part in the management of the business. (73)

double bottom That part of a charted time series which shows two lows. Some interpreters of economic charts contend that business activity or prices of stocks or commodities generally have a second bottom before recovery and thus a double bottom is assumed to be an indicator of recovery.

double bottom (top) Refers to the price action of a security or market average whereby it has twice declined to the same approximate level. Technically, this indicates the existence of a support level, and the possibility that the downward trend has ended. (105)

double budget A system of segregating capital expenditures from recurring expense items so that an annual income statement will not be distorted during those years of heavy capital investment.

double endorsement A negotiable instrument or other document which contains two endorsements which means that recourse can be made to the two firms or individuals which endorsed the instrument.

double entry A system of bookkeeping which requires for every entry made to the debit side of an account or accounts an entry for a corresponding amount or amounts to the credit side of another account or accounts.

NOTE: Double-entry bookkeeping involves the maintaining of a balance between assets and other resources on the one hand and liabilities, other obligations, and surplus on the other. To maintain this balance it is necessary that entries for equal amounts be made in each group. Moreover, if a transaction affects only one group of accounts (for example, the asset group of accounts), the amount within the group must be offset by a credit for another account or accounts within the group for a corresponding amount or amounts (for example, a debit to Cash would be offset by a credit for a corresponding amount to Taxes Receivable or some other asset). (29)

double indorsement See Double Endorsement.

double liability A term used to refer to the liability of the stockholders of banks before banking legislation of the 1930's brought about the elimination of this feature for all national banks and most state banks. Under the double liability provision, the stockholders of a bank, in the event of its liquidation, were held legally responsible for an amount equal to the par value of their stock in addition to the amount of their original investment. (90)

double option Two options in one contract, such

as a spread which combines a Put and Call at different prices; or a Straddle which combines a Put and a Call at identical prices. (105)

double posting The posting of a debit amount or a credit amount to two accounts. (73)

doubtful assets Those assets which would probably not bring full value upon liquidation. (105)

dower The interest or life estate of a widow in the real property of her husband. At common law a wife had a life estate in one-third (in value) of the real property of her husband who died without leaving a valid will or from whose will she dissented (See Dissent). In many states common law dower has been abolished by statute or has never been recognized. (88)

Dow Jones Averages Those averages of industrials, transportation, and utilities which are published by The Wall Street Journal and periodicals using their service. The figures refer to stock market quotations of the securities which make up the averages. There is a considerable amount of statistical processing of the averages through the use of what is called a divisor. The divisor is an attempt to adjust the data for such factors as stock splits and stock dividends. See Dow Theory.

down gap An open space formed on a security chart when the lowest price of any market day is above the highest price of the following day. (105)

down payment A cash sum of money required at the outset of an installment sales credit transaction; sometimes a used item of durable goods is traded in and accepted in lieu of part or all of the down payment. (131)

downstream borrowing The obtaining of credit or funds by a holding company from or because of the credit standing of a subsidiary or subsidiaries.

down tick See Up Tick. (2)

Dow Theory A theory of market analysis based upon the performance of the Dow Jones industrial and transportation stock price averages. The Theory says that the market is in a basic upward trend if one of these averages advances above a previous important high, accompanied or followed by a similar advance in the other. When the averages both dip below previous important lows, this is regarded as confirmation of a basic downward trend. The Theory does not attempt to predict how long either trend will continue, although it is widely misinterpreted as a method of forecasting future action. Whatever the merits of the Theory, it is sometimes a strong factor in the market because many people believe in the Theory—or know that a great many others do. See Technical Position. (2)

drachma Monetary unit of Greece.

draft A draft is an order in writing signed by one party (the drawer) requesting a second party (the drawee) to make payment in lawful money at a determinable future time to a third party (the payee). Drafts may occasionally be written so as to be non-negotiable, in that they will not meet all the requirements of the Uniform Negotiable Instruments Act. Drafts generally arise out of a commercial transaction, whereby the seller makes an agreement with a buyer in advance for the transfer of goods. The draft may be made out by the seller (the drawer) ordering the buyer (the drawee) to pay his bank (the payee) for the goods purchased. The draft may be accompanied by a bill of lading for the goods, whereby the bank will surrender the bill of lading to the buyer upon payment of the draft. The buyer can then claim the goods at the office of the carrier who transported the goods to the buyer's place of business. Drafts may be classified as to time element, such as sight or presentation drafts, or demand drafts; arrival drafts; or time drafts. A time draft is presented at sight, accepted, and then paid on the agreed upon date, which may be 30, 60, 90 days or longer after presentation and acceptance. (1)

drawback The return to an importer of the duties collected on imported goods which were intended for and are reshipped to another nation.

drawee Any party or company upon whom a draft is drawn and from whom payment of the draft is expected. (83)

drawer Any party, such as an individual, proprietorship, partnership, or corporation who draws a draft or check upon another "legal entity" for the payment of funds is known as the drawer of a draft, or the maker of the instrument. (1)

drawing account Money available to owners or salesmen to be used for expenses which will be deducted from future earnings. (93)

drawn securities Any securities such as bonds and preferred stock which have been called for redemption. The term "drawn" arises from the fact that such a redemption is accomplished by the use of lots which are "drawn" or chosen by chance.

dried up To come to a halt, cease. In the securities business it usually refers to the disappearance of either buying or selling orders. (105)

drive 1. A concerted upward or downward movement in security prices. 2. An attempt to manipulate prices of securities or commodities by the concerted efforts of sellers to force prices down. Such action is illegal if proven. (105)

drive-in bank Because of traffic congestion and lack of parking space, many banks now have tellers' windows facing the outside of the building for the convenience of depositors. The depositor drives up to the bank's "Drive-In" teller's window, attracts the teller's attention by means of a bell, and completes his transaction while still seated in his car. The system has every feature of the normal over-the-counter operation, just as though the depositor had been in the bank's lobby. (1)

drop A decline in price or activity.

dry run Another name used by banks for the machine pay plan of journalizing the posting media before posting to the statement. See also Machine Pay. (1)

dry trust See Passive Trust. (74)

dual exchange market Exists when the authorities operate two exchange markets, prescribing the use of one market for exchange transactions relating to specified types of underlying transactions and the use of the other permitted dealing in foreign exchange. Such arrangements have often involved a market where the value of foreign exchange is kept relatively stable and in which the bulk of all transactions takes place, and another, a "free market," where foreign currencies fluctuate freely or with a high degree of freedom. In the secondary market foreign exchange may be either more or less expensive than in the main market, depending on the regulations governing access to each. Official intervention in the form of purchases or sales of foreign currency by the authorities may be resorted to in order to affect fluctuation in the secondary market. (130)

dual listing A security listed on more than one exchange. (105)

dual savings plan A plan whereby a savings deposit or withdrawal requires two separate operations to post an account. The savings teller enters the transaction in the depositor's pass book, verifies the depositor's withdrawal ticket, and sends the media to a "bank-office" bookkeeping department, where the entry is posted to the depositor's ledger card. See Unit Savings Plan. (1)

dual standard plan cost system See Cost Systems, Dual Standard Plan. (28)

due (annuity) Annuity payments to commence immediately. (42)

due bill A statement of an amount that is owed. Frequently used in security sales when a stock has gone ex-dividend but the dividend has not yet been disbursed. The buyer, in the above illustration signs a "due bill" stating the amount of the dividend that is owed to the seller. This amount is to be paid to the seller.

due date The date upon which a note, draft, bond, coupon, etc., becomes payable; the maturity date. (83)

due diligence meeting A bringing together of the officials of a firm whose securities are to be issued with the executives of the underwriting syndicate in compliance with the Securities Act. The underwriters question the firm's officials about the material in the registration statement, the prospectus and related financial statements.

due from banks Title of an asset account in the general ledger. Subsidiary accounts under this title include each account of funds that a bank has on deposit with other banks. Legal reserve funds and funds placed on deposit with correspondent banks are among these accounts. (83)

due to banks Title of a liability account in the general ledger. Includes subsidiary accounts of funds that one bank has on deposit with another bank. (83)

dull That state of business activity which is below normal.

dummy An individual, such as a director elected to a board who simply acts for some other individual. The dummy has no material ownership in the company and permits the individual who has sponsored his election to control his vote on the issues before the board of directors.

dump The sale of a large amount of goods or securities in a disorganizing way, frequently with little regard to price or impact on the market.

dun A term generally used in credit work (but not recommended) describing any form of reminder to customer about past-due obligation. (26)

Dun & Bradstreet A credit and collection agency which is the largest general mercantile agency in the United States. This company provides for its subscribers a periodic reference work which lists the Standard Industrial Classification, the firm's name and city location, and if formed within the last ten years this is indicated with some designation of credit rating as to net worth and how payments are made. They also publish Dun's Review and other economic studies on bankruptcy, collections and terms of trade.

duopoly A market situation in which there are only two producers or sellers of a similar product.

duosony A market situation in which only two buyers are seeking a similar product.

duplicate deposit ticket A copy, usually in carbon, of an original deposit ticket. In business practice, many businesses require that their bookkeepers retain a carbon duplicate of the daily deposit ticket made in a bank. Chain store organizations generally insist upon duplicate deposit tickets, and usually one copy is mailed daily to the "home office" of the chain store group for auditing purposes.

When a depositor fails to bring in a pass book when making a deposit, the bank issues a duplicate deposit ticket as a temporary receipt. The depositor should present this duplicate along with the pass book on his next visit to the bank. The teller will enter the amount in the pass book, and should retain the duplicate ticket for the auditor's use.

In savings department operations where the "Unit Savings Plan" (See definition) is in use, duplicate entries are posted by machine, and a locked storage total protects both the depositor and the teller, giving the audit control. (1)

durable good Commodities which are useful to the consumer over an extended period of time, such as automobiles, furniture, and appliances. (131)

duress Compulsion or constraint by force or fear of personal violence, prosecution, or imprisonment which induces a person to do what he does not want to do or to refrain from doing something he has a legal right to do. Sometimes the word is used with reference to the making of a will, as that it was made under duress. (74)

dutch auction A sale by an auctioneer in which he offers the merchandise at a high price and lowers the price until a bidder responds and purchases.

duty card Same as tickler. Common term used in many trust departments. (74)

dynamiter The expression for a nomadic "securities" salesman who attempts to sell fraudulent securities over the telephone. (105)

E

E. E. Errors Expected.

E.F.F. Exchange for futures.

EIB Export-Import Bank.

Encl. Enclosure.

End. Endorsement.

End. Guar. Endorsement guaranteed.

EOF End of File. (104)

EOM End of Month. (67)

E. P. T. Excess profits tax.

Equ. Equity.

Equiv. Equivalent.

E/R Earnings Record. (67)

Est. Estate; Estimated.

E/T Estate tax.

Evid. Evidence.

Ex. Without.

Exch. Exchange; Exchequer.

Exctr. Executor.

Ex D. Ex dividend or without dividend.

Ex Div. Ex dividend.

Exmr. Examiner.

Exor. Executor.

Exp. Expense; export; express; exporter.

Ex R. Ex Rights.

Ext. External.

Extd. Extended.

each way A transaction in which the broker executes the buying and selling, receiving a commission for each of the two functions. (105)

earmarked A product or territory held aside for a later use or development.

earmarked gold Gold in the fiduciary possession of one nation's central bank for another nation's central bank; treasury or stabilization fund.

earned income The amount received for goods or services delivered and for which no future liability is anticipated.

earned income credit A percentage of the individual taxpayer's earned income which he may subtract from his net income in the computation of his income tax. (73)

earned surplus (or undistributed profits or retained income) The balance of net profits, income, gains and losses of a corporation from the date of incorporation (or from the latest date when a deficit was eliminated in a quasi-reorganization) after deducting distributions therefrom to shareholders and transfers therefrom to capital stock or capital surplus accounts. (17)

earnest A sum paid as part of the price of property sold, or of money due upon an agreement, for the purpose of binding the bargain. (5)

earning assets (bank terminology) Loans and investments which together are the assets responsible for most of the bank's earnings. (103)

earning-capacity standard The Capitalized Value Standard. The annual earnings of a business divided by an appropriate interest rate. The rate is estimated by the risk involved in the business. A very risky business would be capitalized at a higher percentage than a more stable business. At 5%, annual earnings of 1,000 units would be worth 20,000 units while at 10% the same earnings would be worth only 10,000 units.

earning power The demonstrated ability of an individual or firm to show a profit for a period of time.

earnings 1. Synonym for "net income", particularly over a period of years. In the singular, the term is often combined with another word in the expression "earning power", referring to the demonstrated ability of an enterprise to earn net income. 2. *per Common Share*—Net income after all charges, including preferred dividend requirements, divided by the number of common shares outstanding. Net income does not include profits from the sale of securities—these are considered separately as capital gains. 3. *per Preferred Share*—Net income after all charges, including any prior preferred dividend requirements, divided by the number of shares outstanding. Net income does not include profits from the sale of securities—these are considered separately as capital gains. (17, 3)

earnings price (e/p) ratio Earnings per share of common stock outstanding divided by the closing stock market price (or the mid-point between the closing bid and asked price if there are no sales) on a day as close as possible after the publication of the earnings. (21)

earnings report A statement—also called an income statement—issued by a company showing its earnings or losses over a given period. The earnings report lists the income earned, expenses and the net result. See Balance Sheet. (2)

ease off A slow decline in prices. (9)

easy money That condition in which interest rates are low and loans are relatively readily obtained. The condition may be the result of the natural forces of a market such as an inflow of money from abroad or the condition may result from the monetary policy of the monetary and fiscal authorities through such actions as changing rediscount rates and open market operations.

econometric model A set of related equations used to analyze economic data through mathematical and statistical techniques. Such models are devised in order to depict the essential quantitative impact of alternative assumptions or government policies, and for testing various propositions about the way the economy works.

The Office of Business Economics has developed a quarterly econometric model of the U.S. economy. This model consists of 70 equations (excluding identities) and is designed to be used for structural analysis and forecasting. As the model itself is still being tested and improved, the results are not presently being published. (124)

economies of scale Efficiencies which result from the producer having the proper proportions of land, labor and machinery to meet a given market.

effective date Date on which the contract or agreement commences. (42)

effective demand The ability to pay for goods or services that are desired.

effective exchange rate Is any spot exchange rate actually paid or received by the public, including any taxes or subsidies on the exchange transaction as well as any applicable banking commissions. The articles of agreement envisage that all **effective exchange rates shall be situated within permitted margins around par value.** (130)

effective gross revenue Total income less allowance for vacancies, contingencies, and sometimes collection losses, but before deductions for operating expenses. (54)

effective interest rate or yield The rate or earning on a bond investment based on the actual price paid for the bond, the coupon rate, the maturity date, and the length of time between interest dates; in contrast with nominal interest rate. (29)

eighth stocks Stocks on which the odd-lot differential, added to a buy order or subtracted from a sell order, of one-eighth of a point is applied to the next round-lot sale. Eighth Stocks are those selling below 60, those selling above 60 are called Quarter Stocks. (105)

ejectment The name of an action wherein the plaintiff seeks to recover from the defendant the possession of real property, with damages for the unlawful detention of the same. (5)

elastic currency See Elastic Money.

elastic demand Demand which fluctuates at a greater proportionate rate than the rate of change of price for a product. A 10% price decrease which stimulated a more than 10% increase in sales would be elastic demand.

elasticity of demand See Elastic Demand.

elastic money A currency or money supply which increases or decreases with the needs of the economy. The elasticity can be provided by action of the monetary authorities or by making the currency related to bank loans by the rediscount device.

elastic supply Supply which fluctuates at a greater proportionate rate than the rate of change of price for a product. A 10% price increase which stimulated a more than 10% increase in supply would be elastic supply.

election The choice of an alternative right or course. Thus, the right of a widow to take the share of her deceased husband's estate to which she is entitled under the law, despite a contrary provision in the will, is known as the widow's election. (88)

eleemosynary Pertaining or devoted to legal charity; as an eleemosynary institution. (74)

elevator receipt The document given by an elevator company as a receipt for grain deposited with it for storage. It is a warehouse receipt given by an elevator company.

eligible acceptance See Eligible Paper.

eligible bill See Eligible Paper.

eligible paper Those documents, securities, notes and bills which are acceptable by a financial institution such as the Federal Reserve Bank for rediscounting purposes. The technical provisions are in the amended Federal Reserve Act.

embezzlement The fraudulent appropriation to one's own use of the money or property entrusted to his care. (29)

eminent domain The inherent right of certain legally constituted governing bodies to take title to a possession of real property, with just compensation to its owner, for the public good. (29)

emolument The remuneration connected with a service or office such as fee, or salary.

emphyteutic lease A perpetual lease in which the grantee has the right of alienation or descent provided that payment of the rent is maintained in a prompt manner.

employees trust A trust established by an employer (usually a corporation) for the benefit of employees. (74)

employment trust A trust in which an employee is the beneficiary such as a pension trust.

emporium The chief market of an area or products.

encode 1. To place magnetic ink characters of the E 13B type font specified by the A.B.A. on the face of a document during the processing of items through an (encoding) machine. 2. To apply a code, frequently one consisting of binary numbers, to represent individual characters or groups of characters in a message. Synonymous with encipher. Inverse of decode. 3. To substitute letters, numbers, or characters for other numbers, letters, or characters usually to intentionally hide the meaning of the message except to certain individuals who know the enciphering scheme. Synonymous with encipher. (83, 104)

encumbrance A lien or claim against title to property which, unless removed, prevents the passing of full and complete title. (89)

end money That money or fund that may be used should an activity or project exceed the original budget. A contingency fund.

endorse The act of placing one's name on an instrument, usually on the back, either by signing or by rubber stamping, so as legally to pass title of the instrument to another party. May also refer to the endorsing of a note by a second party guaranteeing payment in the event of default by the maker. (83)

endorsee The holder of a negotiable instrument to whom it has been transferred.

endorsement When a party writes a legal signature (any signature recognized by law) upon the back of an instrument, this constitutes an endorsement. An endorsement is required on a negotiable instrument in order to transfer and pass title to another party, who becomes a "holder in due course." An endorsement, in the terms of the Negotiable Instruments Act, has a serious legal significance. The endorser, in signing the endorsement, guarantees that he is the lawful owner of the instrument; that he knows of no infirmity in the instrument (that he received it in good faith for value received) and that he is a holder in due course, and has the legal capacity to transfer title to another party in the normal course of business. A holder in due course has the legal right to look to any prior endorser of the instrument in case the instrument is dishonored by the maker. Endorsements are of six types:

1. Blank endorsement—A general endorsement, showing only the signature of the endorser. 2. Special endorsement—The endorser writes in the names of the party to whom he is conveying title, as "Pay to the order of John Doe—(signed) Richard Roe." 3. Qualified endorsement—The endorser writes the words "Without Recourse" after the endorsement signature. This type of endorsement is not frequently used, although it does not harm the negotiability of the instrument. The endorser "assigns" the instrument, certifies that he is a holder in due course, but restricts the endorsement in that he cannot be called upon for any financial responsibility in case of infirmity in the instrument. 4. Conditional endorsement—

An infrequent use of the endorsement in which the endorser places a condition in the endorsement requiring the completion of some act before the endorser can be held financially responsible. 5. Restricted endorsement—This endorsement destroys further negotiability of an instrument. It is frequently seen in endorsements, such as "Pay to the order of the Blank Bank and Trust Company FOR DEPOSIT ONLY." The endorsing bank can collect on this endorsement, if drawn on another bank, but this is the only way that title may be transferred—for collection purposes only. 6. Absolute endorsement—This type of endorsement limits the liability of the endorser, in that he will not be financially responsible unless all prior parties have failed to pay the holder in due course, and unless he has been duly notified by the holder that all prior parties have dishonored their endorsement. (1)

endorser One who signs his name to a note, a check, or other similar instrument for the purpose of transferring it to another person. (73)

endorsing The act of signing a note, check, or other similar instrument for the purpose of transferring it to another person. (73)

endowment Gift given to an institution for a specific purpose such as money or property given to hospitals for research purposes. (93)

endowment, pure Insurance plan providing for payment of the face amount to the insured only upon survival to the end of a fixed period. Does not allow for payment of benefits to a beneficiary on prior death of the insured. (42)

endowment term Period of time from date of issue to maturity of an endowment contract. (42)

enforced liquidation Condition caused by the failure of a security owner to maintain sufficient equity in his margin account. (105)

entity That which exists as separate and complete in itself. For example, a corporation is a legal entity, separate and distinct from its stockholders. (74)

entrepreneur One who assumes the financial risk of the initiation, operation and management of a given business or undertaking. (1)

entry 1. The record of a financial transaction in its appropriate book of accounts. 2. The act of recording a transaction in the books of account. (29)

equalization fund See Exchange Stabilization fund.

equation price The price reached by the adjusting action of competition in any market at any time, or in a unit of time, such that the demand and supply become equal at that price. (19)

equilibrium Economic or physical condition which tends to maintain itself in the same situation.

equimarginal principle The amount of money, or the quantity of a good or service that an individual feels he should receive for some other good or service.

equipment obligations Equipment bonds, equipment notes, or car-trust notes secured only by lien on specific equipment. (19)

equipment trust 1. A corporate trust established for the purpose of financing the purchase of equipment; commonly resorted to by railroads for the purchase of rolling stock. 2. A device or trust which is used to help firms obtain equipment by either the Philadelphia-Lease Plan or the New York Conditional Sales Plan. See Equipment Trust Certificate. (74)

equipment trust certificate A type of security, generally issued by a railroad, to pay for new equipment. Title to the equipment, such as a locomotive, is held by a trustee until the notes are paid off. An equipment trust certificate is usually secured by a first lien on the equipment. (2)

equitable ownership The estate or interest of a person who has a beneficial right in property, the legal ownership of which is in another person. For example, a beneficiary of a trust has an equitable estate or interest in the trust property. (74)

equitable title A right to the benefits of property which is recognized by and enforceable only in a court of equity; to be distinguished from legal title. (74)

equities A term used synonymously with common stocks or capital stocks to designate securities that are owned capital rather than owed capital. The Stockholders' Equity in a company may be stated inclusive or exclusive of preferred stock. (103)

equity 1. The ownership interest of common and preferred stockholders in a company. Also refers to excess of value of securities over the debit balance in a margin account. 2. The residue of value for the owner of an asset remaining after deducting prior claims. The equity of a corporation may be divided into common shares alone or may include preferred shares as well. In calculating the equity of a common stock, preferred stock as well as debt must be deducted from total assets. 3. A system of principles and rules developed to supplement and correct a system of law that had become too narrow and rigid in scope and application. Its characteristic is flexibility and its aim is the administration of justice. (2, 3, 74)

equity capital Money furnished by owners of the business. (93)

equity earnings Indirect or unreported earnings of a subsidiary which have not been carried upstream to the parent company.

equity financing The acquisition of money for capital or operating purposes in exchange for a share of shares in the business being financed. (118)

equity income Net operating income less loan interest. (Gross is before taxes and net is after taxes.) (120)

equity of redemption The right of an owner of a mortgaged or encumbered property to recover the rights transferred by the mortgage or other lien upon satisfaction of the debt either before or after foreclosure. (89)

equity receivership Rarely found non-statutory proceeding against insolvent debtor.

equity security Technically, term refers to all securities other than debt, but is used sometimes to denote common stocks alone or preferred stocks of a quality which renders them subject to market fluctuations similar to those of common stocks. (3)

equity trading See Leverage.

erratic An irregular trend in the price action of a security, or a general market average, whereby the price moves both up and down in an indefinite fashion. (105)

error account A suspense account which serves as a place to record errors such as till overages or shortages.

escheat The reversion of property to the state (in the United States) in case there are no devisees, legatees, heirs, or next of kin; originally applicable only to real property but now applicable to all kinds of property. (74)

escheat law The reversion to the state of certain funds after a stated period of inactivity pertaining to them, or of other property, the ownership of which is unknown or in doubt. (83)

escrow A written agreement or instrument setting up the allocation of funds or securities deposited by the giver or grantor to a third party, called the escrow agent, for the eventual benefit of the second party, called the grantee. The escrow agent holds the deposit until certain conditions have been met. The grantor cannot get the deposit back except if the grantee fails to comply with the terms of the contract, nor can the grantee receive the deposit until the conditions have been met. A common example of escrow today is the escrow fund carried in relation to mortgages. The property holder, or mortgagor, pays to the financial institution (either the mortgagee or agent for the mortgagee) who in this case is the escrow agent, certain funds for the payment of taxes, assessments, insurance, etc. These escrow funds are for the future benefit of the collector of taxes, etc. At tax collection time, the escrow agent pays the tax collector the funds held in escrow. The mortgagor is relieved of this problem, the tax collector has collected his taxes, and the financial institution has fulfilled its obligations as escrow agent. (1)

escrow funds As applied to mortgage loans, represents reserves established for the payment of taxes and insurance when due. Reserves are collected monthly by the mortgagee as part of the regular payment. (83)

escrow officer An officer of a financial institution designated as the escrow agent or the custodian of the funds, securities, deeds, etc., deposited until their release by agreement upon the completion of the agreed-upon act. (1)

escudo Monetary unit of Portugal.

estate The entire group of assets owned by an individual at the time of his death. The estate includes all funds, personal effects, interests in business enterprises, titles to property (real estate and chattels), and evidences of ownership such as stocks, bonds and mortgages owned, notes receivable, etc. All claims against an estate must be duly filed with the "Executor" or "Administrator" (see definitions) of the estate, and approved by the court of law under which the will is being probated or the line of heritage is being determined before these indebtednesses may be satisfied. (1)

estate account An account in the name of the estate of a decedent, administered by the executor or administrator of the estate. (90)

estate in common See Tenancy in Common. (74)

estate in reversion The residue of an estate left in the grantor, to commence in possession after the termination of some particular estate granted by him. Not to be confused with remainder estate. (54)

estate plan A definite plan for the administration and disposition of one's property during one's lifetime and at one's death; usually set forth in a will and one or more trust agreements. (74)

estate tax The tax levied by the federal government on a decedent's estate as a whole; more specifically known as a federal estate tax. (74)

estimate To form an opinion regarding the value, size, weight, or quantity of. (93)

estimated balance sheet An estimate of the assets, liabilities, and proprietorship at the end of a future fiscal period. (73)

estimated profit and loss statement An estimate of the income, expenses, and net profit for a future fiscal period. (73)

estoppel The legal principle which precludes a person from alleging in an action what is contrary to his previous action or admission or which bars him from denying a misrepresentation of a fact when another person has acted upon that misrepresentation to his detriment. The person so precluded or barred is said to be estopped. (88)

estoppel certificate An instrument which shows the unpaid principal balance of a mortgage and the rate and amount of interest thereon. (5)

evening up 1. When for any reason traders are completing their transactions by selling in the case of longs or by purchasing in the case of shorts, they are said to be evening up. 2. Straddling or liquidating a contract. (123)

even lot A round lot. A board lot.

even up Condition existing when buying and selling strength in a security are about equal. When describing the market before the opening, it indicates that opening prices will be little changed from the previous day's closing. (105)

ex Out of, or without. See Ex-Dividend.

exact interest Interest computed on the basis of 365 days, as opposed to ordinary interest computed on the basis of 360 days. (105)

ex-all A security sold "Ex-all" means that the seller has sold the security but has reserved for himself the right to all pending advantages such as to rights, warrants, dividends in money or kind which may be granted to the security.

examination A detailed check-up made of an association each year by a supervising authority. (31, 92)

examine for bank endorsement An act performed generally in a bank's proof department or bookkeeping department whereby clerks examine the back of all checks to see that the bank which forwarded the items has properly endorsed them. The bank endorsement is very important because banks use it to trace the path of an item through the banks through which it has passed. The whole system of returning items for infirmity through the channels from which they came relies to a great extent upon clear, legible bank endorsements. (1)

examine for endorsement An act performed to determine whether an item has been properly endorsed so as to complete its negotiability. Tellers, or clerks who receive the items from tellers, check endorsements so that the depositor of any item can be readily determined. It is the responsibility of bookkeepers to see that items are properly endorsed before they are paid by the bank. Many cases involving the negotiability of an instrument have arisen because of improper, incomplete, or faulty endorsements on the instrument. (1)

examine for mis-sorts Bookkeepers are required to examine checks before posting them, to determine that they are drawn on accounts in their particular ledger, or that they are actually drawn on the drawee bank. There are, two types of mis-sorts: checks sorted to the wrong ledger, or checks drawn on another bank where a depositor may maintain another account, but using a similar style of check. (1)

excess equity The condition of a margin account when the cash, or liquidating value exceeds the amount required for margin. (105)

excess interest The difference between the minimum rate of interest contractually guaranteed on dividends or proceeds left with the company and the interest actually credited. (58)

excess loan State and national bank acts prohibit banks from making loans in excess of stated legal relationships to capital and surplus. A loan in excess of such relationships results in the directors of the institution being personally liable in the event of such a loss.

excess reserves A term used to designate the amount of funds held in reserve in excess of the legal minimum requirements, whether the funds are on deposit in the Federal Reserve Bank, in a bank approved as a depository, or in the cash reserve carried within its own vaults. (1)

exchange This term has several meanings. See Clearings.

One term commonly used in banking is the "clearing house exchange". Banks in a community who have formed a Clearing House Association exchange the items in their possession but draw on other banks in the community with these other banks at the daily meeting of the Clearing House Association. Settlement of all items exchanged is simplified, because the exchange is settled on a "net basis" wherein the "losing banks" pay the "winning banks" the net difference in the exchange of items.

The term is also used to denote a service charge, or exchange fee, made by banks for cashing checks, usually items drawn on distant points. "Exchange" in financial circles also describes meeting places where stocks, bonds and commodities are bought and sold or traded in. Examples: stock exchange, curb exchange, grain exchange, and cotton exchange.

"Foreign exchange" refers to trading that involves foreign currencies. The principal foreign exchange markets are in New York City where many banks have private wires to all foreign countries. By this communication service, these

banks are able to buy and sell for immediate or even future delivery funds of foreign countries, these funds to be used to pay for imports or exports in the currency desired by the seller of the goods. (1)

exchange acquisition A method of filling an order to buy a large block of stock on the floor of the exchange. Under certain circumstances, a member-broker can facilitate the purchase of a block by soliciting orders to sell. All orders to sell the security are lumped together and offset with the buy order in the regular auction market. The price to the buyer may be on a net basis or on a commission basis. (106)

exchange charge The term "exchange charge" has a variety of meanings. Sometimes it refers to a remittance charge which is a charge that some banks deduct in paying checks drawn upon themselves when they are presented through the mails from out-of-town points for the service of remitting the proceeds to these distant points. Also it refers to a charge for drafts on other cities or to a charge which banks make for collecting out-of-town items. Generally called collection charges. (85)

exchange controls Various governmental restrictions limiting the right to exchange one nation's currency into another nation's currency.

exchange depreciation The decline in terms of a foreign currency or currencies which a currency experiences. This is frequently caused by the reduction in the base, such as gold, of the currency but may be caused by other factors such as monetary funds, stabilization or legislation.

exchange distribution A method of disposing of large blocks of stock on the floor of the Stock Exchange. Under certain circumstances, a member-broker can facilitate the sale of a block of stock by soliciting and getting other member-brokers to solicit orders to buy. Individual buy orders are lumped together and crossed with the sell order in the regular auction market. A special commission is usually paid by the seller; ordinarily the buyer pays no commission. (2)

Exchange Equalization Fund The stabilization fund of Great Britain, originally established for the purpose of helping the British Treasury meet the problems which arose from the suspension of gold in 1931. Was of great value during World War II in meeting the needs of the British Empire which resulted from the financial dislocation. See Exchange Stabilization.

exchange for futures The transfer to the seller of a cash commodity of a long futures position by the buyer of a cash commodity. The difference between the spot and futures contract is settled with cash.

exchange for physical See Exchange of Spot or Cash Commodity for Futures.

exchange of securities Normally occurs in a merger, or consolidation, of two corporations, whereby the securities of one firm are exchanged for those of another on a mutually agreeable basis. (105)

exchange of spot or cash commodity for futures The simultaneous exchange of a specified quantity of a cash commodity for the equivalent quantity in futures, usually due to both parties carrying opposite hedges in the same delivery month. Also known as "Exchange for physical" or against actuals. In grain the exchange is made outside the "pit". (9)

exchanges Clearing House exchanges. Checks and similar drafts which are collected through a clearing house.

exchange stabilization (or) equalization fund The sum of money, or the organization handling the money, used to purchase or sell gold, foreign exchange and domestic currency for the purposes of keeping the exchange rate within a very limited range. See Exchange Rate.

exchequer That account of the Chancellor of the Exchequer of the United Kingdom which is used to handle the revenues and payments of the kingdom. The account is maintained in the Bank of England. It roughly corresponds with the United States Treasury Department's account in the twelve Federal Reserve Banks.

ex-coupon 1. A security without the interest coupon, i.e., the current interest coupon has been detached. 2. A bond which has had its next maturing coupon detached and is sold on a "flat" basis because of this. (105)

exculpatory provision A provision in a will or trust instrument relieving or attempting to relieve an executor or trustee from liability for breach of trust; sometimes called an immunity provision.

ex-dividend When a dividend is declared by a corporation, it is payable on a designated date to stockholders of record as of a stated date. When stock is sold prior to the stated date, the dividend belongs to the buyer and not to the seller. When the stock is sold subsequent to the stated date and prior to the date of payment, the dividend belongs to the seller and not to the buyer. It is then said to sell ex-dividend. (The New York Stock Exchange, however, has a special rule to the effect that the stock becomes ex-dividend three business days prior to the stated date. Most other Exchanges follow the New York rule.) (74)

ex-dividend date The day on and after which the right to receive a current dividend is not transferred automatically from seller to buyer. (74)

execute Accomplish, to carry out, to do. (93)

execute an order The fulfillment of a buy or sell order. Each execution must be accompanied by a confirmation from the broker to the customer. (105)

executor An individual or a trust institution nominated in a will and appointed by a court to settle the estate of the testator. If a woman is nominated and appointed, she is known as an executrix. (88)

executor de bonis non The individual or corporation named in the will to take over and complete the settlement of an estate in those cases in which the original executor, for one reason or another, has failed or been unable to do so. Unless the testator himself names such a successor executor, the court appoints an administrator de bonis non. (74)

executor de son tort One who, without legal authority, assumes control of a decedent's property as if he were executor and thereby makes himself responsible for what comes into his possession. (74)

executor of an estate The person appointed by a testator to execute his will or to see its provisions carried into effect after his decease. (35)

executor's deed A deed given by an executor. (54)

executrix A woman appointed to perform the duties of an executor. (5)

exemplified copy A copy of a record or document witnessed or sealed certified to as required by law for the purpose of a particular transaction. (74)

exempt Free from burden or liability. (5)

exempt security The Securities Act of 1933 requires all new issues to comply with the regulations of the act with certain exemptions. Those securities are known as Exempt Securities and include issues of governmental units in the United States and their instrumentalities, national banks, federal savings and loan associations, common carriers, court approved certificates of receivers or trustees in bankruptcy, intra-state issues sold to residents of that state, insurance policies, most common carriers and securities of eleemonsynary institutions.

exercise The action by a stockholder in taking advantage of a privilege offered to him by the company, such as, subscribing to additional stock, bonds, or converting securities into another form. (105)

ex gratia payment Settlement of a claim, which the insurance company does not think it is legally obligated to pay, to prevent an even larger expense of defending itself in the courts. Strike suits or threats of suit may result in an ex gratia payment. (5)

exhaust price That price at which a broker is forced to sell a security which was margined and subsequently has dropped in price. Prior to reaching the exhaust price, the broker will request his customer to provide additional margin or cover. In the event that the customer does not provide the needed margin, the security will be sold by the broker when the stock drops to the exhaust price so that the broker himself will not suffer any loss.

exhibit 1. A balance sheet or other principal financial statement. 2. Any statement or other document that accompanies or is part of a financial report. (29)

ex-interest Without interest, sometimes referred to as Flat. (105)

expansion That phase of a business cycle or fluctuation in which there is an increase in industrial activity. Periods of expansion are associated with recovery and prosperity.

ex parte Upon, from, or in the interest of, one side only. Ordinarily implies a hearing or examination in the presence of, or on papers filed by one party and in the absence of, and often without notice to, the other. (19, 35)

expense In its broadest sense it includes all expired costs which are deductible from revenues. Narrower, use of the term refers to such items as operating, selling or administrative expenses, interest, and taxes. (17)

expense account An account carried in the general ledger where all operating expenses are deducted from gross profits, or the total of all income accounts, to compute the net profit of the business for the period. Large banks have a very detailed expense ledger as a subsidiary to the general ledger. Large banks also maintain an expense distribution and analysis section where expenses are distributed to departments and analyzed for control purposes. Expenses should not be confused with capital expenditures, where funds are invested in fixed assets. Expenses are the regular charges incurred in doing business. Salaries, payroll, stationery and supplies, heat, light, and power, rent paid on equipment, etc., are expense items. (1)

expense, accrued Expenses which have been incurred but not as yet taken up on the formal books of account. This condition is common at the close of an accounting period when anticipated. Invoices covering expense items have not been received. At that time, the following entry is made to accurately reflect expenses:

      Expense Accounts   XX
      Accrued Expense   XX

This entry is reversed after the books have been closed. (28)

expense, administrative Expenses chargeable to the managerial and policy phases of the company. These are distinct from manufacturing expense (burden charges) and selling expense. They include: financial expenses, officers' salaries, general accounting expenses, etc. (28)

expense constant A flat amount added to the premium of a risk below the experience rating size. Designed to offset the fact that the expense loading on the smaller risk does not yield enough money to cover the minimum cost of issuing and servicing a policy. This term is found in a workmen's compensation policy. The charge is supposed to equate the cost to the insurance company if issuing and servicing the policy of a very small risk. (50+)

expense, controllable An Expense incurred by the authority who will ultimately be charged with it. For example, the foreman controls the number of material move men (but not their rate) in his department; he controls the allowable spoilage, etc. Generally speaking, Controllable Expenses are variable. See Expense, Variable. (28)

expense, direct Any expense which can be directly charged to the department or cost center which incurred it. For example, machine repairs and set-up time are charged directly on job tickets. Indirect material is charged directly on a material requisition, etc. (28)

expense, distribution (primary) The allocation of total indirect expenses (see Expense, Indirect) by expense accounts to the detail expense accounts of both direct departments and indirect departments. For example, total rent to individual departments on the basis of departmental fixed asset valuation, total medical expense on the basis of number of employees in each department, etc. (28)

expense distribution (secondary) The allocation of the total cost of operating indirect departments to the benefiting direct departments. For example, the total cost of operating the power house is distributed to the direct departments on the basis of connected horsepower, the total cost

of the maintenance department is distributed on a combination of floor area and number of employees, etc. (28)

expense, fixed Expenses which remain the same regardless of fluctuations in factory output or plant capacity. For example, rent, property insurance, depreciation, etc. Generally speaking, these expenses are uncontrollable. (28)

expense, indirect Expenses such as rent, taxes, insurance, etc., which cannot be specifically charged to the department or cost center which benefit from them. They are generally accumulated for a period and the total then distributed on some equitable basis. See Expense Distribution, Primary. (28)

expense, uncontrollable An expense which is not under the direct control of the authority who will ultimately be charged with it. For example, the foreman has no control over the amount of rent, taxes, depreciation, etc. charged to his department. Generally speaking, uncontrollable expenses are fixed. See Expense, Fixed. (28)

expense, variable Expenses which vary with the level of factory output or plant capacity. For example, power, oils and lubricants vary with the number of machines in operation; material moving and compensation insurance vary with the number of employees in the department, etc. Generally speaking, variable expenses are controllable. See Expense, Controllable. (28)

expense, variance The difference between actual and budgeted expense. (28)

expiration notice Slip or letter advising the customer, broker, or agent that a policy will terminate in the near future. (5)

ex-pit transaction The purchase of cash commodities at a specified basis outside of the designated exchange.

explicit interest The amount of money or goods paid on a loan.

export credit A commercial letter of credit issued for the purpose of financing a shipment of goods to a foreign country. (85)

Export-Import Bank That governmental agency formed in 1934, and expanded in 1945, to engage in the general banking business but not to compete with private banking activities in helping exports and imports of the United States. Most of such help is tied to price-supported agricultural products.

export license The document issued by a government which will permit a stated amount of the described commodity to be exported. Items such as gold, arms, munitions and drugs may require such a license.

Express Company money order Those money orders, similar to postal money orders and bank money orders. See those terms. In the United States these orders are sold by hotels, travel agencies and banks as agents for the American Express Company. The express money orders have an advantage over postal money orders in that they have no limitation on the number of endorsements and on time of presentation.

express trust A trust stated orally or in writing, with the terms of the trust definitely prescribed; to be distinguished from a resulting trust and a constructive trust. (74)

ex-rights Without the rights. Corporations raising additional money may do so by offering their stockholders the right to subscribe to new or additional stock, usually at a discount from the prevailing market price. The buyer of a stock selling ex-rights is not entitled to the rights. See Ex-Dividend; Rights. (2)

extend To stretch out. (93)

extinguishment fund A Sinking Fund.

extra The short form of "extra dividend." A dividend in the form of stock or cash in addition to the regular or usual dividend the company has been paying. (2)

extra dividend A supplementary dividend in cash or stock. See Extra. (105)

extrapolation A method of estimating a value which is outside the known values.

ex-warranty Without warrants. A security trading ex-warrants indicates that the warrants have been retained or exercised by the seller. (105)

F

F. When printed on the ticker tape following the symbols of a foreign stock, it indicates that it has been sold by a foreign owner. (105)

F. Franc, Flat, folio.

F. & A. Semi-annual interest payments or dividends in February and August.

FCS. Francs.

FCU Federal Credit Unions. (67)

Fd. Fund.

Fdg. Funding.

F.D.I.C. The initials of the Federal Deposit Insurance Corporation. This corporation guarantees the deposits of each depositor of a member bank up to $40,000.00. (83)

F.F. & C. Full faith and credit.

F.H.A. Federal Housing Administration. A government agency formed to carry out the provisions of the National Housing Act approved June 27, 1934. The F.H.A. promotes the ownership of homes, and also the renovation and remodeling of residences through government guaranteed loans to home owners. (1)

F.H.A. Mortgage Loan A loan insured against loss by the Federal Housing Administration. (89)

FHLBB Federal Home Loan Bank Board.

F.I.C.A. Federal Insurance Contributions Act. (5)

Fid. Fidelity, fiduciary.

Fin. Finance, financial.

F. M. A. N. Quarterly interest payments or dividends in February, May, August and November.

F.N.M.A. Federal National Mortgage Association; Fannie May. (5)

Fol. Folio, following.

Forg. Forgery.

F.P. Faithful performance. (5)

Fr. Franc.

F.R.B. Federal Reserve Bank.

FRS Federal Reserve System.

F/S Financial statements. (5)

F.S.L.I.C. Federal Savings and Loan Insurance Corporation. (5)

F.T.C. Federal Trade Commission. (5)

F.X. Foreign Exchange.

FY Fiscal Year. (67)

FYI For your information. (67)

face amount (face value) Principal sum of an instrument.

face of the note The amount stated on the note. It is also known as the principal. (73)

face value The par value, the monetary value, or the principal value of an instrument is known as its face value. It is upon the face value that interest is computed on interest-bearing obligations, such as notes, bonds, mortgages, etc. The individual or other legal entity who issued a note, bond, or other obligation, contracts to repay the face value of the obligation at maturity. Bonds, as an example, when issued, are purchased either at a premium, at par (or face value), or at a discount. The theory of bonded indebtedness is, that regardless of what the purchase price may have been, the confidence in the maker should be such that the market value and the face or par value should converge and meet at maturity, when the face value of the obligation is to be paid in full. (1)

facilitating agency Organization which assists but does not take title to goods. A stock exchange or common carrier is a facilitating agency.

facsimile A system of telecommunication for the transmission of fixed images with a view to their reception in a permanent form. (63)

facsimile broadcasting station A broadcasting station utilizing facsimile primarily. (63)

factor 1. A type of commission merchant who often advances funds to the consignor, identified chiefly with the raw cotton and naval stores trade. 2. A specialized commercial banker, performing the function of financing for producers of and dealers in many varieties of products and occasionally combining this function with that of selling.
    Comment: The term "factor" was formerly synonymous with "commission merchant." (13)

factorage The earnings or commission of a factor.

factor cost The market price of a product from which are deducted all costs that are not factors of production such as transfer payments and depreciation.

factoring A means of advancing credit whereby the factor purchases at a discount and without recourse the accounts receivable of a firm. The factor assumes complete responsibility for credit investigation and collection.

factors Generally speaking, factors are limited to agents to whom property is consigned for sale. They frequently sell in their own name without disclosing the name of their principal. Within the textile industry, they perform a function known as "factoring". Factoring consists of extending financial services to clients by discounting their notes and by advancing funds upon the delivery of duplicate invoices as evidence of sale and delivery of the goods. Those performing such a factoring service for the textile trade are also known as "textile banks." Factors frequently perform all the accounting functions in connection with accounts receivable, in which case purchasers are notified to remit directly to the factor who reimburses the manufacturer after deducting his "fee" or commission for the services rendered. (1)

factor-78th A method commonly employed by the installment loan and other departments of a bank for computing the amount of interest to be refunded or credited due to a 12-month loan being liquidated prior to maturity. Also, a method used for accruing Earned Discount.

This factor is obtained by adding the consecutive number of months (1,2,3,4, etc.) the loan was originally scheduled to run.

The fractional part of the original interest charge to be refunded can be determined by the use of a special pre-computed chart, or by an accounting machine having the ability to automatically compute and schedule the individual amounts of the refundable interest.

The factors involved for loans of different periods of time are as follows:

Number of months:	Factor:
3	6
6	21
9	45
12	78
15	120
18	171
etc.	

(1)

factory, ledger A subsidiary ledger used to reduce the number of required accounts in the general ledger. It contains all cost, inventory, payroll, and other accounts pertaining to the manufacturing end of the business. It is controlled by a single control ledger account entitled "Factory Ledger." (28)

fair market value A legal term variously interpreted by the courts but in general connoting a price obtainable in the market which is fair in view of the conditions currently existing. A price that would induce a willing seller to sell and a willing buyer to buy. (5, 74)

fair return An income on invested capital used in the activity that will permit the business to raise additional capital for normal growth. Courts have held rates between 5% and 9% on total capital invested in public utilities to be fair.

fair value Under the Investment Company Act, value determined in good faith by the board of directors for those securities and assets for which there is no market quotation readily available. (3)

fallout of bed A sudden and sharp price decline of a security for no apparent reason. (105)

false pretense Refers to any untrue statements or representations made with the intention of obtaining property or money. (52)

false statement A financial statement which is untrue. The use of false financial statements for the purpose of obtaining goods or credit is illegal.

fancies Nickname for widely fluctuating, highly priced stocks. (105)

Fannie Mae Nickname. See Federal National Mortgage Association.

Fas-Cash A copyrighted system designed to expedite the handling of cash by the teller. Currency is precounted and strapped by the teller before banking hours. The currency is strapped in packages of from $2 through $9, and from $10 through $100. This permits the teller to select rapidly nearly any combination of precounted packages of currency, and he is only required to get the correct change from an automatic cashier. Example: A check is cashed for $38.75. The teller selects a $30 and an $8 package of currency and selects 75¢ from the automatic cashier. This is a very fast method of handling customers at the teller's window. (1)

fas price An amount charged an importer which includes such expenses as insurance, warehousing, trucking, and lighterage up to the loading tackle of the ship. All risk of ownership rests with the seller up to the loading on the vessel. (5)

feature Refers to the more active stocks in the general list. (105)

federal bonds The promissory notes of a central government. (59)

Federal Credit Union A cooperative association organized under the Federal Credit Union Act for the purpose of accepting savings from its members, making loans to them at low interest rates, and rendering other financial services to its members.

NOTE: Cooperatives offering similar services also operate under state charters. (1)

Federal Deposit Insurance Corporation A government corporation which insures the deposits of all banks which are entitled to the benefits of insurance under Section 12B of the Federal Reserve Act. The F.D.I.C. was created through the Bank Act of 1933, and was affected by amendments contained in the Bank Act of 1935. The F.D.I.C. is managed by certain members called the Board of Directors. One of the members is the Comptroller of the Currency, and the others are appointed by the President of the United States with the approval of the Senate. The F.D.I.C. was created with an appropriation from the United States Treasury whereby $150,000,000 in capital stock was established and sold to the United States Treasury. In addition to this, each Federal Reserve Bank was required to subscribe to capital stock in the F.D.I.C. equivalent to 50% of the surplus of each Federal Reserve bank as of January 1, 1933.

Every national bank, and state banks that are members of the Federal Reserve System, are required by law to be members of the F.D.I.C. For current specific details, see a copy of the present law pertaining to this Act. (1)

Federal farm loan bonds Obligations on a joint and several basis of the twelve Federal Land Banks which are instrumentalities of the United States Government.

Federal home loan banks The system of regional banks to serve the members of the Federal Home Loan Bank System. The members include Federal Savings and Loan Associations, and other home financing-thrift institutions. The F.H.L. Banks in many ways provide for the S.&L. field as the Federal Reserve Banks provide for the commercial bank field.

Federal Home Loan Bank System A system established in 1932 to serve as a mortgage credit reserve system for home mortgage lending institutions. Members may obtain advances on home mortgage collateral and may borrow from home loan banks under certain conditions. (89)

Federal intermediate credit banks Twelve regional banks established by Congress for the purpose of providing intermediate credit for ranchers and farmers by rediscounting the agricultural paper of financial institutions.

Federal land banks Twelve regional banks established by Congress for such purposes as providing long-term mortgage loans to farmers through National Farm Loan Associations.

Federal National Mortgage Association A secondary mortgage market for F.H.A. and G.I. insured mortgages. (5)

Federal Open Market Committee The Board of Governors of the Federal Reserve System plus the President of the New York Federal Reserve Bank and four of the remaining F.R. Bank Presidents from the other eleven F.R. Banks. The four are chosen on a rotating basis. The committee determines the broad policy of open market operations which are conducted through the FRB of N.Y. as agent for the system.

Federal Reserve Act As amended, this act establishes and provides for the operation of the Federal Reserve System. See Federal Reserve Banks; Federal Reserve System.

Federal Reserve agent The Class "C" director and Chairman of the board of directors of a Federal Reserve District Bank whose major function is safeguarding the collateral for Federal Reserve Notes in his possession.

Federal Reserve banks (Twelve in number plus branches.) Federal banking corporations that deal principally with their member banks and with the government. They deal with the general public only to a limited extent. (85)

Federal Reserve Bank System The Federal Reserve System consists of 12 Federal Reserve banks, their 24 branches and the national and state banks which are members of the system. All national banks are stockholding members of the Federal Reserve Bank of their district. Membership for state banks or trust companies is optional. (83)

Federal Reserve Board The seven-member Board of Governors of the Federal Reserve System located in Washington, D.C. Members are appointed for fourteen-year terms by the President with Senate approval and devote their full time to board business. No two members come from the same district. One term expires every two years. (105)

Federal Reserve Bulletin Monthly publication of the Board of Governors of the Federal Reserve System which contains articles of current interest in banking, interpretation of banking ruling and many statistical series of a banking and economic nature.

Federal Reserve Chart Book Monthly and semi-

annual study published by the Board of Governors of the Federal Reserve System which gives in chart form many series of a banking and economic nature.

Federal Reserve cities The head office and number of each of the twelve Federal Reserve Banks follows: 1. Boston, 2. New York, 3. Philadelphia, 4. Cleveland, 5. Richmond, 6. Atlanta, 7. Chicago, 8. St. Louis, 9. Minneapolis, 10. Kansas City, 11. Dallas, 12. San Francisco. These are known as the twelve Federal Reserve Cities.

Federal Reserve note A noninterest-bearing promissory note of a Federal Reserve Bank issued for general circulation as money and payable to the bearer on demand. (85)

Federal Reserve notes of other banks The total amount of Federal Reserve notes held by Reserve Banks other than the Reserve Bank which issued them. (4)

Federal Reserve routing symbol See A.B.A. Number. (83)

Federal Reserve System The central banking system of the United States, created by an act of Congress (Federal Reserve Act) in 1913. It consists of regional bankers' banks (twelve Federal Reserve banks and their branches), which are controlled and supervised by the Board of Governors in Washington, and national and state member banks. (85)

federals A name given to items drawn on banks in a large city in which a Federal Reserve bank is located, but where these banks do not belong to the city's Clearing House Association. The exchange of these items is accomplished by the other banks in the city clearing these "Federal" items through the local Federal Reserve bank. The Federal Reserve bank therefore performs the function of a clearing house for these banks, by debiting and crediting the exchange balances between the clearing house banks and the "federals." Another name also associated with the same condition is "Non-clearing banks" or "Run banks." (1)

Federal Savings and Loan Association The title given to one of the associations established by the Home Owners Loan Act of 1933 and amended in the Home Owners Loan Act of 1934, approved on April 27, 1934. This Act permitted existing and newly formed mutual savings banks and building and loan associations to come under a federal charter. Under the federal charter, these institutions are governed and regulated by the Federal Home Loan Bank Board. (1)

Federal Savings and Loan Insurance Corporation An organization created in 1934 for the purpose of insuring the shares and accounts of all federal savings and loan associations and of such state-chartered savings and loan associations as apply for insurance and meet the requirements of the corporation. (90)

fee 1. In trust terminology, a fixed amount which a trust institution receives as compensation for its services; to be distinguished from allowance, charge, and commission. 2. An estate of inheritance in real property, sometimes referred to as an estate in fee. (88)

fee checking account A type of checking account

on which a fixed fee is charged for each check written or item deposited. This distinguishes it from the regular checking account plan which sometimes requires a minimum balance and the service charge is computed on a measured activity analysis of the account. The fixed fee may be charged before any checks are written, in which case the book of blank checks is sold to the depositor. The fixed fee may be charged at the time the checks or deposits are posted to the account, in which case the bookkeeper posts the service charge immediately after posting the check or deposit to the account. (1)

fees and royalties from direct investments Are reported by companies with direct investments abroad. They represent income received by U.S. parent companies from their foreign affiliates for patent royalties, licensing fees, rentals, management services, other home office charges, and research and development. (124)

feverish market That condition of a commodity or securities market in which prices are rapidly changing and the direction is uncertain.

FHA loan A mortgage insured by the Federal Housing Administration usually with constant periodic payments which pay the interest and amortize the principal during its term. (5)

FHA mortgage Mortgage made in conformity with requirements of the National Housing Act and insured by the Federal Housing Administration. (121)

fiat money Inconvertible and irredeemable money issued by a government but given the status of being legal tender.

fiduciary An individual or a trust institution charged with the duty of acting for the benefit of another party as to matters coming within the scope of the relationship between them.

The relationship between a guardian and his ward, an agent and his principal, an attorney and his client, one partner and another partner, a trustee and a beneficiary, each is an example of fiduciary relationship. (74)

fiduciary money or standard Currency not secured in full by precious metals. Credit money.

fiduciary relationship A relationship between persons based on trust and confidence. A fiduciary, such as a trustee, owes a duty of upmost good faith.

fiduciary return An income tax return prepared by a fiduciary on behalf of a trust or estate, as distinguished from an "individual return." (74)

fiduciary service A service performed by an individual or a corporation acting in a trust capacity. A banking institution authorized to do a trust business may perform fiduciary services, for example, by acting as executor or administrator of estates, guardian of minors, and trustee under wills. (85)

fifo See First In, First Out.

file A collection of items of information or records of information sequentially arranged for easy reference by some classification. (83)

fill or kill Also called an immediate order, or one that must be cancelled if it can not be executed at the stipulated price upon arrival at an exchange's trading floor. (105)

finance As a noun, the system by which the income of a company is raised and administered. As a verb, to conduct financial operations or to furnish money. Deals with methods for supplying capital needed to acquire, develop and operate real property. (5)

finance and control Planning, directing, and measuring the results of company monetary operations. (20)

finance bill A draft drawn by a bank on a bank in another country against securities held by the foreign bank.

finance capitalism A period in the United States from about 1865 to 1929 when great industrial empires came into the possession of a relatively few bankers and investors.

finance company 1. One that specializes in the purchase of installment contracts from merchants who sell merchandise on the installment plan. 2. A discount house or commercial credit company. At times it is also used to refer to a personal loan company. (73)

finance lease A lease transaction in which the lessor's service is a financial one (the financing of the equipment, directly or through others). The lessee assumes all other responsibilities (maintenance, taxes, insurance, etc.) related to the possession of the equipment. Finance leases tend to be full-payout agreements.

financial counseling Expert advice given to a family with respect to money and credit management. (131)

financial guaranty A type of bond in which the insurer guarantees that it will pay a fixed or determinable sum of money. (5)

financial insolvency That situation in which a firm is not able to pay its debts as they mature even though the assets may exceed the liabilities.

financial investment The purchase of sound stocks or bonds as compared to real investment in a capital asset such as real estate or plant machinery.

financial reports Reports of union financial affairs required to be filed with the Secretary of Labor by the Taft-Hartley Act. (12)

financial services Those financial organizations established to rate securities, publish investor services, etc., such as Moody's Investor's Service and Standard & Poor's Corporation. (105)

financial solvency That situation in which a business is able to meet its current debts with its current assets.

financial statement A summary of figure facts showing the financial condition of a business. It is an itemized listing of assets (what the business owns), liabilities (what the business owes), and net worth of capital account (the owners' equity in the business). A balance sheet of a bank is called a statement of condition. (85)

financier A person who is engaged in financing through underwriting, promoting and lending.

financing The practice of an enterprise selling stocks, bonds or notes; or securing bank loans to raise money for working capital or to get back into satisfactory financial condition. (105)

finder's fee The amount an intermediary between a lender and a borrower obtains for bringing the two together, provided that financing is consummated.

fine metal The degree of purity of precious metals.

finished goods journal A book of original entry that contains a record of the total cost of each job completed. (73)

firm Describes the market position of a security or market average which is holding steady with a tendency to advance. (105)

firm bid or offer In the over the counter market a number of bids are nominal or informational and may vary with the size of the order. To make certain that the bid or offer which is quoted is for a given size transaction the inquirer may request a firm quotation which is binding upon acceptance as distinguished from the informational quotation.

firm-commitment offering An issue whereby the risk of selling the entire issue is assumed by the underwriting brokers. Some agreements specify only a "best efforts" approach without the assumption of risk by the underwriters. (105)

firming of interest rate A period during which interest rates are rising and the supply of money tends to become less plentiful. (103)

firming of the market A period when security prices tend to stabilize around a certain level after a downward movement. (103)

firm price An obligation to the maker of a stated price which he must meet if accepted within a specified time. (105)

first in, first out Accounting method of valuing inventory on the basis of first in, first out. That is, the entire inventory may have been acquired at slightly different prices. The accountant upon receiving the notice of a sale of part of that inventory will compute his cost and profit on the oldest or first price for his mark up.

In periods of inflation this will result in high profits being shown at first (and higher taxes since the replacements will have to be acquired at increased prices). For contrast see LIFO.

first lien The best and highest claim against an asset. Certain legal claims such as taxes and some wages may take precedence over a first lien.

first mortgage A legal instrument that creates or conveys a lien on or a claim against an owner's rights in property prior to a lien created by any other mortgage. See also Junior Mortgage. (89)

first notice day The day notices of delivery of spot commodities can first be made against a futures contract. The day will vary from exchange to exchange and from commodity to commodity.

first preferred stock A preferred stock which receives dividends before other preferred stock of the same corporation, if any, as well as ranking ahead of the common stock. (105)

first teller In those banks which have separate tellers for receiving and paying, the paying teller is at times designated as the first teller.

fiscal agent A bank or trust company acting under a corporate trust agreement with a corporation. The bank or trust company may be appointed in the capacity of general treasurer of the corporation, or may be appointed to perform special functions as fiscal agent. The principal duties of a fiscal agent include the disbursement of funds for payment of dividends, redemption of bonds and coupons at maturity, the payment of rents, etc. (1)

fiscal period Any period at the end of which a unit determines its financial condition, the results of its operations and closes its books.

NOTE: It is usually a year, though not necessarily a calendar year. (29)

fiscal policy In a general sense the government activities concerned with taxes, receipts, debt expenditures, currency, and trust funds. In a more limited sense it is concerned with the policy of the U.S. Treasury whereas the Federal Reserve Board is concerned with monetary policy.

fiscal year A corporation's accounting year. Due to the nature of their particular business, some companies do not use the calendar year for their bookkeeping. A typical example is the department store which finds December 31 too early a date to close its books after the Christmas rush. For that reason many stores wind up their accounting year January 31. Their fiscal year, therefore runs from February 1 of one year through January 31 of the next. The fiscal year of other companies may run from July 1 through the following June 30. Most companies though, operate on a calendar year basis. (2)

Fitch Investor's Service A financial organization, with home office on Wall Street, founded by John K. Fitch in 1913, which rates securities, publishes investor services and supervises investment funds. (105)

fixed capital Capital invested in fixed assets, such as land. buildings, machinery, etc. (1)

fixed charges 1. The financial expenses that must be paid when they become due and payable. 2. Those expenses or charges that are normal for a given type of business, and which must be paid in order to engage in that type of business. Example: Certain enterprises must obtain certain licenses each year in order to begin and continue business. (1)

fixed cost Those indirect or overhead expenses of a business activity which do not vary with the volume of activity. A real estate tax is an example of a fixed cost.

fixed debt A permanent debt extending over a length of time, such as that represented by bonds. (105)

fixed income Any constant income which does not fluctuate over time, such as that from bonds, annuities and preferred stocks. (105)

fixed income security A preferred stock or debt security with a stated percentage or dollar income return. (3)

fixed investment Measures additions to and replacements of private capital brought about through purchase of durable equipment and structures for business and residential purposes.

Fixed investment expenditures are reflected in GNP in two ways. First, capital investment increases GNP by the value of the asset in the period in which the investment is made. Second, the effects of previous years' fixed investments show up in the products produced with the help of the capital. These products are of all types: consumer goods, additional capital goods, exports, and government purchases. (124)

fixed investment trust An investment company established as a nondiscretionary trust and which is limited to a stated and agreed upon list of securities.

fixed liabilities Includes all liabilities which will not mature within the ensuing fiscal period. Example: Mortgages due 20 years hence, bonds outstanding, etc. (1)

fixed price A minimum price below which purchases of a new security issue cannot be made, as established by an underwriter of the new issue. (105)

fixed price contract An agreement by which the buyer pays the seller or producer a stipulated amount.

fixing the price The computation of the price at which a spot commodity will be billed. The price is determined after a call sale permits a differential to be established with a specific futures contract.

fixtures Attachments to buildings which are not intended to be removed and which cannot be removed without damage to the latter.

NOTE: Those fixtures with a useful life presumed to be as long as that of the building itself are considered a part of such buildings; all others are classed as equipment. (29)

flash prices A method used whenever the ticker tape runs five or more minutes late. The latest prices of two groups of 50 stocks are printed at five minute intervals. (105)

flat This term means a bond is being traded without any accrued interest included. It is applied to bonds which are in default of interest. Flat means that the market price is the full price. Income bonds, which pay interest only when earned, are usually traded flat. All other bonds are usually dealt in "and interest," the seller receiving the market price plus interest accrued since the last payment date. When applied to a stock loan, flat means without premium or interest. See Short Sale. (2)

fleece The taking advantage of a poorly informed individual by a person conversant with security market conditions.

flier A speculation to buy or sell short a security in which one does not have any material, factual, objective information such as obtained through security analysis but rather has acted from impulse or rumor.

flight of capital The movement of capital, which has generally been converted into a liquid asset, from one place to another to avoid loss or to increase gain. When war or punitive taxes look probable, the owners of capital will seek to protect it by such devices as conversion and movement.

float Checks, in the process of being collected and converted into cash, which represent funds not available to the bank for investment purposes, although immediate credit is usually given to the depositor. Float is an important factor in analyzing customer accounts in order to compute service charges. (83)

floating capital Capital which is identified as being in the form of current assets rather than fixed assets.

floating currency Is one whose value in terms of foreign currency is not kept stable (on the basis of the par value or a fixed relationship to some other currency) but instead is allowed, without a multiplicity of exchange rates, to be determined (entirely or to some degree)) by market forces. Even where a currency is floating, the authorities may influence its movements by official intervention; if such intervention is absent or minor, the expression "clean float" is sometimes used. (130)

floating debt 1. (Municipal bond terminology.) Temporary or shifting debt that has not been funded on a permanent basis. The term is used in connection with a municipality's current cash deficit or tax anticipation warrants. 2. Liabilities (except bonds) payable on demand or at any early date; for example, accounts payable, bank loans, notes or warrants. See Current Liabilities. (103, 29)

floating supply (Municipal bond terminology.) The overall amount of securities believed to be available for immediate purchase, in the hands of dealers and speculators who wish to sell as distinct from investors who may be willing to sell only for a special reason. (103)

floor The huge trading area where stocks and bonds are bought and sold on the stock exchange. (2)

floor broker Any person who, in or surrounding any pit, ring, post, or other place provided by a contract market for the meeting of persons similarly engaged, engages in executing for others any order for the purchase or sale of commodity or security on or subject to the rules of any contract market and who for such services receives or accepts a prescribed fee or brokerage. (9)

floor partner A brokerage firm partner who is a member of a stock exchange, and transacts his firm's business on the floor of that exchange. (105)

floor plan insurance Protection taken out by finance companies on equipment such as automobiles or electrical appliances which they have financed for retail dealers. The articles are in the possession of the dealer but are collateral for the loan by the finance company. (5)

floor report The confirmation of an executed order on an exchange trading floor such as price, number of shares, and name of the security. (105)

floor trader Any member of the Stock Exchange who trades on the floor for his own account. An exchange member who executes his own trades by being personally present in the pit or place provided for futures trading. (2, 9)

flow chart A visual device which shows the movement of some product, item, authority or other economic factor from one point or place to another. A flow chart of an agricultural product would start at the farm, move to the country elevator, thence to the terminal elevator, to the processor, wholesaler, retailer and consumer.

fluctuation harnessing A term applied to the investment formula known as dollar cost averaging because a constant dollar amount is invested at regular intervals, regardless of price. (105)

fluctuations Refers to the price action of securities, either up or down. (105)

fluid capital See Circulating Capital; Working Capital; Floating Capital.

fluid savings Savings in a liquid form such as cash or demand deposits which may be used at the discretion of the holder.

flurry A movement of short duration but rapid price change for a security or a commodity.

folio column of the account The column that provides space for writing the number of the journal page from which the entry in the account has been posted. (73)

for a turn A speculative transaction made to obtain a quick, and frequently small, profit on the sale of securities.

for cash Cash transactions generally require the purchaser to pay for the product or item prior to delivery. In most cases checks as well as currency are considered to meet the cash requirement though in some business lines transfer of title or possession may be delayed until a check which is tendered as payment has cleared or been collected. In some lines of business, such as security brokerage a "for cash" transaction requires seller to deliver the purchased securities on the same business day as the "for cash" sale.

forced loan A sum of money borrowed against the will or judgment of the lender. A draft, drawn against uncollected funds but honored by the bank on the assumption that the uncollected funds will clear, will become a forced loan if the uncollected funds should not clear for any reason such as forgery or insufficient balance. The bank would then probably attempt to collect from the debtor but, failing to do this, convert the returned draft into a loan by having the bank's client sign a note.

forced sale The act of selling property under compulsion as to time and place. Usually a sale made by virtue of a court order, ordinarily at public auction. (54)

forced sale value Amount that may be realized at a forced sale. That price that could be obtained at immediate disposal. An improper use of the word value. The term forced sale value is used erroneously to designate forced sale price. (54 +)

forecasting Business forecasting is an attempt by economists and managers of business firms to evaluate the forces affecting the economy, an industry, a company, a commodity, nation, or security and on the basis of the evaluation come to some conclusion as to probable movements which may develop in the future. All people and business executives forecast or try to anticipate the future. Some forecasts may be short run, covering a brief span of time, others may be quite extended.

foreclosure The act of selling property under a mortgage, deed of trust, or assignment securing an obligation preparatory to applying the pro-

ceeds of the sale to the liquidation or reduction of the obligation. (74)

foreign agency An agency of a domestically domiciled firm which is located outside the country. The major consideration is that the legal relationship is one of agency as compared to branch or subsidiary operation.

foreign bank Any bank other than the subject bank. Items of other banks included with the bank's are considered to be on a "Foreign Bank." The term may also refer to a banking concern outside the continental limits of the United States. (83)

foreign bill A bill drawn in one state and payable in another state or country.

foreign bill of exchange 1. The system by which the balances arising out of transactions between countries are settled. 2. The currency used in making the settlement. (85)

foreign collections Those bills of exchange which either originated abroad and are import or incoming collections or those which are export or outgoing collections in that they are payable in another country.

foreign company Incorporated or organized under the laws of some other state or territory of the United States, such as a company organized under the laws of Louisiana doing business in Texas. This corporation is a foreign company in Texas. It would be an alien company if it were incorporated in Canada doing business in Texas. The term may also be applied to a company writing or soliciting business in the jurisdiction in which it is not admitted to transact business, in which case such companies are also referred to as nonadmitted. Technically an insurance company chartered in a foreign country is described as an alien company while a company chartered in another state than in which it is doing business is a foreign company. (52 +)

foreign correspondent 1. The firm or individual in a foreign nation which acts for a principal as an agent. 2. A reporter of news from a foreign source.

foreign currency The currency of any foreign country which is the authorized media of circulation and the basis for record keeping in that country. Foreign currency is traded in by banks either by the actual handling of currency or checks, or by the establishment of balances in foreign currency with banks in those countries. (1)

foreign currency account An account maintained in a foreign bank in the currency of the country in which the bank is located. Foreign currency accounts are also maintained by banks in the United States for depositors. When such accounts are kept, they usually represent that portion of the carrying bank's foreign currency account that is in excess of its contractual requirements. (1)

foreign department The section or department of a firm which performs the necessary functions for a firm to engage in foreign activities of a business nature such as exports, imports or foreign exchange.

foreign direct investments The flow of foreign capital into U.S. business enterprise in which foreign residents have significant control.

Hence, the capital movements are regarded as foreign extensions of the management interests of the parent corporation. The distinction between long-term investment in the U.S. is made on the basis of ownership. Investment is considered direct when the foreign individual or company owns more than 25 percent of the U.S. concern.

The flows included in the balance-of-payments report are: a) Short- and long-term funds invested by the foreign parent corporation. b) Transfers by the foreign corporation to the U.S. affiliate (or to U.S. residents as compensation for the acquisition of equity interests) of funds that had been borrowed in the U.S. by the foreign parent or its foreign affiliates.

The flows not included in the balance-of-payments report (although they affect the net worth of the investment) are: a) Depreciation allowances and reinvested earnings of U.S. subsidiaries. b) Changes in U.S. assets that result from political actions or natural causes in the United States. These latter transactions involve no transfer of funds between the foreign parent and its U.S. affiliate. A flow in the opposite direction appears in Direct investments. (124)

foreign exchange 1. The system by which the balances arising out of transactions between countries are settled. 2. The currency used in making the settlement. (90)

foreign exchange broker The individual, firm or bank which engages in the business of buying and selling foreign exchange such as foreign currency or bills.

foreign exchange markets Those in which the monies of different countries are exchanged. Rates of exchange are the prices of currencies quoted in terms of other currencies. As with other organized markets, transactions are either "spot" (for prompt settlement) or "future" (contracted for settlement as a stated future date).

The financial instruments exchanged are all current, that is, money in the form of notes and coin, or bank deposits denominated in different currencies, or near-money in such forms as bank drafts and bills of exchange.

Foreign exchange holdings—sometimes referred to as foreign exchange—are holdings of current or liquid claims denominated in the currency of another country. (124)

foreign exchange rate The price relationship between the currencies of two countries. (85)

foreign inquiry Inquiry made to credit bureau for information on person or firm from other than normal service area of bureau. (26)

foreign items 1. Transit items payable at an "out-of-town" bank. 2. Bills of exchange, checks and drafts, etc., which are payable at a bank outside the jurisdiction of the United States government. (1)

foreign money See Foreign Currency.

foreign trade zone A free port or area where foreign merchandise may be imported without being required to pay duties on the condition that it is not used domestically and is shipped to some other country.

forfeit Lose, let go, as giving up to a creditor some security when an obligation is not met. (59)

forged check One on which the drawer's signature has been forged. (85)

forgery The alteration of any document or instrument with the intent to defraud or prejudice any individual constitutes forgery, which is a statutory crime, punishable by imprisonment. The most common concept of a forgery is false signature placed on an instrument. However, raising the amount, altering the payee, changing the number, or writing a true signature on an instrument known to be false, or changing an entry in a deposit pass book constitutes forgery. (1)

forint Monetary unit of Hungary.

formula clause The provision of a will or trust agreement stating a formula whereby the executor or trustee can determine the federal estate-tax value of property; usually employed in connection with the marital deduction under the Revenue Act of 1954. (74)

formula investing An investment technique. One formula calls for the shifting of funds from common shares to preferred shares or bonds as the market, on average, rises above a certain predetermined point—and the return of funds to common share investments as the market average declines. See Dollar Cost Averaging; Scaling. (2)

forward buying The purchase of an actual or spot commodity in which delivery is for a future or forward date as distinct from a current delivery.

forward commitment Investor's agreement to make or purchase a mortgage loan on a specified future date. (121)

forward exchange A means of hedging against the fluctuation of a foreign exchange rate by purchasing a bill of foreign exchange that is payable at some future or forward period of time.

forward exchange transaction Is a purchase or sale of foreign currency for future delivery. Standard periods for forward contracts are one, three, and six months. (130)

forwarding agent That individual or company which handles the function of collecting and shipping merchandise for others.

forward movement The rising or upward tendency in the price of a security or commodity or an average.

forward sales Sales for shipment or delivery in the future that are not on a standardized futures contract by a trader in cash or spot goods.

forward selling The sale of an actual or spot commodity in which delivery is for a future or forward date as distinct from a current delivery.

foul bill of lading A bill of lading indicating that a damage or shortage existed at the time of shipment. (19)

foundation A permanent body of property established by contributions from one source (as the Carnegie Foundation) or from many sources (as the Cleveland Foundation) for charitable, educational, religious, or other benevolent uses or purposes. See also Community Trust. (74)

founders' shares See Founders' Stock.

founders' stock Stock which is issued to the promoters or founders for their services in forming a new corporation. Also known as deferred stock, or promoter's shares. The meaning in the United States differs somewhat from its use in England in that in the United States certain delayed features of British founders' stock are not commonly used.

fraction A term generally applied to holdings of less than one share, resulting from rights and stock dividends. Since they are not entitled to dividends, they are usually disposed of by sale or rounded out, by the purchase of additional fractions, to full shares. (74)

fractional currency Coins in the United States that have a value of less than one dollar. Also called Fractional Coins or Fractional Money.

fractional lot Less than a round lot. With the exception of stocks traded at post 30, most round lots on the New York Stock Exchange are of 100 shares. A fractional lot would be less than 100 shares.

fractional reserve The present system of commercial banking in the United States in which any bank is legally required to only maintain a part of any deposit in the form of reserves such as till cash or deposits with a central bank. The difference between the required reserves and the actual reserves may then be lent to borrowers.

franc Monetary Unit of Albania, Belgium, France, Luxemburg, and Switzerland.

franchise A legal right extended to a corporation or individual by a governmental agency permitting the holder of the franchise to do something. The right might be for such purpose as to use the property of a city for such purposes as furnishing electricity to the residents of the city. If the holder of the franchise is the only one permitted to do so it then is known as an Exclusive Franchise.

fraud, perpetration of Intentional deception for the purpose of personal gain. (42)

fraudulent Cheating, trickery, deceitful, dishonesty. (93)

free and open market A market in which supply and demand are expressed without restraint in terms of price. Contrast with a controlled market in which supply, demand and price may all be regulated. (2)

free balance The smallest or minimum balance which a bank will permit a checking account to average and still not be charged a service fee. The Free Balance will vary from bank to bank and upon the activity of the account.

free banking Concept that any group of incorporators of a bank that can meet certain standards should be issued a charter. Since 1933 the concept of free banking has been altered to showing necessity for the service.

free coinage The situation where the mint must coin all designated metals presented to the mint for that purpose. There may be a charge for minting the coin, and, in this sense, Free Coinage is not necessarily free of expense.

free crowd That group of brokers in bonds which are traded in the active bond section of the New York Stock Exchange. Also known as the Active Group or Active Crowd.

free economy A term describing the American system of privately owned and operated enterprise, whose prices are set by reasonable competition of supply and demand—free under the rules of law and free within socially accepted limits. (59)

free market The area where buyers and sellers may trade without price or quantity regulations.

free ride The situation where an individual is in a position to take advantage of circumstances to obtain a profit without exposing himself to risk. If an issue is being brought out by an underwriter and stabilized or supported at a higher price than the original offering, knowledge of this will permit an individual to buy at the original price and sell at the higher support price before he has tied up his own funds.

free riding 1. The practice of collecting the proceeds from a very rapid purchase and resale of a security without using any personal funds in the original purchase. 2. The witholding by brokerage firms of offerings of new securities expected to rise to a premium from the underwriter's initial fixed public offering price. 3. A practice prohibited by the NASD whereby a member firm would bypass unfilled orders for a security from the public, to permit sales of that security to preferred individuals. (105)

free silver See Free Coinage.

free working capital Also known as Working Capital or Net Current Assets.

friendly counter A newer trend in bank lobby design. The friendly counter is an open counter where depositors and customers of a bank may transact business with the teller. The counter has no grille work other than a gate that the teller may open for the depositor to pass large packages over the counter. The friendly counter has a ledge constructed over the counter. Forms, working supplies, etc. are under this ledge, and are beyond the reach of persons who might try to perpetrate illegal acts in the bank. (1)

frozen account An account that has been suspended in payment until a court order or legal process again makes the account available for withdrawal. An account which has been attached by court order pending the outcome of a legal action is a frozen account. The account of a deceased person is frozen, pending the disbursement by a court order grant to the new lawful owners of the account. An account is frozen to preserve the existing assets until legal action can determine the lawful owners of the asset where a dispute has arisen regarding the true ownership. (1)

frozen credits Loans which would normally have been called and matured, but, due to economic conditions, it is recognized by the creditor that such a step would precipitate the bankruptcy of the debtor and thus preclude any substantial payment. As a result, such credits may be carried or extended with the hope of liquidation when the debtor has recovered. Also described as Frozen Loans.

frozen out An action taken by one party to a transaction which prevents or forces a withdrawal from that transaction by a second party who is then described as being "Frozen Out."

full faith and credit A pledge of the general taxing power for the payment of obligations.

NOTE: Bonds carrying such pledges are usually referred to as "general obligation bonds" or "full faith and credit bonds". (29)

full faith and credit debt Usually state debt for which the credit of the government, implying the power of taxation, is unconditionally pledged. (7)

full lot A "round" or "board" lot. Generally, 100 shares of stock traded on the New York Stock Exchange.

full stock An equity security with the par value of one hundred dollars.

fully paid stock Legally issued stock for which the corporation has received at least the amount of the par value in goods, services or money.

fully registered A term generally applied to bonds which are registered as to principal and income. In this form, a bond is not negotiable and interest is remitted by the disbursing agent to the registered owners. (74)

functional obsolescence The reduction in the value of a real estate property because that property does not possess the technological features of more efficient or newer property. (5)

fund 1. Monies set aside to meet a future need as Contingency Fund, Mortality Fund, Reserve Fund, Sinking Fund. 2. Cash or currency; to be distinguished from other kinds of property. As distinguished from a reserve, an asset or group of assets segregated for some specified purpose. 3. A sum of money or other resources segregated for the purpose of carrying on specific activities or attaining certain objectives in accordance with special regulations, restrictions, or limitations and constituting an independent fiscal and accounting entity.

NOTE: A fund is both a sum of resources and an independent accounting entity. A self-balancing group of accounts must be provided for each fund to show the assets and other resources on the one hand and obligations, surplus and other credits on the other. Accounts must also be set up to permit the identification of revenues and expenditures and receipts and disbursements with the fund to which they apply. Although the General Fund is available for all legally authorized purposes, the definition also applies to it, for the fund can be used for governmental purposes only and expenditures cannot be made from it without legal authorization. Moreover, frequently the General Fund cannot be used for those purposes for which special funds have been established. (42, 74, 29)

fund accounts All accounts necessary to set forth the financial operations and financial condition of a fund.

NOTE: Sometimes the term is used to denote budgetary accounts as distinguished from proprietary accounts but each usage is not recommended. (29)

fundamental factors Those basic economic conditions such as production, employment and sales which influence the level of business or the stock market. This is to distinguish the market conditions from those which are technical in origin such as a change in margin requirements.

fundamentalist A statistician, or trained financial analyst, who uses mathematical data for developing opinions about the status and future of securities and the general market. (105)

fundamentals Basic underlying economic factors, such as financial conditions, corporate developments, and industrial statistics, used in ascertaining the state of business. (105)

funded debt Usually interest-bearing bonds of a company. Could include long-term bank loans. Does not include short-term loans, preferred or common stock. (2)

funded debts to net working capital Funded debts are all long term obligations, as represented by mortgages, bonds, debentures, term loans, serial notes, and other types of liabilities maturing more than one year from statement date. The funds for paying Funded Debts at maturity normally arise from three sources, namely: refunding (i.e., borrowing new money to re-pay the old), or raising new capital, or accumulating earnings into Working Capital over a period of time. Since the likelihood of obtaining new equity capital or re-funding at maturity date can be affected by a number of variables—such as the prevailing business conditions or the financial condition of the business—analysts tend to compare Funded Debts with Net Working Capital in determining whether or not long term debts are in proper proportion. Ordinarily, this relationship should not exceed 100 per cent. (61)

funded debt unmatured Unmatured debt (other than equipment obligations), maturing more than one year from date of issue. (19)

funded deficit A deficit eliminated through the sale of bonds issued for that purpose. See also Bonds, Funding. (29)

funded insurance trust An insurance trust in which, in addition to life insurance policies, cash and securities have been placed in trust to provide sufficient income for the payment of premiums and other charges on or assessments against the insurance policies. (88)

funded pension plan A systematic method used by the insurer to accumulate the amount or fund which will be needed to meet the claims of the plan. A plan may be funded by purchasing insurance annuity contracts from insurance companies. This is known as an insured plan. It may also be funded by depositing funds with a trustee, frequently a bank. In this case it is known as a self-administered or uninsured plan. (5)

funding 1. Providing for pension or welfare and health benefits by putting aside money over a period of years in a trust account or insurance program. 2. The conversion of judgments and other floating debt into bonded debt. 3. The act of converting a shorter maturity debt into a longer maturity. Some authorities use the term to refer to the conversion of debt into equity but they appear to be in the minority. (12, 29)

funds A sum of money or stock convertible to money; assets. (93)

fungible Interchangeable, such as a certain type and grade of wheat stored in a public elevator. Thus a claim may be settled by tendering the same amount, type, and grade but not necessarily the original material. (5)

future estate of interest Any fixed estate or interest, except a reversion, wherein the right of possession and enjoyment is postponed until some future date or until the happening of some event. See also Remainder; Reversion. (74)

future exchange contract A contract for the purchase or sale of foreign exchange to be delivered at a future date and at a rate determined in the present. (85)

futures Agreements to buy and receive or to sell and deliver a commodity at a future date, with these distinguishing features: 1. All trades in the same contract, such as the grain contract, have the same unit of trading, e.g. 5,000 bushels; 2. The terms of all trades are standardized; 3. A trade, therefore, may be offset later by an opposite trade through the same Clearing member; 4. All trades must be made by open outcry in the pit within the hours prescribed; 5. The contract has a basic grade but more than one grade is deliverable; 6. Delivery is made during a single calendar month; 7. The trades are cleared through a Clearing House daily. (9)

futures commission broker A firm or party engaged in soliciting or accepting and handling orders for the purchase or sale of any commodity for future delivery on or subject to the rules of any contract market and who, in or in connection with such solicitations or acceptance of orders, accepts any money, securities, or property (or extends credit in lieu thereof) to margin any trades or contracts that result or may result therefrom. They must be licensed under the Commodity Exchange Act when handling business in commodities covered thereby. (9)

futures commission merchant See Futures Commission Broker.

futures contract Refers to a contract for commodities which requires delivery on or before a stated month in the future. Similar to a share of stock in some ways in that every futures contract for a specific commodity is identical in its provisions for quantity; for example, cotton is traded in 50,000 pound units; and for quality, where a commodity is separated into grades. (105)

futures exchange A Commodity Exchange in which futures are traded.

futures market A Commodity Exchange in which futures are traded.

G

G.A. General agent; General average. (5)
GAO General Accounting Office.
GC General Counsel. (67)
G.D. Good Delivery.
Gen. Led. General Ledger.
Gen. Mtge. General Mortgage.
"G.I." Loan An abbreviation given to one part of Public Law No. 346 of the 78th Congress, entitled "The Serviceman's Readjustment Act of 1944." This Act, commonly called the "G.I. BILL," offers certain benefits to veterans of certain wars. For current specific information, see a copy of the present law pertaining to this Act. (1)
G/T Gift tax.
G. T. C. Good till cancelled.
Gtd. Guaranteed.

G.T.M. (Good This Month) order An order to be entered on a specialist's books to buy or sell at a specific price limit. Unless executed, changed, or cancelled, the order is effective until the close of business on the last day of the month in which the order was placed. (105)

G.T.W. (Good This Week) order An order to be entered on a specialist's books to buy or sell a security at a specific price limit. The order is effective until the close of business on the last day of the week in which the order was placed, unless executed, changed or cancelled. (105)

Guar. Guarantee.

gambling Random buying and selling of securities without intelligently investigating prospects. (105)

garage, the Brokers' nickname for the annex to the New York Stock Exchange trading floor where Post 30, for inactive stocks, and six of the other eighteen trading posts are located. (105)

garnishment A writ from a court directing one party (the bank) to withhold funds from the party owing (depositor) and to pay such funds to the court or to the plaintiff in the action (the person to whom the depositor is indebted). (83)

gateway A basing point on or near the boundary of a rate or classification territory on which rates are constructed. (19)

gather in the stops Refers to the uncovering of stop orders known to be entered at a certain level in a security. The price of the security can be driven down to this level by continuous selling. When the stop price is reached, these stop orders automatically become market orders to sell which, in turn, may depress the price even more. Traders might use such a situation to their advantage, therefore this practice is closely supervised to prevent manipulation. (105)

general asset currency See Asset Currency.

general audit An audit which embraces all financial transactions and records and which is made regularly at the close of an accounting period.
NOTE: The above definition should not be construed to mean that all the transactions are necessarily examined. The number to be examined will depend on the auditor's judgment in the light of the particular conditions encountered. However, the auditor is expected to certify concerning all of the transactions and records, even though he has examined only some of them, subject to such audit is known as may seem necessary. Such an audit is known as a limited audit; on the other hand, if all transactions are examined the audit is known as a complete audit. (29)

general banking law The banking law of an individual state under which the banks organized in that state are authorized to do business. (85)

general bonded debt All of the outstanding bonded indebtedness of a governmental unit with the exception of utility and special assessment bonds. Each specific type of bond should be set up separately rather than showing all bounded indebtedness under one grouping. (29)

general deposit Those bank deposits of deposit currency or money which are commingled by a bank as distinguished from special deposits which are not commingled and for which the bank acts as a bailee.

general depository A bank which is member of the Federal Reserve System and which is permitted to handle deposits of the United States Treasury.

general fund The fund to which are credited all receipts not earmarked by law for a specific purpose and to which are charged expenditures payable from appropriations and from the proceeds of borrowing. (7)

general gift A gift, by will, of personal property which is not a particular thing as distinguished from all others of the same kind. (88)

general journal A journal in which are made all entries not recorded in special journals. (29)

general ledger The bank auditor's or comptroller's detailed accounting records, the functions of which are: a) To provide in summary form a record of changes in the bank's financial status. b) To provide control accounts for the detailed records maintained by the various operating units of the bank (bookkeeping, loans, and discounts, etc.). c) To provide a basis for statements of condition and operation for the bank's management, supervisory authorities, stockholders, and the public. (83)

general legacy A gift of personal property by will which is not a particular thing as distinguished from all others of the same kind; to be distinguished from specific legacy. (74)

general loan and collateral agreement A continuing agreement under which a broker borrows on the security of stocks and bonds which are listed on an exchange. A Broker's Loan.

general management trust A trust not limited to a specific list of securities in which to invest.

general mortgage bond A bond which is secured by a blanket mortgage on the company's property, but which is often outranked by one or more other mortgages. (2)

general obligation That type of debt which is unsecured and the creditors claim on the debtor is general and subject to such prior claims as mortgages, wages mechanics liens and various taxes.

general obligation bonds Bonds for whose payment the full faith and credit of the issuing body are pledged. More commonly, but not necessarily, general obligation bonds are considered to be those payable from taxes and other general revenues. See Full Faith and Credit. (29)

general obligation special assessment bonds See Special Assessment Bond. (29)

general partnership A firm formed by two or more people, each having the power to bind the firm and all partners by his actions and in which all partners are fully liable for the debts of the partnership.

general power of appointment The power of the donee (the one who is given the power) to pass on an interest in property to whomsoever he pleases, including himself or his estate. See Power of Appointment. (74)

gentlemen's agreement A verbal understanding not enforceable at law between two or more businessmen or firms to engage in certain practices, generally for the purposes of increasing the profit of those members of the agreement.

gestor One who acts for another—in law. (93)

G.I. bill of rights The popular term for those privileges that veterans possess under the Servicemen's Readjustment Act of 1944 as amended. (5)

gift The value of a donated asset acquired without cost to the recipient or regard to its donor. The use of the gift may or may not be restricted. (29)

gift causa mortis A gift of personal property made by a person in expectation of death, completed by actual delivery of the property, and effective only if the donor dies; to be distinguished from gift inter vivos. (74)

gift inter vivos A gift of property between living persons. To make such a gift effective, there must be actual delivery of the property during the lifetime of the donor and without reference to his death. (88)

gift tax A graduated tax imposed by the Federal Government since 1932 and by some states on transfers of property by gift during the donor's lifetime. Gifts, under this law, may include irrevocable living trusts. (74)

gilt-edged High-grade bond issued by a company which has demonstrated its ability to earn a comfortable profit over a period of years and pay its bondholders their interest without interruption. (2)

give The transferring to another; a yielding or bestowing. One of the important words in deeds of conveyance of real estate. (5)

give an indication To express an interest in a new security issue by entering a firm buy order for a stated amount. (105)

give an order An instruction to a broker to buy or sell a security in a certain amount which may, or may not, include specifications of a price or time limit. (105)

give up A term with two different meanings. For one, a member of the Exchange on the floor may act for a second member by executing an order for him with a third member. The first member tells the third member that he is acting on behalf of the second member and gives the second member's name rather than his own. For another, if you have an account with Doe & Company but you're in a town where Doe has no office, you go to another member firm, tell them you have an account with Doe & Company and would like to buy some stock. After verifying your account with Doe & Company, the firm may execute your order and tell the broker who sells the stock that the firm is acting on behalf of Doe & Company. They "give up" the name of Doe & Company to the selling broker. Or the firm may simply wire your order to Doe & Company who will execute it for you. In either case you pay only the regular commission. (2)

give-up order Those securities not accepted for direct sale by a participating underwriter. (105)

going concern An enterprise that is already established and engaged in business. (73)

going-concern value An intangible value said to inhere in an operating plant or common carrier or utility with business established because it is an actual operation, as distinguished from one newly constituted and not yet in operation which has yet to establish its business. (19)

going short The act of selling short a commodity or a security.

gold bar See Bullion. (1)

gold brick 1. In a bullion sense, a bar of gold which is nine tenths fine and which probably is embossed with data such as weight and producer as well as assay.

2. In a derisive sense, a worthless and fraudulent transaction in which an uninformed investor is misled into thinking he is making a very profitable investment when in fact it is not.

gold bullion standard Sometimes called the rich man's standard because the paper currency of the nation which is on the gold bullion standard may be exchanged into gold freely but only in sizeable amounts such as a gold bar which might be worth over $5,000.

gold certificate account Gold certificates on hand and due from the Treasury. The certificates, on hand and due from the Treasury, are backed 100 percent by gold owned by the United States Government. They count as legal reserve, the minimum the Reserve Banks are required to maintain being 25 percent of their combined Federal Reserve note and deposit liabilities. (4)

gold clause See Gold Bond.

gold coinage Since 1934 gold has not been coined nor has it circulated as currency in the United States because of such legislation as the Emergency Banking Acts of 1933 and the Gold Reserve Act of 1934.

gold exchange standard The monetary system in which a nation ties its currency to another nation's gold standard by providing that its currency may be exchanged for the currency of the nation that is on the gold standard. The exchange is pegged at a fixed rate which is maintained by the monetary authorities. This makes the one nation's gold do double duty but will also permit the gold exchange nation to earn interest on funds which are not tied up in gold bullion or coin by purchasing bonds of the nation which is on the gold standard.

gold points The upper and lower limits in the rates of foreign exchange between two nations which are on the gold standard. When these limits or points are reached, it then becomes profitable to ship gold rather than purchase foreign exchange.

gold production The Federal Reserve Bulletin which is issued monthly gives the estimated production of gold in the nations of the free world.

gold reserves That amount of gold either in coin or bullion which is held by a nation's monetary authorities as backing for the currency which it has issued. The Federal Reserve Bulletin which is issued monthly provides an excellent source of authoritative data on gold.

gold settlement fund The Interdistrict Settlement Fund.

gold standard The monetary system in which gold of a stated weight and fineness is designated to be the monetary unit. This unit and multiples of it are coined in unlimited amounts and all other forms of the money in circulation such as silver and paper money may be freely converted into gold at the option of the holder. The gold may be exported or imported without restriction.

gold stock Value of gold owned by the government. (4)

gold supply See Gold Production; Gold Reserves.

gold suspension See Gold Coinage.

gold tranche position in I.M.F. (International Monetary Fund) The gold tranche position in the IMF represents the amount that the United States can draw in foreign currencies virtually automatically from the International Monetary Fund if such borrowings are needed to finance a balance-of-payments deficit. The gold tranche itself is determined by the U.S. quota paid in gold minus the holdings of dollars by the IMF in excess of the dollar portion of the U.S. quota. Transactions of the IMF in a member country's currency are transactions in monetary reserves. When the Fund sells dollars to other countries to enable them to finance their international payments, the net position of the U.S. in the Fund is improved. An improvement in the net position in the gold tranche is similar to an increase in the reserve assets of the United States. On the other hand, when the U.S. buys other currencies from the Fund, or when other countries use dollars to meet obligations to the Fund, the net position of the U.S. in the Fund is reduced. (124)

go long The actual buying of a security for investment or speculation as contrasted with "going short" or selling a security one does not own, or owns but does not deliver. (105)

good delivery A term used to describe the conditions that must exist to effect the transfer of ownership of property by means of an instrument or document bearing evidence of title. These conditions are: 1. that the instrument or document is genuine, 2. that the person making the transfer has title to the property, and 3. that the instrument or document is in negotiable form. (85)

good faith Trust. (59)

good through An order to buy or sell a security at a stipulated price limit which is valid through the close of business on some definite future date, such as this week or this month, unless changed, cancelled or executed. (105)

good till cancelled See Good Until Cancelled.

good until cancelled An order or instruction given by the customer to his broker to be effective until the customer rescinds the order. (G.T.C.)

goodwill An intangible asset that represents the difference between the book value of a business and its purchase (or sale) price when the latter is greater than the book value; an asset representing the value of the proprietorship of a business in excess of the amount of proprietorship appearing on the books; the amount by which the price that a corporation pays for the assets of a business exceeds the proprietary interest of the owners. (73)

go public The public offering of securities for sale to raise money, get a market valuation for the stock, or distribute the holdings of the major stockholders. If the offering is large enough, it may come under Security and Exchange Commission regulation. (105)

go short The selling of a security 'short", i.e., selling a security one does not own, or owns but does not deliver. The opposite of "go long," or buying a security. (105)

gourde Monetary unit of Haiti.

governing committee The title for the governing body of a recognized stock exchange. (105)

government depository Any bank which has been selected and approved to receive deposits of a government or agency of a government. Generally the term is used to distinguish a bank which is designated as a depository for the United States government.

government deposits Funds of the United States government and its agencies (such as the Collector of Internal Revenue, the Post Office Department, the Veterans' Administration, and other departments), which are required to be placed in depositories designated by the Secretary of the Treasury. The depositories are required to deposit securities as collateral for the safekeeping of the government deposits they hold. The securities that are eligible as collateral are published periodically by the Treasurer of the United States. Government obligations, state and municipal bonds, and certain approved rail, public utility, and industrial bonds are the usual listed securities chosen as required collateral for depositories holding government deposits. (1)

governments As used in the United States, all types of securities issued by the federal government (U.S. Treasury obligations), including, in its broad concept, securities issued by agencies of the federal government. (103)

grace See Days of Grace. (1)

grace period Period of time, usually 31 days, following the premium due date during which payment of life insurance premiums may be made without loss or penalty. This privilege is extended to accident health policies held in combination with life insurance. (42)

graduate school of banking A school of advanced study in banking, for bank people of officer rank. (1)

grain bill A bill of exchange which is drawn against grain shipments.

grain exchanges Those commodity exchanges upon which trading in spot and futures of grain takes place.

grain futures See Futures.

grain pit That portion of the trading area of a commodity or grain exchange in which the pit traders or commodity brokers transact their business. The physical appearance is of a series of concentric rings with each ring representing a different contract period.

grandfather clause A clause inserted in legislation which exempts those, who before a specified cutoff date, were engaged in the activities made illegal by the legislation. (128)

grantee A person to whom property is transferred by deed or to whom property rights are granted by means of a trust instrument or some other document. (88)

grantor A person who executes and delivers a deed or other instrument by which property rights are conveyed or otherwise transferred to another. The instrument is usually under seal. The grantee is the person to whom the property rights are granted. (31, 92)

gratuitous coinage The monetary system of unlimited coinage at no expense to the owner of the bullion which is presented for coinage at the mint. In contradistinction, seigniorage coinage results in a profit to the mint on the coins minted.

gravelled The term for "bottom out" on the London Stock Exchange. Means the gradual leveling of market prices after a relatively extended decline. (105)

graveyard market Describes a market situation in which those who are in can't get out, and those who are out don't care to get in. (105)

gray market A legal market in which goods in short supply can be purchased at premiums over normal trade prices.

greenbacks Technically only the inconvertible notes issued during the Civil War period which were legal tender for all public and private debts except interest on national debt or import duties. Today, the term is used to refer to any of the paper money issues of the Federal Reserve banks or the United States Treasury.

Gresham's Law This term comes from a principle set forth by Sir Thomas Gresham, who was Master of the Queen's Mint in the reign of Queen Elizabeth. It is known in economic circles as "Gresham's Law." The general theory is that if two kinds of money of equal nominal value are in circulation, the general public may prefer one over the other, because of metal content or because one is more easily mutilated or debased, and will tend to hoard the "good money" and spend the "bad money." This drives the "good money" out of circulation, while keeping the "bad money" or inferior money in circulation. The term also applies to available balances in depositor's account. (1)

gross bonded debt The total amount of direct debt of a governmental unit represented by outstanding bonds before deduction of Sinking Fund assets. See Direct Debt. (29)

gross earnings The total income of a business, usually segregated as to types in financial income statements. (1)

gross estate All of a person's property before debts, taxes, and other expenses or liabilities have been deducted; to be distinguished from net estate which is what is left after these items have been taken into account. (74)

gross income Used as the equivalent of revenue; in public utility practice it is commonly used in referring to net income before deducting interest and other income charges. (17)

gross income, estimated The total anticipated earnings from property without deduction for vacancies, uncollectable rents, etc. (89)

gross income multiplier A figure by which effective gross income is multiplied to obtain an amount that indicates the capital value of property. (89)

gross interest The total price paid for the use of a thing which includes the cost of the capital and the cost of the administration of the transaction.

gross lease A lease of property under which the lessor agrees to meet all charges which would normally be incurred by the owner of that property. (54)

gross national product Expresses in dollars the market value of goods and services produced by the Nation's economy within a specified period of time. It is almost always estimated for a calendar or fiscal year, or expressed at an annual rate. Raw materials, components, and intermediate products are not counted separately in GNP. However, their value is included in the value of finished goods sold to consumers and governments, in investment goods sold to business, or in inventory accumulation. GNP is a "gross" measure because no deduction is made to reflect the wearing out of machinery and other capital assets used in production. Net national product is estimated by subtracting capital consumption allowance from GNP. (124)

gross profit Operating revenue less the cost of goods sold. (17)

gross profit on sales The amount by which the net sales exceed the cost of the merchandise sold. (73)

gross rate See Flat Rate. (50)

gross receipts The same as gross revenues of a business, or total receipts before deducting expenses. (105)

gross revenue Total revenue from all sources before deduction of expenses incurred in gaining such revenue. (54)

gross sale The total of the sale before subtraction of such things as returns, allowances, and taxes. (54)

gross savings by individuals Consists of the current savings of individuals, nonprofit institutions and private pension, health, welfare and trust funds. Included are all personal savings (see definition below) plus changes in holdings of government insurance and consumers' durables and without deduction for depreciation on individual's homes and other durables. This series also differs from personal savings in that it excludes the nonfinancial investments of unincorporated business and farms. (7)

gross variance The total difference between actual and standard attainment under a Standard Cost System. Gross Variance is generally broken down into the Volume and Efficiency components. (28)

gross yield The return obtained from an investment before deduction of costs and losses involved in procuring and managing the investment. See Net Yield. (89)

group banking A term used to describe a form of banking enterprise whereby a group of existing banks form a holding company. The holding company supervises all the banks in the group, and co-ordinates the operations of all banks in the group through uniform procedures. Each bank in the group has its own directorate and

group of officers, with the holding company having a staff of officers and employees to carry out the function of the holding company. A majority of the capital stock of each bank in the group is owned by the holding company. (1)

growth rate Percentage of appreciation estimated for a property (as in securities), times the FMV, divided by the owner's equity. (National economic growth rate for past five years has been in excess of two per cent per year.) (120)

growth stock Stock of an issuer which has shown better than average growth in earnings and is expected to continue to do so—either through discoveries of additional resources, development of new products or expanding markets. (3)

guarani Monetary unit of Paraguay.

guarantee To make oneself liable for the debt of another. (93)

guaranteed account An account, the prompt and full payment of which is guaranteed by a responsible agency or person. Usually guaranteed accounts are those for minors whose legal credit responsibility is deemed insufficient for granting unsupported credit or individuals whose payment record or other factors make necessary the guarantee of a more responsible person. (26)

guaranteed debt Obligations of certain semi-public corporations which are guaranteed by the federal government as contingent liabilities. (7)

guaranteed deposits Prior to the establishment of the Federal Deposit Insurance Corporation in 1935 some states had systems of guaranteed bank deposits. Since 1935 the F.D.I.C., an instrumentality of the United States government has insured limited amounts of deposits in those banks which have applied for such insurance coverage and have met their standards. The vast majority of commercial and mutual savings banks are under the F.D.I.C. program.

guaranteed interest 1. Rate of interest return specified in the policy as the rate at which reserves will be accumulated. 2. Rate of interest paid on funds deposited with the company, either for advance premium deposits or in accordance with the Settlement Options. (42)

guaranteed letter of credit A term used to describe those travelers' letters of credit or commercial letters of credit where the party requesting the credit issuance does not pay the bank in cash for the equivalent amount of the credit upon its issuance. Reimbursement to the bank is guaranteed by the applicant for this accommodation and is often backed by collateral security or the merchandise itself. (1)

guaranteed mortgage A mortgage on which there is a guarantee of payment of principal or interest or both. In years prior to 1930 this was frequently done by a mortgage guarantee corporation. Today most such mortgages are of the Federal Housing Administration or Veterans Administration variety. (5)

guaranteed stock A form of stock on which the dividends are guaranteed by some company other than the issuer. Such stocks are confined almost entirely to the railroad field. (74)

guarantee of signature A certificate affixed to the assignment of a stock certificate or registered bond or to other documents by a bank or stock exchange house, vouching for the genuineness of the signature of the registered holder. (74)

guarantees against price decline Guarantees given by a manufacturer to distributors that if his price to them declines within a given period after purchase, he will reimburse them for the amount of the decline on remaining stocks. (24)

guaranty A written promise by one person (the guarantor) to be liable for the debt of another person (the principal debtor) in the event that the principal debtor fails to perform his obligation and provided the guarantor is notified of that fact by the creditor. A guaranty must be in writing to be enforceable at law. (85)

guaranty fund A fund which a mutual savings bank in certain states must create through subscriptions or out of earnings, in order to meet possible losses resulting from decline in value of investments or from other unforeseen contingencies. In other states such a fund is known as the surplus fund. (90)

guaranty stock Basic stock which is not withdrawable and which protects the interest of all other investors against losses. (31, 92)

guardian An individual or a trust institution appointed by a court to care for the property or the person (or both) of a minor or an incompetent person. When the guardian's duties are limited to the property, he is known as a guardian of the property; when they are limited to the person, he is known as a guardian of the person; when they apply both to property and to the person, he is known merely as a guardian. In some states the term committee, conservator, curator, or tutor is used to designate one who performs substantially the same duties as those of a guardian. (74)

guardian ad litem A person appointed by court to represent and defend a minor or an incompetent person in connection with court proceedings; sometimes called a special guardian. (74)

guardian de son tort One who, although not a regularly appointed guardian, takes possession of an infant's or an incompetent person's property and manages it as if he were guardian, thereby making himself accountable to the court. (74)

guardianship account An account in the name of a guardian who acts on behalf of and administers the funds for the benefit of the ward. (90)

guilder Monetary unit of Netherlands.

gutter market The outdoor securities market that developed when the exchange was closed during WWI in 1914. Business was conducted on New Street near the New York Stock Exchange building. (105)

H

HHFA Housing and Home Finance Agency.

H.H.G. Household goods. (5)

H in D.C. Holder in due course.

H.O. Home Office, Head Office.

HOLC Home Owners' Loan Corporation. Now defunct.

Hon'd. Honored.

habeas corpus A common-law writ by which one restrained of liberty is brought before a court for judicial inquiry as to the lawfulness of his restraint. (93)

haggle To be difficult in bargaining. A situation in which the purchaser offers a low price and the seller asks a high price and, through bargaining, a third price somewhere between the two is arrived at to the agreement of the buyer and the seller. (93)

half stock A common stock or preferred stock having a par value of fifty dollars.

hallmark The indented mark made on gold and silver which shows the degree of purity and fineness of the metal.

hammer Selling pressure frequently accompanied by short sales.

hand signals System used by some of the oldtime brokers on the American Stock Exchange to communicate executions and quotations to their clerks. This practice originated from the days of the outdoor "curb market." (105)

hand-to-mouth operation The technique of operating a business with the smallest amount of goods, labor, machinery, capital and other facilities adequate to take care of current and immediate requirements.

hang-out-loan A loan whose term is longer than the lease.

hard currency See Hard Money.

harden A firming of prices of stocks or commodities after a period in which prices have declined.

hard money Has three different meanings. The context will indicate which one to use. 1. A situation in which interest rates are high and loans are hard to arrange. 2. Metallic currency. 3. A nation's currency which is desired by foreigners in lieu of a "soft" currency which may be the domestic or other foreign currency. In recent years the United States Dollar, Swiss Franc, Portuguese Escudo and the West German Mark have been the major hard currencies or hard monies.

hard spot A security or commodity which either has advanced in price or stayed stable during a market trading period characterized by a general softness or decline in average prices.

head office Principal office in which executive and supervisory offices are located. Need not be the Home Office. (42)

head teller A teller in a bank who sometimes has the title of assistant cashier. The head teller is usually custodian of the reserve cash in the bank's vault. It is his responsibility to see that an "economical" quantity of cash is on hand at all times to meet the normal demands of the banks customers. It is his responsibility to assemble the cash figures for all tellers at the end of the business day, and prepare the cash report for the general ledger. He is also responsible for the work of all tellers in the bank, and he must recount cash for a teller who comes up with a difference at the end of the day. He must fully report any overage or shortages that may appear, and assist where possible to locate the difference. (1)

heart attack market Refers specifically to the market's reaction after President Eisenhower's heart attack in 1955. When the Dow-Jones Industrial Average dropped 31.89 points, or 6.5%. (105)

heavy market A market where there is an apparent number of selling orders overhanging the market without a corresponding amount of buying orders. (9)

hedge To offset. Also, a security which has offsetting qualities. Thus, one attempts to "hedge" against inflation by the purchase of securities whose values should respond to inflationary developments. Securities having these qualities are "inflation hedges." See Arbitrage; Puts and Calls; Selling Against the Box; Short Sale. (3, 2)

hedging The sale of futures against the physical commodity or its equivalent as protection against a price decline; or the purchase of futures against forward sales or anticipated requirements of the physical commodity as protection against a price advance. (123)

heir A person who inherits real property; to be distinguished from next of kin and from distributee. An heir of the body is an heir in the direct line of the decedent. A son, for example, is the heir of the body of his father or mother. See also Collateral Heir; Direct Heir; Next of Kin; Heir at Law. (74)

heir at law An individual who has been designated by a will, or by a legal authority in the event of an intestate estate, to receive some or all of an estate of a deceased person.

hereditament Any type of property which may be inheritable, including such things as real and personal property, as well as corporal and incorporal property. (54)

hidden assets Those assets publicly reported at different value than their true worth. May involve the risk of tax penalty as well as being merely misleading. (105)

hidden inflation That phase of inflation which is not revealed by economic indicators. Generally, hidden inflation takes the form of a reduction in quality. A price index might include an air conditioning unit at the same price for two different dates. If on the first delivery date, installation and service for a period of time were included but were discontinued at the second date hidden inflation would have taken place, or the unit could have been constructed of prime grade materials at the first time the index was used and of inferior materials and workmanship at the later date.

hidden tax A governmental levy of which the ultimate user is unaware. Generally, an indirect tax.

higgling See Haggle.

high credit Highest amount of credit extended to particular customer at one time. (26)

high finance 1. Very complicated financial transactions such as associated with recapitalization of a complicated corporate structure as distinguished from low or simple financial transactions such as a small bank loan. 2. Borrowing to the maximum of one's credit. 3. The use of others funds in a speculative way which may

result in a loss to the owner of the funds.

high grade Those securities, commodities and things which are above average in quality.

high volume accounts An account whose activity is so unusually large as to warrant special handling. (83)

hi-lo index A moving average of individual stocks that reach new highs and new lows each day. Often indicates a change in the market that some of the other market indicators will not show. Variations in the average of the new highs and lows may indicate a deteriorating or rebounding market in general while an average such as the Dow-Jones Industrials might show a neutral or even opposite action in the Blue Chip issues. (105)

hit the bid An instruction by a client to his broker to sell at the highest quoted bid price for a security rather than to wait for a better bid and perhaps have the old bid filled, lowered, or cancelled. (105)

hoarding The acquisition and maintenance of goods by an individual, family or company at a level above their normal rate of use. It may be caused by fear of a later scarcity of the item or of an increase in price.

hokey Slang term for Home Owners Loan Corporation. Now defunct.

hold A term used to indicate that a certain amount of a customer's balance is held intact by the bookkeeper until an item has been collected, or until a specific check or debit comes through for posting. (83)

holder in due course As defined in the Uniform Negotiable Instrument Act: — "A holder in due course is a holder who has taken the instrument under the following conditions: 1. That it is complete and regular upon its face; 2. That he became a holder of it before it was overdue, and without notice that it had been previously dishonored, if such was the fact; 3. That he took it in good faith and for value; 4. That at the time it was negotiated to him, he had no notice of any infirmity in the instrument, or defect in the title of the person negotiating it." See Negotiable Instrument. (1)

holder of record The owners of a corporation's securities as they appear in the records of the firm's transfer agent on a certain date. These individuals or organizations are then entitled to any benefits or dividends declared. (105)

holding company A corporation which exercises control over other companies through title to their securities, primarily voting issues. (19)

holding company affiliate A legal term fully defined in the Banking Act of 1933. Generally, it pertains to any organization which owns or controls any one bank either through stock ownership or through any means that allows it to elect a majority of the bank's directors. (128)

holding company (multiple-bank) A bank holding company, however defined, that owns or controls two or more banks. (128)

holding company (one-bank) At present there is no legal definition of a one-bank holding company. A very broad definition would be any company that owns or controls a single bank. Several alternative legal definitions have been proposed in the bills now pending before Congress. One would simply replace the words "each of two or more banks" with the words "any bank" in the present legal definition of a "bank holding company." Others would define a "single-bank holding company" as a company that owns or controls 51 percent or more of the stock of a single bank. (128)

holding the market A stabilization or support of a particular security or commodity. The Securities Exchange Commission considers attempts to manipulate prices by "holding" or "stabilization" to be illegal with the exception of reported stabilization of a new issue which has been cleared by the Securities Exchange Commission.

hold-overs A term used, usually in large banks, to describe a portion of work that has to be processed by a twilight shift or a night force. The forty-hour work week makes it frequently necessary for the bank to employ three shifts. Since the business day starts officially at midnight, work which has not been processed by the twilight force is "held over" to the night force, who start processing the remaining work. The work, for control purposes, is credited to the twilight force, and re-charged as "hold-overs" to the night force. (1)

hold the line As used in price stabilization it means the use of many devices to stop price increases.

holographic will This type of will is written entirely in the handwriting of the testator but is not witnessed. Although the holograph will is valid in some states, it is invalid in the majority of jurisdictions and should be avoided.

home debit A check or draft drawn upon a bank and presented to the same bank for deposit or payment. A self-check.

home loan bank See Federal Home Loan Banks.

Home Loan Bank Board This board roughly parallels for the Federal Home Loan Bank System the functions of the Board of Governors of the Federal Reserve Bank System.

homestead An artificial estate in land devised by the sovereign federal or state government to protect the possession and enjoyment of the owner against the claims of his creditors by withholding the property from the execution and forced sale so long as the land and building are occupied as a home. From one state to another the protection of the possessions that are considered as part of the homestead varies. (5)

honeycombed with stops A market where many stop orders have been entered. (105)

honor 1. To accept a time draft or other time instrument when it is presented to the drawee for acceptance. 2. To pay a check or demand draft when it is presented to the drawee for payment. A bank honors a check when it pays the instrument. Items which are not so accepted or paid are said to be dishonored. See Dishonor. (90)

honored A term, when it refers to a draft or a note, meaning that the paper was either accepted or paid. (73)

hot issue Refers to a new issue, or one being initially offered for public sale, that has a great demand. Usually such an issue will rise to a

premium and the original holders have an opportunity for quick profit. (105)

hot money Funds which move from investment situation or institution to investment situation or institution in a short period of time generally to obtain a higher rate of return or greater safety and at times to avoid taxes or regulation. It may also be a designation for currency which was illegally acquired and subject to being traced.

hot stuff An expression for good selling propaganda within literature pertaining to a stock issue, whether truthful or not. (105)

house 1. In the securities business, this usually refers to a firm, but may also apply to an individual conducting his own business. 2. The London Stock Exchange is also known as the House. (105)

house account A customer who is serviced by the home office or executive of the home office as distinguished from one who is solicited by a salesman of the territory in which the customer operates. Typically the salesman does not receive any or a regular commission for "house account" sales even though the account is in his territory.

house bill A bill of exchange drawn by a head office against an agency or branch.

house of issue An investment banking firm which offers for public sale a new issue of securities it has underwritten. (105)

hung up A situation in which an individual or firm has overextended his purchases, frequently at higher than prevailing prices and thus cannot sell except at a loss.

hypothecary value The value assigned by a lender to the collateral pledged to secure a loan.

hypothecate To give to a creditor the right to cause personal property of his debtor to be sold in satisfaction of a debt. If the property offered as security is delivered to the creditor (lender), the hypothecation is generally called a pledge. In a true hypothecation, the debtor (borrower) usually retains possession of the property until such time as he defaults in meeting his obligation. (85)

hypothecated account An account which is pledged or assigned as collateral for a loan. Savings accounts, trust accounts, etc., may come in this category. (83)

hypothecated stock 1. Stock which has been pledged as collateral for a loan. 2. Pawned stock. (105)

hypothecation Originally, a pledge to secure an obligation without delivery of title or possession; now, generally any pledge to secure an obligation, such as the hypothecation of securities for a loan. (88)

I

I.&B. Improvements and betterments.

I.B.A. Investment Bankers Association of America.

IBRD International Bank for Reconstruction and Development.

IBS Report Report of selected income and balance sheet items filed monthly with the Interstate Commerce Commission. (19)

Ident. Identification.

IMF International Monetary Fund.

Imp. Importer; Imports; Improvement.

Inc. Income; Incorporated.

Ind. Led. Individual Ledger.

Indent. Indenture.

Indm. Indemnity.

Inj. Injunction.

Ins. Insurance.

Inst. Instant (of the present month); installment; instrument.

Instl. Installment.

Int. Internal; Interest.

Intermed. Intermediate.

Intl. International.

Inv. Invoice.

I. O. U. I Owe You.

IRC Internal Revenue Code. (67)

Irred. Irredeemable.

I.R.S. Internal Revenue Service. (7)

I/T Income tax.

identification The procedure by which a bank teller or other employee assures himself as far as possible (through documents, contact with another bank, and other means) that the person with whom he is dealing is the person he or she claims to be. (90)

idle money Uninvested, available funds. (1)

illiquid An asset which cannot easily be converted into cash.

immediate and deferred credit Items sent to a Federal Reserve bank are generally divided into separate cash letters which contain items for immediate credit and items for deferred credit. When a transit letter is received from a member bank in time for the Federal Reserve bank to collect payment for the items that day, the reserve account of the member bank is immediately credited with the total of the cash letter. Immediate credit is given only in those cities that have Federal Reserve banks or branches. Cash letters received beyond the deadline, or containing checks drawn on banks outside a Federal Reserve bank city, cannot be collected that day, so the total amount is credited to a deferred account and the member bank is notified as to the date the funds will be available. Schedules of availability of funds are prepared for each Federal Reserve bank, showing the approximate, not actual, time required for the collection of cash items. The maximum period for which credit is deferred by the Federal Reserve bank on any check received for collection is presently two business days, regardless of the time actually required for collection. (83)

immediate beneficiary (Also called present beneficiary or primary beneficiary) A beneficiary of a trust who is entitled to receive immediate benefits from the trust property, whether or not limited to income; opposed to ultimate beneficiary. (74)

immediate credit Cash and home debit items are given immediate credit, that is the depositor may draw on them in the form of withdrawal or check, while checks drawn on other banks are subject to "deferred availability" until such time as they are collected, by the bank in which they have been deposited.

immediate delivery Arrangement whereby an investor selects mortgages, generally from a mortgage banker's off the shelf inventory, for delivery, acceptance and payment within a limited period, usually 30 days. (121)

immediate order Also called a "fill, or kill" order, or one that must be executed at a stipulated price as soon as it reaches the exchange floor, or be cancelled. (105)

immigrant remittances Any funds which immigrants may send out of the country. Generally, such remittances are minor factors in a nation's balance of payments.

impaired capital A condition in which the capital of a business is worth less than its stated capital. This may be caused by inability to raise the capital initially or due to losses which the business has suffered. If the impairment is material a firm may fail.

impaired credit A condition in which a borrower or debtor has experienced some development which has resulted in creditors refusing to extend their normal line of credit.

impaired risk A risk that is substandard or under average. (5)

impair investment A money, or near-money, expenditure which does not result in capital formation being either for consumption or a transfer and acquisition of existing capital.

impersonal account An account in a set of books of record which is other than that of an individual or firm. A real estate account, and insurance account, a tax account are all impersonal accounts while J. Jones or X Company are personal accounts.

implied covenant One which infers by the context of a deed, or related instrument. (5)

implied trust A trust created by operation of law or by judicial construction to be distinguished from an express trust which is created by express language, oral or in writing. (74)

import credit A commercial letter of credit issued for the purpose of financing the importation of goods. (85)

import letter of credit See Import Credit; Letter of Credit.

import license Permission obtained from a government to import stated quantities of enumerated goods.

import quota The amount of a product which a nation will permit to be imported during a stated period.

imports of goods and services Represent the sum of all payments for merchandise imports, military expenditures, transportation and travel costs, other private and U.S. Government services, and income and service payments to foreign parent companies by their affiliates operating in the United States. By far the largest component of this category is merchandise imports, which includes all goods bought or otherwise transferred from a foreign country to the United States. However, military and foreign travel expenditures, international transportations payments, and income payments on foreign investments in the U.S. are also of considerable significance.

Military expenditures are those payments abroad that are connected with our military programs in foreign areas. Expenditures for travel by Americans abroad include payments closely connected with travel such as lodging, food, amusements, gifts, and other purchases. International transportation payments consist principally of payments to foreign carriers of U.S. imports, payments for charter hire of foreign flag vessels, and travel fares paid to foreign international airlines by U.S. residents traveling to and from abroad. (124)

impound To seize and retain in custody of the law. (93)

imprest system A system for handling minor disbursements whereby a fixed amount of money, designated as petty cash, is set aside for this purpose. Disbursements are made from time to time as needed. At certain intervals, a report is rendered of the amount disbursed, and the petty cash is replenished for the amount of the disbursements ordinarily drawn by check on the fund or funds from which the items are payable. The total of petty cash plus unreplenished disbursements must always equal the fixed sum of cash set aside. See Petty Cash. (29)

imprinting To place on the face of a document the magnetic ink characters specified by the American Bankers Association. (83)

imputed An estimate of value in the event that a cash payment is not made for a good or service.

imputed interest An estimate of value, charge or interest due for the use of capital even though a cash payment is not made. Implicit interest.

inactive account No items to post to the account on the given day. An account which has little or no activity. (83)

inactive corporation One which neither operates property nor administers its financial affairs. If it maintains an organization, it does so only for the purpose of complying with legal requirements and maintaining title to property or franchises. (19)

inactive market The condition in a market characterized by a lower volume of activity than is customary.

inactive post A trading post on the floor of the N. Y. Stock Exchange where inactive securities are traded in units of 10 shares instead of the usual 100-share lots. Better known in the business as Post 30. See Round Lot. (2)

inactive security See Inactive Stock. The security may be a debt instrument as well as an equity as well as either listed or traded over-the-counter.

inactive stock An issue traded on an exchange or in the over-the-counter market in which there is a relatively low volume of transactions. Volume may be no more than a few hundred shares a week or even less. On the N. Y. Stock Exchange most inactive stocks are traded in 10-share units

rather than the customary 100. See Round Lot. (2)

inactive trust A trust in which the trustee has no duty except to hold title to the property. (74)

in-and-out Purchase and sale of the same security within a short period—a day, week, even a month. An in-and-out trader is generally more interested in day-to-day price fluctuations than dividends or long-term growth. (2)

in balance Term meaning that the total of the debits is the same amount as the total of the credits. (73)

inchoate Not yet completed. Contracts are inchoate until executed by all the parties who should join in their execution, and a widow's right to dower is inchoate so long as her husband lives. (5)

in-clearing items Items received by a bank as a result of a clearinghouse exchange are commonly called incoming clearings, or shorted to "in-clearings." (83)

income 1. A stream of benefits generally measured in terms of money as of a certain time; a flow of services. It is the source of value. Loosely, the money a person or company has coming in from any source. Exactly, income is made up of the amount received from both earnings and investments. 2. General Term: A general ledger account having subsidiary accounts which describe the aggregate and analytical analysis of a bank's sources of revenue. 3. Bookkeeping: In the account analysis procedure the credit given toward the service charge determined from the available balance. (54 +, 83)

income and profit Income and profit involve net or partially net concepts and refer to amounts resulting from the deduction from revenues, or from operating revenues, of cost of goods sold, other expenses, and losses, or some of them. The terms are often used interchangeably and are generally preceded by an appropriate qualifying adjective or term such as "gross," "operating," "net . . . before income taxes," and "net." The terms are also used in titles of statements showing results of operations, such as "income statement" or "statement of profit and loss," or, sometimes, "profit and loss account." (17)

income available for fixed charges Total income less miscellaneous deductions, which consist of expenses of miscellaneous operations, taxes on miscellaneous operating property, miscellaneous rents and tax accruals, loss on separately operated properties, maintenance of investment organizations, income transferred to other companies, and miscellaneous income charges. (19)

income beneficiary A person who, by the terms of a will or a trust instrument, is entitled to receive income from property for a specified number of years or for life. (74)

income coverage 1. Direct—The extent to which net income from portfolio investments (after deduction of any prior interest or preferred dividend requirements) covers the requirements of a specific senior obligation, whether bank loans, debentures or preferred stock; in computing the coverage for bank loans or debentures, interest actually paid is added back to net income. The coverage figure may be expressed in dollars, as a percentage, or as a ratio. 2. Overall—The amount by which net income from portfolio investments plus interest actually paid covers total interest charges, if any, senior preferred dividends, if any, and the dividend requirement of the subject issue. (3)

income deductions Includes interest on long-term debt, amortization of debt discount, expense and premium-net, taxes assumed on interest, interest on debt to associated companies, other interest charges, interest charged to construction (Credit), miscellaneous amortization and miscellaneous income deductions (any nonrecurring income deductions of a material amount should be noted). (21)

income fund Investment Company whose primary objective is generous current income. May be Balanced Fund, Common Stock Fund, Bond Fund or Preferred Stock Fund. (3)

income, gross 1. Total periodic income collectible from the operation of a property on the basis of existing rent schedules; in this sense, often designated "Actual Gross Income." 2. Total periodic income collectible from the operation of a property on the basis of current economic (as opposed to existing or contract) rents; in this usage, frequently designated "Reasonable Gross Income." In either case, miscellaneous income from advertising signs, limited yard parking, coin operated laundry equipment, etc., is included only when consideration is given to it in the market place. (66)

income, gross effective Actual or reasonable gross income less allowance for vacancies, noncollectibles, and possible declining rent levels; very frequently called Stabilized Income. (66)

income, gross operating Gross scheduled income minus vacancy and collection loss. (Net operating income is gross operating income minus operating expenses but before loan payments.) (120)

income, gross scheduled Projection of anticipated annual income from the property fully rented. (120)

income, gross spendable Net operating income minus total loan payments (principal and interest). (120)

income group People grouped according to how much they earn per year. Usually broken down into low, medium and high income groups. (93)

income, net 1. The remainder after deduction of expenses of operation from effective gross income; in this sense, better termed "Net Income Before Depreciation." This is the "net income" which is capitalized directly into property value in the Property Residual Technique. 2. Interest or return on capital value, estimated as the remainder after subtraction of annual depreciation charge-off for wasting assets (buildings, etc.) from net income before depreciation; better designated "Net Income After Depreciation." (66)

income, personal A measure of the actual current income receipts of persons from all sources (as generally used, the term is for a year). (24)

income portfolio An aggregate of securities held mainly because they generate a steady income. (105)

income property A property in which the income is derived from commercial rentals or in which the returns attributable to the real estate can be so segregated as to permit direct estimation. The income production may be in several forms; e.g., commercial rents, business profits attributable to real estate other than rents, etc. (54)

income return 1. The amount of annual income paid on an investment. 2. The per cent obtained by dividing the amount of annual income paid on an investment by the cost or purchase price.

income statement 1. The profit and loss statement of a given concern for a particular period of time. 2. A copy of the Income Cash Ledger for a particular trust account. (1)

income tax That tax, federal, state or local, which is levied on the income of individuals or firms.

incoming clearings Checks and drafts received from other banks in the same city. (83)

incoming mail Checks and drafts received through the mail for deposit from other banks and depositors. (83)

incoming, outgoing exchanges See Clearings; Clearing House.

incompetent One who is incapable of managing his affairs because of mental deficiency or undeveloped mentality. Children and idiots are incompetents in the eyes of the law. (54)

inconvertible money Irredeemable money. Money which may not be converted into the standard. U.S. money is inconvertible since it is not redeemable in gold.

incorporate To form into a corporation; become a corporation. (93)

incorporated trustee A bank or trust company which by law and its charter may act as a fiduciary.

incorporation by reference Reference in one document to the contents of another document in such a manner as to give legal effect to the material to which reference is made. (88)

increases Additions to an amount. Increases are debits to asset accounts and credits to liability accounts or the proprietorship account. (73)

increasing costs A production situation in which the cost per production unit goes up as production volume goes up.

increasing returns A situation in which production is increased even though there has been no increase in the various factors of production such as land, labor, capital or management. This may be due to a more efficient utilization of one or more of the factors. The term is also used to describe a situation in which an additional unit of any of the factors or production results in an increase in production more than was caused by a prior unit of the same factor.

incremental cost The cost of one more unit; marginal cost.

incumbrance A lien or liability attached to real property. (35)

incur To become liable for a loss or expense. (5)

indefeasible Incapable of being annulled or rendered void; as, an indefeasible title to property. (74)

indemnity agreement A written instrument by which the signer guarantees to protect another against loss. If the written instrument has a surety or bondsman and is under seal, it is called a bond of indemnity. (31, 92)

indent A foreign order for merchandise with or without restrictions such as price, quality of mode of shipment.

indenture A written agreement under which bonds or debentures are issued, setting forth maturity date, interest rate, security and other terms. (2)

independent bank An independent bank is one which operates in one locality. The directors and officers are generally local men of the community. If the local bank operates branches, these will be located in the same city as the central office, except in states where state-wide branches are permitted, in which case the independent bank may have state-wide branch offices. Independent banks are to be distinguished from chain or group banks. (1)

independent executor An executor of a will, who, after filing his inventory, does not make further accounting to the probate court; recognized by statute in only a few states. (74)

index A statistical yard stick expressed in terms of percentages of a base year or years. For instance, the Federal Reserve Board's index of industrial production is based on 1947-49 as 100. In January, 1957, the index stood at 146, which meant that industrial production that month was 46 per cent higher than in the base period. An index is not an average. See Average. (2)

index number (prices, freight rates, wages, etc.) A means of measuring relative changes, by arranging data in comparable form, including suitable weighting where composite results are considered, and computing percentages according to a base, usually a year or an average of several years in the case of a time service. (19)

indicated interest Also called open interest, or the willingness to buy a new securities issue by the investing public shown through their orders to the underwriter. (105)

indicated market The price at which a trader thinks a security might be bought or sold when there is not a firm bid or offer upon which to base a more definite opinion. (105)

indicated yield 1. Preliminary crop reports at times estimate what the harvested yield will be on the basis of the state or condition of a crop which has not fully matured. Such reports are based upon the "indicated" or estimated yield.

2. The yield, either expressed as current yield or yield to maturity which is based upon the assumption that future payments on the security will be on the same basis as the dividends or interest payments of the recent past. A stock which is selling at $100 and has paid two quarterly dividends of $1 each would have an indicated current yield of 4% since it would be anticipated that the next two quarterly dividends would be at the same rate and amount unless additional information indicated otherwise.

indirect control Control of an individual, a corporation, or other legal person, as exercised through an intermediary. (19)

indirect cost Also called Overhead, Fixed Cost or Supplementary Cost. A cost which does not vary with the volume of activity. A real estate tax is an example of an indirect cost.

indirect earnings See Equity Earnings.

indirect exchange The technique used in arbitrage of foreign exchange in buying foreign exchange in one market and promptly selling it in another market at a rate that will yield a profit over the purchase price plus the expenses of the transaction.

indirect export An export which is handled by a middleman rather than the producer. The reasons why this is done may be that the middleman is more familiar with the exporting situation or because the volume of a producers exports are not large enough to support the staff needed to provide the specialized skills involved.

indirect liability A secondary, or contingent liability assumed by the endorsement or guaranty of an obligation for which another party is primarily liable. It becomes an absolute liability only upon the failure of the primary party to live up to his agreement. (83)

indirect standard The monetary system which does not directly convert its currency into a standard metal such as gold or silver but permits, as a right of ownership, the exchange of the domestic currency into the currency of a nation that is on a metal standard. The ratio of exchange is established and maintained with only infrequent changes.

indirect tax A levy by a governmental unit which can easily be passed on to some other individual or firm. To the individual or firm that bears the final burden of the tax it is an indirect tax.

individual account An account in the name of one individual, as contrasted with an account of a corporation, a partnership, or an account in two or more names. (85)

individual banker An unincorporated bank, a private banker. Found only in a few states.

individual policy pension trust A type of pension plan, frequently used for small groups, administered by trustees who are authorized to purchase individual level premium policies or annuity contracts for each member of the plan. The policies usually provide both life insurance and retirement benefits. (53)

individual proprietorship A business owned by one person. The individual owner has all the rights to profits from the business as well as all the liabilities and losses.

indorse See Endorse.

industrial bank A financial institution that derives its funds through a form of savings known as "investment shares" and invests these funds by specializing in the financing of businesses through the assignment of pledge accounts receivable. (1)

industrial credit Debt incurred by industrial or business firms to meet payrolls, buy raw materials, build new plants. (131)

industrial loan commitments Amount of loans to industrial borrowers which have been approved but the funds have not yet been advanced to them. (4)

industrial loans Loans outstanding to industrial

115

borrowers under an amendment to the Federal Reserve Act which authorized the Federal Reserve banks to make loans to certain business firms unable to get credit from other financial institutions on reasonable terms. This authority was terminated in August 1959. (4)

industrials In an investment connotation the word includes not only companies in production and industry but includes distribution and extractive business activities. In fact the term may best be described by what are *not* industrials. Investments literature groups securities into several main classifications—Rails, Utilities, Banks & Insurance, Investment Companies, Municipals, Government Bonds—the remainder and catch-all is Industrials. The three major investment averages are Transportation, Utilities and Industrials.

industrial stock See Industrials.

inelastic demand Demand which does not change at a proportionate rate with the rate of change in price. Necessities of life tend to be relatively inelastic in their demand. Table salt is an item frequently cited as being subject to inelastic demand.

inelastic supply Supply which does not change at a proportionate rate with the rate of change in price.

infant A person not of legal age, which at common law was 21 years but which in some states has been changed by statute; the same as a minor. (74)

infirmity Any known act, or visible omission in detail, in the creation or transfer of title that would invalidate an instrument is known as an infirmity. Common examples of infirmities that would invalidate an instrument and cause a bank to refuse payment, if detected, are endorsement missing, signature missing, amount missing, amount conflicting in written and numerical figures, any alteration, or forgery. (1)

inflation A substantial rise in prices caused by undue expansion in paper money or bank credit. (93)

ingot A metal bar.

inheritance That estate in property, technically real property but in general usage any property, which has come about through a bequest by will or devise or through intestate descent.

inheritance tax A tax on the right to receive property by inheritance; to be distinguished from an estate tax. (74)

inheritance tax return The return that the executor or administrator is required to make to the state on the basis of which the inheritance tax due the state is calculated and paid; to be distinguished from the federal estate tax return. (74)

initiation fee The initial membership levy for all newly elected members to an exchange. Thereafter most exchanges have annual dues. (105)

inland bill A bill drawn and payable within one state in a technical sense but in a common usage any domestic bill as distinguished from a foreign bill.

inland bill of exchange A bill drawn and payable in the same state. (90)

in loco parentis (In the place of a parent.) A phrase referring to a person who takes the place of a child's parent. While it sometimes refers to a guardian, a person who has not been legally appointed guardian may also stand "in loco parentis." (88)

insanity A mental condition, or impairment, which results in a person's being declared legally incompetent. (42)

inscribed Those particular government bonds such as Series E savings bonds whose records are maintained by the Federal Reserve banks rather than the United States Treasury.

in shape for sale A term describing the condition in which a security will make a good delivery. (74)

inside board of directors See Board of Directors.

insider An individual who is conversant with developments concerning a company prior to the time when such information becomes available to the general stockholders or public.

insider reports The monthly reports required by the Securities and Exchange Commission that must be filed by the officers, directors and stockholders who own more than 10% of any corporation whose securities are listed on a national securities exchange. Included are records of all purchases and sales made during the previous month and the total number of shares held at the end of the month. These reports, along with information on what action investment funds are taking, make it possible to know which securities have gained or lost favor with people who are close to the market. (105)

insolvency The inability to pay one's debts as they mature. Even though the total assets of a business might exceed its total liabilities by a wide margin, the business is said to be insolvent should the nature of the assets be such that they cannot be readily converted into cash to meet the current obligations of the business as they mature. See Bankruptcy. (1)

inspection report Information gathered by a mercantile source, and compiled in report form to be used to supplement underwriting material in the selection of risks. The primary purpose of the report is to verify information given on the application. (42)

inspection slip Written form of reporting on the examination of a risk. (5)

installment A partial payment on a debt or purchase. One of several parts of a thing which is presented at intervals.

installment accounts receivable The title of the controlling account in the general ledger that controls the installment ledger. (73)

installment cash credit Money loaned directly to an individual and repaid through periodic payments over a specified length of time. (131)

installment contract A contract that sets forth the conditions of an installment sale and the payments on it. (73)

installment loan See Personal Loan. (1)

installment loans Loans which are repayable in periodic installments. (83)

installment payments Periodic payments to discharge an indebtedness. Sometimes used synonymously with amortization payments. (5)

installment settlement A clause in a policy permitting the beneficiary to elect to receive death proceeds in installments over a period of time. (5)

institutional investors An organized group which invests. (93)

instrument A legal document; a note, contract, agreement, when in writing. (59)

instrumentalities A term often applied to agencies of the federal government and whose obligations are not the direct obligation of the federal government. However, there is an implied support; for example, Federal Land Bank bonds. (74)

instrumentality A subordinate agency.

insufficient funds (sometimes abbreviated N.S.F., not sufficient funds). A term used by a bank to indicate that the drawer's deposit balance is smaller than the amount of a check presented for payment. (85)

insurance, accounts receivable Pays for loss of records showing how much is due the insured. Insurance against loss due to inability to collect outstanding accounts receivable because of damage to or destruction of records by a peril insured against. (5)

insurance, credit life Life insurance issued by a life insurance company on the lives of borrowers to cover payment of loans (usually small loans repayable in installments) in case of death. It is usually handled through a lending office and is written on either a group or an individual basis. (5)

insurance trust A trust whose corpus is either life insurance contracts, life insurance proceeds, or both.

insurance trust expenditures Cash payments to beneficiaries of contributory social insurance programs, such as employee retirement, unemployment compensation, workmen's compensation, sickness insurance, etc. Excludes cost of administration, intergovernmental expenditures for social insurance, and other non-contributory payments to former employees. (7)

insurance trust revenue Revenue from contributions required of employers and employees for financing social insurance programs operated by the state plus earnings on assets help for such systems. (7)

insured bank A bank that subscribes to the deposit insurance plan of the Federal Deposit Insurance Corporation. A state banking institution which does not subscribe to this plan is referred to as a non-insured bank. (85)

interbank demand deposits Deposits held for other commercial or savings banks; the breakdown shows the amounts for domestic (United States) and foreign banks. (4)

inter-branch A term associated with any action or function that takes place between or among the various branches of a bank. As an example, an inter-branch memorandum would be sent to all branches within a banking organization to inform them of some action, function, or decision to be instituted. All branches would receive the same message, so that all would be coordinated and put the action into effect at the same time in the same manner. (1)

interdistrict settlement fund That part of the Federal Reserve System, located in Washington, D.C., which serves as a clearinghouse for the twelve Federal Reserve banks in settling the difference between the debits and credits each of the banks has with the other eleven, thus minimizing the need to transfer funds. The fund is settled daily.

interest The cost of or charge made for the use of wealth. It may be an income or an expense item. When it is computed only on the original investment it is termed Simple Interest, but when it is added to the principal and the interest for the next period is reckoned on this enlarged amount it becomes Compound Interest. Not to be confused with "credit service charge," which includes interest but consists of several other charges for services rendered in making credit facilities available. (66, 59)

interest accrued Interest which has been earned but is not due or payable.

interest and debt expense The interest and other costs which the company and subsidiary companies must pay on money borrowed in the form of notes, bonds, and debentures.

interest bearing Any debt instrument such as a note bond or mortgage upon which interest is computed is "interest bearing" as distinguished from equities upon which dividends are declared.

interest-bearing note A note in which the maker has agreed to pay the face of the note with interest. (73)

interest charges The carrying charge on a client's margin account that compensates a broker for the responsibility and expense of obtaining the funds necessary to maintain it. This rate is ordinarily slightly higher than a broker's rate at the bank. (105)

interest earned but not collected Another name for "Interest Receivable." This represents interest on loans which has not been collected in advance, but is due and payable at specified times. Interest on demand loans usually comes into this class, collection being made each month, each quarter, or longer period of time, based upon bills being sent to the borrower for interest due. This is an asset (resources) account in the general ledger. (1)

interest expense The expense incurred for interest on any debt. (73)

interest income The income realized from interest on any claim against others. (73)

interest on long-term debt Interest on outstanding bonds (mortgage and debenture), receivers' certificates and miscellaneous long-term debt, notes, etc. issued or assumed by the utility and which are due one year or more from date of issuance. (21)

interest payable A liability representing accrued interest owed by the business. (73)

interest rate A percentage that expresses the relationship between the interest for one year and the principal. (73)

interest receivable An asset representing accrued interest to be collected. (73)

interest table A broad term given to any mechanical indexing device, or chart, permitting independent calculation of simple or compound interest, the discount or present value, etc., on varied amounts for certain or varied intervals of time. (1)

interest warrant The document used by the debtor to notify and direct the paying agent of a bond or note to pay the registered holders of a bond or note issue.

inter-fund accounts Accounts in which transactions between funds are reflected. See Inter-Fund Transfers. (29)

inter-fund loans Loans made by one fund to another. (29)

inter-fund transfers Amounts transferred from one fund to another. (29)

interim borrowing The sale of short-term paper in anticipation of bond issuance. See also Bond Anticipation Notes. (29)

interim certificate A temporary document which serves the purchaser of a new issue of securities as proof of ownership until such time as the engraved certificate is available.

interim dividend A dividend declared and paid by a corporation during the fiscal or calendar period in anticipation of a major or final dividend at the end of the period.

interim loan Short-term construction loan made to finance improvements on real property. (121)

interim report A monthly, quarterly or semiannual report issued to corporate stockholders to inform them of current developments and results. Serves as a supplement to the annual report. (105)

interlocking directors Directors of two or more similar corporations who simultaneously hold office in the corporations. The inference generally is that this device will tie the policies of the two companies together and reduce the competition between them.

intermediate credit bank Shortened designation for one of the twelve Federal Intermediate Credit Banks established in 1923 to provide banks and similar financial institutions with a rediscounting facility for agricultural paper of an intermediate term.

intermediate trend Movements within the framework of the primary or major trend. The price of the security may move in one direction ten to thirty points and then back the other way. It is made up of many smaller movements in price. (105)

internal audit A routine and continuous check on the accuracy of all accounting records. It is generally carried out under the supervision of the Comptroller's Office. Additional responsibilities frequently include that of setting up accounting systems designed to minimize the possibility of fraud and collusion. (28)

internal control A plan of organization under which employees' duties are so arranged and records and procedures so designed as to make it possible to exercise effective accounting control over assets, liabilities, revenues and expenditures. For example, under such a system the employees' work is subdivided so that no one employee performs a complete cycle of operations. For instance, an employee handling cash would not post the accounts receivable records.

Again, under such a system, the procedures to be followed are definitely laid down and such procedures call for proper authorizations by designated officials for all action to be taken. (29)

internal items Debit or credit memoranda prepared by or for an officer of the bank to adjust the balance in the general ledger and for a customer's account. Examples: corrections, loan proceeds, special customer charges, certification entries, etc. (83)

International Bank for Reconstruction and Development See World Bank.

international banking Those actions of banks involving handling of foreign exchange, making of foreign loans or acting as investment bankers for foreign nations, provinces, municipalities and companies.

international cheques Those travelers checks which are acceptable and payable in the various nations of the world. The American Express Travelers Cheque is one of the more widely known types of international cheques.

international exchange See Foreign Exchange.

international gold bullion standard A gold bullion standard with the limitation that gold may be freely obtained in the form of bullion only for purposes of export. This prevents it from being hoarded for domestic purposes and gives a central bank greater control over the limited amount of gold.

International Monetary Fund A companion institution to the World Bank established in 1945 to provide its member nations with foreign exchange to meet temporary needs in their balance of international payments and thus avoid nationalistic trade barriers and currency depreciation.

international money order See Money Orders. A money order issued by a bank, express company or post office which is payable abroad.

international postal money order A money order issued by a post office which is payable in foreign countries.

international securities Securities which are traded in the major securities markets of the world. The trading may be on a listed or unlisted basis.

international trade The foreign trade expressed in terms of the merchandise exports and imports of a nation for a given period such as a year.

international unit A statistical device used to put data from various nations on a uniform base so that the different economies may be compared.

interpleader A court procedure under which a bank or other stakeholder, in order to be protected from possible double liability, acknowledges his obligation to make payment, or to turn over property, and compels the rival claimants to litigate their respective rights. (90)

in terrorem clause A provision of a will or trust agreement intended or, at any rate, calculated to frighten a possible beneficiary into doing or refraining from doing something at the peril of forfeiting his possible benefits—such as a provision that would disinherit any named or potential beneficiary who contested the will. (74)

inter-sympathy between stocks The tendency for price action of securities within the same group to be similar. (105)

intervention currency Is the foreign currency a country uses to ensure by means of official exchange transactions that the permitted exchange rate margins are observed. Intervention usually takes the form of purchases and sales of foreign currency by the central bank or exchange equalization fund in domestic dealings with commercial banks. Under the temporary regime of central rates and wider margins mentioned above, members must communicate an intervention currency to the Fund, which is then used to determine the limits around the par value of central rate within which spot exchange transactions should take place. For purposes of this regime, a floation currency cannot be communicated as the intervention currency. (130)

inter vivos "Between living persons" In the term trust inter vivos or inter vivos trust, the same as living trust. See also Gift Inter Vivos. (88)

intestacy The condition resulting from a person's dying without leaving a valid will. (88)

intestate To die without a valid will.

intestate succession The descent and distribution of property of a person who dies without a valid will. (74)

in the black (red) To be operating in the black means to be operating profitably. Operating in the red means to be operating at a loss. (105)

intimidation A contract procured by intimidation or force is void. The use of undue pressure or force to obtain what may appear to be consent. (5)

intra-branch A term used to express an action or function that is ordered to take place within an individual branch or office, and does not affect the action of other branches or offices of an organization. Example: A personnel problem such as tardiness or absenteeism that applies only to one office or branch of an organization. An intra-branch memorandum would be sent to all departments within the one office or branch involved. (1)

intra-city An action or function taking place within one city. As an example, intra-city clearings between banks within one city. This is to be distinguished from inter-city clearings or collections, which means the exchange of items through transit between different cities. (1)

intraday high and low The highest and lowest price attained by a security during a particular market session which defines the trading range for that day. (105)

intrastate commerce Business activities confined within the borders of any one state.

intrastate securities Over-the-counter securities that are issued and distributed solely within one state. Often issued by companies just getting into business and therefore usually sold only on a best efforts basis by underwriters. (105)

intrinsic value The value possessed by a particular thing considered in itself. (1)

inventory An account, schedule, or catalogue, made by an executor or administrator of all goods and chattels, and sometimes of the real property, of a deceased person. A list of the property of a person or estate. An itemized list of goods or valuables, with their estimated worth. (74)

inventory control 1. An internal system for keeping adequate inventory at hand. 2. A governmental device used in emergencies to regulate inventories for the purpose of better utilization of the goods and to prevent hoarding.

inventory, finished goods Materials which are fully manufactured and ready for shipment. As articles are completed, work in process inventory is credited by the three elements of direct labor, direct material and burden applied. Finished goods inventory is debited with the total of the three. When these articles are ultimately shipped, finished goods inventory is credited and cost of sales is debited. (28)

inventory, maximum & minimum Pre-determined high and low limits for quantities of material on hand. The low limit is set to insure reasonable quantities available for production. The high limit is set to prevent excessive investment in Inventory and to insure against obsolescense, deterioration, etc. (28)

inventory of estate A complete listing of all the assets—funds, property (real and chattel), evidences of holdings (stocks, bonds, mortgages owned, notes receivable, other securities, personal effects of value), which must be distributed to the lawful heirs or other beneficiaries as designated in the will of a testator, or through the legal line of heritage as determined by a court of law where the decedent died intestate. (1)

inventory, perpetual A running book record of individual balances of material on hand. Before final closings can be effected, these balances must be adjusted to the actual balances on hand as reflected by taking a physical inventory. (28)

inventory, physical The actual verification of material on hand balances as reflected in the book inventory. This is accomplished by counting, weighing, measuring, or occasionally estimating, the quantities of materials on hand. Physical Inventories are generally taken near the close of a fiscal accounting period or during the vacation shutdown. Occasionally they are made on a continuous rotating basis. In this manner, the inventory can be taken with a considerably smaller inventory crew and with no shut-down of the normal production flow. (28)

inventory plans, first in, first out A method of pricing material requisitions and valuing book inventory based on the assumption that the oldest items in stock should be requisitioned first. This plan has the advantage of adhering to sound stores-keeping policy (move the oldest items first). It also reflects the truest value of material on hand (since it is the newest, it more nearly reflects current market value). It has the disadvantage of distorting cost of sales since the value of the oldest items is used in pricing material requisitions. In practice, it requires considerable "keying off" of the book inventory which can become very cumbersome with fast moving items. (28)

inventory plans, last in, first out A method of pricing material requisitions and valuing book inventory based on the assumption that materials entering into manufacturing cost should as nearly as possible reflect current market value. This plan has the advantage of providing a truer cost of sales, but distorts the asset value of material on hand (since the inventory on hand is always carried at the oldest price). In practice, it requires considerable "keying off" of the book inventory which can become very cumbersome with fast moving items. (28)

inventory plans, moving average A method of pricing material requisitions and valuing book inventory which is a variation of the Weighted Average Inventory Plan (see Inventory Plan, Weighted Average). It is designed to provide a maximum reduction in the effect of market fluctuations on the cost of sales and the asset value of material on hand. Moving averages are figured on a long term basis (for example, six months or a year). Every month a new average is figured which drops the oldest month and adds the newest. This spreads any market fluctuations over a much wider base. (28)

inventory plans, normal or base stock A method of pricing material requisitions and valuing book inventory based on the theory that there is always a residual or minimum inventory on hand. This is priced at a long term average value. Quantities over and above this amount are carried at cost or market value (whichever is lower). This plan finds its widest application where process cost systems are in use. For example, steel mills, oil refineries, chemical industries, etc. (28)

inventory plans, periodic average A method of pricing material requisitions and valuing book inventory which is a variation of the Weighted Average Inventory Plan (see Inventory Plans, Weighted Average). It is designed to reduce the number of clerical calculations necessary. New average prices are obtained once a month regardless of the number of purchases made. This plan is only practical where certain process cost systems are in use and costs are figured at the end of the month only. (28)

inventory plans, specific cost A method of pricing material requisitions and valuing book inventory based on actual costs of material purchased for specific orders in work in process inventory. This plan (usually associated with some other inventory plan) finds its widest application in metal working and job shops where a wide variety of unusual material must be purchased. (28)

inventory plans, standard cost A method of pricing material requisitions and valuing book inventory based on pre-determined standard costs for each type of item. This plan has the advantage of simplicity, reduction in clerical effort and the elimination of fluctuations in value. When used, material variance accounts must be maintained which reflect the difference between actual and standard price of material purchased. This plan finds its widest application in industries making continuous repetitive purchases of the same items. (28)

inventory plans, weighted average A method of pricing material requisitions and valuing book inventory designed to reduce the effect of market fluctuations on the cost records. Requisitions are costed at an average price until new purchases are made. At this time a new average price is computed. This average is obtained by dividing the new total value of material on hand by the new total quantity of material on hand. This method is particularly advantageous where a small volume of large quantity purchases is

made and a large volume of small quantity material requisitions are issued. (28)

inventory, raw material Materials on hand upon which no manufacturing operations have been performed. For example, sheet steel, bars, tubes, pigs, purchased parts, etc. (28)

inventory, reserve account An off-setting account designed to reduce the value of the book inventory to market value; or to provide for estimated shrinkage of the perpetual inventory so that it will conform with the results of taking a physical inventory. (28)

inventory, semi-finished parts Materials which have been partially manufactured, then withdrawn from work in process inventory and placed in a Stores Crib. They are subsequently withdrawn from Stores on a Material Requisition or Bill of Material and again placed in Work in Process Inventory for final completion. (28)

inventory valuation adjustment A method of removing the influence of price inflation from inventories stated in monetary units. This may be done by the use of various price indexes. (28)

inverted market A situation in which the nearer months of a futures market have higher prices than months that are more distant.

investment The use of money for the purpose of making more money, to gain income or increase capital, or both. Safety of principal is an important consideration. Securities, including those issued by the governmental unit, or other property in which money is invested either temporarily or permanently. See Speculation. (2, 29)

investment adviser An individual or firm which makes a business of advising clients on investments and is required to register under the Investment Advisers Act of 1940 with the Securities Exchange Commission.

Investment Advisers Act of 1940 A law requiring certain persons or firms who advise for compensation, other people with respect to their securities' transactions, to register with the Securities Exchange Commission. This is similar to the Securities Exchange Act governing the conduct of brokers and dealers. Registration of investment advisers may be denied, suspended, or revoked if a statutory disqualification is found to exist. The law also contains anti-fraud provisions. The original Act was amended in 1960. (105)

investment banker Also known as an underwriter. He is the middleman between the corporation issuing new securities and the public. The usual practice is for one or more investment bankers to buy outright from a corporation a new issue of stocks or bonds. The group forms a syndicate to sell the securities to individuals and institutions. Investment bankers also distribute very large blocks of stocks or bonds—perhaps held by an estate. Thereafter the market in the security may be over-the-counter, on a regional stock exchange, the American Exchange or the N.Y. Stock Exchange. See Over-the-Counter; Primary Offering; Syndicate. (2)

Investment Bankers Association The national association of investment bankers comprised of individuals, firms and corporations who have or are engaged in investment banking. It was formed in 1912.

investment banking A term used to describe the financing of the capital requirements of an enterprise rather than the current "working capital" requirements of a business. Investment bankers buy and sell securities, such as stocks, bonds, and mortgages. They act as the "middle men" between the corporation who wishes funds for new buildings, new equipment, plant expansion, etc., and the investor, who wishes to invest his savings. Investment bankers may promote a new industry; they may handle the finances of a corporation for expansion purposes; and they may act as brokers with other investment bankers in the floatation of stocks and bonds. (1)

investment banking house One which engages in the merchandising of corporate and government securities by purchasing them in large blocks and selling them to investors. It helps to finance the capital, or long term, credit requirements of business organizations, whereas the commercial bank finances their short term credit requirements. (85)

investment bill A discounted bill of exchange held to maturity as an investment.

investment certificate Certificate issued by associations which shows the amount of money an individual has invested with them. They do not carry any stockholders' liability and have no voting rights. Not to be confused with investment accounts. (31, 92)

investment club A group of individuals who collect on a periodic basis sums of money from their members. The collected money is then used to purchase securities generally on the basis of a report or review of the prospects of the company which is made by the club members on a rotating basis. The National Association of Investment Clubs, which is located in Detroit, Michigan serves as the focal point for information, legislation proposals and forms for establishing such an association.

investment company A corporation or trust which provides a medium through which members of the public may combine their funds for the purpose of having those funds invested in a broad portfolio of securities. The securities held in the portfolio are generally widely diversified, and the investment company provides professional supervision of those securities. (65)

Investment Company Act Federal statute enacted in 1940 for the registration and regulation of investment companies. (3)

investment counselor One who is professionally engaged in rendering investment advisory and supervisory services. (2)

investment credit The long term extension of funds for purchase of such fixed assets as machinery, buildings or land as compared with the furnishing of working capital credit for inventory or accounts receivables and wages.

investment income The revenue which results from investments rather than income from operations or production of goods or services. The income may be from investment return such as interest or dividends. Technically, price appreciation of a sold investment over the acquisition price is considered income if the investment has been held less than six months and is considered to be capital gains if held six months or over.

investment in default Investment in which there exists a default in the payment of principal or interest. (29)

investment in fixed assets The book value (q.v.) of fixed assets. (29)

investment market 1. Place where securities and other investments are sold. 2. The state or condition of trade in investments. The area around Wall Street probably comprises the greatest investment market in the world.

investment media Any area in which capital may be invested such as securities, notes, certificates, time deposit accounts, insurance, real estate, commodities, annuities and business ownership.

investment objective The goal—e.g. long-term capital growth, liberal current income, etc.— which an investor (whether an individual, an investment company or other institution) pursues. (65)

investment policy The means employed in pursuit of an investment objective. (65)

investment portfolio The list of securities owned by a bank, an individual, or a business enterprise. In banks the investment portfolio is a title given to the complete list of securities held by the bank for investment purposes. In the general ledger the investment portfolio is in reality a control account entitled "Investments" supported by subsidiary accounts, each of which contains the title and complete description of each investment held by the bank. (1)

investment powers The power of a fiduciary regarding the investments in the account. (74)

investment property The property which is within itself a business enterprise consisting of all tangible and intangible assets considered as integral with the property, assembled and developed as a single unit of utility for lease or rental, in whole or in part to others for profit. (54)

investment ratings A number of investment services such as Moody's, Fitch's, Standard & Poors, Value Line, etc. rate securities by various devices such as letters, numbers or similar devices. In addition, bank examiners and "legal list" states assign investment classifications to securities. These ratings attempt to assign securities to certain general classes of quality or investment attributes.

investment stocks See Blue Chip.

investment trust A company which uses its capital to invest in other companies. There are two principal types: the closed-end and the open-end, or mutual fund. Shares in closed-end investment trusts, some of which are listed on stock exchanges, are readily transferable in the open market and are bought and sold like other shares. Capitalization of these companies is fixed. Open-end funds sell their own new shares to investors, stand ready to buy back their old shares, and are not listed. Open-end funds are so-called because their capitalization is not fixed; they issue more shares as people want them. (2)

investor An individual whose principal concerns in the purchase of a security are regular dividend income, safety of the original investment, and, if possible, capital appreciation. See Speculator. (2)

invoice A bill prepared by a seller of goods or services and rendered to the buyer. The invoice usually itemizes all items making up the bill for the convenience of the buyer, and to prevent disagreements regarding the amount of the bill. Invoices are used as posting media by the seller in his accounts payable. Invoices are also used in preparing shipments by the seller, and in receiving goods by the buyer. (1)

involuntary alienation The transfer of title or ownership of property against the will or without the exercise of the will of the owner, such as a sale of property for taxes. (74)

involuntary bankrupt That individual or firm which is unable to meet its debt obligations and has been decreed as bankrupt by a competent court of jurisdiction because of an involuntary act of bankruptcy and who owes at least one thousand dollars.

involuntary investor A person who normally trades in securities; but becomes an "investor" after buying at the top of a rise, and then not being able to sell without taking a loss. (105)

irish dividend A trade term which refers to the imposition of an assessment on a security rather than a dividend.

irredeemable bonds Bonds issued which contain no provision for their being "called" or redeemed prior to their maturity date. (1)

irredeemable money Inconvertible money which cannot be exchanged for standard money.

irregular That condition in a commodity or security market in which some prices or averages advance while others decline with no generally recognized movement of the overall market in any particular direction.

irrevocable beneficiary The stated beneficiary of a policy that cannot be changed without the permission of the beneficiary or by his death. (5)

irrevocable letter of credit A contract by the issuer to accept drafts as conditioned by the contract and to charge them against their account. The letter is good (irrevocable) for a stated period of time.

irrevocable trust A trust which by its terms 1. cannot be revoked by the settlor or 2. can be terminated by him only with the consent of someone who has an adverse interest in the trust—that is, someone to whose interest it would be in for the trust not to be terminated, such as a beneficiary; to be distinguished from a revocable trust with consent or approval. (74)

issue 1. Any of a company's securities, or the act of distributing such securities. 2. Legal term for offspring. (2, 42)

issued stock That portion of the authorized stock which is Treasury Stock or outstanding in the possession of the stockholders as distinguished from unissued stock.

issue price The price which an underwriter offers a new security issue to the public.

issuer With reference to investment company securities, the company itself. (3)

issue value The value of a share of stock at which it is issued by the corporation. (73)

items (as used in bank collections) A flexible term broad enough to include instruments payable in money generally. The term is often used in combinations such as cash items, non-cash items, collection items, city items, and out-of-town items. (85)

J

J Judgment.

J/A Joint account.

J.A.J.O. Quarterly interest payments or dividends in January, April, July, and October.

J. & D. Semi-annual interest payments or dividends in June & December.

J. & J. Semi-annual interest payments or dividends in January and July.

J. O. J. A. Quarterly interest payments or dividends in July, October, January and April.

Jour. Journal.

Jr. Junior.

J. S. D. M. Quarterly interest payment or dividends in June, September, December and March.

Juris. Jurisdiction.

jacket A wrapper or enclosure for an official document. (29)

job lot A form of contract having a smaller unit of trading than the regular contract. (9)

john doe A name given in legal proceedings to a party whose true name is unknown. (93)

joint account An account in which two or more persons have and may exercise equal rights. See Tenancy in Common; Alternate Account; Survivorship Account. (83)

joint and last survivor (annuity) Payments made jointly to two or more annuitants, and continuing until death of the last survivor. (42)

joint and several Obligations which are enforceable against each and all of several persons. (35)

joint and several account with right of survivorship Where two or more persons desire to deposit in a jointly owned account, and where the account is drawn against either by check or withdrawal, the signature of any ONE of the owners may be honored. Agreements are usually signed by all parties relieving the bank of all liability, and permitting payment to any of the survivors. This type of account is usually distinguished by the wording "either/or" or "and/or" shown in the agreement or signature cards used in establishing the account. (1)

joint costs The manufacturing costs of more than one product which, by the nature of production, are processed together. A meat packer must dress a hide to produce cuts of meat. He also has by-products such as bones and tissue. While total costs can be computed it becomes a matter of judgment to split up the total costs among the various items.

joint demand The type of demand in which two or more products or services must be brought together if utility is to be produced. Many manufactured goods are examples of joint demand. A television set requires many types of products such as glass, copper and other metals.

joint deposit See Joint Account.

joint endorsement Some instruments, such as a tax refund on a joint tax return, require joint endorsement which is the endorsement of the two or, at rare times, more individual payees.

jointly and severally This term is more frequently used in loan transactions where several persons sign a note for a loan. When the term "jointly and severally" is used, it becomes the legal obligation of each person to become individually liable for the payment of the note, as well as the group involved to become liable. If the wording "we jointly promise to pay" is used, the legal status is on the parties jointly, but not individually. (1)

joint note A note with more than one maker. In the event of default, the holder sues all of the makers on a joint basis as distinguished from a "joint and several" action which may be against one or all of the makers.

joint ownership Ownership in Joint Tenancy as distinguished from "Tenancy in Common." Joint ownership designates the right of survivorship to the remaining tenant upon the death of the other tenant and does not need a will for the descent of ownership.

joint stock company A form of business organization in which the capital contribution of the partners are represented by transferable shares. It differs from the corporate form of organization in that each of the partners has unlimited liability and is similar from the standpoint that death or transfer of membership does not terminate operations. (105)

joint tenancy An estate held by two or more persons in which the interest of anyone dying passes to the surviving tenant. (35)

joint venture Something undertaken by two or more people. (93)

joint wills An attested will which is executed by two or more persons. Many times a husband and wife will make a joint will to avoid the time and cost involved with separate instruments. However, if either estate is large, or there is the likelihood of changing circumstances, a joint will may be more difficult to change than a separate will. Furthermore as each testator to a joint will dies, the will must be probated.

journal A record of original entry. This record may be written in pen and ink at the time a transaction is made, or may be created either in original printing or carbonized as the posting of the entry is made by machine. The journal is a chronological record of the transactions as they transpire or a chronological record of the posting media posted after a "fine sort" has been made. The all-important point is that EVERY ENTRY is recorded each day to the journal. (1)

journalizing The process of recording a transaction in a journal. It consists of two steps: the mental process of determining the debits and the credits and, the recording of the entry in the journal. (73)

journal voucher A voucher provided for the recording of certain transactions or information in place of or supplementary to the journals or registers. The journal voucher usually contains an entry or entries explanations, references to documentary evidence supporting the entry or entries, and the signature or initials of one or more properly authorized officials. (29)

judgment The conclusion of the law, delivered by a court of justice or other competent tribunal. Also means an adjudication for the payment of money. (5)

judgment bonds Bonds issued to fund judgments. See Funding. (29)

judgment creditor The creditor who has been granted a judgment against a debtor by an appropriate court of jurisdiction.

judgment debt Any debt contested in a suit at law and proved to be valid. (1)

judgment debtor The debtor against whom a judgment has been obtained, which has been recorded.

judgment lien A charge rendered in a state or federal court on a piece of land or personal property against one who owes a debt. When applied to personal property it is generally termed an attachment. (31, 92)

judgment note A note given by debtor to a creditor acknowledging the debt and one which, if remaining unpaid at maturity, authorizes the creditor to appear in a court at law and confess judgment without process to the maker. (1)

judgment rates Rates established by the judgment of the underwriter without application of a formal set of rules or schedule. (50)

judicial Belonging to the office of a judge; as judicial authority. (93)

judicial accounting An account of proceedings prepared for submission to a court having jurisdiction. (74)

judicial settlement The settlement of an account in accordance with the order, judgment or decree of a proper court, the effect of which in many states is determined by statute. (88)

junior advance refunding An operation where the securities eligible for exchange mature in from one to five years. (112)

junior interest A mortgage participation junior to another participation. A legal right that is subordinate to another interest. (5)

junior lien A lien placed upon a property that has a senior lien made and recorded. The rights are enforceable only after the previous liens have been satisified. (54+)

junior mortgage A claim against or a lien on the title to a property which is subordinate to that created by a prior mortgage. See First Mortgage. (89)

junior refunding An exchange by holders of securities maturing within one to five years for issues with original maturities of five or more years. (115)

junior securities Common stocks and other issues whose claims to assets and earnings are contingent upon the satisfaction of the claims of prior obligations. (3)

jurat That part of an affidavit in which the officer certifies that the same was sworn to before him. (5)

jurisdiction Legal right, power, or authority to hear and determine a cause; as the jurisdiction of a court. (74)

justified price The price which an informed and prudent purchaser would be warranted in paying. (89)

K

K.D. Knocked down.

K. D. L. C. L. Knocked down in less than carload lots.

kaffirs London Stock Exchange term for South African mining securities. (105)

key industry a dominant industry in its field or the general economy. (105)

killing An exceptionally profitable transaction.

kin Persons of the same blood or members of the same family. (74)

kind In the phrase "distribution in kind," distribution of the property itself and not the cash value of the property. (74)

kite A term used in banking circles to describe the malpractice of individuals in taking advantage of the time element of check collections by the bank. The individual either has a cohort in a distant city, or another account in another city himself. He deposits a check drawn on a bank in a distant city, and then draws from this uncollected balance while the check is in the process of collection. The same individual also sends a check drawn upon this bank, and deposits it in the bank, where he also draws against uncollected funds by issuing checks against this out-of-town bank. In this manner he uses both bank accounts to his advantage to draw against "Non-Existent" true balances. (83)

kiting Technique of drawing checks against deposits that have to clear through the banking system. Kiting takes advantage of the time needed for checks to clear and permits the kiter to use funds that are not his. (5)

kiting stock A manipulative attempt to push up prices by such techniques as matched orders, rumors and similar devices.

koruna Monetary unit of Czechoslovakia.

krona Monetary unit of Iceland and Sweden.

krone Monetary unit of Denmark and Norway.

L

L/C Letter of Credit.

L. & D. Loans and Discounts; loss and damage.

Ld. Gt. Land Grant.

Led. Ledger.

L.F. Ledger Folio.

Li. Liability. (5)

Lir. Italian Lira.

Lshld. Leasehold.

Ltd. Limited.

Ltr. Letter.

labor bank One of a relatively small number of banks which were formed and owned by unions or union members.

labor, direct Labor specifically identified with an order or process affecting the manufactured product. Thus labor expended in producing parts for inventory is direct labor because the parts so produced ultimately find their way into the finished product. (28)

laches A defendant in a law suit may plead laches as his defense if he can prove that he has suffered from the fact that the plaintiff delayed in bringing suit. (5)

lamb A novice at speculation, inexperienced and quite likely to be "shorn," or lose on his investments.

lame duck 1. A speculator whose venture has not succeeded. 2. An elected official who is still in office but whose position has been filled by another who will take over at a later date.

land bank 1. An agricultural program which has as its purpose the retirement of land from active agricultural purposes by a government subsidy to encourage the transfer of use into such activities as tree cultivation. Also called "Soil Bank." 2. A Federal Land Bank. 3. A state cooperative to assist savings and loan associations. 4. A bank which instead of having capital uses land as the basis for issuing currency and extending credit such as the Land Bank founded in New England in 1740.

land trust An unincorporated association for holding real property by putting the title in one or more trustees for the benefit of the members whose interests are evidenced by land-trust certificates. (74)

land trust certificate An instrument which grants participation in benefits of the ownership of real estate, while the title remains in a trustee. (5)

lapping Theft from one customer being covered by theft from another, generally by means of false entries in books of accounts. (5)

lapse The falling of a gift into the residuary estate by reason of the death of the donee during the testator's lifetime. Such a gift is known as a lapsed legacy or a lapsed devise. (74)

la salle street The financial center of Chicago. La Salle street is to Chicago what Wall Street is to New York.

last in, first out An expression which means that, in the usual course of business, the most recently purchased raw materials are the first to be processed into finished products, and the goods most recently acquired for resale in substantially the same form are the first to be sold. In its practical application, this is a system of assessing inventories, as follows: 1. Manufacturers' inventories; i.e., the contribution to the total value estimate of stocks on hand, materials used in the goods in process and in the finished goods on hand, is based upon the cost to the owner of the last purchased raw materials available for processing. 2. Wholesalers' inventories; i.e., the value estimate is based upon the cost to the owner of the most recently purchased goods on hand. See also First In, First Out. (66)

last sale Refers to the last price in the transacting of a security during the trading day or at the end of the day. (105)

last trading day That time when futures trading ceases for a specific delivery month and all the futures contracts that have not been balanced out must have spot or actual delivery of the physical commodity.

last will and testament A legally enforceable declaration of a person's wishes regarding matters to be attended to after his death and not operative until his death; usually but not always relating to property; revocable (or amendable by means of a codicil) up to the time of his death or loss of mental capacity to make a valid will. Originally, "will" related to real property; "testament," to personal property; but at the present time, "will" is equally applicable to real and personal property. (74)

late charge A special fee demanded in connection with any payment on a mortgage loan or other obligation that is not made when due. (89)

late tape The condition of the ticker tape when transactions on the exchange floor are at such a pace the ticker can not report sales fast enough. When the tape runs five or more minutes late, devices such as flashing prices, reducing symbols, etc. may be used to alleviate time lag. (105)

law, common Those principles which have their origin in the decisions of the court of chancery and are not founded on statute. (66)

lawful money All forms of money which, by federal law, are endowed with legal tender for the payment of all debts, both public and private. See Legal Tender. (1)

lawful reserve Banking laws establish the lawful reserves that must be maintained by banks for the protection of depositors' accounts. These reserves were established by the Federal Reserve Act of 1933 and 1935 for national banks, and by the banking laws of the various states for state-chartered banks. The Federal Reserve Board is vested by law with power to change the lawful reserve for national banks in order to control the supply of credit throughout the United States. This Board may increase the reserve requirements in order to curtail the extension of credit, or it may decrease the reserve requirements in order to permit the expansion of credit. The various state laws follow a similar pattern, being more strict in some respects and less strict in others. The lawful reserves are required to be available at all times in the form of cash, and under certain conditions, government securities, either in the vaults of the bank, or in lawful bank depositories authorized by government or state officials. (1)

laws of descent Laws governing the descent of real property from ancestor to heir; to be distinguished from laws, rules, or statutes of distribution governing the disposition of personal property. (88)

law, statutory Law created by legislative enactment. (66)

lawsuit A claim in a court of law. (93)

layoff loan Generally considered to be one within the legal limit of the country bank but taken by the city bank to assist a country bank that is highly loaned up. (89)

lease A contract by which an owner of property grants to another party the right of use, tenancy, or occupancy of that property. The property may be land, buildings, equipment, or other chattel property. The lease agreement describes the rights of the owner and of the renter and recites the terms of periodic payment and the tenure of the lease. The property leased reverts to the owner at the expiration of the lease agreements. (89)

leaseback A technique of financing and handling

real estate. The original owner sells the property and simultaneously leases it back. There are a number of advantages and disadvantages of such a practice. Advantages include frequent tax savings; disadvantages include loss of a hedge in a period of inflation.

lease broker A person who is in the business of obtaining leases for speculation and resale in areas where land plays or exploration work is being done. He may act on his own or as an agent for others, including oil companies. (125)

leased fee A property held in fee with the right of use and occupancy conveyed under lease to others. A property consisting of the right to receive ground rentals over a period of time, and the further right of ultimate repossession. (54)

lease, gross A lease under which the lessor pays all expenses of operation of the property, as well as capital charges. (66)

lease ground A lease which provides for occupancy and use of a parcel of unimproved land often, though obviously not always, for the construction of a building. In the event the lessee is to assume all property charges, more descriptive terminology would be Net Ground Lease. (66)

leasehold An estate or right in real property limited to a definitely ascertainable period of time, obtained and held with the consent of the owner of the estate or right and on the payment of a stipulated consideration. (89)

lease, percentage A lease which provides that the rental shall be based on a percentage of the volume of business done on the premises, usually with a guaranteed minimum and occasionally a maximum rental regardless of business volume. (66)

lease-purchase Method for obtaining new post offices and facilities under a long term purchase contract (10 to 25 years) substantially like purchasing a home in monthly payments. (39)

lease (regular or commercial) Agreement to occupy and use space for a definite term at a fixed monthly rental. (39)

lease, sandwich 1. A lease in a middle position between a prime lessor and a third party. 2. A lease in which the original or prime lessee re-leases the property to a subsequent lessee. Ordinarily a Sandwich Lease involves the subletting of the entire premises so that the prime or first lessee is no longer the occupant. (66)

ledger A record of final entry in bookkeeping. An account is established for every type of transaction, and a ledger account is posted with every transaction affecting this particular account. The term ledger also applies to a group of accounts, all of a similar nature, such as an accounts receivable ledger, an accounts payable ledger, etc. When accounts of a similar nature become too large, they are taken from the general ledger and placed in a subsidiary ledger, with a control ledger card in the general ledger. The control ledger card contains the balance of the entire subsidiary ledger that it represents. Subsidiary ledgers are established for control, and to facilitate more than one person posting to the ledger whenever the volume of a ledger control becomes more than one person can handle. (1)

ledger control card A monthly record to date of

the total debits, credits, and balances of the customer accounts it represents. In Demand Deposit Accounting, this card is the final record of its group to be updated. (83)

ledger proof card A record prepared daily containing total debits and credits affecting a given group of accounts. In Demand Deposit Accounting, this card follows the customer account cards. Its reconciliation with the daily updating totals is the control for its group. (83)

legacy (Bequest) A gift of personal property made by a decedent (testator male, or testatrix female) in his or her will. The party receiving the gift is called a legatee. There are four common types of legacies: 1. Specific legacy—a gift of a particular piece of property, as an automobile, a chair, or an investment which has been specifically described. 2. Demonstrative legacy—one payable in cash out of a particular designated fund. 3. General legacy—a gift of money of a certain sum. 4. Residuary legacy—includes all the remaining personal property after the payment of all obligations (debts), charges against the estate, and all the other legacies. A residuary legatee receives "all the rest, residue, and remainder" of the personal estate. (1)

legal Counseling on, preparing documents required by, and representing the company in connection with governmental controls, requirements and statutory obligations. (20)

legal charity One that comes within the legal definition of a charity. (74)

legal common trust fund A common trust fund invested wholly in property that is legal for the investment of trust funds in the state in which the common trust is being administered. The term is employed most often in or with respect to common trust funds in states that have a statutory or court-approved list of authorized investment for trustees where the terms of the trust do not provide otherwise. (74)

legal entity Any individual, proprietorship, partnership, corporation, organization, or association which has, in the eyes of the law, the capacity to make a contract or an agreement, and the ability to assume an obligation and to discharge an indebtedness. A legal entity is a responsible being in the eyes of the law, and can be sued for damages if the performance of a contract is not met according to the contract or the agreement.

legal fees Amounts charged to or collected from clients for legal counsel or services. (73)

legal holiday A public holiday which has been proclaimed by competent authority or made by law. In addition to Sunday, New Year's Day, Washington's Birthday, Independence Day, Labor Day, Thanksgiving Day and Christmas which are celebrated in all states certain other days may be observed ranging from Columbus Day, Jefferson Davis's Birthday through Lincoln's Birthday, depending upon the state which has jurisdiction within its own area. From a business point of view such days are not valid for legal or judicial service of process of instruments or protest of non-payment of negotiable instruments.

legal interest That maximum interest rate established by state law which is used in contracts which have omitted mention of a rate.

legal investments 1. Investments which savings banks, insurance companies, trustees, and other fiduciaries (individual or corporate) are permitted to make by the laws of the state in which they are domiciled, or under the jurisdiction of which they operate or serve. The investments which meet the conditions imposed by law constitute the legal investment list. 2. Investments which governmental units are permitted to make by law. (29)

legal list (Often abbreviated to "Legals".) A list of investments selected by various states in which certain institutions and fiduciaries, such as insurance companies and banks, may invest. Legal lists are restricted to high quality securities meeting certain specifications. See Prudent Man Rule. (2)

legal obligations A debt or promise to perform, that can be enforced by legal means if necessary. (59)

legal opinion 1. The opinion of an official authorized to render it such as an attorney general or city attorney, as to legality. 2. In the case of municipal bonds, the opinion, usually of a specialized bond attorney, as to the legality of a bond issue. A preliminary legal opinion is made in advance of the original sale of the bonds, a final opinion, after the bonds have been issued and sold. (29)

legal ownership An estate of interest in property which is enforceable in a court of law; to be distinguished from equitable ownership. (74)

legal person Description of a corporation's condition of being subject to laws just as if it were a person.

legal rate of interest The maximum rate of interest that is permitted by the laws of the state having jurisdiction over the legality of a transaction. Interest in excess of this legal rate is termed usury. See Usury. (1)

legal reserve A bank's legal reserve is the portion of its deposits (demand and time) which it is required by law to maintain in the form of cash or readily available balances to meet the demands of depositors. Members of the Federal Reserve System must keep their legal reserves on deposit with the Federal Reserve banks of their respective districts. (85)

legal security That stock or bond which a fiduciary such as a trust company or trustee may purchase and hold for beneficiaries. In some states these are published in a Legal List.

legal tender The Gold Act of 1934 (48 Stat. 337) says in part: Sec. 15:—"The term 'currency of the United States' means currency which is legal tender in the United States, and includes United States notes, Treasury notes of 1890, gold certificates, silver certificates, Federal Reserve notes, and circulating notes of the Federal Reserve banks and national banking associations." Legal tender means any money that is recognized by law as being lawfully used by a debtor to pay a creditor who must accept same in the discharge of a debt, unless the contract between the parties specifically states the type of money to be used. (1)

legal title Title to property recognized by and enforceable in a court of law; to be distinguished from equitable title. (74)

legatee A person who receives a gift of personal property by will.

lempira Monetary unit of Honduras.

lender One who makes a trade of putting money to interest; a money lender. (93)

lending flat When a security which has been sold short is borrowed for purposes of delivery it is said to be lent flat if the borrower does not have to pay a charge for the privilege of borrowing it. When a security is lent flat no fee is charged the borrower.

lending institution One set up to lend money, making its livelihood out of advancing funds to others. (59)

lending rates Those interest rates charged by lenders to borrowers. The rates will vary by class of borrower, collateral, and maturity of loan as well as the availability of funds and the actions of the monetary authorities.

lending securities Those securities which may be borrowed by the broker representing a short seller.

lessee An entity (company, individual, etc.) that leases equipment from a lessor. The lessee enjoys the use of the equipment but does not own it.

lessor An entity that leases equipment to a lessee. Title to the equipment is vested in the lessor.

let To lease, demise or convey; thus a sign "to let." (5)

letter of administration Evidence of appointment issued by a court to an individual or a trust instruction to settle the estate of a decedent who failed to name an executor. (74)

letter of advice A note giving instructions.

letter of allotment An "Allotment Notice." See that term.

letter of attorney A written instrument which evidences the authority of an agent who is known as an attorney-in-fact. (74)

letter of conservatorship A certificate of authority issued by the court to an individual or corporate fiduciary to serve as conservator of the property of a person; corresponds with letters of guardianship. (74)

letter of credit An instrument or document issued by a bank on another bank or banks, foreign or domestic, or upon itself. The letter of credit gives the buyer (probably unknown to the seller) the prestige and the financial backing of the bank who issues the letter of credit in his behalf. The acceptance by the bank of drafts drawn under the letter of credit satisfies the seller and his bank in the handling of the transaction. The buyer and the accepting bank also have an agreement as to payment for the drafts as they are presented. (1)

letter of identification A note or letter given by the maker to the bearer which will serve to introduce him to the one to whom it is addressed. On the basis of the identification the firm or individual addressed is in a position to rely on the identity of the bearer, such as honoring drafts or orders for material.

letter of intention A pledge to purchase a sufficient amount of open-end investment company shares within a limited time (usually 12 or 13 months) to qualify for the reduced selling charge that would apply to a comparable lump-sum purchase. (3)

letter of introduction A note or letter given by the maker to the bearer which serves to introduce the bearer to the one to whom it is addressed.

letter of lien See Letter of Trust.

letter of trust A letter of lien. A letter which states that the signer-agent is holding merchandise for a seller until such times as the seller is paid for the goods.

letter patent A sealed and signed document from a government which grants a special right, privilege, property, or title such as the exclusive right to make or sell an invention.

letters testamentary A certificate of authority to settle a particular estate issued by the appointing court to the executor named in the will; to be distinguished from letters of administration. (74)

leu Monetary unit of Rumania.

lev Monetary unit of Bulgaria.

level charge plan An accumulation plan under which the selling charges are spread over the entire life of the program; i.e., a sales charge obtains on each separate purchase, the amount varying with the size of the purchase. (3)

level-payment plan An amortization plan that provides for equal monthly payments covering both principal and interest during the term of the mortgage. Part of each payment is applied to interest as earned, and the rest of the payment is credited to principal. (89)

leverage The effect on the par share earnings of the common stock of a company when large sums must be paid for bond interest or preferred stock dividends, or both, before the common stock is entitled to share in earnings. Leverage may be advantageous for the common stock when earnings are good but may work against the common stock when earnings decline. Example: Company A has 1,000,000 shares of common stock outstanding, no other securities. Earnings drop from $1,000,000 to $800,000 or from $1 to 80 cents a share, a decline of 20 percent. Company B also has 1,000,000 shares of common but must pay $500,000 annually in bond interest. If earnings amount to $1,000,000, there is $500,000 available for the common or 50 cents a share—a drop of 40 percent. Or suppose earnings of the company with only common stock increased from $1,000,000 to $1,500,000— earnings per share would go from $1 to $1.50, or an increase of 50 percent. But if earnings of the company which had to pay $500,000 in bond interest increased that much—earnings per common share would jump from 50 cents to $1 a share, or 100 percent. When a company has common stock only, no leverage exists because all earnings are available for the common, although relatively large fixed charges payable for lease of substantial plant assets may have an effect similar to that of a bond issue. (2)

leveraged lease A lease transaction in which the financing of the equipment is divided into debt and equity portions and placed separately with different investors. The debt portion has a fixed return and is secured by the equipment. The equity portion, the ownership of the equipment, may represent no more than 20-25 percent of the original equipment cost. The equity investor enjoys the tax advantages of equipment ownership, and those benefits may be reflected in the lease rate itself, reducing the lessee's rental payments. The equity investor assumes the normal ownership risks.

leverage factor Ratio of working assets to price of the leverage security. (3)

leverage stock Junior security of a multiple-capital-structure company, generally a common stock, but the term may also be applied to a warrant, or to a preferred stock if the latter is preceded by funded debt or bank loans. (3)

levy An exaction of payments or services by a public authority. (89)

liabilities 1. In banking, liabilities are the funds a bank owes. By far the largest items on the liability side of a bank's financial statement are the time and demand deposits. 2. All the claims against a corporation. Liabilities include accounts and wages and salaries payable, dividends declared payable, accrued taxes payable, fixed or long-term liabilities such as mortgage bonds, debentures and bank loans. See Assets; Balance Sheet. (83, 2)

liability Something represented by a credit balance that is or would be properly carried forward upon a closing of books of account according to the rules or principles of accounting, provided such credit balance is not in effect a negative balance applicable to an asset. Thus, the word is used broadly to comprise not only items which constitute liabilities in the popular sense of debts or obligations (including provision for those that are unascertained), but also credit balances to be accounted for which do not involve the debtor and creditor relation. For example, capital stock and related or similar elements of proprietorship are balance-sheet liabilities in that they represent balances to be accounted for, though these are not liabilities in the ordinary sense of debts owed to legal creditors. (17)

liability, capital A comprehensive term which includes all long-term indebtedness of a corporation which is represented by the outstanding capital stock (liability to owners) and mortgages and bonded indebtedness (liability to outside creditors). Generally, a long-term indebtedness is considered as one which, during the normal course of the business, will not fall due or be liquidated during the ensuing fiscal period. (1)

liability, central The grouping together on one record of all liabilities of a borrower, such as loans both direct and indirect, consumer credit, letters of credit, guarantees, and other accommodations. The purpose of this record is to prevent over-extensions of credit to the borrower. (1)

liability, common law The responsibility for injuries or damage imposed upon a party because of his actions, by that part of the law based upon custom and usage as established by the courts, as distinguished from liability under statutes passed by a legislative body. Such law is known as statutory law. Liability of one party to an-

other, other than liability which is covered under a specific legislated law. (5)

liability, contingent Liability for damages arising out of the acts or omissions of others, not employees nor agents. (51)

liability, contractual Liability over and above that which would be imposed by law which a person assumes under the terms of a contract. For example, manufacturers in selling their products may agree to protect the purchaser against claims which may arise out of the use of the products. (52)

liability, corporate profits tax Federal and state taxes levied on corporate earnings of a given year. This measures taxes for the year in which they are incurred, not necessarily for the year in which they are paid. (7)

liability, cumulative When one bond is cancelled and another issued to take its place and the first bond has a discovery period, the surety company is exposed to the possibility of a loss equal to the aggregate sum of the two bonds. For instance, an employee of the insured could take an amount equal to the full penalty of the first bond while the first bond is in force and also steal the full amount of the second bond during its currency, and the whole loss could be discovered before the discovery period under the first bond has elapsed. Unless required by statute to afford such cumulative liability the surety company generally attaches a superseded suretyship rider. This not only picks up liability for undiscovered loss under the prior bond, but, in the case where both the bonds are written by the same company, bars the possibility of an accumulation of losses as between two bonds. (50)

liability, current Those pecuniary obligations ordinarily intended to be paid in the usual course of business within a relatively short time, normally within a year, out of earnings. (66)

liability, deposit The total of time, demand and certificate of deposits as well as other special deposits such as Christmas Club, Vacation Club and escrow accounts which a bank owes its customers.

liability, direct A known primary obligation requiring the payment of a certain sum of money either now or at some determinable future date. See Prime Maker. (1)

liability, fixed Long term debt—recurring expenses. (93)

liability, indirect A secondary, or contingent, liability assumed by the endorsement or guaranty of an obligation for which another party is primarily liable. It becomes an absolute liability only upon the failure of the primary party to live up to his agreement. (85)

liability, indirect business tax and nontax All tax liabilities incurred by business, except for corporate income and social insurance taxes, plus general government nontax revenues for business. Nontax liabilities consist mainly of certain charges for government products and services, of fines and penalties, of donations, and of special assessments by state and local governments. Note that tax and nontax liability consists of payments incurred, not payments made. (7)

liability, joint Liability for which more than one person or company share responsibility. (5)

liability ledger One of the most important records of the bank is the liability ledger. In this ledger is the record of all outstanding loans made by the bank to every borrower. Each borrower has an individual ledger card, wherein is recorded each loan the borrower may have with the bank, and the total of all outstanding loans made to each borrower. The aggregate of all outstanding loans make up the liability ledger, which is the record of the bank's largest "earning asset" account. (1)

liability, legal An obligation enforceable by law most often considered in a monetary sense. Broadly, any legally enforceable obligation. The term is most commonly used in a pecuniary sense. For example, if you own an automobile you may have a legal liability, or liability under the law, to reimburse anyone who may be injured through your negligence in the operation of that automobile. (52+)

liability, limited Responsibility in event of bankruptcy limited to the amount invested in the business. (93)

liability, primary A direct liability as differentiated from an indirect or contingent liability.

liability, secondary A contingent liability.

liable Bound or obliged in law; responsible. (93)

license The document embodying the formal permission from a legally constituted governing authority to carry on a certain activity the conduct of which would otherwise be illegal. The rates charged for licenses and permits are established by legislative action, such as by the passage of an ordinance or by statute. Such rates generally are not established each year, but are revised or adjusted from time to time as the need arises. The expected revenue from licenses and permits should not be considered until it is received in cash, since the amount cannot be known until the license and permits are issued. (29)

licensed lender A consumer finance office which is authorized to conduct business in the state in which it is located. (131)

lien The right of a legally constituted governing body, or a legal right granted to an individual by the authority of a court, to control or to enforce a charge against one's property until some legal claim is paid or otherwise satisfied. (29)

lienee The person who possesses a right of lien on property of another. (66)

lienor The person on whose property the right of lien exists. (66)

life beneficiary A person who receives benefits from an estate, generally in the form of income, during his lifetime; sometimes called a life tenant if the estate consists of real property. (74)

life contingency Probability of living or dying. Tables relating to life contingency may be found in the rate manuals. (42)

life, economic 1. The length of time over which it is estimated a building will enhance the value of the land. 2. The length of time during which a building will produce a net income over and above the income attributable to the land. (66)

life estate A freehold interest in land, the duration of which is confined to the life of one or more persons or contingent upon certain happenings. (54)

life in being A beneficiary living at the time a trust is created.

life-tenant A beneficiary under a will or trust who has been left a legacy from the testator or donor in the form of income derived from the principal or "corpus" (see definition) of a trust. The income accruing to the life-tenant must come from the earnings of the corpus—the life-tenant has no interest in the corpus other than the income derived from it, unless otherwise specified in the will or trust instrument. (1)

lifo See Last In, First Out.

lift check A check that is not drawn on a bank but through the bank against the maker. Many corporations issue payroll checks in the form of "lift checks." The bank through which the items are drawn accumulates a group of these items and delivers them to the maker upon receipt of a regular check in payment of the total. (83)

limit In commodities, the maximum permitted price fluctuation in any one day before trading is suspended, also the restriction on the number of futures contracts any one person or company may hold.

limited (ltd) A corporation. While mostly associated with British or Canadian business firms using the corporate form and thus having limited liability the term is sometimes used in the United States and has the same meaning.

limited audit An audit in which the effectiveness of the system of internal control and the mathematical accuracy, legality, propriety, and completeness of all transactions are determined by examining only selected items. The assumption is that the transactions selected for examination are representative of the entire group from which selected and therefore if no errors are found in them the unchecked items in the group are also correct. See also Complete Audit. (29)

limited check A check which is limited as to the amount. Such checks have inscribed on their face a legend that the item is "void" if more than a certain amount. Limited checks are frequently used in payroll payments by check, with the maximum amount shown on the face. This is done to frustrate attempts to raise the amount of the check. The date by which a check must be presented for payment also constitutes a limitation. (1)

limited depositary A Federal Reserve System member bank which under stated restrictions may receive governmental deposits.

limited general audit A limited audit of the transactions of an accounting period, usually a year. See Limited Audit; General Audit. (29)

limited liability The extent of the liability of the owners of a business (financial or other) to outside creditors. The liability of the stockholders of a commercial (as opposed to financial) corporation is limited to the par value of the stock they have subscribed for or own. In certain states, the liability of the stockholders of stock in a state-chartered bank is double the amount of the par value of the stock they have subscribed for or own. (1)

limited open-end mortgage An indenture under

which additional bonds may be issued, but which establishes certain limits, or measures, of maximum amounts that may be issued. (88)

limited order An order in which the client has set restrictions as contrasted to a market order. See Market Order. (9)

limited partner A member of a partnership who as a result of giving up an active voice in management and publicly announcing in the legally required way that he is a limited partner acquires limited liability.

limited partnership A partnership consisting of both general and special partners, with at least one member, the manager, being fully responsible for all debts. (105)

limited power of appointment A power of the donee (the one who has the power) to pass on an interest in property that is limited in some way—as to or for whom or to the time within which he must exercise the power; also known as special power; the opposite of general power of appointment; all powers that are not general are special or limited powers. (74)

limited tax bond A bond which is secured by a tax which is limited as to rate and amount.

limit order A customer's order to a securities broker to buy or sell at a specific price or better. The order can be executed only at that price or a better one. See Stop Order; GTC; Market Order. (2)

limping standard A monetary standard in which designated silver coins are considered as unlimited legal tender and thus do not have to be redeemed in gold though the paper currency is so redeemable.

lineal descendant A person in the direct line of descent, as child or grandchild; opposed to collateral heir. (74)

line chart Also referred to as a bar and line chart, constructed on graph paper by recording the price range of a particular security for a day, week or month. The closing price is usually denoted and a separate chart of volume is also recorded. The patterns formed over a period of time help the chartists attempt to predict future price action. (105)

line graph A graph that uses a single line to indicate increases and decreases in an item from one period to another. (73)

line of credit An agreement between a bank and a customer whereby the bank agrees to lend the customer funds up to a previously agreed maximum amount. The bank has the option to withdraw from the agreement if the financial status of the borrower changes, or if the borrower fails to use the line of credit for its intended use as per the agreement. The customer may borrow as much of the "line" as is required and pays interest on the borrowed portion only. A line of credit is widely used by large organizations for the future commitments and purchases of inventory. The bank is fully entitled to periodic financial reports from the borrower so as to be constantly informed on his credit status. (1)

line of stocks The systematic purchase or sale of a large amount of stocks, for example, by scale orders. (105)

liquidate To discharge, to pay off, to convert into cash by selling. (93)

liquidating dividend A distribution of assets, as distinguished from a distribution of earnings. The term is generally used in connection with the dissolution of a corporation, but it may also be applied to payments of a going concern resulting from the disposition of wasting assets, such as mining property or timber. (74)

liquidating market The condition of a commodity or security market in which strong selling pressure is present. A bear market.

liquidating value The anticipated value of a particular asset that will be realized in case of liquidation of a business. (1)

liquidation The process of paying the liabilities of a business, selling the assets, and distributing the remaining cash to the owner or owners of the business. (73)

liquidator The individual chosen by an appropriate court of jurisdiction or named by statute for the purpose of liquidating or winding up a business.

liquidity 1. The ability of the market in a particular security to absorb a reasonable amount of buying or selling at reasonable price changes. Liquidity is one of the most important characteristics of a good market. 2. The quality that renders an asset convertible into cash on short notice by sale in the open market or by rediscount, usually at a minimum of loss. (2, 89)

liquidity preference The tendency for people to keep their assets in a form that is cash or easily converted into cash rather than in a frozen form.

liquid saving Individuals' saving consisting of, or easily and quickly convertible into, cash. These consist of currency, bank deposits, shares in savings and loan associations and securities. Included are holdings of persons, unincorporated business, trusts, and non-profit institutions. (7)

liquid securities Stocks, bonds, etc., easily marketable and converted to cash. (59)

lira Monetary unit of Italy and Turkey.

lis pendens Notice of a pending suit. (66)

list A column of figures listed on an adding machine tape or piece of paper. Lists are used to obtain a total of large volumes of items in the same category, such as checks drawn on the same account. (83)

listed securities The term applies to any bonds or stocks which have been admitted for trading on the stock or curb exchanges and whose issues have complied in every way with the listing requirements of the exchange. Listing requirements are very stringent and are primarily designed to protect the public from trading in bonds or stocks of unscrupulous corporations. (1)

listed stock The stock of a company which is traded on a national securities exchange, and for which a listing application and a registration statement, giving detailed information about the company and its operations, have been filed with the Securities & Exchange Commission and the exchange itself. The various stock exchanges have different standards for listing. Some of the guides used by the N.Y. Stock Exchange for an original listing are national interest in the company and its stock, at least 1,500 share owners,

300,000 shares outstanding in the hands of the public, an earning power at the time of listing of at least $1,000,000 annually. (2)

listing The record of a property for sale or lease by a broker who has been authorized in writing by the owner to act as his agent. (54+)

listing requirements Requirements of stock exchanges that must be satisfied before a company will be admitted to listing. Requirements (1964) of the New York Stock Exchange include: a minimum of 500,000 common shares outstanding exclusive of concentrated or family holdings; a total market value or net tangible assets applicable to common stock of $10 million at least 1,500 round-lot holders and demonstrated earning power of $1 million annually after all charge and taxes under competitive conditions. Other general guides include requirements that the company must be a going concern; a national interest in company; and agreement to submitting public reports. (105)

list price The posted, published price which may at times be reduced by such devices as volume discounts, commissions, discounts for prompt payment or cash or other rebate.

list, the The total list of names of all the securities listed on a particular exchange. (105)

litigation The act of carrying on a lawsuit. (5)

little board The American Stock Exchange, The New York Stock Exchange is called the Big Board.

little steel All steel manufacturers in the United States except United States Steel Corporation.

lives in being Lives in existence at a given time. See Rule Against Perpetuities. (74)

living trust A trust instrument made effective during the lifetime of the creator, in contrast to a Testamentary Trust, which is created under a will. (3)

load The portion of the offering price of shares of open-end investment companies which covers sales commissions and all other costs of distribution. The load is incurred only on purchase, there being, in most cases, no charge when the shares are sold (redeemed). (2)

load charge The commission charged to the buyer of many mutual fund shares to cover sales, promotion and distribution costs. The price of mutual fund shares consists of net asset value plus commission, which averages about 8½%. (105)

load up To be long in a commodity or security more than one would normally be.

loan The lending of a sum of money by a lender to a borrower, to be repaid with a certain amount of interest. May be either secured or unsecured, on a time, demand, or installment basis. Secured loans are backed by collateral which the bank may claim in case of default by the maker; time loans have a fixed or determinable maturity; demand loans are terminable at the option of either the lender or the borrower; installment loans are repaid in regular installments at fixed intervals. (83)

loanable funds interest theory Theory that the supply and demand of money determines interest rates.

loan application A form used by banks to record the formal request for a loan by a borrower. The form is specially designed by each bank to incorporate the necessary information that the bank desires having on record. The loan application may be a simple form or a more complex form containing information relative to the assets, liabilities, income, insurance, and contingent obligations of the borrower, as well as the purpose for which the loan is intended. (1)

loan capital The capital of a business which is in the form of debt as distinguished from equity capital. It would include bonds, notes, bank loans and all debt of a formal or instrument nature as distinguished from open account debt.

loan crowd Those members of a stock exchange who will lend securities for those who have sold short.

loan department The department of the bank where all the paper work as well as the actual loan transactions are handled. All notes and other negotiable instruments are filed in this department. All collateral securities are also filed in this department, which is bailee or custodian of these instruments and securities. The "Loans Made Register," the record of original entry for all loans, is created here. The note notice and maturity tickler are filed here for ready reference. The liability ledger containing the complete loan record of each borrower is made and kept in this department. This department is the principal source of revenue for the operations of the bank. (1)

loaned flat When stocks are sold short the seller must borrow them to make delivery. If he is able to borrow them without making a payment of interest for them he is dealing in a stock that is "loaned flat."

loaned stock Stock which has been loaned to a short seller or his broker in order to fulfill the terms of a short selling contract by delivering shares. The borrower pays the lender of the security the market value of the stock in money. The lender may have to pay interest on that money, or may receive a premium for lending it. Many times, however, the securities are loaned flat. (105)

loan function The processing of a loan, covering each step necessary to furnish all required information. The following steps in the processing of a loan come under the loan function:

1. Interview between customer and loan officer.

2. Credit information assembled and placed in the customer's credit file.

3. Review of the credit information by the loan officer or loan committee.

4. Decision to extend credit to the customer.

5. Note processed by the loan teller and disbursement made to the borrower.

6. Loan recorded in the "Loans Made Register."

7. Customer's liability ledger, note notice, and maturity tickler recorded.

8. Note notice filed by customer; maturity tickler filed by due date.

9. Collateral and note filed for ready reference and accessibility.

10. Note and collateral, if any, surrendered to customer upon payment of loan.

11. Payment recorded in liability ledger; customer's ledger card kept for reference for future credit extension. (1)

loan interest Explicit interest. The amount paid for the use of capital or money.

loan ledger The "Liability Ledger." See that term.

loan market Those places such as banks, finance companies, factors, trust companies and similar financial institutions including wealthy individuals' places of business where loans are made.

loan officer An officer of the bank who is designated with the responsibility of interviewing customers who may become borrowers. Certain officers have the power to grant loans. Large loans are approved by a loan committee consisting of appointed officers and directors of the bank. (83)

loan participation See Participation Loan.

loan price The price at which growers may obtain loans from the government.

loan program The federal government price support program on agricultural products. The government will lend money to farmers on the basis of the collateral of the covered crop based on a schedule announced by the Department of Agriculture.

loan rate The charge at which loan funds can be had at a given time and at a given lending source. (59)

loan register A loose-leaf or bound journal in which the details of loans are entered, usually in the order in which they are granted. (1)

loans adjusted Face value of customers' notes held (including bankers' acceptances and commercial paper purchased in the market) less interbank loans and reserves for losses on loans. (4)

loans and discounts Used by banks to designate all funds outstanding on loans. (83)

loans and investments adjusted Total of loans adjusted, U.S. Government securities and other bank eligible securities. (4)

loans and notes payable Obligations outstanding in the form of loans and notes payable or other similar evidences (except interest coupons) of indebtedness payable on demand or within a time not exceeding one year from date of issue. (19)

loans and notes receivable Obligations in the form of demand or time loans and notes receivable, or other similar evidences (except interest coupons) of money receivable within a time not exceeding one year from date of issue. (19)

loans and other long-term assets A part of total transactions in U.S. Government assets, this account includes the flow of capital abroad resulting from all loans and credits with an original maturity of more than one year made by the federal government to foreign countries. Most of these credits finance U.S. exports of goods and services.

In 1968 long-term dollar loans under the defense and economic development programs administered by the Agency for International Development accounted for less than one-third of total U.S. Government long-term foreign lending; Export-Import Bank dollar credits ac-

counted for over 40 percent; and dollar and foreign currency loans extended under Public Law 480, about 25 percent. The remaining long-term credit transactions include principally credits related to the sale of military equipment. (124)

loan shark A lender of funds at a rate higher than the maximum legal rate.

loans to nonbank financial institutions Loans outstanding to nonbank financial institutions subdivided as follows:

Sales finance, personal finance, factors, and business credit companies.

Other—including mortgage companies, mutual savings banks, savings and loan associations, insurance companies, and federal agencies. (4)

loan teller An employee in the loan department who handles loan transactions. This teller is the custodian of cash in the loan teller's cash till (except in the larger banks), and handles all direct transactions involving loans for the loan officer, upon the officer's recommendations and approval. The teller usually computes the interest based upon the rate set by the loan officer, accepts collateral over the counter, and performs all duties of a regular teller, but dealing specifically with the functions of the loan department. (1)

loan value The largest amount that can be borrowed by the insured on the security of the cash value of his life insurance. Generally, the loan is from the life insurance company but at times may be made by other lenders. (5)

loan-value ratio The ratio between the amount of a loan and the appraised value of the collateral. (89)

lobby The main banking room of a bank where depositors and customers of the bank may transact business with the bank. The ordinary business is transacted through the teller, while loans, credit extensions, trust operations, and the more complex matters of finance are handled in privacy in offices away from the bank lobby. (1)

local clearings See Local Items. (83)

local items Term referring to checks drawn on other banks in the same city as the bank currently holding them. Synonym: Local clearings. (83)

lock boxes Rental boxes for public use in post office lobby, with key or combination lock. (39)

locked in An investor is said to be locked in when he has a profit on a security he owns but does not sell because his profit would immediately become subject to the capital gains tax. See Capital Gain. (2)

lock up Refers to securities that have been withdrawn from circulation and placed in a safe deposit box for purposes of long-term investment. (105)

lombard loan A loan by a central bank based upon collateral such as bonds and stocks.

Lombard Street The London financial area similar to Wall Street in New York or LaSalle Street in Chicago.

long 1. One is said to be net "long" of the futures market if he has bought more contracts than he has sold—the opposite of "short". Long hedges are purchases of futures made as a hedge against the sale of the cash commodity; long interest—the sum total of all long contracts (or in the plural, the owners of such interest). 2. Signifies ownership of securities. "I am long 100 U. S. Steel" means the speaker owns 100 shares. See Short. (9, 2)

long account The aggregate of securities held by traders and investors in expectation of rising prices. Also may refer to specific securities held by a broker for his client, either for cash or on margin. (105)

long bill A bill of exchange drawn for more than the customary period of time. Generally over 30 days' sight.

long draft A draft that is drawn for more than the customary period of time. See Long Bill.

long interest The holders of a security who have long positions as distinguished from short interests which are bearish in action.

long market A market which has experienced a rise which leaves it technically weak due to the tendency of some of the long interests to take profits from their selling of the securities.

long on the basis One who has bought cash or spot goods and has hedged them with the sale of the futures. He has therefore bought at a certain basis on or off futures and expects to sell at a better basis with the future for a profit. (9)

long position A market attitude of one who actually owns securities, that is, one who is expecting a rise in prices or holding for income as opposed to one who has a short position. (105)

long pull The purchase of a product, security or contract expecting higher prices eventually, although declines may occur meanwhile. (9)

long side A bull. A long interest.

long stock Securities which have been purchased in expectation of rising prices. (105)

long term A period of six months or more as opposed to the short or near-term period of less than six months. Long-term securities profits are accorded a more favorable tax treatment than short term gains. (105)

long-term financing The issuance and sale of debt securities with a maturity of more than one year, and preferred and common stock for the purpose of raising new capital, refunding outstanding securities or for the divestment of investments in securities not permitted to be held under the Public Utility Holding Company Act of 1935. (21)

long-term liabilities reported by U.S. banks Include long-term deposits—in excess of one year—by foreigners in U.S. banks, mainly by foreign official or international agencies. Some of these liabilities consist of deposits used to finance U.S. imports, plant expansion, and other financial transactions which would involve U.S. banking services, such as a foreign government's line of credit to a U.S. bank.

The flow in the opposite direction appears in claims reported by U.S. banks: long-term. (124)

long term receivables and investments A group of assets which includes money owed to the company on a long term installment basis, plus the company's investments in affiliated and other companies.

long-term trend The basic direction in which market prices seem likely to move over a period of time in the future. (105)

look back A term used in banks to describe the act of auditing past records in order to locate errors that have come to the attention of the bank's auditing department. (1)

loss The excess of all expenses, in the broad sense of that word, over revenues for a period, or the excess of all or the appropriate portion of the cost of assets over related proceeds, if any, when the items are sold, abandoned, or either wholly or partially destroyed by casualty or otherwise written off. (17)

loss on bad debts An expense that results from failure to collect amounts due from charge customers. (73)

loss on fixed assets A term applied to the loss, or expense, that results when the book value of a fixed asset is greater than the actual value at the time the asset is sold. (73)

loss on sale of assets An expense account used for recording losses that result when assets are sold for less than the book value. (73)

loss outstanding Tabulation of losses that an insurance company has in the form of claims but which it has not settled. (5)

loss ratio Ratio between losses incurred and premium income during any given period. (42)

lost certificates Owners of certificates which have been lost must notify the transfer agent of the company concerned. The certificates must be positively identified and usually a security bond posted before new certificates will be issued. (105)

lot A unit of trading in securities. A round-lot is normally 100 shares; an odd-lot an amount less than a round-lot. (105)

lowest offer The lowest price that will be accepted for something being offered for sale. (105)

lump sum Full payment made in one sum, and at one time. (42)

lump sum appropriation The provision of an amount of money for some purpose or agency without detailed and itemized allocation.

M

Maj. Majority.

M. A. N. F. Quarterly interest payments or dividends in May, August, November, and February.

Mat. Maturity.

Max. Maximum.

MBA Mortgage Bankers Association of America.

Mfst. Manifest.

MICR Magnetic Ink Character Recognition.

Min. Minimum; Minority; Minute.

MIP Monthly Investment Plan. A pay-as-you-go method of buying N.Y. Stock Exchange listed shares on a regular payment plan for as little as $40 a month, or $40 every three months. Under MIP the investor buys stocks by the dollars' worth if the price advances, he gets fewer shares and if it declines, he gets more shares. He may discontinue purchases at any time without penalty. The only charge for purchases and sales is the usual commission for buying and selling, plus the regular odd-lot dealer differential. The commission ranges from 6 per cent on small transactions to slightly below 1½ per cent on larger transactions. See Dollar Cost Averaging; Odd Lot Dealer. (2)

M. J. S. D. Quarterly interest payments or dividends in March, June, September and December.

Mk. Marks.

Mkr. Maker.

Mkt. Market.

M. & N. Semi-annual interest payments or dividends in May and November.

M.O. Money Order.

Mos. Months.

M/P Mail Payment.

M. & S. Semi-annual interest payments or dividends in March and September.

Mshp. Machine shop.

Mtge. Mortgage.

Mun. Municipal.

machine pay A plan of checking account posting whereby all media, both checks and deposits, are posted to a journal only on the first "run" of the media. The old balances of all affected accounts are picked up, the media posted, and new balances extended as in any posting run. The affected accounts may or may not be offset, depending upon the using bank's preference. The machine pay journalizing mechanically shows up items to be returned for insufficient funds, or paid as overdrafts. The run also establishes totals for checks, deposits, and new balances of affected accounts. The subsequent run on the depositor's statements must then prove to the machine pay run for checks, deposits, and new balances, verifying that the items were posted correctly, checks as checks, deposits as deposits, and the right accounts selected. (1)

magnetic ink character recognition See Common Machine Language. (83)

mail deposit A deposit received by the bank through the mail rather than over the counter. The bank credits the customer's account and mails a receipt back to customer. (83)

mail teller This name is used to designate the teller or division which handles deposits received by mail. (83)

maintenance The total of cash or securities deposited in a brokerage account to meet a broker's margin requirements. (105)

maintenance of investment organization The charges to income for the directly assignable organization and administration expenses which are incident to carrier's investments in leased or non-operating physical property, and in stocks, bonds, or other securities. (19)

majority control In a de jure sense a slight fraction of over fifty percent of the voting stock of a corporation is needed to control a corporation. In a de facto sense control may be achieved with a much smaller percentage if the stockholders are in small units and widely scattered and management is not strongly opposed.

majority stockholders Those stockholders who own controlling interest in a corporation, that is, they control a majority of the outstanding stock. (105)

major trend The basic direction in which stock prices are moving over a period of time regardless of temporary movements contrary to trend. Also called the primary movement. (105)

make a market To stand ready to buy or sell, adjusting bid and offer prices to balance purchases and sales. (103)

maker Any individual, proprietorship, corporation, or other legal entity who signs a check, draft, note, or other type of negotiable instrument as a primary responsible party is known as the maker. (1)

making a line The price pattern of a stock which fluctuates within a relatively narrow range for some time. This may indicate either accumulation or distribution of the security; therefore, chartists watch these formations carefully for clues of which direction the price may finally take. (105)

making a market 1. Creating or stimulating interest in a security by publicity or possibly listing on an exchange which will increase its marketability. 2. Action by a broker in naming a price at which he will purchase a security, while another broker names a price at which he will sell the security. 3. Action of a dealer in the over-the-counter market in acquiring an inventory in a new issue security whereby he stands ready to buy and sell for his own account. His profit is then made from the "spread," or difference in what he pays for the security and what he can sell it for. (105)

managed currency A manipulated money. The currency is not permitted to respond to "natural laws" of such factors as gold points or supply and demand. Instead the monetary authorities control the supply and velocity by various devices, one of such would be removal of free convertibility into gold.

management The Board of Directors, elected by the stockholders, and the officers of the corporation, appointed by the Board of Directors. (2)

management fee The charge made to an investment company for supervision of its portfolio. Frequently includes various other services and is usually a fixed percentage of average assets at market. (3)

management stock 1. The stock owned by the management of a corporation. 2. Stock which having extra voting privileges can control a corporation.

manifest A document listing the contents, value, origin, destination, carrier and time a cargo is shipped.

manipulation An illegal operation. Buying or selling a security for the purpose of creating false or misleading appearance of active trading or for the purpose of raising or depressing the price to induce purchase or sale by others. (2)

manual A book published by an agency, company, or rating bureau for the guidance of its users. In it are found rates, classifications, specifications, and rules governing the subject covered. (52)

manual of operation The written instructions, usually prepared by, or with the approval of the accounting, auditing, comptroller's or methods department, covering the procedure to follow and the responsibilities of the party or parties in the handling of the transactions within and affecting the operations of a given business or financial institution. (1)

margin The amount deposited by a client with his broker to protect the broker against loss on contracts being carried or to be carried by the broker. A margin call is a request to deposit either the original margin or to maintain margin with added cash. The margin may be set by such bodies as The Federal Reserve Board, The Board of Governors of the Exchange or by the broker. In any event the minimum margin would be the highest of the requirements of the various organizations. (9)

margin account An account of a customer of a brokerage firm which is used by the customer for purchasing securities or commodities on margin.

marginal activity A commercial venture which is just able to meet its expenses from its revenues and which would probably fail if expenses increased or revenue dropped.

marginal borrower The individual or firm which will cease to borrow if the loan rate of interest is increased.

marginal buyer A buyer who will quit the market if the price is raised.

marginal cost That amount of money one extra unit of production will add to the total cost of production.

marginal efficiency of capital The relationship between the return and the cost of an additional unit of capital.

marginal lender The individual or firm which will cease to lend if the loan rate of interest is decreased.

marginal revenue The gross income, or sale price of an additional unit of production.

marginal seller The individual or firm which will drop out, or refuse to sell in the event that the price of the product or service is reduced.

marginal trading The purchasing of a security or commodity in which the buyer does not pay for the transaction entirely with his own funds but rather borrows part of the purchase price. The amount of buyers equity is his margin.

margin buying The use of margin or borrowing for the purpose of purchasing securities or commodities. The percentage of the loan is determined by several different agencies such as the Federal Reserve Board, the respective exchange, the policy of the broker and lender.

margin call A demand upon a customer to put up money or securities with the broker. The call is made when a purchase is made; also if a customer's equity in a margin account declines below a minimum standard set by an exchange or by the firm. (106)

margined securities Securities bought on credit or held as collateral in a margin account which cannot be withdrawn until the debit balance owing in the account has been paid in full. (105)

margin notice Same as Margin Call.

margin of safety The safety factor of a thing or transaction. A bond issue which has income available of twice the interest charges would have a 100% margin of safety. A structural device which is tested and known to be able to support a stress of twice the anticipated stress in use would have a 100% margin of safety.

margin requirements May refer to any of several different requirements or to all requirements of such agencies as the Federal Reserve Board, the stock exchange, the individual brokerage office.

margins Are the limits around the par value within which the spot exchange rate of a member country's currency is permitted to move in actual exchange market dealings and in transactions with the public. The Articles of Agreement prescribe that these margins shall not exceed one percent either side of par, but somewhat wider margins around a central rate or a par value are provided for under conditions specified for a decision taken by the Executive Directors of the Fund in 1971. (130)

marital deduction The portion of a decedent's estate that may be given to the surviving wife or husband without its becoming subject to the federal estate tax levied against the decedent's estate; a term that came into general use under the Internal Revenue Act of 1954. (74)

marital rights The rights that a husband and wife have in each other's property. (74)

mark-down To change the offering price or valuation to a lower level. To reduce the price.

market 1. An aggregate composed of a prospective buyer (or buyers), and a seller (or sellers), that brings to focus the conditions and forces which determine prices. 2. The aggregate demand of the potential buyers of a commodity or service. 3. The place or area in which buyers and sellers function. 4. (as a verb) To perform business activities which direct the flow of goods and services from producer to consumer or user. (13)

marketability The rapidity and ease with which a given asset (particularly stocks, bonds, and other securities) can be converted into cash. (1)

marketable securities Securities which have available a ready, active market. (105)

marketable title A title which a reasonably prudent man, knowing all the facts, regards and accepts as good. (74)

market analysis A subdivision of marketing research which involves the measurement of the extent of a market and the determination of its characteristics. The activity consists essentially in the process of exploring and evaluating the marketing possibilities of the aggregates described in (2) of the definition of "market". (13)

market averages Any of a number of well known averages of securities such as Dow-Jones Industrial Average, Standard and Poor's Average of Stock Prices, The Security Exchange Commission's Averages. Since all of these are collections of representative stocks the fact that they fluctuate up or down permits the analyst to gage the movement of the market.

market cycle When referring to securities, a cycle consists of a period of rising prices including accumulation and advance followed by a period of lower prices including distribution and decline. These phases correspond roughly to the business cycle of recovery, prosperity, recession and depression. (105)

market demand The total quantity of a good which is demanded at any one time at a given price.

market factors Statistical series such as population, number of families, and income, which are used for setting sales potential for any selection of the market. (24)

market financing That part of the general business function of providing and managing funds and credit which is directly related to the transactions involved in the flow of goods and services from producer to consumer or industrial user.

Comment: This definition includes the provision and management of funds needed to finance the carrying of stocks and the granting of mercantile and retail credit, including installment credit. It does not include the provision of funds to purchase a building in which to carry on a marketing enterprise, nor does it embrace consumer borrowing on a personal basis.

Roughly it embraces financial operations that are undertaken to control or modify the direction of the flow of goods and services in marketing but excludes those which are of a more general nature. (13)

market index Data expressed as a percentage of a base in which a portion of the market is stated as a percentage of the whole market.

market indicators Economic factors for measuring the relative sales opportunities in various geographical units such as states, counties, trading areas, or any other physical subdivision. The data for individual parts of the market usually are reduced to a percentage of the total for the entire United States. (24)

marketing faciliating agencies Those agencies which perform or assist in the performance of one or a number of the marketing functions but which neither take title to goods nor negotiate purchases or sales. Common types are banks, railroads, storage warehouses, commodity exchanges and markets, stockyards, insurance companies, graders and inspectors, advertising agencies, firms engaged in marketing research, cattle loan companies, furniture marts, and packers and shippers.

Writers on marketing at one time classified these agencies as functional middlemen, including also in that classification all types of nontitle-taking middlemen. This mixture of incongruous elements hardly seems desirable. (13)

marketing quota The amount of a covered commodity that a producer is permitted to sell based upon the acreage allotment of the government.

market instinct Term referring to the capability of rather accurately interpreting the significance of the price and volume changes in securities. (105)

market is off An analysis of the condition of the market which indicates that prices are down from the previous closing.

market leaders The securities of major companies such as American Telephone and Telegraph Company, Standard Oil of New Jersey,

and General Motors which, because of their importance in their own industry are considered to be significant indicators of the economic health of the economy in general and the security market in particular.

market letter Those printed sheets sent out by brokerage firms and investment advisory services which attempt to interpret the conditions in the market and to make recommendations for the recipient reader to follow regarding specific investment opportunities and as to general portfolio practice.

market off When referring to securities, means that the prices of a particular market average or group of stocks is selling lower for the day than the previous market session. (105)

market order An order to buy or sell stocks or bonds at the price prevailing when the order reaches the market. (1)

market penetration Extent to which a given establishment, firm, or plant shares or dominates the sales in a given market area. The measurement of performance or efficiency is usually defined in terms of a penetration ratio which is found by dividing a firm's sales in a given area by the market potential set for that area. (24)

marketplace Common term for any place where business is done, where trading is carried on and where prices develop out of the forces of supply and demand. (59)

market potential The expected sales of a commodity, a group of commodities, or a service for an entire industry in a market during a stated period.

Comment: The use of this concept should be considered in relation to that of "sales potential." (13)

market price In the case of a security, market price is usually considered the last reported price at which the stock or bond sold. (2)

market report 1. Technically, it means the verbal or written report from the trading floor of an exchange that a particular transaction has been executed at the stated price in the report. 2. Generally, this term might refer to any news about or condition of the securities market. (105)

market securities 1. Market used as a verb, means to offer securities for sale on the market. 2. Market used as an adjective means those securities traded in a public market as opposed to those with a limited market. (105)

market sentiment The feeling or tone of a market as illustrated by the activity and price movement of the securities. A bullish market sentiment would be indicated by rising prices while a bearish sentiment would be indicated by falling prices.

markets, law of Also known as Say's Law. The greater the offerings of goods and services for sale the greater sales each good and service will enjoy because of unlimited human wants.

market stabilization An attempt to prevent the working of the full and free forces in a market by some agency such as the underwriter of an issue or a sponsoring investment banker. Generally attempts to stabilize prices are considered to be manipulative acts and as such are prohibited by the Securities Exchange Commission; exception is made to an initial offering which is registered with the S.E.C. and has received their permission to "peg" or stabilize prices of an issue. At times a secondary offering may receive such permission.

market swing Those movements of the average prices of a security or commodity market which are of a cyclical or secondary trend.

market value The quantity of other commodities a property would command in exchange; specifically the highest price estimated in terms of money which a buyer would be warranted in paying and a seller justified in accepting, provided both parties were fully informed, acted intelligently and voluntarily, and further, that all the rights and benefits inherent in or attributable to the property were included in the transfer. At any given moment of time, market value connotes what a property is actually worth and market price what it can be sold for. The amounts may or may not coincide, since current supply and demand factors enter strongly into market price. (54)

marking time The condition of a commodity or security market in which no trend or direction appears to be indicated by the prices of the various transactions.

markka Monetary unit of Finland.

mark to the market To check the last sales of a security held in a margin account to determine if the current value of the account meets the minimum margin requirements of an exchange or firm. More specifically, in the case of a short sale, where the borrower (short-seller,) of stock must ordinarily deposit cash equal to 100% of the market value of the stock; mark to the market means a formal notice that additional cash must be deposited by the short seller because the market value of the stock has gone up, or if the market value has gone down, the lender of the stock must return cash to keep the protection at 100% of market value. (105)

mark up The monetary amount or percentage representing the difference between the item cost of the seller and the price he receives for an item. Also called price spread.

mark x signature See X Mark Signature.

massachusetts rule A term frequently applied to a rule for the investment of trust funds enunciated by the Supreme Judicial Court of Massachusetts in 1830; not commonly referred to as the prudent man rule. See Prudent Man Rule for Trust Investment. (88)

massachusetts trust An unincorporated organization created for profit under a written instrument or declaration of trust, by the terms of which the property held in trust is managed by compensated trustees for the benefit of persons whose legal interests are represented by transferable certificates of participation or shares; also called business trust. (88)

master's deed A deed issued by a master in chancery in satisfaction of a judgment and under a court order. (5)

matched and lost When two bids to buy the same stock are made on the trading floor simultaneously, and each bid is equal to or larger than the amount of stock offered, both bids are consi-

dered to be on an equal basis. So the two bidders flip a coin to decide who buys the stock. Also applies to offers to sell. (2)

matched orders 1. A form of manipulation whereby the same person enters an order to buy a particular security with one broker and an order to sell the same security simultaneously with another broker. This practice is prohibited as a method of trying to either increase or decrease security prices. 2. A specialist in a stock may match orders to buy and sell that security in order to arrange an opening price that is reasonably close to the previous day's close. Market conditions and any special circumstances are taken into consideration. (105)

material fact Statement of something that is done or exists of such importance that disclosure of it would alter an underwriting decision or loss settlement. (5)

materialmen's lien A lien in favor of those who have supplied materials for a building. (31, 92)

matured Fully paid up, fully carried out as to terms, completed as to time or as to contract. (59)

maturity The date upon which a note, time draft, bill of exchange, bond, or other negotiable instrument becomes due and payable. Notes, time drafts, and bills of exchange drawn for a future date, have a maturity date which is set, starting with the date of the loan or acceptance, and running the specified number of days from date of loan or acceptance to maturity. Presentation and request for payment of the instrument are made on the maturity date. (1)

maturity date The date upon which a financial obligation becomes due for payments. (31, 92)

maturity distribution of loans and securities Shows the amounts of loans, holdings of acceptances, and government securities that mature or are payable within the various periods specified. (4)

maturity index Same as "Maturity Tickler." See that term.

maturity tickler A form made and used in the loan department of a bank. The maturity tickler is usually a copy of the "Note Notice" (see definition) and contains all information as to the amount, due date, maker, address, collateral, etc. It is filed according to the due date of the note. This permits ready access to the number and total value of all notes maturing on any day. The maturity ticklers are generally used by bank officials and the loan committee in daily meetings when the maturing notes are under review and discussion for official reference and action. (1)

maturity value The amount that must be paid on the date the note becomes due. (73)

mechanics lien The legal, enforceable claim which a person who has performed work on, or provided materials for, a given asset is permitted to make, by statute law in certain states, as a lien against the title to the property, or which may grant him a degree of preference in the case of liquidation of an estate or business. (1)

medium of exchange Any commodity (commonly money) which is widely accepted in payment for goods and services and in settlement of debts, and is accepted without reference to the standing of the person who offers it in payment. (90)

medium other than cash Checks, notes, credit. (93)

meeting bond interest and principal An expression indicating that payments are being made when due. (103)

melon Slang financial term meaning extraordinary profits waiting to be divided. (105)

member A person owning an account in an association, or a person borrowing from or obligated to an association. (31, 92)

member bank All national banks, and any state bank that has applied for membership, and has been accepted as a member of the Federal Reserve System is called a member bank. Member banks are required to purchase capital stock in the Federal Reserve bank in their district equal to 6% of the total paid-in capital and surplus of the member bank. Fifty percent of the capital stock purchased is paid for and carried 'on the books of the member bank as an asset. The remaining fifty percent is not recorded on the books, but this subscribed portion may be called by the Board of Governors of the Federal Reserve System at any time. (1)

member corporation A securities brokerage firm, organized as a corporation, with at least one member of the N.Y. Stock Exchange who is a director and a holder of voting stock in the corporation. (2)

membership dues The annual fee paid to an exchange by its members as distinguished from the initiation fee. (105)

member's rate The amount of commission charged a member of an exchange who is not a member of the clearing association. This amount is less than the regular charge which the average customer pays.

memorandum account The record of an account maintained by a bank which is not included in its assets or liabilities. An example is the record of a bad debt written off, on which subsequent recoveries are anticipated. (1)

mercantile agency That organization such as Dun and Bradstreet or local credit bureau which supplies credit information on applicants for credit to its members. In addition the agency may also perform other functions such as collection of past due accounts and trade collection statistics.

mercantile paper Commercial paper such as notes, bills and acceptances which originate from such mercantile sources as wholesalers, retailers or jobbers.

merchandise turnover The ratio of sales to merchandise. An inventory of one million dollars and annual sales of ten million dollars would indicate a merchandise turnover of ten times. By comparing the ratio for similar establishments some idea of efficiency of sales force may be obtained. In turn this should have important bearing on the profitability of the various establishments.

merchantable Saleable in the ordinary way; fit for ordinary uses to which it is put. (5)

merchantable title That condition of title which is acceptable in the market. (89)

merger The combination of two or more enterprises. If the enterprises are of the corporate type, the merger involves the exchange of securities or the issuance of new securities or both. (74)

middle of the road policy To be noncommittal about the future trend of security prices, that is, neither optimistic nor pessimistic. (105)

milling A corrugated edge on a coin. Milling is performed at the mint to reduce attempts by people to clip coins, that is, wear away the edges so that the abrazed metal may be used for bullion.

minimum The least amount. (93)

minimum balance The lowest balance. The term is generally used in reference to checking accounts in banks in that those accounts with lower than the minimum balance are charged by the banks for the services which the banks perform. Accounts with average balances above the stated dollar amount of minimum balance are not charged for their activity such as deposits or checks drawn.

minor A person below the age of legal capacity. A minor is incapable of making a contract. A parent or guardian must sign any application for insurance for a minor unless state law permits an earlier age limit. (5)

minor coins The five cent and one cent pieces.

minority stockholders In a de jure sense, stockholders representing less than fifty per cent of the voting stock. In a de facto sense, stockholders who have not been able to obtain control of a corporation though by means of cumulative voting in some cases may have representation on a board of directors.

minor trend The day-to-day fluctuations in security prices as opposed to the longer intermediate and primary trends. These minor movements are held to be insignificant under the Dow Theory. (105)

mint The establishment or place where coins are made from metal under the supervision of an authorized governmental official.

mintage The fee collected by the mint for making coins from metal.

mint mark A small letter on a coin or similar device which shows at which mint a coin was produced. A "d" would stand for the mint at Denver.

mint par of exchange The figure derived by dividing the pure gold or silver weight of the monetary unit of one nation by the pure similar metal weight of the monetary unit of the other nation.

mint ratio The ratio of the weight of gold which is in a monetary unit to the weight of silver in the same monetary unit provided that the nation is on a bimetallic standard.

minute book A book in which is kept a record of the proceedings of stockholders' meetings and board of directors' meetings. (73)

mis-sent item An item which has been sent in error to another bank is called a mis-sent item. Banks return mis-sent items to the sending bank, marking the return ticket with a legend showing the reason, such as "Sent in Error." Banks usually prefer not to forward the item to the correct paying bank because they do not wish their own bank endorsement on the item. Clearing house associations frequently exact fines for mis-sent items. (1)

mis-sort Generally, a check drawn by a depositor which is wrongly sorted to a "book" or bank other than that in which the account is kept. (83)

miss the market To allow any particularly attractive opportunity to buy or sell a security slip by. (105)

mixed accounts Accounts whose balances are part asset and part expense or part liability and part income. (73)

mixed collateral Property of different types such as stocks, bonds, notes and certificates which are put up as security for a loan.

modernization loan Loans for repair and modernization purposes made by private institutional investors, frequently guaranteed and insured by the Federal Housing Administration. The monthly payments include interest, part of principal, and insurance. (5)

monetary The coinage or currency of a country. (93)

monetary commission A body of experts in money and banking who are appointed by legislative action to prepare an analysis and recommendation of changes in the banking and monetary area.

monetary indemnity A specified amount benefit as contrasted to expense reimbursement. (5)

monetary reserves The amount of gold and silver held by the Treasury or Monetary Authorities to secure the issue of credit money in circulation.

monetary standard The standard upon which a country's money is issued.

monetary system Description of the legal standard money of a nation and the related legislation on reserves, coinage and methods of redemption and conversion.

monetary unit A country's unit of money.

money Any form or denomination of coin or paper currency of legal tender which passes freely as a medium of exchange. See Legal Tender. In bank operations, money refers to cash and includes both currency (paper money) and coin (metallic money). (1, 85)

money broker An individual or firm, sometimes called a "finder" who brings those needing money to those who lend money and for this expects a fee. See Finder's Fee.

moneyed corporation A financial institution such as a bank, trust company or insurance company and as such subject to the banking or insurance code.

money in circulation Total amount of currency and coin outside the Treasury and the Federal Reserve banks. (4)

money management Financial planning with the aim of gratifying long-range as well as immediate needs and of maintaining a sound relationship between income, savings, and spending. (131)

money market The financial area. Rather than being a place, the money market is made up of many types of financial institutions such as commercial banks, savings banks, trust com-

panies, insurance companies, stock brokerage firms, investment bankers, mortgage bankers. There is no place such as the stock exchange which is the money market but rather it is all the financial institutions who may participate in a financial area, thus banks throughout the country by virtue of the use of telephone and teletype and their correspondent relationship may participate in the money market.

money market securities High quality and generally accepted senior securities whose market prices expressed on a yield basis relate more closely to the prevailing interest rate for money than to the risks in a company's operations or in general business conditions. (103)

money of account The unit in which monetary records are kept. In the United States entries are made in U.S. dollars and cents. In Canada the Canadian dollar and cent is used. In Mexico the money of account is the Mexican peso.

money orders Money orders are instruments commonly purchased for a fee by people who do not maintain checking accounts, but who wish to send money to distant points. The name of the purchaser as well as the payee is shown on the face of the money order. Postal money orders are drawn on the post office in the city where the payee is located, while bank money orders are drawn either on the issuing bank or on its correspondent. (1)

money rates Those rates of interest which lenders are charging various classes of borrowers. This would include such money rates as the prime rate, the call money rate.

money stock See Money in Circulation.

money transfer While money may be physically transferred by such facilities as armored car and registered mail the term is generally associated with the use of telephone or telegraph to credit an account in one place and debit it in another location. The Federal Reserve District Banks provide extensive transfer facilities for their member banks as do most large banks for their correspondents and customers.

monometallism A single standard monetary system in which one metal, generally gold, is given free and unlimited coinage.

monthly investment plan (mip) A methodical investment technique introduced by members of the New York Stock Exchange in 1954 to allow a public investor to acquire stock on a regular convenient basis, with payments ranging from $40 every three months to $1000 every month. (105)

monthly statement In the securities business, an account issued by brokerage firms to their clients stating the date, amount, prices, etc., of any transactions for the month; plus a listing of dividends, interest, securities received or delivered, and the existing debit or credit balance. (105)

mooch A slang financial term for anyone who is lured into buying securities because of hopes of big profits, without first making a careful investigation. (105)

Moody's Bond Ratings and Stock Quality Groups
Bonds:

Aaa—Best quality, generally referred to as "gilt edge".

Aa—High quality by all standards, generally known as high grade bonds.

A—Possessing many favorable investment attributes and considered as high medium grade obligations.

Baa—Considered as lower medium grade obligations, i.e., neither highly protected nor poorly secured. Such bonds lack outstanding investment characteristics as well.

Preferred and Common Stocks:

High Quality—High quality by all standards.

Good Quality—Possesses many favorable high-grade investment attributes.

Medium Quality—Medium grade equity securities. (21)

Moody's Bond Yield (Annual Averages of Monthly Yield) Represents the average yield on 40 operating utility companies' bonds (10 each of Class Aaa, Aa, A & Baa) as determined and rated by Moody's Investors Service. This "yield" is the arithmetical average of 12 months and is calculated on the basis of market price, coupon rate, and on being "held to maturity". (21)

Moody's Investor's Service A publisher of financial statistics. Founded by John Moody in 1900 who was the first analyst to rate the investment quality and character of bonds. The company is located in New York City and is a subsidiary of Dun and Bradstreet, Inc. (105)

moral hazard Any deviation of personal habits from accepted social standards. (42)

moral obligation A debt or responsibility whose payment or fulfillment is not based on legal rights or action. (59)

moral risk See Moral Hazard. All credit extensions in addition to insurance are concerned with the moral risk or hazard.

moratorium That period of time, generally some emergency such as war, depression or bank holiday during which the payment of interest or principal or both may be postponed. The moratorium will be declared by such government official as a governor or president and will describe what payments fall under the proclamation.

more or less Those words, when used in a contract, are intended to cover only a reasonable excess or deficit. (5)

morning loan Loans made by banks to stockbrokers on an unsecured basis for the purpose of the broker handling his stock deliveries until reimbursed by his customer.

morris plan bank A bank which concentrates on relatively small loans and consumer credit involving insurance on the life of the debtor.

mortgage An instrument by which the borrower (mortgagor) gives the lender (mortgagee) a lien on property (commonly real property) as security for the payment of an obligation. The borrower continues to use the property, and when the obligation is fully extinguished the lien is removed. If the subject matter of the lien is personal property other than securities (such as machinery, tools, or equipment), the mortgage is known as a chattel mortgage. (88)

mortgage administration The part of a mortgage banker's service involving all clerical and supervisory functions necessary to ensure prompt repayment of mortgage loans, and to protect and enforce all rights of investors thereunder. (121)

mortgage banker A banker who specializes in mortgage financing; an operator of a mortgage financing company. Mortgage financing companies are mortgages themselves, as well as being mortgage agents for other large mortgagees. Serving as mortgage agents, these mortgage bankers collect payments, maintain complete mortgage records, and make remittances to the mortgagees for a set fee or service charge. They also disburse funds for taxes, insurances, etc., as escrow agents. (1)

Mortgage Bankers Association of America, (mba) The professional and business organization of persons operating under the correspondency system whose major purpose is continuing improvement in the quality of service to investors. (121)

mortgage bond A direct loan secured by real estate in which all of the dollars are provided and all of the rental income is used to retire the loan within the terms of the loan.

mortgage certificate An interest in a mortgage evidenced by the instrument, generally a fractional portion of the mortgage, which certifies as to the agreement between the mortgagees who hold the certificates and the mortgagor as to such terms as principal, amount, date of payment, place of payment. Such certificates are not obligations to pay money, as in a bond or note, but are merely a certification by the holder of the mortgage, generally a corporate depository, that he holds such mortgage for the beneficial and undivided interest of all the certificate holders. The certificate itself generally sets forth a full agreement between the holder and the depository, although in some cases a more lengthy document, known as a depository agreement is executed. (54)

mortgage clause Clause in an insurance policy which makes the proceeds payable to the holder of a mortgage on the insured property to the extent of his interest in that property. (52)

mortgage company Mortgage financing companies are mortgages themselves, as well as being mortgage agents for other large mortgagees. Serving as mortgage agents, these mortgage bankers collect payments, maintain complete mortgage records, and make remittances to the mortgagees for a set fee or service charge. (1)

mortgage credit Money which is owed for the acquisition of land or buildings (frequently, of a home) and which is paid back over an extended period of time; hence, long-term debt. (131)

mortgage debenture A Mortgage Bond.

mortgage department A department in banks, building and loan, savings and loan associations, and trust companies, where mortgage counselors, mortgage loan officers, and mortgage recording personnel handle all phases of mortgage work for mortgagors. This department may also act as "escrow agents" (see definition) for mortgagors, in that they collect in the monthly payment from the mortgagor a portion of the real estate taxes, assessments on real estate, and hazard insurance. They hold these in escrow funds until payable, and then disburse the funds for the benefit of the mortgagor, and also the mortgagee, to prevent the development of liens against the property. In some states, they administer escrow funds in connection with closing mortgages, whereas in other states mortgage closings are required to be handled by attorneys-at-law. (1)

mortgagee The source of the funds for a mortgage loan and in whose favor the property serving as security is mortgaged. A person or company to whom property is conveyed as security for a loan made by such person or company. The creditor. (54+)

mortgagee clause A clause in an insurance contract making the proceeds payable to a named mortgagee, as his interest may appear, and stating the terms of the contract between the insurer and the mortgagee. Preferable usage but same as mortgage clause. (51+)

mortgagee in possession A mortgagee creditor who takes over the income from the mortgaged property upon default of the mortgage by the debtor. (5)

mortgage loan A loan made by a lender, called the mortgagee, to a borrower, called the mortgagor, for the financing of a parcel of real estate. The loan is evidenced by a mortgage. The mortgage sets forth the conditions of the loan, the manner of repayment or liquidation of the loan, and reserves the right of foreclosure or repossession to the mortgagee. In case the mortgagor defaults in the payment of interest and principal, or if he permits a lien to be placed against the real estate mortgaged due to failure to pay the taxes and assessments levied against the property, the right of foreclosure can be exercised. Mortgage loans fall into four general categories: Regular mortgages (National Banks); Regular mortgages (State Banks). See local state banking laws; F.H.A. mortgages; Veterans' "G.I." mortgages.

For current specific information, refer to copy of the present law or laws pertaining to rules and regulations regarding these mortgages. (1)

mortgage origination The part of a mortgage banker's service involving performance of all details concerned with the making of a real estate loan. (121)

mortgage pattern The arrangement or design of payments and other terms established by a mortgage contract. (89)

mortgage portfolio The aggregate of mortgage loans or obligations held by a bank as assets. (89)

mortgage risk The hazard of loss of principal or of anticipated interest inherent in an advance of funds on the security of a mortgage. (89)

mortgaging future income Pledging, income not yet earned. (59)

mortgagor The borrower or borrowers in a mortgage transaction. (31, 92)

multiple banking The offering of all types of banking services to a bank's customers, as distinguished from specialization in a few services as offered by certain types of banks. Multiple banking has even been termed "department store" banking, in that the customer has at his disposal all types of banking services, such as checking accounts, savings accounts, loan advice and service, mortgage service, trust services, safe deposit facilities, etc. (1)

multiple currency practice Arises when two or more effective exchange rates exist simultaneously, at least one of which, as the result of official action, is more than 1 percent higher or lower than the par value. Such practices are usually to be found where a dual exchange market exists (q.v.) or where the monetary authorities set different exchange rates for imports, exports, current invisibles, and capital. They often result from taxes or subsidies on specified exchange transactions. (130)

multiple currency securities Those securities—mostly bonds—which are payable in more than one currency at the election of the holder. The holder in the event of devaluation of a currency may elect to be paid in the currency of a nation which has not devalued its currency.

multiple currency system A method of control for foreign exchange. The domestic currency may only be exchanged for foreign currency through a government agency or controlled bank. The rate of exchange will vary according to the product or use being made of the exchange. Generally, essentials such as farm machinery and tools are given a more favorable rate than luxuries.

multiple expansion of deposits (or credit) The nature of operation of a fractional reserve commercial banking system such as is found in the United States. A bank, with excess reserves, makes a loan and thus creates a deposit; when the deposit is withdrawn and spent it tends to be deposited in a bank creating excess reserves which in turn may be lent and cause a multiple expansion of credit or deposits. The rate of expansion being determined by the reserve requirement. A 10% reserve requirement in theory could have an expansion of ten times while a 20% would have a five times expansion potential.

municipal An adjective applying to any governmental unit below or subordinate to the state. (29)

municipal corporation An incorporated political subdivision such as a town, county or city.

municipal improvement certificates Certificates issued in lieu of bonds for the financing of special improvements.

NOTE: As a rule, they are placed in the contractor's hands for collection from the special assessment payers. (29)

municipals In investments this term has been broadened to include not only the securities of any political subdivision of a state such as a town, county or city but also to take in state bonds. Probably the latter are included because they have the same federal tax exemption feature as the bonds of cities, towns and counties.

mutilated currency Coin and paper currency which is not in shape or condition for further circulation and thus is withdrawn. Where the mutilation is such that less than three fifths of the paper bill is presented it is not redeemed at face value without an affidavit from the holder that he certifies that the missing portions have been destroyed.

mutual fund The shorter and more popular term for an open-end investment company. (65)

mutual savings bank A banking organization without capital stock which receives deposits. Its earnings are distributed, within legal limits to its depositors. Mutual savings banks are set up to encourage thrift by small savers, primarily. (8)

mutual wills Separate wills executed by different persons but having reciprocal provisions. In most situations mutual wills are unilaterally revocable by one testator without consent of the other. This feature is a strong argument against having mutual wills.

N

N.A.S.D. National Association of Security Dealers.

Nat. National.

Natl. National.

N.C.I. No common interest. (5)

N/E Net Earnings. (67)

Negb. Negotiable.

Neg. Inst. Negotiable instrument.

Negl. Negligence.

N.F. No funds.

N.G. An abbreviation used in banks, principally in the bookkeeping department, to designate that a check is "NOT GOOD"; that there are insufficient funds in the balance of the account to pay the item. (1)

N.&M. Semi-annual interest payments or dividends in November and May.

No. Number.

No A/C No account.

No Adv. No advice.

Non-Can Noncancellable. (5)

Non-Cum Non-cumulative.

Non-Par Nonparticipating. (5)

N.O.S. Not otherwise specified. Relates to commodities not specifically named in tariffs or I.C.C. freight commodity classes. (19)

N/P Notes Payable.

N.P. No Protest.

N.P.N.A. No protest non-acceptance.

N.Q.A. Net quick assets. (5)

N/R Notes Receivable.

N.S.F. See Insufficient Funds. (85)

NTE Not to exceed. (67)

narrow market A thin market. A condition in the securities market characterized by low volume of trading and slight variation in quotations.

National Advisory Council on International Monetary and Financial Problems Comprised of the Secretary of State, the Secretary of the Treasury, The Secretary of Commerce, Chairmen of the Board of Governors of the Federal Reserve System, and the Export-Import Bank. Its function is to coordinate the policies of the United States in the World Bank and the International Monetary Fund.

National Association of Securities Dealers A voluntary association of brokers and dealers handling over-the-counter securities, formed after the Maloney Act of 1938, special legislation passed to regulate the over-the-counter market. The association has importance to members because they receive reduced commission from each other. (105)

National bank A corporation organized under a federal banking law (National Bank Act) and authorized to do a general or commercial banking business—that is, receive deposits subject to check and make loans. It usually performs a variety of other functions as well. A national bank must have the word "national" in its corporate title. (85)

National Bank Act The legislation under which national banks were formed and operate. See National Bank.

National bank call report National banks are required by the Comptroller of the Currency to submit a report or statement of condition of their bank a minimum of three times a year. The act of the Comptroller in directing that these reports be submitted is known as the "call report." The information disclosed by the reports provide vital economic information for not only the Comptroller but for monetary policy decisions as well.

National bank examination A minimum of twice during each year all national banks are subject to an examination by the staff of a National Bank Examiner for purposes of checking their records and making sure that the bank is being operated within the National Bank Act.

National Banking Association The same as a National Bank.

National banking system Prior to 1863, the system of banking was mostly confined to state charted banks (with the exceptions of the First and Second Banks of the United States). After that date banks could, if they complied with the requirements of the National Bank Act, obtain federal charters. This has led to our present dual banking system in which both the states and the federal government may issue charters to banks.

national bank note A type of currency issued in the United States. National bank notes are backed by two types of United States government bonds—2% consols of 1930, and the 2% Panama Canal bonds of 1916-36 and 1918-38. These bonds were called for redemption by the Bank Act of 1935, and no further issuance of national bank notes was authorized. They are being retired from circulation. National bank notes are in denominations of 5, 10, 20, 50, and 100 dollars, and each has a brown seal and the issuing bank's charter number on its face. (1)

national bank report See National Bank Call Report.

National Bankruptcy Act This act, as frequently amended has established uniform laws on bankruptcy in all the states. In its present state it contains numerous chapters covering the procedures for handling the various bankrupt organizations ranging from individual to corporate, municipal and railroad reorganization.

national currency Federal Reserve Bank Notes and National Bank Notes, now retired.

National Farm Loan Association Agricultural cooperative of local operation formed as a result of Federal Farm Loan Act. Upon subscription to shares of the Federal Land Bank in its area the association may obtain financing for farm mortgages.

National Housing Act Legislation in 1934 which created the Federal Savings and Loan Insurance Corporation, and made major changes in federal activities in the housing area including insurance of modernization loans, insurance of mortgage loans and financing of housing projects.

national income The total earnings of labor and property from the production of goods and services. It is the income earned—but not necessarily received by—all persons in the country in a specified period. This aggregate measure may be estimated directly by totaling the various forms of income of persons and income retained in business firms. Or it may be derived by subtracting indirect business taxes, business transfers, and capital consumption allowances from GNP and making adjustments for the activities of government enterprises. (124)

National Monetary Commission Body of experts in money and banking which reports to the Congress on the state of the banking structure and which makes recommendations as to changes. In 1908 as a result of the obvious distress in our monetary system the National Monetary Commission was formed. Since then recommendations have been made that similar commissions be formed.

National Mortgage Association See Federal National Mortgage Association.

National Quotation Bureau Primary quotation source for securities traded over the counter. The Bureau publishes its quotations in sections. The major section is called the Eastern Section or the "Pink Sheets". The Western Section, contrary to its name, originates out of Chicago and covers securities popular in that area. The San Francisco or Coast section covers securities popular on the Pacific Coast markets.

National Security Exchange An exchange classified as such by the Securities Exchange Commission. Included are most of the larger exchanges in the United States. Only a few small exchanges are not designated as National Security Exchanges. Not to be confused with National Stock Exchange.

national wealth 1. The monetary sum of all the material assets owned by citizens and institutions of a country as of a stated time and which are within the borders of the nation, plus the material assets owned outside the nation. 2. A number of nations assume a balance between assets owned abroad and assets within a nation owned by foreigners and thus count all material assets, irrespective of ownership within their borders. Material asset is used to prevent duplication of counting assets such as currency or securities.

natural guardian The parent of a minor; originally the father but now either the father or the mother. Natural guardianship relates only to the person of a minor. (74)

nearby delivery Delivery during the nearest active month. (9)

near money Time deposits in commercial banks, Savings and Loan shares, Treasury bills and other very liquid assets are considered near money since they may be converted into cash very easily.

near-term Meaning short-term as opposed to long-term, i.e., the near future or less than two months usually. (105)

negative investment See Disinvestment.

negative pledge clause A covenant in an indenture to the effect that the corporation will not pledge any of its assets unless the notes or debentures outstanding under the particular indenture are at least equally secured by such pledge; also called the covenant of equal coverage. (74)

negative verification Many banks have a legend printed on the statement form going to the depositor to the effect that "if no difference is reported within ten days, the account will be considered correct." If the bank does not hear from the depositor, it assumes that the depositor has "negatively verified" the account. (1)

negligence Failure to do what a reasonable prudent individual would ordinarily do under the circumstances of a particular case, or doing what a prudent person would not have done. Negligence may be caused by acts of omission, commission, or both. (53 + 50)

negotiable Refers to a security, title to which, when properly endorsed by the owner, is transferable by delivery. (2)

negotiable instrument A written order or promise to pay money, which can be transferred from one person to another by delivery or by endorsement and delivery. Upon such a transfer, the new party receives the full legal title to the property. Negotiable instruments are usually in the form of checks, drafts or bills of exchange, promissory notes and acceptances. To be negotiable, the instrument must: (1) Be in writing and signed by the maker or endorser, (2) Contain an unconditional promise or order to pay a certain sum of money, (3) Be payable on demand or at a fixed or determinable future time, (4) Be payable to order or to bearer. (31, 92)

negotiable paper Negotiable documents and negotiable instruments. The term is generally used to refer to such pieces of paper as they are used in borrowing and as used for collateral.

negotiable securities Bearer instruments which result in transfer of title by means of assignment or delivery. Bearer bonds, bearer notes, bearer warrants, stock certificates and coupons may be negotiated as distinguished from registered securities.

negotiate To arrange by bargain or agreement. To transfer a written obligation such as a note or bond. To successfully handle.

net A fixed price at which a person agrees to deliver or receive a security. (105)

net bonded debt Gross bonded debt less applicable cash or other assets. (29)

net change The change in the price of a security from the closing price on one day and the closing price on the following day on which the stock is traded. In the case of a stock which is entitled to a dividend one day, but is traded "ex-dividend" the next, the dividend is considered in computing the change. For example, if the closing market price of a stock on Monday—the last day it was entitled to receive a 50-cent dividend—was $45 a share, and $44.50 at the close the next day, when it was "ex-dividend," the price would be considered unchanged. The same applies to a split-up of shares. A stock selling at $100 the day before a 2-for-1 split and trading the next day at $50 would be considered unchanged. If it sold at $51, it would be considered up $1. The net change is ordinarily the last figure in a stock price list. The mark 1 ⅛ means up $1.125 a share from the last sale on the previous day the stock traded. See Ex-dividend; Point; Split. (2)

net demand deposits Excess of demand deposits, including deposits, due to other banks and the United States Government, over demand balances due from other domestic banks with the exception of Federal Reserve Banks, foreign banks or branches, foreign branches of domestic and private banks and such cash items that are in the process of collection.

net earnings In banks, net earnings or net operating earnings for a given period represent the excess of gross earnings over the normal operating expenses before taking into consideration the gain or loss on the sales of securities, other losses, and charge-offs. In financial institutions, Net Earnings usually refer to earnings made prior to considering federal income taxes. (1)

net for common stock Net income less dividends on preferred stock applicable to the period on an accrual basis. (21)

net foreign investment The net change in the nation's foreign assets and liabilities, including the monetary gold stocks, arising out of current trade, income on foreign investment, and cash gifts and contributions. It measures the excess of (1) exports over imports, (2) income on U.S. public and private investment abroad over payments on foreign investment in the U.S., (3) cash gifts and contributions of the U.S. (public and Private) to foreigners over cash gifts and contributions received from abroad. (7)

net free or net borrowed reserves Excess reserves less member bank borrowings from Federal Reserve banks. The resulting difference is called net free when positive and net borrowed when negative. (117)

net income after dividends Net income less dividends on preferred stock applicable to the period and dividends declared on common stock during the period. (21)

net income or net profit Results of operations after deducting from revenues all related costs and expenses and all other charges and losses assigned to the period. These deductions do not include dividends or comparable withdrawals. (17)

net interest Measures the excess of interest payments made by the domestic business sector over its interest receipts from other sectors, plus net interest received from abroad. Interest paid by one business firm to another business firm is a transaction within the business sector and has no effect on the overall interest payments or receipts of the sector. The same is true of interest payments within other sectors as from one individual to another, or one government agency to another. (124)

net investment income per share The net amount of dividends and interest earned during an accounting period on an investment company's portfolio securities (after deduction of operating expenses) divided by the number of shares outstanding. (65)

net lease A lease where, in addition to the rental stipulated, the lessee assumes payment of all property charges such as taxes, insurance, and maintenance. (54)

net option A written instrument which grants the right to purchase property at a specified price to the owner. (5)

net position The difference between the open contracts long and the open contracts short held in any one commodity by an individual or group. (123)

net profits on net sales Obtained by dividing the net earnings of the business, after taxes, by net sales (the dollar volume less returns, allowances, and cash discounts). This is an important yardstick in measuring profitability. (61)

net profits on net working capital Net Working Capital represents the equity of the owners in the Current Assets, as obtained by subtracting total Current Debt from Total Current Assets. This equity, or margin, represents the cushion available to the business for carrying inventories and receivables, and for financing day-to-day operations. To illustrate how Net Working Capital is computed: If a concern has Current Assets of $1,000,000 and Current Debt of $400,000 its Net Working Capital is $600,000. (61)

net profits on tangible net worth Tangible Net Worth represents the equity of owners, partners, or stockholders in the business, as reflected by the figure which results from subtracting total liabilities from total assets, and then deducting such intangibles as goodwill, trademarks, patents, copyrights, leaseholds, mailing lists, treasury stock, organization expenses, and underwriting discount and expense. (61)

net realized capital gain per share The amount of net capital gains realized on the sale of portfolio securities during an accounting period after deducting losses realized, divided by the number of shares outstanding. (65)

net sales to inventory Obtained by dividing annual Net Sales by Merchandise Inventory as carried on the balance sheet. This quotient does not yield an actual physical turnover. It only provides a yardstick for comparing stock-to-sales ratios of one concern with another or with those for the industry. When the ratio of Net Sales to Inventory is too high, it may expose a chronically under-stocked condition in which sales are being lost because of lack of adequate inventories in stock, and failure to offer proper depth of selections to customers. If the ratio is too low, compared with figures which are more or less typical of those for the industry, it may be that inventories are top-heavy, stagnant, or obsolete. (61)

net sales to tangible net worth Obtained by dividing Net Sales by Tangible Net Worth. The result gives a measure of the relative turnover of capital. If capital is turned over too rapidly, liabilities build up excessively, as amounts owed to creditors become a substitute for permanent capital.

And if capital is turned too slowly, funds become stagnant, and profitability suffers. (61)

net sales to working capital Similar to the concept above, except that the Net Sales are divided by the Net Working Capital (or net equity in Current Assets). If the ratio is too high, the tendency of the business is to owe too much, because it depends on credit granted by suppliers, the bank, and others as a substitute for an adequate margin of current operating funds. (61)

net worth 1. The proprietor's equity in a given business represented by the excess of the total assets over the total amounts owing to outside creditors at a given moment of time. 2. The worth of an individual as determined by deducting the amount of all his personal liabilities from the total value of his personal assets. (1)

net yield The Yield to maturity. The total income received each year if the bond has been purchased exactly at par at no cost or commission. The yield is generally expressed as a percent. Since most securities are not purchased exactly at par at no cost the amount paid as a premium must be amortized to earliest maturity and thus reduce the gross yield by the amount of the amortization. If a discount from face amount of bond has been paid, an accumulation is present and must be added to the annual rate.

neutral money A plan whereby various commodities could be exchanged for a fixed amount of money. The objective being the elimination of price level fluctuations.

new business department That section of a bank which has as its major function the obtaining of new accounts. It does this much as the sales promotion department of a commercial, industrial or mercantile firm obtains new customers for their firm.

new high A description of the price movement of a commodity, a security or of an average meaning that the price is at the highest level for some stated duration such as a year, month. An all time new high would be a price higher than had ever prevailed. Students of the Dow theory and chartists infer bullish tendencies to a market or average exhibiting new highs.

new housing authority bonds Bonds issued by a local Public Housing Authority to finance public housing and backed by federal funds.

new issue A stock or bond issued by a corporation for the first time. Proceeds may be used to retire outstanding securities of the company, for new plant or equipment or for additional working capital. (2)

news ticker Also called a Broad Tape, which is a machine operated by Dow-Jones & Co. Many broker's offices and banks have these machines to receive important financial news as quickly as possible. (105)

New York Clearing House Oldest and largest check clearing facility in the United States. See Clearing House.

New York Curb Exchange Former title of the American Stock Exchange. (105)

New York dollars Those funds payable in New York City as differentiated from dollars in other financial centers such as Chicago or San Francisco. Since movement of funds requires some expense either for telegraph or registered mail, foreign correspondents of country banks in the United States tend to prefer drawing against their deposits in their correspondent bank in the desired geographic area such as New York.

New York Exchange Any check which is drawn upon a commercial bank located in New York City.

New York funds Same as "New York Exchange" or "New York Dollars." See those terms.

New York Stock Exchange See Stock Exchanges. The major security exchange in the world. It is an unincorporated association in which membership is limited in number and may be obtained only upon acceptance by a membership committee. Such membership is called "a seat."

next friend One who, although not regularly appointed a guardian, acts for the benefit of a minor or incompetent person or, in some instances, a married woman or for any person who, for some legal reason, cannot appear for himself. (74)

next of kin The person or persons in the nearest degree of blood relationship to the decedent. As the term is usually employed, those entitled by law to the personal property of a person who has died without leaving a valid will (such persons do not include the surviving husband and wife except where specifically so provided by statute); to be distinguished from the heirs, who take the real property. (74)

night depository A small vault located on the inside of a bank, but accessible to the street-side of the bank. To use this vault depositors are given a passkey to the outer door of the night depository vault. When this door is opened, the package of money properly identified by the depositor is dropped down a chute into the night depository vault. This convenience is used by merchants who do not wish the day's receipts to remain in their place of business, and so have this means of protecting their deposits after the regular business hours of the bank. The vault is opened by a bank attendant, and the deposits properly counted and credited to the depositor's account. (1)

no account A notation or stamp put on a check which has been presented for collection and has been returned by the bank upon which it has been drawn for the reason that it has no account or depositor by the name of the drawer. Such checks probably are no good and may have been fraudulently made out. At times it is caused by an individual using a check drawn upon a bank other than his own. In the later case a new and properly made out check is substituted for the returned check.

no funds A notation or stamp put on a check which has been presented for collection and has been returned by the bank upon which it has been drawn for the reason that the drawer of the check does not have sufficient collected funds or balance for the check to be paid. Since the bank is unwilling to pay it as an overdraft the check is returned unpaid to the bank of the individual or firm which deposited it. This bank in turn advises its depositor that the check has been returned.

no limit order Means the opposite of a limit order, in other words, it is a market order because it has no stipulation as to prices. May be either a buy or sell order. (105)

no load fund A mutual fund which has no sales organization, but whose sponsor sells shares directly to the public for little or no commission (loan charge). (105)

nominal account A ledger account which is closed out when the books are balanced.

nominal capital The par value of the issued shares of a corporation as differentiated from the book or market value. Since shares are taxed on the par value many corporations issue low par value stock which is sold at substantially higher amounts.

nominal exchange rate The Mint Par of Exchange. See that term.

nominal interest rate The contractual interest rate shown on the face and in the body of a bond and representing the amount of interest to be paid, in contrast with the effective interest rate. See Coupon Rate. (29)

nominalist An individual who holds that money is the standard money defined by a government. Most economists today consider money to be inclusive not only of the currency in circulation but to include deposits which are subject to demand withdrawal.

nominally issued Capital stock, funded debt, and other securities when they are signed and sealed or certified and placed with the proper officer for sale and delivery, or pledged or placed in some special fund of the issuing corporation. (19)

nominally outstanding Securities reacquired by or for the issuing corporation under each circumstance as requires them to be considered as held alive, and not cancelled or retired. See Actually Outstanding. (19)

nominal partner One who represents himself or permits others to represent him to the public as a partner, but who in reality is not a partner. (73)

nominal price or nominal quotation Price quotations on futures for a period in which no actual trading took place. (123)

nominal purchase option This is a purchase option given at the inception of a lease which does not necessarily relate to the true expected residual value. It may be as little as $1 or as much as 10%. However, if the "nominal purchase option" is obviously less than the true expected residual, then the lease will not be a true lease for accounting purposes. This type of lease is sometimes referred to as a purchase option lease.

nominal quote The probable price of a security, based upon an evaluation of previous prices of the security or similar securities. A broker may be asked for a quotation on an inactive stock which sells within a narrow range, even though there has been no recent transaction he may hazard an estimate in the form of a nominal quote. If interest is expressed at that price he may later change the nominal quote into a firm or binding quotation through an actual transaction.

nominal rate of exchange The posted rate of exchange which permits the concerned individual to have a good idea of about what the foreign exchange rate is and which is actually used for small foreign exchange transactions. However, on large trades or sales of foreign exchange it is customary for the rates to fluctuate during the day in response to forces of supply and demand. For this reason a foreign exchange nominal or posted rate may vary from the actual rate.

nominal yield The amount of interest stated on an instrument's face. The amount of dividend stated on the face of the stock (if preferred).

nomination The naming or proposal of a person for an office, position, or duty; to be distinguished from appointment. Thus, the testator nominates but the court appoints the executor under a will. (88)

nominee An official of a bank or Trust Company, or an appointed agent into whose name securities or other funds are transferred by agreement. This is done to facilitate the purchase or sale of securities, when it may be inconvenient to obtain the signature of the principal to make such transfers. It also facilitates the collection and distribution of income from securities when these securities are held in the name of a nominee. Nominee arrangements also apply to custodianships. (1)

no more credit Instruction to authorizers that no further credit be allowed a particular customer. (26)

nonassented securities Securities whose holders have not agreed to some change in the terms or status of a defaulted security. See Assented Securities.

non-assessable stock A type of security which cannot be assessed in the event of insolvency or failure, i.e., it is fully paid for. Most stocks are of this nature, thus the holder cannot be assessed. (105)

nonborrowed reserves Total reserves less member bank borrowings from Reserve Banks. (117)

non-callable bond A bond that cannot, under the terms of the issue, be called by the obligor (the corporation) for redemption or conversion. (74)

non-callable securities A security not subject to call cannot be paid off before maturity, even if the company can afford to do so. (105)

nonclearing house stock Those securities which do not clear through the New York Stock Exchange Clearing Corporation. These would include stocks traded on other exchanges or over the counter.

non compus mentis "Not of sound mind" A term that includes all forms of mental unsoundness. (74)

non-contingent preference stock Cumulative preferred stock. See that term.

non-cumulative A preferred stock on which unpaid dividends do not accrue. Omitted dividends are, as a rule, gone forever. See Cumulative Preferred. (2)

noncupative will See Nuncupative Will.

nondiscretionary trust A fixed investment trust. See that term.

no near bid-offer Term meaning that the highest bid or lowest offer is relatively far below or above the price of the last sale. (105)

none offered A condition which usually occurs only in the over-the-counter market, indicating a current lack of stock being offered for sale. (105)

non-expendable disbursements Disbursements which are not chargeable as expenditures; for example, a disbursement made for the purpose of paying off an account payable previously recorded on the books. (29)

non-expendable fund A fund the principal and sometimes also the earnings, of which may not be expended. See also Endowment Fund. (29)

nonguaranteed debt Debt payable solely from pledged specific sources which does not constitute an obligation on any other resources of the government if the pledged sources are insufficient. (7)

non-installment credit A financial obligation which is met through a single payment. (131)

noninsured fund Pension or other fund invested through channels other than deposit with an insurance company. (121)

non-interest-bearing note A note in which the maker is not required to pay interest. (73)

non-legal investment An investment which is outside the classes designated by statute or by some governmental agency as proper for the investment of trust funds. (74)

nonlegals Securities that do not conform to the requirements of the statutes, in certain states, concerning investments for savings banks and for trust funds; opposed to Legals. See Legal List. (103)

nonmarketable liabilities of U.S. Government United States Government liabilities associated with specific transactions are mainly advance payments by foreign governments to special subscription securities issued to the Department of Defense in anticipation of future delivery of military procurement shipments. Other institutions for securities transactions include the International Development Association, the Inter-American Development Bank, and the United Nations. Payments are in the form of noninterest-bearing, nonmarketable securities issued in lieu of cash payments. In the past, these special securities were issued to these international institutions until such time as they were spent.

nonmarketable liabilities of U.S. Government (including medium-term securities). Other medium-term securities include foreign holdings of nonmarketable, medium-term U.S. Government securities, payable before maturity only under special conditions. Examples of these are nonconvertible "Roosa Bonds" issued by the Treasury, and Certificates of Participation representing Export-Import Bank loans sold mainly to foreign governments and central banks. (124)

non member bank A bank which is not a member of the Federal Reserve System.

non negotiable instrument First see Negotiable Instrument for distinction. An instrument may be non negotiable because of the very nature of not fulfilling all the requirements of the Uniform Negotiable Instrument Law. In addition a negotiable instrument may be made non negotiable by endorsement restriction. Other instruments may become non-negotiable by action of law. Some paper may be non negotiable but not classified as instruments such as bills of lading. The latter would be classified as non-negotiable paper.

non negotiable paper See Non Negotiable Instrument for technical distinctions between paper and instrument.

nonoperating expenses Decreases in the proprietorship of a business that are incurred through the financial control of the business. They are also known as financial expenses, nonrecurring income, or other income. (73)

non-operating income Income of municipal utilities and other governmental enterprises of a business character which is not derived from the operation of such enterprises. An example is interest on investments or on bank deposits. (29)

non-par item A check which cannot be collected at the par or face value when presented by another bank. All checks drawn on member banks of the Federal Reserve System, and non-member banks that have met the requirements of the Federal Reserve System, are collectible at par. Some non-member banks in certain regions of the United States levy an exchange charge against the check presented for collection and payment. These banks are called non-par banks, and deduct the exchange charge when remitting the payment to the bank requesting collection and payment. See Par List. (1)

non participating preferred First see Preferred Stock. Participating stock participates in the earnings of a corporation within the stated terms of the participation clause and will vary from security issue to security issue. In a general sense the participating preferred stock first receives a stated amount or percent of its par value from the earnings available for dividends. The common then receives a determinable amount. If there are earnings still available then the participating preferred shares in some proportion with the common stock.

nonpayment Failure to pay as agreed. (59)

nonpayout lease A cancellable contract that does not obligate the lessee to make payments that equal the equipment's cost. A lease of this nature is usually cancellable after the first 12 months on 60-90 days notice, with the equipment being returned to the lessor. Primary risk to the lessor is the lessee's continued use of the equipment, plus the lessor's ability to sell or re-lease the returned equipment. Most computer leases belong in this category.

nonprofit institutions Enterprises set up to do some useful service and seek no profit, e.g. colleges, schools, churches). Also such as foundations established to better business relationships and understanding with and by the public, etc. (59)

nonrecourse A situation in which the holder of an instrument does not have the legal right to compel a prior endorser or drawer to pay the amount of the negotiable instrument if it is dishonored. This may be because of a prior endorsement having the term "nonrecourse" as part of the endorsement. Or it may be the holder is not "in due course".

non-recurring expense Cost involved with putting a facility into operation for the first time, called start-up costs; or an unusual expense or loss that is unlikely to be repeated, e.g. that caused by fire or theft. (105)

nonstock money corporation A corporation operating either under the banking law or the insurance law which does not issue stock. This includes mutual savings banks, credit unions, mutual insurance companies and similar organizations.

non-taxable dividend A distribution which constitutes a return of capital for federal income tax purposes, and is not subject to normal federal income taxes by the recipient, but must be applied to reduce the cost of his stock. (3)

nontaxable securities Securities which have certain tax exempt features. The most common is the exemption holders of municipal securities have in their federal income tax in reporting the income from their holdings of municipals.

nonvalidating stamp The stamp which banks put on the back of all domestic drafts accompanying bills of lading which removes the bank from certain liability. The stamped words state that the bank is not responsible nor does it guaranty the documents stamped.

non-voting stock All stock of a corporation classified as other than voting stock. Under NYSE listing requirements, a non-voting stock cannot be listed. (105)

no par stock Stock which has no par value. Most stock is assigned a par value for such purposes as establishing the capital structure of the corporation or for tax purposes. When no-par stock is issued today it must pay the tax of one hundred dollars par stock; as a result most stock does not have the no par feature.

no-par value Having no face value. (73)

no-par-value stock Stock that does not have a value for each share printed on the stock certificate. (73)

no protest A term used in banks whereby one bank can instruct another collecting bank not to protest items in case of non-payment. The sending bank will stamp on the face of the item the letters "N.P." with its A.B.A. number (transit number). If the item cannot be collected, the collecting bank will return the item without protesting it. This will save the notary public's protest fees against the check. See Protest. (1)

no record Report given to credit granter by credit bureau when no record exists in bureau files be allowed particular customer. (26)

normal price That price which will balance the supply and demand for a product for an extended period of time and to which the price will tend to return to upon fluctuation up or down. Sometimes called the equilibrium price.

nostro account The name applied to an accounting record of an account maintained by one bank with another. The bank owning the account maintains this record and makes entries to it in reverse order to the manner in which they will appear on the statement which it will receive from the carrying bank. The term is used mainly in connection with foreign currency accounts. When both foreign currency and dollars are shown on the account, balances in both the

foreign currency and dollar equivalents are maintained. (1)

nostro overdraft The designation on a bank's statement that it has sold more foreign bills of exchange than it has purchased and thus the domestic bank owes funds to foreign banks in the amount of the Nostro (our) Overdraft.

not a delivery Commodity and security exchanges have rules for delivery of the item in the transaction such as a stock certificate. If the delivery and instrument or document meets with the rules it is described as a good delivery while if there is some fault it is called "Not a delivery."

notarial acknowledgment The acknowledgment of the due execution of a legal instrument before a notary public. The statement of the notary public as to the fact and date of the acknowledgment, with the notary public's signature and seal of office and date of expiration of commission to serve as notary public. (74)

notarial certificate The certificate of the notary public as to the due acknowledgment of the instrument. (74)

notarial protest certificate See Notice of Dishonor. (1)

notarized draft A withdrawal order signed and acknowledged before a notary public, who affirms that the person who signed the draft personally appeared before him, was known to be the person indicated, and executed the draft for the purpose indicated. (90)

notary public A person commissioned by the state for a stipulated period of time—with the privilege of renewal—to administer certain oaths, to attest and certify documents thus giving them authenticity in the eyes of the law, to take affidavits and depositions, and who is authorized to "protest" negotiable instruments for non-payment or nonacceptance. See also Notice of Dishonor. (1)

note An instrument, such as a promissory note, which is the recognized legal evidence of a debt. It is an instrument signed by the maker, called the borrower, promising to pay a certain sum in money on a specified date at a certain place of business, to a certain business, individual, or bank, called the lender. It should meet all requirements of the Uniform Negotiable Instruments Act. See Negotiable Instrument; Loan. (1)

note broker See Bill Broker.

note liability The liability which a Federal Reserve bank has for the notes it has outstanding.

note notice A form which is made and used by the loan department of a bank. The note notice contains all information as to the amount, due date, maker's name and address, securities pledged, if any, etc. It is mailed to the borrower several days before the maturity of the note, as a reminder of the due date of the note. If the bank is posting the "liability ledger" by machine, the "Loans Made Register," customer's liability ledger card, Note Notice, and maturity tickler are all created in one posting operation. (1)

note payable 1. In general, an unconditional written promise signed by the maker, to pay a certain sum in money on demand or at a fixed or determinable future time either to the bearer or to the order of a person designated therein. 2. Promissory notes issued by a business. 3. An accounting term for a ledger heading for notes to be paid. See Temporary Loans. (29, 73)

note payable register A special book in which a detailed record of all notes and acceptances payable may be recorded. (73)

note receivable A note payable of another held by a governmental unit as designated payee or by endorsement.

NOTE: While in a legal sense, a note receivable may be merely a promise to pay and is not necessarily negotiable, the term "notes receivable" when used in a balance sheet means negotiable notes which the holder has received in the course of business. (29)

note receivable register A special book in which a detailed record of all notes and acceptances receivable may be recorded. (73)

note teller Another title for "Loan Teller." See definition. (1)

not held A term describing a customer's instruction accompanying a market order to his broker which gives the broker some discretion over the execution and relieves him of any responsibility if he temporarily misses the market. (105)

notice, constructive The party is presumed to have knowledge of the act. (66)

notice day The business day that notices of delivery of actual commodities are made. The actual commodities are against short positions in the spot month.

notice of dishonor When a "holder in due course" (see definition) presents an instrument for payment, or acceptance by a drawee, and the maker of drawee dishonors the instrument, the holder in due course gives it to a Notary Public. The Notary Public also presents the instrument to the maker or drawee as a legal formality. If the maker or drawee again dishonors the instrument by refusing to pay for, or to accept it, the Notary Public prepares a "Notice of Dishonor," or as is termed in some states, a "Mandate of Protest," or a "Notarial Protest Certificate." This notice is made out in a copy for each endorser and maker or drawee evidence in courts of law that the instrument was duly presented for payment or acceptance; that the instrument was dishonored by the maker or drawee; and that the notice serves to notify all parties interested in the instrument of the dishonor. They are then legally placed on notice that the holder in due course can look to these parties to meet their obligation of repayment on the instrument. (1)

notice of withdrawal A notice which may be required by a mutual savings bank or other recipient of savings deposits before a withdrawal of funds is permitted. The length of time required before the notice becomes effective varies in the several states. (90)

notice to creditors The notice in writing by posting in public places or by notice in newspapers to creditors of an estate to present their claims for what the executor or administrator owes them; it usually is also a notice to debtors to come in and pay what they owe the estate. (74)

no-ticket savings plan A variation of the "Unit-Savings Plan" whereby the normal savings account transaction, either deposit or withdrawal, is accomplished without the use of either a deposit ticket or a withdrawal slip. A deposit is recorded just as in the "Unit-Savings Plan," but the depositor is not required to make out a deposit ticket under this machine-printed entry plan. In place of a withdrawal slip, the depositor merely writes his signature on the same line as the machine-printed entry of withdrawal. As in the Unit Savings Plan, the pass book, ledger card, and lock-protected audit tape are posted in original printing in one operation directly in front of the depositor, who is the "auditor" of the transaction. (1)

notification Notice given in words or writing, or by other means. (93)

not subject to call Meaning not callable, designation for securities which cannot be paid off and retired before their maturity date. (105)

nuisance value This is not a true value but is the amount that someone, other than the owner of a property will pay for it, not for its own sake but because in its present hands it is an annoyance or is actually damaging to the prospective buyer. (5)

numerical transit system See A.B.A. Number. (1)

numismatic Pertaining to coins and the collection of coins and medals.

nuncupative Verbal, oral as distinguished from being in writing such as a will.

nuncupative will An oral will made by a person on his deathbed or by one who is conscious of the possibility of meeting death in the near future—as by a person in active military service. It is declared in the presence of at least two witnesses and later reduced to writing by someone other than the testator and offered for probate in the manner prescribed by statute. (74)

O

O.&A. Semi-annual interest payment or dividends in October and April.

OAA Old Age Assistance. (67)

OAIB Old-Age Insurance Benefit.

O.B. Ordered Back.

OC Office of Commissioner. (67)

O/D On demand.

OD. Overdrawn or overdraft.

OIC Officer in Charge. (67)

O. J. A. J. Quarterly interest payments or dividends in October, January, April and July.

O.K. Correct.

Opt. Option; optional.

Outstdg. Outstanding.

objective value The price which an economic good can command in terms of other goods in the market. (89)

obligation The legal responsibility and duty of the debtor (the obligor) to pay a debt when due, and the legal right of the creditor (the obligee) to enforce payment in the event of default. (1)

obligator Commonly called principal; one bound by an obligation. Under a bond, strictly speaking, both the principal and the surety are obligors. The surety. Another word for Obligor.

obligee A firm or person protected by a bond similar to the insured under a policy of insurance. The creditor on an obligation such as a bond or note. (52+50)

obligor Commonly called principal; one bound by an obligation. Under a bond, strictly speaking, both the principal and the surety are obligors. The surety. Another word for Obligator. (50+)

obsolescence The decrease in value of a Fixed Asset brought about by invention of newer and more efficient machines, or the abandonment of the process for which the machine was originally intended. The term is also frequently applied to Material On Hand which has been superseded by new items, or is no longer necessary to the manufacture of a product. (28)

obsolete securities 1. The securities of an abandoned or defunct corporation. 2. A bond which has matured or been retired. (105)

odd lot An amount of stock less than the established 100-share unit or 10-share unit of trading: from 1 to 99 shares for the great majority of issues, 1 to 9 for so-called inactive stocks. See Round Lot; Inactive Stocks. (2)

odd-lot dealer A broker or a dealer who assembles orders to buy or sell smaller quantities of a security than the normal trading unit and who consolidates such orders into a round-lot transaction. See Round Lot. (103)

odd-lot differential The compensation for an odd-lot broker's services amounting to ⅛ point (12½¢) per share on stocks selling below $55., and ¼ point (25¢) per share on stocks selling above $55. This differential is added to the price of the effective round-lot sale on buy orders and subtracted from the price of each share on sell orders. (105)

odd-lot house A brokerage firm which specializes as a dealer in handling orders from investors for amounts less than 100 shares (round-lots). As a dealer the brokers must take positions in the market and draw on their own inventory to satisfy demand for securities. (105)

odd-lot index A measurement of public psychology in the securities market. It is computed by dividing total odd-lot sales by odd-lot purchases on a ten-day moving average. If sales outnumber purchases, this is interpreted as unfavorable because the public is reluctant to buy. When purchases outnumber sales, the reverse is true. (105)

odd lot orders The unit of trading for shares on the exchange is in 100-share lots. Any purchase or sale of stock in less than 100-share units is called an "Odd Lot Order." (1)

odd-lot trader One who buys and sells securities in less than 100 share lots, as distinguished from professional investors and people of substantial means who deal in larger, more economical amounts. (105)

odds The probable number of incidents that will occur within a statistical universe. For example, the odds are one in two that a head will come up on any given toss of a coin. Insurance actuaries compute their tables on the basis of past experience and other factors including the odds of probability. (5)

off The amount the cash price is under a futures price. In commodity trading this is expressed in number of points below the month of the future. The point generally is 1/100 of a cent but in some futures it is 1/10 of a cent and in grains it is ⅛th of a cent. A quotation of 50 points off X month could thus have at least three different meanings until the commodity is mentioned.

off-board This term may refer to transactions over-the-counter in unlisted securities, or, in a special situation, to a transaction involving a block of listed shares which was not executed on a national securities exchange. See Over-the-Counter; Secondary Distribution. (2)

offer The price at which a person is ready to sell. Opposed to bid, the price at which one is ready to buy. See Bid and Asked. (2)

offered ahead A condition which might exist when a security order to sell is entered at a stipulated price, but other similar or lower offers have been previously submitted on the same stock, and have precedence over this order. (105)

offered down A price which is lower than the last transaction's price.

offered firm A firm offer. An offer by a seller to sell a stated amount of a commodity or security at a stated price for a stated period of time. A product may be offered firm to a specific firm or individual or it may be made general in the form of a publication of the offer to the trade or market.

offering book See Offering List.

offering list A document or documents upon which the price, amount and description of the article are printed by the seller or dealer and are used as a reference.

offering price The price per share at which mutual fund shares are offered to the public. The offering price usually consists of the net asset value per share plus a sales charge. Synonymous with "asked price." (65)

offering sheet See Offering List.

offer wanted A request by a willing, and often anxious, buyer of a security to find a seller with whom he can trade when no apparent market exists. (105)

office See Head Office; Home Office. (42)

office paper Finance Bill. See that term.

officer One who is appointed or elected to fill an official position in a company or body such as a president, vice president, treasurer, secretary.

officer's check Same as cashier's check. (85)

official check A check drawn by an official of a commercial bank on the bank itself, used by a bank to pay its bills and other obligations; sometimes provided to the bank's customers for transactions in which a personal check might not be acceptable (also called cashier's or treasurer's check). (8)

official exchange rate The rate at which the monetary authority of a nation will exchange its currency for the currency of another nation.

offset 1. Any entry which, when posted, has the effect of restoring the balance to its original condition, or changes it to reflect only the new entry as the balance is known as an offsetting entry. It is merely a debit offsetting a credit, or a debit or credit being offset by the previous balance of the account. This use of the term is best known in general ledger work. 2. The right of a bank to take possession of any balances that a guarantor may have in the bank to cover a loan in default which has been guaranteed by the guarantor. This is called the "right of offset" accruing to the bank. 3. A depositor who has both a deposit credit balance and a loan balance is denied the right of offset in case the bank becomes insolvent and closes. This right is denied a depositor for the reason that it would make him a "preferred" creditor, which is in conflict with banking laws. The loan must stand as an asset to be liquidated, whereas the deposit balance must be treated as being owned by a general creditor of the bank. 4. A term used in connection with the "sight-pay" plan of posting checking accounts. Affected accounts sheets are usually extended or "offset" to the right of account sheets not affected. This permits the bookkeeper to refer to them quickly when making a "pre-list" of the balances. 5. A straddle or balance of an opposite position from a previous long or short position. A broker's offset exists when he has executed a short position in a specific commodity contract for one of his customers which balances a long position in the same commodity and month for another customer. It may also refer to the sale and thus liquidation of either a long or short position. (1)

offsets to long-term debt Cash and investment assets of sinking funds, bond reserve and other reserve funds which are specifically held for redemption are pledged to redeem debt incurred to finance loan activities of such funds. (7)

of record As shown by the record; usually employed in such entries as "attorney of record," showing that the one named is the recognized representative of the party at interest. (74)

"o.k." packages A list or package of checks that has been processed in a branch office, proved for accuracy, checked for date and endorsement, and considered OK by the branch office. The total on the package is used at the main office for final consolidation of totals without the main office having to rerun the items in the package. (1)

old and new balance proof A method of proof used in a bank, especially in savings departments, to prove the correct pick-up of old balances, and to establish the net amount of increase or decrease to ledger controls. An adding machine tape, or a columnar journal sheet is used as a permanent record of this proof. All affected ledger cards are sorted by account number, and then run on an adding machine. Generally, the new balances are run in the first column. In the next column the old balances are run so that the old balances appear opposite the new balances and the old balances must equal the difference in the totals of the deposits and the withdrawals. If these two differences agree, it is proof that the old balance was picked up correctly on every account affected in the day's business. (1)

old lady of threadneedle street The Bank of England.

oligopoly A condition of partial monopoly in which there are so few sellers of a product or service that each may affect the price and market and in view of this can judge the probable impact of his actions on the other sellers.

oligopsony A condition of partial monopoly in which there are so few buyers of a product or service that each may affect the price and market and in view of this can judge the probable impact of his actions on the other buyers.

omnibus account An account carried by one futures commission merchant with another in which the transactions of two or more persons are combined rather than designated separately and the identity of individual accounts is not disclosed. (9)

on The number of points a cash commodity is higher than a specific futures month. See Off.

on account 1. A payment made toward the settlement of an account. 2. A purchase of sale made on "open account." (1)

on a scale A system of purchasing securities or futures contracts for commodities in which as a market price drifts downward purchases are made at regular intervals either in even amounts or according to some formula or proportion. As prices rise sales are made at regular intervals. It is a technique for acquiring or distributing a portfolio without the risk of buying at the high or selling at the low.

on balance The excess over previous sales or purchases of security. For example, if a trader has bought 400 shares of a security earlier in the day, and now sells 500 shares of the same; he has sold 100 shares on balance. (105)

on bid, or offer A method by which an odd-lot trader can transact in a listed security without waiting for an actual round-lot trade in the security to take place. A transaction can be made by selling at the bid price or buying at the offering price. (105)

on consignment Goods sent to an agent with payment to be made after sale is made. (93)

one bank The bank that is owned or controlled by a one-bank holding company.

one hundred per cent reserve A banking system which would be substituted for the fractional reserve system. Commercial banks would be required to maintain reserves of the entire amount of their deposits and thus could not make loans with any funds except those available from paid-in capital and surplus. Loans would be made by some other agency or financial institution such as an investment bank.

one hundred percent statement A technique used by statement analysts in which all the individual items in a balance sheet are converted to a per-cent of the total assets. When this is done for several periods the proportionate change is more readily revealed. It also permits statements to be compared of different sized companies in the same industry.

one name paper Single name paper. Straight paper. An instrument which is signed by only one party, individual or firm as distinguished from obligations which have two or more obligors.

on margin Securities which have been purchased by a customer who borrowed part of the purchase price from the broker, i.e., they are not fully paid for. (105)

on opening A term used to specify execution of an order during the opening call. (123)

on the brink of financial failure Not enough money to carry on. (93)

on us check Any depositor's check drawn on and payable at the bank wherein the account is carried, is termed an "on us" check when presented for payment to the drawee bank. (1)

open account Credit extended to an individual, firm, corporation or other legal entity based on an estimate of the general ability to pay, as distinguished from credit extended that is supported by a note, mortgage, or other formal written evidence of indebtedness. (1)

open book account See Open Account.

open contract 1. An oral or written contract between two or more parties, the terms, or duration of which remain unfilfilled. 2. In the commodities markets, it means a transaction which has not yet been completed by the sale or repurchase of a contract previously bought or sold, or by the actual delivery or receipt of the commodity. (105)

open credit See Open Account.

open end contract The contract of a supplier to furnish all the required designated material to a purchaser for a stated period of time even though the total volume is not known at the time the contract is signed.

open-end investment companies Generally referred to as "mutual funds", are obligated to repurchase on demand their outstanding shares at prices determined by their current net asset value, which may be more or less than the investor paid for them. In most cases open-end companies continuously offer new shares through securities brokers and dealers and, in some cases, directly or through the agents of the company. (65)

open-end investment trust An investment trust in which the trustee, by the terms of the trust, is authorized to invest in shares of stock other than those in the trust at the time of the inception of the trust or of the participation in the trust. (74)

open-end mortgage A loan reduced by amortization which can be increased to the original amount and secured by the original mortgage. A mortgage that by mutual agreement may have the balance or maturity extended to provide for modernization or improvement of the property. (5)

open fund An open-end investment company or mutual fund, so designated because it does not have a fixed capitalization. It raises money by selling its own stock to the public and invests the proceeds in other securities. As many shares can be issued as necessary to satisfy demand. (105)

opening The time or price at which trading begins in a commodity or security. Some orders to buy or sell are to be executed at the "opening".

opening entry An entry that is made in the general journal to record the assets, liabilities, and proprietorship of a new business at the time the business is organized, or of a going concern at the time a new set of books is opened; the first entry that is made in opening a new set of books. It is recorded in the general journal and presents a complete record of the assets, the liabilities, and the proprietorship as of the date of the entry. (73)

opening price The price of the first transaction in the security during the day is termed the Opening Price and constitutes one of the important quotations carried in financial publications. See Opening; Opening Range.

opening range Commodities, unlike securities, are often traded at several prices at the opening or close of the market. Buying or selling orders at the opening might be filled at any point in such a price range for the commodity. (9)

open interest In a contract market it is the total position on one side of the market shown by all clearing brokers at any given time. In any one delivery month the short interest equals the long interest, in other words, the total number of contracts sold equals the total number bought. (9)

open letter of credit An Open Letter has no restrictions on the presenting of documents such as bills of lading against drafts and is paid simply on a valid draft. See Letter of Credit.

open market A highly competitive and broad market without limitations as to the qualifications of either the purchaser or seller.

open market committee The committee is composed of the Board of Governors of the Federal Reserve System plus the presidents of five of the Federal Reserve District Banks. See Open Market Operations.

open-market operations The actions of the Federal Reserve Bank of New York in carrying out the instructions of the Federal Open Market Committee to buy and sell government securities as one of the major tools of monetary policy. In most cases Bills are bought or sold for the accounts of the twelve Federal Reserve Banks. Buying creates excess reserves and eases the interest rate structure. Selling Government securities reduces reserves and firms interest rates.

open market paper Short-term high grade promissory notes sold in the open market.

open mortgage A mortgage of which the date of maturity has passed but the unamortized balance has not been called. (5)

open order An order to buy or sell a security at a specified price. An open order remains in effect until executed or cancelled by the customer. See GTC; Limit Order; Market Order; Specialist. (2)

open outcry Required method of registering all bids and offers in the ring. (123)

open price system The practice of one or more companies in an industry in keeping the other producers informed about the prices and trends of their products.

open to buy The currently unused portion of a total dollar credit limit agreed upon. (59)

open trade A transaction which has not yet been closed. (105)

operating company A company whose officers direct the business of transportation and whose books contain operating as well as financial accounts. (19)

operating cost Cost of maintenance, utilities, office supplies, salaries and such required to keep the business running. (93)

operating expense Any expense incurred by a bank in the normal operation of the business. This is to be distinguished from capital expenditures, which are disbursements that are capitalized and depreciated over a period of years. Many large banks have as many as fifty major expense classifications, and maintain subsidiary ledgers for these major classifications. Monthly departmental expense reports are made out and forwarded to department heads, who can analyze their expenditures and budget requirements. Smaller banks do not require such elaborate bookkeeping, the expense accounts being carried as a part of the general ledger. (1)

operating income Income to the bank produced by its operating assets. The bank's source of income lies in the judicious use of the assets (resources) it owns. The bank must rely upon its directors and officers to exercise this good judgment to produce sufficient income to pay all expenses and produce a profit that will justify the operation of the bank. (1)

operating lease A lease transaction in which the lessor or an associated manufacturer provides maintenance or other supervisory and supportive services in connection with the agreement. Nonpayout leases tend to be operating leases.

operating losses Losses incurred in the normal operation of the bank. Such losses may be incurred when a loan becomes uncollectable—when a borrower becomes insolvent and cannot pay his loan. Such a loan is charged off against the undivided profits account. (1)

operating officer The officer who heads up an operating department in a large bank. He is in complete charge of the operations of his department. This distinction is made from the other officials, such as the vice-presidents, who are specialists in their fields. The cashier of the bank can be construed as being the senior operating officer in charge of the over-all operations of the bank in its routine work. The vice-presidents are specialists in the field of loans, credits, investments, and trusts. In the smaller banks, it is not uncommon for vice-presidents to be in charge of certain operations as well as being specialists in their field. Any decision regarding the operation of a department is usually left to the operating officer in charge of the department. His recommendations regarding personnel requirements, equipment purchases, type and quantity of supplies used, etc., carry great weight with higher officials. (1)

operating profit (for purposes of marketing) Gross margin (gross profit), less operating expenses (including salaries of managers, whether proprietors or employees), fixed plant and equipment cost, and sometimes interest on invested capital.
Comment: Obviously this definition includes only the profit accruing from the trading operations of a mercantile business. (13)

operating ratio The ratio of the operating expenses to the operating revenues. (19)

operating statement A tabulation of data, generally of a financial nature such as income and outgo for a stated period such as week, month or year.

operating surplus The profit remaining after deducting all costs of operating a business for a given period of time. (105)

operator 1. An individual who makes a career in speculation on the prices of securities or commodities. 2. A skilled worker on a machine. 3. The symbol which indicates a mathematical process.

opportunity cost A concept of cost which includes not only the amount paid out but also the amount of income lost as the cost of a course of action.

option A right to buy or sell specific securities of properties at a specified price within a specified time. A term sometimes erroneously applied to a future contract, because the seller has the option of fixing the day during the delivery month on which delivery may be made, also the option of the grade to be delivered and the warehouse where delivery is to be made. See Puts and Calls. (2, 9)

optional dividend A dividend in which the shareholder has the right of choice of a cash dividend or a stock dividend.

option day A put, call, or straddle option on a security must be exercised or declared by the option day given in the stock option.

option period Most options to buy or sell are for a stated period of time and are not indefinite. In cases of individual negotiation any legal period may be elected as the option period. In the cases of institutionalized purchases or sales it is customary for the agency such as the stock exchange, commodity exchange or auction to have stated periods during which options may be exercised.

option writer A person, usually an investor with a large portfolio, who writes stock option contracts for put and call brokers, who, in turn, resell these to the investing public. The options are written as promises to buy or sell certain securities at a set price within a specified time with the primary purpose to obtain capital gain or purchase stock at lower-than-market prices. Large financial institutions have shown interest in this function as a way of earning more and establishing prices at which they will buy or sell stocks. (105)

order 1. A written instruction or commission to do something such as buy, sell, negotiate or supply. 2. A direction from a proper court of jurisdiction. 3. Regulation.

order bill of lading A special form of bill of lading that is used in C.O.D. freight shipments. It is negotiable and is good only to the person in whose favor it is drawn or the person to whom it is endorsed. (73)

order instrument A negotiable instrument which contains the words "pay to the order of——" or "Pay to (the name of payee) or order" and thus requires endorsement and delivery prior to negotiation.

orderly marketing Control of the distribution of products in such a way that the market equilibrium of supply and demand are not adversely affected.

order of distribution An order by a probate or other court having jurisdiction of an estate directing distribution of estate property to persons or others entitled thereto. (74)

order room The department of a brokerage firm which is responsible for transmitting buy and sell orders to and receiving reports of executions from the trading floor of a stock exchange. (105)

orders Any type of verbal or written instruction to a broker to buy, or sell, securities or commodities. For example, market order, limit order, stop order. (105)

ordinary interest Interest computed on the basis of 360 days to the year—12 months of 30 days each. (105)

ordinary shares Common or equity stock. In England has different meaning and includes deferred and preference shares.

ordinary stock Common or equity stock.

organization expenses Costs of organizing a corporation, such as the incorporation fee and attorneys' fees. (73)

organized market A group of traders, operating under recognized rules for the purpose of buying and selling a single commodity or a small number of related commodities.

Comment: Examples are the Chicago Board of Trade, the New York Cotton Exchange, and the New York Produce Exchange. (13)

original Many business papers such as bills are issued with copies. These copies are used for several purposes such as record keeping and to provide an identical memorandum to all parties directly concerned with the transaction. The "original" document is the major paper and is most important while the copies permit efficient handling and notification.

original balance The beginning debt or obligation before any payment has been made on it to reduce it. (59)

original cost The actual cost of construction or acquisition or, in other words, the actual original cost of property to the carrier at the time of its initial dedication to public use. (19)

original investment An investment received by the trustee as part of the decedent's estate or from the settlor of a living trust. (88)

original issue stock Those shares which were initially issued at the time the corporation was formed and are part of the starting capitalization.

original margin Margin required at the onset of a transaction. (123)

originator The investment banker or banking house first to promote a new security issue for a corporation.

orphan's court In many states the court that has jurisdiction over matters pertaining to the settlement of estates and sometimes over guardianships and trusts. (74)

ostensible partner One who is openly recognized by the public as a partner. (73)

other expense An expense not considered to be one of the regular operating expenses of a business. (73)

other income A general heading on the income statement under which are grouped revenues from miscellaneous operations, income from lease of road and equipment, miscellaneous rent income, income from non-operating property, profit from separately operated properties, dividend income, interest income, income from sinking and other reserve funds, release of premiums on funded debt, contributions from other companies, miscellaneous income and delayed income credits. (19)

other liabilities and accrued dividends Miscellaneous liabilities plus dividends accrued but unpaid on Federal Reserve bank stock owned by the member banks. (4)

other loans Mostly loans to individuals, except farmers, for consumption purposes. (4)

other loans for purchasing or carrying securities Loans to others than brokers and dealers for the purpose of buying or carrying securities. (4)

other long-term debt Long-Term Debt other than Mortgage Bonds and Debentures. This includes Serial Notes and Notes Payable to Banks with original maturity of more than one year. (21)

other real estate The real estate held by a bank which has been acquired in satisfaction of a defaulted debt. The term arises from the fact that such real estate is usually recorded on a bank's books separate from the real estate which is used, or is intended to be used, for the transaction of the bank's business. (90)

other securities All securities other than U.S. Government obligations i.e., state, municipal, and corporate bonds. (Member banks are generally not permitted to invest in stocks other than Federal Reserve bank stock.) (4)

out card A card which is substituted for a ledger card when the latter is removed from the file. The out card should contain the balance, the date the ledger card was removed, by whose authority, and the person in whose possession the ledger card is held. There are occasions when ledger cards must be removed from the ledger trays for reference. One such instance is when a borrower who already is borrowing funds from the bank requests a large loan. The ledger card is the record that must be used to review the borrower's use of credit, how the loans in the past were liquidated, and when the customer had last completely liquidated his borrowings. This information supplements other available credit information held by the bank and is used by the loan committee in arriving at decisions. (1)

out-go Expenses. (93)

outlays Synonymous with Expenditures. See Capital Outlays. (29)

out of line A security which is selling at what appears to be a very high or low price when that security is compared with other securities of relatively similar quality.

out-of-town-business The aggregate of security orders from areas other than the immediate business location of the main office of a brokerage firm. (105)

out-of-town checks See Out of Town Item; Foreign Item; Transit Letter.

out-of-town-item See Foreign Item; Transit Letter. (1)

outside board of directors See Board of Directors.

outside broker A broker who does not belong to the local board or exchange.

outside collector Person employed by store or firm. Makes personal calls on debtors for purpose of securing payment or promise of payment. (26)

outside market Means over-the-counter, or a market where unlisted securities are traded. (105)

outsider One without special association or inside information on a transaction.

outside securities Those securities which are unlisted, i.e., they have no trading privileges on a regular exchange. (105)

outstanding Still owing, still unperformed. (59)

outstanding checks Checks that have been issued by the depositor but that have not yet been paid by the bank. (73)

outstanding securities That part of the authorized capital stock of a corporation which has been issued and sold to the public and is still publicly owned, as opposed to that stock which may have been issued but later cancelled or reacquired by the corporation. (105)

out-the-window Designation for a new security issue which was quickly sold to the public by underwriters. (105)

overall coverage The relationship of income available for payments on corporate obligations divided by the amount of such annual charges. This ratio gives an analyst an appreciation of how sound the various obligations are. The better the coverage over a period of time the sounder the issue.

overall market price coverage The ratio of net assets to the sum of all prior obligations at liquidating value plus the issue in question taken at market price. (3)

over and short account An account carried in the general ledger. Overages and shortages from all sources, and their nature, are posted to this account, which is also termed a "suspense" or "differences" account in banks. At the end of the fiscal period, this account is closed out to profit and loss, and becomes either an increase or a decrease to the undivided profits account in the general ledger. In larger banks a subsidiary ledger is carried on this account, so that the overages and shortages of all departments are carried as separate accounts. In this way, the frequency of any differences can be localized to a department and this department brought under control. (1)

over-bought An opinion as to price levels. May refer to a security which has had a sharp rise or to the market as a whole after a period of vigorous buying, which, it may be argued, has left prices "too high." See Technical Position. (2)

overbought market See Oversold Market.

over capitalized 1. A corporation whose capital is valued at less than the property which secures it. 2. A corporation whose assets exceed the need of the business. The business has too much capacity for the market for its production. Since these two meanings of the same term vary so

much, care must be taken to be sure of the context. See Watered Stock.

overcertification The certification by a bank of a customers check in those cases where the collected balance in the customers account is less than the amount of the check. It is less common today than prior to 1933 when stock brokers would use this device to obtain securities which in turn would be left with the bank as collateral for overcertification and until such times as their collected balance was sufficient to cover the overcertification. Members of the Federal Reserve System are prohibited from making any "overcertification."

overcheck An overdraft. A check drawn against an insufficient or uncollected balance.

over-commitment Same as Over Extension. See that term.

overdraft When a depositor draws a check for more than the balance on deposit in his account with a bank, he is said to be "overdrawn." The bank can either return the check to the bank from which it came, or to the depositor who presented it for payment, marked "Insufficient Funds"; or the bank may elect to render the customer a service and pay the check. When the bank pays the check, it creates an overdraft in the depositor's account. The account ceases to become a deposit liability, and becomes an asset, since it is in effect a loan to the depositor. This type of "loan", however, does not find favor with bank officials or bank examiners, because it is an unauthorized and illegal "loan" without a note as evidence. Overdrafts are infrequent and a depositor's credit is impaired when checks are presented that would, if approved by the banker, create overdrafts in his account. Some banks exact heavy service charges for checks returned for insufficient funds. Interest is often charged on overdrawn accounts. (1)

over due A debt or obligation which has not been met on time.

over-estimate To value or judge too highly. (93)

overexpansion That stage of business characterized by greater productive capacity and inventory than the existing conditions warrant. A business, an industry or an economy may at times experience overexpansion. In a growing economy the growth will correct this condition but in a mature economy correction of overexpansion is difficult and characteristically accompanied by business failures and liquidation.

over-extension 1. Credit received or extended beyond the debtor's ability to pay. 2. The condition where a dealer in securities obligates himself for an amount beyond his borrowing power or ability to pay. 3. The expansion of buildings, equipment, etc., by a business concern which is in excess of its present or prospective future needs. (1)

overhead Charges of a fairly fixed nature which do not vary with the volume of activity. Light, water, rent, and some taxes are overhead items. (5)

overhead expenses Term applied to certain costs that do not vary much, regardless of business conditions, sales, etc.; such as rent, heat, the salaries of office clerks, officers of a company

—as contrasted to the wages of those who are paid for what they make or sell. (59)

overimprovement An addition or alteration which is not in the highest and best use for the site on which it is placed, thus a very expensive building on a very poor or cheap site. (5)

overissue An amount in excess of the authorized or ordered amount.

overlying bond A junior bond which subject to the claim of a senior underlying bond which has priority of claim.

overlying mortgage A junior mortgage which is subject to the claim of a senior mortgage which has priority of claim.

overproduction A supply of goods greater than can be sold within a reasonable time at a price sufficient to keep a business or industry manufacturing or growing the product.

override A commission paid to managerial personnel in addition to their basic compensation. (93)

oversavings A situation where there are more liquid assets than can be profitably invested. When capital-savings have been used to produce more goods than can be profitably sold.

over-sold An opinion—the reverse of overbought. A single security or a market which, it is believed, has declined to an unreasonable level. (106)

oversold market When the speculative long interest has been drastically reduced and the speculative short interest increases, actually or relatively, a market is said to be oversold. At such times, sharp rallies often materialize. On the other hand, when the speculative short interest decreases sharply, a market is said to be overbought. At such times, the market is often in a position to decline sharply. (9)

overspeculation That situation in a market in which the activity is abnormally high caused not by the normal requirements of legitimate buyers and sellers but by speculators.

overstayed the market That condition of an individual who is either long or short of a market and who has experienced a theoretical or paper profit and who is not content with the profit and thus expects to "ride" his position to even higher profits but finds that the movement of the market has reversed itself and his profits are cut and may even have been converted into losses by the time he withdraws from the market.

oversubscription The situation in which for a given issue of securities more orders have been received then can be filled. In such cases the syndicate manager and the underwriters scale down the orders to the amount of the issue. Such scaling down is not always proportionate since one of the goals is wide distribution; thus small orders may receive their full allotment but larger orders may be cut down.

over-the-counter A market for securities made up of securities dealers who may or may not be members of a securities exchange. Over-the-counter is mainly a market made over the telephone. Thousands of companies have insufficient shares outstanding, stockholders, or earnings to warrant application for listing on a stock exchange. Others may prefer not to make public all the information which listing requires. Securities of these companies are traded in the over-the-counter market between dealers who act either as principals or as brokers for customers. The over-the-counter market is the principal market for U.S. Gov't. bonds, municipals, bank and insurance stocks. See NASD; Off-Board. (2)

over-the-counter market This is the market operated by security dealers for thousands of stocks which are not listed on stock exchanges. Also, many listed stocks are traded by security dealers offboard, i.e., in the over-the-counter market. (116)

over-the-counter securities Securities not listed or traded on any of the regular exchanges are called "Over-the-counter" securities. The method of trading such securities is through traders and dealers in unlisted stocks. Sales or purchases are arranged by these dealers or through a chain of them until the desired securities and prices are obtained. (1)

overtrading An attempt to do more volume of business than can be safely handled with the given amount of capital available. In securities this may involve pyramiding; in other areas it may involve excessive use of margins.

owner Includes his duly authorized agent or attorney, a purchaser, devisee, fiduciary, and a person having a vested or contingent interest in the property in question. (11)

owner of record The individual or organization whose name appears on a corporation's transfer agent's book as the owner of securities in that corporation as of a certain date. This name is then identified to be entitled to receive any benefits or dividends declared. (105)

ownership certificate A form required by the government and furnished by the Collector of Internal Revenue which discloses the real owner of stocks registered in the name of a nominee. Such a form must also accompany coupons presented for collection on bonds belonging to nonresident aliens, or partially tax-free corporate bonds issued prior to January 1, 1934. (74)

P

P Partnership.

P Payee; Peso; Purchaser.

P/A Power of attorney. (5)

PA Per Annum (used after figures); Public assistance. (67)

P.A.P. Pension Administration Plan. (5)

Part. Participating.

Pat. Patent.

Payt. Payment.

P. C. Per cent; petty cash.

PC Payment Center. (67)

P. & C. Puts and calls.

PCC Production Credit Corporation.

P/D Per Diem. (67)

Per Cap. Per capita.

Per Pro. Per procuration.

Perp. Perpetual.

Pers. Personal.

Pf. or Pfd. Preferred.

P. & L. Profit and loss.

PM Push money.

P. O. R. Payable on receipt.

Pot. Potential.

Pr. Principal.

P.R. Pro rata. (5)

P.R.D. See Pay Roll Deduction. (42)

Pr. Ln. Prior lien.

Prec. Precedent.

Prem. Premium.

Pres. President.

Pro. Protest.

Proc. Procedure.

Prop. Property.

Pt. Pd. Part paid.

Ptas. Pesetas (Spain).

P.V. Par value.

Pwnbkr. Pawnbroker.

package mortgage A loan by which not only the real property is financed but also certain personal property such as washing machine, dishwasher, etc. (5)

packet London Stock Exchange term meaning block, as in a block purchase of securities. (105)

paid checks Checks which have been cancelled and paid.

paid-in-capital Capital contributed by stockholders and credited to accounts other than Capital Stock. (21)

paid in surplus That amount of surplus which was not earned but contributed to the corporation. Paid in surplus has several advantages to a business. 1. In a superficial way it makes a financial statement look better. 2. Some companies such as banks may not be permitted to pay dividends until they have a surplus in some relationship to their capital. By having the surplus paid in at the time of initial sale of stock by the technique of selling the stock at a premium over par the bank may pay dividends much sooner.

paid up capital The part of the authorized capital which has been paid for and issued as distinguished from the authorized and unsubscribed capital.

paid up shares See Paid up Stock.

paid up stock Capital stock upon which the initial purchaser from the issuing corporation has paid in goods, services or money an amount at least as much as the par value. There is little question about a stock being paid up when the payment is in cash or money of an amount at least as much as the par value. It is however a question of fact in those cases where a promoter or other purchaser renders services in exchange for the stock.

paid vouchers file An alphabetic file for paid vouchers. (73)

painting the tape 1. A form of manipulation, currently illegal, which involves constant trading in a security by a manipulator who wishes to excite the investing public's curiosity and interest in a particular security when it appears frequently on the ticker tape. 2. Any condition involving the frequent appearance of a particular stock on the ticker tape—indicating active trading and an unusual public interest. (105)

panic That part of a business cycle characterized by a very sharp drop in prices and general confidence in the economy and a high increase in business failures.

paper Commercial paper, short-term evidences of debt.

paper gain or loss An expression for unrealized capital gains or losses on securities in a portfolio, based on comparison of current market quotations and the original costs. (103)

paper money Those pieces of paper which a sovereign designates to be money. Such paper money may be also designated as being fiduciary, representative, convertible, irredeemable, fiat or otherwise depending upon its characteristics.

paper profit An unrealized profit on a security still held. Paper profits become realized profits only when the security is sold. (2)

par In the case of a common share, par means a dollar amount assigned to the share by the company's charter. Par value may also be used to compute the dollar amount of the common shares on the balance sheet. Par value has little significance so far as market value of common stock is concerned. Many companies today issue no-par stock but give a stated per share value on the balance sheet. Par at one time was supposed to represent the value of the original investment behind each share in cash, goods or services. In the case of preferred shares and bonds, however, par is important. It often signifies the dollar value upon which dividends on preferred stocks, and interest on bonds, are figured. The issuer of a 3 per cent bond promises to pay that percentage of the bond's par value annually. See Capitalization; Transfer Tax. (2)

par clearance A check which clears at par as distinguished from one which is non par. See Par.

par collection That system of collection of checks made possible by the "par collection requirement" of the Federal Reserve Act. See Par.

parent company The oldest, or controlling, of two or more companies. Usually, such companies are under common ownership or management. (42)

Pareto's Law A generalization which states that regardless of the form of a nation's institutional structure its income distribution will be the same.

par exchange rate The rate or price in gold designated by the International Monetary Fund in cooperation with a nation's monetary authorities at which that currency may be exchanged for the currency of another member nation of the IMF whose currency is computed on the same basis. The nations need *not* be on a gold standard for in this case gold is used only as the common denominator for all the IMF members currency.

Paris Bourse The Paris Stock Exchange, officially named Company of the Paris Bank, Exchange, Trade and Finance Brokers. The seventy broker-members of the Bourse cannot trade for their own account, but serve the several hundred "curb brokers" who deal for investors. (105)

par item Any item that can be collected upon presentation at its par or face value is known as a par item. Items drawn upon all national banks and state banks which are members of the Federal Reserve System, and non-member banks which have met the requirements of the Federal Reserve System, are called par items, in that no service charge is levied against the item upon payment. See also Non-Par Item. (1)

parity The relationship of one foreign currency to another as indicated by their exchange value in gold or silver. The relationship of agricultural prices in covered commodities such as wheat and corn to a base period of prices which farmers had to pay. The base period is used to measure the increase in prices for the commodities which the farmer purchases. Different base periods are used for various commodities, generally 1910-14.

par list The Board of Governors of the Federal Reserve System periodically issues lists of cities and towns wherein banks are located through which checks are collectible at par. All banks located in these cities and towns are known as par banks, EXCEPT where the listing specifies that only national banks in the city or town are par banks. The par list also shows banks throughout the nation in what Federal Reserve district the cities and towns are located. The par list is in constant use in transit departments of banks. (1)

parol Oral, as distinguished from written. (5)

parol evidence Testimony or evidence which is oral, as contrasted to written or documentary evidence. (74)

partial audit See Limited Audit. (29)

partially amortized mortgage A mortgage which is partly repaid by amortization during the life of the mortgage and partly repaid at the end of the term. (5)

partial monopoly A condition of partial monopoly in which there are few sellers of a product or service that each may affect the price and market and in view of this can judge the probable impact of his actions on the other sellers.

partial payment. 1. A payment on open account which is not equal to the full amount owed, and which is not intended to be accepted as the full payment thereof. 2. The amount of the payment on a debt that is accepted by the creditor as being satisfactory for the full discharge, or full payment of the obligation of indebtedness, as evidenced by the creditor's surrender of the instrument bearing the proper endorsement, or the creditor's issuing a receipt stipulating that a certain specified debt is paid in full. (1)

partial release The giving up of a claim to a portion of the property held as security for the payment of a debt. (31, 92)

participant Any bank, investment house, or brokerage firm which has agreed to sell an issue of securities to the public as a member of a selling syndicate. (105)

participating preferred stock Preferred stock that has the right to share with the common stock in profits above a fixed amount. (73)

participation An ownership interest in a mortgage. (31, 92)

participation agreement An understanding, the terms of which are usually specified in writing between institutional investors by buy or sell partial ownership interests in mortgages. (31, 92)

participation certificate An instrument that evidences a proportionate interest in a security or group of securities held by a trustee for the benefit of a group of investors. (89)

participation dividends Earnings of a cooperative that are distributed to each member in proportion to the amount of business he has done with the co-operative during the fiscal period. (73)

participation loan Limitations have been set up by banking laws whereby banks are not permitted to lend more than a fixed percent of their capital and surplus to any one borrower. (In most states, this fixed percent is approximately 10%.) This limitation causes banks to invite other banks to participate in making a large loan. If the financial background and credit position of the borrower warrants the large loan, several banks may each lend a portion of the amount to the borrower. The participating banks work together in handling the loan, and work out a joint agreement as to the liquidation program of the loan, since some of the banks may wish to be paid off ahead of other banks. (1)

partition Division, apportionment, and allocation of property between or among two or more persons who are entitled to fractional interests in the whole property, frequently used in connection with a parcel of real property which must be sold in order to satisfy interests of the parties owning unallocated shares in such property. (74)

partition proceedings A legal procedure by which an estate held by tenants in common is divided and title in severalty to a designated portion passed to each of the previous tenants in common. (54)

partition suit A court action to separate common interests in real estate and to assign full ownership of a designated portion of the property to each of the parties previously holding an interest in common. (89)

partly paid In the securities business usually refers to those securities held in a margin account, i.e., a balance is owed by the investor to his broker on the full amount of the securities purchased. (105)

partner A person who is a member of a partnership; one who has entered into a verbal or written agreement with one or more persons to operate a business. (73)

partnership A form of business organization in which two or more persons combine their property or their skill, or both, in one venture and agree to share in the profits or the losses of the business. (73)

partnership certificate A certificate filed with a bank showing the interest of each partner in a business enterprise operating as a partnership. This certificate also shows the limited partners

(partners who specify a maximum amount for which they may be held responsible in settlement of obligations incurred by the partnership), and also "silent partners" (partners who have invested funds in the partnership, but who, for certain reasons, do not wish to be publicly known as partners). (1)

part-paid stock A stock on which part of the amount owed the corporation has not been paid.

par value 1. The value printed on the face of an instrument of credit (bonds, etc.) representing the amount which the debtor agrees to pay upon maturity. 2. The value expressed on a share of stock which represents the holder's proportionate equity in the corporation. (1)

par value (of currency) Is its value in terms of gold as formally proposed to the International Monetary Fund, normally subject to Fund concurrence. The Fund's Articles of Agreement envisage that each member country shall have an effective par value, i.e., a unitary, fixed exchange rate for spot transactions that is established and maintained in accordance with the provisions of the Articles. (130)

passbook In general a book supplied by a bank to a depositor for record purposes. A savings passbook contains a complete record of the customer's account, showing deposits made and withdrawals as well as the interest credited at regular periods; it must be presented to the bank for proper entry of these transactions. A checking account passbook is the customer's deposit receipt book, in which the teller receipts for deposits as they are made. (85)

passed dividend Omission of a regular or scheduled dividend. (106)

passive trade balance A trade deficit, an unfavorable balance of trade.

passive trust A trust regarding which the trustee has no active duties to perform; the same as bare, dry, or naked trust; opposed to an active trust. (74)

pass no more See No More Credit. (26)

past due An account on which payment has not been made according to agreement and owes a given amount which is in arrears. (26)

past-due item A note or acceptance which has reached maturity without payment being offered by the maker (in case of a note); or the drawee—the buyer of goods (in case of an acceptance). Past-due items are usually protested for non-payment at the discretion of the banker. See also Dishonor; Protest. (1)

pawn An item pledged as security for a loan.

pawnbroker The businessman who will lend on items which are pledged as security for the loan. He is generally licensed by the local political subdivision and must report to police periodically those items which are pawned. If the loan is not repaid within the statute of limitations for such loans the pawnbroker may sell the security to compensate for nonpayment.

pay 1. To pay a check in cash, as when a check is paid by the paying teller. 2. To charge a check against a customer's account, as in the case of a check coming through the clearings. (85)

payables A bookkeeping designation for any and all accounts or notes payable total.

pay-as-you-go accounts A variation of "Special Checking Accounts" or "Special Fee Accounts." Under the "Pay-As-You-Go" plan, the special checking account depositor purchases a check book, usually at the rate of five or ten cents per check. The fee or service charge is therefore prepaid to the bank, and the depositor can control the cost of his checking account by the number of checks he writes. In this plan no service charge is posted as checks are posted against the account. (1)

payee The legal entity who is named in an instrument as the recipient of the amount shown on the instrument. In a check, the maker of the check orders the drawee bank to pay an amount to the payee whose name is written after the words "Pay to the Order of" on the face of a check. In a draft, the drawer of the draft orders the drawee to pay an amount to the payee whose name appears after the words "Pay to the Order of" or "At Sight, Pay to the Order of," etc. The payee is the party who will benefit by the payment of an instrument. (1)

payer The party primarily responsible for the payment of the amount owed as evidenced by a given negotiable instrument. (1)

paying agent An agent to receive funds from an obligor to pay maturing bonds and coupons, or from a corporation for the payment of dividends. (74)

paying teller A representative of the bank who is responsible for the proper paying or cashing of checks presented at the window. See Unit Teller System. (85)

payment stopped A negotiable instrument such as a check upon which a Stop Payment has been issued. See Stop Payment.

payment voucher Usually upper part of customer's monthly statement presented or mailed together with remittance. Becomes the posting media for Accounts Receivable bookkeeper. (26)

payroll A special form listing all employees entitled to pay, with the amounts due each. (73)

payroll clerks In large businesses, office workers who spend all or most of their time keeping payroll records. In smaller businesses the bookkeeper usually keeps the payroll records. (73)

payroll deduction (p.r.d.) Withholding of a regular portion from an employee's earnings for the purpose of making direct payment on behalf of the employee. (42)

pay to bearer See Bearer Instrument.

pay to order Any negotiable instrument containing such words is negotiable by endorsement of the within named payee and his delivery to another. A similar meaning is obtained from the use of "Pay to (the named individual) or order."

peak An exceptionally busy period of time in the banking business. A peak is reached daily, weekly, monthly, and seasonally. The daily peak generally begins the last business hour and continues a few hours after the bank is closed. At this time, all departments are working at "peak load" to get all the day's work processed and settled. In most communities, the weekly peak loads are on Mondays and Fridays. The monthly peaks are the first few business days of the month, and again between the 10th and the 15th of the month. The seasonal peaks vary according to geographical location. They differ in urban and rural communities; in normal business centers and resort centers; and of course occur after banking holidays and the Christmas and Easter seasons. (1)

pecuniary exchange The use of money for purchasing things as compared with barter which does not use money.

pecuniary legacy A gift of money by will. (74)

pegged price 1. The agreed, customary, or legal price at which any commodity has been fixed. 2. A price level for a particular security at which buying support nearly always develops and prevents a decline—thus "pegging" the price. (105)

pegging An attempt to keep the price of a commodity or a security within a narrow range by buying when the price drops and selling when the price increases. During WWII the United States Treasury through the Federal Reserve banks pegged the price of United States government bonds that were negotiable.

penalty A punishment imposed or incurred for a violation of law or rule. (93)

pendente lite During the continuance of a suit at law or in equity. (74)

Pennsylvania Rule A rule that requires credit of extraordinary dividends received in trust on the basis of the source of such dividends; to income if declared from earnings of the corporation during the life of the trust, and to principal if from earnings accumulated before commencement of the trust. (74)

penny stocks Low-priced issues often highly speculative, selling at less than $1 a share. Frequently used as a term of disparagement, although a few penny stocks have developed into investment-caliber issues. (2)

pension A regular allowance made to someone who has worked a certain number of years, attained a certain age, suffered some injury, etc. (93)

pension fund A fund out of which pensions are to be paid either to those entitled thereto under specific agreement or to those who may be selected by persons in control of the fund.
    NOTE: A pension fund is a Trust Fund. (29)

pension plan A system frequently using insurance companies, for the payment of annuities or pensions to qualified individuals. Sections 165 and 23 of the Internal Revenue Code establish requirements for taxes based upon pension plans. (5)

pension pool A system for the payment of pensions to workers in a limited geographic area in which subscribing employers all contribute according to some formula to a common fund or pool for their employees pensions. In the event that any employee transfers from one of the subscribing employer's firm to another subscribing employer's firm he has not lost any of the pension rights.

pension trust A trust established by an employer (commonly a corporation) to provide benefits for incapacitated, retired, or superannuated employees, with or without contributions by the employees. (74)

peppercorn rent A nominal rent, paid in order to give formal recognition to the landlord's position.

per capita (by the head) A term used in the distribution of property; distribution to persons as individuals (per capita) and not as members of a family per stirpes). For example, "I give my estate in equal shares to my son A and to my grandsons C, D, and E (the sons of my deceased son B) per capita." C, D, and E take as individuals (not as the sons of B), each taking the same share as A, namely, one-fourth of the estate. (74)

percentage Rate of interest or commission on each hundred. (93)

percentage bar graph A bar graph in which each bar, representing 100 percent, is divided to indicate the proportions of the items that make up the total. For example, a bar representing total income may be divided into percentage proportions to indicate cost of merchandise sold, operating expenses, financial expenses, federal income taxes, and net income. (73)

percentage lease A commercial lease of property in which the rental is determined as a percentage of the receipts from certain or all of the sales conducted by the lessee. It may be expressed as the percent of the gross revenues. When sales are low the return is low. When business improves and sales are higher the rent increases. (54+)

per cent return on investment Profit received from the business as compared to the money and property invested in the business. (93)

per contra item A ledger account which exactly offsets some other ledger account.

per diem Per day.

perfect competition The market situation where no one trader can materially affect the market for a product.
    In addition each trader is considered to be fully informed as to all the forces in the market. Pure competition.

period of digestion A period immediately following the issuance of a large or a new security offering during which sales are being effected to more or less permanent investors. (103)

period of redemption The length of time during which a mortgagor may reclaim the title and possession of his property by paying the debt it secured. (31, 92)

perjury False statement made under oath. (5)

permanent certificate As distinguished from a "Temporary Certificate" which is printed and is an "Interim Certificate" most "Permanent Certificates" are engraved for the purpose of making counterfeiting more difficult and to observe the requirements of most of the security exchanges.

permit A document giving the right to perform some action.

perpetual inventory A system whereby the inventory by units of property at any date may be obtained directly from the records without resorting to an actual physical count. An account is provided for each item or group of items to be inventoried so divided as to provide a running record of goods ordered, received, and withdrawn, and the balance on hand, in units and frequently also in value. (29)

perpetuity Duration without limitation as to time. See Rule Against Perpetuities. (88)

per procuration The signature of a principal made by his agent. The agent instead of having power of attorney is given limited authority by the principal. The words "Per Procuration" call attention to the limitation and the holder of the instrument is within his rights in requesting a statement in which the authority for the signature is given.

perquisite Any incidental gain or profit from work beyond monetary wages. Meals or clothing furnished an employee are examples of such benefits.

person Either a human being or a corporation, unless the context shows that one or the other is intended. (88)

personal account An account carried in the name of an individual or business. If the account has a debit balance it shows how much the individual or business owes while credit entries indicate payments on the debt. When the debits equal the amounts of the credits the personal account is in balance.

personal check A check drawn by an individual. (1)

personal credit That credit which an individual possesses as differentiated from credit of a firm, partnership or corporation.

personal estate Personal Property. See that term.

personal exemption An amount determined by the taxpayer's status as a single person, married person, or head of a family which he may subtract from his net income in the computation of his income tax. (73)

personal finance company A personal loan company which lends individuals relatively modest amounts of money at rates of interest which are generally higher than bank rates.

personal holding company A device used by individuals for tax minimization. The Internal Revenue Code defines the conditions under which a corporation is considered to be a Personal Holding Company and thus subject to special surtaxes.

personal income The income received by all individuals in the economy from all sources. It is made up of wage and salary disbursements, proprietor's income, rental income of persons, dividends, personal interest income, and the difference between transfer payments and personal contributions for Social Security. (124)

personal liability The sum owed by a natural person. (5)

personal loan A type of loan generally obtained by an individual borrower in small amounts, usually under $1,000. The purpose of the personal loan is often for the consolidation of debts, the payment of taxes or insurance, or a large hospital bill. It is not usually secured by collateral—the integrity of the borrower and his wife being sufficient. In some cases a guarantor may be required. The loan is made upon the agreement by the borrower to repay it in equal monthly payments, the tenure of the loan usually running between six and twenty-four months. The interest is computed and handled in either of two ways: 1. Interest may be added to the principal or face of the note and the total divided by the number of monthly payments. The ledger posting used with this method will usually be a descending balance showing the net amount actually owed after each payment. 2. The other plan is posted as an ascending balance of a hypothecated account known as a "deposit ledger account." In this plan the interest may be added to the face of the note, but more frequently is deducted as a discount. The regular monthly payment is posted as a "deposit," and when the total deposit reaches the total of the note, the account is closed as being fully liquidated. (1)

personal outlays Are made up of personal consumption expenditures, interest paid by consumers, and personal transfer payments to foreigners. They represent the disbursements made by individuals of that portion of personal income available after payment of personal taxes. The residual is personal saving. (124)

personal property That property that is bequeathed by will to a party known as a legatee; or all moveable property or possessions, both tangible and intangible, accumulated by individual effort. Also, such property received from another in the form of a gift. (1)

personal representative A general term applicable to both executor and administrator. (74)

personal saving The difference between disposable personal income and personal consumption expenditures. Personal saving includes the changes in cash and deposits, security holdings, indebtedness, reserves of life insurance companies and mutual savings institutions, the net investment of unincorporated enterprises, and the acquisition of real property net of depreciation. Personal saving includes saving by individuals, nonprofit institutions, and private pension, health, welfare, and trust funds. (7)

personal security That unsecured accommodation in which the net worth and the business stature of the borrower are relied upon rather than some collateral which is pledged.

personal surety Surety provided by an individual as compared to surety provided by an insurance company. (5)

personalty Property which is movable. All property is either personalty, realty, or mixed. (54)

per stirpes (By the branch) A term used in the distribution of property; distribution to persons as members of a family (per stirpes) and not as individuals (per capita). Two or more children of the same parent take per stirpes when together they take what the parent, if living, would take. For example, "I give my estate to my son A and to my grandsons C, D, and E, (the sons of my deceased son B). My grandsons are to take per stirpes." C, D, and E take as the sons of B (not as individuals), each receiving one-sixth of the estate (one-third of the one-half to which B would be entitled if living), while A receives one-half of the estate. Taking per stirpes is also known as taking by right of representation. (74)

peseta Monetary unit of Spain. ·

peso Monetary unit of Argentina, Colombia, Cuba, Dominican Republic, Mexico, Phillipine Republic, and Uruguay.

petition A written prayer or request to a court or to a judge for the granting of some remedy or relief. (74)

petty cash A sum of money, either in the form of currency or a special bank deposit, set aside for the purpose of making change or immediate payments of comparatively small amounts. See Imprest System. (29)

petty cash book A memorandum book for keeping a record of, sorting, and summarizing the miscellaneous small cash payments paid out of a special office fund rather than through the regular checking account. (73)

petty cash fund A small fund of cash that is kept on hand to provide the money needed for making small payments or for making change at the beginning of the day. (73)

petty cash record A term used to describe the classified record that is kept of payments made by cash in situations where it is the practice to deposit all cash receipts in the bank and to make all major disbursements by check. (73)

petty cash voucher A written form that provides an immediate record of a petty cash payment. (73)

physical depreciation A term that is frequently used when physical deterioration is meant. In a broad concept it may relate to those elements that are inherent in the physical property itself, as distinguished from other and external circumstances that may influence its utilization. Not a clear or proper term without qualification and explanation. Deterioration due to the adverse changes in the physical condition of property such as the loss of top soil, the rotting or wearing away of buildings, as well as damage caused by physical elements—rain, storm, sleet. (54+)

physical value A term erroneously used to designate an estimate of reproduction or replacement cost, or the estimated value of physical assets as distinct from nonphysical assets. (54)

physiocratic economics French 18th century economic system emphasizing productivity of land and contending that non-agricultural activities are relatively less productive.

pictorial graph A graph that makes use of pictures, drawings, or cartoons to make the figures or proportions more interesting. (73)

pilferage Any petty thievery or the theft of a portion of property such as theft of a tire from an automobile. (52+)

pinch A condition in the market when short interests have been forced to cover as a result of an unanticipated increase in prices.

pink sheets The popular designation for the pink or eastern section of the quotations of over the counter securities published each business day by the National Quotation Bureau.

pit The trading point in some exchanges. In a number of commodity exchanges there are either rings, or a restraining rail around the pit. In other exchanges the rings are raised at a higher level as the distance from the pit increases. Each level or ring may stand for a different contract time for delivery.

planning network A logic network developed during the early planning phase at a gross level of detail to give subsequent detailed planning a dis-ciplined approach. By this method, a gross assessment of alternative approaches, associated deadlines, and rates of funding buildup can be established. Generally, this type network is not adequate for management control and is supplanted by more detailed control networks as soon as possible. (99)

pledge The transference of property such as the cash value of a life insurance policy to a creditor as security for a debt. (5)

pledged securities Securities issued or assumed by the accounting company that have been pledged as collateral security for any of its long term debt or short-term loans. (19)

pledgee The individual or company to whom the security for a loan is pledged.

pledgor The individual or company which makes a pledge of real or personal property as the collateral for a loan.

plow back To retain and reinvest most of the earnings in a business as opposed to paying earnings out in dividends. (105)

plum A melon or unexpected earnings or dividends either in the form of cash or stock.

plunge Reckless speculation.

plunger One who plunges, engages in reckless speculation.

plus tick Means that a security has been traded at a higher price than the previous transaction. This is an indicator for short sales, because they can only be made on an up (plus) tick, i.e., when the effective round-lot price is higher than the previous price. (105)

point In the case of shares of stock, a point means $1. If General Motors shares rise 3 points, each share has risen $3. In the case of bonds a point means $10, since a bond is quoted as a percentage of $1,000. A bond which rises 3 points gains 3 per cent of $1,000, or $30 in value. An advance from 87 to 90 would mean an advance in dollar value from $870 to $900 for each $1,000 bond. In the case of market averages, the word point means merely that and no more. If, for example, the Dow-Jones industrial average rises from 470.25 to 471.25, it has risen a point. A point in the averages, however, is not equivalent to $1. See Averages. (2)

point and figure charting A technique for graphically plotting price changes in relation to previous price changes. The "point" refers to the price unit chosen for the security or commodity. Each such price change is indicated by a figure or mark such as an "X". The result appears as a line of varying vertical dimensions made up of "X"s. These charts are used by market analysts as a means of judging the price action of the item being charted.

point of ideal proportions That theoretical balance of the capital, land, labor and entrepreneural ability in a business which would provide the greatest profit.

point of indifference That theoretical balance of capital, land, labor and entrepreneural ability in a business where one additional unit of any of the productive factors would just equal the probable return from such factor. At this point the business manager is indifferent in increasing his volume because his profit will not increase.

policy loan, cash Loan granted to make a cash amount available to the insured. The total loan is usually for an amount more than sufficient to pay any premiums due, cancel previous loan, if any, and pay interest to the next premium due date. The insured then receives a check for the balance or proceeds of the loan. (42)

pool A group of individuals or companies who have joined together for the purpose of buying or selling stock, stocks, commodity or commodities with the intent of manipulating the price up or down for the purposes of making profits or of obtaining control. There are many different types of pools, almost all of which are illegal under the Securities Exchange Acts or the Commodity Exchange Acts.

pooling To put money, etc., into a common fund. (93)

pooling of wealth Putting together the money of different people so that enough will be available for some special purpose. (93)

portfolio Holdings of securities by an individual or institution. A portfolio may contain bonds, preferred stocks and common stocks of various types of enterprises. (2)

position An interest in the market in the form of open commitments. (123)

position sheet The daily accounting summary of a firm which shows what its commitments are either in sales, orders or other relationships such as inventory or state of production.

positive verification See Direct Verification. (1)

post Strictly speaking, this term describes the recording onto detailed subsidiary records (ledgers) amounts that have been originally recorded in chronological records of original entry (a blotter or journal).

In the more general sense, considering the simplification developed through modern mechanization, the term "post" is used to describe the recording of records, while in the same operation creating a chronological record of original entry, either in original machine printing or by creating a carbon copy record of the individual account posting. Posting to accounts may be made from the original entry listed on a blotter or journal, or from posting media such as deposit tickets, withdrawal slips, checks, debit or credit memoranda, etc. (1)

post-audit An audit made after the transactions to be audited have taken place and have been recorded or have been approved for recording by designated officials, if such approval is required. See Pre-audit. (29)

post-closing trial balance A trial balance of the ledger made after the adjusting and the closing entries have been posted and the accounts have been balanced and ruled. (73)

postdate To date an instrument a time after that on which it is made. (93)

postdated check A check dated ahead. It is not an effective order on the bank until the future date is reached. Thus, if a check dated July 15 is issued on July 1, it cannot be collected from the bank until July 15. (85)

posthumous child A child born after the father's death; to be distinguished from after-born child. (74)

postil A notation in a journal or in a ledger which has been made by the bookkeeper or accountant to explain an entry. Some ledgers provide a postil space, in other cases it may be a memorandum type of entry lightly inscribed for informational purposes.

posting The transferring of accounts to a ledger. (93)

posting reference column of the journal The column that provides space for writing the number of the ledger page to which a debit or a credit amount in a journal entry has been posted. (73)

post-list A term used generally in the bookkeeping department of banks. Many banks use a posting plan whereby the old balances are listed AFTER a posting run to prove the correct pickup of old balances, and to catch any "high posting" (posting over or above the last previous balance). When this type of proof is used, the bookkeeper is said to create a post-list of the previous old balances. The total of the post-list is the total of all old balances of accounts affected by the posting run. (1)

post 30 The trading post at the NYSE where usually inactive security issues are traded in 10-share units, rather than the normal 100-share round-lots. No odd-lot differential is involved on purchases or sales. It is located in the annex, commonly called the "garage", of the NYSE. (105)

potential demand A loose term signifying an estimation of how much demand would or will exist at some time in the future. It is generally based on projection of economic trends and relationships.

potential stock The difference between the total authorized capital stock and the actually issued stock.

potential value A loose term signifying a value which would or will exist if and when future probabilities become actualities. (54)

pound Monetary unit of Australia, Egypt, Irish Republic, Israel, Lebanon, Syria, Union of South Africa and the United Kingdom.

pour-over A term referring to the transfer of property from an estate or trust to another estate or trust upon the happening of an event as provided in the instrument. (74)

power Authority or right to do or to refrain from doing a particular act, as a trustee's power of sale or power to withhold income. (74)

power in trust A power which the donee (the trustee) is under a duty to exercise in favor of the beneficiary of the trust. (74)

power of alienation The power to assign, transfer, or otherwise dispose of property. (74)

power of appointment A right given to a person to dispose of property which he does not fully own. A power of appointment may be general or special. Under a general power the donee may exercise the right as he sees fit. A special power limits the donee as to those in favor of whom he may exercise the power of appointment. A wife who is given the power to appoint among her children has a special power of appointment. (74)

power of attorney A written document authorizing a named person to perform certain acts in place of the signer. It is usually acknowledged before a public officer or witness and is void on the death of the signer. (31, 92)

power of retention Power expressed or implied in will or trust agreement permitting the trustee to retain certain or all of the investments comprising the trust property at inception, even though they may not be of a type suitable for new investments made by the trustee. (74)

power of sale Power expressed or implied in will or trust agreement permitting the trustee to dispose by sale of investments comprising the trust. (74)

power of substitution A document or entry which authorizes a person or firm appointed under a power of attorney to substitute or appoint substitute.

pre-audit An examination for the purpose of determining the propriety of proposed financial transactions and of financial transactions which have already taken place but have not yet been recorded, or, if such approval is required, before the approval of the financial transactions by designated officials for recording.

NOTE: There is frequently confusion between the audit as a whole and the auditing of individual transactions. For example, if we speak of an audit as a whole, then an independent auditor may be said to be performing a post-audit, since most of the transactions whose propriety he examines have already been approved for recording. The independent auditor may, however, also have to deal with transactions which have not been approved for recording (for example, accrued salaries and wages) but in speaking of an audit as a whole we may ignore these and say that the audit under consideration is a post-audit. On the other hand, if the audit of individual transactions is involved, the independent auditor, in the case illustrated, would be performing a post-audit with respect to most of the transactions, but a pre-audit with respect to some of them. Sometimes the term "pre-audit" is used as a synonym for "internal audit" but such usage is not recommended. See Post-Audit. (29)

precatory words Expressions in a will praying or requesting (but not directing) that a thing be done or not done. (74)

precedence of orders This refers to the priority of buy and sell orders in securities. Priorities for bids at the same price are determined by time, first come, first served; and by size according to amount of bid (in numbers of shares). The same determination is made for offers at the same price. Restrictions are placed upon stock exchange members operating on the floor as to how much priority they might have over orders originating off the floor. (105)

preclusive buying The purchase of goods and services, not for the purpose of own normal use but rather for the purpose of depriving someone else from buying them.

predatory price cutting The competitive device of selling merchandise or a service below purchase price or cost of production. This term does not include the sale at below-cost prices of seasonal or perishable merchandise. Comment: This term is frequently used to include the two

ideas of selling below cost and of selling at such levels with the motive of injuring a competitor. In a given case it is practically impossible to tell whether a price cutter is attempting merely to increase his own business, thereby incidentally injuring a rival, or is primarily endeavoring to hurt a competitor with only incidental benefit to his own business. The mingling of these two motives is inevitable under our competitive economic system. In view of the impossibility of dissecting out the motive behind any given instance of price cutting it seems best to adhere to the more objective test of the relation between cost and price as the basis for the definition of the term. The soundness of this conclusion is supported by the "price floor" legislation adopted during the 1930's. (13)

preemptive right A prior right or privilege, such as the right of a stockholder to be offered the privilege of buying additional shares before the stock is offered to others. (74)

preference share Preferred Stock. See that term.

preferred capital stock Capital stock to which preferences or special rights are attached (i.e. preferred as to dividends and/or proceeds in liquidation) as compared to another class of stock issued by the same company. (21)

preferred creditor A creditor whose claim takes legal preference over the claim of another (such as government taxes over the amount owed to an individual). (1)

preferred dividends payable An account that contains a record of the amount owed to the preferred stockholders for dividends. (73)

preferred stock A class of stock with a claim on the company's earnings before payment may be made on the common stock and usually entitled to priority over the common stock and to dividends at a specified rate—when declared by the Board of Directors and before payment of a dividend on the common stock—depending upon the terms of the issue. See Cumulative Preferred Stock; Participating Preferred Stock. (2)

preferred stock, cumulative A stock having a provision that if one or more dividends are omitted, the omitted dividends must be paid before dividends may be paid on the company's common stock. (2)

preferred stock (non-cumulative) Provides that dividends, if passed, do not have to be paid later. (116)

preferred stock (participating) Under certain conditions shares in earnings beyond the stated dividend. (116)

preferred stock (prior) Ranks ahead of any other preferred and the common as to claim on dividends and assets. (116)

preliminary prospectus An advance report, often called a Red Herring because of red ink notation that it is a preliminary report, which gives the details of an expected offering of corporate securities. The issue is still in the process of being registered by the Securities and Exchange Commission, and cannot be sold until cleared. (105)

pre-list A term used generally in bookkeeping in a bank as a part of the bank's posting plan. After offsetting the ledger sheets to be affected by a posting run, the bookkeeper makes a pre-list run of the balances, thus creating a total of all balances which will be affected by the run to be made. This is the opposite of Post-list, but has the same effect in the proof of pick-up of old balances. (1)

premises The part of a legal paper which states the subject material and parties to it. The legal papers such as a deed or mortgage have an introduction which is known as the premises.

premium on bonds The amount or percentage by which bonds are bought, sold, or redeemed for more than their face value. (74)

premium on capital stock Excess of the cash or cash value of the consideration received from the sale of capital stock (excluding accrued dividends) over the par or stated value of such stock. (21)

premium on funded debt The excess of the actual cash value of the consideration received for funded debt securities (of whatever kind) issued or assumed over the par value of such securities and the accrued interest thereon. (19)

premium on securities The amount by which a security (a bond or a share of stock) is bought or sold for more than its face or par value; opposed to discount on securities. (74)

premium stock 1. A stock which lends at a premium, i.e., an amount has been charged for loaning it to someone who borrowed it to make delivery on a short sale. 2. Also may denote an above average, superior stock, an established leader. (105)

prepaid charge plan An accumulation plan under which the major deductions for selling charges are made during the first year or two of the program. Investor must complete program in order to minimize purchasing expenses.

prepayment Privilege to make any payment on a note before its due date which must be specifically authorized by the note's terms which may also require payment of an additional charge for exercise of the privilege. (121)

prepayment penalty A special charge, provided for in a mortgage contract, which may be collected from the mortgagor if he repays all or a part of the loan in advance of the due date. (89)

pre-refunding An exchange by holders of securities maturing in less than one year for securities of longer original maturity, usually due within ten years. (115)

prescription A title to property or means of obtaining title based upon uninterrupted possession.

presentation A legal term used in connection with negotiable instruments (see definition). The act of presentation technically means the actual delivery of a negotiable instrument by a holder in due course to the drawee for acceptance, or to the maker for payment. Upon presentation, the holder in due course requests acceptance of a draft, or requests payment of the instrument from the maker of a note, check, etc. See Negotiable. (1)

present beneficiary The same as immediate beneficiary. (88)

present capital The proprietorship at the end of the fiscal period. (73)

presentment Same as Presentation.

present value Immediate worth. Also, the amount which if increased at interest will in a given time accumulate to a specified sum. See Tables, Interest; Tables, Discount. (42)

presumption of death A common-law presumption, later incorporated in many state statutes, to the effect that a presumption of death arises from a person's continuous and unexplained absence from home or place of residence without any intelligence from him or concerning him for a period of years—usually seven years. (74)

pretermitted child A child to whom the parent's will leaves no share of his or her estate without affirmative provision in the will showing an intention to omit. It frequently is an after-born child, a posthumous child, or a child erroneously believed to be dead or one unintentionally omitted. (74)

price Quantity of one thing obtainable or paid in exchange for another. Generally expressed in terms of money. (5)

price consumption curve Using indifference curves shows the various amounts of two goods which will be purchased if the ratio between their prices is varied.

priced out of the market A market situation in which the price asked for a product has eliminated many potential buyers and thus the volume of sales has declined.

price-earnings ratio The price of a stock divided by its earnings per share.

price fixing or stabilization Holding prices at a certain level. Often attempted by governments, but generally illegal if attempted by private firms.

price index A statistical device for showing the percentage change in the price of a thing or a group of things from the base period which is assigned the value of one hundred.

price leadership A situation in which a major producer of a product establishes a price and other producers in the same field adopt that price as their own.

price level A relative position in the scale of prices as determined by a comparison of prices (of labor, materials, capital, etc.), as of one time with prices as of other times. (54)

price limit The maximum fluctuation in price of a futures contract permitted during one trading session, as fixed by the rules of the Exchange. (123)

price loco The price at the location where the product or service was purchased.

price, market The amount actually paid, or to be paid, for a property in a particular transaction.

It differs from market value in that it is an accomplished fact which can be proved, whereas market value is and remains an estimate until proven. In market price, there is no assumption of prudent conduct by the parties, lack of undue stimulus, or any of the other conditions basic to the market value concept. (66)

price range The area bound by the highest and lowest prices of a security under discussion, or the general market, over any specified time such as a day, week, or year. (105)

price sovereignty The concept that the individual or firm that can pay the highest price has the right to buy merchandise. While in capitalistic systems such as in the United States this is believed to normally provide the best allocation of resources. During an emergency such as a war, some form of priority system is adopted so that the poor may obtain access to the limited supply. This may be done by rationing or some other priority system.

price spread See Markup.

price supports Any of many ways to keep prices from falling below some preconceived level. Agricultural prices in the United States are in many cases supported by such devices as subsidies, loans, government purchases, soil banks and school lunch programs.

price system An economy in which goods and services are produced for profit and the amounts produced and consumed are determined by price.

price taker Relatively small purchaser or seller who has no influence on the market price.

prima beneficiary See Beneficiary, Primary. (5)

prima facie At first view. Prima facie evidence is such as in law sufficient to establish a fact, unless rebutted. (5)

primary beneficiary One whom the insured designates as first in order of time, or development, in the payment of policy benefits. See Beneficiary. (42)

primary deposit A deposit in a bank which is created by an inflow of cash or checks as compared with a deposit created by the commercial bank making a loan and crediting the account of the borrower with a deposit for the amount of the loan. The latter is a derivative deposit. However, a derivative deposit, when withdrawn by check may become a primary deposit in the receiving bank.

primary market Market for new issues of municipal bonds.

primary money Standard Money.

primary movement The long-term, at least a year or longer, movement of a security price as classified by Charles H. Dow in his Dow Theory. The intrinsic value of the security is proposed to be the controlling factor in the long run prices, and hence in investment and speculation. (105)

primary offering Also called a primary distribution, or the first time a corporation's securities are offered for public sale either directly or by an underwriting group. (105)

primary points Major trading centers for agricultural commodities such as Chicago, Minneapolis, Kansas City. The centers will vary with the commodity under discussion.

primary receipts The amount of a commodity that has been received at the major trading centers for the commodity during a period such as day, week, or agricultural marketing season.

primary reserves Those assets of a bank, consisting of cash and balances on deposit with other banks, which are immediately available for the payment of liabilities. (89)

prime A very high grade or quality.

prime bill of exchange A draft or trade acceptance which states on the face of the instrument that it was created through a business transaction involving the movement of goods. Bankers' acceptances are considered prime bills of exchange, although smaller banks must generally have the endorsement without recourse of a large bank enjoying high financial recognition in order to give the instrument "prime status." Prime bills of exchange are acceptable for rediscount with the Federal Reserve bank, and therefore can be construed as a "secondary reserve" for banks. (1)

prime investment Any investment considered to be sound, safe and conservative, i.e., high-grade with unquestioned dividend or interest payments. (105)

prime maker The party (or parties) who signs his name to a negotiable instrument and who becomes the original primary responsible party for its payment. See Liability, Direct. (1)

prime rate The minimum interest rate on bank loans as set by Commercial Banks and granted to only top business borrowers. The rate is influenced by the size of the loan—larger loans receiving better rates; and by general business conditions, geographical area, availability of reserves, etc. (105)

primogeniture The status of being the first-born or eldest. (74)

principal 1. An individual or company whose performance of certain obligations is covered by a bond. 2. The money due under the policy; the party to a transaction, as distinguished from the broker or agent. 3. A sum lent or employed as a fund or investment, as distinguished from its income or profits. 4. The original amount (as of a loan) of the total due and payable at a certain date. 5. A party to a transaction as distinguished from an agent. (52, 54)

principal beneficiary 1. The beneficiary who is ultimately to receive the principal of the estate. 2. The beneficiary who is the settlor's primary concern. (74)

principles An accepted or professed rule of action or conduct. (93)

priority Legal preference. (5)

priority system A technique for distributing a limited supply of goods among the members of the society on some basis other than complete reliance on price sovereignty. In periods of emergency where supplies are abnormally limited it may be deemed more socially desirable to have a distribution of products that are scarce based on allocation. Ration books, ration stamps and similar devices are used in the consumer area. Certificates of necessity and quotas may be used in the production area.

prior preferred stock Preferred stock which has preference as to dividends of a corporation over other preferred stock or common stock of the same company. (105)

prior redemption An obligation which the debtor has paid before stated maturity.

prior redemption privilege A privilege frequently extended by a debtor to the holders of called bonds permitting them to redeem their holdings prior to the call date or maturity date. There are chiefly three types of offers—prior redemption (1) with interest in full to the call date; (2) with interest in full to the call date less a bank discount (usually ¼ per cent per annum) based on the period from the date of collection to the date of call; and (3) with interest to the date of collection only. (74)

prior sale When the supply of a good or commodity is limited the owner or his broker may offer it at a price subject to the fact that more than one buyer may wish the article. Thus the first bid for the article will buy it. The public is advised that bids after the first may not be effective because of some prior sale.

prior stock A preferred stock.

private bank An unincorporated institution which is owned and operated by an individual or a partnership. It may or may not be subject to supervision by the banking authorities, depending on the laws of the particular state in which it is located. (85)

private debt The monetary amount owed by the people and businesses of a nation and not including the amount owed by the governmental units, federal, state or local.

private enterprise Those profit seeking activities carried out by private individuals in any business form. Activities of government agencies even if producing profits do not come under the heading of private enterprise.

private financing A method of raising capital by which a corporation places a new issue of securities with institutions such as insurance companies rather than with the public. A non-public issue does not have to be registered with the Securities and Exchange Commission, and is not as costly to either the issuer or institutional investor as is a public offering. (105)

private remittances Represent transfers or transmissions of cash and goods by individuals and by charitable and nonprofit institutions to individuals or groups residing abroad.

Personal remittances include all noncommercial transfers of funds abroad by means of customary bank drafts and money orders. The remittances include gifts, inheritances, and tax orders. In addition to these cash remittances, an estimate is included for the value of goods forwarded abroad as gifts. In the case of gifts mailed abroad, an equal export entry (an offsetting credit) is made to the merchandise account.

Institutional unilateral transfers of cash and goods arise from foreign relief work in the developing nations of the world. Approximately 135 religious and charitable agencies are currently reporting such transfers. Included also are receipts by U.S. residents—principally German and Austrian—of indemnifications of losses sustained as a result of actions by the German government prior to and during World War II. (124)

private trust 1. A trust created for the benefit of a designated beneficiary or designated beneficiaries; as, a trust for the benefit of the settlor's or the testator's wife and children; opposed to a charitable (or public) trust. 2. A trust created under a declaration of trust or under a trust agreement; as, a living trust or an insurance trust; opposed to a trust coming under the immediate supervision of a court. See Court Trust. (88)

private trust fund A Trust Fund which will ordinarily revert to private individuals or will be used for private purposes. For example, a fund which consists of guarantee deposits. (29)

private-wire house A brokerage firm that leases telegraph wires to various cities especially financial and commodity centers.

privilege Synonymous to a stock option contract, such as a call or put, which permits one of the parties to exercise some right or privilege stated in the contract during the specified time period. (105)

privilege broker See Privilege Dealer.

privilege dealer A dealer or broker who is in the business of selling puts and calls and variations of such options which are also known as privileges.

privileges Options such as puts, calls and straddles. See those terms.

privity Exists where heirs, executors, and certain others succeed to the rights of a contract. This permits them to have the same rights as the original party. Privity may be a factor in action of negligence. (5)

probability The likelihood that a future event will take place. (5)

probate The legal act of admitting a will before a competent court of law to establish official proof that the instrument presented is the last will and testament of a deceased person it purports to be. A will is probated to establish its prima facie validity both as to manner and form of execution, and as to the testator's capacity to make the will. The term also applies to the right or jurisdiction of hearing and determining questions or issues in matters concerning a will; or legal interpretation of the line of heritage complying with the state's laws by the court having jurisdiction over the administration of a decedent's estate, the decedent having died intestate (without a will). Courts of law having jurisdiction in the probating of wills and the interpretation of the legality of claims in lines of heritage are given different names in different localities—some titles for such courts of law are the Surrogate's Court, the Probate Court, and the Orphan's Court. (1)

probate court A court having jurisdiction of the proof of wills, the settlement of estates, and usually, of guardianships. In some states it is the district court. (5)

probate in solemn form The probate of a will in a formal proceeding after notice to the interested parties; opposed to probate in common form which is an informal proceeding without such notice. (74)

probate of will Presentation of proof before the proper officer or court that the instrument offered is the last will of the decedent. (74)

procedure A simple, systematic way of accomplishing an objective, which is usually applicable only in the situation for which it was designed. (20)

proceeding A measure or step taken in business; transaction. (93)

proceeds A very general term used to designate the total amount realized or received in any transaction, whether it be a sale, an issue of stock, the collection of receivables, or the borrowing of money. (17)

process effects That increase in consumer expenditures which has come about because of an increase in governmental expenditures.

produce exchange 1. A spot market for such items as perishable agricultural products. 2. A contract market in which futures contracts are bought and sold for products of agriculture.

producer Term commonly applied to an agent, solicitor, broker, or any other person who sells insurance; producing business for the company and for a commission (if so paid) for himself. He also creates the insurance product; namely, security and relief from risk for the insured. (50)

production function A curve or schedule which shows how total quantity of a product will vary with changing proportions of factors of production such as labor and machinery.

productivity theory That attempt to explain wage rates in terms of the value or productivity of work performed.

professional In the securities business, a student of the market or a person who makes a living buying and selling securities. A professional may direct the investments of a pension fund or other institution, or be a member of a brokerage firm who advises or acts for his firm's clients. (2)

profit 1. The excess of the selling price over all costs and expenses incurred in making the sale. 2. The reward to the entrepreneur for the risks assumed by him in the establishment, operation and management of a given enterprise or undertaking. See Entrepreneur. (1)

profit and loss account Account transferred from Accounts Receivable to separate ledger. Amount deducted from Accounts Receivable balance. An account deemed to be uncollectable or a certain number of months past due, becomes eligible for transfer to "Profit and Loss Account" ledger. (26)

profit and loss reserve Amount set aside by firm to provide for anticipated "P & L Accounts" during fiscal period. Usually calculated as given percentage of total "Accounts Receivable." (26)

profit and loss statement Same as income statement. (85)

profit and loss summary account An account to which balances of all the income and all the expense accounts are transferred at the end of the fiscal period. (73)

profit, gross (or margin, gross) Net sales less cost of goods sold (before consideration of selling and administrative expenses). Gross profit is expressed in dollar figures; gross margin is expressed as a percentage of net sales. (24)

profit, net (or income, net) Revenue remaining after deduction of all costs, but before taxes; usually designates the final figure on Profit and Loss Statement. (24)

profit on fixed assets A term applied to the profit that results when the book value of a fixed asset is less than the actual value at the time the asset is sold. (73)

profit sharing securities Such securities as Participating Bonds or Participating Preferred Stock.

profit-sharing trust A trust established by an employer (usually a corporation) as a means of having the employees share in the profits of the enterprise. (74)

profit taking Selling to take a profit, the process of converting paper profits into cash. (2)

pro forma The term for a statement of facts adjusted as of one date to reflect some past circumstance or proposed change in a company's capitalization or operating conditions. For example, past and current earnings may be shown to reflect the effect of an increased number of shares of common stock. (103)

promisor The individual or firm responsible in keeping a promise such as an acceptor or a maker of a note or bill.

promissory note A negotiable instrument which is evidence of a debt contracted by borrower from a creditor known as a lender of funds. If the instrument does not have all the qualities of a negotiable instrument, it cannot legally be transferred from one person to another. See Negotiable Instrument. (1)

promoter An individual, who acting as a middleman, brings together the various needed factors of a venture in business, especially as they are associated with a new firm.

proof 1. An operation for testing the accuracy of a previous operation, as relisting the checks and adding their amounts to determine the accuracy of the total shown on a deposit slip. 2. Applied to the proof sheet, the record on which the test is made. 3. Also used to describe the method by which a type of transaction is proved, as transit proof. Proof is generally effected when a total agrees with another total of the same items arrived at in a different manner; it is then said to be in balance. (85)

proof department A department of a bank which is charged with the duties of sorting, distributing, and proving all transactions arising from the commercial operations of the bank. The proof function involves the creation of adequate records of all transactions, showing the proper distribution of all items going to other departments for further processing, and proof of the correctness of all transactions passing through the bank. The records created by the proof department are of vital importance, since examination of these records may be made months after a transaction occurs, in order to substantiate the accuracy of deposits made by customers, and the legal fact that deposits were made by certain individual depositors. (1)

propensity to consume The relationship between total income and the total of consumer expenditures. The propensity thus is expressed as a percentage of consumer expenditures divided by income.

propensity to invest That proportion or percentage of national income which is invested in new capital formation.

propensity to save That proportion or percentage of national income which is not used for consumption. It is derived by subtracting consumption from income and dividing the result by income.

property capital Stocks, bonds, mortgages and notes are representative examples of property capital but currency and bank deposits are excluded as being money capital.

property dividends Dividends paid by a corporation in the form of securities of another corporation as opposed to cash or stock dividends of the issuing company. (105)

property search report Type of credit bureau report. Deals specifically with details of real property owned by subject of inquiry. Frequently involves search of county courthouse records for details of purchase, title, mortgage, or other encumbrance on property. (26)

proprietary accounts Those accounts which show actual financial condition and operations such as actual assets, liabilities, reserves, surplus, revenues, and expenditures, as distinguished from budgetary accounts. (29)

proprietorship Also called Individual Proprietorship. See that term.

proprietorship certificate A certificate filed with a bank showing the ownership of a business enterprise privately owned. The Secretary of State in the state in which an individual is operating a business under a "trade name" authorizes the individual to use this name in conducting his business. Since the trade name is not considered a legal entity but the individual owner is, the individual proprietor is held fully responsible for all obligations incurred under the trade name. Example: "John Doe D.B.A. the ABC Company" means John Doe, the proprietor (a legal entity) doing business as "The ABC Company" (a trade name authorized by the Secretary of State in the state where this firm is doing business). (1)

pro rata In proportion. (31, 92)

pro rata rate A premium rate charged for a short term at the same proportion of the rate for a longer term as the short term bears to the longer term. See "Short Rate." (51)

prorate To divide proportionately. (19)

prospectus The official circular which describes the shares of an investment company and offers them for sale. It contains definitive details concerning the investment company issuing the shares, the determination of the price at which the shares are offered to the public, etc. (65)

prosperity That business state or condition in which employment and production are at high levels. It is generally preceded by a period of recovery and is followed by a recession.

protected check A check that is prepared in such a manner as to prevent alterations. For example: Machine protection—perforating the paper with pressure and in indelible ink. Paper protection —any erasure of matter written in ink, by rubber eraser, knife or chemical eradicator, will remove the sensitive color and show instantly that an alteration has been attempted.

Machine printing protection—machine automatically prints stars or asterisks between the dollar sign and first digit of the amount. Use of indelible ink ribbon, or ribbon treated with a

special acid which eats into the paper upon impression. (1)

protective committee A committee formed to represent security holders in negotiations on defaulted securities. (90)

protective stocks The equities of seasoned companies which emphasize stability over growth. Usually unattractive to speculators and traders, thus enhancing their safety. (105)

protest A written statement by a notary public, or other authorized person, under seal for the purpose of giving formal notice to parties secondarily liable that an instrument has been dishonored, either by refusal to accept or by refusal to make payment. (85)

protest fee The charge made by a notary public for protesting a negotiable instrument which has not been honored.

protest jacket Another name for Notice of Dishonor. See Definition.

prove In banking, the act of creating a record, to show by a list or run of the items, the accuracy of a list or deposit created by another person. The list shows that each item is listed correctly as to amount, and that the amounts listed add up to an exact total. The two lists, one made by the bank as a record, and the other created by another person, such as a depositor, must agree in total to be "in proof." (1)

proving cash Ascertaining that the cash on hand is equal to the original balance plus the receipts minus the payments. (73)

proxy A power of attorney by a stockholder to an individual or individuals to exercise his rights to vote at meetings of a corporation. (1)

proxy statement Information required by SEC to be given stockholders as a prerequisite to solicitation of proxies for a listed security. (2)

prudent investment cost The amount arrived at in valuation of a business or property which considers original cost of the property but deducts from that amount those expenses or frills which a prudent man would not accept.

prudent-man rule for trust investment A rule originally stated in 1830 by the Supreme Judicial Court of Massachusetts in Harvard College v. Amory, 9 Pick. (Mass.) 446, that, in investing, all that can be required of a trustee is that he conduct himself faithfully and exercise a sound discretion and observe how men of prudence, discretion, and intelligence manage their own affairs not in regard to speculation, but in regard to the permanent disposition of their funds considering the probable income as well as the probable safety of the capital to be invested. (74)

public administrator In many states, a county officer whose main duty is to settle the estates of persons who die intestate, when there is no member of the family, creditor, or other person having a prior right of administration who is able to administer the estate. (88)

public authority A public agency usually created to perform a single function which is financed from tolls or fees charged those using the facilities operated by the agency; for example, a bridge or tunnel authority. (29)

public credit The credit of a government or subdivision of a government as distinguished from the private credit of private firms or individuals.

public debt A term that sometimes is restricted to the debt of the federal government and at other times represents the debt of the federal government plus the debt of the states, municipalities, and other political subdivisions. (103)

public finance Those financial activities which are associated with any phase of government. Taxes, customs, public debt, public expenditures and related fields all comprise public finance.

public good Those economic goods or services which the government, federal, state or local makes available without direct costs to its citizens. It would include such things as public roads, public health programs, public libraries, public parks and education.

public ownership The control and ownership of some productive facility for providing some good or service to the citizens of a community or nation by an agency of government. Public ownership is not uncommon in the public utility fields.

public property That property which is owned by other than the individual or individuals or private corporations; that is, property whose ownership is vested in the community. This would include such things as public buildings, such as post offices, town halls, county courthouses. (54+)

public relations department A department within a bank or other business institution created and maintained to promote and encourage better harmony and relationships between that particular institution and the general public by offering a wide variety of services—educational and other—to the public without cost to the recipient. Such departments operate under a variety of names such as "Courtesy," "Customer's Service," "Public Aid," "Public Service," etc. (1)

public space Any area where the public may freely enter in the normal course of business and during business hours. A private establishment such as a store or bank has a space for the public and customers to transact their business. Such an area is called public space.

public trust The same as a charitable trust; opposed to a private trust. (74)

public trust fund A Trust Fund whose principal, earnings, or both must be used for a public purpose; for example a pension fund. (29)

pull To lower the bid price or raise the offering price for a security, or cancel entirely. (105)

pull the plug on the market To cancel or remove the supporting bids which had previously been entered just below the market prices prevailing for certain leading issues. (105)

punch card check A check which has perforations either in the body of the check or around a portion of its border. These perforations are used to re-sort and correlate the checks after they have been cancelled and returned with the bank statement. This type of check must be cancelled in some special manner agreed upon by the banker and the depositor. Punch card checks are used to correlate the checks by number or some other coding, thus facilitating the reconcilement of the depositor's bank statement. (1)

pup A low priced, inactive stock. (105)

purchased paper Commercial paper bought through brokers or others with whom the purchaser has no direct business relations.

purchase money mortgage A mortgage executed by the buyer in lieu of the complete payment in cash for the real estate. For example, a $10,000 house purchased by a man who can put up only $4,000, the seller is issued a $6,000 mortgage by the purchaser. (5)

purchase option "Fair Market": This is an option given to the lessee to purchase the equipment at the end of the lease. "Fair Market" normally means that the price will be determined at the end of the lease through appraisals or open bidding. It can be predetermined and stated at the beginning of the lease, if you can properly document the file and justify the amount.

purchase outright To pay the full amount in cash for securities purchased. (105)

purchases account An account in the general ledger where the total purchases for the month as shown in the purchases journal are recorded as debits. (73)

purchases budget An estimate of the purchases that will provide for the anticipated sales of a future fiscal period. (73)

purchases journal A special journal that brings all credit purchases transactions together in one book. (73)

purchasing power of the dollar A measurement of the quantity (not quality) of goods and services that a dollar will buy compared with the amount that it could buy in some base period. It is obtained by taking the reciprocal of a price index, usually the consumers' price index. (7)

pure competition The market situation where no one trader can materially affect the market price of a product.

pure endowment See Endowment, Pure. (42)

pure interest A theoretical concept that excludes all costs for risk and overhead from the cost paid for capital. See Consols.

put A contract to have the option to sell a security within a stated time and amount to the drawer of the option. It is the opposite of a Call. See Call.

put and call broker A broker who deals in options or privileges, which are contracts to exercise some right or privilege during the specified time. Put and Call Brokers are not permitted on a stock exchange floor. (105)

put out a line Term meaning to sell short a substantial amount of securities of one or more companies, usually over a period of time, in expectation of declining prices. The opposite of take on a line. (105)

puts and calls Options which give the right to buy or sell a fixed amount of a certain stock at a specified price within a specified time. A put gives the holder the right to sell the stock; a call the right to buy the stock. Puts are purchased by those who think a stock may go down. A put obligates the seller of the contract to take delivery of the stock and pay the specified price to the owner of the option within the time limit of the contract. The price specified in a put or call is usually close to the market price of the stock at the time the contract is made. Calls are purchased by those who think a stock may rise. A call gives the holder the right to buy the stock from the seller of the contract at the specified price within a fixed period of time. Put and call contracts are written for 30, 60, or 90 days, or longer. If the purchaser of a put or call does not wish to exercise the option, the price he paid for the option becomes a loss. (2)

pyramiding 1. A situation where a series of holding companies own stock in related holding or operating companies. Generally the holding is for control and speculative profit and does not serve as an improvement in the operating efficiency of the individual companies. 2. The use of the increased value of a purchased security above the margin requirement is used as the collateral to purchase additional securities, also on margin. In turn if these increase in price over the margin required additional purchases are made. It tends to magnify profits in a bull market and magnify losses in a bear market. In fact, in a bear market the pyramider is frequently wiped out since he has no funds to cover his required margin.

Q

Q Quarterly.

Q/C Quasi-contract.

Quar., Qtr. Quarter.

qualification A portion of a report by an auditor, underwriter, claims investigator accountant, or actuary, that calls attention to the limitations of his report. (5)

qualified acceptance In reality, a counter offer. To be binding, acceptance must be unqualified. Since a condition or qualification is made by one party the other must accept the qualification before the contract has both offer and acceptance.

qualified endorsement An endorsement, such as "without recourse" which relieves the endorser from liability to a subsequent holder of the instrument in the event it is not paid. An endorsement such as "for deposit" which restricts the negotiability.

qualified plan or trust An employer's trust or plan that qualifies under the Internal Revenue Code of 1954 for the exclusive benefit of his employees or their beneficiaries in such manner and form as to entitle the employer who makes the payments to the plan or trust to the deductions and income tax benefits as set forth in that Code. (74)

quality Fineness. (93)

quality stock A superior stock representing a high grade industry as indicated by unquestioned dividends and earning power; a blue chip. (105)

quantity theory of money The belief that prices are related directly to the quantity of money in circulation. As the quantity of money increased, prices increased, as the money in circulation decreased, prices too decreased. Modern economists add additional factors to the equation of exchange and various formulas express the idea.

quarterly dividend Today many corporations pay dividends to their stockholders on a quarterly basis or every three months. Such a payment is called a quarterly dividend.

quarter stock Stock with a par value of twenty five dollars per share.

quetzal Monetary unit of Guatemala.

quick assets 1. Those assets which, in the ordinary course of business, will be converted into cash within a reasonably short period of time (as within one year). 2. Those assets which can be readily converted into cash without appreciable loss. (1)

quick ratio The ratio between the quick assets and the current liabilities. (73)

quick turn A speculative security transaction carried out in relatively short time involving both a purchase and a sale. (105)

quiet enjoyment clause Provision of lease or deed that gives the new owner or tenant the right of not being disturbed in his possession. (5)

quieting title Removing a cloud from a title by a proper action in court. (5)

quit claim To release or relinquish a claim whether valid or invalid in conveyancing a deed. Quit claim is generally associated with the term quit claim deed and conveys no warrantee. (5)

quit-claim deed A deed by which the owner of real estate conveys to another whatever title or interest he has to the property, but which makes no representation that the property is free from encumbrances, except those created by the owner himself. (31, 92)

quit rent A rent paid by a freeholder for release from some service.

quotation Often shortened to "quote". The highest bid to buy and the lowest offer to sell a security in a given market at a given time. If the broker is asked for a "quote" on a stock, he may come back with something like "45¼ to 45½." This means that $45.25 is the highest price any buyer wanted to pay at the time the quote was given on the floor of the Exchange and that $45.50 was the lowest price which any seller would take at the same time. See Bid and Asked. (2)

quotation board An electrically operated board on the wall of a brokerage firm or other financial business. Many of the leading and most active stocks occupy a certain panel on the board; information, such as price range, dividend payments and current transactions, is automatically entered as it occurs. (105)

quotation ticker The machine which prints quotations of prices and transactions in securities or commodities. This electrically operated instrument is found in the board or customers room of brokers offices and may be attached to a "translux" device so that the tape on which the price quotations appear may be enlarged and shown on a screen so that many in the office can view the results.

quote To repeat from a book, or a speech. (93)

quoted price The price at which the last purchase and the last sale took place in the market by a particular security. (105)

quote wire The direct wire from a brokerage firm to the Quotation Department of the NYSE by which a firm can learn the highest bid and lowest offer for any listed stock. A quotation can be obtained during regular business hours by dialing the number assigned to the stock. The quotation department is in constant contact with special clerks at each post on the exchange floor. This is soon to be automated by using recorded voice announcements. (105)

R

RC Report of Contact. (67)
R.E. Real Estate.
Rec. Receipt.
Recap. Recapitulation.
Redisc. Rediscount.
Ref. Refunding; referee.
Reg. Registered; registrar; regular.
Rem. Remittance.
Reqn. Requisition. (67)
Res. Reserve.
RFC Reconstruction Finance Corporation. Defunct.
Rfg. Refunding.
R.I.L. Res ipsa loquitur.
RIR Request Immediate Reply. (67)
R/N Requisition number. (67)
R/O Regional Office.
R.O.G. Receipt of goods.
Rt. Right.
Rts. Rights.

rack 1. Term is used in some banks to describe the "rack department," which sorts, distributes, and proves items in the commercial operations of the bank. See description of Proof Department. 2. An open cabinet with built-in bins in which to sort items according to a sorting classification. This is called a sorting rack. Many banks use sorting racks for clearing house, transit, bookkeeping, and other sorts. Items are listed after these sorts have been made, and prove to an established central control total. (1)
rack rent A very high contract rent for a property which equals or exceeds the economic rent of the property.
raid Concerted and heavy activity in buying or selling a security or commodity with the expectation that the marginal holder will be shaken and the price fluctuation will permit a profit for the members of the raiding group, the raid may be "bears" who expect to force the price down or by "bulls" who expect to force the price up.
raised check A check on which the amount has been illegally increased. To deter checks from being raised, they are designed so that the amount is clearly shown in two places. In one place, near the right margin and after the payee's name, the amount of the check is written in numerical figures. Below the payee's name, the check amount is either spelled out, or protected by machine printing or perforation. See also Protected Check. (1)

raising funds Financing or acquiring money or credit from surplus earnings of the corporation, the stockholders, the public, creditors, customers, or employees. (105)
ratable distribution The proportionate distribution of an estate according to a percentage. For example, if all the legacies cannot be paid in full and each of them is reduced by the same percentage, there is ratable distribution. (74)
rate of estimated depreciation The annual depreciation of a fixed asset expressed as a percentage of the cost price; a percentage obtained by dividing the annual depreciation of a fixed asset by the original cost. (73)
rate of exchange The ratio at which foreign currency exchanges for a domestic currency. See Foreign Exchange.
rate of interest The percentage of the principal amount which is annually charged for use of money. While charged annually, the interest may be paid at other periods such as monthly, quarterly, or semi-annually.
rate of return 1. The yield obtainable on a security based on its purchase price or its current market price. This may be the amortized yield to maturity on a bond or the current income return. 2. The income earned by a public utility company on its property or capital investment, expressed as a percentage. (103)
rate war A destructive type of competition in which the various sellers of a good or service progressively decrease their prices even below their costs for the purpose of driving their competitors out of business.
rating The evaluation of the moral or other risk of an individual or organization. Dun & Bradstreet, Hooper-Holmes, Retail Credit Bureau, as well as trade rating bureaus may be used by insurance companies to obtain an external source of information on a risk. The investment department of an insurance company may use Standard & Poor's, Moody's, or Fitch's to obtain an idea of the evaluation of specific securities. The making of insurance rates. (5)
rating (bonds) System of rating to provide the investor with a simple system of gradation by which the relative investment qualities of bonds are indicated. (21)
ratio This term refers to the various analysis made by a money, or credit, lending agency of the financial statements of a given individual, company, or other business enterprise seeking credit to determine the feasibility of granting the requested credit. Some of the most common ratios used are as follows:
1. Current Assets to Current Liabilities, or Working Capital Ratio.
2. "Acid Test" Ratio. See definition. The ratio that is determined by using the following formula:

$$\frac{\text{Cash plus Receivables plus Marketable Securities divided by Current Liabilities}}{\frac{C+R+M.S.}{C.L.}}$$

Frequently, a 1 to 1 ratio is deemed satisfactory.
3. Ratio of Notes Receivable to Accounts Receivable. Should the financial statement disclose a large amount of notes receivable, as compared with other firms in a similar line of business,

there is a possibility of a lax credit policy or the firm's extending credit to customers whose ability to pay promptly might not be too strong.

4. Ratio of Notes Payable to Accounts Payable. Three factors are frequently considered when determining whether the resulting ratio is desirable: (a) Notes issued in payment of merchandise. (b) Notes issued to banks and brokers. (c) Notes issued to others.

If a relatively large amount of the outstanding notes were issued to merchandise creditors, it might indicate that the firm is unable to take advantage of the cash discounts offered in the trade and also, that other lending agencies might consider the firm's credit not too favorably.

5. Ratio of Fixed Assets to Fixed Liabilities. This ratio tends to indicate the margin of protection to the present mortgage and bond holders, if any. If the ratio does not meet the minimum requirement, it frequently suggests that additional funds should be raised from the owners (stockholders) rather than by mortgaging fixed assets.

6. Ratio of Owned Capital to Borrowed Capital. This ratio is considered important in determining the advisability of extending additional long term credit to an applicant. If this ratio is not considered favorable, it frequently suggests that the sought funds should be raised from the owners (stockholders) of the business rather than through the additional pledging of any assets.

7. Ratio of Capital to Fixed Assets. This ratio is usually determined for a number of years to ascertain whether there is a trend toward converting the investment of the owners into fixed assets, thereby possibly relying upon creditors for furnishing the required working capital.

8. Ratio of Accounts Payable to Purchases. This ratio determined for the present period and compared with a similar ratio for previous periods will indicate the trend towards the prompt payment of current obligations.

9. Ratio of Raw Material Inventory to Cost of Manufacture. This ratio is determined by dividing the Cost of Goods Manufactured by the average Raw Material Inventory. The resulting figure is the number of times the investment in the Raw Material Inventory has turned over during the period under consideration. The present ratio is compared with a similar ratio for previous periods as it will tend to portray the trend and steadiness of production, or a possible over-stated or expended inventory.

10. Ratio of Finished Goods Inventory to the Cost of Goods Sold. This ratio is determined by dividing the Cost of Goods Sold by the average Finished Goods Inventory. The resulting figure is the number of times the investment in the Finished Goods Inventory has turned over during the period under consideration. The present ratio is compared with a similar ratio for several previous periods as it will tend to portray the stability and trend of sales, or the possible over-stated or expanded inventory. These ratios serve as only one of the many tools used in determining the advisability of granting the requested credit and the type of credit considered best for the applicant and the lending institution. Many other factors also are given consideration,

among these being the Economic Cycle or trend, the continued consumer demand for the particular product being manufactured or sold, etc. (1)

ratio chart A logarithmic or semilogarithmic graphic device to show rates of changes in data rather than absolute variations in data.

rationing of exchange A system which requires exporters to sell all foreign exchange to the government for domestic currency. The government then sells foreign exchange to those importers engaged in approved activities.

reacquired securities Securities, once outstanding, that have been acquired by the issuing corporation and are legally available for reissue or resale (in some states reacquired securities cannot be reissued without approval of regulatory authorities). (21)

reaction A rapid decline in prices following an advance. (9)

readjustment The business conditions associated with a current rate of economic production which is lower than the preceding period. During the readjustment period inventories which were excessive are worked off and business policies evolved to meet the lower level of business. When this phase is finished it leads to recovery.

readjustment plan A voluntary plan worked out by the creditors and a debtor corporation outside the framework of the bankruptcy courts generally for the purpose of avoiding going through formal bankruptcy.

read the tape 1. To watch the price action of various securities as printed on the ticker tape. 2. To predict the near-term action of securities by studying volume and price changes as printed on the ticker tape. (105)

real estate The right, title, or interest that a person has in real property, as distinguished from the property itself, which is the subject matter of the interest. (88)

real estate loans Loans secured by real estate, regardless of the purpose. See Mortgage. (4)

real estate owned A term that applies to all real estate directly owned by a bank, usually not including real estate taken to satisfy a debt. (89)

real investment Capital Formation. The production or creation of new capital.

realization value That amount actually received from the sale of a thing as differentiated from the other types of value such as par, book, etc.

realized profit or loss A profit or loss resulting from the sale or other disposal of a security, as distinguished from a paper profit or loss. (103)

realizing When a profit is realized either by a liquidating sale or the repurchase of a short sale. (123)

realizing sale A sale to convert a paper profit into an actual profit. The term is most frequently used in the securities and commodity fields.

real money Money, the composition of which contains one or more metals having intrinsic value, as distinguished from representative money such as currency issued by a realm, and checks, drafts, etc., issued by legal entities in society. (1)

real property The property that is devised by will to a party known as the devisee; or all property of a fixed, permanent, immovable nature, such as land, tenements, etc., accumulated by individual effort. Also, such property received from another in the form of a gift. (1)

real stock Long stock as differentiated from stock which is sold short.

rebate A portion of unearned interest which may be given back to a borrower if his loan is paid off prior to the maturity date. (1)

rebated acceptance An acceptance which is paid prior to its due date. An Anticipated Acceptance.

recap An abbreviated term for "recapitulation" (or assembling) of totals taken from "batch proof" sheets or from proof machines which must be assembled in proper order so as to build up control totals for the various departments charged with the items. Recap sheets may be used in all departments of the bank, and all recap sheets assembled into a final recap sheet for the settlement of the entire bank. See also Settlement Clerk. (1)

recapitalization Replacement of outstanding capital stock with a new issue during a corporate reorganization to change the amount and priority of different stock issues and/or to reduce the amount, or change the character, of bonds outstanding. (105)

recede A price decline.

receipt 1. A machine-printed or hand-written, dated, legally validated acknowledgment of receiving a given sum of money as full or part payment of an amount owing, which the creditor gives or forwards to the party responsible for the payment. 2. A machine-printed or hand-written, dated, legally validated acknowledgment of receiving a given sum of money or items of stated value to be placed on deposit or to be held in trust to the credit of the party parting with the money or items. See Warehouse Receipt. (1)

receipt book A bound book of blank receipt stubs with detachable blank receipts. (73)

receipts outstanding for funded debt Receipts for payments on account of subscriptions to funded debt. (19)

receipts outstanding for installments paid Receipts for payments on account of subscriptions to capital stock. (19)

receivables Accounts receivable owned by a borrower which are pledged as collateral for a loan made with the bank. See also Assigned Account. (1)

receiver A person appointed by a court as its agent, usually for the purpose of taking over the assets of a going concern and either continuing its operation or liquidating it under court direction in the best interests of all its creditors and savings account holders. (31, 92)

receivers' and trustees' securities Evidences of indebtedness (other than equipment securities or obligations) issued by a receiver or trustee acting under orders of a court. (19)

receiver's certificate A note issued by a receiver for the purposes of obtaining working capital to keep a distressed corporation in operation. The

note is generally for a short term and given a priority over other open book accounts. The exact priority is determined by authority of the court.

receivership The office or function of a receiver appointed by a court or under a statute. (35)

receiving teller A bank employee assigned to the duties of accepting deposits from depositors. This teller is responsible for counting all cash received, and for verification of the count to the customer's deposit. The teller should also see that all checks deposited are properly endorsed by the depositor. The receiving teller enters the amount of the deposit in the depositor's pass book, or issues a receipt from a teller's machine for the depositor's record. (1)

recession That phase of a business cycle characterized by a reduction in the level of production from the previous phase.

reciprocal business An order to buy or sell securities given by one person or firm to another in return for a more or less equivalent order, or business favor, previously granted. Quite often, brokerage firms will have a correspondent relationship with another firm which may be a member of a particular stock exchange, and orders brought in may be repaid by another type of business in return. (105)

reciprocal statutes Similar statutes in two or more states providing mutual provisions or reciprocal treatment within the states affected concerning the subjects treated in such statutes; e.g., similar provisions with regard to corporations or inheritance taxes, a trust institution, bank, or business in another state. (74)

reclamation 1. A negotiable instrument such as a check or note which has incorrectly been posted through a clearinghouse and now is to be corrected or reclaimed. 2. The process of making a heretofore unproductive asset, such as eroded land, productive by restoring through terracing and good land management.

recognized quotations Statements regarding the highest bid and lowest offer prevailing for a particular security listed on a stock exchange. These may be obtained by a direct quote to the quotation department of the exchange during regular business hours. (105)

reconcilement of accounts Any of several methods of verification of accuracy of accounts. This may involve the use of certain control figures or in the case of accounts of customers a form requesting customers to advise if the statement amounts do not agree with the customers records.

reconciliation (of a bank statement) The process of bringing into agreement the bank balance as shown by the monthly bank statement and the balance as shown by the depositor's record on his check stubs. (73)

record To place a document on public record. (31, 92)

recordation In connection with a mortgage, the recording of the fact that a lien has been created against certain property, described in the mortgage, such entry usually being made in the appropriate public record of the county or other jurisdiction in which the particular property is located. (74)

record date Dividends are declared payable to stockholders of record on a specified date. The date on which the dividend is payable may be later than the date on which a stockholder must have officially owned shares in order to participate in the dividend. The date of ownership specified by Board of Directors is known as the "Record Date." (1)

recording Entering a document into the public records. Deeds and mortgages are recorded with the county register of deeds, and most liens are recorded with a clerk of the circuit court.

recourse A term used to define the rights of a holder in due course of a negotiable instrument to force prior endorsers on the instrument to meet their legal obligations by making good the payment of the instrument if dishonored by the maker or acceptor. The holder in due course must have met the legal requirements of presentation and delivery of the instrument to the maker of a note or acceptor of a draft, and must have found that this legal entity has refused to pay for, or defaulted in payment of the instrument. See also Notice of Dishonor. For distinction in terms, see also Endorsement—Qualified Endorsement for use of the term Without Recourse. (1)

recovery 1. Money or other valuables that the insurance company obtains from subrogation, salvage, or reinsurance. 2. An advance in price after a decline. 3. That phase of a business cycle characterized by improvement in the level of business. Recovery is generally preceded by recession or depression but precedes prosperity. (5, 9)

redeem To buy back. (93)

redeemable stock A preferred stock which is callable.

redemption The liquidation of an indebtedness whether on maturity or prior to maturity, such as the retirement of a bond issue prior to its maturity date. See Repurchases. (1, 3)

redemption agent A firm which redeems obligations. These obligations may be securities, mutilated currency, trading stamps or similar claims.

redemption fund A fund created for the purpose of retiring an obligation maturing serially or purchased as they become available, (i.e. a fund created to redeem or retire bonds on or before maturity). (1)

redemption notice That information which is mailed to concerned holders of securities being redeemed or which is published in financial periodicals according to the requirements of the indenture of the issue. The notice gives the time and terms of the redemption.

redemption price The price at which a bond may be redeemed before maturity, at the option of the issuing company. Redemption value also applies to the price the company may pay to call in certain types of preferred stock. (2)

redemption value 1. The price at which bonds may be redeemed; old bond issues often were redeemable at par value. 2. The cash-in value of investment company shares. (105)

red herring An advance or preliminary prospectus which gives the details of an expected offering of corporate securities. A statement in red

ink stamped on the prospectus indicates the issue cannot be sold until the Securities and Exchange Commission finishes the process of registering and clearing it for sale. (105)

rediscount A negotiable instrument which has been discounted by a bank, and subsequently "sold" or discounted a second time by a Federal Reserve bank or another bank for the benefit of the bank which originally discounted the instrument. A prime bill of exchange may be "sold" to the Federal Reserve bank, if the bank holding the prime bill wishes to build up its lawful reserve balance in the Federal Reserve bank. The Federal Reserve bank will rediscount prime paper for banks, and the rate of interest for the rediscount is one of the methods employed by the Federal Reserve System to control the expansion or contraction of credit. (1)

rediscount rate The interest rate charged by one of the twelve Federal Reserve banks to a member bank on eligible commercial paper which the member bank has used as collateral for a loan.

redraft A Cross Bill. When a check or other bill of exchange which has been presented for payment is dishonored and as a result is protested, the holder of the instrument may draw a bill of exchange for the original amount of the obligation plus the cost of the notary and other protest expenses. This new instrument is known as a Redraft or Cross Bill.

refer authorizer Person in credit office with authority to approve or disapprove credit transactions which need special attention. Person is usually supervisor of section. (26)

referee A person appointed in court proceedings for the judicial settlement of a trustee's accounts to conduct hearings with the interested parties and report his findings to the court. (74)

re-finance The changing of a loan from one financial institution to another or the rewriting of the contract within the same institution. (31, 92)

refinancing Same as refunding. New securities are sold by a company and the money is used to retire existing securities. Object may be to save interest costs, extend the maturity of the loan, or both. (2)

reflation An increase or decrease in the quantity of money by action of the monetary authorities in an attempt to return to a previous level of prices.

reformation of contract Proof in a court of equity that the contract does not state the true intentions of both parties will permit reformation of contract to correct the contract. (5)

refund 1. An amount paid back of credit allowed because of an over-collection or on account of the return of an object sold. 2. To pay back or allow credit for an amount because of an over-collection or because of the return of an object sold. 3. To provide for the payment of a loan through cash or credit secured by a new loan. 4. To replace one bond issue with another, usually in order to extend the maturity, to reduce the interest rate, or to consolidate several issues. Advance Refunding, offer to exchange new securities for outstanding securities prior to their maturity dates. (29, 103)

refundable interest The return to the debtor (maker of a note) of the unearned portion of interest previously charged due to the indebtedness being liquidated prior to maturity. See Factor 78th. (1)

refunding The refinancing of an indebtedness on or before its maturity in order to reduce the fixed interest charge; to reduce the amount of fixed payment, or due to the inability to conveniently liquidate an indebtedness when it matures. (1)

regional bank One of the twelve Federal Reserve District or Regional Banks. Each bank is numbered as follows: 1-Boston, 2-New York, 3-Philadelphia, 4-Cleveland, 5-Richmond, 6-Atlanta, 7-Chicago, 8-St. Louis, 9-Minneapolis, 10-Kansas City, 11-Dallas, 12-San Francisco.

regional exchange Any organized securities exchange located outside New York City. Three major ones are Philadelphia-Baltimore-Washington Stock Exchange, the Midwest Stock Exchange, and the Pacific Coast Stock Exchange. All of the regional exchanges together account for less than 10% of all stock trading. (105)

register A record for the consecutive entry of a certain class of events, documents, or transactions, with a proper notation of all the required particulars.
NOTE: The form of register for accounting purposes varies from a one-column to a multi-columnar sheet of special design whereon the entries are distributed, summarized, and aggregated usually for convenient posting to the accounts. (29)

register check The title given to a check used in parts of the United States in lieu of cashier's checks or bank drafts. The check is preprinted. The purchaser writes in the name of the payee and his own name as purchaser, and the amount of money desired to be transmitted. The purchaser then presents the check to the teller, who protects it with the issuing bank's name, the amount, and a number. The check has two stubs—one for the purchaser, and the other which the bank uses as a credit to the checks outstanding liability account. (1)

registered as to principal A term applied to a coupon bond, the name of the owner of which is registered on the bond and on the books of the company. Such bonds are not negotiable and cannot be sold without an assignment. (74)

registered bond A bond whose owner's name is registered with the issuer or its agent.

registered check See Register Check. (85)

registered coupon bonds Most registered bonds are of one of two types: 1. Those bonds in which interest is paid to the registered owner in the form of a check mailed to the owner and 2. Registered coupon bonds, those bonds in which interest is paid by the means of coupons attached to the bonds. As the coupons come due the holder clips the coupons from the bonds and has his bank collect them from the obligor or his agent.

registered exchange A security exchange which has registered and subscribed to the regulation of the Securities Exchange Commission. A commodity exchange which has registered and subscribed to the regulation of the Commodity Exchange Commission.

registered investment company An investment company which has filed a registration statement with the Securities and Exchange Commission, fulfilling the requirements of the Investment Company Act of 1940. (3)

registered representative Present name for the older term "customers' man." The registered representative is an employee of a Stock Exchange member firm, registered with the Exchange as having passed certain tests and met certain requirements, authorized to serve the public customers of his firm. Also known as "customers' broker." (2)

register of wills In some states (Delaware, for example), the name of the officer before whom wills are offered for probate and who grants letters testamentary and letters of administration. (88)

registrar An agent for a corporation, usually a bank, who has the responsibility of registering the ownership of all bonds within an issue. The registrar also certifies on the bond that it is a genuine bond of the issuing corporation, and is one of the authorized issues within the limits of the total bond issue. The registrar pays the coupons on "bearer" bonds, and issues interest checks on registered bonds for the corporation. (1)

registration Before a public offering may be made of new securities by a company, or of outstanding securities by controlling stockholders—through the mails or in interstate commerce—the securities must be registered under the Securities Act of 1933. The application must be filed with the SEC by the issuer. It must disclose pertinent information relating to the company's operations, securities, management and purpose of the public offering. Securities of railroads under jurisdiction of the Interstate Commerce Commission, and certain other types of securities, are exempted. On security offerings involving less than $300,000, only limited information is required.
Before a security may be admitted to dealings on a national securities exchange, it must be registered under the Securities Exchange Act of 1934. The application for registration must be filed with the Exchange and the SEC by the company issuing the securities. The application must disclose pertinent information relating to the company's operations, securities and management. Registration may become effective 30 days after receipt by the SEC of the certification by the Exchange of approval of listing and registration, or sooner by special order of the Commission. (2)

registration statement A statement which sets forth certain facts as prescribed by statute and by rules and regulations issued there-under and which (subject to certain exceptions) must be filed with the Securities and Exchange Commission prior to a public offering of new securities. (88)

regular dividend A dividend of a fixed sum or sums declared periodically on the same date or dates each year. (19)

regular lot The unit of trading which is customary for the line of activity. See Round Lot; Full Lot; Board Lot.

regular way delivery Unless otherwise specified, securities (other than governments') sold on the N.Y. Stock Exchange are to be delivered to the buying broker by the selling broker and payment made to the selling broker by the buying broker on the fourth business day after the transaction. Regular way delivery for government bonds is the following business day. See Delivery; Transfer. (2)

regular way sale A term designating a transaction that is not a short sale. (105)

regulated commodities Those commodities over which the Commodity Exchange Authority has supervision are known as "regulated." This does not mean that the prices are controlled. The C.E.A. simply concerns itself with the orderly operation of the futures market and, at times, investigates abnormal price movements. Under the Commodity Exchange Act, approved June 15, 1936, definite regulations are established providing for the safeguarding of customers' money deposited as margin. Commodities currently supervised by the C.E.A. are wheat, cotton, corn, rice, oats, barley, rye, flaxseed, grain sorghums, bran, shorts, middlings, butter, eggs, potatoes, onions, wool tops, wool futures, lard, tallow, soybean oil, cottonseed meal, cottonseed, peanuts, soybeans and soybean meal. (9)

regulated investment company A term applied in the Federal Internal Revenue Code to an investment company which is registered under the Investment Company Act of 1940 and meets certain specified Internal Revenue Code requirements. Special provision of the Internal Revenue Code apply to regulated investment companies and their shareholders. (65)

regulation F A regulation issued by the Board of Governors of the Federal Reserve System under authority of Section 11 (k) of the Federal Reserve Act, as amended, relating to the conduct of fiduciary business by national banks. The full title of the regulation is Regulation F—Trust Powers of National Banks. (74)

regulation Q A requirement of the Federal Reserve Board which limits the amount of interest that may be paid by covered commercial banks to their depositors on time deposits.

regulation T The Federal regulation governing the amount of credit which may be advanced by brokers and dealers to customers for the purchase of securities. See Margin. (2)

regulation U The Federal regulation governing the amount of credit which may be advanced by a bank to its customers for the purchase of securities. See Margin. (2)

rehypothecate To transfer to another a note which is secured by the hypothecation of property. See Hypothecate. (85)

rehypothecation The use of collateral which has been pledged as security for a loan by the original lender who in turn uses it as collateral for a loan. Stock brokers obtain the consent of their customers to rehypotecate the securities left as collateral on margin accounts.

reimbursement Cash or other assets received as a repayment of the cost of work or services performed or of other expenditures, made for or on behalf of another governmental unit, or department, or for an individual, firm or corporation. (29)

reinvestment The use of the proceeds of dividends, interest or sale of securities for the purpose of purchasing other securities. A popular feature of some securities of investment companies is that the proceeds may be reinvested at favorable terms.

reject To refuse or decline a risk. (42)

related funds Funds of a similar character which are brought together for administrative and reporting purposes; for example, Sinking Fund. (29)

release 1. The act of surrendering checks from one department to another for further processing; surrendering collateral to a borrower upon payment or acceptance as to a future fixed date of payment made between the drawee (a borrower) and the bank. 2. The giving up of a claim by the person entitled to it, to the person against whom the claim exists. A written statement that an obligation has been satisfied. (1, 31, 92)

release of mortgage 1. The act of releasing or relinquishing the claim against property established by a mortgage. 2. The instrument by which such a release is effected. (89)

release of premiums on funded debt A credit to income each fiscal period of a proportion of the premium realized at the sale of funded securities, based on the ratio of such fiscal period to the remaining life of the securities. (19)

reloader A slang expression in finance for one who is adept at selling more securities to someone who has so far made only a small commitment. (105)

remainder A future estate or interest in property which will become an estate or interest in possession upon the termination of the prior estate or interest created at the same time and by the same instrument. For example, A conveys Blackacre to B for life and upon B's death to C in fee simple. C's interest is a remainder. The term remainder over is sometimes used in such phrases as "To A for life, with remainder over to B," calling attention to the fact that there is a prior estate or interest. To be distinguished from reversion. (74)

remainder beneficiary The beneficiary of a trust who is entitled to the principal outright after the prior life beneficiary or other prior beneficiary has died or his interest has been terminated. (88)

remainder estate An estate in property created simultaneously with other estates by a single grant and consisting of the rights and interest contingent upon and remaining after the termination of the other estates. (54)

remainder interest A future interest which will become an interest in possession after the termination of a prior interest created at the same time and by the same instrument as the future interest. For example, H leaves his estate in trust with income to be paid to W, and on her death the trust is to terminate and the property is to be delivered to C. C has a remainder interest. (74)

remainderman The person who is entitled to an estate after the prior estate has expired. For example, "I devise Blackacre to A for life, remainder to B." A is the life tenant; B, the remainderman. Originally the term applied, and in most states still does apply, to real property only. (74)

remargining The act of putting up additional margin against a loan. When securities have dropped in price, brokers may require their customers who have margin accounts to provide additional collateral either in the form of other securities or of cash.

remise An archaic term found in deeds of release and quit claim meaning to remit or give up. (5)

remittance Any payment in part or in full on a debt, or obligation.

remittance letter A transit letter containing a list of checks sent for collection and payment by a sending bank to a receiving bank. The sending bank does not maintain an account with the receiving bank, and hence, requests the latter to remit payment for the items sent. The receiving bank pays for the checks by remitting a bank draft to the sending bank. This is to be distinguished from a cash letter for credit, in which case the receiving bank credits the account of the sending bank in its "Due to Banks" Ledger. (1)

remitting Paying, as in remitting a payment; also cancelling, as in remitting a debt. (59)

remonetize To reinstate as standard, lawful money a type of money which had been demonetized.

remoteness of vesting See Rule Against Perpetuities. (74)

renewal The liquidation of an existing loan, as evidenced by a note, on or before its maturity by permitting the borrower to execute and to substitute a new note with a different maturity date in lieu of the original note, thus creating a new obligation and extending the term of credit. (1)

renounce 1. An act by which an individual or trust institution named under a will as executor or trustee declines to accept such appointment. 2. The act of a surviving husband or wife under the decedent's state law declining to take the provision made for him or her under the other's will and taking his or her share of the estate had the other died without a will. 3. Any action by which the beneficiary of any interest in real or personal property therewith refuses to accept such interest. (74)

rent The return in money, labor, or chattel provisions which are given by the rentor to the owner of the land in compensation for the use or right of use of the real estate. (5)

rentier An individual whose income is derived from real estate, securities and annuities.

rentes Generally used to refer to certain French Government perpetual bonds though other European governments also issue bonds with the same designation. Technically the term refers to the annual interest payable on the bonded debt of certain European governments.

renunciation As the term is employed in trust business, an act, in accordance with prescribed procedure, by which an individual or a trust institution named in a fiduciary capacity declines to accept the appointment. (88)

reorganization The changing of the capital structure of a corporation which is in distress financially under the appropriate legislation such as the National Bankruptcy Act. The objective is to remove the cause of the failure, make a fair settlement with the creditors and to permit the corporation to stay in business.

reorganization committee Any committee representing creditors or investors which prepares plans for the reorganization of a distressed corporation. The National Bankruptcy Act, as amended, establishes strict conditions under which such committees operate.

repatriation The liquidation of foreign investments and return of the proceeds to the nation of the investor. In a broader sense it means the return to ones own country either persons or things.

repledge Rehypothecate. See that term.

replevin The writ by which or the action in which personal property wrongfully taken is returned to the rightful owner. (35)

report (or certificate) The report (or certificate) of an independent accountant (or auditor) is a document in which he indicates the nature and scope of the examination (or audit) which he has made and expresses the opinion which he has formed in respect of the financial statements. (17)

reporter Person employed by credit bureau. Makes reports on credit inquiries. (26)

report to stockholders A periodic statement of financial conditions made by a corporation to its stockholders. Sometimes the reports are quite comprehensive, but always include a balance sheet and profit and loss statement. (105)

repossession Legal procedure where seller of goods on installment basis repossesses goods because of failure of purchaser to fulfill agreement. (26)

representative 1. A general term designating either an executor or an administrator. 2. The person who acts or speaks for another under his authority. (74)

representative good Those evidences of ownership of wealth such as notes, bonds, stocks, and money are considered to be representative goods.

representative money Those paper monies which have full standard money backing or are freely redeemable in the standard such as gold or silver.

reproduction cost Normal cost of the exact duplication of a property as of a certain date. (5)

reproduction value The sum of money which would be required to reproduce a building less an allowance for depreciation of that building. (89)

repudiation The intentional and willful refusal to pay a debt in whole or in part. The term usually refers to the willful act of a government or a subdivision thereof. (1)

repurchase agreement An agreement by one individual or firm to buy back, under certain terms, the thing which it originally sold to the second party of the transaction. Such agreements are fairly common in certain types of underwriting of security issues. The Federal Reserve Authorities enter into repurchase agreements with certain government bond dealers for the mutual advantage of both.

repurchases In closed-end companies refers to voluntary open market purchases by investment companies of their own securities, usually for retirement, in open-end funds, term represents stock taken back at approximate liquidating value. (3)

request for a report A request about the status of a security order made through the order room of a brokerage firm to the broker concerned on the stock exchange floor. (105)

request for proposal (RFP sometimes referred to as RFQ, Request for Quotation) The official document which requests from prospective contractors—industrial, universities, or other government agencies—a description of the manner in which they would achieve the objective specified by the RFP if they were awarded a contract to do so. This plan normally includes the proposer's estimate of total cost and required schedule. (99)

required reserves Those liquid assets state charted banks are required to maintain by the state Superintendent of Banking and which member banks are required to maintain by the Federal Reserve Authorities. Member banks must maintain their reserves mostly in the form of deposits with their regional Federal Reserve bank depending upon the type of deposits, time or demand, and the type of bank, Central Reserve, Reserve or Country Bank. In addition, certain till cash may be counted as being part of the required reserves.

res In the phrase trust res, the same as trust property. The corpus of the trust. (74)

rescind To cancel a contract so that both parties may be put as far as possible in the same position as before making the contract. (35)

rescission of contracts The abrogating or annulling of contracts. (5)

reservation That reservation or right reserved by an owner in selling or leasing a property, a common reservation being in the use of the attic or basement for the storage of personal property of the owner. (54+)

reservation price In auctions some products are conditionally offered with a reservation price which means that the initial bid must be at least that high or the auctioneer will withdraw the item.

reserve A portion of the bank's funds which has been set aside for the purpose of assuring its ability to meet its liabilities to depositors in cash. Minimum reserves to be maintained against demand and time deposits are usually specified by banking law. See Legal Reserve. (85)

reserve bank One of the twelve Federal Reserve banks.

reserve city bank A member bank of the Federal Reserve System which is located in cities designated by the Federal Reserve Act as amended as reserve cities. Banks are divided for reserve requirements by the Act into two classes: Reserve City banks and Country Banks.

reserve for bad debts Same as Allowance for Bad Debts; the amount recorded on the books that represents the estimated reduction in the value of the accounts receivable because of estimated uncollectable accounts; an account that shows the estimated decrease in the value of the accounts receivable because of anticipated losses on bad debts. (73)

reserve for retirement of sinking fund bonds A reserve which indicates the amount of cash and other resources which should have been accumulated at a certain date in order eventually to redeem bonds outstanding.

NOTE: In a Utility or Other Enterprise Fund, the reserve may equal the actual resources in the fund rather than the amount which should have been accumulated, since a Utility or Other Enterprise Fund is accounted for the same way as a like private enterprise. However, the amount which should have been accumulated should also be shown on the balance sheet either in parentheses following the reserve account or in a footnote. See also Sinking Fund. (29)

reserve fund An asset such as cash or highly liquid securities which was created to meet some expense.

reserve ratio The proportion of deposit liability which a bank keeps as reserves. The ratio required by member banks of the Federal Reserve System varies by type of deposit, time or demand and by location of bank in country or reserve city. It is in the form of deposits with the regional Federal Reserve bank and a minor amount may be vault cash.

reserve requirement That proportion of the deposits as classified into demand and time deposits which the appropriate banking authority requires to be held by the bank as reserves. In the case of banks which are members of the Federal Reserve System these reserves are deposited with the district Federal Reserve bank though a proportion of till cash may now be included by bank. See Reserve Ratio.

reserves with federal reserve banks Deposits of reporting member banks with the Federal Reserve banks. Member banks are required by law to hold an amount equal to a percentage of their deposits as reserve (a deposit) in the Reserve banks. (4)

residual The estimated sale or release value of the equipment at the end of the base lease term. In the case of all leasing companies, the residual is a management estimate. Since a residual is taken into earnings over the life of a lease, it is a most important factor in evaluating earnings. An overly optimistic residual valuation, for example, would tend to overstate earnings.

residual ownership What is left after claims. (93)

residual value The estimated sale or release value of the equipment at the end of the base lease term. Currently, most leasing companies book this estimated amount and take it into earnings over the life of the lease. Most bank leasing functions do not.

residuary clause The provision in the will or trust agreement that disposes of all of the decedent's property remaining after the payment of all taxes, debts, expenses, and charges and the satisfaction of all other gifts in the will or trust agreement. (74)

residuary devise A gift by will of the real property remaining after all specific devises have been made. (74)

residuary devisee The individual named by a will to receive real property left after those specific pieces of real property have been devised.

residuary estate The property that remains after all other gifts in the will have been satisfied. Those who take the residuary estate are known as residuary legatees (as to personal property) and residuary devisees (as to real property). (74)

residuary legatee A person to whom is given the remainder of testator's personal property after all other legacies have been satisfied. (74)

residuary trust A trust which is composed of the property of the testator, remaining in the estate after the payment of all taxes, debts, expenses, charges, and the satisfaction of all other gifts under the will. (74)

residue (Rest, residue, and remainder) That portion of a decedent's estate remaining after the payment of all debts, expenses, and charges and the satisfaction of all legacies and devises. (74)

resistance points Those points or areas of price fluctuation at which a security or security average comes to a resistance or stop prior to moving in a direction. Technically a resistance point may be caused by a standing order by a large institution to buy or sell at certain levels. Other theories such as the Dow theory hold that charted resistance points must be penetrated and confirmed by another average before a break out from the resistance points will result in a new market movement.

resolution A formal document expressing the intention of a board of directors of a corporation. (74)

resources The bank's title for Assets Owned. The resources of a bank are offset by the liabilities and capital accounts as listed on the Daily Statement of Condition. The major resources of a bank are: Cash on hand and due from banks; investments held; loans and discounts; and buildings, furniture, fixtures, and equipment. (1)

resting order One which, if an order to buy, is limited to a price below the market, or which, if an order to sell, is limited to a price above the market. The order may be open or good until cancelled. (9)

restraint on alienation of property A limitation on the right of a person to transfer title to property or property rights. (74)

restricted account Account on which certain instructions have been given as to authorization, etc.

restrictive endorsement An endorsement on a negotiable instrument which limits the negotiability of it. The words "For Deposit Only" is a common type of restrictive endorsement. Also known as Qualified Endorsement.

resulting trust A trust which arises in law from the acts of the parties, regardless of whether they actually intend to create a trust—as when a person disposes of property under circumstances which raise an inference that he does not

intend that the person taking or holding the property shall have the beneficial interest in it; to be distinguished from an express trust and a constructive trust. (88)

retained income (earned surplus) The Retained Income Account is the collective title for a group of accounts which forms the connecting link between the income account and the balance sheet. The several accounts are designed to show the changes in retained income or deficit during each calendar year resulting from (a) the operations and other transactions during the period as reflected in the income account, (b) appropriations of other reservations of retained income for specific purposes, (c) accounting adjustments not properly attributable to the period, (d) miscellaneous gains and losses not accounted for elsewhere, and (e) appropriations for dividends. (21)

retirement plan trusts Trusts established to enable the employees on retirement to receive a pension from funds created out of payments made by the employees, their employers, or both. (74)

retreat A drop in the price level of securities or commodities.

return Income received from investments, usually expressed in terms of percentage of market price, also referred to as yield. (3)

return item A negotiable instrument, principally a check, which has been sent to another bank for collection and payment and returned unpaid for one reason or another to the sending bank. A returned item will have a ticket attached to it showing the reason for its return. Return items are sent back through the same channels from which they came. This is done by the reading of bank endorsements on the back of the item. (1)

revalorization The revaluation or restoration of purchasing power to an inflated currency. See Revaluation.

revaluation The revaluation or restoration of purchasing power to an inflated currency. See Devaluation. (130)

revenue The increase in ownership equity during a designated period of time. If the accounts are kept on an accrual basis this term designates additions to assets which do not increase any liability, nor represent the recovery of an expenditure, and the cancellation of liabilities or a decrease in assets. The same definition applies in its entirety to those cases where the accounts are kept on a cash basis except that the additions must be to cash only. (29)

revenue bonds Bonds payable from and secured by stated revenues from a specific project or group of projects.

revenue expenditures Those expenditures that do not increase the value of the fixed assets but that are necessary to maintain the assets in an efficient operating condition. (73)

revenue stamps (Documentary stamps) Adhesive stamps issued by the federal or state government, which must be purchased and affixed, in amounts provided by law, to documents or instruments representing original issues, sales, and transfers of stocks and bonds, deeds of conveyance, and certain types of foreign insurance policies. (74)

reverse split Also called a split down; the opposite of a stock split. The number of outstanding shares of the corporation is reduced and the market price of these remaining shares is increased. For example a 1-for-4 reverse split by a company with 4 million outstanding shares would leave 1 million shares outstanding. Such a strategy is rarely used and then usually only when the price of the stock is relatively low. Stockholders normally must approve this proposal of the corporation's directors. (105)

reversing entries General journal entries made at the beginning of a new fiscal period to reverse the adjusting entries that were recorded at the end of the preceding period. (73)

reversion The interest in an estate remaining in the grantor after a particular interest, less than the whole has, been granted by the owner to another person; to be distinguished from remainder. The reversion remains in the grantor; the remainder goes to some grantee. (88)

reversionary right The right to receive possession and use of property upon the termination or defeat of an estate carrying the rights of possession and use and vested in another. (54)

reverter The interest which the grantor retains in property in which he has conveyed an interest less than the whole to another party. If the grantor makes the conveyance subject to a condition which may or may not be broken sometime in the future, he retains a possibility of reverter. (74)

revocable beneficiary A beneficiary whose rights in the policy are subject to the insured's right of change. See Beneficiary. (42)

revocable letter of credit A letter of credit which may be cancelled.

revocable trust A trust which may be terminated by the settlor or by another person; opposed to an irrevocable trust. (74)

revocable trust with consent or approval A trust which may be terminated by the settlor or by another person but only with the consent or approval of one or more other persons. For example, A creates for his son B a trust which may be revoked by B with C's consent (in this case C may be B's mother). To be distinguished from an irrevocable trust. (74)

revocation 1. The act of recalling a power or authority conferred, as the revocation of a power of attorney, a license, etc. 2. The act of annulling or making inoperative a will or a trust instrument. (5)

revolving letter of credit A letter of credit issued for a specific amount which renews itself for the same amount over a given period. Usually the unused renewable portion of the credit is cumulative, so long as drafts are drawn before the expiration of the credit. (1)

rial Monetary unit of Iran.

rialto Term sometimes applied to stock exchanges and other busy centers. (105)

ricardian theory of rent Theory ·that held that differences in rent resulted from differences in the productivity of land.

rich An expression applied to security prices when the current market quotation appears to be high (or the income return low) in comparison

with either the past price record of the individual security or the current prices of comparable securities. (103)

rigging The manipulation or attempt to manipulate the market in a commodity or security. Illegal manipulation such as matched orders, wash sales and certain types of stabilization of prices are prohibited by blue-sky and Securities Exchange Act legislation.

right of election The right of a surviving husband or wife, under the decedent's estate law, to take his or her intestate share in preference to the provision made in the deceased person's will. (74)

right of redemption See Equity of Redemption. (89)

right of withdrawal Privilege of an insured or beneficiary permitting withdrawal of funds placed on deposit. (42)

rights When a company wants to raise more funds by issuing additional securities, it may give its stockholders the opportunity, ahead of others, to buy the new securities in proportion to the number of shares each owns. The piece of paper evidencing this privilege is called a right. Because the additional stock is usually offered to stockholders below the current market price, rights ordinarily have a market value of their own and are actively traded. In most cases they must be exercised within a relatively short period. Failure to exercise or sell rights may result in actual loss to the holder. See Warrants. (2)

rights off Without the rights, i.e., a security is selling at a price and on a basis which excludes the privilege to buy a pro rata amount of additional securities being offered. Also called ex-rights. (105)

rights on Term indicating that a security is selling at a price and on a basis which includes the privilege to buy a pro rata amount of the additional securities being offered. (105)

ring 1. A prohibited form of manipulation in the securities business whereby a combination of individuals working for their own account attempt to change the price of a security by buying or selling it simultaneously. This is similar to a clique, but differs from a pool which acts collectively under a pool manager for the united risk of its members. 2. A place on the trading floor of an exchange where orders are executed. On many exchanges a physical ring of wood or metal is used to control the location of the traders who form around the area. (105)

risk analysis An examination of the elements or sources of risk in a mortgage loan and of their efforts both·separately and in combination. (89)

risk capital Venture capital. That proportion of a total capitalization which is not secured by a lien or mortgage, common stock in a new enterprise.

risk category A class or group into which related elements affecting mortgage risk are placed for purposes of convenience in analysis. (89)

rock bottom A financial term which indicates that security prices will fall no further. (105)

roll back A governmental attempt to reduce a price to some previous level either through verbal request to manufacturers or distributors to lower their profit margins or by a subsidy or tax rebate.

rollover Refunding an issue to the same holders of the issue which has been refunded. The effect is that the new issue replaces the old issue and the same holders are to be found for the new issue as were holders of the old issue.

round lot A security transaction for the number of shares that constitute the normal trading unit, which may be 10 shares, 25 shares, or 100 shares depending on the particular issue. On the N. Y. Stock Exchange the unit of trading is generally 100 shares in stocks and $1,000 par value in the case of bonds. (103, 2)

round turn The offsetting sale or purchase to a previous purchase or sale thus completing the transaction and resulting in a profit or loss.

routing symbol See Check Routing System.

royalty That amount or percentage of the selling price of a thing which has been copyrighted, patented or contracted which is given to the owner of the royalty for the use of his property or right. In the case of extraction rather than being a percentage of a selling price it may be a fixed amount per unit extracted such as one dollar a ton.

ruble Monetary unit of Union of Soviet Socialist Republics.

rubricated account A term applied by bankers to any "earmarked" account. The practice of marking accounts in red to indicate that they were intended for a specific purpose was no doubt responsible for this term. (1)

rule against accumulations The limitation imposed by common law or by statute upon the accumulation of income in the hands of a trustee. (74)

rule against perpetuities A rule of common law that makes void any estate or interest in property so limited that it will not take effect or vest within a period measured by a life or lives in being at the time of the creation of the estate plus 21 years and the period of gestation. In many states the rule has been modified by statute. Sometimes it is known as the rule against remoteness of vesting. (74)

rule in Shelley's case A rule of law which nullifies a remainder interest in heirs of grantee. For example, A conveys Blackacre to B for life, remainder to heirs of B. Under this rule, B's heirs received nothing and B took a fee simple absolute interest in Blackacre. This rule has been abolished by statute or judicial decision in many states. (74)

rule of reason Interpretation of a rule or law in which consideration of the reasonableness of a situation or act is taken into the basis of judgment.

rumor In the securities business, hearsay or unfounded gossip intended to cause a rise or fall in security prices. Stock Exchange members are restricted from circulating any information which might be detrimental to the interest and welfare of the exchange. (105)

run The action by a large number of people doing the same thing. A run on a bank is caused by an abnormally large number of withdrawals. A run

on a product or commodity may be caused by some scare such as war or strike.

runaway inflation A very sharp increase in the general price level. The severe inflation becomes part of an inflationary spiral in which higher prices lead to higher demands for wages which in turn leads to higher prices.

runner An employee of the bank who delivers items to other banks in the same community, and who in turn may receive and bring back to his bank the items that the other banks may wish delivered there. The runner's duties may involve all types of messenger service for his bank. (1)

running a book One of the duties of a person who specializes in certain stocks on the trading floor of a stock exchange. A list of orders that are limited to a price other than that currently prevailing is kept in the books. (105)

running in the shorts Buying various stocks in which there is a known short position in an attempt to raise the price and force the "shorts" to cover, i.e., buy in to complete their short selling contracts and thereby spark a further advance in price. (105)

run off The last sales, or final prices, as printed by the stock ticker after the market is closed for the day. The run off may last much past the last actual transaction if volume was particularly heavy near the close of the session. (105)

run on a bank A condition existing when depositors become concerned over the safety of their money and suddenly seek to withdraw their deposits simultaneously; often associated with panic. (105)

rupee Monetary unit of Burma, Ceylon, India, and Pakistan.

rupiah Monetary unit of Indonesia.

S

S Servant; settler; seller; sold.

S Shilling.

S. 7 Seller's delivery within seven days.

S. A. Semi-annual.

SA State Agency. (67)

SANO Senior Assistant Nurse Officer. (67)

SBA Small Business Administration.

S.B.L.I. Savings bank life insurance. (5)

S/D Sight draft.

S. D. Co. Safe Deposit Company.

S. D. M. J. Quarterly interest payments or dividends in September, December, March and June.

Ser. Series; serial.

S/F Statute of frauds.

S. F. Sinking fund.

S. & F. Stock and fixtures. (5)

S/H Shareholder, stockholder.

Shs. Shares.

Sig. Signature.

Sig. Mis. Signature Missing.

Sig. Unk. Signature Unknown.

S. & L. Assn. Savings and Loan Association.

Sld. Sold.

S. & M. Semi-annual interest payments or dividends in September and March; Stock and machinery. (5)

S.O.P. Standard operating procedure; Statement of policy.

S/P Specific performance.

S.P. Stop payment.

S.R. Short rate. (5)

SSA Social Security Administration.

Stg. Sterling.

Stk. Stock.

Stk. Ex. Stock Exchange.

Stpd. Stamped.

S/U Statute of uses.

Substn. Substitution.

SUB Supplementary Unemployment Benefit Plan.

Suby. Subsidiary.

Sur. Surplus.

saddled The position of someone who owns an undesirable security that he bought at a price higher than the prevailing market price. (105)

safe deposit box A metal container kept under lock and key in a section of a bank's vault for customer use. The boxes are kept in small compartments, each with a separate lock. These boxes are rented with the compartment to depositors and customers for an annual rental. Each customer has an individual key to the safe deposit box that he rents. The bank also has a separate key to each box. The box cannot be opened unless both keys are used, the customer's key opening one set of tumblers, and the bank's key opening another set to release the lock. (1)

safe deposit vault A section of the bank's vault set aside for the use of customers who may rent space in the vault for the safekeeping of valuable securities, papers, and small objects of value. See also Safe Deposit Box. (1)

safekeeping A service rendered by banks, especially banks in large metropolitan areas, where securities and valuables of all types and descriptions are protected in the vaults of the bank for the customer for a service fee. (These valuables may include securities, precious gems, valuable paintings, collection pieces of great value, silver and gold services, etc.) Many of these items are too large to be placed in safe deposit boxes. In the case of securities, some customers "buy" security counselor services of large banks, requesting the banks to handle their securities to the best advantage. The banks will buy and sell, collect dividends and interest, and credit the depositor's account with this income. Many clients of this type are foreign citizens, and wealthy Americans who spend a good portion of their time abroad, traveling or living in foreign countries. Since they cannot have constant access to safe deposit boxes, they appoint banks to act as their fiscal agents to protect and control their holdings for them in their absence. (1)

safekeeping account An agency account concerning which the duties of the agent are to receipt for, safekeep, and deliver the property in the account on demand of the principal or on his order; to be distinguished from a custody account and a managing agency account. (88)

safekeeping (deposit for) The receipt by a bank of custody of specific property to be returned as contrasted with an ordinary deposit to be repaid in money and with a safe deposit where the property is placed in a safe deposit box, rented to a customer, to which the renter rather than the bank has access. (85)

safety of income-principal A quality associated usually with bonds and preferred stock, as opposed to common stock. However, some common stocks are recognized to be of superior merit and their owners also enjoy safety of income and principal. (105)

sag A small price drop in commodity or stock price.

sale and lease-back A transaction in which used equipment is purchased from a company by a lessor, with title passing from the user to the lessor. The lessor then leases the equipment back to the company, who now becomes the lessee.

sales agreement A written document by which a seller agrees to convey property to a buyer for a stipulated price and under specified conditions. (89)

sales charge The amount charged in connection with the issuance of shares of a mutual fund and their distribution to the public. It is added to the net asset value per share in the determination of the offering price. (65)

sales journal A special journal that provides columns for recording all charge sales in one book. (73)

sales literature Literature used by an issuer, underwriter or dealer to inform prospective purchasers concerning an investment company the shares of which are offered for sale. Such literature is governed by the S.E.C.'s Statement of Policy and various State regulations. (65)

salt down stock To buy securities and put them away, holding them for an extended period. (105)

sandwich lease A leasehold in which the interest of the sublessor is inserted between the fee owner and the user of the property. The owner A of a fee simple leases to B, who in turn leases to C. The interest of A may be called the leased fee; that of B the sandwich lease, and that of C the leasehold. (54)

satisfaction of judgment Legal procedure followed when debtor pays amount of judgment, together with interest and costs. "Satisfaction of judgment" then entered on records of Court of Record. (26)

satisfaction piece An instrument acknowledging payment of the indebtedness due under a mortgage. (5)

saturation The condition of a market in which the supply of a commodity or security is so large that price reductions are necessary to absorb any additional offerings.

saturation point That point in the securities market when the supply of stocks begins to exceed the demand. This coincides with the peak of a market cycle. (105)

savings Money, or goods and other valuable property set aside from earnings, investments, etc.—left over after the costs of living have been met. (59)

savings account An account which is deposited in a bank usually in small amounts periodically over a long period of time and not subject to check. Savings accounts are also known as Time Deposits. The depositor is generally required to present his pass book upon making either a deposit or withdrawal. Banks use the savings account plan to encourage the methodical habit of thrift in customers. Savings accounts are usually interest bearing, and some banks also levy a service charge for excess withdrawal activity in an account. (1)

savings and loan association A financial corporation organized under state or federal statute for the primary purpose of selling shares to individuals, the proceeds of which are largely invested in home mortgages. The return to the investor is in the form of a dividend on shares and not as interest on deposits. (89)

savings bank A banking association whose purpose is to promote thrift and savings habits within a community. This organization may be either a stock organization (a bank with a capital stock structure), or a mutual savings bank. It usually has little or no commercial functions, but specializes in savings accounts, with an investment of these savings in long-term bonds and investments for the benefit of all the depositors.

NOTE: Some banks today have the word "savings" in their titles but are in fact commercial banks. (1)

savings bank life insurance Insurance written in several states through mutual savings banks. Characterized by having no agents to sell the insurance. It is purchased over the counter and is available in statutory limited amounts in the form of whole life, limited-payment life, endowment, term, and annuities on a participating basis. (5)

Savings Bank Life Insurance Council Voluntary association of issuing savings banks formed in 1938 in Massachusetts. It furnishes mutual savings banks and their policyholders with various services. (5)

savings deposit (Savings Account) A fund which a person gradually accumulates from earnings and on which the bank usually pays interest. See also Time Deposit (Open Account.) (85)

savings function A curve or schedule in which savings is related to some other function such as consumption, income, investment.

scale buying Also called Buying on Scale. See Scaling.

scale order A mechanical formula plan for averaging cost prices down or selling up. This method is based on preconceived strategy and standing orders which are useful for accumulating stocks in a bull market, or distributing them or selling short in a declining market. The purchase or sale of shares of the stock are made at

fixed intervals and to a prescribed point above or below the price of the initial commitment; for example, a scale order to sell 1,000 shares on a ¼ point scale up from 36 would involve ten separate sell orders of 100 shares, each beginning with 36 and continuing to 38¼. (105)

scaling A technique of trading in commodities or securities by placing orders for purchase or sale at intervals of price rather than placing the order in full at the market or at a price.

scalping A speculative attempt to obtain a quick profit by purchase of a security at an initial offering price with the expectation that the issue being oversubscribed will then advance in price at which time the security may then be sold. In some cases the sale will be consumated by the scalper before he is required to pay for his purchase. Thus, no capital was tied up or little capital in terms of the total transactions. Scalping is also found on commodity exchanges where the scalper buys and sells during the trading day in equal amounts so that at the end of the trading period he has no position either long or short.

scarcity value The rate of worth of a thing which is fixed in supply. (There can only be one picture of Mona Lisa and partly because of this it possesses scarcity value.)

scheduled payment A payment promised at a particular time, or one of several payments scheduled as to due date. (59)

schedule of accounts payable A list showing the account titles and the balances in the accounts payable ledger. (73)

schedule of accounts receivable A list showing the account titles and the balances in the accounts receivable ledger. (73)

schedule of distribution A form of accounting which sets forth in detail the estate property contained in each share to be distributed. (74)

schilling Monetary unit of Austria.

school savings A plan designed to promote the lesson of thrift in children in schools. A bank representative will call at the school one day a week, and assist teachers in accepting deposits in any small amount for the account of the pupil. (1)

scrip Any temporary document which entitles the holder or bearer to receive stock or a fractional share of stock in a corporation, cash, or some other article of value upon demand, or at some specified future date. Some industries, in remote sections, issue scrip to their employees for services performed in order to diminish the amount of cash which would otherwise be required. (1)

scrip certificate A certificate representing ownership of a fractional share of stock, which may be converted into a full share when presented in amounts equal to a full share. (105)

scrip dividend A type of dividend issued by a corporation to its stockholders entitling the holder or bearer to receive cash, stock or a fractional share of stock, or one or more units of the product manufactured, upon presentation, or at a specified future date. (1)

seal An impression, device, sign, or mark recognized by statute or by judicial decision as having the legal effect of a common-law seal. The letters L.S. or a scroll made with a pen is a recognized seal, as is a seal of wax or gummed paper or one embossed on the paper itself. (74)

sealed bid A technique for submitting an offer to buy or perform something. All interested parties are invited to submit in a sealed envelope their bid to buy or perform something such as a construction of a building or other type of work. The bids are all opened at one time and the most attractive bid is accepted. To insure good faith a bond may be required in connection with the bid. Many municipalities require that their bond issues be handled on a sealed bid rather than a negotiated basis.

seasoned security A stock or bond which has been publicly held at relatively even prices and which has a consistent record of earnings and dividends.

seasoned stocks The stocks of well established companies with unquestioned earning power and dividend paying ability. (105)

seat A traditional figure-of-speech for a membership on a securities or commodity exchange. Price and admission requirements vary. (2)

secondary beneficiary A beneficiary whose interest in a trust is postponed or is subordinate to that of the primary beneficiary. (74)

secondary distribution Also known as a secondary offering. The redistribution of a block of stock sometime after it has been sold by the issuing company. The sale is handled off the Exchange by a securities firm or group of firms and the shares are usually offered at a fixed price which is related to the current market price of the stock. Usually the block is a large one, such as might be involved in the settlement of an estate. The security may be listed or unlisted. Exchange approval is required for member firms to participate in a secondary distribution of a listed stock. See Exchange Distribution, Investment Banker; Special Offering; Syndicate. (2)

secondary financing See Junior Mortgage. (89)

secondary market A term for the sale and purchase of securities under a special offering or away from the regular channel of transactions, whether the trading is on a recognized securities exchange or over the counter. See also Dealer. (103)

secondary movement Security price movements consisting of sharp rallies in a bear market and sharp reaction in a primary bull market, as classified by Charles H. Dow in the development of his Dow Theory. Dow considered a bull period to continue as long as the highs attained in the secondary movements exceeded the preceding high points, and a bear period when the low points reached on a subsequent reaction were lower than the previous low points. (105)

secondary reserves Those assets of a bank that are convertible into cash on short notice by sale in the open market or by rediscount. (89)

second mortgage A mortgage which is made on property which has already had a mortgage placed upon it. The first mortgage has priority of claim over the second mortgage. See Mortgage.

second preferred stocks A security issue of a corporation which ranks just behind any first preferred stock, but ahead of any other preferred or common stocks in order of priority for dividends or assets. (105)

secretarial and legal Performing or causing to be performed such duties as are required by law or by-laws of the corporation and appraising and advising the company on all phases of its operations and relations from a legal viewpoint. (20)

secretary An officer of a trust company whose signature is necessary on all official documents. In large trust companies where a secretary's duties are too numerous, the board of directors may appoint assistant secretaries to perform specific duties in connection with his official functions. (1)

secret partner One whose membership in the firm is not known to the public, although he may have an active part in the management of the business. (73)

secular stagnation The long term period in which there has been little or no rate of economic growth and a relative equilibrium at substantially less than full employment.

secular trend A long term trend as compared with a seasonal variation or business cycle movement.

secured Guaranteed as to payment by the pledge of something valuable. (59)

secured creditor An individual or firm that has a claim on the debtor's assets in the form of definite collateral such as a real estate mortgage on the debtor's land.

secured deposits Bank deposits of state or local government funds which, under the laws of certain jurisdictions, are secured by the pledge of acceptable securities or by a surety contract (known as a depository bond) for the direct protection of these funds. (103)

secured loan A loan which is secured by marketable securities or other marketable valuables. Secured loans may be either time or demand loans. See Hypothecation. (1)

securities Defined in section 20a(2) of the Interstate Commerce Act as "any share of capital stock or any bond or other evidence of interest in or indebtedness of the carrier." Defined in section 77(b) of the Bankruptcy Act as including "evidences of indebtedness either secured or unsecured, bonds, stock, certificates of beneficial interest therein, certificates of beneficial interest in property, options, and warrants to receive, or to subscribe for, securities." (19)

securities acts The aggregation of federal laws enforced by the Securities and Exchange Commission to protect investors. The acts include the Investment Advisers Act, Investment Company Act, Securities Act of 1933, Securities Exchange Act of 1934, Trust Indenture Act, and the Public Utility Holding Company Act. (105)

Securities and Exchange Commission Established by Congress to help protect investors. The SEC administers the Securities Act of 1933, the Securities Exchange Act of 1934, the Trust Indenture Act, the Investment Company Act, and the Public Utility Holding Company Act. (2)

securities trading A term applied to the selling or buying of securities. Anyone who sells or buys securities through recognized channels (such as brokers) is said to engage in securities trading. The term also applies to the operations of brokers in the various exchanges. (1)

security What the borrower puts up to guarantee payment of the loan. This normally is his house but might also include other real estate, corporate stock or bonds and life insurance policies. Real estate is mortgaged, stock is pledged and life insurance is assigned.

security analysis The application of comprehensive examination of the factors concerning a security. This would include consideration of growth of sales and earnings, ratio analysis of the financial statements, evaluation of the trends which will affect a security.

security capital That proportion of a total capitalization which is relatively secured by a lien or mortgage. The rest of the capitalization consists of risk capital.

security exchange See Stock Exchange.

security loan A loan made for the purpose of acquiring a security which in turn is included as collateral for the loan.

security price level The price level prevailing at any particular time for a specific security, a group of securities, or the general market. (105)

security ratings Ratings placed on securities according to the degree of investment risk to purchasers. (21)

security record This term is applied to any accounting record relative to the custody of securities, whether it be for safekeeping, collateral, or trust ownership. (1)

segregated account A term used to describe funds which have been segregated to meet obligations which the bank has assumed for a customer. Usually it applies to cash set aside to meet drafts drawn under a letter of credit issued by the bank. It may also apply to funds set aside to honor checks certified by the bank. It is a liability account. (1)

seigniorage The difference between the value of bullion such as gold or silver and the face value of the same metal when it has been coined less the actual cost of coining. If one ounce of metal cost fifty cents and is coined into a dollar at the minting cost of ten cents then the seigniorage would be forty cents.

seisin Frequently spelled seizin. Possession whether of land or chattels; the possession of a freehold estate in land by one having the title thereto. The act of delivery of the land to the new freeholder. (5)

self liquidating A transaction such as a loan in which the proceeds are used to purchase or make something which, in turn, when sold provide the funds to repay the loan.

self-liquidating loan A short term commercial loan, usually supported by a lien on a given product or commodities, which is liquidated from the proceeds of the sale of the product or commodities. (Example: Loans granted for the growing of crops.) (1)

self-supporting of self-liquidating debt Debt obligations whose principal and interest are payable primarily or solely from the earnings of the municipal utility or enterprise for the construction or improvement of which they were originally issued. (29)

sell (or buy) at the close An order to be executed at the market (best price obtainable) at the close of the market on the day the order is entered. (105)

sell (or buy) at the opening An order to be executed at the market (best price obtainable) immediately after the stock exchange opens for business. (105)

seller's market A market in which goods are scarce so that buyers compete among themselves to obtain supplies. (93)

seller's option A special transaction on the Stock Exchange which gives the seller the right to deliver the stock or bond at any time within a specified period, ranging from not less than five business days to not more than 60 days. See Delivery. On a commodity transaction, the seller's right to choose the place, day of delivery, and grade within the limitations established by the regulations of the exchange. (2)

seller's surplus That amount which is the difference between the price a seller receives and the lowest price he would accept.

seller's 30 A security contract which gives the seller the option of delivering a security which has been sold at any time within thirty days of the date of sale. (105)

selling against the box A method of protecting a paper profit. Let's say you own 100 shares of XYZ which has advanced in price, and you think the price may decline. So you sell 100 shares short, borrowing 100 shares to make delivery. You retain in your security box the 100 shares which you own. If XYZ declines, the profit on your short sale is exactly offset by the loss in the market value of the stock you own. If XYZ advances, the loss on your short sale is exactly offset by the profit in the market value of the stock you have retained. You can close out your short sale by buying 100 shares to return to the person from whom you borrowed, or you can send him the 100 shares which you own. See Hedge; Short Sale. (106)

selling below the market An expression indicating that a security is currently quoted for less than similar securities of comparable quality and acceptance. (103)

selling charge See Load. (3)

selling flat Securities such as bonds are described as selling flat when the buyer does not have to pay an additional sum beyond the purchase price of the principal of the bond. This additional sum is the payment for accrued interest which the issuer will pay the holder. The bonds which typically sell flat are bonds which are in default or income bonds.

selling group A combination of securities dealers operating under the leadership of a syndicate department of an underwriting firm, and participating in the public sale of an issue of securities. (105)

selling off Refers to a decline in price by a specific security, a group of securities, or the general market caused by the supply of sell orders outnumbering the demand or buy orders. (105)

selling on balance That period of time such as a day or week during which a broker of commodities or securities processes more selling orders than buying orders.

selling on scale See Scaling.

selling out 1. A liquidation sale of a product, a line or a firm. 2. The Exhaust Price at which point a broker in a declining market liquidates a margin account.

selling short See Short Sale.

sell out notice An urgent notice which is sometimes sent by a brokerage firm to a client stating that an amount due must be immediately paid or the firm will be obliged to sell enough of the client's securities to satisfy the liability. This final warning is normally used when a client has not paid for securities purchased, or needs to deposit cash or securities to maintain adequate margin in his account. (105)

semi annual Twice a year at intervals six months apart.

senior interest A participation senior or ahead of another participation. (5)

senior issue A security which has a prior claim before another security issue.

senior lien The lien which has prior claim before other liens.

senior refunding An exchange by holders of securities maturing within five to twelve years for issues with original maturities of fifteen years or longer. (115)

senior securities Notes, bonds, debentures, or preferred stocks. These issues have a prior claim ahead of common stock to assets and earnings. (3)

sensitive market Those market conditions in which prices show considerable fluctuation considering the volume of trading and information received by the market.

sequestered account A term used to describe an account that has been impounded under due process of law. Since disbursement of such an account is subject to court action, the account is usually set up in a separate control. See Attached Account. (1)

serial issue A bond issue with a staggered maturity, usually due in equal annual amounts over a period of successive years. See Term Issue. (103)

service charge A fee which is charged by a bank against a depositor for services rendered in the bookkeeping of the depositor's account. This may be a "flat" monthly fee, regardless of activity, or it may be a "measured analysis" in which the service charge is levied against the activity of the account. Under the last plan, the depositor is permitted a credit based upon the average or minimum balance maintained. If his activity is small, he may not be charged for the maintenance of the account. If, however, he makes several deposits, and draws many checks against the account, the service charge on the basis of a few cents per item may become much larger than

the amount credited, and he may therefore be charged for this activity. Other types of service charges are made on the basis of a "flat" rate per check, or per checks and items deposited. Service charges are also made for other banking transactions, such as the safekeeping of securities, issuance of bank drafts, and excessive withdrawal activity in savings accounts. (1)

service value The difference between the ledger value of a unit of property and its salvage value. (19)

servicing 1. In connection with bonded indebtedness, the payment by the obligor of the interest and principal as they become due. 2. In mortgage financing, the performance by the mortgagee or his agent of the many services which must be taken care of while the mortgage is held by the institution, such as searching of title, billing, collection of interest and principal payments, reinspections and reappraisals of the real property, readjustment of the terms of the mortgage contract when necessary, tax follow-up work, etc. (90)

session In the securities business, a period of trading activity which ordinarily coincides with a stock exchange's hours of business, e.g., volume was five million shares in today's session. (105)

settlement 1. The winding up and distribution of an estate by an executor or an administrator; to be distinguished from the administration of an estate by a trustee or a guardian. 2. A property arrangement, as between a husband and wife or a parent and child, frequently involving a trust. (74)

settlement check A memorandum issued by the manager of a Clearing House Association to settle the results of a clearing house exchange between the member banks. This memorandum is sent to the local Federal Reserve bank, which adjusts the accounts of the clearing house banks to settle the debits and credits, or "wins and losses" in the exchange each day. The term may also be used with reference to checks and drafts received in payment of items sent for collection under Remittance Letters. (1)

settlement clerk A senior clerk in the proof department of a bank who is responsible for assembling totals obtained in the proof department. These totals showing all credits and charges to all departments are assembled and written on a "settlement sheet," or recap sheet of the proof department. It is from this source that the proof department shows a settlement of the day's work. The settlement sheet then becomes a subsidiary record for the general ledger, and the general ledger bookkeeper may use all final totals shown on this record. (1)

settlement date In the securities business, the date on which a securities transaction is finally consummated, normally four full business days following the date of trade. (105)

settlement day See Account Day.

settlement price The daily price at which the Clearing House clears all the day's trades. It may also refer to the price established by the Exchange to settle contracts unliquidated because of acts of God, such as floods or other causes. (9)

settlor A person who creates a trust, such as a living trust, to become operative during his lifetime; also called donor, grantor, and trustor. Compare Testator. (74)

shade A small reduction in price or terms.

shading The act of granting a small reduction in price or terms.

shake out A sudden flurry of security selling which often causes the ticker tape to run late in printing out the transactions. (105)

shaking out The removal of marginal traders or business men by the operation of increased competition or of the business cycle.

share Stock. A share may be designated as being common, preferred, A, B, founders or capital.

share capital The equity or portion of total capital which is represented by shares which may be either common, classified or preferred as differentiated from the portion of capital in the form of bonds and debt.

shareholder(s) Co-owners, of specific percentages of the whole. (59)

share of stocks Units of ownership in a company or corporation. (59)

shares The equal interests into which the capital stock of a corporation is divided, the ownership usually being evidenced by certificates called stock certificates. (90)

share turnover Means the same as volume in the securities business, or the aggregate number of shares traded during a given period for the security, a group of securities, or a market group. (105)

sheared An individual who has traded in securities or commodities in a very unsuccessful way.

sheltering trust A Spendthrift Trust. See that term.

sheriff's deed An instrument drawn under order of court to convey title to property sold to satisfy a judgment at law. (54)

sheriff's sale A sale of real or personal property made by a sheriff or other like ministerial officer, in obedience to an execution or other similar mandate of the court. (5)

shifting taxation The ability of an individual or firm which is taxed to transfer the incidence of the tax to some other person or body. A landlord who succeeds in raising his rent upon notification of an increase in his real estate tax has shifted the incidence of the tax.

shoestring A very small amount that is probably inadequate.

shoestring trading Similar in meaning to skating on thin ice, i.e., operating on thin or barely sufficient margin. The trader is putting up only the minimum amount of capital required to legally buy securities, borrowing the remainder. (105)

short One who has sold a futures contract that does not liquidate a previously bought contract for the same delivery month. In other words, he sells in expectation of buying back at a lower price. Short hedges are sales of futures made as hedges against holdings of the spot commodity, or products thereof. Short interest is the sum total of all short contracts or the owners of such contracts. (9)

short account The account of a firm or individual who is short. See Short.

shortage Deficiency in quantity. (93)

short and intermediate term credit Debt which is repaid over a relatively short span of time. (131)

short certificate A certificate by the proper officer of a court as to the appointment and authority of a fiduciary, as distinguished from a full certified copy of letters testamentary, administration, or trusteeship. (74)

short covering Buying stock to return stock previously borrowed to make delivery on a short sale. (2)

short form credit report Type of credit bureau report. Usually combining certain features of Oral Report and Written Report in abbreviated form. (26)

short interest The total of the short sales in a security or a commodity or on an exchange which are outstanding. Typically short interest figures are released by exchanges on a weekly basis.

short of the basis This is said of a person or firm who has sold cash or spot goods and has hedged them with purchases of futures. He has therefore sold at a certain "basis" and expects to buy back at a better basis for a profit. (9)

short of the market The situation which a short seller is in until he has covered his short position with a long purchase.

short position Stocks sold short and not covered as of a particular date. On the N. Y. Stock Exchange, a tabulation is issued a few days after the middle of the month listing all issues on the Exchange in which there was a short position of 5,000 or more shares, and issues in which the short position had changed by 2,000 or more shares in the preceding month. This tabulation is based on reports of positions on member firms' books. Short position also means the total amount of stock an individual has sold short and has not covered, as of a particular date. Initial margin requirements for a short position are the same as for a long position. See Margin; Up Tick; Short Sale. (2)

short rate The charge required for insurance or bonds taken for less than one year and, in some cases, the earned premium for insurance or bonds canceled by the insured before the end of the policy period or term of bond. (50)

short run A period which will vary from situation to situation. In a business it is the time within which a company can change price or production with a given fixed plant but not change the size of its plant or terminate operations.

shorts Those bear traders on the short side. See Short Sale.

short sale A person who believes a stock will decline and sells it though he does not own any has made a short sale. For instance: You instruct your broker to sell short 100 shares of ABC. Your broker borrows the stock so he can deliver the 100 shares to the buyer. The money value of the shares borrowed is deposited by your broker with the lender. Sooner or later you must cover your short sale by buying the same amount of stock you borrowed for return to the lender. If you are able to buy ABC at a lower price than you sold it, your profit is the difference between the two prices—not counting commissions and taxes. But if you have to pay more for the stock than the price you received, that is the amount of your loss. Stock Exchange and federal regulations govern and limit the conditions under which a short sale may be made on a national securities exchange. See Margin; Premium; Up Tick. (2)

short seller In the securities business, one who is a pessimist, i.e., bearish on the trend of securities prices and substantiates this opinion by selling short; for example, selling a security not owned at one price, hoping that the price will later fall and it can be bought back at a lower price to make delivery, and profit from the transaction. (105)

short selling The act of selling short. See Short Sale. (105)

short side Those bear traders whose trading is based on the expectation that prices of securities or commodities will decline.

short squeeze A situation in which the short seller, who has sold a security or commodity is forced to cover or repurchase the security or commodity. Under these circumstances there is a rapid increase in prices.

short stock A stock which has been sold short as differentiated from a long sale.

short term debt Interest-bearing debt payable within one year from date of issue, such as bond anticipation notes, bank loans, and tax anticipation notes and warrants. It includes obligations having no fixed maturity date if payable from a tax levied for collection in the year of their issuance. (7)

short term securities Securities payable on demand or which mature not more than one year from date of issue. (19)

short-term trust An irrevocable trust running for a period of ten years longer, in which the income is payable to a person other than the settlor, and established under the provisions of the Revenue Act of 1954. The income from a trust of this kind is taxable to the income beneficiary and not to the settlor. The agreement may provide that on the date fixed for the termination of the trust, or on the prior death of the income beneficiary, the assets of the trust shall be returned to the settlor. (74)

sibling Children of the same parents. (74)

sick market In the securities business, a weak, seemingly wobbly, tremulous market, giving the appearance of being sick. Previous over-speculation often causes this period of uncertainty and discouragement, and only good news or developments justify taking a position in this market. (105)

sight bill of exchange Any bill of exchange that becomes due and payable when presented by the holder to the party upon whom it is drawn. See Draft. (1)

sight credit Popular designation for a Sight Letter of Credit.

sight draft A draft which is payable on presentation to the drawee—in other words, on "sight" or demand. (85)

signature A person's name or a mark representing it, as signed or written by himself or by deputy, as in subscribing a letter or other document. (93)

signature by mark See X Mark Signature.

signature card A card signed by each depositor and customer of the bank. The signature card is technically a contract between the bank and its customer, in that it recites the obligations of both in their relationship with each other. The principal use of the signature card is that of identification of the depositor. Signature cards are made out in at least two sets, one for the signature file department, where all signatures are kept for ready reference, and the other for the file at the teller's window where the depositor will most frequently transact his business. (1)

signature file department This department is the custodian for all signature cards. The employees of this department issue daily reports on all accounts opened and all accounts closed. As a part of the public relations and "new business" work, the signature file department may write "thank you" letters to new depositors. (1)

signature guaranteed The requirement in the securities business to have a registered owner of a security have a brokerage firm or a bank guarantee his signature so that a good delivery or transfer of the security may be made. (105)

signed instrument Any legal agreement, or note which is written and signed. (59)

silent partner One who is known to the public as a member of the firm but who does not take an active part in the management of the business. (73)

silver certificates United States paper money which was in circulation until 1967. The certificates were redeemable for silver.

simple interest The interest arising from the principal sum only. (5)

simple trust A term known only in tax laws to describe a trust that is required to distribute all of its income currently and that does not provide for any charitable distribution; opposed to complex trust. (74)

simulation The process of imposing various hypothetical conditions on a model in order to observe their effects on certain variables. (126)

single capital structure company Company having only one class of security outstanding. (3)

single debit reporting Normal method used by mortgage bankers for reporting the current status of its mortgages when making a regular remittance to an investor. (121)

single name paper A note for which only one legal entity—the maker—is obligated to make payment at maturity. A legal distinction exists in single name paper, in that if the obligation is incurred for one purpose, or one common interest, the paper may have more than one maker or endorser, and still be termed single name paper. Such a case would be two or more partners making a note for a loan to the common partnership, or a subsidiary company making a note endorsed by the parent company. Single name paper is also frequently termed "Straight Paper." (1)

single option A put or a call option on stock.

single posting system A plan of posting used in the bookkeeping department of a bank. Single posting generally means the posting of a depositor's statement only. The ledger record may be either a carbonized ledger created with the posting of the statement, or a photographed record of the statement (under the Unit-Photographic Plan made on microfilm. This posting plan is to be distinguished from the Dual Plan where the statement is posted in one run and the ledger is posted in another. (1)

single standard Monometallism, a monetary system in which one metal, generally gold is given free and unlimited coinage.

sinking fund A voluntary, or contractually required, fund created by the actual setting aside from earnings a certain sum of money, for a certain number of stated periods of time, in order to accumulate a sufficient sum of money to liquidate or discharge a certain known obligation on the date of its maturity. Such a fund requirement is frequently a part of the obligation of an indebtedness and the contract covering the indebtedness. Such contract may or may not stipulate that such periodic payments be placed in the custody of a third party known as a "Trustee." (1)

sinking fund depreciation method A plan for depreciating fixed assets through the medium of establishing an actual cash fund in the hands of a trustee to be used for subsequent replacement of the assets. The actual interest earned on this fund is credited to the depreciation reserve account. This plan is objectionable because it overstates the burden charges accounts and treats interest earned as an addition to the reserve account instead of as income. (28)

sinking fund requirements The amount by which a Sinking Fund must be increased periodically through contributions and earnings so that the accumulation thereof will be sufficient to redeem Sinking Fund bonds as they mature.

NOTE: The amount required periodically should be calculated on an actuarial basis unless another basis is provided by law. (29)

sinking fund reserve See Reserve for Retirement of Sinking Fund Bonds. (29)

size of the market In the securities business, this term describes the number of round-lots bid for at the highest price showing on the specialist's book and the total number being offered for sale simultaneously at the lowest price quoted, at any specific moment. An answer to a request for the size of the market might be "4 and 2," which means that four hundred shares have been bid for at the highest price and two hundred shares are offered at the lowest price on the book. (105)

skewness Refers to a distribution curve which is not symmetrical.

skip Person owing money who has moved leaving no forwarding address. (26)

skyrocketing A sharp rise in security prices within a short period of time. (105)

slaughter The indiscriminate selling of securities at very low levels, often unnecessarily low. (105)

sleeper An item, individual, or security which has not displayed any unusual characteristics but which is believed to be undervalued and that

increase in value or productivity should develop in the near future.

slide A term used in bookkeeping to describe a posting error by which an amount is wrongly recorded by the bookkeeper's unintentionally placing the decimal one or more digits to the right or left of the true decimal position. Example: Posting $5.03 as $50.30 or as $503.00. (1)

slid off In the securities business, means dropped in price. (105)

slipping A downward movement in the prices of securities or commodities which is not severe.

slow asset Any thing of value which cannot be liquidated at close to its book value within a year.

slump A decline in activity and prices of an economy, a commodity, a security or industry.

small business There are many different definitions depending upon the source of the term. The Small Business Administration, The Census Bureau, The National Industrial Conference Board, The Investment Bankers Association and others have defined the term with somewhat different characteristics. Some definitions permit as many as 500 employees to work for a small business. Others use sales of less than 200,000 dollars a year. Others use relative size in an industry. Still others consider public financing and corporations that are not closed to indicate a business that is not small. For exact meaning, one must know the source using the term and even the time since the Small Business Administration has modified their original definition.

Small Business Investment Company (SBIC) A form of company designed to provide capital to small businesses, licensed and regulated by the Small Business Administration as authorized by Congress in 1958. The SBIC's may make long-term loans or buy convertible debentures or stock in small enterprises, as defined as having less than $5 million in assets, net worth of less than $2 ½ million and average net income after taxes the previous two years not exceeding $250,000. Investor's in SBIC's put up their own money; the SBA matches this amount, and four times this amount (initial capital) can be borrowed to relend to small firms. Investors in SBIC's enjoy a tax advantage in that any loss can be deducted from the taxpayer's ordinary income, not just to offset capital gains taxes. (105)

small loan law A regulatory code covering cash installment loans, administered by the state, and protecting both the borrower and the lender. (131)

small loans Most states have small loan laws which define the size of small loans in their state. Industrial states frequently permit larger amounts to be considered small loans than do agricultural states. Small loans are generally classed separately in the usury laws and may be charged higher rates. Typical interest rates on small loans are 36% + per year on a simple interest computation. Typical small loan maximums by state definition are 300 dollars though the trend is upward.

snowballing The financial term describing the condition occurring when a conglomeration of stop orders around a certain price level are "touched off" successively, causing either an advance or a decline. Stop orders become market orders, i.e., orders to sell at the price prevailing in the market, when a transaction has been consummated at the same price as the stop order. If there are a number of stop orders close together, and the price falls or rises to the first of these, the result often is that the market orders "uncovered" will cause the next stop order price to be reached and so on. This can cause sharp trading swings, thus floor governors of a stock exchange have the authority to suspend stop orders in individual securities if that action seems to be warranted. (105)

Society of Savings and Loan Controllers Formed in 1950 under the sponsorship of the American Savings and Loan Institute as a professional organization, the Society is devoted to improving the professional status of accounting and auditing officers through the development of better accounting methods and new aids to management. The Society presently exists as a separate organization closely allied to the Institute activities and interests. This organization consists of more than 1,500 of the principal accounting and chief auditing officers in savings associations. The society's technical publications are available on a subscription basis to non-members. (31, 92)

soft The condition of a commodity or security market characterized by falling prices with little buying support of the market.

soft money 1. A situation in which interest rates are low and loans are easy to arrange. 2. A paper rather than metallic currency. 3. A nation's currency which is not desired by foreigners in lieu of a "hard" currency which may be domestic or other foreign currency. In recent years nations with unfavorable trade balances or currency restrictions have tended to have soft money.

soft spot A sudden decline in prices by certain stocks amidst a firm or strong general market. (105)

sol Monetary unit of Peru.

sola bill A type of foreign bill of exchange. See Bill of Exchange.

sold out market A market in which liquidation of weakly held contracts has largely been completed and offerings have become scarce. (9)

special administrator An administrator appointed by the court to take over and safeguard an estate pending the appointment of an executor or administrator; sometimes known as a temporary administrator. (74)

special assessment bond(s) Bonds payable from the proceeds of special assessments. If the bonds are payable only from the proceeds of special assessments levied against the properties presumed to be benefited by such improvements or services. (29)

special assessment liens Claims which governmental units have upon properties until special assessments levied against them have been paid.

NOTE: The term is sometimes limited to those delinquent special assessments for the collection of which legal action has been taken through the filing of liens. (29)

special assessment roll The official list showing the amount of special assessments levied against such property presumed to be benefited by an improvement or service. (29)

special bid A method of filling an order to buy a large block of stock on the floor of the Exchange. In a Special Bid, the bidder for the block of stock—a pension fund, for instance, will pay a special commission to the broker who represents him in making the purchase. The seller does not pay a commission. The Special Bid is made on the floor of the Exchange at a fixed price which may not be below the last sale of the security or the current bid in the regular market, whichever is higher. Member firms may sell this stock for customers directly to the buyer's broker during trading hours. (2)

special deposit A fund established for the payment of interest, dividends or other debts, or to insure the performance of contracts, and other deposits of a special nature as distinguished from sinking funds. (19)

special depository A bank authorized by the United States Treasury to receive as deposits the proceeds of sales of government bonds.

special devise A gift, by will, of a specific parcel of real property. (88)

special dividend Might be called an extra dividend; declared in addition to any regular payments of cash or stock. (105)

special endorsement A negotiable instrument made out to the order of John Jones would have a special endorsement if he endorsed it with the words: "Pay to the order of Frank Brown" and then signed it "John Jones". This is an unqualified endorsement which limits the negotiability to Frank Brown or his order.

special guardian A guardian appointed by a court for a particular purpose connected with the affairs of a minor or an incompetent person; sometimes a guardian ad litem is known as a special guardian. (74)

special indorsement See Special Endorsement.

special interest account A term used by commercial banks to describe a savings account. Some states do not permit a commercial bank to accept "savings" accounts. They may, however, accept deposits on which interest is paid and under the same conditions as a savings bank, but under another name such as "Special Interest Accounts," "Thrift Accounts," and the like. (1)

special issues Securities issued by the Treasury for investment of reserves of government trust funds and for certain payments to veterans. (7)

specialist A member of a stock exchange who assumes two responsibilities: First, to maintain an orderly market, insofar as reasonably practicable, in the stocks in which he is registered as a specialist. In order to maintain an orderly market, the specialist must be prepared to buy or sell for his own account, to a reasonable degree, when there is a temporary disparity between supply and demand. Second, the specialist acts as a broker's broker. When a commission broker on the Exchange floor receives a limit order, say, to buy at $50 a stock then selling at $60—he cannot wait at the particular post where the stock is traded until the price reaches the specified level. So he leaves the order with the specialist, who will try to execute it in the market if and when the stock declines to the specified price. At all times the specialists must put his customers' interests above his own. There are about 350 specialists on the N.Y. Stock Exchange. See Limit Order. (2)

specialist block purchase Purchase by the specialist for his own account of a large block of stock outside the regular market on the Exchange. Such purchases may be made only when the sale of the block could not be made in the regular market within a reasonable time and at reasonable prices, and when the purchase by the specialist would aid him in maintaining a fair and orderly market. (2)

specialist block sale Opposite of the Specialist Block Purchase. Under exceptional circumstances, the specialist may sell a block of stock outside the regular market on the Exchange for his own account at a price above the prevailing market. The price is negotiated between the specialist and the broker for the buyer. (2)

specialist's book Also called simply, "the book". It is composed of orders that have come to the specialist in a security on the stock exchange floor at prices limited to other than the prevailing market price. The orders are kept in a book, to be executed at such time as the market price reaches their limitations. A specialist will have a book on each security he specializes in standing ready to accept orders from brokers who are unable to execute them. (105)

specialized management trust An investment company whose investment policy is confined to securities of businesses found in one industry such as oils, electronics or aircraft.

special loan A loan involving unusual collateral hence a higher rate of interest is often required. Over-the-counter securities usually are classified in this category. (105)

special offering Occasionally a large block of stock becomes available for sale which, due to its size and the market in that particular issue, calls for special handling. A notice is printed on the ticker tape announcing that the stock will be offered for sale on the floor of the Exchange at a fixed price. Member firms may buy this stock for customers directly from the seller's broker during trading hours. The price is usually based on the last transaction in the regular auction market. If there are more buyers than stock, allotments are made. Only the seller pays a commission on a special offering. See Secondary Distribution. (2)

special partner The same as a limited partner and is one whose liability for the debts of the firm is limited. (73)

special power of appointment See Limited Power of Appointment; Power of Appointment. (74)

special situation Usually describes venture capital type of investment, but may also refer to conservative but relatively unknown investment or to heavy commitments in investments which, in the opinion of the management, are temporarily undervalued by the market. (3)

special stock That stock which is issued for a special, and probably not recurring, purpose.

specialty or specialized fund Investment company concentrating its holdings in specific industry groups (insurance, oil, aviation stocks, etc.). (3)

specialty stock A stock which advances independently of the general market; attracts attention even though it does not belong to any particular industry group. (105)

special warranty deed A warranty only against the acts of the grantor himself and all persons claiming by, through, or under him. (54)

specie Coined money.

specie payment Payment in coin rather than with paper money.

specific bequest See Specific Legacy. (74)

specific devise A gift, by will, of a specific parcel of real property. (74)

specific legacy A gift, by will, of a specific article of personal property, such as a watch. (88)

speculate To invest in securities with the intention of making a profit over a relatively short period of time. Although not gambling, speculation involves few of the decisions of true investment, which considers growth possibilities and income producing capacity of the company concerned. (105)

speculation Buying or selling at a large risk—large profit or large loss results. (93)

speculative securities A classification for securities which have a relatively large risk.

speculator One who is willing to assume a relatively large risk in the hope of gain. His principal concern is to increase his capital rather than his dividend income. The speculator may buy and sell the same day or speculate in an enterprise which he does not expect to be profitable for years. See Investor. (2)

spendthrift provision A provision in a trust instrument which limits the right of the beneficiary to dispose of his interest, as by assignment, and the right of his creditors to reach it, as by attachment. (88)

spendthrift trust A trust designed to protect the beneficiary from his own improvidence or lack of ability in handling the estate. The principal is typically kept under the control of a trust company and periodic payments of income from the trust are made.

spilling stock To dispose of securities out of necessity, throwing the stocks on the market for sale. (105)

spin-off Division of a corporate business into two or more companies by the original corporation transferring certain of the properties to another corporation formed for that purpose and then distributing the new corporation's stock to the original corporation's stockholders in proportion to their holdings.

split The division of the outstanding shares of a corporation into a larger number of shares. A 3-for-1 split by a company with 1 million shares outstanding would result in 3 million shares outstanding. Each holder of 100 shares before the 3-for-1 split would have 300 shares, although his proportionate equity in the company would remain the same, since 100 parts of 1 million are the equivalent of 300 parts of 3 million. Ordinarily splits must be voted by directors and approved by shareholders. See Stock Dividend. (2)

split close 1. Term referring to the range of prices in commodities traded at the close of any market session. 2. Also would describe the situation existing, when, at the close of a market session; at least one of the Industrial Utility or Rail market indices closed higher or lower than the others when compared with the previous session's closing averages. For example, a split close is indicated if the Rail average closes at a higher price than the previous session, while the Industrial and Utility averages close lower. (105)

split commission A prohibited practice under New York Stock Exchange rules whereby a broker would split his commission with his customer or someone else who solicits business for him. A Registered Representative could lose his license for life. This practice should not be confused with the legal practice of members "giving-up" the name of another member for whom they executed the transaction. (105)

split down The opposite of a stock split. In this situation the number of outstanding shares is reduced and the market price is increased. This rare practice is also known as a reverse split. (105)

split opening That situation on a commodity or security exchange in which a security or a commodity has simultaneous opening prices which are spread or different. This can occur when a number of traders at a trading post break up into groups and the sales take place in two groups at the same time but at different prices.

split order An order to buy or to sell a given commodity or security which, because of the large size of the transaction might cause a material price fluctuation, is "split" or executed in smaller units over a period of time.

split quotation A quotation for a security or a commodity which is expressed in a different unit than the adopted standard quotation. Most stocks on the New York Stock Exchange are normally quoted in ⅛th of a point units. For such securities to be quoted in 1/16th of a point would be split quotations.

split schedule loan A mortgage which sets up interest only for a few years and then a complete amortization schedule. It also is more generally accomplished through split amortization schedules on the loan.

split stock The new outstanding stock resulting from a corporation's stock split. (105)

sponsorship The market support or interest which is known to be associated with a particular security; for example, Underwriters of a security issue generally stand behind it, ready to support it in the open market. (105)

spot In commodity trading and foreign exchange, this term indicates ready delivery as compared with some future time.

spot cash Immediate cash payment as distinguished from payment at some later date.

spot commodity The physical commodity.

spot exchange transaction Is a purchase or sale of foreign currency for ready delivery. In practice, market usage normally prescribes settlement within two working days. For purposes of the Fund's Articles of Agreement, the term excludes transactions in banknotes or coins. (130)

spot news Any kind of abrupt news or condition which will have temporary effect on general market action. (105)

spot price The selling price of the physical commodity.

spot sale The sale of a product for cash and current delivery rather than for at some future date.

spotted market That condition of a market for securities or commodities characterized by little price movement while some are up some are also down and no general price trend or movement is observed.

spouse A husband or wife.

spread 1. The difference between the bid and asked price. 2. The use of both a put and a call on a specific security. 3. The purchase of one futures contract and the simultaneous sale of the same commodity but in a different month with both the sale and purchase remaining open until one of the contracts matures.

spurt A rapid increase in prices on a commodity or security exchange.

squeeze In the monetary sense, a shortage of available cash due to such factors as tight money, irregular cash flow or difficulty in being able to borrow. It may also refer to a situation where short sellers are forced to cover, that is, buy long to balance the short sale.

stabilization fund Fund established 1934 as result of the devaluation of the dollar with two billion dollars to stabilize exchange values of the United States Dollar, to deal in such things as foreign exchange and gold and to invest in direct obligations of the United States government. Under the Bretton Woods Agreement much of the assets of the Fund were used to contribute to the International Bank for Reconstruction and Development and the International Monetary Fund. See World Bank.

stabilized dollar Plan proposed by Fisher of Yale to provide constant purchasing power for the dollar by making it into a commodity standard by means of changing the weight of the gold content of the dollar in order to compensate for the changing prices.

stable money Money which does not fluctuate much in purchasing power. One of the goals of the Federal Reserve Authorities is to maintain a stable level of prices.

stag A term used at the London Stock Exchange to describe anyone who subscribes to a new security issue with the intention of selling for a profit in the "after offering" market. Such a person has not invested for the long term, but hopes that the price will rise to a premium. (105)

staggered election An election of a board of directors in which only part of the board stands for election in any one year. A board of twenty-five could have five members only elected in any one year and, thus, it would take five years to have a completely new board. This has the advantage of providing continuity of service but the disadvantage of preventing the stockholders from unseating unsatisfactory directors within a feasible period.

stale check Generally any check dated 90 days prior to presentation for payment is considered stale. However, the time element is usually determined by local regulations. Such checks are marked "stale" and are returned unpaid to the bank from which they were received. This is done principally for the protection of the depositor, who will be informed of the return, and may elect to write out a new check to replace the "stale check." (1)

stamped security See Bonds, Stamped.

stamps (tax) Instruments representing the amount of tax levied on the issue, sale or transfer of a security by the federal government (Commissioner of Internal Revenue) or by a state commission. (105)

Standard & Poor's Corporation A leading organization in the field of financial service which provides corporate information such as dividend, stock, and bond reports as well as other pertinent records. (105)

standard bullion Bullion which is composed of the same proportions of metals and the same degree of purity as the standard gold and silver coins and, thus, is ready for coinage without further refining.

standard money Primary Money. A monetary unit which is made of the standard such as gold. A coin which is worth as much as its face value—if used as a commodity.

standard of living Those luxuries and necessities which an individual or class of people generally possess or use.

standard of value The function of serving as a gage or model of value. This is one of the major functions of money since the monetary value is expressed in units of the standard.

standard securities Stocks and bonds of established companies of good reputation and experience.

standby commitment Commitment for a limited period made, for a fee, as security for a construction lender by an investor who stands ready to make or purchase the committed loan at above-market terms in the event that a take out commitment cannot be obtained on market terms. (121)

standby controls Those actions legally permitted to be instituted by the government in the event of some emergency but which are not enforced during normal periods.

standstill agreement That agreement between a debtor and his creditor or creditors under which new conditions of a loan or loans are reached. In most cases this will involve a postponement of payments and may also include a reduction in the principal due. Such agreements are the result of adverse economic developments in which the debtor obviously cannot meet the terms of the loan and the creditor or creditors recognize that it is to their and the debtors best interest to accept terms which have some probability of being met rather than possessing a claim of a debtor in default.

state bank A corporation organized under the general banking law of a state and authorized to do a commercial banking business—that is, receive deposits subject to check and make loans.

It usually performs a variety of other functions as well. In a broader sense, a state bank is any bank chartered by the state. (85)

state banking department The organization in each state which supervises the operations and affairs of state banking institutions. The chief officer of this department is designated superintendent of banks or commissioner of banks or is given some comparable title. (90)

state bonds A division of municipal bonds; or the promissory notes of a state. (59)

stated value The value given to a corporation's stock and carried on the books if there is no assigned par value. (105)

statement analysis The application of ratios such as Current Ratio, Turnover Ratio and other accounting and credit measuring techniques for the purpose of reaching a decision on the outlook of a company or a security.

statement, annual See "Annual Statement". (42)

statement clerk An employee in the bookkeeping department of a bank. This title has two different meanings as applied to the duties of the clerk. In some banks the statement clerk posts the statements for depositors' checking accounts under the Dual System. In other banks this title is used in describing an employee who is responsible for verification of all paid checks listed on a depositor's statement to see that the statement is complete before it is mailed to the depositor. (1)

statement of condition A detailed listing of a bank's resources, liabilities, and capital accounts showing its condition on a given date. On requests (calls) by supervisory authorities several times a year, banks are required to submit sworn statements of condition. In general accounting, this type of financial report is known as a balance sheet. (85)

statement of income and expenses A summary report which shows the amount and sources of the income, the amount and kind of each expense, and the net increase in proprietorship. (73)

statement of operations A summary of the financial operations during a given period showing the sources of income and its allocation to the payment of operating expenses, dividends to holders of savings accounts and allocations to reserves for the protection of savers. (31, 92)

statement of policy A guide issued by the Securities and Exchange Commission to assist issuers, underwriters, dealers and salesmen in complying with statutory disclosure standards as applied to sales literature, reports to shareholders, and other communications "addressed to or intended for distribution to prospective investors." (3)

State Street The financial area of Boston corresponding to Wall Street in New York.

static economy An economy which is at equilibrium. That is, the forces of supply and demand which are equated by price are such that little change in production or demand is created.

statute A law established by the act of the legislature. (5)

statute of frauds A statute, first enacted in England in 1677, designed to prevent many fraudulent practices by requiring proof of a specific kind, usually in writing, of the important transactions of business, declaring that no action shall be brought or that no contract shall be allowed to be good when the transaction is not so evidenced. For example, the original statute declared that all trusts of land shall be in writing. While each state has its own statute of frauds designed to serve the same general purpose as the original statute, many of these statutes differ greatly from the original statute, but the general purpose of all of them is to prevent fraudulent transactions by requiring that obligations to be enforceable be in writing. (74)

statute of limitations A statute which bars suits upon valid claims after the expiration of a specified period of time. The period varies for different kinds of claims. In most states there is a twenty-year limitation on judgments; ordinarily contract claims expire in six years; and claims for torts (injuries to persons or property) expire within a shorter time. Each state has its own statute or statutes of limitations. (88)

statute of uses An English statute enacted in 1536 which provided that the legal as well as the beneficial title to land held for the use of a person vested in that person. There were certain exceptions to this vesting which opened the way for the development of the law of trusts. (74)

statutes of descent Laws, rules, or statutes governing the descent of real property under intestacy. (74)

statutes of distribution Laws, rules, or statutes governing the distribution of personal property under intestacy. (74)

statutes of mortmain Several early English statutes, dating back as far as the Thirteenth Century, restricting the alienation of land to a corporation, particularly to an ecclesiastical corporation. Mortmain means dead hand. In the early English law an ecclesiastic was deemed civilly dead; hence, the origin of the term dead hand. (74)

statutes of will Statutes (the first one passed in 1541) providing that no will shall be valid and no devise or bequest shall be valid unless the will is in writing, signed and attested in the manner provided by the statute. (88)

statutory exemptions Specified articles of personal property and a specified amount of cash left by decedent which are set apart for his immediate family and which may not be subjected to the claims of creditors. (74)

statutory investment An investment which a trustee is specifically authorized to make under the terms of the statutes of the state having jurisdiction of the trust. (74)

statutory receivership Most commonly found proceeding against insolvent debtor brought generally under Federal Bankruptcy legislation though state statutes may at times be applicable.

statutory warranty deed A warranty deed form prescribed by state statutes. (54)

stay law A statute which restricts the use of certain legal remedies, generally in the form of a postponement.

steady The condition of a business, industry, economy security or commodity in which activity is at normal levels and prices do not fluctuate much.

sterilized gold A technique for preventing newly imported gold from expanding the credit base of a nation. One method of gold sterilization is to have the Treasury of the United States pay for the gold with a draft on a commercial bank in which it has an account rather than drawing upon the Federal Reserve System and then issuing gold certificates. This reduces the multiple expansion potential and sterilizes or prevents the normal inflation which would usually result.

sterling That which has a standard of fineness or value such as established by the government of Great Britain for silver or gold or bank notes.

sterling area Those nations since 1939 which have been closely tied to the British pound and the monetary policies of the British Empire.

sterling credit A letter of credit denominated in British pounds sterling.

sterling exchange A bill or check denominated in pounds sterling and payable through a bank in Great Britain.

stiffened The condition of a commodity or security price movement characterized by a modest increase in price or prices.

stipend A salary.

stock 1. The capital stock of a bank is determined by established banking laws, such as the Bank Act of 1933 and the Bank Act of 1935, and various state banking laws. All bank capital stock must be issued with some stated par value, although the par value is not fixed. See National Bank (for regulations on capital stock in National banks). 2. A certificate evidencing ownership in a corporate enterprise. The stock of a corporation is usually divided into two classes, common and preferred. The former represents the basic ownership and its holders' claims to income and assets are subordinate to the claims of bondholders, creditors, and preferred stockholders. Common stock usually has the voting privilege. The holder of preferred stock always enjoys priority as to income and generally as to assets, however, his income is usually limited to a definite percentage, regardless of earnings. (1, 74)

stock ahead Sometimes an investor who has entered an order to buy or sell a stock at a certain price will see transactions at that price reported on the ticker tape while his own order has not been executed. The reason is that other buy and sell orders at the same price came in to the specialist ahead of his and had priority. See Specialist's Book. (2)

stock allotment The amount of stock which the manager of an underwriting syndicate sets aside as the portion for a member of the syndicate to distribute.

stock assessment The levy which is made upon a share holder to make up a capital deficiency caused by adverse economic developments in the corporation's operation.

stock-bonus trust A trust established by a corporation to enable its employees to receive benefits in the form of the corporation's own stock as a reward for meritorious service or as a means of sharing in the profits of the enterprise. (74)

stock borrowed Stock borrowed by one broker from another. Often used to effect delivery in short sales. A premium and/or interest may be charged for the use of the borrowed stock. (105)

stockbroker An individual or firm engaged in the business of selling securities.

stock certificate An evidence of ownership in the form of a certificate. A stock certificate shows the number of shares owned in the name of the owner. It shows the corporation issuing the capital stock and states whether or not the stock is a par value or a non-par value stock. It names the par value, if the stock issued has such value. It cites the rights of the stockholder, such as voting or non-voting rights. In the case of preferred stock, it stipulates the dividend rate which is paid on the preferred stock, and tells whether it is cumulative or not. It also states whether the preferred stockholder has voting rights, and how many dividends can be passed before the stockholder exercises voting rights. (1)

stock certificate book A book of blank stock certificates. (73)

Stock Clearing Corporation A subsidiary of the N.Y. Stock Exchange which acts as a central agency for security deliveries and money payments between member firms of the Exchange. (2)

stock dividend A dividend paid in securities rather than cash. The dividend may be additional shares of the issuing company, or in shares of another company (usually a subsidiary) held by the company. See Ex-Dividend; Split. (2)

stock exchange 1. An association of brokers and dealers engaged in the business of buying and selling securities. 2. The place where such brokers and dealers meet to do their trading. (85)

stock exchange broker See Stockbroker.

stock exchange seat Membership in a stock exchange.

stock exchanges Organizations which provide a market for the purpose of trading in bonds and stocks. Regulations for the admission of securities for trading on the stock exchanges are very stringent, thus, securities traded on stock exchanges have a "Grade A" value to investors and others. (1)

stockholder The owner of shares in a corporation which entitles him to a proportionate share of the company's undivided assets, declared dividends, proportionate voting power, and quite frequently a preemptive right which enables the stockholder to subscribe to additional shares before the general public. (105)

stockholder list The list of all stockholder's of a corporation entitled to vote in corporation affairs. Each name in the alphabetical list contains the corresponding address and number of shares held. (105)

stockholder of record A stockholder whose name is registered on the books of the issuing corporation. See Record Date; Ex-Dividend; Ex-Rights. (2)

stockholders annual report Report compiled annually for stockholders showing financial position and progress, etc., during the fiscal year. (19)

stockholders' ledger A subsidiary ledger that contains detailed information about the stock owned by each stockholder. (73)

stock loaned That stock loaned with interest by one broker to another. (105)

stock markets Those security exchanges such as the New York Stock Exchange, The American Stock Exchange, The National Stock Exchange. In addition to dealing in stocks most exchanges also trade in other securities such as bonds, rights, warrants.

stock option See Option.

stock option contract A negotiable instrument, also called a "paper" or "privilege", which gives the purchaser the right to buy (call) or sell (put) the number of shares of stock designated in the contract at a fixed price within a stated period of time. (105)

stock power A form of assignment executed by the owner of stock which contains an irrevocable appointment of an attorney-in-fact to make the actual transfer on the books of the corporation. See Power of Attorney. (74)

stock purchase option A privilege whereby specified securities in a given amount and at a given price may be purchased within a specified period of time. The details are set forth normally in contract form. (118)

stock purchase trust A trust under which a surviving stockholder of a close corporation may purchase the stock of a deceased stockholder; usually, but not necessarily, an insurance trust. (74)

stock purchase warrant An instrument granted by a corporation which gives the holder the privilege of purchasing more shares in the corporation at a stipulated price and at a predetermined date. A warrant may have a market value of its own depending upon the outlook of the stock it is associated with. Some warrants are detachable and can be bought and sold in the open market. A non-detachable warrant may be traded only with the security of which it is a part. (105)

stock quotation The price of the stock. Generally the quotation is in terms of a round lot and expressed in eighths or units of 12½ cents. Quotations are frequently found in the financial section of newspapers and business publications. In addition brokerage offices subscribe to a service which provides the quotations from the covered exchanges in the form of a ticker tape or translux projection.

stock quotation instrument The original name for the stock ticker. (105)

stock registrar The bank or trust company designated by the corporation to control the issuing of certificates to the amount properly authorized by the process of registering the certificates as they are issued by the transfer agent. Since the signature of an official of the registrar is required in addition to the identification of the registrar and the certificate number it is easy to make certain that more stock is not issued than that which has been authorized.

stock rights See Rights; Warrant.

stock split The division of shares of stock of a corporation which goes to increase the number of outstanding shares but does not increase the capitalization of the company. (74)

stock transfer The act of recording the change in ownership of stock on the records of a corporation's stock transfer book. This includes the maintenance of records for a corporation of the complete list of stockholders; the certificate identification evidencing the ownership of each stockholder; and the total number of shares owned by each stockholder. The stock transfer agent must maintain a record of all transfers of title to stock from one stockholder to another. It is the responsibility of the stock transfer agent to furnish a complete list of the stockholders and the number of shares held by each, whenever a dividend is declared. In the declaration of dividends, the board of directors stipulates the date of record in which stockholders shall participate. Transfers of stock after this date of record do not carry the right of dividend to the new owner except by agreement with the stockholder who gave up the title through the transfer. (1)

stock-transfer agent The agent of a corporation appointed for the purpose of effecting transfers of stock from one stockholder to another by the actual cancellation of the surrendered certificates and the issuance of new certificates in the name of the new stockholder. (74)

stock transfer book A special journal that is used to record transfers of stock. Its entries are posted to the stockholders' ledger. (73)

stock transfer tax The federal and/or state tax on sale or transfer and, in some cases, loan of stock.

stock trust certificate A trust certificate which is exchanged for stock. Typically the certificate has a limited life during which a trustee has sole voting authority for the stock and has physical possession of the certificate. The beneficial owner is issued the trust certificate which entitles him to the income of the security. If not used in violation of the antitrust laws the certificate may be used for control purposes.

stock warrants See Rights; Warrant.

stock watering The act of issuing stock in exchange for overvalued assets. In effect, this dilutes the equity of those owners who were issued stock for properly valued assets.

stock yield The rate of return on a stock based upon its market value as of a particular date and the dividend being currently paid by the company. (74)

stop limit order A form of a stop order by which a specific price limit is set. Any price below this will not be accepted if it is a sell order, or any price above this will not be accepted if this is a buy order. One danger is that such an order may miss the market since the stop order becomes a market order when the stop price is reached or passed through. For example, a stop limit order to sell at 60 means that if the price passes through 60, the order has missed it. By placing the stop at 60 and the limit at 59 ½ the chances for the order to be effective are enhanced. (105)

stop loss Any provision in a policy designed to cut off the company's loss at a given point. A stop loss may be an aggregate payable under the policy, maximum payable for any one disability, or the like. (50+)

stop loss order or stop order An order entered to buy or sell when the market reaches a specified point. A stop order to buy becomes a market order when the commodity sells (or is bid) at or above the stop price. A stop order to sell becomes a market order when the commodity sells (or is offered) at or below the stop price. The purpose of a stop loss order is to limit losses or protect profits. (9)

stop payment If a depositor issues a check and for some reason wishes to rescind the payment, he has the right to request the bank to stop payment of this item. The depositor must make his request either in writing or by a personal call. A stop payment notice is prepared and signed by the depositor giving a complete description of the item to be stopped. This includes the number of the check, the date of issue, the payee and amount, and the reason for stopping payment. If this check is presented for payment, it is the responsibility of the bank to refuse payment and to return it to the holder. The holder must then seek his repayment from the maker who stopped payment. The most common and valid use of a stop payment is where a check has been lost en route to the payee. The maker will stop payment on the original check and issue a duplicate in settlement of his debt to the payee. A disagreement over a purchase may cause the maker of a check to stop payment to a payee. The bank should refuse payment of a check through the authorized stop payment order, and let the parties involved settle their own disagreement. Many banks exact service fees for each month a stop payment is in effect. Other banks try to exercise due care in the matter of stop payment by carrying the stop payment jacket on the account for 90 days, after which the stop payment is placed in another ledger, where it is isolated and where better control can be maintained over it. If the item is then presented, its date will show it to be a stale check. See Stale Check. (1)

stopped at A guaranteed price given by the Specialist in a stock to a buyer or a seller of the same security. By this method the execution price will be better than or equal to the price "stopped at", or guaranteed. (105)

stopped out Condition forced by the execution of a round-lot sale in a security at a price at or below the stop price of an order on the books. The stop order became a market order at this point and was executed at the best obtainable price. (105)

stopped stock A service performed in most cases by the specialist-for an order given him by a commission broker. Let's say XYZ just sold at $50 a share. Broker A comes along with an order to buy 100 shares at the market. The lowest offer is $50.50. Broker A believes he can do better for his client than $50.50, perhaps might get the stock at $50.25. But he doesn't want to take a chance that he'll miss the market—that is, the next sale might be $50.50 and the following one even higher. So he asks the specialist if he will stop 100 at ½ ($50.50). The specialist agrees. The specialist guarantees Broker A he will get 100 shares at 50 ½ if the stock sells at the price. In the meantime, if the specialist or Broker A succeeds in executing the order at $50.25, the stop is called off. See Specialist. (2)

stop price That price where a stop order becomes a market order. (105)

straddle The simultaneous purchase of options to buy and sell a specific security. The exercising of both a put and a call in the same security. In commodities, the simultaneous sale of one futures month with the purchase of the same commodity in a different month.

straddle the market The simultaneous purchase of an option to buy a specific security and the purchase of an option to sell a different security. The assumption is that if the market moves in either direction that what is gained or lost by the put option is about balanced by the gain or loss by the call option.

straight amortization plan An amortization plan that provides for the payment of a fixed amount of principal at specified intervals, with interest payable on the remaining balance of the loan. (89)

straight bill of lading A bill of lading which states a specific person to whom the goods should be delivered and which is not negotiable.

straight letter of credit An irrevocable letter of credit which has been confirmed. See Letter of Credit.

straight-line depreciation Depreciation figured at a fixed percentage of the cost basis of the property over a given life of the property, as opposed to the declining balance method, or the sum-of-the-digits method; a term frequently found in tax returns. (74)

straight loan A loan granted an individual, or other legal entity, where the basis for granting the credit is the general ability to pay unsupported by any form of collateral security. See Unsecured Loans. (1)

straight term mortgage loan A mortgage loan granted for a fixed term of years, the entire loan becoming due at the end of that time. (89)

strap A Stock Option Contract combining two Calls and one Put. See Strip. (105)

street The New York financial community concentrated in the Wall Street area. (2)

street broker An over-the-counter broker as distinguished from a broker who is a member of an exchange.

street certificate A security or stock certificate which has been made out to a broker and which the broker has endorsed so that it is negotiable and thus may be transferred to others.

street loan See Call Loan.

street name Securities held in the name of a broker instead of his customer's name are said to be carried in a "street name." This occurs when the securities have been bought on margin or when the customer wishes the security to be held by the broker. (2)

street orders Form of order used by representative of one carrier to secure tickets of another carrier's issue, settlement of which is made direct or through accounting office. (19)

street, the A designation for financial centers in general or more specifically, the New York financial center (known as Wall Street). (103)

strike from the list The action taken by a stock exchange in suspending a security from further dealings and canceling its trading privileges on that exchange. (105)

strike suit A legal action brought mostly for nuisance value. See Ex Gratia Payment. (5)

striking price The fixed price at which a stock may be bought in a Call contract, or sold in a Put contract. (105)

stringency The condition in the money market characterized by difficulty in obtaining credit and increasing rates of interest.

stringent terms Severe or strict terms. (93)

strip A Stock Option Contract combining two Puts (obligations to accept delivery of stock) and one call (obligation to deliver). (105)

strong The condition of a market characterized by a volume of activity above normal and an upward trend in prices.

strong hands or weak hands The technical terms applied to security holders. Strong hands are considered to be ones in which securities are held for investment purposes over a period of time, such as institutions. Weak hands include those "investors" who will sell at the slightest chance of profit or sell out during reactions, and include the general public, traders and other speculators. (105)

stub 1. The portion of a document such as a check or security certificate used for making a record of data on the instrument. The term is generally preceded by the name of the document such as a check stub. 2. In statistical tables the stub describes the data found in the rows of the table and are found at the left in the body of the table.

subchapter M The sections of the Internal Revenue Code which provide special tax treatment for "regulated investment companies." (3)

subject bid A bid which is not firm but rather exploratory in the expectation that it may induce an offer which will permit negotiation.

subjective value The value which an individual may place upon goods for his own purposes. (89)

subject offer An offer which is not firm but rather exploratory in the expectation that it may induce a bid which will permit additional negotiation on price.

subject to call Securities such as preferred stocks and various bonds may be callable at the option of the company debtor for redemption. They are thus described as being subject to call.

subject to check The demand deposits of a commercial bank are "subject to check" withdrawal as differentiated from the time deposits which are not payable on demand as a legal right though in practice most banks will honor drafts on time deposits.

subject to prior sale Underwriters of securities and merchants advertising goods for sale recognize that if the market is strong and the supply is limited that there may be more buy orders than merchandise. The disclaimer "subject to prior sale" thus warns late bidders that the product may have already been sold. In addition such a statement may at times serve as a stimulant for submitting early bids.

subject to redemption See Subject to Call.

submission Mortgage banker's offering of mortgages for purchase by an investor. (121)

subordination Acknowledgement by a creditor in writing that the debt due him from a specified debtor shall have a status inferior or subordinate to the debt which the debtor owes another creditor. (89)

subordination agreement Where more than one legal entity has an interest or claim upon the assets of a prospective borrower, a bank may require that the other interested parties sign subordination agreements before a loan will be granted. The subordination agreement is an agreement in which another interested party grants the bank a priority claim or preference to the assets of the borrower ahead of any claim that he may have. (1)

subpoena A writ or order commanding the person named in it to appear and testify in a legal proceeding. (93)

subrogation The substitution of one person for another with reference to a lawful claim or right and frequently referred to as the doctrine of substitution. It is a device adopted or invented by equity to compel the ultimate discharge of a debt or obligation by him who in good conscience should pay it. (74)

subscriber One who agrees in writing to purchase a certain offering such as a certain number of shares of designated stock of a given corporation, or a certain number of bonds of a given stipulated (par) value. (1)

subscribers' ledger A subsidiary ledger that contains all information about the subscription and the payments of each subscriber. (73)

subscribing witness One who sees a document signed or hears the signature acknowledged by the signer and who signs his own name to the document, such as the subscribing witness to a will; to be distinguished from an attesting witness. (74)

subscription The offer to purchase a certain offering as a certain number of shares of stipulated stock, or bonds, for a stipulated amount of money. Such offer is not binding unless accepted by the proper authorized representatives of the issuing firm or corporation. See Subscriber. (1)

subscription book A book consisting of the subscription blanks that have been turned over to the bookkeeper. It contains the information that serves as a basis for recording the subscriptions receivable in the general journal. (73)

subscription cash record A memorandum cash record of down payments and installment payments received from subscribers to capital stock. (73)

subscription list An agreement signed by subscribers indicating the amount of stock that each subscriber has agreed to purchase. (73)

subscription price The offering price at which new or additional security issues of a corporation may be purchased. (105)

subscription rights A privilege to the stockholders of a corporation to purchase proportionate amounts of a new issue of securities, at an established price, usually below the current market price; also, the negotiable certificate evidencing such privilege. (21)

subscriptions receivable A current asset account that shows the amount to be collected from subscribers to capital stock in a corporation. (73)

subscription warrant The document delivered to the shareholder of record which evidences his right to subscribe to new shares under stated terms and conditions as to price, time and amount.

subsidiary coins Any coin with the denomination of less than one dollar including minor coins such as pennies or cents.

substituted trustee A trustee appointed by the court (not named or provided for in the trust instrument) to serve in the place of the original trustee or of a prior trustee; to be distinguished from a successor trustee. (88)

substitution, law of Economic concept that if one product or service may be readily exchanged or substituted for another that the prices of the two must be relatively close.

substitution of collateral The act of exchanging or replacing one portion of collateral such as a block of stock with another block of stock or notes.

subvene A grant such as a subsidy.

succession The act or fact of a person's becoming entitled to property of a deceased person, whether by operation of law upon his dying intestate or by taking under his will. (88)

succession tax 1. A tax upon the transmission of property by a deceased person, in which case it will be charged upon the whole estate, regardless of the manner in which it is to be distributed, in which case it is called a probate or estate tax. 2. The more common form of a tax on the privilege of taking property by will or by inheritance or by succession in any other form upon the death of the owner, and in such case it is imposed upon each legacy or distributive share of the estate as it is received. It is then usually called a legacy or succession tax. (74)

successive beneficiaries 1. Beneficiaries who take one after another by succession. Thus, under a will in which property is left to A for life, then to B for life, and then to C outright, B and C are successive beneficiaries. 2. The inheritance of property by descent or transmission to the next in a succession—as from parent to child and so on down the direct line. (74)

successor trustee A trustee following the original or a prior trustee the appointment of whom is provided for in the trust instrument; to be distinguished from a substituted trustee. (88)

sucre Monetary unit of Equador.

summons A legal notice requiring a person to answer a complaint within a specified time. (93)

superintendent of banks See state banking department. (90)

superseded suretyship rider A continuity of coverage clause in the form of a rider attached to a new fidelity bond, taking the place of another bond and agreeing to pay losses that would be recoverable under the first bond except that the discovery period has expired. Losses caused by dishonest employees frequently have been found to have occurred at various times stretching over a period of years. This may involve a chain of several bonds, each one superseding a prior obligation. These losses will be covered if the chain of bonds is unbroken and each has included the superseded suretyship rider. (50, 52)

supervisory authority The official or officials authorized by law to see that associations are operated in conformity with the charter, statutes and by-laws governing the operation of associations. (31, 92)

supply To offer or provide for sale. The supply of securities, along with the demand, affect price movements. A large supply may have a price depressing effect. (105)

supply and demand, law of The theory that the price of a product fluctuates in the same direction as demand and in the opposite direction of the supply.

supply area The price area on a security or market average chart which indicates a resistance level, or a place where previous advances have been extinguished. (105)

support Action by an individual, firm or agency such as the Federal Reserve banks in purchasing government securities in the open market or of the Department of Agriculture in buying agricultural commodities in the market. Such purchases then tend to push up prices of the products or items so purchased or supported.

supporting orders Any orders which may be entered to support the price of a particular security. These buy orders may be by a Specialist in his stabilizing function, or entered by selling organizations to support the price of their underwritten issue. (105)

supporting schedules Additional lists of facts or financial reports that are used with the balance sheet or profit and loss statement as supplementary reports. (73)

support level A technical term indicating an area of repeated demand on the price chart of a security or market average. This area has stopped price declines in the past, and promoted rallies. (105)

support the market The entering of buy orders at or slightly below the prevailing market level to support and stabilize the existing prices and promote a rise in prices if possible. (105)

surcharge Used as a noun an amount in excess of the value of the property held by a fiduciary, or in excess of the proceeds thereof constituting a loss from the value of the property when originally acquired by the fiduciary, which the fiduciary is required by law to make good because of negligence or other failure of duty. The term is also used as a verb; as, the court surcharged the trustee. (88)

surety 1. An individual who agrees, usually in writing, to be responsible for the performance of another on a contract, or for a certain debt or debts of another individual. 2. An insurance, bond, guaranty, or other security which protects a person, corporation, or other legal entity in case of another's default in the payment of a given obligation, proper performance of a given contract, malfeasance of office, etc. (1)

suretyship All forms of obligations to pay the debt or default of another. The function of being a surety. (50, 51)

suretyship, personal The giving of a bond by an individual. (51)

surplus The surplus account is a part of the capital structure of a bank, and is carried in the general ledger. Before a bank can open for business as a national bank, it must have a beginning surplus equal to 20% of the paid-in capital stock. A state bank must conform to whatever the laws of the state require as pertaining to surplus. After a bank has opened, the surplus account is made up of all past earnings less the dividends declared and paid from the profits. National banks are required to carry a minimum of 10% of each previous six months' earnings to their surplus account before the Comptroller of the Currency will approve the payment of a dividend. State laws deal with surplus requirements in various ways. The surplus is a part of the net worth or ownership of the bank, and in case of liquidation, any remaining portion of surplus after all creditors have been satisfied, will be divided in the same related percent as the capital stock held by the stockholders. (1)

surplus equity That amount of difference between the market value of securities and the amount needed to satisfy margin requirements of a brokerage account. (105)

surrogate A probate judge.

surrogate's court See Probate Court. (74)

survivorship account An account in the names of two or more persons, each signature alone being sufficient authority for the withdrawal of funds, the balance in the account belonging to the survivor or survivors on the death of the other or others. See Alternate Account; Joint Account. (85)

suspend trading An action which can be taken if there is evidence an orderly market may be threatened because of some unusual event. Might be invoked if there is a sudden influx of buy or sell orders, and continued so long as necessary. (105)

suspension The stopping of a firm or activity because of such reasons as legal prohibition by an appropriate agency such as a Superintendent of Banking, Insurance, and by Exchanges or because of some other action such as suit, bankruptcy or insolvency.

sweating 1. To reduce the metallic content of gold coins so that the coin can later be used and the gold dust can be recovered. 2. To employ people in a sweatshop.

sweetening The act of adding some additional attractive feature to an offer or transaction.

swimming market A buoyant market in which there is strength and confidence. (105)

swindle The act of cheating and defrauding.

swindlers Unscrupulous people who distort facts and deal in worthless and doubtful securities. (105)

swing The analogy of the similarity of business conditions to a pendulum. Business has its ups and downs which seem to somewhat correspond to the movements of the pendulum.

switch The liquidation of a position in one future of a commodity and the simultaneous reinstatement of such position in another future of the same commodity. It may be done at the market price that is current or at a specified difference. (9)

switching Simultaneously buying a contract for future delivery in one month while selling a contract of the same commodity in another delivery month, on the same exchange, also known as "straddle". (123)

symmetallism 1. A monetary system in which the paper currency is redeemable in two or more metals which are paid in a fixed and proportionate combination. 2. A standard coin which is a combination of two or more precious metals.

syndicate A group of bankers who, by agreement among themselves, have joined together for the purpose of distributing a particular lot of securities. The syndicate manager is usually the bank that has made a successful bid for the wholesale purchase of the securities as a lot. The other banks in the syndicate agree to distribute a specified amount of the securities and the manager allots the securities to them on a pro rate basis. Upon final distribution of all securities, the syndicate is closed and the obligation of all members is terminated. (1)

syndicate agreement The document used to join together the members of an underwriting or loan syndicate.

syndicate loan See Participation Loan. (1)

syndicate manager That firm or investment bank which has been chosen to direct the handling of the underwriting of a security issue by the members of the joint adventure.

syndicate member An investment banker, brokerage firm, or bank which participates with others under the direction of a syndicate manager in the process of underwriting and distributing a security issue.

system unit A bargaining unit in some communications, transportation, and utility systems. (12)

T

T Testator.

T.D. Treasury Department. (7)

T/D Time Deposit.

T/E Total Earnings. (67)

Tee. Trustee.

Temp. Ctfs. Temporary Certificates.

TI Temporary Instructions. (67)

T/L Time Loan.

T.N. Transferable Notice.

T/O Travel Order. (67)

Tr. Trust.

T/R Trust Receipt.

Tr. Co. Trust Company.

Treas. Treasurer; Treasury.

Trf. Transfer.

T.T. Telegraphic transfer.

tables, annual investment accumulation Shows amounts to be invested yearly at a given rate of interest which will accumulate to $1,000 in a given number of years. (42)

tables, discount Tables showing the present value of a unit of money due at the end of various periods of time, or the present value of one unit per period for various periods of time at various rates. (42)

tables, interest Tables showing the amount to which a unit principal sum, or a unit periodic payment, will accumulate at the end of various periods of time, at various interest rates. (42)

tabular standard of value A theoretical monetary standard in which a price index of representative commodities would be used. A unit of value would be represented by a given quantity of each of the component commodities.

tacit collusion Conspiracy without evidence except from the results. In cases of oligopoly when one buyer or seller takes an action such as changing a bid or asked price and the same action is promptly taken by another in a consistent pattern, courts of law may hold that tacit collusion exists.

take a bath The incurring of a large loss, i.e., to be run through the "financial wringer." (105)

take a flier To make a highly speculative investment in a security with hope of a large profit, while fully understanding the possibility of a substantial loss. (105)

take a position An expression for the activities of a principal or a dealer (occasionally a broker acting as a principal) in purchasing a block of a specific security as inventory in the expectation of resale at a profit. (103)

take it The term used by brokers on the floor of an exchange to indicate their willingness to buy a particular security at a stipulated amount. (105)

take on a line To systematically acquire over a period of time the securities of one or more companies in the expectation of higher prices. (105)

takeout loan Permanent loan on real property which takes out the interim, construction lender. (121)

take profits To realize a capital gain by selling a security; to be distinguished from retaining a paper gain. (103)

take up 1. The retirement of an obligation such as a bond or note. 2. The payment at the time of delivery for an item previously ordered.

tale The counting, or numbering of things as differentiated from the weighing of things.

talon 1. That portion of a debt instrument which remains on an unmatured bond after the interest coupons which were attached have been presented. The talon is then exchanged for a new certificate with coupons. 2. An extended bond, rente or consul which has had all its coupons presented but has still not matured has a portion of the original document, called a talon, which is exchanged for the new bond.

tap To collect mail from a deposit box. (39)

tape 1. The narrow tape refers to the slip of paper or plastic which has quotations of prices of securities or commodities. This tape is found most frequently in the customers' room of brokers offices and represents the telegraphed quotations from the exchange floor. 2. The broad tape refers to the wider slip of paper which Dow-Jones, publisher of the Wall Street Journal uses to release to subscribing brokers news of an economic nature.

tape price The price printed on the ticker tape which indicates the last sale of a particular security. (105)

tape reading The practice of using only the price, volume, activity and other factors indicated on the ticker tape to forecast the price action of securities. (105)

taxable value The value set upon the property by which the tax levy is computed. In some cases the tax value may have but small relationship to the market value since the market value will fluctuate more rapidly and is not set in a fairly arbitrary manner. (54+)

tax anticipation notes Notes (sometimes called "warrants") issued in anticipation of collection of taxes, usually retirable only from tax collections, and frequently only from the proceeds of the tax levy whose collection they anticipate. (29)

tax anticipation warrants See Tax Anticipation Notes. (29)

tax avoidance The use of legal means to minimize one's taxes. (The use of illegal means is known as tax evasion.)

tax certificate A certificate issued by a governmental unit as evidence of the conditional transfer of title to tax delinquent property from the original owner to the holder of the certificate. If the owner does not pay the amount of the tax arrearage and other charges required by law during the specified period of redemption, the holder can foreclose to obtain title. Also called in some jurisdictions, "tax sale certificate" and "tax lien certificate". See also Tax Deed. (29)

tax deed A deed issued by a public authority as a result of a tax sale of the property. (5)

tax exemption The excuse of freedom and immunity from tax. The exemption may be in whole or in part. Individual tax payers are permitted to take legal dependents as an allowance or tax exemption on their income tax up to a stated amount per dependent. Charitable, educational and religious organizations frequently are granted some tax exemption. The income from state and municipal bonds is exempt from federal income taxation.

tax notes See Tax Anticipation Notes. (29)

tax selling The practice of effecting securities that will realize a capital gain or loss which is desired as an offset to the losses or gains realized in the same tax period. The purpose of this practice is to minimize the tax impact of the seller's capital transactions during a tax period. (103)

technical decline The drop in price of a security or commodity because of conditions within the market itself and not attributed to external forces of supply and demand.

technical divergence The condition existing when one of the market averages fails to follow, or confirm, the action of the other as described in the Dow Theory. (105)

technical market action As opposed to the psychological factors that influence the market, this term refers to the market's overall price performance as it is affected by the technical factors such as volume, short interest, odd-lot transactions, and the highs and lows of individual stocks. (105)

technical position A term applied to the various factors affecting the market; opposed to external forces such as earnings, dividends, political considerations and general economic conditions. Some internal factors considered in appraising the market's technical position includes the size of the short interest, whether the market has had a sustained advance or decline without interruption, a sharp advance or decline on small volume and the amount of credit in use in the market. See Over-Bought; Over-Sold. (2)

technical rally The increase in the price of a security or commodity because of conditions within the market itself and not attributed to external forces of supply and demand.

technician Also called a Chartist because his analysis of a particular security or market is based primarily upon the technical, or chart formation, aspect of the changes taking place. (105)

telegraphic transfer The use of telegraph or cable to remit funds. The physical money does not move but rather the order is telegraphed to the cashier of the company to make payment to an identified individual or firm.

teller An employee of a bank who is assigned the duty of waiting on depositors and customers of the bank. The teller's principal responsibility is to handle cash for the depositor and the bank and to serve the depositor or the customer as far as his duties will permit. The teller is the "personal" contact between the customer and the bank. See also Head Teller; Loan Teller; Paying Teller; Receiving Teller. (1)

teller proof A system of individual teller control whereby the teller balances and settles his own cash position daily. If the teller is using a bank teller's machine, this proof is very simple, because the machine will carry totals for Cash Received and Cash Paid Out. Otherwise the teller will maintain his own cash settlement sheet, listing all cash taken in and all checks cashed. Teller proof consists of using the teller's starting cash total, adding his cash received, and subtracting his cash paid out, to arrive at his cash on hand. The cash counted must agree with this cash ending total for proof. (1)

teller's cash ticket For description, see Cash Release Ticket. (1)

teller's check A check drawn by a bank on another (drawee) bank and signed by a teller or tellers of the drawer bank. Tellers' checks are used in payment of withdrawal orders and, in lieu of savings bank money orders, are sometimes sold to depositors in exchange for cash. (90)

teller's stamp A rubber stamp, usually showing the teller's number or initials and the bank's name or transit number, which the teller uses to identify deposits, cashed checks, or other posting media that he handles. (1)

temporary administrator An individual or a trust institution appointed by a court to take over and safeguard an estate during a suit over an alleged will, or over the right of appointment of an executor or administrator, or during the period that probate is delayed for any reason, such as difficulty in finding or citing missing heirs. (88)

temporary certificate See Temporary Receipt.

temporary loans Short-term obligations representing amounts borrowed for short periods of time and usually evidenced by notes payable or warrants payable. They may be unsecured, or secured by specific revenues to be collected. See Tax Anticipation Notes. (29)

temporary receipt The printed or lithographed acknowledgement used until the engraved certificate is ready to be issued which is exchanged for the definitive security by the holder of the temporary receipt.

tenancy at sufferance A tenancy in which the tenant comes into possession of real property under a lawful title or interest and continues to hold the property even after his title or interest has terminated. (74)

tenancy at will That estate which may be terminated by either the lessor or the lessee at any time. (54)

tenancy by the entirety Tenancy by a husband and wife in such a manner that, except in concert with the other, neither husband nor wife has a disposable interest in the property during the lifetime of the other. Upon the death of either, the property goes to the survivor. To be distinguished from joint tenancy and tenancy in common. (74)

tenancy for years A tenancy for a definite period of time—for example, a year or ninety-nine years. It cannot be terminated by either party alone except at the expiration of the time agreed upon. (88)

tenancy in common Form of estate held by two or more persons, each of whom is considered as being possessed of the whole of an undivided part.

tenant One who holds or possesses real estate by any kind of title, either in fee, for life, for years, or at will. In a more limited and popular sense, a tenant is one who has the temporary use of real estate which belongs to another. (5)

tendency The inclination for a security or market average to move in a certain direction, either up, down, or sideways over a period of time. (105)

tender The unconditional offer of payment by a debtor to the creditor of the amount owed. To deliver against futures.

tenderable A commodity that will fulfill the standards of quality established by the commodity exchange or exchanges as well as the requirements as to time and place of delivery.

term bond A bond which has a single maturity.

term issue A bond issue that matures as a whole in a single future year. (103)

term loan Usually a long-term loan with a tenure running up to ten years. These loans are made generally by the larger commercial banks and insurance companies to large, well-established business enterprises for capital expenditures such as plant improvements, purchase of equipment, etc. An amortization program is worked out in the loan agreement for the liquidation of the loan over its tenure. Generally, the amortization is moderate during the life of the loan, with a large final payment, termed a "balloon" payment, scheduled in the last year of the loan. The loan agreement generally calls for certain restrictions in further loan commitments by the borrower, dividends can only be paid from current earnings, and also provides that certain ratios (such as working capital ratio) be maintained at an agreed-upon level. (1)

term mortgage See Straight Term Mortgage Loan. (89)

terms of trade 1. Those discounts from the list price which may be taken if payment is made within a stated period. There are many terms of trade but probably the most common is expressed 2/10/ net 30, which means that the purchaser may deduct 2% of the face amount of the bill if he pays within ten days of the presentation or date of the bill. In the event he does not pay within the ten day period he is to pay the full amount within the period from the tenth to the thirtieth day. After the thirtieth day the account, if un-paid, is considered to be past due.

tertiary movement The insignificant daily fluctuations in price caused by trifling developments as classified by Charles Dow in his Dow Theory. (105)

testament Under the early English law, a term that referred to the disposition of personal property at the death of the owner. The words "and testament" are no longer necessary since a will now relates to both real and personal property. (88)

testamentary Any instrument, including a will and codicil, which is only effective after death.

testamentary capacity Mental capacity to make a valid will.

testamentary disposition The disposition of property by deed, will or otherwise in such a manner that it shall not take effect unless or until the grantor dies. (74)

testamentary guardian A guardian of a minor or an incompetent person named in the decedent's will. (74)

testamentary trust A trust which is established through a will. The executor or some other legal entity, such as a Trust Company, is specified in the will to take possession of certain property of the deceased, and to carry out this administration for the benefit of the parties named in the will as beneficiaries. (1)

testate To dispose of one's property by a valid will. (5)

testator or testatrix (Female) The maker of a will.

thin margin That condition in which the owner of a thing such as a security or other property has a very small equity. As a result, a small drop in the price or value of the thing will result in a condition in which the debtor owes more than the value of the collateral put up for the loan.

thin market A market in which there are comparatively few bids to buy or offers to sell or both. The phrase may apply to a single security or to the entire stock market. In a thin market, price fluctuations between transactions are usually larger than when the market is liquid. A thin market in a particular stock may reflect lack of interest in that issue or a limited supply of or demand for stock in the market. See Bid and Offer; Liquidity. (2)

third market Trading in the over-the-counter market of securities listed on an exchange. To the distress of exchange officials, the practice is growing. (106)

third-party insurance Protection for the insured against liability arising out of bodily injury to others or damage to their property. Insurance other than life against loss due to liability to third parties, or for the benefit of third parties. (51 + 50)

thirty days after date Phrase meaning that the amount is due for payment on a time draft thirty days after the date of the draft. (73)

Threadneedle Street The financial area in London which corresponds to Wall Street in New York.

thrift account A time deposit in a bank, savings and loan, cooperative or other financial institution for the purpose of savings. Generally such accounts have interest computed and credited according to some formula.

through bill of lading That type of bill of lading which is used in the event more than one carrier will be handling a shipment so that processing of documents is minimized at the intermediate connecting stations. See Bill of Lading.

ticker The instrument which prints prices and volume of security transactions in cities and towns throughout the U.S. within minutes after each trade on the floor. (2)

ticker symbol Abbreviations for the names of stocks. They are to aid in speeding information on transactions, and are associated as closely as possible to the actual names, using as few letters as possible. (105)

ticker tape The device used by stock exchanges to transmit reports of transactions. It is a narrow band of paper imprinted with the reports only minutes after the execution of the transactions on the exchange floor. (105)

tickler Any record established to serve as a reminder of action to be taken on a fixed future date. It is always arranged in the order of dates on which such action is to be taken. (74)

tied in scale A sale that is conditioned upon the purchaser also purchasing a specific item to qualify for purchasing a different item. The advertised product for sale generally is priced very attractively while the product it is tied to probably is not.

tied loan A loan in which the granting of the loan is conditioned (tied) to the borrower using the proceeds for a very specific purchase from a named supplier.

tight credit That condition in an economy in which credit accommodations are difficult to obtain and in which interest rates tend to increase.

tight money See Tight Credit.

tight money market An expression relating to conditions when the supply of money is less than

the demand for it, with a resulting tendency for a firming of interest rates. See Firming of Interest Rate; Easy Money. (103)

till money Money set aside for use by a teller at his window as distinguished from money in the vault, on deposit in other banks, etc. See Cash Till. (1)

time bill A bill of exchange that has a fixed or determinable date of payment as contrasted with a sight or demand bill.

time certificates of deposit A time deposit evidenced by a negotiable or nonnegotiable instrument specifying an amount and a maturity. Savings bonds and savings certificates are merely forms of nonnegotiable time certificates of deposit. (119)

time deposit A deposit from which the customer has the right to withdraw funds at a specified date thirty or more days after the date of deposit, or from which, if the bank so requires, the customer may withdraw funds only by giving the bank written notice thirty days or more in advance of the contemplated withdrawal. (89)

time deposit (open account) A deposit with respect to which there is in force a written contract with the depositor that neither the whole nor any part of the deposit may be withdrawn within thirty days after the date of the deposit or prior to the expiration of the period of notice given by the depositor in writing not less than thirty days in advance of withdrawal. (85)

time draft A draft which is payable a specified number of days (30, 60, or 90 days, for example) after its date of issuance or acceptance. (1)

time loan A loan made for a specified period of time. The maturity date generally is 30, 60, 90, or 120 days after the date of the loan. Interest is usually collected in advance, at the time the loan is made, in the form of a discount. This type of loan is distinguished from a Demand Loan in that the bank cannot demand payment at any time, but is obligated to permit the borrower the use of the money loaned until maturity of the note. (1)

time lock The device used on some safes and vaults which prevents the door of the safe from opening until a certain time has passed. This makes certain types of robbery more difficult.

time money Same as Time Loan.

time of the note The number of days or months from the date of issue to the date of maturity. (73)

time open accounts A time deposit evidenced by a written contract specifying a maturity but leaving open the amount involved. (119)

time order An order for the purchase or sale of a security which, unless executed before the end of a certain day, expires automatically. (74)

timing Refers to the art of selecting the proper time to purchase or sell securities. Good timing results in selling before a decline and purchasing before an advance. Unprofitable transactions are often caused by poor timing. (105)

timing of notes The function of calculating and marking the maturity date on notes and other evidences of debt. Also the number of days which a loan must run until maturity for interest calculations. (1)

tips Supposedly "inside" information on corporation affairs. (2)

tipster An individual who gives tips. See Tips.

tipster sheet An advertisement or propaganda sheet which claims to have "information" concerning profitable information about certain stocks. (105)

title 1. The right to ownership of property. 2. Evidence or proof of ownership. (89)

to arrive Portion of a sales contract which defines how the price of the commodity will be computed after the commodity reaches a stated destination.

to come—to go The term which refers to the exact number of shares in a transaction which are to be sold, but still remain (to go); or the number in a buying transaction which are yet to be bought (to come). If 200 shares of a 500 share buy order have been purchased, it is reported that there are 300 "to come". (105)

token coins Those coins which have a commodity value less than their face value. Coins which if smelted down and sold for metal would not sell as metal for as much as the amount at which they circulate as money.

token money See Token Coins.

took a bath An investment or underwriting that was not successful.

top The condition of a price series such as of securities or commodities in which the series shows a high compared with some other period of time.

topheavy The condition of a price series such as one of securities or commodities in which the series while being high compared with some other period is considered to be vulnerable for a reaction downward.

topheavy market The existence of technical or fundamental conditions which indicate that the market seems too high and is likely to react. (105)

top price Refers to the highest price reached by the general market, a particular stock, or a group of stocks during an arbitrary period of time. (105)

toppy Topheaviness in a market, or stock, which often indicates a possible decline. (105)

top out The gradual leveling off of market prices after an extended upward climb. Also may refer to a temporary peak in the market or in a particular stock which is unlikely to be surpassed in the near future. (105)

total reserves Member bank deposits with Federal Reserve banks plus member bank vault cash. The sum of required and excess reserves. (117)

totten trust Trust created by deposit of one's own money in his own name as trustee for another. Title is vested in the record owner (trustee), who during his life holds it on a revocable trust for the named beneficiary. At the death of the depositor a presumption arises that an absolute trust was created as to the balance on hand at the death of the depositor. (74)

touch off the stops Refers to the point at which stop orders become market orders because the price at which the stop orders were placed has been reached. A situation described as "snowballing" may result if prices continue to decline and successive stop orders are hit or "touched off", i.e., become market orders, and thus create even more selling pressure. (105)

trade The buying, selling or exchanging of commodities either by wholesale or by retail, within a country or between countries. (93)

trade acceptance A bill of exchange that is drawn by the seller of goods or materials at the time of the purchase and which is accepted by the purchaser. (1)

trade creditor The individual or business firm which is owed on an open account basis as a result of a transaction by a trade debtor.

trade debtor The individual or business firm which owes on an open account basis as a result of a transaction with a trade creditor.

trade discount A deduction, usually expressed in a percentage, or a series of percentages, from the quoted or published list price that is used in commerce to adjust fixed quoted or printed prices to the current market price of a given commodity. Trade discount should not be entered in the books of account, or considered as a type of earnings. (1)

trade house A firm that buys and sells futures and actuals for the accounts of customers as well as for its own account. (123)

trade paper Short term negotiable instrument such as an acceptance, bill or note that originated out of the purchase of merchandise.

trader One who buys and sells for his own account for short-term profit. See Investor; Speculator. (2)

trade reference The name and address of the credit applicants supplier or suppliers. In addition, it is common to extend permission for the requester of a trade reference to inquire as to such factors as promptness of payment, highest credit and period of time the debtor had transacted business with the one whose name was given as reference.

trade report See Credit Report. (50)

trader's market An advantageous market for active trading whereby the fluctuation is relatively narrow without extended movements. (105)

trading flat See Flat. (103)

trading floor See Floor. (2)

trading limit In most all North American commodity contract markets there is a maximum price change permitted for a single session. These limits vary in the different commodity markets. After prices have advanced or declined to the permissible daily limits, trading automatically ceases unless, of course, offers appear at the permissible upper trading limit, or on the other hand, bids appear at the permissible lower limit. (9)

trading market That market condition in securities or commodities in which the major volume of transactions is attributed to professional traders as distinguished from trades attributed to the general public. As a result volume is off and low with only narrow fluctuations in prices.

trading post One of 18 horseshoe-shaped trading locations on the floor of the N. Y. Stock Exchange at which stocks assigned to that location are bought and sold. About 75 stocks are traded at each post. See Inactive Post. (2)

trading temper The condition of the general public with regard to its capacity to be influenced and persuaded toward certain actions. (105)

trading unit The unit adopted by an exchange or association in which transactions are regularly expressed. The unit will vary with the exchange and may vary between the spot or futures market, as well as by the commodity.

transcript A copy made from an original. (35)

transfer 1. The delivery of a stock certificate from the seller's broker to the buyer's broker and legal change of ownership, normally accomplished within a few days. 2. To record the change of ownership on the books of the corporation by the transfer agent. When the purchaser's name is recorded on the books of the company, dividends, notices of meetings, proxies, financial reports and all pertinent literature sent by the issuer to its securities holders are mailed directly to the new owner. See Delivery; Registrar; Street Name. (2)

transferable notice A written announcement issued by a seller signifying his intention of making delivery in fulfillment of a futures contract. The recipient of the notice may make a sale of the future contract and transfer the notice within a specified time to another party, on some exchanges directly, and on others through the Clearing association. The last recipient takes delivery of the commodity tendered. Notices on some exchanges are not transferable. (9)

transfer agent An agent of a corporation to effect the transfer of its stock or bonds from one owner to another. A transfer agent for bonds usually is known as a registrar. (74)

transfer books The transfer agent maintains certain records or books for the corporation for which he is acting as transfer agent. These books are usually open, but are closed at certain periods so that dividends may be sent to those shown as the owners of record.

transferee The person or corporation to which property has been transferred. (74)

transfer in contemplation of death A transfer of property by gift made in apprehension of death arising from some existing bodily condition or impending peril and not the general expectation of eventual decease commonly entertained by all persons. (74)

transferor The person or corporation which conveys or transfers property. (74)

transfer payments Payments to individuals by government and business for which no goods or services are currently rendered. Examples are benefits from social insurance funds, relief payments, military pensions, mustering-out pay, corporate gifts to non-profit institutions. (7)

transferred title To turn over the legal title, right or ownership to another. (93)

transfers—mail, wire, cable Mail Transfer is the remittance of money by a bank to be paid to a party in another town or city. The instructions to pay such funds are transmitted by regular mail, hence the term "mail transfer." Wire Transfer is used to designate a transfer of funds from one point to another by wire or telegraph. Cable Transfer is used to designate a transfer of funds to a city or town located outside the United States by cable. Commissions or fees are charged for all types of transfers. When transfers are made by wire or cable, the cost of transmitting the instructions to pay by wire or cable is charged to the remitter in addition to the commission. (1)

transfer tax A tax imposed by New York State, a few other states, and the Federal Government when a security is sold or transferred from one person to another. Paid by the seller. The present New York tax ranges from one cent a share on stock selling below $5 a share to 4 cents a share on stock selling at $20 or more. The present Federal tax is based on par value with no-par considered $100 par for tax purposes. In odd-lot transactions both buyer and seller pay the federal tax; the state tax is paid only by the seller. (2)

transit department A department of a bank whose function is the processing of all out-of-city items. The transit department writes all transit letters, both cash letters and remittance letters and forwards these letters to the Federal Reserve bank, correspondent banks, and other banks for collection and payment. (1)

transit items Cash items which are payable outside the town or city of the bank receiving them for credit to customers' accounts. (85)

transit letter A letter or form of deposit slip on which a bank lists and describes transit items. (85)

transit number See Check Routing System. (85)

trans-lux The electrical device used to project the quotations of a commodity or security exchange upon a screen in the board room of a brokerage firm.

transmittal letter A letter accompanying a shipment of securities, documents, or other property usually containing a brief description of the securities, documents, or property being forwarded and an explanation of the transaction. (74)

transposition An error caused by the interchanging of digits in an amount. (73)

travel department A department in a bank established to render service to the bank's customers in any matter relative to travel or foreign transactions. In the larger coastal banks, all foreign transactions are handled by the Foreign Department of the bank. In interior banks, the Travel Department deals directly with their coastal banks correspondents in handling foreign transactions. The Travel Department will arrange accommodations for domestic or foreign travel, plan vacation trips, handle foreign transactions, etc., for its customers. (1)

travelers checks A form of check especially designed for travelers or persons on vacation trips. Many of the large banks issue and sell their own travelers checks to customers planning such trips. The checks are preprinted in certain denominations, such as $10, $20, $50, and $100. The customer must sign his name on the face of each check in a designated place in the presence of an employee of the issuing bank. When the check is cashed at a distant point, the purchaser must again sign the check on its face. The bank, hotel, or other party cashing the check thereby has ready comparison of signatures for proper identification. The use of these checks protects purchasers from loss which might result from carrying large amounts of currency with them while traveling. The checks are readily accepted by banks throughout the United States and Canada. (1)

travelers cheques See Travelers Checks.

traveler's letter of credit A letter addressed by a bank to its correspondent banks either in the same country or in foreign countries, authorizing the person named in the letter to draw drafts on the correspondent banks to the extent of the credit specified. The person in whose favor the letter of credit is issued deposits with the issuing bank a sum of money equal to the total amount of the credit plus the bank's charges for this service. (85)

treasurer One who handles the financial transactions of an organization. (73)

treasurer of the United States The cabinet ranking executive who heads the Treasury Department.

treasurer's check See Cashier's Check. (85)

treasury bills Non-coupon obligations; sold at discount through competitive bidding; generally having original maturities of three months, and one year. (115)

treasury cash holdings Currency and coin held by the Treasury. (4)

treasury certificates of indebtedness Usually mature in 9 to 12 months from date of issue. (4)

treasury currency outstanding Currency such as United States notes and silver certificates, and coin in the hands of the public for which the Treasury is responsible. (4)

treasury notes Coupon obligations having original maturities of from one to five years. (115)

treasury notes and U.S. bonds From date of issue, notes usually mature in 1 to 5 years and bonds in over 5 years. Holdings are classified according to time remaining before maturity— within 1 year, 1 to 5 years, and over 5 years. (4)

treasury obligations Treasury certificates and bills are short-term federal securities; certificates maturing in one year, bills in 90 or 91 days. Treasury notes are federal securities with maturities ranging from two to five years. Treasury bonds are federal securities with maturity dates ranging from six to fifty years. (7)

treasury stock The title to previously issued stock of a corporation which has been reacquired by that corporation by purchase, gift, donation, inheritance, etc. The value of such stock should be considered as a deduction from the value of outstanding stock of similar type rather than as an asset of the issuing corporation. (1)

trend The direction prices or other indicators are taking.

trial balance A list of the balances of the accounts in a ledger kept by double entry with the debit and credit balances shown in separate columns are equal or their net balance agrees with a controlling account, the ledger from which the figures are taken is said to be "in balance". (29)

triangular arbitrage Arbitrage between the exchange rates of three foreign currencies. See Arbitrage.

true discount rate An installment finance method by which the Rate is computed on the total note. It is based on deducting the charge at the time the loan is made. The Factor for each maturity *is not* pro rata per annum of the Rate but is figured by deducting the dollar charge (which *is* pro rata per annum of the rate) from $100, and computing the percent of this charge on the remainder which is the advance. 6% True Discount means $6 per $94 for 1 year, $9 per $91 for 18 months, $12 per $88 for 24 months, etc., on monthly and seasonal contracts. (70)

true interest See Pure Interest; Net Interest.

true lease This term is an abbreviation for the intended meaning that a certain lease has been structured so as to meet the tests of the Internal Revenue Service and certified public accountants. Therefore, the lease can be accounted for as a "true lease for accounting purposes" and the lessor can claim the allowable tax depreciation and ITC and the lessee can charge the rental payments as expense and footnote the lease obligation.

trust An equitable right or interest in property distinct from the legal ownership thereof. A property interest held by one person for the benefit of another, usually under temporary or conditional terms such as that ownership transferred to a trustee until an heir becomes of legal age. (5)

trust account A general term to cover all types of accounts in a trust department, including estates, guardianships, and agencies as well as trusts proper. (74)

trust administrator A person in the employment of a trust institution who handles trust accounts in the sense of having direct contacts and dealings with trust customers and beneficiaries. (74)

trust agreement Arrangement with a bank or trust company providing for methodical distribution of an estate. (42)

trust authority The legal right of a corporation to engage in trust business. (88)

trust business A trust company, or a trust department of a bank, which settles estates, administers trusts, and performs agency functions for individuals, corporations, governments, associations, public or educational or related institutions, is said to engage in the Trust Business. (1)

trust by declaration See Declaration of Trust. (74)

trust by order of court A trust created by an order of a court of competent jurisdiction. (74)

trust charges The charges made by a trust institution for its trust and agency services. See Commission; Fee. (88)

trust committee A committee of directors or officers or both of a trust institution charged with general or specific duties relating to its trust business. (74)

trust company A corporation chartered by the state to engage in the trust business for both individuals and business organizations. It may or may not perform banking functions as well, depending on the powers granted in its charter. (85)

trust, corporate The name applied to that division of a trust company which handles the business of corporations. These functions may cover stock transfer, bond registrar, fiscal agent, coupon-paying agent, and many others. (1)

trust costs The costs to a trust institution of rendering trust and agency services; opposed to trust charges, which are the cost to trust institution customers or beneficiaries for obtaining trust and agency services. (88)

trust deed That deed which establishes a trust, conveying legal title of property to a trustee, states his authority and conditions which bind him in dealing with the property held in the fiduciary capacity as a means sometimes to secure the lenders against loss; thus it may serve a similar function to a mortgage. The term is usually and peculiarly applied to such a deed when made to secure a debt. (54 +)

trust deposit The deposit made by a trustee under a trustee account agreement.

trustee The person charged with the proper administration of property or funds in accordance with the wishes of the donor. Trust companies usually perform this function in the administration of estates, trusts, and the like. (1)

trusteed fund Any accumulation of capital held in trust for retirement, religious, educational, research, profit-sharing or other purposes. (121)

trusteed pension plan A pension plan in which the corporation's contributions to the plan are placed in a trust for investment and reinvestment, as distinguished from a plan in which the benefits are secured by life insurance. (74)

trustee in bankruptcy A qualified person elected by the creditors to take charge of the property of the bankrupt. (35)

trustee shares In an investment company formed under the business organization form of a Massachusetts Trust, the certificates of beneficial interest are referred to as Trustee Shares.

trusteeship The status of a carrier's property while in charge of trustees appointed under Section 77 of the Bankruptcy Act, approved March 3, 1933. Reorganization proceeding under trustees differs from receivership equity proceeding chiefly in the fact that the former may be instituted by a railroad as well as by creditors and must follow a detailed prescribed procedure in regard to the presentation, consideration, and adoption of plans of reorganization, involving participation by the Interstate Commerce Commission as well as by the court. (19)

trustees' securities See Receivers' and Trustees' Securities. (19)

trust estate All the property in a particular trust account. (74)

trust for support A trust which provides that the trustee shall pay or apply only so much of the income or principal as in its judgment is necessary for the support, including education, of the beneficiary. (74)

trust function The fiduciary capacity in which an individual or a trust institution may act, such as executor, administrator, guardian or trustee. (74)

trust fund A fund consisting of resources received and held by the governmental unit as trustee to be expended or invested in accordance with the conditions of the trust. See Endowment Fund; Private Trust Fund; Public Trust Fund. (29)

trust funds, federal Those funds which are established to account for receipts which are held in trust by the government for use in carrying out specific purposes and programs in accordance with a trust agreement or a statute. Trust transactions are excluded from federal budget expenditures. (7)

trust indenture An instrument in writing which contains a description of all property originally placed in the trust, the agreement as to the rights of the trustee in administering the property, the rights of all beneficiaries named, along with their proportionate share in the trust, the duration of the trusteeship, the distribution of income from the trust principal to the life-tenants, and the distribution of the trust property to the remaindermen at the termination of the trust. (1)

trust institution The same as Trust Company. (1)

trust instrument Any writing—will, trust agreement, declaration of trust, deed of trust, or order of court—under which a trust is created. (74)

trust instrument committee A committee of directors or officers (or both) of a trust institution charged with specific duties relating to trust investments; duties other than those relating to investments may be imposed by the board of directors. (74)

trust inter vivos See Voluntary Trust; Living Trust. (74)

trust investments The property in which trust funds are invested; a broad term which includes all kinds of property, not securities alone. (74)

trust officer The administrative officer of a trust company, or of the trust department of a bank. He is responsible for the proper administration of trust, the investment of trust funds, and the administration of agencies for trust clients. (1)

trustor A person who creates a trust; a broad term which includes settlor and testator. (74)

trust or commission clause A clause extending the coverage of the insurance contract to the insured's interest in a legal liability for property belonging to others and held by the insured in trust, on commission, on storage, for repairs or otherwise held. (51)

trust, personal That branch of a trust company whose function is connected with the handling of trusts for individuals. Some of the functions performed are those of executor of estates, administration of trust funds, investment services, guardianships, etc. Detailed records are maintained and statements mailed to beneficiaries of every transaction affecting a trust. (1)

trust powers As the term is used in the Federal Reserve Act, authority to engage in the trust business; to be distinguished from the powers of a trustee. (74)

trust receipt A receipt in the form of an agreement by which the party signing the receipt promises to hold the property received, in the name of the bank delivering such property. It further agrees that the property shall be maintained in a form that it can be readily identified. If the property is further fabricated in a manufacturing process, it must be properly identified to the trust receipt. Trust receipts are used mostly to permit importers to obtain possession of merchandise for resale. Arrangements for this financing are usually completed before the issuance of letters of credit. The trust receipt is used as collateral security for the advance of funds by the bank to meet the acceptances arising out of the letter of credit. Under the terms of the agreement, the importer is required to pay to the bank proceeds from the sale of merchandise as soon as they are received. The importer is also required to keep the merchandise insured, and the bank may take possession of the merchandise at any time without due process of law. Federal Reserve banks do not recognize trust receipts as good collateral, and the legal status of the trust receipt has not been clearly defined by the courts. (1)

trust relationship When an individual or other legal entity takes over legal title to certain property to hold it in trust for another individual or other legal entity as specified in the trust indenture, a trust or fiduciary relationship is established. The legal entity taking possession of the property is the trustee—the legal entity who will benefit from the relationship is the beneficiary. The beneficiary has an equitable title to the property, and may bring suit in courts of equity to maintain his rights as set forth in the trust agreement, and to prevent mishandling of the property by the trustee. (1)

trust under agreement A trust evidenced by an agreement between the settlor and the trustee; the same as a trust inter vivos or living trust. (88)

trust under decree A trust evidenced by a decree of a court of equity. (74)

trust under deed A trust evidenced by a deed of conveyance, as distinguished from an agreement; originally confined to real property but now frequently applied to personal property as well. (74)

trust under will A trust created by a valid will, to become operative only on the death of the testator; opposed to a living trust and the same as testamentary trust. (74)

turn The completed transaction of a purchase and sale of a commodity or a security. It may be a long purchase followed by a sale, or a short sale followed by the long purchase. The last transaction completes the "turn."

turning the corner The change in the prevailing direction of a business index or time series, either up or down.

turnover The volume of business in a security or the entire market. If turnover on the N. Y. Stock Exchange is reported at three million shares on a particular day, 3,000,000 shares changed hands. Odd-lot turnover is tabulated separately and ordinarily is not included in reported volume. The number of times stock is sold out within a given time. (2, 93)

tutor Under civil law, a person legally appointed to care for the person and the property of a minor; the equivalent of a guardian. (74)

two-dollar broker Members on the floor of the N. Y. Stock Exchange who execute orders for other brokers having more business at that time than they can handle themselves, or for firms who do not have their Exchange member-partner on the floor. The term derives from the time when these members received $2 per hundred shares for executing such orders. The fee is paid by the broker and today it varies with the price of the stock. See Commission Broker. (2)

two name paper A loan contract which has been signed by two people or companies making either or both liable for payment. The second name is frequently an accommodation endorsement. See Accommodation Endorsement.

U

U. K. United Kingdom.

ULT. Last.

UN United Nations.

U. & O. Use and occupancy. (5)

U. P. Unearned premium. (5)

U. S. United States.

ultimate beneficiary A beneficiary of a trust who is entitled to receive principal of the trust property in final distribution; also called principal beneficiary; opposed to immediate beneficiary and income beneficiary. (74)

ultra vires An act beyond the powers legally granted a corporation. (5)

unassented security A security such as a stock or bond which has not had its owner agree to a change in the terms or conditions affecting the security. Typically the issuer of the security is financially embarrassed and requests assention to his proposal which generally reduces either principal or interest payments. Those accepting the terms present their securities which are stamped "Assented" with a description of the new terms. Those not accepting the terms do not present their securities and thus securities are traded on an assented or unassented basis.

unauthorized investment A trust investment that is not authorized by the trust instrument; to be distinguished from a non-legal investment. (74)

uncalled capital The amount of a capital subscription less the amount already paid. In financing a new venture the promoters may sell securities on an installment basis. The amount subscribed for but not as yet paid is the "uncalled capital."

unclaimed balances The balances of the accounts for funds on deposit which have remained inactive (without being legally debited or credited), for a period of time. See Dormant Account; Escheat Law. (1)

uncollected cash items Checks in the process of collection for which payment has not yet been received from the banks on which the checks are drawn. (4)

uncollected funds A term used to describe a portion of a deposit or deposit account which has not been collected or paid because the items deposited are en route in transit to the drawee bank for payment. Check drawn against uncollected funds are returned by banks, where they are presented. These checks will not be paid by a bank until it knows that the deposit account is fully available and all deposits fully collected. See Float; Kite. (1)

unconfirmed letter of credit A letter of credit in which the issuing bank has processed all the necessary documents and advised the financial institution upon which the letter is drawn but the institution has not confirmed acknowledgement and accepted the advice of the letter. See Letter of Credit.

uncovered paper money Paper money which is irredeemable because it is not backed by specie or bullion.

uncover the stops To create selling pressure in a stock to depress it to a level where there are a relatively large number of stop orders on the books. Whenever a round-lot of this stock sells at the stop price, the stop orders become market orders; and additional selling pressure is brought to bear. Further declines will hit more stop orders at lower prices creating more downward pressure. This process is closely supervised because it could lead to manipulative practices. (105)

underestimate To judge the value too low. (93)

underlying lien A claim, which has priority over some other claim which is junior to it.

underlying mortgage A mortgage which has priority over some other mortgage.

underlying movement Same as the primary movement in the Dow Theory. (105)

underlying syndicate The original members of the underwriters of a new issue of securities as distinguished from the distributing syndicate which may include some members of the underlying syndicate and also additional brokerage firms.

under the rule When a member of an exchange does not complete delivery of a security in terms of the rules of the exchange, the security is purchased by an official of the exchange who makes the delivery under the rule.

undertone Refers to the technical basis of the market—strong or weak. (105)

underwriter One who arranges for the distribution and sale of a large block of securities and who assumes responsibility for paying the net purchase price to the seller at a predetermined price. In most instances the underwriter deals in a new issue and with the issuing company. (103)

underwriter, principal See Distributor. (3)

undigested securities Securities that have not been absorbed by the market. When an issue has been brought out and only partly sold with the remainder meeting selling resistance at the issuing price, that portion which remains is described as being "undigested".

undistributed profits The portion of a corporation's profit remaining after taxes and dividends have been paid. It is one of the two main components of the corporate cash flow (gross retained earnings of business); the second is capital consumption allowances.

undistributed profits tax A tax which for a brief time was levied during the great depression. Besides a regular income tax and additional tax, Undistributed Profits Tax was made on that excessive amount of a firms' profits which were not paid out as dividends. The idea was that by such a tax, business firms would be stimulated to avoid the tax and to pay out larger dividends which in turn would be used to purchase things and thus stimulate business.

undivided interests See Tenancy in Common; Joint Tenancy; Tenancy by the Entirety. (88)

undivided profits Undistributed earnings available for dividends and for the writing off of bad debts or special losses. (85)

unearned discount In firms operating under an accrual system, the term Unearned Discount applies to interest which has been received in advance by deduction from the face value of the loan, but which is still unearned until the note matures. Example: A 90-day note has been discounted for $6.00. After 30 days, the firm has earned $2.00 of the discount; the $4.00 remaining is the unearned discount. (1)

unearned income Income that has been collected in advance of the contract to be performed, or consideration to be met in order to earn the income. See Unearned Discount. Also the unused portion of a fee charged on a traveler's letter of credit, which is refunded by the bank to the purchaser. (1)

unearned increment The increase in the value of property that can be attributed to changing social or economic conditions beyond the control of the title-holder as distinguished from that increase in value that can be attributed to the improvements made or additions added by the labor of the title-holder. (1)

unearned interest Interest which has been received before it has been fully earned.

uneven lot Another name for odd-lot. (105)

uneven market A market condition characterized by widely fluctuating prices.

unfunded debt Debt which is short term and not represented by formal securities such as bonds. See Floating Debt.

unfunded insurance trust An insurance trust in which the premiums on the policies are to be paid by the insured or by some third person and not by the trustee; to be distinguished from a funded insurance trust. (74)

unissued stock That portion of the authorized capital stock of a corporation which is not outstanding or issued.

unit bank A single independent bank which conducts all its operations at one office. (85)

unit banking A term used to refer to the type of banking in which an individual bank is separate and distinct from every other bank in operation, management, and control. (85)

United States government deposits All deposits in reporting member banks held for the account of the United States Government or one of its departments or bureaus. (4)

United States treasury check See Government Check. (1)

unit of trading The minimum basic quantity in which a security may be traded in accordance with stock exchange rules. (105)

unit savings plan A plan whereby savings deposits and withdrawals are posted by machine to the depositor's pass book, the bank's ledger card, and the auditor's detailed audit tape, all in original printing in one simultaneous operation. The ledger card is posted at the teller's window by the teller in the same machine operation that posts the entry in the depositor's pass book. The entry must be identical, because of the simultaneous machine printing. This assures complete protection to the depositor (who can "audit" his account at the window,) the bank teller, and the bank. See also No Ticket Savings Plan; Dual Savings Plan, for distinction in posting methods. (1)

unit teller An employee of a bank who is charged with the duties of both a paying and receiving teller. This teller may receive deposits or pay out funds to depositors. His cash balance at the end of the business day will be the NET of his cash received, less his cash paid out. See Paying Teller; Receiving Teller. (1)

unit teller system An arrangement for the convenience of customers who wish to make deposits and withdrawals at the same time. When this system is in use, the bank representative at each window handles both receiving and paying operations. (85)

universal numerical system The system of numbering checks with a code to indicate the city, state and the bank. In this way checks may be rapidly sorted by use of the numbering system. With the introduction of magnetic ink this system becomes even more important because it permits mechanical sorting.

unlimited mortgage A mortgage with an open-end. This permits the borrower to finance under a single mortgage rather than being forced to issue several. While the mortgage has an open-end, it generally has certain restrictions such as the ratio of debt instruments to the total value of the assets securing the debt.

unlisted market The market made by person-to-person transactions, usually between brokers, for securities which are not listed on an organized stock exchange. (85)

unlisted securities A security not listed on a stock exchange. See Listed Securities; Over-the-Counter. (103)

unlisted trading privileges On some exchanges a stock may be traded at the request of a member without any prior application by the company itself. The company has no agreement to conform with standards of the exchange. Companies admitted to unlisted trading privileges prior to enactment of the Securities Exchange Act of 1934 are not subject to the rules and regulations under that Act. Today, admission of a stock to unlisted trading privileges requires SEC approval of an application filed by the exchange. The information in the application must be made available by the exchange to the public. No unlisted stocks are traded on the N. Y. Stock Exchange. See Listed Stock. (2)

unload The sale of securities or commodities in expectation of a price decline.

unparted bullion Bullion which contains base metals in addition to the precious metal.

unrealized profits The existence of paper profits which have not yet been made actual. (105)

unregistered exchanges Those small volume stock exchanges which have been exempted from complying with the registration requirements of the Securities Exchange Commission. Typical of such exchanges are the Richmond Stock Exchange, the Colorado Springs Exchange and the Honolulu Stock Exchange.

unsatisfied judgment funds A fund created by state law in several states. Reimbursement is made to persons having claims arising out of automobile accidents who have been unable to collect from the party responsible for the accident because the party is not insured or is financially not in a position to pay. (5)

unseasoned securities The opposite of seasoned securities. See Seasoned Securities. (103)

unsecured creditor A general creditor such as the tradesman who sold the merchandise to the debtor on open book account. His claim is subordinate to the claim of a creditor who has priority because of such features as a mortgage or other security.

unsecured loan A loan made by a bank based upon credit information on the borrower and his integrity to repay his obligations. The loan is not secured by collateral, but is made on the signature of the borrower. A man's wife may be asked to sign the note, and the bank may also request a guarantor, if the borrower is not well known in the community. (1)

unsteady market The condition of a security or commodity market in which prices fluctuate widely but no discernable trend is noted.

unvalued stock Stock which has no par or stated value. The term is a misnomer since it must have value to be bought and sold but the unvalued reference is to the value which the issuer of the stock carries it on the books. The trend in recent years is away from unvalued or no-par stock because it is generally taxed as if it had a value of $100 par.

upside gap An open space formed on a security chart when the highest price of one day is lower than the lowest price of the following day. (105)

up tick A term used to designate a transaction made at a price higher than the preceding transaction. Also called a plus-tick. A stock may be sold short only on an up tick, or on a zero-plus tick. A zero-plus tick is a term used for a transaction at the same price as the preceding trade but higher than the preceding different price.

Conversely, a down tick, or minus tick, is a term used to designate a transaction made at a price lower than the preceding trade. A zero-minus tick is a transaction made at the same price as the preceding sale but lower than the preceding different price.

A plus sign, or a minus sign, is displayed throughout the day next to the last price of each company's stock traded at each trading post on the floor of the N. Y. Stock Exchange. See Short Sale. (2)

use As a noun, the beneficial ownership of property the legal title to which is in another; the forerunner of the present-day trust. (88)

usury The amount paid for the use of another's money, or for credit extended, the rate of which exceeds the legal limit allowed for that type of transaction by the state whose laws govern the legality of the transaction. (1)

V

V. P. Vice President.

V. T. C. Voting Trust Certificates.

Vtg. Voting.

vacancy Unoccupied, empty. (93)

valuation Appraised or estimated worth. The process of determining a company's liabilities under its policy obligations is policy (reserve) valuation. The process of determining the value of a company's investments is "asset valuation." Minimum valuation standards are prescribed by state laws. (42)

value Ability to serve useful purposes or to command goods, including money, in exchange; utility; desirability; the quantity of goods including money, which should be commanded or received in exchange for the thing valued; the present worth of all the rights to future benefits arising from ownership of the thing valued. See Actual Cash Value. (50, 51, 54)

value, book The amount at which an asset is carried on personal, partnership, or corporation books and which may or may not represent market value; except under unusual circumstances, computed as historical cost less reserves for accrued depreciation. (66)

value, capitalized A value indication produced by discounting anticipated future income at the going rate; more properly, "an indication of value by the net income capitalization approach." (66)

value compensated This term is applied to contracts for the delivery of foreign exchange by cable transfer when it is agreed that the purchaser will reimburse the seller for the dollar equivalent on the date payment is due abroad.
     Under the Value Compensated arrangement, the bank assumes a credit risk. For example, if it is the seller, the cable ordering payment is dispatched one business day before receipt of the dollar equivalent, thus involving extension of at least overnight credit to the purchaser. If the bank is the purchaser, payment is made to the seller prior to receipt of confirmation from the bank's correspondent abroad that the foreign currency payment has been received. In this case, the credit risk may vary from a few hours, in the case of a cable advice, to a few days or more, in the case of mail advice. (1)

value date The date on which an entry made on an account is considered effective. The value date has no relation to the entry date, since it is based on the collection or payment of items which may be received from a depositor, or sent to a depository bank. Its use is generally associated with foreign accounts maintained with, or by a bank. (1)

value, face The state worth, in terms of money, of formal, written evidences of indebtedness such as bonds, mortgages, or notes; synonymous with par value of capital stock. (66)

V.A. mortgage Mortgage made in conformity with requirements of the Servicemen's Readjustment Act, and guaranteed to an amount specified in the act by the Veterans Administration. (121)

variation margin The portion of additional margin required because of a price decline in the commodity or security. Payment required upon margin call.

vault A large room or rooms in a bank, frequently subterranean, where the cash on hand is stored. A section of the vault is also set apart for safe deposit boxes. The vault is constructed so as to be impregnable to theft or damage by fire or water. Banks take pride in the construction of their vaults, and the time lock doors which protect their most valued assets. (1)

vault cash That portion of the Cash on Hand which is not required for immediate use, and is left in the vault of the bank as an immediate reserve. The remainder of the Cash on Hand is carried in the cash busses and cash tills under the custodianship of the tellers. (1)

velocity of circulation The rate at which money and those substitutes such as checks are transferred from one holder to the next.

velocity of money See Velocity of Circulation.

velvet An easily obtained profit.

vend To sell, to market in a small way. (93)

vendee The party who purchases, or agrees to purchase, an item or a piece of property owned by another. (1)

vendor The person who sells, or agrees to sell, an item of property. (74)

vendor's lien An equitable lien which the vendor of land has thereon for the unpaid purchase money. (5)

venture capital See Risk Capital.

venue The place or county where a suit is brought. (35)

verify To prove to be true. (93)

verifying the extensions Proving multiplication and addition on a purchase invoice. (73)

vertical bar graph A bar graph in which the bars are plotted vertically. (73)

vertical expansion The establishment of facilities to permit a firm to expand its business from the basic raw material, through processing, manufacturing, and distribution to the sale to the ultimate consumer. Vertical expansion may start at any level of activity be it production or distribution. The main feature is that control is maintained by one firm at all the levels. Naturally there are degrees of less than full vertical expansion.

vertical integration Ownership or control of the various levels of production and distribution for a class of merchandise generally from raw material to the ultimate consumer.

vest As a verb, to confer an immediate, fixed right of immediate or future possession and enjoyment of property. (74)

vested Giving the rights of absolute ownership, although enjoyment may be postponed.

vested interest An immediate, fixed interest in real or personal property although the right of possession and enjoyment may be postponed until some future date or until the happening of some event; to be distinguished from a contingent interest. (74)

vested remainder A fixed interest in real property, with the right of possession and enjoyment postponed until the termination of the prior estate; to be distinguished from a contingent remainder. (74)

vested renewals Future commissions for business placed to become due to a soliciting agent or general agency if the business remains in force. (42)

vesting The right of an employee who is covered by a contributary retirement plan or noncontributary retirement plan to acquire the employer's contribution upon severance of employment providing certain qualifying conditions have been met. (5)

vicinity of the exchange Defined by the New York Stock Exchange as that part of New York City south of Fulton Street. (105)

vie probable Denotes the number of years a person has an even chance of living. (42)

vis major An act of God. An accident for which no one is responsible. (5)

void Of no legal effect; not binding. (35)

voidable contract A valid contract that may be rescinded by one of the parties due to such grounds as fraud, duress, insanity, incompetency, or minority. (5)

volatility A measure of the rapidity with which a security changes in value as compared to the market generally. (3)

volume Refers to the aggregate number of shares traded during a given period. (105)

volume of trading Represents a simple addition of successive futures transactions. It is the total of the sales (or of the purchases), and not of the sum of both. Also known as Volume of Sales. (123)

voluntary bankruptcy That state of insolvency of an individual, corporation or other legal entity in which the debtor has petitioned a competent court and been judged insolvent and has had his property assigned for the benefit of his creditors.

voluntary plan A type of accumulation plan for investment on a regular basis but without any total time period or ultimate investment amount specified. The sales charge is applicable individually to each purchase made. (65)

voluntary trust A deed of transfer of certain property made voluntarily by an individual or other legal entity to a trustee for a specified purpose will establish a voluntary trust. Voluntary trusts may be made as a living trust for one's children or relatives, or for benevolent reasons, such as the establishment of a trust fund for medical research, libraries, institutions of learning, homes for the aged, or orphanages, etc. Voluntary trusts are also created to meet certain contractual agreements, such as the appointment of trustees to take title to certain property and to perform certain duties agreed upon under a bond issue, for the benefit of bondholders. (1)

vostro account This term is used in connection with Foreign Exchange. It applies particularly to the accounts of foreign banks or businesses maintained in United States currency on the books of United States banks. (1)

voting right The stockholder's right to vote his stock in the affairs of his company. Most common shares have one vote each. Preferred stock usually has the right to vote when preferred dividends are in default. The right to vote may be delegated by the stockholder to another person. See Cumulative Voting; Proxy. (2)

voting stock Stock in a corporation in which the holders are entitled to vote for the directors. (105)

voting trust A device whereby the owner of shares turns over the control of the stock to a trustee who exchanges a voting trust certificate for the stock. The certificate gives the holder all the rights he previously had as to dividends and equity but transfers the right to vote to the trustee for a stated period of time. At the end of that time the trust may be dissolved and the shares re-exchanged for the trust certificates or the trust may be renewed.

voting trust certificate See Voting Trust.

voting trustee See Voting Trust.

voucher check A form of check to which is attached another form termed a voucher. The voucher portion of the check is used to itemize or otherwise designate the purpose for which the check is drawn. When a voucher check is received from a buyer by a seller, the seller detaches the voucher from the check before presenting the check for payment. The voucher is then used as the posting medium to credit the seller's accounts receivable ledger, thereby showing payment received from the buyer. The buyer who created the voucher along with the check for payment of goods or services, uses it as a "remittance advice" for the convenience of the seller, and uses the voucher as the basis for his accounts payable posting. Many businesses use copies of the voucher check as their accounts payable ledger, since the record created lists both the evidence for which the indebtedness is incurred and the copy of the check showing the date, amount of payment, discount taken (if any), and the payee (seller or vendor), which discharges the debt. (1)

W

Warr. Warrants.

W/E Wage Earner. (67)

Whl. Wholesale.

Whous. Warehouse.

W. I. When issued.

Wit. Witness.

W. N. P. Wire non-payment.

W. P. Wire payment.

W/R Wage Record; Warehouse Receipt. (67)

W&R Wholesale & Retail.

W.W.A. With will annexed. (5)

wage Payment for services rendered, especially the pay for workers by hour, day, week or month.

waiver The voluntary relinquishment of a right, privilege, or advantage. The instrument evidencing such an act frequently is known as a waiver. (89)

waiver of citation A document executed by an interested party in an accounting proceeding by which he relinquishes his right to the formal issue and service of a citation. (74)

waiver of demand The right which parties who are secondarily liable on a defaulted negotiable instrument have to being served with a notice of demand or a protest may be waived. This is known as waiver of demand.

waiver of protest See Waiver of Demand.

wall street The geographic area of the financial district of New York City which includes all the major banks, insurance companies, exchanges and other financial institutions located not only on Wall Street but also the surrounding area.

ward The infant or incompetent person who is the beneficiary of an estate of a deceased person. The ward is under the care of a guardian who is appointed by a court of law to administer the affairs of the ward with the sanction of the court having such jurisdiction, until such time as the court finds that the ward has reached majority or has become fully competent to handle his own affairs. (1)

warehouse receipt A receipt for goods stored in a warehouse and an agreement between the warehouseman and the person storing the goods. By its terms the warehouseman promises to keep the goods safely and to redeliver them upon the surrender of the receipt, properly endorsed, and payment of the storage charges. The receipt is also evidence that the owner or holder has title to the stored goods. (85)

warehousing Hypothecation of mortgage to a commercial bank as security for repayment of short-term loans. (121)

warrant A form of draft which, in itself, is not negotiable, but which can be converted into a negotiable instrument. Warrants are considered "cash items" by banks. Warrants are evidences of indebtedness incurred by legal entities, and which will be duly redeemed for cash or check when presented to the drawee of the warrant. State and municipal agencies pay their indebtedness by warrants. These warrants state that the payee has performed a service for the governmental agency, and requests that the funds due be paid by the treasury of the governmental agency against some appropriation. The warrant, when presented to the treasury, is paid either by check or in cash. A claim draft on an insurance claim is a warrant issued by the insurance adjustor as evidence that the claim is valid.

It authorizes the treasurer of the insurance company to pay the claim. See Warrants (Securities). (1)

warrants payable The amount of warrants outstanding and unpaid. (29)

warrants (securities) There are several types of warrants. In general they represent the right of a holder to exchange them for cash or securities according to the purpose for which they are issued.

Dividend warrant—A document which entitles a shareholder to a specified dividend.

Interest warrant—A document authorizing payment of interest on bonds or notes to a registered holder.

Stock purchase warrant—In some respects this warrant is similar to Rights, permitting the holder to acquire common stock of the issuer at some future date at a specified price. Unlike "Rights," however, warrants usually have no value when issued. They are usually issued with bonds or preferred stock in order that a corporation may be able to increase its capital structure at some future date and to add attractiveness to the investment value of the bonds or preferred stock. (1)

warranty deed The deed by which a freehold is guaranteed in writing by the grantor and his successors. Instrument, in writing, by which a real estate is created or alienated and whereby the freehold is guaranteed by the grantor, his heirs, or successors. (54+)

warranty, implied A warranty assumed to be a part of the insurance contract even though not expressly included. In connection with products liability insurance, the warranty assumed to be made by one who sells a product that is fit for the purpose for which it is sold. (51)

wash sale An illegal security manipulation where a security is bought and sold by the same interest to give the impression of market activity and price rise. This may be done by using different brokers and instructing one to buy and the other to sell at the same time.

wasting trust A trust composed of property which is gradually being consumed. (74)

watch my number A request by one broker on an exchange floor to another broker to watch for the first broker's assigned number on the annunciator board if he should happen to be off the floor. If a broker's number is flashed on the board, it means that he is requested to go to his firm's booth on the edge of the floor. (105)

watered capital See Watered Stock.

watered stock When the actual value of the assets behind the stock is less than its par value. Securities whose value has been reduced or diluted by any of many techniques such as granting a block of stock to a promoter for services he has performed when the services are overvalued in terms of his efforts. The innocent purchaser pays for the security on the assumption that the company received value for what it has acquired. If the promoter's services are not worth the services performed the result is watered stock. (93)

weak The condition in a securities or commodity market characterized by declining prices.

weak holdings Securities which are usually held in margin accounts by speculators and traders, and vulnerable to their profit taking during short rallies or sales on the slightest decline. (105)

weak market Selling pressure which is forcing a declining trend in the market. (105)

wealth An economic term designating the value of one's total possessions or rights in property. (1)

went to the wall Term describing individuals or corporations that have failed. (105)

when, as, and if issued See When Issued.

when issued (WI) A short form of "when, as, and if issued." The term indicates a conditional transaction in a security authorized for issuance but not as yet actually issued. All "when issued" transactions are on an "if" basis, to be settled if and when the actual security is issued and the Exchange or National Association of Securities Dealers rules the transactions are to be settled. (2)

when issued basis A term applied to securities that are traded in before they are actually issued, the transactions to be null and void if the securities are not issued; usually abbreviated to W.I. following a market quotation of such securities. (103)

whipsawed The condition when a holder of securities or commodities has bought long at a high in the market price but sold long at a subsequent low. He then, anticipating a further drop sells short but the market going up causes him to take an additional loss when he is forced to cover.

wholesale price index A measure of the average change in the prices of 2,000 commodities at the primary market level (usually the level at which the commodity is first sold commercially in substantial volume). (7)

wide market 1. As opposed to a close Bid and Asked market, a situation where price quotations are relatively far apart. 2. A market where there are a relatively great number of investors. (105)

wide opening The situation in a security or commodity market in which the bid and asked price is separated by a greater spread than is normal.

widow and orphan's risk A designation for a class of securities in which the investor is supposed to not be able to assume any important risk because of lack of business background and need for security. See Businessman's Risk, for further clarification.

widow's allowance The allowance of personal property made by the court or by statute to a widow for her immediate requirements after her husband's death. (74)

widow's exemption The amount allowed as a deduction in computing the state inheritance tax on the widow's share of her husband's estate. (74)

wildcat banking The period after 1836 under Jackson in which many small banks were formed generally for the purpose of issuing bank notes which the wildcat banks tried not to redeem.

wildcat scheme A highly speculative venture with little apparent hope of success. (105)

will A document in writing in which an individual having full mental faculties sets forth his desires and bequests regarding the disposition of his total wealth after his death. A good will, to be properly drawn, is usually prepared by an attorney-at-law for his client. The will must be signed by the individual making the will. The laws of the various states differ regarding the requirements of witnesses to wills—in some states wills can be probated with only the testator's signature on the will; in other states the law may require one, two, or more individuals to affix their signatures as witnesses to the signing of the will by the testator. (1)

windfall profit An unexpected and unusually high profit.

wiped out The loss of one's wealth. The connotation is that the loss was fairly rapid such as caused by some act of God or drop in price.

wire fate items Checks or other items sent for collection or in transit letters to out-of-town banks, accompanied by instructions to notify the sending bank by wire as to whether the item is paid or not paid. This enables the sending bank to ascertain quickly whether or not the item is paid. Such items are referred to as wire fate items. (1)

wire house A member firm of the Stock Exchange with branch offices linked together by a communications network. (2)

wire off Telegraphic instructions to an agent to cancel a specific policy on receipt of the telegram. (5)

wire transfer An order to pay or to credit money transmitted by telegraph or cable. (85)

withdrawal The manner in which funds on deposit in savings accounts may be paid out by the bank. The depositor must present his pass book, and sign either a withdrawal slip or the ledger card (No-Ticket savings Plan) before the bank can pay out funds against the deposit account. The signature on the withdrawal slip or signed on the proper line of the ledger card should always agree with the signature on file in the bank to insure that the right person is receiving the withdrawn funds. (1)

withdrawal plan Arrangement provided by certain open-end companies by which an investor can receive monthly or quarterly payments in a designated amount that may be more or less than actual investment income. (3)

with exchange A designation on a check or draft of Payable With Exchange or With Exchange indicates that any collection or exchange charges will be against the payer in the event it is a check or the drawee in the event it is a draft.

without interest Securities and other debt instruments which are in default sell on a "flat" or "without interest basis" which means that the buyer does not make an additional payment for the accrued interest. Income bonds, while not in default, since the interest is not required to be paid unless earned, sell on a flat or without interest basis. See With Interest.

without par value Same as No Par Value. See that term.

without prejudice Part of a nonwaiver agreement that holds that the insured who signs the agreement cannot legally construe certain actions, such as the determination of the value of a claim by the insurance company to be an admission of liability on their part. (5)

without recourse Words used in endorsing a note or bill to denote that the future holder is not to look to the endorser in case of nonpayment. (5)

won Monetary unit of Korea.

worked off A slight, fractional decline in the price of a security or commodity.

working capital 1. That portion of the capital of a business enterprise which is not invested in fixed assets but is kept liquid to care for day-to-day working needs. 2. In an accounting sense, the excess of current assets over current liabilities. (90)

working control Theoretically ownership of 51 percent of a company's voting stock is necessary to exercise control. In practice—and this is particularly true in the case of a large corporation—effective control sometimes can be exerted through ownership, individually or by a group acting in concert, of less than 50 percent. (2)

World Bank Formerly The International Bank For Reconstruction and Development. Formed in 1945 for the purposes of helping finance the reconstruction of productive facilities destroyed during World War II and the development of member nations. It does not compete with regular commercial banks since the loans it makes are to governments or to business firms which have the backing of their government by the endorsement of their loan contract. The World Bank also will participate with commercial banks in making loans.

wrap-around mortgage Mortgage which permits a lender to advance funds to a borrower in excess of an existing first mortgage without requiring the discharge of the existing mortgage. This type of mortgage is reverse leverage or reverse trading on equity.

writ An order of a court commanding that the will of the court be obeyed. (35)

write down The reduction in the quotation of a thing or a ledger account to bring the present quotation in line with current values.

write-offs An instrument which has been determined to be uncollectable, since there are no known visible assets available with which to liquidate the obligation. Write-offs are charged as losses to either the surplus or the undivided profits account. (1)

write up The increase in the quotation of a thing or of a ledger account to bring the present quotation in line with current values.

writ of execution A court order issued to an officer of law commanding him to take certain action. (35)

written notice A notification in writing delivered in person to the individual or to the parties intended or delivered at or sent by registered mail to the last business address known to the party giving the notice. (11)

written off See Write-Offs. (73)

X

X No protest.

X-C Ex Coupon.

X.C. L. Excess current liabilities. (5)

X-D Ex Dividend.

X-I Ex Interest.

X-Rts. Ex Rights.

X-Warr. Ex Warrants.

X mark signature When people are unable to sign their names because of illiteracy or injury, provision may be made for them to "sign" with an X. In these cases, his name is inserted by another and the notation "his mark" is put next to the "X" and then witnessed by a person who in addition signs the instrument with the notation that he witnessed the "X".

xmas club account See Christmas Club Account. (1)

Y

Yr. Year.

yachts fire coverage A fire coverage rather than marine risk that is written on a standard fire insurance policy but issued through the marine department of the insurer, which has an endorsement covering the ship ashore or afloat. (5)

yankees Term for American securities on the London Stock Exchange. (105)

yen Monetary unit of Japan.

yield Also known as return. The dividends or interest paid by a company expressed as a percentage of the current price—or, if you own the security, of the price you originally paid. The return on a stock is figured by dividing the total of dividends paid in the preceding twelve months by the current market price—or, if you are the owner, the price you originally paid. A stock with a current market value of $40 a share which has paid $2 in dividends in the preceding twelve months is said to return 5 percent ($2.00 ÷ $40.00). If you paid $20 for the stock five years earlier, the stock would be returning you 10 percent on your original investment. The current return on a bond is figured the same way. A 3 percent $1,000 bond selling at $600 offers a return of 5 percent (30 ÷ $600). Figuring the yield of a bond to maturity calls for a bond yield table. See Dividend; Interest. (2)

yield, current That rate of return expressed in percentage that is calculated by dividing the annual dividend, coupon, or payment, such as rent, by the price paid for the investment. (5)

yield test Measurement applied to bond investments in the portfolios of insurance companies. It is the relationship of the yield of bonds the insurance company has in its portfolio individually to the yield of fully taxable United States Government bonds of the same maturity. Yields of such corporate bonds of over 1½ percent higher than the United States Government bonds require that they be valued at market price rather than amortized value. (5)

yield to lessor In financial language, this normally means the internal rate of return generated from the lease transaction alone. The first step is to determine the after-tax cash flow of the lease. This means netting the rentals against the tax depreciation and interest expense (the latter if you have a leverage lease). Once you determine the net after-tax cash flow, you find the internal rate of return that will discount these cash flows to equal the amount of equity investment. This gives the after-tax yield, which you then convert to a before-tax equivalent and this yield is the yield most commonly referred to as the "yield to lessor."

yield to maturity That rate of return expressed in a percentage that will be obtained on an investment if the investment is held to maturity. It takes into consideration that few investments are bought exactly at par and thus have a capital gain or loss in addition to the rate of return stated on the face of the instrument. For example, a bond with a face interest of 4% bought at 95 (that is $950) and maturing in one year will actually yield to maturity 9.41% as follows: 4% of $1,000 (the face value of the bond) equals $40, appreciation on the bond between purchase price of $950 and redemption value of $1,000 equals $50. The $40 interest and the $50 capital gain equals $90. Thus a return of $90 on the original investment of $950 or a yield to maturity of 90 divided by 950 or 9.4 plus %. Most insurance companies have tables of yields based on various interest tables. (5)

yo-yo stocks A relatively wide fluctuating, volatile, high-priced specialty issue. (105)

yuan Monetary unit of China.

Z

zero plus tick A price that is higher than the last difference price in a continuing series of round-lot sales. Used frequently by odd-lot dealers and in short-sale transactions. (105)

zero proof A mechanical method of posting records in such a manner as to prove that the previous balance on each line of posting was made correctly. This is accomplished simply by utilizing a posting plan in which the first pick-up of the previous balance adds into a second balance mechanism, and the "proof" pick-up of the previous balance subtracts, thus reducing the mechanism to zero.

Zero proof is also utilized effectively on machines used for distributing and proving items in the proof department of banks. When the total amount of a group of items is recorded in the machine, it adds into a classification total and also into a second "proof" balance total. As the separate items making up the total are distributed, they add into their individual classification totals, but subtract from the second "proof" balance total. This mechanical function thus reduces the second "proof" balance total to zero, and permits the machine to continue to operate if all items were added and listed correctly by the depositor or other party who established the total being proved. (1)

zloty Monetary unit of Poland.

ORGANIZATIONS AND AGENCIES
RELATED TO THE FIELD
OF
BANKING AND FINANCE

BANKING ORGANIZATIONS

AMERICAN BANKERS ASSOCIATION
1120 Connecticut Ave., N.W.
Washington, D.C. 20036

Serving banking industry through banker committee structure in areas of banking professions, education, government relations, communications and special activities.

AMERICAN INSTITUTE OF BANKING
1120 Connecticut Ave., N.W.
Washington, D.C. 20036

Carries on educational program for bank employees. A division of American Bankers Association.

ASSOCIATION OF REGISTERED BANK HOLDING COMPANIES
730 15th St., N.W.
Washington, D.C.

A group of registered bank holding companies.

ASSOCIATION OF RESERVE CITY BANKERS
135 S. LaSalle Street
Chicago, IL 60603

Executive officers of banking institutions located in a designated Reserve or Central City having deposit accounts with and/or from other banks or banking institutions and transacting, what is commonly known as a "correspondent" business.

BANK ADMINISTRATION INSTITUTE
303 South Northwest Hwy.
Park Ridge, IL 60068

Banks organized to conduct research and foster education in bank operating methods, production control, personnel administration, accounting practices, auditing methods and internal controls.

BANKERS ASSOCIATION FOR FOREIGN TRADE
1101 16th St., N.W.
Washington, D.C. 20036

A group of bankers organized in the interest of international trade.

INDEPENDENT BANKERS ASSOCIATION OF AMERICA
P.O. Box 267
Suak Centre, NM 56378

Provides legislative information and representation for community or "main street" banks and opposes "concentration of banking and credit powers" in chains, branch systems, or holding company combines of banks.

MORTGAGE BANKERS ASSOCIATION OF AMERICA
1125 Fifteenth St., N.W.
Washington, D.C. 20005

Through industry education and cooperation with federal agencies and regulatory bodies, seeks to improve methods of originating, marketing, and servicing first-mortgage loans on residential and income producing properties.

NATIONAL ASSOCIATION OF MUTUAL SAVINGS BANKS
200 Park Avenue
New York, NY 10017

Serves Mutual Savings Bank members and Sponsors Graduate School of Savings Banking at Brown University and Management Development Program at University of Massachusetts and compiles statistics.

ROBERT MORRIS ASSOCIATES
(National Association of Bank Loan and Credit Officers)
Philadelphia National Bank Building
Philadelphia, PA 19107

Conducts research and activities in areas of loan administration, asset management, commercial lending, and credit in commercial banks.

CREDIT UNIONS
AND
CONSUMER CREDIT ORGANIZATIONS

ASSOCIATED CREDIT BUREAUS
6767 Southwest Freeway
Houston, TX 77036

International association of credit reporting and collection service offices.

CREDIT RESEARCH FOUNDATION
3000 Marcus Avenue
Lake Success, NY 10040

Credit and financial executives of manufacturing concerns. Conducts surveys on credit condition trends, policies, practices, theory, systems & methodology.

CREDIT UNION EXECUTIVE
SOCIETY
P.O. Box 431
Madison, WI 53701

Purpose is to put members in touch with the most creative thinking in the credit union management field. Conducts conferences, seminars and workshops.

CREDIT UNION NATIONAL
ASSOCIATION
1617 Sherman Avenue
Madison, WI 53701

Aims to promote organization of new credit unions and to perfect credit union laws; researches the needs and accomplishments of credit union and investigates pertinent new technical development. Aids in the training of credit union officials and employees. Principal source of educational tools for new credit unions.

INTERNATIONAL CONSUMER
CREDIT ASSOCIATION
375 Jackson Avenue
St. Louis, MO 63130

Conducts home study courses and collects statistics on consumer credit; offers personalized assistance on consumer credit problems to members.

NATIONAL ASSOCIATION OF
CREDIT MANAGERS
475 Park Ave., South
New York, NY 10016

To promote sound credit practices and legislation; to exchange credit information. Credit and financial executives rep. manufacturers, wholesalers, financial institutions, insurance companies, utilities and other businesses interested in commercial credit.

NATIONAL CONSUMER FINANCE
ASSOCIATION
1000 Sixteenth Street, Northwest
Washington, D.C. 20036

Consumer finance, industrial banks, and industrial loan companies that deal with families and individuals with financial needs. Provides an educational service to interested parties.

NATIONAL FOUNDATION FOR
CONSUMER CREDIT
1819 H St., N.W., Suite 510
Washington, D.C. 20006

Manufacturers, retailers, wholesale distributors, bankers, sales and consumer finance companies, insurance companies with interests in consumer financing facilities.

FINANCE ORGANIZATIONS

AMERICAN FINANCE
  ASSOCIATION
100 Trinity Place
New York, NY 10006

A group of professional people interested in financial affairs.

NATIONAL COMMERCIAL
  FINANCE CONFERENCE
29 Broadway
New York, NY

Commercial finance companies and factors, lending money on a secured basis to small and medium business firms.

INSURANCE ORGANIZATIONS

AMERICAN SOCIETY OF PENSION
  ACTUARIES
1112 Sinclair Blvd.
Fort Worth, TX 76102

Aims are: to provide a center for the exchange of information and ideas; to provide an education center; to provide a liaison office between government and the society; to promote high standards in the profession.

NATIONAL ASSOCIATION OF
  INDEPENDENT INSURERS
2600 River Road
Des Moines, IA 60018

Through its independent statistical service, collects, compiles and files statistics and develops simplified statistical plans.

NATIONAL ASSOCIATION OF
  INSURANCE BROKERS
1511 K Street, N.W., Suite 316
Washington, D.C. 20005

"Sole proprietors, partnerships, and corps." acting as insurance brokers, primarily in the areas of commercial, industrial and institutional risks and related insurance.

NATIONAL INSURANCE
  ASSOCIATION
2400 South Michigan Avenue
Chicago, IL 60616

Conducts annual Institute in Agency Management. Sponsors: National Insurance Week

INVESTMENTS ORGANIZATIONS

INVESTMENT COMPANY
  INSTITUTE
Suffridge Bldg.
1775 K Street, N.W.
Washington, D.C. 20006

Represents members in matters of legislation, taxation, regulation, economic research, marketing and public information.

INVESTORS LEAGUE
One the Crescent
Montclair, NJ 07042

Investors organized "to protect their interest" from government encroachment (taxes, regulations, etc.).

NATIONAL ASSOCIATION OF
  SECURITIES DEALERS
1735 K Street, N.W.
Washington, D.C. 20006

Organized under federal law to enable its members to enforce standards of ethical conduct, by self-regulation in over-the-counter securities market. Major current project, National Association of Securities Dealers Automated Quotations, a nationwide automated quotations systems for over-the-counter market.

NATIONAL INVESTOR RELATIONS
  INSTITUTE
1629 K St., N.W.
Washington, D.C. 20036

"To protect a free and open market with equity and access to investors of all kinds; to improve communication between corporate management and shareholders, present and future."

SECURITIES INDUSTRY
  ASSOCIATION
20 Broad
New York, NY 10005

"To represent and serve all segments of the securities industry; provide a unified voice in legislation, regulation, and public relations."

SAVINGS AND LOANS ORGANIZATIONS

AMERICAN SAVINGS AND LOAN
  INSTITUTE
111 E. Wacker Drive
Chicago, IL 60601

Nationwide educational organization conducting courses of study for personnel of savings & loan associations and cooperative banks.

AMERICAN SAVINGS AND LOAN
  LEAGUE
5505 5th St., N.W., Suite 403
Washington, D.C. 20011

Undertakes programs to increase the income of and savings flow into the association including a direct solicitation effort; provides counseling and technical assistance; provides consultant services to assist individual associations and groups wishing to organize new associations.

NATIONAL LEAGUE OF INSURED
  SAVINGS ASSOCIATIONS
1200 17th St., N.W.
Washington, D.C. 20036

Holds committees on accounting, attorney, constitution and bylaws; credentials and resolutions, education, ethics, Federal Association Regulations, FHLB System, and FSLIC regulations. Also publishes several weekly, monthly, and annual reports.

SAVINGS & LOAN FOUNDATION
111 E. Street, N.W.
Washington, D.C. 20004

Conducts national advertising program through magazines, newspapers, radio and television programs to increase public knowledge of savings and loan institutions, attract new customers, and encourage thrift and homeownership.

UNITED STATES LEAGUE OF
  SAVINGS ASSOCIATIONS
111 E. Wacker Drive
Chicago, IL 60601

Conducts studies of operating procedures; provides accounting consultation; gathers information on business trends and conditions; sponsors management and legislative conferences; analyzes federal rules, regulations and laws pertaining to taxation and housing legislation.

FEDERAL AND STATE
ORGANIZATIONS AND AGENCIES

COUNCIL OF STATE
  GOVERNMENTS
Iron Works Pike
Lexington, KY 40511

To serve governmental progress within the individual states, among the states working together, and by the states in their relations with the federal government.

COMPTROLLER OF THE
  CURRENCY
490 L'Enfant Plaza East, S.W.
Washington, D.C. 20219

Safeguards bank operations and the public interest by examining every national bank on an unannounced basis at least three times every two years. Examiners analyze the operation of trust departments. Emphasis is given to the review, analysis and evaluation of bank management decisions.

CONFERENCE OF STATE BANK
  SUPERVISORS
1015 Eighteenth Street, N.W.
Washington, D.C. 20036

Primary purpose is to assure the maintenance of a viable, decentralized dual banking system with its inherent checks and balances.

EXPORT-IMPORT BANK OF THE
  U.S.
811 Vermont Avenue, N.W.
Washington, D.C. 20571

Purpose is to help finance and facilitate exports and imports.

FEDERAL DEPOSIT INSURANCE
  CORP.
550 17th St., N.W.
Washington, D.C. 20429

Insures bank deposits up to $40,000.

FEDERAL HOME LOAN BANK
  BOARD
320 1st Street, N.W.
Washington, D.C. 20552

Regulates savings and loans, and has a legislative mandate to promote them. Assisted in the creation and maintenance of a secondary mortgage market through the Federal Home Loan Mortgage Corp. Has taken an active role in widening the competitive opportunities of federally chartered savings and loans.

FEDERAL RESERVE BOARD
20th St. and Constitution Ave., N.W.
Washington, D.C. 20551

Functions include setting of monetary policy, the discount rate, influencing the cost and availability of credit, bank regulation, bank holding company supervision, and the overseeing of international banking operations.

FEDERAL SAVINGS AND LOAN
  INSURANCE CORP. (FSLIC)
c/o FHLB Board
101 Indiana Ave., N.W.
Washington, D.C. 20552

Insures savings deposits up to $40,000.

HOUSE COMMITTEE ON BANKING,
  CURRENCY, & HOUSING
(House Committee)

Oversees banking and currency generally.

NATIONAL CREDIT UNION
  ADMINISTRATION
2025 M Street, N.W.
Washington, D.C. 20456

Supervises and regulates federally chartered credit unions.

SENATE BANKING, HOUSING &
  URBAN AFFAIRS COMMITTEE
(Senate Committee)

Oversees banking and currency generally.

THE TREASURY DEPARTMENT
Fifteenth Street and Pennsylvania
  Avenue, N.W.
(Main Treasury Bldg.) Washington, D.C.
  20220

Prints the money (Bureau of Engraving and Printing), provides the coinage (Bureau of the Mint), copes with counterfeiters (U.S. Secret Service), comes to market to sell debt securities, and wrestles with the national debt.

BIBLIOGRAPHY OF REFERENCE BOOKS ON
BANKING AND FINANCE

Banking (Journal of American Bankers
    Association)
A Banker's Guide to Washington
January 1976
pp. 38-65

Book of the States
Council of State Governments
Iron Works Pike
Lexington, Ky., 1976-1977

Business Information
How to Find and Use It
Manley, Marian C.
New York: Harper & Brothers, 1955

Directory of Business and Financial
    Services
McNierney, Mary A.
New York: Special Libraries
    Association, 1963

Encyclopedia of Associations
Vol. 1 National Organizations of the
    U.S.
Vol. 2 Geographic 7 Executive Index
Vol. 3 New Associations 7 Projects
Margaret Fisk, Editor
Detroit: Gale Research Co.,

Encyclopedia of Business Information
    Sources
Vol. 1 General Subjects
Vol. 2 Geographic Sources
Wasserman, Paul
Detroit: Gale Research Co., 1970.

Executive Guide to Information Sources
3 Volumes
Business Guides Co.
Detroit: 1965.

Federal Home Loan Bank Board Digest
U.S. Federal Home Loan Bank Board
101 Indiana Ave., N.W.
Washington, D.C.

Federal Reserve Bulletin
U.S. Board of Governors of the Federal
    Reserve System,
Federal Reserve Building
Washington, D.C.

Money Management and Institutions
Richard W. Lindholm
Totowa, N. J.: Littlefield, Adams & Co., 1978

U.S. Government Organization Manual
Office of the Federal Register
U.S. Government Printing Office
Washington, D.C.

ACKNOWLEDGEMENTS

The author gives special thanks for permission given to quote from the works, studies, and definitions by many authorities, agencies, individuals, and others.

The following is a listing of all sources arranged numerically by the key numbers which appear in parenthesis after entries.

(1) The National Cash Register Company: *Bank Terminology*
(2) New York Stock Exchange: *The Language of Investing—A Glossary*
(3) Arthur Wiesenberger and Company: *Investment Companies*
(4) Federal Reserve System—*Terms*
(5) Littlefield Adams & Company: *Dictionary of Insurance—Davids*
(6) U.S. Department of Labor: *Glossary of Currently Used Wage Terms*
(7) Tax Foundation Inc.: *Glossary—Facts and Figures*
(8) Federal Reserve of New York: Glossary—*The Story of Checks*
(9) The Association of Commodity Commission Merchants: *Trading in Commodity Futures*
(11) The National Board of Fire Underwriters: *National Building Code*
(12) Commerce Clearing House, Inc.: *Federal Tax Course*
(13) American Marketing Association: *Report on Definitions; SBA Mgt. Aids #127*
(16) National Industrial Conference Board: *Economic Almanac*
(17) American Institute of Certified Public Accountants: *Institute Terminology Bulletins*
(19) Association of American Railroads: *Definition of Terms, Units, and Phrases*
(20) Association of Consulting Management Engineers, Inc.: *Common Body of Knowledge Required by Professional Management Consultants*
(21) Edison Electric Institute: *Glossary of Electric Terms, Financial and Technical*
(24) U.S. Department of Commerce: *Selected U.S. Marketing Terms and Definitions*
(26) National Retail Credit Association: *Definitions of Terms Used in Retail Credit and Collection Operations*
(27) Commerce Clearing House, Inc.: *Federal Tax Course*
(28) The National Cash Register Company: *Industrial Accounting Terminology*
(29) Municipal Finance Officers Association: *Municipal Accounting Terminology*
(31) American Savings and Loan Institute: *Handbook of Savings and Loan*
(32) Municipal Finance Officers Association: *Public Employee Retirement Terminology*
(33) National Retail Merchant Association: *Glossary—The Display Manual*
(35) Associated Credit Bureaus of America: *Glossary*
(37) U.S. Department of Commerce, National Bureau of Standards: *Definitions and Tables of Equivalents*
(39) Post Office Department, Bureau of Operations: *Postal Term Glossary*
(40) National Association of Securities Dealers, Inc.: *Over the Counter Trading Handbook*

227

(42) Mutual of Omaha: *Glossary of Insurance Terms*
(44) U.S. Department of Labor, Bureau of Labor Statistics: *Glossary of Current Industrial Relations Terms*
(45) Chamber of Commerce of the U.S.: *Revised American Foreign Trade Definitions*
(50) Hartford Fire Insurance Company: *Glossary of Insurance Terms*
(51) Chamber of Commerce of the U.S.: *Dictionary of Insurance Terms*
(52) Employers Mutual Liability Insurance Company of Wisconsin: *Dictionary of Insurance Terms*
(53) Institute of Life Insurance: *Life Insurance Fact Book*
(54) National Institution of Real Estate Brokers: *Real Estate Salesman's Handbook*
(58) The Macmillan Company: *Modern Life Insurance by Mehr & Osler*
(59) National Foundation for Consumer Credit: *Using Credit Intelligently*
(61) Dun and Bradstreet, Incorporated: *Glossary—How Does Your Business Compare?*
(63) Federal Communication Commission: *Rules and Regulations of the FCC*
(64) National Association of Investment Companies: *Glossary of Investment Company Terms*
(65) National Association of Investment Companies: *An Aid to Bankers and Trust Officers*
(66) Society of Residential Appraisers: *Real Estate Appraisal Principles and Terminology*
(67) U.S. Department of Health, Education and Welfare, Social Security Administration: *Standard Abbreviations; Government Regulations*
(69) U.S. Department of Agriculture: *Marketing Service Definitions*
(70) American Charts Company: *Identification of Method*
(73) South Western Publishing Company: *Dictionary of Bookkeeping and Accounting Terms*
(74) American Bankers Association: *Glossary of Fiduciary Terms*
(83) Burroughs Corporation. Marketing Division: *Glossary of Financial and Data-Process Terms*
(84) Ralph Hogan: *Definitions and Terms*
(85) American Institute of Banking: *Principles of Bank Operations*
(88) American Institute of Banking: *Trust Department Service*
(89) American Institute of Banking: *Home Mortgage Lending*
(90) American Institute of Banking: *Savings Banking*
(92) American Savings and Loan Institute: *Glossary of S&L Terms*
(93) Cities Service Company. Business Research and Education Department: *Words Often Used in Business*
(95) International Business Machines:Glossary for Information Processing
(98) American Institute of Certified Public Accountants: *Glossary of Statistical Terms for Accountants*
(99) National Aeronautics and Space Administration: *NASA-PERT and Companion Cost System*
(103) American Institute of Banking: *Investments*
(104) U.S. Bureau of the Budget: *Automatic Data Processing—Glossary*
(105) Ron Cowan: *Investment Terms*
(106) New York Stock Exchange: *Stock Exchange Terms*
(111) FRB of Philadelphia: *What Are Federal Funds?*
(112) FRB of New York: *Definitions*
(115) FRB of Cleveland: *Terms—Economic Review, January 1967*
(116) Pacific Coast Stock Exchange: *Stocks and Bonds—Glossary*

(117) FRB of St. Louis: *Review—Definitions*

(118) Small Business Administration: *The SBIC—Glossary*

(119) FRB of Boston: *Pandora's Box?—Glossary of Terms*

(120) National Institute of Real Estate Brokers: *Exchange Systems and Procedures*

(121) Mortgage Bankers Association of America: *Mortgages for Retirement and Endowment Funds*

(123) New York Coffee and Sugar Exchange: *How Businessmen Use Commodity Futures Trading*

(124) U.S. Department of Commerce: *Dictionary of Economical and Statistical Terms*

(125) Resources Programs Institution: *A Glossary of Oil Terms*

(126) FRB of Atlanta: *Econometric Models*

(128) FRB of Chicago: *Definitions*

(129) Chicago Board of Trade: *Jargon of the Marketplace*

(130) International Monetary Fund: *Glossary of Exchange Concepts*

(131) National Consumer Finance Corporation: *Glossary*